# English G 21

## D4

Erweiterte Ausgabe
für differenzierende
Schulformen

Cornelsen

# English G 21 • Band D 4 • Erweiterte Ausgabe


*Im Auftrag des Verlages herausgegeben von*
Prof. Hellmut Schwarz, Mannheim

*Erarbeitet von*
Susan Abbey, Nenagh, Irland
Barbara Derkow Disselbeck, Köln
Allen J. Woppert, Berlin
*sowie* Laurence Harger, Wellington, Neuseeland

*unter Mitarbeit von*
Wolfgang Biederstädt, Köln
Joachim Blombach, Herford
David Christie, Banbury, England
Helmut Dengler, Limbach
Claire Lamsdale, Bristol, England
Martina Schroeder, Stedtlingen
Jennifer Seidl, München
Udo Wagner, Voerde
Herbert Willms, Herford
*sowie* Ulrike Flach, Köln; Silke Lehmacher, Monheim

*in Zusammenarbeit mit der Englischredaktion*
Dr. Christiane Kallenbach (Projektleitung);
Dr. Eva Grabowski (verantwortliche Redakteurin);
Susanne Bennetreu (Bildredaktion); Stefanie Bayer;
Britta Bensmann; Dr. Philip Devlin; Gwendolyn Düwel;
Cornelia Frisse; Bonnie S. Glänzer; Mara Leibowitz;
Anne Linder; Nathalie Schwering; Kathrin Spiegelberg;
Uwe Tröger; Klaus G. Unger *sowie* Olivia Gruver

*Beratende Mitwirkung*
Walter Droste, Spenge; Manuela Feierabend-Vonhausen,
Rossfeld; Birgit Heinemann, Neu Wulmstorf;
Ivette Huxol, Wilkau-Haßlau; Bernd Jost, Salzbergen;
Heike Jurenz, Neukirch/Lausitz; Heike Meisner,
Bad Klosterlausnitz; Gabriele Rotter, Wiesbaden;
Karl Starkebaum, Diekholzen

*Illustrationen*
Silke Bachmann, Hamburg; Roland Beier, Berlin;
Stéphane Gamain/NB Illustration, London;
Jörn Hennig, Berlin

*Layoutkonzept*
Aksinia Raphael; Korinna Wilkes

*Technische Umsetzung*
Aksinia Raphael; Korinna Wilkes;
Stephan Hilleckenbach; Rainer Bachmaier

*Umschlaggestaltung*
Klein & Halm Grafikdesign, Berlin



www.cornelsen.de
www.EnglishG.de





Druck: Mohn Media Mohndruck, Gütersloh

1. Auflage, 7. Druck 2017
broschiert
978-3-06-031321-1

1. Auflage, 5. Druck 2016
gebunden
978-3-06-031369-3

PEFC zertifiziert
Dieses Produkt stammt aus nachhaltig bewirtschafteten Wäldern und kontrollierten Quellen.
www.pefc.de
PEFC
PEFC/04-31-1033

## Dein Englischbuch enthält folgende Teile:

| | |
|---|---|
| **Introduction** | Hier lernst du die jungen Leute von Band 4 kennen. |
| **Units** | die fünf Kapitel des Buches |
| **Getting ready for a test** | Hier kannst du dich gezielt auf einen Test vorbereiten. |
| **EXTRA: Text File** | viele interessante Texte zum Lesen (passend zu den Units) |
| **Skills File (SF)** | Beschreibung wichtiger Lern- und Arbeitstechniken |
| **Grammar File (GF)** | Zusammenfassung der Grammatik jeder Unit |
| **Vocabulary** | Wörterverzeichnis zum Lernen der neuen Wörter jeder Unit |
| **Dictionary** | alphabetische Wörterverzeichnisse zum Nachschlagen |

### Die Units bestehen aus diesen Teilen:

| | |
|---|---|
| **Lead-in** | Einstieg in das neue Thema |
| **A-Section** | neuer Lernstoff mit vielen Aktivitäten und **Background File** |
| **Practice** | Übungen |
| **Text** | eine spannende oder lustige Geschichte |
| **How am I doing?** | Hier kannst du dein Wissen und Können überprüfen. |

### In den Units findest du diese Überschriften und Symbole:

| | |
|---|---|
| **Looking at language** | Hier sammelst du Beispiele und entdeckst Regeln. |
| **STUDY SKILLS** | Einführung in Lern- und Arbeitstechniken |
| **Dossier** | Schöne und wichtige Arbeiten kannst du in einer Mappe sammeln. |
| **All about ...** | Hier übst du Wortschatz zum Thema der Unit. |
| **READING COURSE** | Lesekurs in vier Kapiteln mit Hilfen zum Lesen von Texten |
| **EVERYDAY ENGLISH** | Übungen zum Bewältigen wichtiger Alltagssituationen |
| **MEDIATION** | Hier vermittelst du zwischen zwei Sprachen. |
| **LISTENING** | Aufgaben zu Hörtexten auf der CD |
| **Now you** | Hier sprichst und schreibst du über dich selbst. |
| **REVISION** | Übungen zur Wiederholung |
| **WORDS** | Übungen zu Wortfamilien, Wortfeldern und Wortverbindungen |
| **Extra** | Zusätzliche Aktivitäten und Übungen |
|  | Partnerarbeit / Gruppenarbeit |
|  | nur auf CD / auf CD und im Schülerbuch |
|  | Textaufgaben |
| 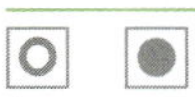 | leichtere Übungen / schwierigere Übungen |
| //○ //● | parallele Übungen auf zwei Niveaus |
| more help | Hier findest du zusätzliche Hilfen für das Lösen einer Aufgabe. |

# Inhalt

# Welcome to the United States of America

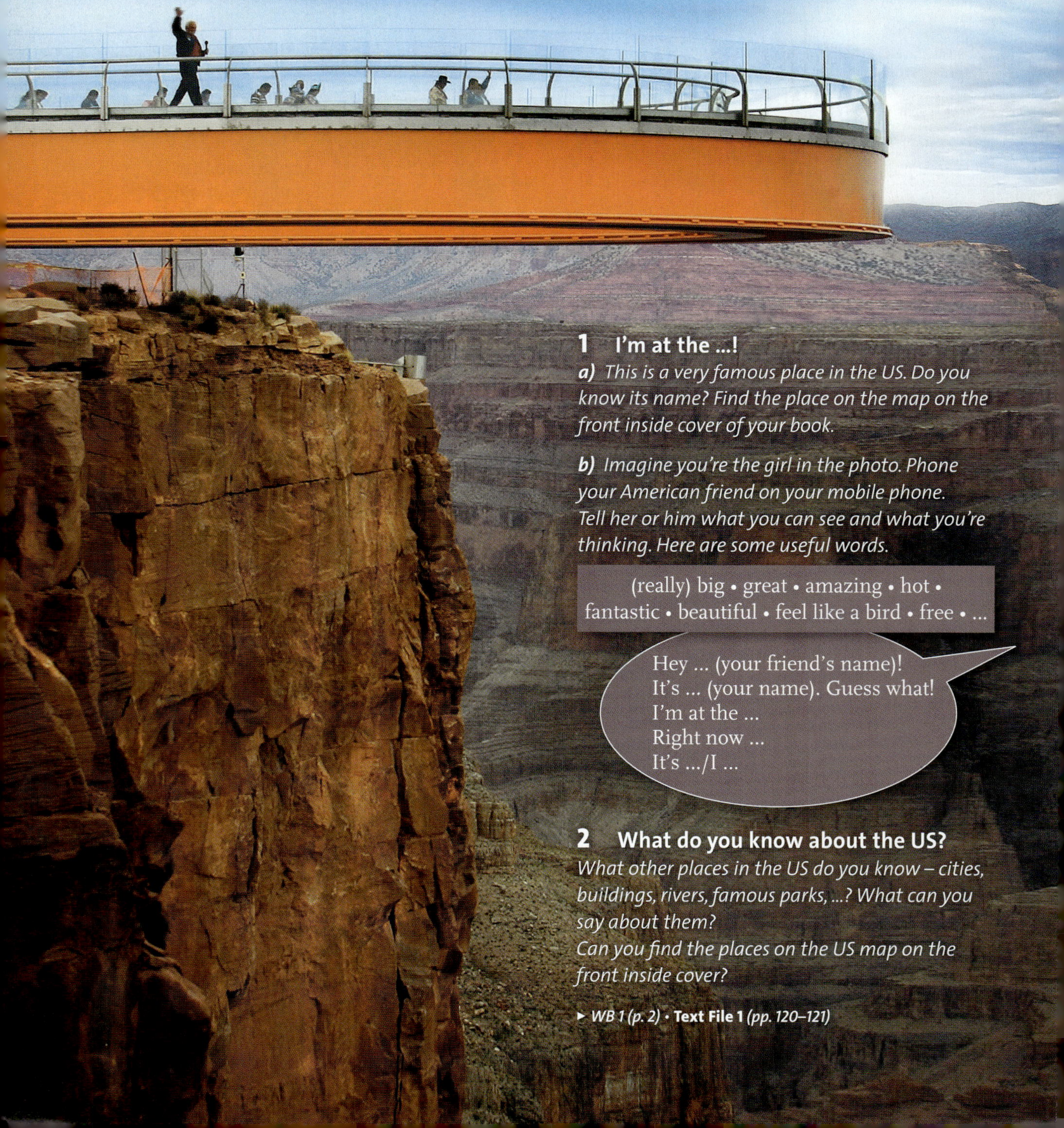

## 1 I'm at the ...!

***a)*** *This is a very famous place in the US. Do you know its name? Find the place on the map on the front inside cover of your book.*

***b)*** *Imagine you're the girl in the photo. Phone your American friend on your mobile phone. Tell her or him what you can see and what you're thinking. Here are some useful words.*

(really) big • great • amazing • hot • fantastic • beautiful • feel like a bird • free • ...

Hey ... (your friend's name)!
It's ... (your name). Guess what!
I'm at the ...
Right now ...
It's .../I ...

## 2 What do you know about the US?

*What other places in the US do you know – cities, buildings, rivers, famous parks, ...? What can you say about them?*
*Can you find the places on the US map on the front inside cover?*

▸ *WB 1 (p. 2)* • **Text File 1** *(pp. 120–121)*

## 1 Four summer holidays

*On pp. 8–11 you can read about four young Americans who all visited the Grand Canyon in their summer holidays. Quickly scan the four pages and find the answers to these questions.*

▸ *SF Scanning (p. 150)*

1. What are the names of the young people?
2. Where are they from?
3. Who lives closest to the Grand Canyon?
4. How did they travel there?
5. Where did they stay?
6. Who wrote about their trip for school?

**Americana ★ ★ ★**

**The Grand Canyon**

In Arizona there's a place where the Colorado River cuts deep into the rocks. This is the Grand Canyon. It's 446 km long, between 6 to 24 km wide and over 1 km deep. It became a national park in 1919, and today about five million people visit it every year.

▸ *SF Learning words (p. 143)*

## 2 It's awesome!

**Caitlin's blog**

About me

Name: Caitlin

Birthday: July 9

Hometown: New York, New York

**August 26**

Hi guys – I'm back from my summer vacation, so you can look forward to more of my daily blogs from New York. Like every year, my mom and dad packed me, my little brother and lots of camping gear into our car and drove, and drove … and drove. We always go to a national park, and this year it was the Grand Canyon. The drive there is long, almost 2500 miles. We crossed three time zones! It took us three and a half days. We camped at two different places on the rim and went on day trips in the car or hiked. The Grand Canyon is awesome! If you haven't been there, go!

**Comments** ➔ *On 8/27 Ruth wrote*

Hi Cait, sounds like an awesome trip! Good to have you back. CU Ruth

▶ *How far is the Grand Canyon from Caitlin's home in kilometres? (1 mile = 1.6 kilometres)*
*Go to the map on the front inside cover. What time is it in the canyon when it's 11 am in New York?*

## 3 Extra Your comment

*What do you think of Caitlin's holidays? Add a comment to her blog.*

## 4 A trip with a youth group

**Shorecliffs Middle School**
San Clemente, California

Student's name: *Luis Morales*

Grade: *8*

Date: *September 3*

*My summer vacation*

*This summer I was very lucky. I was able to go on a trip to Grand Canyon National Park with the youth group at my church. Before we went, we raised money for the trip. We washed cars, cut the grass, cleaned pools and had a bake sale. (Everybody loved my mother's empanadas – they were sold out in two hours!)*

*We were all very excited when the bus came to pick us up. I'm 14 years old, and I've never been so far from home. The ride took about nine hours with a short lunch break. We sang songs in Spanish and English the whole time – till the driver said we had to stop.*

*We stayed at the canyon for three days. We went on long hikes around and into the canyon. The colors were amazing. At night we slept in tents – that was new for me – and cooked our own meals. That was really great.*

*In the park we met some park rangers. They showed us how to use binoculars and other ranger tools and we were allowed to use them for the rest of the day. One of the rangers was a Native American. She told us about the Hualapai who still live in the Grand Canyon. I loved my vacation and learned a lot.*

*How did Luis's group get the money for the trip? Why do you think they sang songs in English and Spanish? What did you learn about the job of a park ranger?*

## 5 Extra Now you

***a)*** *Imagine your class wants to go on a trip. What kinds of things could you do to raise money?*

***b)*** *If your class had € 500, what would you do?*

**Americana ★ ★ ★**

**Park Rangers**

National parks in the US can be forests, mountains, rivers and of course canyons, or famous monuments. Park rangers protect the parks so that visitors don't damage them. They protect the visitors too – in some parks there are dangerous animals. The rangers also tell visitors about the natural and human history of the park.

## 6 On the road with Dad

**Hermann High School,**
**Hermann, Missouri**

Name: Jake Kruger, 14
Grade: 9

MY ROAD DIARY

August 7 – Dad and I said goodbye to Mom at the farm and began our trip from Missouri along the famous highway – Route 66 – to the Grand Canyon. We traveled west – into Kansas and Oklahoma. Dad has always dreamed about this journey. He told me about the old TV series "Route 66" and sang the song "Route 66" – "Well it winds from Chicago to L.A. More than 2000 miles all the way."

We stopped at every gas station and café and Dad bought Route 66 souvenirs. It's the first day and already he has a license plate for the car and a key ring. Tonight we're at a motel outside Tulsa.

August 8 – Early start and another day in the car. Boring! We drove through Oklahoma and Texas and into New Mexico. We're spending the night here in Tucumcari. Dad has added a poster and a cap to his Route 66 stuff. This is so sad!

August 9 – On to Santa Rosa and – guess what – the Route 66 Auto Museum. Dad got a Route 66 bag for Mom. It was already dark when we drove into Arizona, so we stopped at the next motel.

August 10 – At last! Today we arrived at the Grand Canyon – and wow, IT IS GRAND! We left the car at our motel and went to the rim of the canyon to look across it. All you can see for miles and miles are walls of multi-colored rock. Later, when it got cooler, we walked down into the canyon. We saw a condor. What a bird – 9 feet from wing tip to wing tip. Now I forgive Dad for all the hours in the car.

Today was a day I will never forget!

**Americana ★ ★ ★**

**Route 66**
In the US, Route 66 is a modern legend. People often call it the Mother Road because it was one of the first roads that linked the Midwest (Chicago) to the west coast (Los Angeles). It opened in 1926 and was 3940 kilometres long.
The original road closed in 1985. Parts of it, called Historic Route 66, still exist in Arizona and New Mexico.

1. *What souvenirs did Jake's dad buy?*
2. *What did Mr Kruger and Jake see and do on their trip?*
3. *Look at the map on the front inside cover:*
   *– What states did they drive through?*
   *– How many kilometres do you think they travelled?*

## 7 What a fantastic trip!

*Look at the photos. What do you think Madison did in her summer holidays?*

## 8 Madison's trip

*Read the questions below. Then listen, take notes and answer the questions:*

1. How much vacation did Madison's parents take this summer?
2. Did Madison think Las Vegas or the Grand Canyon was more exciting?
3. What was 'the big adventure'?

► *SF Listening (p. 148)*

## 9 Extra Now you

*Write about a summer holiday. Write a blog, an essay, a diary or make a presentation. Brainstorm your ideas. Look for useful phrases on pp. 7–11. Add pictures or maps and put it in your DOSSIER.*

► *WB 2–7 (pp. 3–5)* • *SF Brainstorming (p. 153)* •
**Text File 2** *(pp. 122–123)*

# New York, New York

A The Manhattan skyline with the ... in the middle.

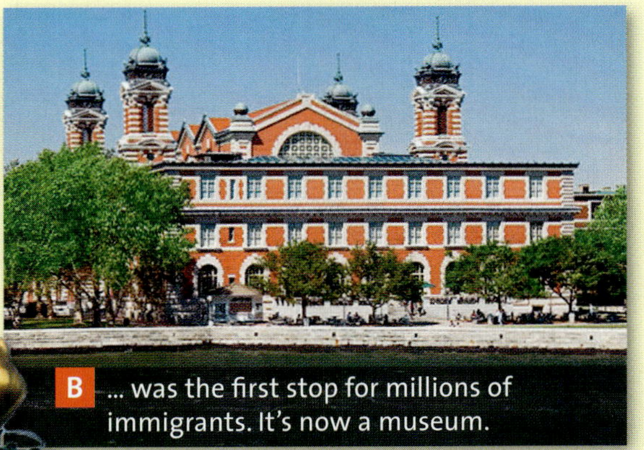

B ... was the first stop for millions of immigrants. It's now a museum.

C Tourists love the ...

## 1 What do you know about New York?

*a) Look at the photos. Complete the captions with the names from the box.*

Brooklyn Bridge • Central Park • Chinatown • Ellis Island • Empire State Building • Fifth Avenue • Statue of Liberty • Times Square

*b) Find the places on the Manhattan map. What else do you know about New York?*

## 2 A visit to New York

*a) Listen to Caitlin and her friend Ruth. In what order do they talk about the sights on these two pages? Write down the sights.*

*b) Listen again.*

– Who's Ryan?
– Which sights do the girls choose for him?
– What else do you learn about each sight?
– What is a deli?

► P 1 (p. 20) • SF Listening (p. 148) • WB 1–2 (p. 6)

D The ... stands on Liberty Island in New York Harbor south of Manhattan.

**E** Skating in ... which lies in the heart of Manhattan.

The five boroughs of New York

The streets go from west to east. They usually have numbers. The avenues go from north to south. Some have names, others have numbers too.

**F** ... is famous for shopping!

**G** ... at night

**H** The busy street life of ... in downtown Manhattan.

## All about ... getting around an American city

### 1 Understanding directions

*Read what the woman tells the tourist. Match the words and the definitions below.*

| | |
|---|---|
| • block | • the corner of 34th Street and Broadway |
| • downtown | • a group of buildings between two streets |
| • 34th and Broadway | • the city centre |

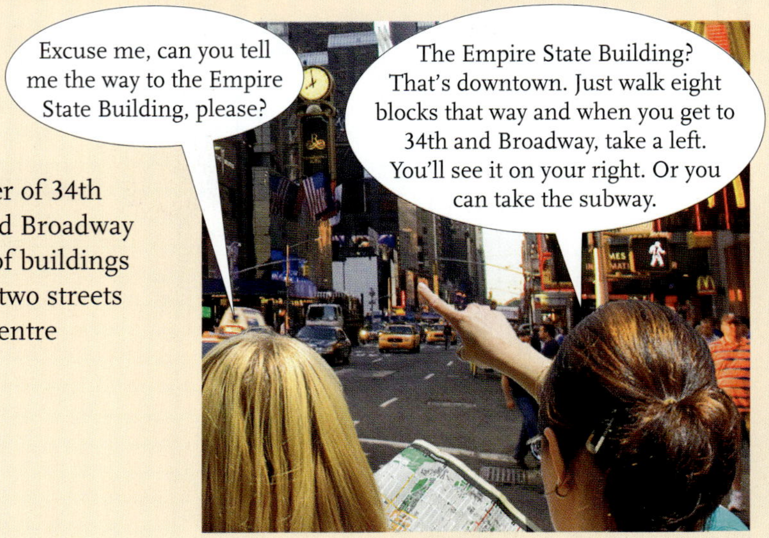


### 2 Understanding signs

***a)*** *Where could you see these signs?*

inside/outside a ... • on the street • ...

***b)*** *What do you think each sign means? Discuss with your partner.*

1

2

3

4

5

6

### 3 American and British English

*Copy and complete the chart below. You can use a German-English dictionary.*

| American English (AE) | German | British English (BE) |
|---|---|---|
| subway | U-Bahn | ... |
| ... | (Stadt)Zentrum | ... |
| ... | Bürgersteig | ... |
| ... | Schlange | |
| ... | Handy | |

► SF Using a dictionary (p. 145) • P 2–3 (pp. 20–21) • WB 3–6 (pp. 7–8)

## 4 Travelling is hard

'You look tired,' Caitlin said as Ryan, her cousin from Ireland, sat down at the kitchen table.

'Well,' said Ryan, 'I had to leave home really early this morning. Getting up at 4 o'clock was hard! Then flying for six hours ...'

'And then there's the five hour time difference between Ireland and New York,' added Caitlin. 'Poor you! But don't go to bed yet. If you sleep now, you'll wake up in the middle of the night and think it's morning. Oh, I know. Let's walk over to the fire station and say hi to Dad.'

'Great idea!' said Ryan. He wanted to know all about his uncle's job as a New York firefighter.

*What took six hours? When it's 5 pm in New York, what time is it in Ireland? Who did Ryan want to know all about?*

## 5 I love being a firefighter

My dad and my grandpa were both firefighters and I can't imagine doing anything else. I love being a firefighter too. Sure, it's hard work. And nobody enjoys getting up in the middle of the night! But it feels good when you put out a fire and maybe save another person's life.

We work 15-hour shifts, but we spend a lot of that time at the station. The men and women on my shift are like family and we enjoy being together. Some of the guys are great cooks. There was this one guy, Ricardo. We all loved his chili con carne. Good old Ricardo. He's not with us any more – he died on 9/11.

*What are the hard things about being a firefighter? What are the good things?*

### Looking at language

**a)** *Write down all the sentences in* **4** *and* **5** *with* **-ing***-forms.*
*Travelling is ...*

**b)** *These* **-ing***-forms are like nouns. They're called* **gerunds***. Translate them into German and compare.*

► GF 1a–b: Gerund (p. 161) • P 4–7 (pp. 21–22) • WB 7–9 (pp. 9–10)

### Americana ★ ★ ★

**9/11 and Ground Zero**

On September 11th (9/11), 2001, nineteen hijackers took over four US planes. They flew two of them into the Twin Towers of the World Trade Center in downtown Manhattan. Both skyscrapers burned and collapsed. Almost 3000 people died, 343 of them were firefighters.
The place where the Towers stood is now called Ground Zero. Every year, on 9/11 the 'Tribute in Light' takes place and people remember the men and women who died there.

## 6 On top of the world

'Well, it's a perfect day for the Empire State Building!' Caitlin said and pointed to a sign. 'Today you can see 45 miles. Come on, the ticket office is one floor up.'

'But here it says it's on the second floor,' said Ryan.

'Right,' said Caitlin. 'This is the first floor, the next one up is the second.'

After buying the tickets the two cousins went to the lifts. 'Do we have to take the lift?' asked Ryan. 'I'm ... er ... scared of going in lifts.'

'So you want to walk up the 86 floors to the observatory?' asked Caitlin and laughed. 'Come on. You'll be OK.'

He was. The lift was fast and in only one minute they were on the 86th floor. Ryan was interested in learning about the city and its boroughs and Caitlin pointed to lots of places and explained them to him.

After about twenty minutes they were tired of looking. 'Let's get some lunch,' said Caitlin. 'I know the perfect place. You can meet my friend Ruth. And there are no elevators!'

*1 Why was it a good day to visit the ESB?*
*2 Ryan was confused about where the 'second floor' is. Why?*
*3 What have these numbers got to do with the ESB?* 86 – 41 – 1454 – 365 – 1930

▸ *GF 1c: Gerunds after prepositions (p. 162)* • *P 8–10 (pp. 22–24)* • *WB 10–13 (pp. 10–12)*

## 7 Extra Group puzzle

***a)*** *Make six groups (A, B, ..., F). Each group finds out more about one of the New York sights in this unit. Take notes.*

***b)*** *Then give each person in the group a number. Form new groups (A1, B1, C1, .../A2, B2, C2, ...). Tell the others about your sight.*

***c)*** *Return to your first group. Share your new information. Plan a day of sightseeing.*

▸ **Text File 3** *(pp. 124–125)*

## 8 At the deli

Caitlin and Ryan met Caitlin's friend Ruth outside a crowded restaurant. They went in.

'Hi, Aaron!' Ruth called.

'Two bagels and cream cheese, one bagel and lox – hi there, Ruthie – and two coffees to go,' shouted the young man behind the counter.

'They know you here, Ruth?' asked Ryan.

'Sure, the local deli waiters know everybody in the area. – OK. You two find a table and I'll order. What do you both want?'

'Ryan must have a bagel,' said Caitlin. 'When you're in New York, you have to eat bagels. What about a bagel and lox, Ryan?'

'Er, lox. What's that?'

'Salmon – in Yiddish,' explained Ruth.

'Sorry, but I don't really like fish,' said Ryan.

'No problem,' Ruth answered. 'I'll get you a bagel and cream cheese.'

'For me too. And water, please, regular, sparkling,' said Caitlin.

'For me too,' said Ryan, 'but large, please.'

Five minutes later they were all at their table with their food. Ryan loved his bagel – and all the friendly people in the deli.

'This is great!' he said to Caitlin and Ruth. 'If I lived in New York, I'd come here every day!'

*What kind of place is a deli?*
*What would you say if you wanted to take a cola with you from a deli?*

► *P 11–14 (pp. 24–25) • WB 14–17 (pp. 13–14)*

**Americana ★ ★ ★**

**Bagels and delis**
Bagels are a kind of roll with a hole in it and they come with lots of different fillings. New Yorkers often eat bagels for breakfast. They run into a deli (the name comes from the German *Delikatessen*) on their way to work and grab a bagel and coffee to go. Jewish immigrants from Europe brought the bagel with them to the US in the 19th century.

► **Text File 4** *(pp. 126–127)*

## 9 Extra SONG A heart in New York

New York
To that tall skyline I come
flying in from London
To your door

New York
Looking down on Central Park
Where they say you should not wander
After dark

New York
Like a scene from all those movies
But you're real enough to me
But there's a heart
A heart that lives in New York

*by Benny Gallagher and Graham Lyle*

– *What is the singer doing in this song?*
– *What sights in New York does he mention?*
– *Would the singer like this sticker? Why (not)?*

Extra | Background File | **A COUNTRY OF IMMIGRANTS**

## America! America!

About 300 million people live in the US. Only four million of them are Native Americans, the people who lived there before Europeans and others arrived. All the rest have their roots in countries around the world.
Until the middle of the last century the main place where immigrants to the US arrived was the port of New York. The first thing they saw was the Statue of Liberty.

## A better life

Immigrants came to America for all kinds of reasons. Many came because in their countries they were not free to practise their religion or take part in politics. But most – like these Irish people – wanted a new life in the US because they were so poor at home.

## Ellis Island

In 1892 the city of New York opened the Ellis Island Immigration Station within sight of the Statue of Liberty and Manhattan Island. More than 12 million immigrants entered the US through Ellis Island. Most of them came between 1892 and 1924. The station finally closed in 1954 and today it's a museum.

## Today's immigrants

Thousands of people still come to the US for a better life every year. And they come from many different countries. In the last century they came mainly from Germany, Ireland, Russia and other European countries. Today they mainly come from Mexico, China and the Philippines.

### 1 America's people

*Read the texts and answer these questions.*

1. How many Americans today are Native Americans?
2. How many people came to America between 1892 and 1924? Where did they arrive? What was usually the first thing they saw in America?
3. Where did immigrants come from in the past? Where do they come from today? Why do you think this has changed?

## Young people's voices

When immigrants arrived at Ellis Island they went first to the Great Hall. On busy days, 12,000 a day went through here.

"I had never seen such a big building. Compared to the size of the houses I had left in my town, this was like a whole city. I almost felt smaller than I was. It looked beautiful."

*Celia Adler, 12, when she arrived from Russia in 1914.*

"America was on everyone's lips. We talked about America; we dreamt about America. We all had one wish – to be in America."

*Louis Sage, 15, from Poland.*

Sometimes people had to wait a long time on Ellis Island. And they ate their first American food.

"[They gave us] big pieces of bread, and then each one had been given a bowl, and they filled it with red stuff. And I [...] told my sister, 'Oh, they're serving bread and blood.' I had never seen tomato soup in my life."

*Sonya Gillick from Sweden*

Immigrants arrived after a long journey by ship.

"Oh, God, I was sick. Everybody was sick. I don't ever want to remember anything about that old boat [...] I didn't care if it went down or not. And everybody else was the same way."

*Bertha Devlin when she arrived from Ireland.*

New York itself amazed the immigrants.

"We walked up Broadway [...]. And I saw the big buildings. We didn't have big buildings in Germany. Then we got on an elevated train, and all of a sudden, we were in the sky."

*William Reinhart from Germany talking about his first day in NY.*

"This is the only country where you're not a stranger because we are all strangers."

*Lazarus Salamon, 16, when he arrived from Hungary in 1920.*

> *What countries were the young people from? What things did they notice in their new country? How did they feel?*

▸ *SF Using a dictionary (p. 145)*

### 2 Now you

*Do a), b) or c).*

***a)*** *Imagine you are one of the young people from this page. Write a short diary entry about your first day in a new country.*

***b)*** *Has anybody from your family ever gone to live in the US? Go to www.ellisisland.org. Put their name into the search engine there.*

***c)*** *Do you know anybody who came to Germany from another country? Find out as many details as you can.*

▸ *WE 18 (p. 15)*

## 1 The five boroughs of New York

*New York has five boroughs. Manhattan is one of them. You can see them on this map.*

***a)*** *Partner B: Go to p. 106.*
*Partner A: Read out the texts below. Your partner must say which boroughs you're describing.*

1 This is the biggest of New York's five boroughs. If you fly to John F. Kennedy Airport, this is where you'll land. On the map it's east of Brooklyn.
2 A famous bridge over the East River links this borough to Manhattan. It's south of Manhattan.

***b)*** *Now listen to your partner. Which of the five boroughs is he/she describing?*

1 The correct answer is 'Queens'. 2 The correct answer is 'Brooklyn'.

## 2 LISTENING British and American English

***a)*** *Look at the pictures. Write down the British English (BE) word for the things (1–11).*
*1 rucksack*
*2 ...*

***b)*** *You will hear two dialogues. Listen for the American English (AE) words in the box. Listen again and write down the AE words next to the BE words on your list from a).*

+backpack • cellphone • +cookies • +eraser • +French fries • +garbage • +pants • +potato chips • +schedule • sidewalk • subway

## 3 WORDS Verbs and nouns that go together

*a) Find one verb that can go with all the nouns in each group.*

1 ... a bus, a photo, the underground *= take*
2 ... a train, a cold, a thief
3 ... a museum, a city, an aunt
4 ... at a bus stop, in a queue, for a friend

*b) Find at least three nouns that go with each of these verbs.*

1 arrive at *a hotel, ...*
2 eat at ...
3 ride ...
4 walk ...

## 4 I/O Getting around New York (Gerund) ▸ D p. 110

*a) Complete the sentences with the verb forms in the box.*

buying • crossing • cycling • driving • going • spotting • taking • visiting • walking

1 ... is a great way to get around New York – but wear good shoes.
2 ... the street in Manhattan's busy traffic is dangerous, so be careful.
3 ... can be dangerous too, so wear a helmet on your bike.
4 ... by bus is a good way to see lots of city sights.
5 ... can be expensive if you have to pay for parking.
6 ... the subway is cheap, but you don't see much of the city.
7 ... a subway ticket is easy if you've got the correct change.
8 ... a taxi is easy because they're all bright yellow.
9 ... New York's museums is fun, but it can be very expensive.

*1 Walking is a great way ...*

**b)** ● **Extra** *Write down three tips for getting around the place where you live. Use gerunds.*

## 5 WORDS Jobs in the city

*a) These are all people who work in a city. What are they?*

1 a person who puts out fires
2 a person who catches thieves
3 a person who helps you in a shop
4 a person who puts on the music at the disco
5 a person in an ambulance who helps people who are hurt
6 a person who works at a national park or monument
7 a person who cuts your hair
8 a person who keeps the city clean
9 a person who helps people who are ill
10 a person who shows people on a bus tour the sights of the city

**b)** **Extra** *Describe two more jobs. Can your partner guess them?*

## 6 //O The life of a paramedic (Gerund) ▸ D p. 110

***a)*** *Complete this interview with a New York paramedic. Use the gerunds from the box.*

being • doing • meeting • saving

driving • getting • waiting • working

**What do you like doing in your job?**
I like *saving* people's lives. That's number one.
I love ... part of a great team. That's important.
I like ... new people every day too. That's great.
And I really enjoy ... different things every day.

**What don't you like so much?**
I hate ... up in the middle of the night. And
I don't really enjoy ... long shifts. That's hard.
I don't like ... for a call. That can be boring.
And I hate ... fast through the city. It's no fun!

***b)*** **Extra** *Look at the people in exercise* **5** *again. What do you think they like doing or don't like doing in their jobs? Write some sentences. Park ranger: I like working outside in summer. But I don't like ...*

## 7 I love chatting ... (Gerund)

***a)*** O *Finish these sentences. Use a gerund.*

1 (+ + +) I love ...
2 (+ +) I really enjoy ...
3 (+) I like ...
4 (–) I don't like ...
5 (– –) I really don't enjoy ...
6 (– – –) I hate ...

*I love chatting with my friends / ...*
*I really enjoy going to ... / ...*

***b)*** *Meet people in your class. Tell them what you like/don't like. Then listen to their ideas. Take notes. Use the symbols.*

*Tim:*
*++ watching TV*
*– – learning English words*

▸ SF Taking notes (p. 149)

***c)*** *Tell the class.*
Tim likes watching ... He really doesn't enjoy ... And he hates ...

## 8 WRITING Taking a break in Central Park

**Remember**

- First brainstorm, then make a mind map or list, or use the 5 Ws.
- Think of a good beginning and ending.
- Start a new paragraph for each new topic.
- Use adjectives, adverbs and linking words.
- Read and correct your text.

*Look at the photo. Imagine you're one of the people. Write 80–100 words about your day in the park. Use questions like these to get ideas for your writing:*
**Who** was in the park with you? **What** was the weather like? **Where** did you sit? **How** did you like it there? **When** did you arrive?

more help ▸ D p. 111

▸ SF The steps of writing (p. 154) • SF Brainstorming (p. 153)

## 9 READING Fire safety (Working out the meaning of words) ► SF p. 150

***a)*** *Read these fire safety instructions. Try to understand them with the help of the tips. Then explain (in German) what you have to do if there's a fire.*

**1** Look at the **pictures**:
What could a *high-rise building* be?

**2** Some words look like **German** words:
What could *second* mean?

**3** Look at the **context** (the words around the word you don't know):
What could *alert* mean?

**4** Sometimes you already know **parts of the word** or phrase:
You know *stairs*, you know *way*. What could *stairway* mean?
You know *direction*. What could *directed* mean?

***b)*** **Extra** *Try to understand the other highlighted words from the instructions (page **1**):* stay low, exit, report a fire, dial.
*Use the tips from a).*

***c)*** *Explain the highlighted words in page **2** of the safety instructions.*
more help ► D p. 111

**1**

### Fire safety in high-rise buildings

FIRE DEPARTMENT CITY OF NEW YORK

#### If the fire is IN your room

- If there is a fire, stay calm and think about what to do. Act quickly because every second counts.
- Get everybody out. Stay low, where air is fresher – smoke rises.
- Use your safest and nearest exit.
- CLOSE ALL DOORS as you leave.
- Knock on other guests' doors on your way out and alert them to the danger.
- DO NOT USE THE ELEVATOR.
- Go down the nearest STAIRWAY.
- To report a fire, dial 911. Firefighters will be directed to your location.

**2**

### Fire safety in high-rise buildings

FIRE DEPARTMENT CITY OF NEW YORK

#### If the fire is NOT in your room

- If the hallways are full of smoke, stay in your room.
- Place a wet cloth over your mouth and nose to facilitate breathing.
- Turn off air conditioners.
- Fill your bathtub with water. If your door gets hot, wet it down.

- If you are in great danger, hang a bedsheet out the window so that firefighters can spot you.

## 10 Lisa is good at ... (Gerund after prepositions)

**a)** Complete the sentences with the gerund of the verb in brackets.

1 Lisa is good at ... (speak) English.
*Lisa is good at speaking English.*
2 She dreams of ... (live) in New York.
3 And she's very interested in ... (learn) hip hop.
4 So she'll ask about ... (join) a dance class when she gets there.
5 And she's thinking of ... (become) a rapper!

**b)** *Complete the following sentences with a gerund. Write them on a piece of paper.*

1 I dream of ...
2 I'm scared of ...
3 I'm good at ...
4 I'm not so good at ...

**c)** *Put the pieces of paper in a box. Take turns to read out a piece of paper. Can the class guess who wrote it?*

## 11 REVISION I might visit New York (*if* and *when*)

**Tip**

**when = sobald, dann wenn** (Zeit) *When I take you to Times Square tonight ... (= es steht fest)*

**if = wenn, falls** (Bedingung) *If I take you to Times Square tonight ... (= es steht nicht fest)*

**a)** *Complete the short dialogues with **if** or **when**.*

1 *A:* I might visit New York this summer.
*B:* ... you come to New York, you can stay with me.
2 *A:* My friend Tom will be in New York in July.
*B:* I'd love to meet him. Ask him to call me ... he's here.
3 *A:* I hope the weather will be OK tomorrow.
*B:* Don't worry. ... it rains we can go to one of the many museums in New York.
4 *A:* We're going to visit the Bronx Zoo today.
*B:* You must see the snakes ... you're there.
5 *A:* Will we have time to go to your local deli?
*B:* Well, ... we don't have time today, we can go tomorrow.
6 *A:* There's a film about New York on TV this evening.
*B:* Great. Can you call me ... it starts?

**b) Extra** *Translate the two sentences into German and explain the difference.*

1 Call me when you come to New York.
2 Call me if you come to New York.

## 12 REVISION If I go to New York ... (Conditional sentences 1 and 2)

**a)** *Complete these conditional sentences.*

1 If I go to New York one day, I'll/I won't ...
2 If it's hot in New York, I'll/I won't be able to ...
3 If I have enough time while I'm there, ...
4 If I see any famous people, ...
5 If I had friends in New York, I'd/I wouldn't ...
6 If I lived in New York, I'd/I wouldn't ...
7 If I was a New York firefighter, ...
8 If I was in a building that was burning, ...

**b)** *Make an if-chain. You can start like this:*

*A:* If I had lots of money, I'd fly to New York.
*B:* If I flew to New York, ...

## 13 MEDIATION At the deli

*a) Imagine you are in a New York deli. You hear another German. Help him to order.*

| | |
|---|---|
| *German man* | Die Frau spricht so schnell. Kannst du sie bitten, ihre Frage zu wiederholen? |
| *You* | Excuse me, can you ... |
| *Woman at deli* | Sure. Is this for here or to go? |
| *You* | Sie will wissen, ... |
| *German man* | Ach so, ich möchte hier essen. Ich hätte gern einen Bagel mit Käse, aber kein Ei, wenn's geht. |
| *You* | It's for ... |

*b) Listen to the rest of the dialogue. Listen again and help the man.*

▸ SF Mediation (p. 152)

## 14 SPEAKING Making plans together

*Partner B: Look at p. 106.*
*Partner A: You and your partner are on holiday in New York. You want to spend the day together, but you have different ideas about what to do.*

### THE BRONX ZOO

The Bronx Zoo is one of the largest zoos in the United States with over 4000 animals.
The zoo is open 365 days a year!
10:00 a.m. – 5:00 p.m.
Admission: Adult $ 14.00, Child (Ages 3–12) $ 10.00

*b) Listen to your partner's plans and take notes.*

▸ SF Taking notes (p. 149)

*a) You want to go to the places below. Read the texts and tell your partner ...*

- *where you want to go*
- *where the places are, what they cost, when you can go there*
- *one reason why you would like to go there*

### SKYSCRAPER MUSEUM

The Skyscraper Museum – the only museum of its kind – explores the history of tall buildings.
It's at 39 Battery Place in Manhattan.
Museum hours are 12–6 p.m., Wednesday–Sunday.
Admission is $ 5, $ 2.50 for students.

*c) Now talk to her/him and decide where you'd like to go together – one place in the morning, one place in the afternoon. You each have $ 20. Check the prices and opening hours.*

## You can tell me From *Kelly 'n' Me* by Myron Levoy (adapted)

The story so far ... *Anthony (15) lives in a poor part of New York with his mother. He often plays his guitar and sings to earn money. One day he meets a girl in Central Park. She says her name is Kelly Callahan and that her family is poor, like Anthony's. She loves music too. Kelly takes Anthony to a beautiful apartment near the park. She says her mother works for the rich Lawrence family that lives there. She also tells Anthony that she wants to go away from New York and her family. Anthony likes spending time with Kelly. One day they decide to play music together in Central Park.*

▸ *SF Working out the meaning of words (p. 150)*

"Hey, Kelly," I said. "There aren't many people here. We could go and play at the zoo."

"How about the subway, Anthony?"

I hate being underground. And the subway is so depressing. But I agreed.

"Okay, if you really want to," I said.

"I do! It's fun. You can sing really loud down there. Come on!"

Kelly said the best station was the IRT at Lexington Avenue and Forty-second Street. We took the downtown train and got off at Forty-second. Kelly was right. There were crowds of people.

We did some of our loudest and liveliest songs. And Kelly was right again; the money was good.

Some people stopped. One of them seemed drunk or on drugs. He was looking at our money. I wanted to move, but Kelly said no.

"Don't worry, Anthony," she said. "If he takes any money, it means he needs it more than we do."

"Aren't you afraid of anybody?" I asked.

"Oh, sure. I'm afraid of you."

"Me? I don't understand."

"I'll explain later," Kelly said. "Come on. Let's sing."

We sang for another hour and a half. But then all the people and the noise and smells were too much for me.

"Please Kelly! I feel sick. Let's get out of here, please!"

*Why does Anthony agree to play in the subway? What kind of person is he? Do you think money is important to Kelly? What kind of person is she?*

I felt better up on the street. As we walked, I started to feel hungry. "Say, Kelly," I said. "How about feeding the body?"

"You want to have a picnic?"

"You mean right here on the street?"

"Come on, Anthony. Don't be dumb. We buy some rolls and cheese and sausage and let's see, chocolate milk, and then we go to the park – I know a nice place there."

Our picnic was in a wild part of the park called the Ramble. I wouldn't go there when it's dark, but it was safe in the evening. I thought.

As Kelly drank the last of the chocolate milk, I put my arm around her.

"Give me a chocolate mustache," I said.

Kelly leaned over and gave me a very good kiss. And I moved closer.

"Anthony, we really should talk," she said.

"You always want to talk."

"Don't you want to know why I'm afraid of you?"

"Okay, why?"

"It's because you're making it hard for me to do what I want to do."

"Huh?"

"To be the new me. To leave everything and take off. I'm nervous enough, and now you've come along ..."

"You don't look nervous to me."

"Well, I am. I'm scared of everything. Of my parents. And of being alone. And ..."

Suddenly there were tears in her eyes.

"Kelly? Why are you crying? What is it? You can tell me. Anything."

"I can and I can't. Why did I have to meet you just now?"

> *What is different for Kelly now that she has met Anthony?*

Suddenly I noticed that Kelly was looking past me, towards the path. "Uh-oh-..."

I followed her eyes. Two guys, one with a red beard and one blond, were watching us. One of them, Redbeard, had tattoos all over his arms.

This didn't look good to me. So I said quietly to Kelly, "Let's, maybe, get up slowly and ..."

"Yo, blondie!" said Redbeard to Kelly. "You got a nice bod. You ever use it?"

"L-leave us alone," I said. It was dumb to be in this part of the park this late!

"I like your guitar, blondie," said Redbeard. "It's nice, just like your ass." He walked slowly towards her.

What Redbeard didn't know is that when I get angry, I don't think. I just go for it. I jumped up and hit him as hard as I could. He wasn't expecting it, and he fell. My hand hurt.

Kelly screamed. And she really can scream! She tried to hit Blondbeard with her guitar, but he jumped away.

Redbeard was getting up, so I kicked him in the head. It wasn't fair, but I didn't care. I just hoped that they didn't have knives. Or guns.

I turned towards Blondbeard, but it was too late. He hit Kelly – just below her right eye. She fell against a tree and hit her head. She was hurt, but I couldn't help her. Blondbeard was coming towards me. And then I heard some people shouting from down the path.

"Let's get out of here," Blondbeard shouted.

As the people got closer, Blondbeard and Redbeard took off – with Kelly's guitar.

I sat down next to Kelly. There was blood on her face. I tore off a piece of my T-shirt and pressed it against her cheek.

> *What does Anthony think when he sees the two men? Was it a good idea to fight with the men?*

We started to walk slowly towards the street.

"Take me to – to Fifth Avenue and I'll get a cab," Kelly said. She still held the piece of my T-shirt against her cheek.

"No, I'm going all the way home with you. I don't care how your house looks."

"Please. Please, Anthony."

"No! Enough's enough, Kelly. If you don't let me go with you, I'll never see you again."

"Okay, let's get out of the park," she said.

As we left the park, I asked Kelly again and again if she was all right.

"It's nothing, Anthony. It's only blood."

"Very nice blood. You were really brave."

"Thanks. You too. Wow! Those guys were dangerous."

"I'm sorry about your guitar," I said.

"I've got another guitar," she said. "No problem."

We got to Fifth Avenue and Kelly said again, "I'll get a cab now. See you tomorrow."

"No! I'm going with you!"

Kelly looked at me. "Okay ... Anthony, could we sit there a minute?"

We went over to one of the benches along the park on Fifth Avenue and sat. Kelly looked out at the tops of some buildings across the street.

"This is what – what I wanted to tell you," she said. "We won't have to walk far. Because I live right there." She pointed to the building across the street, the one with the apartment we had visited a couple of weeks ago.

"But that's just the place where your mother works. Are you, like, using it while they're away?"

"No. It's ... I'm sorry, Anthony. It's that my name isn't really Kelly Callahan. It's Kelsey. You know? Kelsey Lawrence. I'm sorry ... I'm sorry ..."

> *Does Kelly want Anthony to take her home?*
*Where does Kelly live?*
*Why does Kelly say sorry to Anthony at the end?*

## Working with the text

### 1 The story

*Put the headings below in the right order. Which part of the story do they go with? Write in two or three sentences what happens in each part.*

- **A** The attack
- **B** In the subway
- **C** Kelly's real name
- **D** A picnic and an important conversation

*1 B: In the subway (l. 8–39) – Anthony and Kelly ...*

### 2 ○ True or false?

*Read the story again. Which statements are true? Correct the false statements.*

1. Kelly and Anthony played music for money.
2. They didn't get much money in the subway.
3. Anthony was hungry, so they left the subway.
4. Anthony thought the Rambles was a dangerous place for a picnic.
5. The two men took Kelly's guitar.
6. Kelly wanted Anthony to go home with her.
7. Anthony was surprised when he learned where Kelly lived.

### 3 Guess the meaning of the words

**a)** *English words are sometimes like German words. Find these words in the text. Guess what they mean, then check in a dictionary.*

depressing – p. 26, l. 11
drunk – p. 26, l. 24
dumb – p. 26, l. 44
leaned – p. 27, l. 55

**b)** ● *Sometimes you have to think hard about a word or phrase. Look for clues in the text. Think: What could the word mean? Guess these words then check in your dictionary.*

take off – p. 27, l. 66
I just go for it – p. 27, l. 92
I didn't care – p. 27, l. 99

### 4 Extra What will happen next?

**a)** ● *What do you think? Will Anthony be angry with Kelsey? Or will he forgive her? Write a short paragraph.*

**b)** *Go to p. 119 and find out how the story goes on.*

► *WB 19 (p. 16)* • **Checkpoint 1** *WB (p. 17)*

## How am I doing? ▸ SF Check yourself (p. 144)

**STUDY SKILLS** Check yourself

**Remember: Stop – Check – Go!**
Check yourself after every unit. Find out what's giving you problems. Make plans to improve your English in these areas. 'How am I doing?' will help you to do that.

***a)*** *Choose or find the correct answers.*

### New York

1 The city of New York has got five ...
A areas. B parts. C boroughs. D sections.

2 Many of the famous sights in New York (like the Empire State Building) are in ...
A Staten Island. B Manhattan. C Brooklyn. D the Bronx. E Queens.

3 Downtown Manhattan is ...
A under ground. B a poor area. C in the south of Manhattan. D where the airport is.

4 When Americans speak of 9/11, they mean the date when planes flew into ...
A the Empire State Building. B the World Trade Center. C Ground Zero. D Times Square.

5 What can't you get in a deli?
A a bagel with cream cheese B a sandwich C a bagel with lox D a cellphone

6 The place where immigrants came into the USA is called ...
A the Statue of Liberty. B Ellis Island. C Liberty Island. D the Brooklyn Bridge.

### British English (BE) – American English (AE)

7 What are these BE words in AE?
mobile phone – trousers – pavement – crisps

8 What are these AE words in BE?
elevator – line (Warteschlange) – subway – vacation

### Words

9 Which word does *not* mean 'very good'?
A awesome B awful C great D fantastic

10 The job of a firefighter is to ... fires
A put on B put off C put out D put up

11 The library is three ... west of here.
A parks B blocks C corners D sidewalks

12 Where can you *not* sleep?
A motel B tent C hotel D deli

### Grammar

13 ... in the Grand Canyon is very exciting.
A Hike B Hiked C Hiking D Hikes

14 Janet is good at ... the guitar.
A to play B the play of C play D playing

15 Put in *if* or *when*:
a) ... you had lots of money, you could fly to New York in your next holidays.
b) ... I ever go to New York, I want to go up the Empire State Building.
c) ... I was in New York last June, I saw Times Square.

***b)*** *Check your answers on p. 260 and add up your points – one for each correct answer.*

***c)*** *If you had 18 or more points, well done! Maybe you can help students who had fewer points. If you had 17 points or fewer, it's a good idea to do some more work before you go on to the next unit. Where did you make mistakes? The chart below will tell you what you can do to improve your English.*

| No. | Areas | Find out more | Exercises |
|---|---|---|---|
| 1– 6 | New York | Unit 1 (pp. 12–17) | P 1 (p. 20), WB 1–2 (p. 6) |
| 7– 8 | American English | Unit 1 (p. 14) | P 2 (p. 20), WB 3 (p. 7), 5 (p. 8) |
| 9–12 | Words | Vocabulary (pp. 174–178) | WB 6 (p. 8), 8 (p. 9), 17 (p. 14) |
| 13–14 | The gerund | GF 1 (pp. 161–162) | P 4, 6–7 (pp. 21–22), WB 7 (p. 9), 9 (p. 10), 12–13 (p. 12) |
| 15 | if/when | P 11–12 (p. 24) | WB 14 (p. 13) |

## 1 WORDS In a city

*Look at this picture of an American city. Write down words for as many things and people as you can.*

## 2 WORDS Describing towns and cities

***a)*** *Complete the sentences with words that mean the opposite.*

1 A town can be large or *small*.
2 It can be in the east or the ... of a country.
3 It can be exciting or ...
4 It can be noisy or ...
5 The buildings can be old or ...
6 The streets can be clean or ...
7 It can be a safe or a ... city.
8 Life there can be awful or ...

***b)*** *Write a text about the picture in 1.*

– What/Who can you see in the picture?
– Is the city old, clean, ...?
– What things do you think you can do in the city?
– Would you like to live there? Give reasons.

▸ *SF Describing pictures (p. 147)*

## 3 You aren't allowed to park here! (Modal verbs)

*Complete each sentence with an expression from the box.*

you don't have to • you have to • you're allowed to • you aren't allowed to

1 Look at that NO PARKING sign! ... park here!
2 ... drive on the right in the US.
3 But ... drive on the right in England!
4 Can you play football in the park? – Sure, and ... skate there too.
5 ... to take the subway to get to Central Park. It's only two blocks away.
6 If you visit the sports museum on Saturday, ... buy a ticket. It's free at weekends.
7 In many restaurants in the US ... wait until the hostess seats you.
8 Sorry, no cameras, please. ... take photos here.

## 4 What did you do last weekend? (Simple past)

*Rachel is telling her friend what she did last Saturday morning. Finish the sentences with the correct forms of the verbs. Use the* ***simple past****.*

1 On Saturday morning I ... (get up) at 7 o'clock.
*On Saturday morning I got up at 7 o'clock.*
2 I ... (feel) fit, although it ... (be) so early in the morning.
3 After breakfast I ... (take) the bus into town.
4 First, I ... (go) to Jeans World.
5 I ... (want) to buy some jeans but they ... (have) the ones I liked best in my size.
6 Outside in the street, I ... (meet) Karen and Amy from our class. What a nice surprise!
7 They ... (show) me their new magazines and we ... (look at) those and ... (chat).
8 Suddenly I ... (notice) the time! It was 1.30 pm. Unfortunately, I ... (have) to go home.
9 I ... (run) to the bus stop and I just ... (catch) the bus.
10 My parents ... (be) happy because I ... (get) home late. I ... (say) sorry and ... (promise) to come home earlier next time.

## 5 STUDY SKILLS Writing better sentences (Linking words)

*In a test, you might have to write an e-mail or a letter. Remember that* ***linking words*** *can make them more interesting. Link the pairs of sentences with the words in the box.*

although • and • because • but • or • so that • that • who

1 I like my town. It's big and exciting.
*I like my town because it's big and exciting.*
2 I often look at expensive clothes. I never buy them!
3 I often eat chips. I know they're bad for me!
4 We could go to the cinema. We could watch a DVD at home.
5 Yesterday we saw a guy. He sells fun T-shirts.
6 Aaron's is a deli. It sells great bagels.
7 My mum often gives me money. I can go out with my friends.
8 My favourite place in town is the park. It's quiet and really pretty.
9 The film was long. It was boring too.

▸ *SF Writing course (p. 154)*

## 6 What do you like doing? (Gerunds)

**a)** *Work with a partner. Brainstorm ideas about things you like doing. Make a network.*

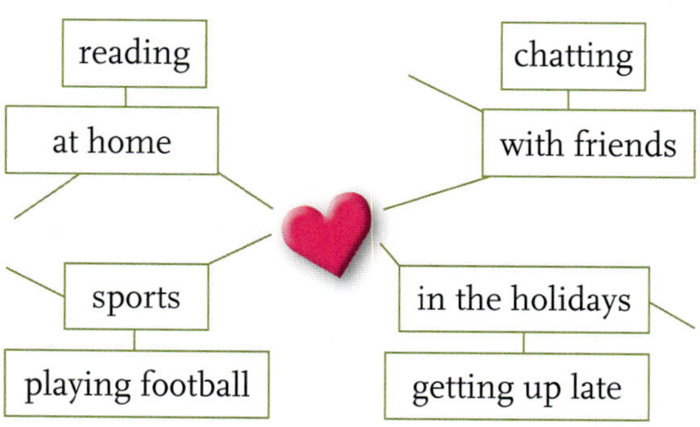


▸ *WB 1–5 (pp. 18–19) • SF How to do well in a test (pp. 158–159)*

**b)** *Make sentences that are true for you with words and phrases from your network.*
– I like ... when I'm at home/with friends.
– I (really) like/love/enjoy ...
– I'm (very) interested in ...
– My hobby/My favourite activity is...

**STUDY SKILLS How to do well in a test**

If you have to take a test, you should
– start preparing a week before
– make sure you understand the instructions
– make sure how to answer multiple-choice questions.
Look for help in the **Skills File**.

## 1 Reading

*Greg Zimmermann is a teenager from New York. Read his blog this week and do the tasks below.*



**New York's yellow taxis are going green!**

Hi! What do you think of when you hear the words New York? Skyscrapers? Delis? Central Park? The Statue of Liberty? I love all those things too, but for me, there's another thing that is so typical of the city. Taxis. The famous yellow New York taxicabs.

Taxicabs are everywhere in New York. In fact, there are 13,000 of them. Over half of all the cars you see in Manhattan are taxis. That's great if you need a cab. You can usually get one easily on the street. But there is a problem. They use a lot of gas – around a gallon every hour (that's 3.8 liters for you guys in Europe!). And all that gas makes the air in New York dirty. Very dirty!

But now something interesting is happening. The cabs are going green. No, I don't mean that people are painting them a different color. The cabs will still be yellow like always. But they'll be 'environmentally friendly'[1]. The old cabs will slowly go, and there'll be new ones.

The new cabs (there are almost 400 of them in the city already), will be 'hybrid cabs'. What does that mean? A normal cab uses gas all the time. A hybrid cab uses gas and electricity. It has a normal gas motor, and then it also has a battery[2] and an electric motor. It uses the electric motor when it's going slowly

– and when it's stopped at a traffic light. And it uses the gas motor when it travels more quickly. Result: cleaner air! Cool.

Everybody is excited about the new cabs. The mayor[3] was on TV yesterday. His idea is that New York's image is really important. When tourists come here, they don't want to visit a dirty city. They want to find a place that's modern and that cares about[4] the environment.

And what do the cab drivers think? Our neighbor, Mr. Janjma, drives one of the new cabs, so I asked him. "Cab drivers have to buy their cabs," he said, "and the new ones cost more than the old ones. But they don't use so much gas. I save about 30 dollars a day now. I'm really happy!"

Until next week! Stay safe!
Greg

**a)** *Choose the right answers:*

1 New York taxicabs …
A aren't typical of the city. B don't use much gas. C make the city's air dirty. D aren't a problem.

2 In future, New York's taxicabs will …
A change colour. B be environmentally friendly. C travel slowly. D only drive in Manhattan.

3 A hybrid taxi …
A has two motors. B has a motor and a battery. C uses only gas. D uses only electricity.

4 The mayor of New York says that the city should be … for tourists.
A dirty B famous C cool D clean

5 Mr Janjma … green taxi.
A pays $ 30 a day for his B likes his C never drives his D hasn't got a

**b)** *Finish the sentences.*

1 There are … taxis in New York and they use about … litres of gas every hour.
2 There are already almost … hybrid cabs.
3 A hybrid cab only uses gas when it …
4 Mr Janjma saves money now because …

[1] environmentally friendly [ɪnˌvaɪrənmentəli 'frendli] *umweltfreundlich* [2] battery ['bætri] *Akku, Batterie* [3] mayor [meə] *Bürgermeister/in*
[4] (to) care about ['keər‿əbaʊt] *achten auf*

## 2 Reading

*Here are some signs that you might see in town. Write a sentence for six of the signs. Use the phrases from the box.*
*Sign 1: You aren't allowed to …*

– You are/aren't allowed to … where you see this sign.
– You (don't) have … when you see this sign.

Signs

## 3 Writing

*Choose one of the tasks below (a or b). Write an e-mail of 100–120 words. Think of a nice beginning and ending for your e-mail. Count your words at the end.*

***a)*** *Chloe is your new American penfriend[1] and she wants to know something about the place where you live. What about the following things.*

Where in Germany? … in/near a village/town? shops and buildings old? famous? What's there to do? Do you like it? Why (not)?

***b)*** *Your British penfriend Robert wants to know what you did last weekend. Tell him:*
*– what you did on Saturday and Sunday*
*– who you did it with*
*– if it was fun/boring/…*
*Use* **time phrases** *(in the morning, after lunch, …) and* **linking words** *(because, although, so that, …).*

## 4 Speaking

*You're starting an internet project with a school in Boston in the US. In your class you are making sound files about yourselves. Say who you are, then talk about 'What I like doing' for about one minute.*

[1] penfriend ['penfrend] *Brieffreund/in*

# California, the 'Golden State'?

## 1 What did you know?

***a)*** *Look at the photos and read the information about California.*
*What did you know already? What didn't you know before?*

I knew/I didn't know that ...
- Hollywood is part of Los Angeles.
- California is near Mexico.
- ...

***b)*** *What else do you know about California?*

**A** Tsunamis and earthquakes can happen here!

**B** Everyone likes to go to the beach. You see lots of homeless people there too.

**C** You can drive 1200 miles along the coast of California on Highway 101.

**D** San Francisco is famous for the Golden Gate Bridge – and for fog!

## 2 California sounds

*a) Listen. Which sound file (1–8) goes with which photo (A–H)?*

*b) Listen again and finish these sentences.*

1 In the afternoon it will be (foggy/sunny).
2 Luis's parents are (Spanish/Mexican).
3 When he came to California the governor had ($ 20/$ 220).
4 One boy met a homeless person (at the beach/in town).
5 The park ranger says the visitors can stay for (one night/two nights).
6 The girls (know/don't know) who Errol Flynn is.
7 If you're at the beach and there's an earthquake, you should (leave/stay).
8 The road will be open again at (9.30/10.30).

► *SF Listening (p. 148)*

## 3 Extra SONG California

*Listen to the song from the TV series 'The OC'.*

*a) How do you feel when you listen to the song? What comes to your mind?*

I feel happy/relaxed/cool ...
I think of ...

*b) Which photo goes best with the song?*

► *P 1–4 (pp. 42–43)* • *WB 1–3 (p. 20–21)* • **Text File 5** *(pp. 128–129)*

**E** This is Yosemite National Park. It's just one of eight national parks in California.

**F** Hollywood is part of L.A. – tourists come here to see the stars.

**G** This man moved from Austria to California. Later he became governor of the state.

**H** They grow fruit and vegetables in California. Lots of Mexicans cross the border to work on the farms.

## 1 Business in California

### General facts

Farmers grow all kinds of fruit and vegetables in California because most of the time the weather is very warm and sunny. Central Valley is California's most important farming area. Strawberries, lettuce and oranges are grown on huge industrial farms. Over 85 % of America's strawberries are produced in California.

A lot of wine is produced there too. Have a look in your local supermarket. Maybe they sell wine from California. Californian wine is sold all over the world.

An area in the Santa Clara Valley near San Francisco is called 'Silicon Valley'. It's the world centre of the computer industry. Lots of famous hi-tech companies are found there. Their products are used by people all over the world at home and at work.

Tourists are very important for California. Theme parks like Disneyland, SeaWorld and Six Flags Magic Mountain are big attractions. Of course the visitors have to eat. Four million burgers are eaten in Disneyland every year.

*Strawberry fields in Central Valley*

*Growing grapes in Napa Valley*

*Hi-tech companies in Silicon Valley*

*Six Flags Magic Mountain, near Los Angeles*

*Scan the text and answer these questions:*
1 What is grown on Californian farms?
2 Where can you buy Californian wine?
3 What kind of companies are there in Silicon Valley?
4 What are the names of two theme parks in California?
5 How many burgers are eaten in Disneyland in one year?

► *SF Scanning (p. 150)*

**Looking at language**

Farmers **grow** all kinds of fruit and vegetables.
Strawberries **are grown** on huge farms.

***a)*** *Which of the two sentences tells you who grows something and which doesn't?*

***b)*** ***are grown*** *is a passive verb form. To make this form you need a form of the verb* ***be*** *and the* ***past participle****. Find more passive forms in* ***1****.*

***c)*** *Make sentences in the passive:*
- Most American strawberries ... (produce) in California.
- Maybe Californian wine ... (sold) in your supermarket too.
- Millions of burgers ... (eat) in California's many theme parks every year.

► *GF 2a–c: Passive (p. 163) • P 5–6 (p. 44) • WB 4–8 (pp. 22–23)*

# All about ... growing up in two cultures

## 2 Letters to the editor

Last week we asked our readers about their attitudes to minorities and immigration. Here are some of the letters we got from California.

### "I don't fit in"

I'm Korean, and I hate being a member of a minority. When I started school some of the students laughed at me because I was different. I didn't look like the others and I spoke almost no English. It was a terrible experience.

I can't take anyone home with me. My mom doesn't speak much English and she only cooks Korean dishes. So people don't invite me to their houses. I just don't fit in because I belong to the wrong ethnic group.

*Kim L. (16), Eureka, CA*

### "Lucky to live in America"

I was born in California, so I'm a US citizen. But I'm proud to be a Latino. I've never thought of it as a disadvantage.

I'm growing up in two cultures, so I speak English and Spanish. In my opinion, being bilingual is an advantage. It will be useful when I look for a job and will help me to be successful at what I do.

Where I live, Latinos and "Anglos" get on well together – I've never experienced any discrimination. I know that isn't true everywhere – there's a lot of prejudice in our country.

I feel very lucky to live in America, where you can succeed if you have the right attitude.

*Luis M. (14), San Clemente, CA*

### "Learn the language"

I'm not prejudiced against immigrants, and I would never discriminate against them. But I believe people who want to live in this country should try and fit in. They should learn the language and act like real Americans!

*Ashley S. (15), Los Angeles, CA*

*Find reasons in the letters why it is important that immigrants learn the language of their new country. What is your opinion? What do your classmates think?*

**Americana ★ ★ ★**

**Californians**

With about 37 million people, California has the largest population of all the 50 American states. One in three Californians is Latino. That means that they, or their families, are from Spanish-speaking countries like Mexico or Puerto Rico. (Another word for Latino is Hispanic.)

## 3 Words and phrases

***a)*** *Find words in the letters which mean:*

- an American – a US ...
- a good thing – an ...
- it will help me – it will be ...
- you can do well – you can ...
- I don't feel happy here – I don't ...
- people think badly about other people without a good reason – there's a lot of ...
- a small group – a ...
- I belong to this group – I'm a ...

***b)*** *Find English phrases for:*

- Ich würde Immigranten niemals diskriminieren.
- Ich finde, ...
- Ich habe es nie als Nachteil empfunden.
- Meiner Meinung nach ...
- Wir kommen gut miteinander aus.

► P 7–9 (pp. 44–45) • WB 9–10 (pp. 23–24)

## 4 How was your day?

After cleaning and cooking in two houses, Mrs Morales took the bus back to Avenida Pico. It was six o'clock now and she had to hurry. Today was one of the days when she had a third job in the evening – as a waitress.

'Hi!' she called out as she opened the front door. Maria ran to her.

Luis turned off the TV. 'Hey, Mom! You look tired. How was your day?'

'Ah, hijo mio! Lots of trouble. At the Whites', the gardener – old Señor Fuentes – was attacked by the dog. And at the Taylors', the twins were sent home from school and ...'

'There was lots of trouble at our school too, Mama,' said Diego. 'Manuel's bike was stolen! And José was bullied by Sam again ... he was taken to the hospital, and ...'

'Oh, look at the time!' Mrs Morales saw the clock on the wall. 'I have to leave again in half an hour. Did you go to the supermarket, Luis?'

'Yes, of course, Mom,' said Luis. 'I bought everything for dinner.'

'Fine, thanks. Then let's hurry and make dinner.'

'First a story, Mama, please,' begged Maria. 'The story about you and Papa when you came across the border to California.'

'First dinner, then, if there's time, a story, bebita mia.'

*How was Mrs Morales's day? And Diego's?*

▸ *GF 2d: Passive with 'by' (p. 164) • P 10–12 (pp. 45–46) • WB 11–15 (pp. 24–26)*

**Americana ★ ★ ★**

**The border**

*Many illegal immigrants are killed in car accidents as they run away from the border patrols.*

The border between the US and Mexico runs from San Diego, California, in the west to Brownsville, Texas, in the east. It's over 3000 km long. Along parts of the border the US government has built a high fence to stop the thousands of illegal immigrants. Almost half (3.8 million) of all Mexican immigrants in the US live in California.
A lot of legal and illegal Mexican immigrants work on farms and in factories, or they do house or garden work. Often the women work as nannies. Most work for very little money.

## 5 A family story

***a)*** *Read the questions on the right. Then listen to Mrs Morales's story and take notes.*

***b)*** *Answer the questions. Then listen again to check your answers.*

▸ *SF Taking notes (p. 149) • P 13–15 (pp. 47–48) • WB 16–19 (pp. 26–27) •* **Text File 6** *(pp. 130–131)*

1. Why did Mr and Mrs Morales leave Mexico?
2. Did she and her husband cross the border as legal or illegal immigrants?
3. Did they find work quickly?
4. Where was their first job?
5. After they arrived in California there was an amnesty. What did that mean for them?

## 6 Extra The California dream

# VISIT COLOMA,

## WHERE THE CALIFORNIA GOLD RUSH BEGAN

**The Marshall Gold Discovery State Historic Park, Coloma, California**

**GOLD!** The Gold Rush started when a piece of gold was discovered by James Marshall in Coloma in 1848. 300,000 people rushed to California to look for gold between 1849 and 1855.

Today Coloma is a state park. A statue of James Marshall can be seen in the park, and lots of houses from the old days can be visited there too.

Learn about the history of California's gold towns and have fun at the same time.

Come and see how people lived in the 1850s. And YOU can look for gold too. These pans can be bought in our shop. You might be lucky! There are special events throughout the summer. Tickets will be sold online. Check our website for details.

Where to find us? Just off Highway 49, about 60 miles north-east of Sacramento

> 1 *Would you like to visit this state park? Skim the brochure, then say why/why not.*
2 *Why is there a statue of James Marshall in Coloma?*

▸ Extra *GF 2e: Passive (p. 164) • P 16 (p. 48) • WB 20–21 (p. 28)*

## 7 Extra Now you

*Say something about your area. The questions below can help you.*

- What is your town/area famous for?
- Who is remembered in your area and why?
- What is grown/produced/made there?
- When were the oldest buildings built?

## 8 Extra PROJECT More on California

**Step 1:** *In groups of four, fill in a placemat with interesting topics about California – jobs, free-time activities, minorities, sights, ... Agree on four topics. Each member of the group takes one.*

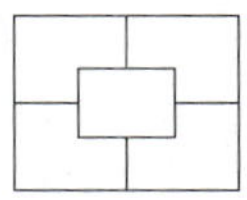

**Step 2:** *Collect information and words and phrases that have to do with your topic.*

**Step 3:** *In your group decide how you will present your project – posters/OHP/... Who will start/be next/...*

**Step 4:** *Prepare your presentation.*

**Step 5:** *Check what you have written.*

**Step 6:** *Practise, and present your information.*

▸ *SF Giving a presentation (p. 147)*

**Extra** Background File **WELCOME TO CALIFORNIA!**

# California, the Golden State,

is the third largest of the fifty states of the US, and it has more people than any other state.
In 1848, gold was discovered in California. People from the East heard the news and crossed America to join the Gold Rush. This made California more attractive to the US and in 1850 it became the thirty-first state of the United States of America.

Today California is very rich. Its money comes from:

- farming: fruit, vegetables and wine
- the computer industry in Silicon Valley
- natural resources – oil, gas and gold
- the entertainment industry – films and TV
- tourism – the national parks, San Francisco, Hollywood and much more.

## *Let's go to San Francisco ...*

... where you can see the Golden Gate Bridge, gateway to the Pacific Ocean. The city is built on hills and known for its beautiful views.
When you're in San Francisco, don't forget to take a ride on a cable car – it's the best way to see the city.

San Francisco is a financial and communications centre, and a centre for trade with Asia. It's one of the richest areas in California. However, not everyone is rich. The city's homeless population is very high.

## *... where the earth moves ...*

One problem for the people in San Francisco – and large parts of California – is earthquakes. In 1906 about 3000 people were killed by a great earthquake and the fire that followed it. More than half of San Francisco's population lost their homes. In the 1989 earthquake 57 people died and again there was a lot of damage.
Remember if there's an earthquake:
'Drop, cover and hold on!'

- drop down under a strong table
- cover your eyes
- hold on to a table leg.

► **Text File 7** *(pp. 132–133)*

## ... or to the world-famous Sequoia National Park ...

There are eight beautiful national parks in California. The Sequoia National Park is where the giant sequoia trees grow – the tallest (up to 110 metres) and oldest trees in the world. Some are over 2000 years old.

## ... and maybe end up in Los Angeles

It's the largest city in California (second largest in the US) and it has a very famous suburb: Hollywood, or 'The Dream Factory'. The first Hollywood movie was made in 1910. The great weather and locations (sea, mountains, deserts) brought movie makers and stars to L. A., and to this day Hollywood dominates the world of film and TV.

### 1 Gallery walk

***a)*** *Make six groups. Each group gets a statement. Write your statement on a piece of paper. Discuss and complete it. Hang your piece of paper on the classroom wall.*

***b)*** *With your group, move from statement to statement, discuss each one and add your own comment.*

***c)*** *When you have added a comment to all the statements, return to your own. Discuss the other groups' comments on your statement.* ► WB 22 (p. 29)

Statements:

1. The place we'd like to visit in California is ...
2. The things we like best that come from California are ...
3. The Hollywood star we'd like to meet is ...
4. The Hollywood star we wouldn't like to meet is ...
5. For us California is the Golden State because ...
6. For us California isn't the Golden State because ...

## 1 WORDS California words

***a)*** *Group the words from the box in a chart or a mind map. You can use the group words on the right or find your own group words. Collect more words as you work through the unit.*

actors • beach • border • career • drive along the coast • destroy • dream of • earthquakes • film stars • foggy • forest fires • Golden Gate Bridge • governor • grow fruit and vegetables • highways • Hollywood • homeless people • hot • immigrants • lettuce • Mexicans • national parks • park rangers • produce movies • put out a fire • relax in the sun • Sacramento • state capital • strawberries • sunny • surfers • tomatoes • tsunamis • warm • wine • Yosemite

California

dangers | people | weather | activity | film | places

***b)*** *Complete the sentences about California. Use words from the box and add as much as you can. Then make other sentences with words from the box.*

1 California has lots of things for tourists. They can go to .../visit .../drive to .../...
2 You see lots of different people in California, for example ... – They/He ...
3 There are some dangers in California. For example, they have ...
4 They grow lots of ... in California, because most of the time the weather is ...

## 2 WORDS Synonyms

***a)*** *Find a word or phrase in the yellow box that means the same as a word in the green box.*

afraid • also • awful • close • correct • difficult • film • great • kid • leave • loud • now • sad • start

at the moment • begin • child • fantastic • go away • hard • movie • near • noisy • right • scared • terrible • too • unhappy

***b)*** *Choose six words from the boxes and make sentences: We had a great time in California.*

***c)*** *Read your sentences to your partner. He/She says the sentence again but uses a synonym.*
*A:* We had a great time in California.
*B:* We had a fantastic time in California.

***d)*** **Extra** *Choose three words from each box and try to write a story that uses all of them.*

## 3 WORDS Word building (-less)

*Add -less to the nouns in the box to make adjectives. Then complete the sentences with them.*

cloud • end • head • help • home • job • sleep • tooth

1 I'm so tired. Last night I had a ... night.
2 Ben never stops talking. I hate his ... stories.
3 The weather was great. The sun shone from a ... sky.
4 He didn't know what to do – he just ran around like a ... chicken.

5 The number of ... people in the town went up after the factory closed.
6 Little babies always look so ...
7 The old man gave us a ... smile.
8 Thousands of ... people sleep on the streets of L. A.

## 4 READING Endless summer surf camp (Skimming and scanning) ▸ SF p. 150

***a)*** *You want to learn to surf. You'd like to find a surf camp where you can have fun, stay overnight and have all your meals.*

***Skim*** *the website.*
*Has the camp got what you're looking for?*

**Remember**

***Skimming*** helps you to find the main ideas of a text quickly.
- Look at the title, words in bold print or in capital letters, pictures and their captions.
- Often it is useful to read the first and last sentence of each paragraph quickly.
- Don't read the whole text word for word.

***b)*** *You think the* Endless summer surf camp *might be right for you, but you have some specific questions (see 1–6 below).*

***Scan*** *the website.*
*What key words in each of these questions might help you to find the information you need?*

1 How many days can I spend at this surf camp?
2 How big are the surf groups?
3 I don't eat meat. Do they have vegetarian meals?
4 Do they do video analysis of students' surfing?
5 Will I be able to watch TV or play games?
6 Can I share a tent with my boyfriend/girlfriend?

**Remember**

***Scanning*** helps you to find specific information in a long text.
- Picture specific words in your mind.
- Don't read. Move your eyes over the page:
  – across the page in an 'S' or
  – down and up the page in a 'U'.

**At our 5-day surf camps we offer**
- **quality surfing lessons**
- **video analysis of your surfing practice**
- **expert surf coaches**
- **great surfing equipment**
- **comfortable tents**
- **delicious meals**

### Surf training

You've never surfed before? You want to learn new tricks and become a better surfer? Then we've got what you're looking for! Our coaches work with you in small groups of 3, so every student gets individual help.

### Relaxing and sleeping

You sleep in large and comfortable tents (boys and girls separate). And at the campsite you'll find a game area with table tennis and beach volleyball. There's also a lounge with sofas where you can watch a movie on TV, read a book or just listen to music and hang out.

### Meals

Three meals a day, plus snacks and drinks! Start the day with a hearty breakfast at the camp. Enjoy a relaxed lunch of sandwiches, summer fruits and other snacks on the beach. And round it all off with a great dinner back at camp every evening. There's a vegetarian alternative at every meal.

## 5 //O A quiz (Passive – simple present) ▸ D p. 112

***a)*** *Write sentences. Choose the correct form of the verb in brackets.*

1 Spanish (is/are) spoken in Portugal (I)/Mexico (H)/Italy (L).
*Spanish is spoken in ...*
2 California (is/are) called the Yellow State (R)/Orange State (Q)/Golden State (Y).
3 Most US strawberries (is/are) grown in Alaska (M)/California (W)/New York (N).
4 Computer software (is/are) made in Napa Valley (K)/Silicon Valley (L)/Central Valley (M).
5 Californian wine (is/are) sold in the US (S)/in Canada (T)/all over the world (O).
6 Park rangers (is/are) found at all American beaches (H)/national parks (O)/stations (J).
7 Most of the big films (is/are) made in Los Angeles (D)/San Francisco (T)/New York (N).
8 Oscars (is/are) given to film stars (O)/good sportsmen or sportswomen (P)/governors (Q).
9 Millions of sausages (C)/burgers (L)/cookies (G) (is/are) eaten in Disneyland every year.

***b)*** *The letters behind the correct answers form a word. Write down the letters and find this word.*

## 6 //O What else do you know about California? (Passive – simple present) ▸ D p. 112

*Make passive sentences.*

1 Some of the best beaches in the US *are found* (find) along California's coast.
2 A lot of rubbish ... (pick up) from California's coast every year.
3 Software from California ... (use) in computers all over the world.
4 Every year lots of animals ... (kill) in large forest fires.
5 California's Death Valley ... (visit) by thousands of tourists every year.
6 Californian strawberries ... (sell) all over the US.
7 Lots of workers ... (need) on Californian farms every summer.
8 Lots of Hollywood movies ... (show) in German cinemas.

*Death Valley: one of the hottest places on earth*

*Forest fires in California*

## 7 WORDS Minorities and ethnic groups

***a)*** *Look back at the letters to the editor on p. 37 and find the English phrases for:*

1 Ich gehöre zur falschen ethnischen Gruppe.
2 Ich bin stolz, ein Latino zu sein.
3 Ich wachse in zwei Kulturen auf.
4 Zweisprachig zu sein ist ein Vorteil.
5 Wir kommen gut miteinander aus.
6 Ich habe keine Vorurteile gegen Immigranten.
7 Sie sollten versuchen sich anzupassen.

***b)*** ● *Complete the text on the right. The phrases from a) will help you.*

I'm white, and I'm ... to be an American. My great-grandfather came from Italy and he didn't speak English. Now our family only speaks English, but I still feel I'm growing ... in two ... We eat Italian food and do lots of traditional Italian things. The different ethnic groups ... where I live. I'm sorry I can't speak Italian, because I think speaking two languages is an ... But in the US you have to speak English if you want to ... Even people who aren't ... against immigrants say that people who come to live in America must learn English.

## 8 WRITING More about 'Growing up in two cultures' (Writing letters)

**STUDY SKILLS Writing letters**

There are different rules for writing letters to your family or friends (informal letters) and writing letters to people you don't know at all or only a little (formal letters). It's very important to know how to ***start*** and ***end*** your (formal) letter.

*Write a (formal) letter to the editor about one of the letters on p. 37 – Kim's, Ashley's or Luis's. Say why you agree or disagree with it. Here are two ideas for how you can start. You can add your letter to your DOSSIER.*

20 April …

Dear Sir or Madam

Ashley writes that people who live in America should 'act like real Americans!' I don't belong to a minority, but I don't think …

…

Yours faithfully

…

…

Dear Ms Winter

I thought the letters about growing up in two cultures were really interesting.
I don't live in the US, but I am a member of an ethnic minority too.
I agree with everything Kim wrote. He says that …

Yours sincerely

…

more help ▸ D p. 113

▸ SF Writing letters (p. 156)

## 9 REVISION Being a student is … (Gerund)

**a)** *Complete the sentences. Use the* ***gerund*** *and an adjective. Give reasons.*

1 (be) a student is …
*Being a student is great because you learn lots of important things.*
2 (have) brothers or sisters is …
3 (get up) early is …
4 (write) e-mails is …
5 (go) to school by bike is …
6 (text) someone is …

**b)** *Make appointments with three partners. Compare your ideas.*

A: I think being a student is great because you you learn lots of interesting things. What about you?
B: I don't agree. I think being a student is horrible because you have to do lots of homework.

**c)** *Tell the class what your partners think.*

## 10 // O California was discovered by … (Passive – simple past) ▸ D p. 113

*Look at the pictures. Write down what happened when. Use* ***by*** *if you need it.*

1 California – discovered – Spanish explorers – 1769

2 Golden Gate Bridge – built – Joseph Strauss – 1933–37

3 first film – made – in Hollywood – 1910

4 gold – found – near Sacramento – 1848

5 first jeans – sold – Levi Strauss – in the Gold Rush

6 fourteen people – killed – forest fires – last summer

## 11 Which came first? (Passive – simple past)

***a)*** *Partner B: Go to p. 107. Partner A: Look at each pair of pictures. Guess which of the two came first. Tell your partner what you think.*

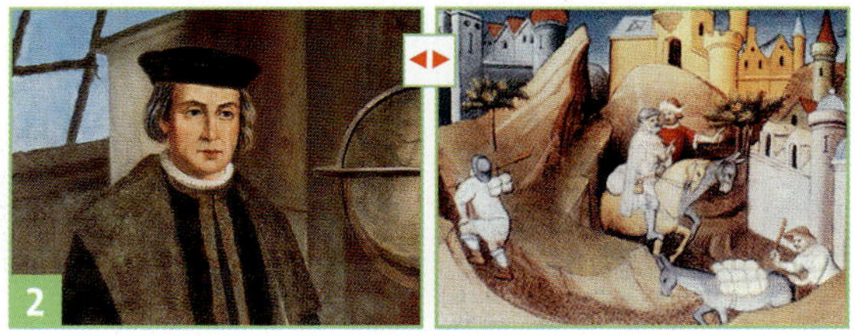

*1* Eiffel Tower (build) first car (make)
*A:* I think the Eiffel Tower was built before the first car was made.
*B:* That's right. / No, that's wrong. The first car was made in ..., the Eiffel Tower was built in ...

*2* North America (discover) by Columbus ◂▸ China (visit) by Marco Polo
*3* first plane (fly) ◂▸ first underground railway (open)
*4* first Mickey Mouse film (show) ◂▸ Ernie and Bert first (see) on TV

***b)*** *Now your partner is going to say what came first. Listen and correct his/her statements if they're wrong. Use these dates.*
*5* popcorn: eaten more than 2000 years ago ◂▸ first pizza: sold in 1889
*6* Golden Gate Bridge: finished in 1937 ◂▸ Empire State Building: built between 1930–1931
*7* first tea bags: sold in 1904 ◂▸ first helicopter: flown in 1907
*8* John F. Kennedy: killed in 1963 ◂▸ Berlin Wall: built in 1961

## 12 An accident – young man crashed into ... (Active and passive)

*Read these notes by a reporter and write his report about an accident. Be careful. Some sentences have to be in the passive.*

- young man on bike crashed into old woman
- old woman fell, hurt her head
- man left quickly, didn't help old woman
- accident seen by young woman
- called ambulance
- woman taken to hospital
- police interviewed young woman
- descriptions sent to all police stations
- same man seen at station minutes after accident
- left bike there
- police didn't find the man

*An accident happened on Park Road yesterday morning.*
*A young man on a bike crashed ...*

more help ▸ D p. 114

EVERYDAY ENGLISH

## 13 MEDIATION Sale! (Understanding and explaining announcements)

*The Walthers from Germany are shopping at a department store in Los Angeles.*
*Listen and explain to Mr Walther in German the important points in each announcement.*

## 14 SPEAKING A picture story

***a)*** *Partner B: Go to p. 108. Partner A: Look at pictures 1–3.*
*Tell the story to your partner. You can use the ideas in the green boxes.*

- Tom and Debbie – new café
- a nice table – in front of the pictures

- ordered – drinks
- laughed – talked
- lots of fun

- suddenly – a bright light
- somebody – shouted
- shocked

***b)*** *Look at pictures 4–6. Listen to your partner's story.*
*Is it the same, or nearly the same, as the story in the orange boxes?*

At that moment Tom and Debbie saw a gun. It was on the floor near their table.

Then a man ran towards them. Debbie screamed loudly. Tom didn't think. He picked up the gun.

Then somebody shouted angrily, 'Cut!' – It was a film director! Tom and Debbie felt really silly.

***c)*** **Extra** *Try and tell the whole story.*

## 15 LISTENING Welcome to San Clemente cinemas

**Tip**

If you call somewhere for information, you might get a recorded message, where you usually have to press buttons on your phone. Don't panic! You can always listen again and you don't have to understand every word.

▸ SF Listening (p. 148)

***a)*** *Imagine you want to take your ten-year-old cousin to the cinema on Saturday afternoon. Listen to **part 1** and fill in a copy of the chart.*

| What numbers do you have to press | |
|---|---|
| – to hear which movies you can see? | ... |
| – to hear the information again? | |
| – to get tickets? | |
| – to listen to the child hotline? | |
| – to find out when the movies start? | |

***b)*** *Look at the poster above. Then listen to **part 2** and find out which of these three movies you may see with your cousin.*

***c)*** *Listen to **part 3**. What time do you have to be at the cinema if you need ten minutes to get your tickets and buy drinks and popcorn?*

## 16 Extra The Golden Gate Bridge (Passive – modals and will-future)

*Match the sentence halves.*

1. For years, San Francisco Bay ...
2. Some engineers wanted to build a bridge, ...
3. When Joseph Strauss started to build it in 1933, people were still sure: ...
4. When the bridge was opened in 1937, ...
5. The bridge had to be closed ...
6. Today the bridge can be used ...
7. The Golden Gate Bridge will always be known ...

... by more than 100,000 cars and lorries a day.
... a couple of times because of strong winds.
... 'That bridge will never be built!'
... as the most famous sight in San Francisco.
... but most people believed it couldn't be done.
... had to be crossed by ferry.
... the bay could be crossed on foot for the first time.

## Santa Monica – Episode 1 of a TV series

*Teen TV*, a new TV station for teenagers in Los Angeles, wants to start with a new teen soap. People are sending lots of scripts. This is one of them.

*Read the start of the script for the series* Santa Monica *and then help to decide if it should become a TV series. Some of the new words in the text aren't in the Dictionary in this book. Try to guess unknown words from the context. Only use your English-German dictionary if you have to.*

▸ *SF Working out the meaning of words (p. 150)* • *SF Using a dictionary (p. 145)*

### Opening titles

*From a helicopter we see the skyscrapers of L.A. We fly out towards the Pacific Ocean and turn down towards Malibu. The series song plays, and as we get near Santa Monica, the opening titles appear.*

### Scene 1 At the beach

*A group of five cool, beautiful rich kids – Brad and Josh, Cindy, Jane and Lara – are walking along the beach in Santa Monica, laughing.*

Lara ... so I'm going to Alaska with my parents in the summer.

Brad You poor thing – I hate the cold.

Lara It's not cold in Alaska in the summer ... is it?

*Brad and Josh look at each other.*

Jane Hey, there's Luke!

*Luke is waving to them from the road.*

Josh He wants us to go surfing with him.

Lara Well, aaaall right! Let's go.

*We see the group walk off the beach.*

### Scene 2 At Luke's car

*Luke, cool like the others, stands by an expensive SUV. On top of it are surfboards. He holds a door open.*

Luke Hey, guys. The surf's good over at Malibu. Make yourselves comfortable and let's go.

Josh Is this the new car?

Luke Sure is.

Cindy Wow! It's real nice, Lukey. *It's clear Cindy likes Luke a lot. He's relaxed.*

Luke Thanks, Cindy.

### Scene 3 On the road

*We're inside the car as it drives along by the sea. Lots of laughter. Josh is in the front with Luke. Brad, Lara, Jane and Cindy are in the back, Jane on Brad's knee, Cindy behind the driver.*

Brad *Pulls out bottle of water from under him, then an orange.* Hey man: You have a lot of stuff in this new car!

Cindy Right!

*She's looking through some clothes she's found on the floor. She holds a T-shirt against herself and shows it to Lara, who is sitting next to her. She throws it into the back. Next a pair of shorts. Both girls laugh. Then she finds a black tie.*

Cindy Even a tie! *From behind she puts the tie round Luke.* Hey, Lukey, I didn't even know you could tie one of these.

Luke *He pushes her away.* Hey Cindy, careful! Sure I can tie a tie!

Josh Look, that girl needs help. *He points to a car at the side of the road. A girl is looking at the engine.* Let's make sure she's OK.

Luke *Stops the car.* Fine, whatever, but make sure you're quick!

*Josh gets out and goes over to the girl.*

Lara Josh is a real nice guy.

Luke Too nice! Look at the car – it's all old and dirty – totally white trash!

*All laugh, except Lara.*

## Scene 4 By the road

*Jenna is looking at the engine. She's puzzled. She's very pretty. She wears the uniform of a coffee shop waitress – a short skirt and blouse. Josh walks over.*

Josh — Hi, can I help you?

*She looks up, sees the SUV, sees Josh.*

Jenna — *Coldly*. Normally I'd say no. But if I don't get to Santa Monica in five minutes I'll lose my job. So, if you know anything about cars ... yes, you can help me.

*Josh quickly begins to check the engine.*

Luke — *Calls from SUV.* Hey, Josh, hurry up!

*Josh looks up.*

Josh — Go on, I'll meet you there.

*He turns back to the car and doesn't look up through the rest of the dialogue.*

Josh — By the way, my name's Josh.

Jenna — I'm Jenna.

Josh — Nice to meet you, Jenna.

*Jenna looks nervously at her watch. Josh stands up straight.*

Josh — There you go!

## Scene 5 A street in Santa Monica

*A café with tables on the street. The old car arrives. Jenna and Josh get out.*

Josh — Go! Go! I'll wait.

Boss — Well, you won't have to wait long!

Jenna, this is the third time you've been late. I warned you: you're fired!

Jenna — Larry, please ...

*The boss goes back into the café. Sadly Jenna turns away and gets back in the car. Josh gets in too.*

## Scene 6 In Jenna's car

Josh — I'm sorry. But it was only a café job.

Jenna — That's what you think!

*Jenna is depressed. Josh looks at her and smiles.*

Josh — Hey Jenna, it's not the end of the world.

Jenna — *Angrily.* Not for you! You and your friends don't have to work for your money – you just ask your parents.

Josh — *Feeling guilty.* I'm sorry.

Jenna — *Still angry.* Yeah. You know... *bitterly* ... I live with my mom in Inglewood – but I guess you never go to that part of town. My dad – at least I think he's my dad – he's in jail. He stole a car, crashed it and then got into a fight. And my mom doesn't have a job. She says that things will change ... But right now I'm the one who has to pay for everything ...

Josh — I'm sorry ...

Jenna — It's not your fault.

Josh — Don't give up, Jenna. I'm sure things will get better. Maybe I can help ...

*Jenna turns off the road. We see Luke's SUV and Josh's friends with their surfboards on the beach.*

Jenna — There are your friends. They're waiting for you.

*Josh opens his door.*

Josh — Do you have a boyfriend, Jenna?

Jenna — *Coldly.* Why?

Josh — *Smiling.* What are you doing tonight?

*Jenna looks at him. She's clearly nervous.*

Jenna — I'm babysitting for our neighbor.

Josh — Give me the address. I might come too.

Jenna — Why?

Josh — Because I want to get to know you.

Jenna — Seriously?

Josh — Seriously.

Jenna — But Mrs Alvarez doesn't want me to bring anyone.

Josh — Just this one time.

Jenna — *Pause.* 41 Hayden Street.

Josh — 41 Hayden Street. *He jumps out.* Thanks for the ride.

*He closes the door and Jenna drives off.*

## Scene 7 The kitchen at Jenna's house

*Jenna is cleaning the small, cheap kitchen. We hear the front door open.*

Mom — *Calling.* Hi baby! I'm home.

Jenna — Hi, Mom.

*She goes through to the living room which is small and shabby.*

## Scene 8 The living room at Jenna's house

*Jenna's mom has just dropped her keys on a table by the phone and is falling onto the sofa.*

Mom — I met this real nice guy ...

Jenna — *Bored.* Who is it this time, Mom?

Mom — Whoever you'd like! *She laughs.* Superman, Batman, Rambo ...

Jenna — Oh, Mom. You're drunk again. You promised ...

Mom — Oh, Jenna baby, don't get angry. *She tries to get up.* Where are my cigarettes? *She sees them on the table next to her, takes one and lights it.*

Jenna — And you promised ...

*Mom closes her eyes as she smokes. Jenna gives up.*

Jenna — I lost my job today.

Mom — *Opens eyes.* My poor baby. Things will change, I'm sure. You'll get another job, I'll get another job – things will work out, baby. Hey, let's go out for a drink tonight, just you and me ...

Jenna — *Sadly.* I'm babysitting for Mrs Alvarez tonight, Mom. *Gets ready to go.*

Mom — Aw, don't go, baby. It's so depressing, here, all alone.

*Jenna kisses her mom.*

Jenna — I'm sorry, Mom. I know. But Mrs Alvarez has to work and since her niece doesn't have time tonight, I promised to help. And it's ten dollars. See you.

## Scene 9 Malibu Beach

*Brad and Jane are in the water. The others are sitting on the beach and talking.*

Cindy — Hey, look at that girl – she's real fat.

Lara — No, she isn't, Cindy. Just because she isn't skinny like you doesn't make her fat.

Luke — I'm not so sure.

*He and Cindy laugh. Lara looks at Josh. He's looking out to sea.*

Luke — So, what are we doing tonight, guys?

Cindy — There's a party over at Melissa's house. We could ...

Josh — *Angry.* Hey Cindy, all you ever think about is parties and surfing ... don't you believe in anything ... in anything more important?

Cindy — Shopping.

*Cindy and Luke laugh. Josh gets up angrily.*

Lara — I believe in lots of things, Josh.

*He looks down at her.*

Josh — I know.

Lara — So, what do you want to do tonight?

Josh — I'm busy. I'll call you tomorrow, OK?

*He walks off. Cindy leans over to Lara.*

Cindy — Don't worry, Lara. He'll be back.

Lara — I'm not so sure ...

## Scene 10 The Alvarez house – the living room

*The front door opens onto the living room, all other rooms open from there. It's very clean and tidy. Jenna stands at a bedroom door, looking in. She turns off the bedroom light and very quietly closes the door – clearly the kids are asleep. Outside somebody knocks at the door. She goes over, checks who it is and opens the door. Josh stands there with boxes of Chinese food.*

Josh — Hi.

Jenna — Oh, it's you. You shouldn't be here.

Josh — Hungry?

Jenna — *Smells the food.* OK, just this one time.

*She lets him come in. They sit down.*

### Scene 11 Party at a rich house

*One of the guests, standing alone, is Lara. We see a young waiter offer her some food.*

Lara — No thanks.

Waiter — *Whispers.* You OK?

Lara — Yeah, sure. *She smiles weakly.* Thanks.

### Scene 12 The Alvarez house – the living room

*The meal is finished. Jenna and Josh are on the white sofa. She's drinking a coffee. Josh suddenly turns to her, the coffee spills on the sofa.*

Jenna — *Jumps up.* Oh, no!

Josh — It's only coffee!

Jenna — Only coffee! Look at the sofa – and it's new.

Josh — *Gets up.* I'll clean it up. Where's the kitchen?

Jenna — No, I'll try to clean it up.

Josh — No, let me ...

*Jenna goes to the kitchen and gets a towel.*

Jenna — *Angry and worried.* I'll do it! You shouldn't even be here.

Josh — Hey, let's not get into an argument over a little coffee.

Jenna — I'll take it from here, Josh. I think you should leave.

Josh — Hey, Jenna. I thought we were having a good time. You're a mystery.

Jenna — This whole thing was a bad idea. Just go, Josh!

*Josh goes to the door, his feelings hurt.*

Josh — Bye Jenna.

Jenna — Bye.

## Working with the text

### 1 The scenes

*Say in 1–2 sentences what each scene is about.*

Scene 1: Brad, Josh, Cindy, Jane and Lara meet at the beach.

Scene 2: Luke invites them to go to Malibu in his car. They want to go surfing there.

Scene 3: They see a girl at the side of ...

### 2 The characters

**a)** *Write a sentence about how each person feels about the other. Why do you think that? Find examples from the script.*

1 Josh and Lara — 3 Luke and Cindy

2 Brad and Jane — 4 Josh and Jenna

**b)** *Discuss the following lines. Why do you think the characters say them?*

1 Cindy (l. 25): 'Wow! It's real nice, Lukey.'
2 Luke (ll. 55–56): 'Too nice! ... white trash!'
3 Josh (l. 113): 'I'm sorry.'
4 Lara (l. 204): 'I'm not so sure ...'
5 Jenna (l. 248): 'This whole thing was a bad idea.'

► *WB 23 (p. 30)* • **Checkpoint 2** *WB (p. 31)* • *Selbsteinschätzung 1–2 WB (pp. 32–33)*

### 3 Teen TV series

**a)** *What do you think makes a good TV series for teens? Think of American and German series you know and like. What do they show?*

romance • divorce • fights • arguments • comedy • music • everyday life • jealousy • social problems • money problems

**b)** *Do you think* Teen TV *should produce the series* Santa Monica *or not? Write a short report or give a talk. Give reasons for your opinion. You can use phrases like these:*

*I think Teen TV should / shouldn't make this soap ...*
*The episode is awesome / boring / difficult to understand / ...*
*I like / don't like that it shows ...*

### 4 Extra And next week ...

**a)** *Write one or two scenes for the start of the next episode of* Santa Monica.

**b)** *Read your scripts. Vote for your favourite. Practise it in your group.*

**c)** *Each group reads its favourite script to the class. Vote for the best.*

## How am I doing? ► SF Check yourself (p. 144)

***a)*** *Find or choose the correct answers.*

### California

1 California is sometimes called ...
A the Golden State. B the Orange State. C the Sunny State. D the Surfing State.

2 There are lots of computer companies in ...
A San Clemente. B Yosemite. C Silicon Valley. D San Diego.

3 Because many of the people in California come from Mexico, they speak ...
A Mexican. B English. C French. D Spanish.

4 People who cross the border from Mexico to the US without papers are called ... immigrants.
A bad B illegal C bilingual D border

5 The famous bridge on the US west coast is ... A the Brooklyn Bridge. B Tower Bridge C the Golden Gate Bridge. D Harbour Bridge.

### Study Skills

6 If you skim a text, you *don't* ...
A look at captions. B look at pictures. C look at the title. D read every word.

7 Scanning helps you to find ...
A the main ideas of a text. B good pictures. C specific information. D a translation.

8 If you write a letter to a person you don't know, you end your letter with:
A Love B Talk soon! C Yours faithfully D CU soon

### Words

9 Lots of hi-tech ... are found in Silicon Valley.
A farms B supermarkets C companies D theme parks

10 Large farms are usually called ... farms.
A industry B industrial C family D process

11 Mexicans are a large and important ... in California.
A ethnic group B majority C attitude D advantage

12 I've never ... any discrimination.
A had B produced C done D experienced

13 I've got lots of Latino friends, but my parents don't like it because they're ...
A prejudice. B prejudiced. C discriminate. D discriminated against.

### Grammar

14 Most American films ... in Hollywood.
A become made B will made C have made D are made

15 Gold ... in California in 1848.
A was discovered B has discovered C discovered itself D is discovered

16 That film was made ... Steven Spielberg.
A from B by C through D after

17 Which means the same as 'My camera was stolen'?
A I stole a camera. B A camera stole me. C Someone stole my camera.

***b)*** *Check your answers on p. 260 and add up your points – one point for each correct answer.*

***c)*** *If you had 14 or more points, well done! Maybe you can help students who had fewer points. If you had 13 points or fewer, it's a good idea to do some more work before you go on to the next unit. Where did you make mistakes? The chart below will tell you what you can do to improve your English.*

| No. | Areas | Find out more | Exercises |
|---|---|---|---|
| 1– 5 | California | Unit 2 (pp. 34–38) | WB 1 (p. 20), 22 (p. 29) |
| 6– 7 | Skimming/Scanning | SF (p. 150) | P 4 (p. 43), WB 3 (p. 21) |
| 8 | Writing letters | SF (p. 156) | P 8 (p. 45), WB 10 (p. 24) |
| 9–13 | Words | Unit 2 (pp. 36–37) | WB 2, (p. 20), 4–5 (p. 22), 9 (p. 23), 21 (p. 28) |
| 14–17 | The passive | Unit 2 (p. 36); GF2, (pp. 163–164) | P 5, 6, 10–12 (pp. 44–46); WB 7–8 (pp. 22–23), 11–13 (p. 24–25), 15 (p. 26), 20 (p. 28) |

# Hermann says 'Willkommen'

**A** Hermann isn't a big place. There's only one traffic light in the whole town!

**C** The town on the Missouri River was founded in 1837 by German immigrants.

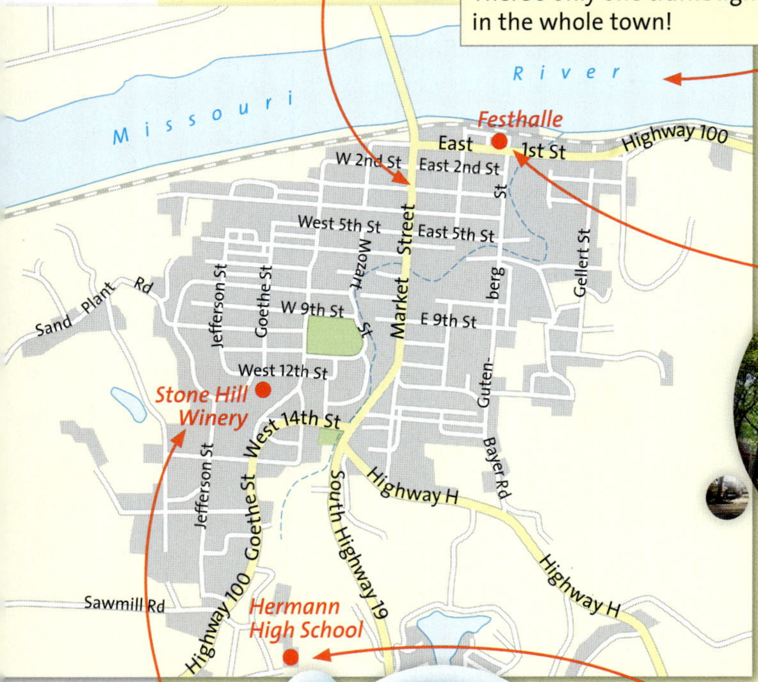

**D** Hermann's Festhalle – keeping German traditions alive

**B** Wineries are one of Hermann's most important industries.

**E** Hermann High School is a modern school with about 400 students.

F German festivals like Maifest and Oktoberfest are very popular with visitors.

G These beautiful old houses were built by Germans in the 19th century.

H Arriving at the Krugers' farmhouse, outside Hermann

## 1 What's Hermann like?

**a)** *Look at the map above and the map on the front inside cover of your book.*

– What state is Hermann in?
– Where is that state in the US?
– What big rivers can you find in the state?

**b)** *Look at the photos. Would you like to live in Hermann for a year? Why (not)? Make notes.*

attractions • buildings • busy • countryside • grapes • hilly • nice • old-fashioned • pretty • quiet • river • sights • shops • tourists • traffic

*I'd like / I wouldn't like to live there because ...*
*I think the town / the countryside is / looks ...*
*There is / are ... in the town.*
*They've got / They haven't got ...*

**c)** *Make appointments with three students. Discuss your ideas about living in Hermann.*

## 2 Arriving in Hermann

**a)** *Listen and find out:*

– Where do the Schmidts arrive?
– Why are they going to Hermann?

**b)** *Listen again and answer these questions:*

1 How many people are in the German family?
2 What's the temperature in St. Louis when they arrive?
3 How long does the drive take?
4 What events take place in the Festhalle?
5 How many people live in Hermann?
6 Why are there lots of restaurants in town?
7 Who's going to start at Hermann High School soon?
8 Where's the German family going to stay at first?

▸ P 1–3 (pp. 62–63) • WB 1–3 (pp. 34–35) • SF Listening (p. 148)

## All about ... American schools

### 1 A brochure about Hermann High School

*If you were in the US, which school and grade would you be in? Who has more school holidays – American or German students?*

Home of the Bearcats

## Hermann High School

Hermann MO

### Information for international exchange students

**The school system**

| | | |
|---|---|---|
| High School | Grades 9-12 | Ages 14-18 |
| Middle School | Grades 6-8 | Ages 11-14 |
| Elementary School | Grades 1-5 | Ages 6-11 |
| Kindergarten | | Ages 5-6 |

**The school year**

The school year starts at the beginning of September and goes to the end of May. It has two semesters. The summer vacation is three months: June, July and August. There is also a week off for Christmas and a week for Easter.

**The school day**

The school day starts at 8:20 a.m. and finishes at 3:00 p.m. Most students come by school bus or drive to school. You can get hot lunches in the school cafeteria, or you can bring your own lunch from home.

**Grades**

At Hermann High we use the same grades that are used in all American schools:

A 'excellent' – B 'good' – C 'average' – D 'below average' – F 'failure'

If you want to take part in extracurricular activities, you can't have any grade below a C.

### 2 Jake's schedule

Hermann High School **Jake Kruger** **Grade: 9**

Monday – Friday

| Period | Time | Subject | Rm. |
|---|---|---|---|
| 1 | 08:20–09:10 | English 1 | 31 |
| 2 | 09:15–10:05 | Science | 36 |
| 3 | 10:10–11:00 | Algebra | 16 |
| 4 | 11:05–11:55 | Health | 28 |
| 5 | Lunch/study hall | | |
| 6 | 01:15–02:05 | American History and Government | 21 |
| 7 | 02:10–03:00 | Boys' PE | Gym |

*How is Jake's timetable different to yours? (times, rooms, subjects)*
*Would you like to have the same timetable every day? Why (not)?*

▸ P 4–6 (pp. 63–64) • WB 4–6 (pp. 36–37)

### 3 From the school bulletin board

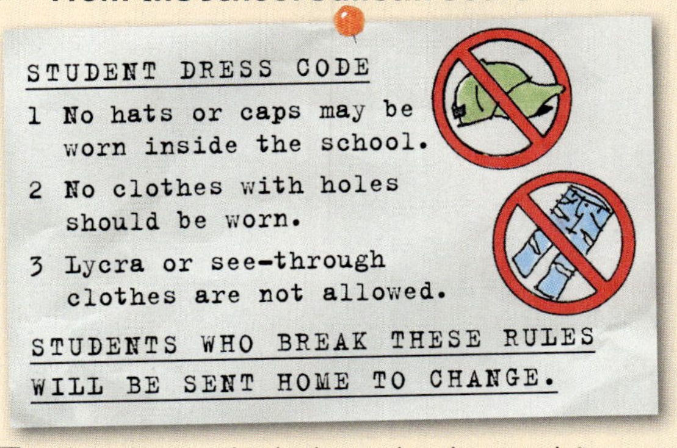

STUDENT DRESS CODE

1 No hats or caps may be worn inside the school.

2 No clothes with holes should be worn.

3 Lycra or see-through clothes are not allowed.

STUDENTS WHO BREAK THESE RULES WILL BE SENT HOME TO CHANGE.

*What do you think about this dress code? Would you like one at your school?*

### 4 School words in Britain and America

*Copy and complete the chart.*

| German | AE | BE |
|---|---|---|
| Jahrgangsstufe | ... | year |
| Stundenplan | ... | ... |
| Unterrichtsstunde | ... | ... |
| (Schul-)Note | ... | grade |
| schwarzes Brett | ... | ... |

## 5 Extracurriculars

'Hey Timo! Come to the FFA meeting with us!'

Timo looked across the hall and saw Jake with his girlfriend Cindy.

'FFA?' he asked. 'What's that?'

'Future Farmers of America,' Cindy explained.

Timo didn't seem very interested. 'A meeting for farmers? Er, no thanks! I should do some homework.'

Jake looked hurt. 'But Timo, we don't have much homework. It won't take much time.'

'And this is an important meeting,' Cindy said. 'There'll be some news about the County Fair on Saturday. Jake and I are going to show our hogs there.'

'Hog? Isn't that a word for a pig? You mean students have their own hogs?' Timo was surprised.

So Timo went to the meeting with Jake and Cindy. Some of the students talked about their hogs: how much money they paid for them, how many hours a week they spent on looking after them, and so on. Timo found the information very interesting.

After the meeting Jake said to Timo, 'You see, not everyone in FFA is a farm kid.'

'You're right,' said Timo. 'One student told me that city kids from New York schools go to FFA ... and there aren't many farms in New York!'

*▶ What is FFA? Do you think students at your school would like it?*
*Do you have extracurriculars at your school?*

**Americana ★ ★ ★**

**Extracurricular activities**

'Get involved!' That's what they say at American high schools, where sports and other extra-curricular activities are just as important as lessons. Students should be 'well-rounded' – good at their school subjects, good at sports and interested in other things. FFA is only one of these activities – there are usually foreign language clubs, debate teams, dance groups, a school band, a drama group, cheerleaders, and teams for every kind of sport from golf to football.

## 6 Now you

***a)*** *Make notes about your school in Germany and Hermann High School. What's the same/different in the two schools? Think about: the school year, school day, timetable, how students get to school, lunch break, activities, ...*

more help ▸ D p. 115

***b)*** **Extra** *Imagine some American exchange students will be in your school next month. Prepare a short talk for them about your school. Each member of your group should give one part of the talk.*

more help ▸ D p. 116

▸ GF 3: Countable/uncountable nouns (p. 165) • P 7–8 (p. 64) • WB 7–9 (pp. 37–38) • SF Giving a presentation (p. 147)

## 7 In Jake's Health class

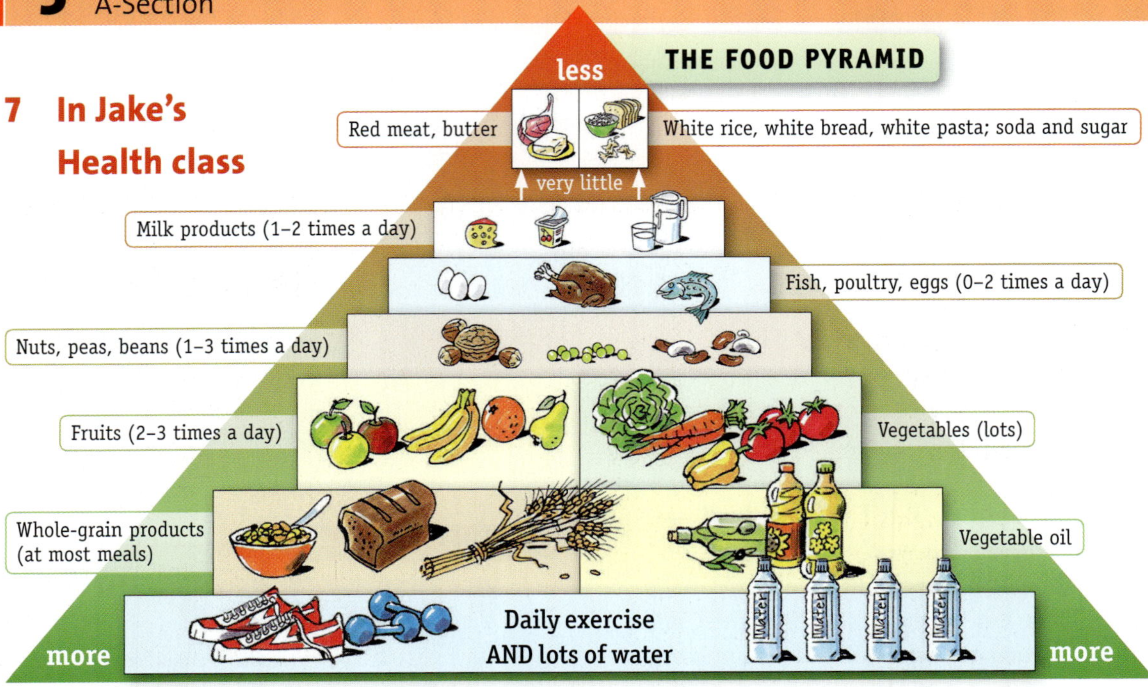


> *Study the pyramid then complete these sentences. Lots of different answers are possible.*

• ... is healthier than ... • You should eat ... more often than ... • You should eat/drink less ...

## 8 Now you

***a)*** *Write down everything you ate and drank yesterday.*

*Morning: muesli, 2 glasses of milk, a banana, ...*

***b)*** *Where do the things you ate go in the pyramid? Some things (like muesli) can go in more than one section.*
*Do you think you ate healthily or unhealthily?*

## 9 Talking about health

'OK, we've talked a lot about food and health all week,' said Ms. Meerbusch, the Health class teacher. 'Now let's talk about the food we eat and the health of the students in this school. Are we healthy? – Yes, Cindy?'

'Well, the food I eat at home is very healthy. Every morning my mom gives me a piece of fruit. And for dinner we always have fresh vegetables or a salad. But school lunches are a problem. Most of the food that students choose is unhealthy.'

'Thank you, Cindy. – Yes, Jake.'

'I think fitness is important too,' said Jake. 'Fact is if you play sports and eat good food, you feel great. But if you sit and watch TV and eat fast food all day, you feel bad.'

'You sound like my mom!' Jenny said.

Timo smiled. 'And Jake, what about that hamburger and fries you had for lunch today?'

**Looking at language**

***a)*** *Look at the word 'food' in the two sentences below. In one sentence it is used in a general way. In the other it is used to talk about specific food.*
– We've talked a lot about food all week.
– Now let's talk about the food we eat.
*Which sentence means food in general?*
*Which sentence means specific food?*
*Tip: Does it answer the question 'Which food?'?*

***b)*** *Look at the text again. Find more sentences with the word 'food'. Is 'food' used in a general or a specific way in these sentences?*

> *Why is Cindy's food healthy? What else is important for your health?*

▸ GF 4: Definite article (p. 166) • P 9–11 (pp. 65–66) • WB 10–14 (pp. 38–40)

## 10 From the local paper

Scrapbook — Hermann Advertiser-Courier — Wedne

### Hermann says a big 'Willkommen!' to new German family

**When Andreas Schmidt first visited Hermann, he had never heard of Missouri wine. So it was a surprise when he discovered that Hermann had so many wineries. Now, 20 years later, he's back again in Hermann to start a new life with his family and to restart the old Hermannthal winery.**

Andreas Schmidt was a member of the first group of high school students that visited Hermann from our sister city of Bad Arolsen over 20 years ago. He stayed with the Kruger family, and he kept in touch with them over the years.

It was the Krugers who told him about the job at the Hermannthal winery. "They read about it in the local paper and told me in a Christmas card," Schmidt says.

That Christmas card changed the lives of the Schmidt family! "We had never thought about moving to the US," Schmidt says. "And now we're here."

His wife Karla says it was "an adventure" to move to the US. "As the day came nearer, I got worried. What about all our friends in Germany? Would I miss them? But we had sold our house in Bad Arolsen, so there was no way back." And now? "Oh, we have found lots of new friends in Hermann," Karla Schmidt says. "I'm even working at Maifest next month."

Son Timo (14) likes his new school. "A lot of things seemed strange at first, like the FFA. And I missed my old soccer team." But Timo is now an active FFA member and he also helped to start a soccer team at Hermann High. "They weren't very good at first," Timo laughs. "You see, they hadn't played soccer before. But they're getting better now!"

Timo's younger sister Anna (12) likes her new school too. She already speaks English with a Missouri accent!

**To Andreas, Karla, Timo and Anna: Hermann says 'Willkommen!'**

*What do the different family members think about their new home?*

▸ GF 5: Past perfect (p. 167) • P 12–13 (p. 66) • WB 15–16 (p. 41)

## 11 Calling Timo

*Jake calls Timo to tell him about the article in the paper. Imagine you're Jake. Tell him the main points of the article. You can start like this:*

Hey, Timo. There's an article about your family in the paper. The first part is about ...
It says that ...
It also says that ...

▸ SF Summarizing texts (p. 157) • P 14 (p. 67) • WB 17–18 (pp. 41–42)

Extra | Background File | **GOING WEST**

## 1 READING Group puzzle (part 1)

*Divide the class into four groups (A, B, C, D). Each person in the group has a number (1, 2, 3, ...). Group A reads text A about Hermann, Group B reads text B about Missouri, etc. Take notes. Then go to **2** on p. 61.*

### A HERMANN

In the 18th and early 19th centuries, many Germans who had come to the New World were unhappy: English traditions and the English language dominated everyday life. The Germans were afraid that their children wouldn't learn their language and traditions. So they founded the *Deutsche Ansiedlungs-gesellschaft zu Philadelphia* in 1836. The following year this group bought land in Missouri and started a German colony there. And so the town of Hermann was founded.

Hermann stayed very German until World War I (1914–1918). The US was fighting against the Germans in Europe, so many Americans worried about Germans in the middle of their country. The school in Hermann was no longer allowed to teach in German. The proud Germans of Hermann stopped speaking their language and gave up their traditions for many years.

*The first settlers in Hermann thought it looked like the Rhine Valley.*

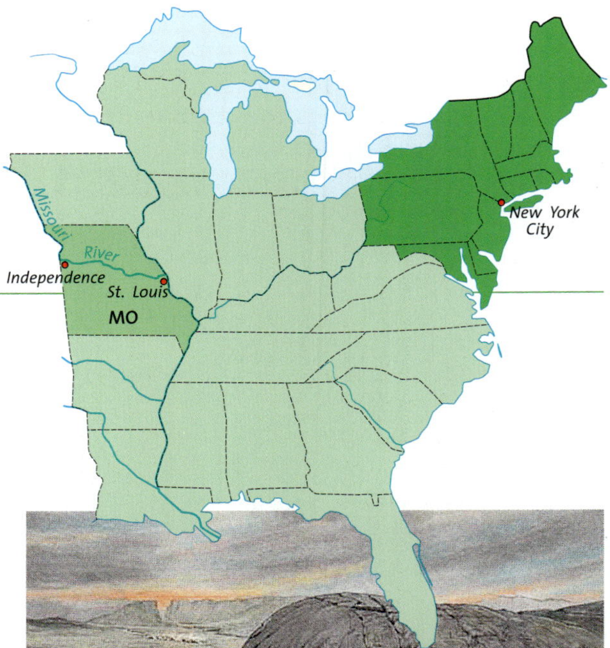


### B THE ROLE OF MISSOURI

The first states in the United States of America were along the east coast. As more and more Europeans came to the US, the country grew towards the west. Missouri became a state in 1821, and by 1840 more than 380,000 people lived there. When gold was discovered in California in 1848, Missouri became the 'Gateway to the West', and the wagon trains to the West started from there. But not everyone went west to look for gold. Thousands went to get free or cheap land where they could start a farm and a new life.

People who wanted to go to California, Oregon or other places in the West travelled to St. Louis, where they bought everything they needed for the journey. Most then took a boat up the Missouri River to Independence, where they joined a wagon train.

*Settlers got off the Missouri river boats and formed wagon trains for the journey to the West.*

## C THE TRAILS TO THE WEST

Wagon trains were the safest way to travel across the continent until a railway was finished in 1869. The wagon trains followed one of many trails to the West: the Oregon Trail is the most famous. It was more than 2000 miles long, and the journey often took five months or more.

Over the years more than half a million people went west this way. Their wagons were full of the things they needed for their new lives in the West. The journey was hard, so only those who were very strong were able to do it. Many of the pioneers walked the whole way. About ten per cent of them died of accidents or illnesses. A few were killed by animals or died in fights with Native Americans. There are many stories about the brave men and women who made the journey, and Americans are still very proud of this 'pioneer spirit'. ■

## D THE NATIVE AMERICANS

When the first Europeans came to North America, the continent wasn't empty. Already millions of people lived there, although no one can say exactly how many.

In the beginning, the meetings between the Europeans and the 'Native Americans' (or 'American Indians') were peaceful, and they often helped each other. But as more and more Europeans arrived, the relationship changed. The white settlers wanted more land and the Native Americans were forced to move to areas called reservations. The whites promised to leave the Indians alone if they agreed to move. But most of these promises were broken. Some tribes tried to fight for their rights, but they were defeated.

At the beginning of the 21st century, there are about four million Native Americans in the US, that's 1.5 % of the population. More than one third of them still live on reservations across the country. Statistics show that they are poorer than the average white American and that more of them are unemployed. ■

### 2 Group puzzle (part 2)

***a)*** *In your group (A,B, C or D), compare your notes. Agree on the most important points.*

more help ▸ *D p. 117*

***b)*** *Make new groups of four (A1, B1, C1, D1; A2, B2, ...). Tell the others the important information from your text. Take notes on the other texts.*

***c)*** *Go back to your first group (A, B, C or D) and compare your information. Did you all understand the same things? If not, read the texts again to check your information.*

▸ *WB 19 (p. 43)* • **Text File 9** *(pp. 136–137)*

EVERYDAY ENGLISH

## 1 MEDIATION American tourists in Germany

*a) You are at the train station in Bad Arolsen, the town where the Schmidt family comes from. On the platform an American tourist asks you for help. Look at the first announcement. What can you say to the man?*

**Announcement 1:**
Bitte beachten Sie: Der Regionalexpress von Bad Arolsen nach Kassel-Wilhelmshöhe fährt heute ausnahmsweise nicht von Gleis 1 ab, sondern von Gleis 4.

*Man* Excuse me, can you help me, please? We're going to Kassel. I think we need platform 1. Is that right?
*You* No, that isn't right. The train to …

*b) Now listen to the announcements and help the tourists.*

**Remember**
You don't need to translate every word. Just give the most important information.

▸ SF Mediation (p. 152)

## 2 WRITING A letter to an exchange student (Letter for information)

*Imagine you're going to a school in the US as an exchange student. You want to write a letter to the American student you'll be staying with. Introduce yourself and ask some questions. Think about what you want to say. The notes below can give you some ideas. (120–140 words)*

***In your letter you should say:***
- who you are and why you're writing

***You can say something about yourself:***
- where you come from in Germany and what it's like there
- what you're interested in
- what kind of school you go to in Germany and what you like about your school
- …

***You can ask things like:***
- what the American student is interested in
- what you can do in his/her town
- when school starts/finishes
- if there's a school dress code
- what clubs or extracurricular activities there are at his/her school
- …

more help ▸ D p. 114

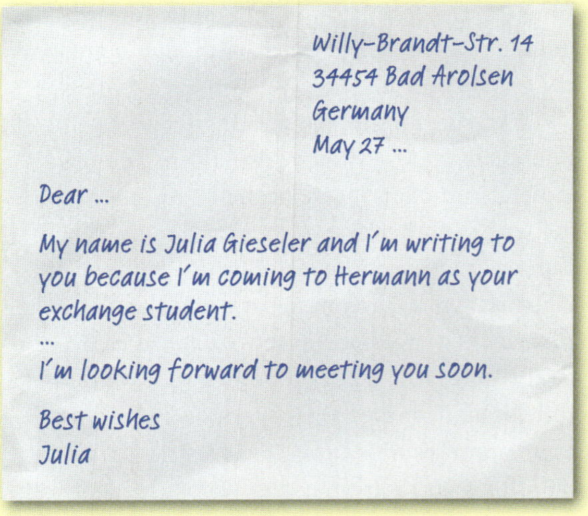


**Tip**
- Write a beginning and ending to your letter.
- Read your letter carefully again.
- Check spelling and grammar of your letter.
- Sign your letter.

*You can put your letter in your DOSSIER.*

▸ SF Writing letters (p. 156)

## 3 WORDS Using numbers

*Partner B: Look at p. 107. Partner C: Look at p. 109.*
**a)** *Partner A: Tell your partners about St. Louis. Then listen to them and fill in the information about Los Angeles and New York in a copy of the chart.*

| | St. Louis | Los Angeles | New York |
|---|---|---|---|
| Founded in | 1764 | | |
| Population | 348,000 | | |
| Area | 171.3 sq km | | |
| Average temperature | – 6° C (winter) 32° C (summer) | | |
| Largest ethnic group | black (52%) | | |

St. Louis, Missouri, with the Gateway Arch

▸ **Text File 8** *(pp. 134–135)*

*A:* St. Louis was founded in 1764. The population ...

**b)** *Which city is the oldest city? Which has got the most Latino people? Which is coldest in winter?*

## 4 //O WORDS School in the US and Britain ▸ *D p. 115*

*Complete the sentences with words from the box.*

bulletin board • dress code • grades • holidays • lessons • notice board • periods • schedule • timetable • uniform • vacation

1 When American students talk about what they do every day at school and when, they say *schedule*. British students say ___.
2 At Hermann High School there are seven of these in a school day and each one is 50 minutes long. They are called ___ in the US. In Britain they are called ___.
3 In every school you can find this on a wall. Teachers and students put information on it so that everyone can read it. In America they use the word ___. In Britain the word is ___.
4 In Britain and America teachers give you ___ to tell you how good or bad a piece of work is.
5 In HHS, they aren't so strict about what students wear to school. They only have a ___. In Britain, students must wear a ___ at school.
6 In the US they talk about the summer ___. In Britain they usually talk about the summer ___.

## 5 WORDS What' s going on at Timo's new school?

**a)** O *Find the words and complete the sentences.*
1 Timo wants to do well in his test. He wants to g___ a good grade.
2 At US schools students go from classroom to classroom for each lesson. That was new for Timo. In Germany students c___ rooms only for some subjects.
3 Timo and Jake have a vocabulary test in French tomorrow. They have to r___ for it tonight.
4 Do you want to be in the school play? All students can t___ p___ in it.
5 Students have to follow the school rules. If they b___ them, they're in trouble.

**b)** **Extra** *Make a school mind map. First think of good headings for your mind map:*
*the school day, the school year, activities, people in school, places in school, tests, ...*
*Then collect as many of the words and phrases from* **4** *and* **5** *as you can.*

## 6 LISTENING School announcements and 'Thought for the day'

***a)*** *Read the statements below. Write down the numbers 1–9. Then listen to the announcements at Hermann High School. Are the statements true (**T**) or false (**F**)? Write **T** or **F** next to each number.*

1. The win against Washington was a surprise.
2. Washington has a bad baseball team.
3. The Hermann High School team is called the Bearcats.
4. The school band will meet in the music room this Saturday.
5. The band is going to play at Maifest.
6. The school play is called 'TV Hour'.
7. The play will be on Friday, Saturday and Sunday evenings.
8. Khalil Gibran wrote today's 'Thought for the day'.
9. It says that not everybody can give something.

***b)*** **Extra** *Listen to the announcements again. Take notes, then correct the false statements.*

## 7 One sandwich – some sugar (Countable/uncountable nouns)

**Tip**

**Countable nouns** have a singular and a plural (sandwich/sandwiches). You can use a/an or one/two/three/..., some or lots of with them.

**Uncountable nouns** have no plural. They describe things you can't count. Use some or lots of with them (some sugar, lots of sugar).

***a)*** *Copy the chart below. Continue the lists with nouns from the green box.*

| Countable (how many? = wie viele) | Uncountable (how much? = wie viel) |
|---|---|
| car / cars | traffic |
| ... | ... |

car • earring • equipment • essay • fact • food • hair • health • homework • information • money • music • news • dollar • sandwich • song • story • sugar • time • traffic

***b)*** *Complete the sentences with words from the chart in a).*

1. There wasn't much ... in the purse, only one or two ...
2. Hundreds of ... drive along this road every day. There's too much ... on our roads.
3. I didn't find much ... about St. Louis on the internet, but I think all the ... are correct.
4. I've done some ..., but I still have to write an ... for our history teacher.

## 8 Can I make a sandwich? (Countable/uncountable nouns)

***a)*** *Complete the sentences. Use a/an with countable nouns, some with uncountable nouns.*

1. Can I make ... sandwich?
   – Sure. There's ... bread in the kitchen.
2. What do you need for the curry?
   – ... beef, ... rice and ... big tomato.
3. I've got to write ... essay for English. And I've got ... French homework for next week.
4. I need ... more information about hogs.
   – Well, I can give you ... book about them.
5. You can go skiing with us if you want. But you'll have to buy ... equipment.

***b)*** *Complete each sentence with all the possible words from the box. Use the plural if you have to.*

apple • bread • milk • juice • potato

1. How much ... do we need?
2. How many ... do we need?
3. We need ten ...
4. We need some ...
5. We need lots of ...
6. We need a kilo of ...
7. We need a bottle of ...

## 9 READING Soft drinks, hard facts (Finding the main ideas of a text) ▸ SF p. 151

You want to find out how healthy soft drinks are. You have found this article on the internet. If you want to find the main ideas of a text, it's often helpful to look at its structure.

**1 Topic:**
Every text has a topic. You'll often find it in the first paragraph.

**2 Main ideas:**
Every paragraph has a main idea. You can often find the main idea of a paragraph in the first or the last sentence.

**3 Reasons and examples:**
There are reasons and examples for each main idea. They say more about the ideas. Sometimes reasons or examples are given with words like 'because, that's why, for example, so, …'.

# SOFT DRINKS, HARD FACTS

(1) **Drinking soda is one of the worst things you can do to your health. But some schools are now beginning to do something about it.**

(2) Experts agree that sugary soft drinks and fast food are the main reasons why so many American teenagers are fat. About 7% of the calories that they take in come from soft drinks alone. And even if this doesn't cause health problems now, there could be serious trouble later in life.

(3) The problem is that you are still hungry after drinking soft drinks, says Wayne Campbell, a professor in the Department of Food and Nutrition at Purdue University. That's because you don't feel full after drinking – although soft drinks contain a lot of calories. So if you drink a cola, for example, you take in 200 calories, but you still want a burger.

(4) American kids and teenagers are drinking more soft drinks than ever before, according to the U.S. Department of Agriculture. Soda has taken the place of other, healthier drinks. Thirty years ago, for example, boys drank more than twice as much milk as soft drinks.

(5) So what can be done? In California, at least, schools aren't allowed to sell soda any more. That's because experts have found out that having or not having soda machines in schools changes how much soda teenagers drink. If it's easy to buy soda, kids will drink more. If it's difficult, they won't.

*a)* ○ *Look at the highlighted sentences in paragraph (3) and (4). Decide which sentence contains the main idea and which sentence gives a reason or example.*

*b) Read paragraph (5). Find the main idea. What examples and reasons support it?*

*c) Here are three main ideas from the text. Write them down and collect reasons and examples from the text for each main idea.*

- *Soft drinks are unhealthy.*
- *Soft drinks are one of the main reasons why kids are fat.*
- *Schools are trying to change the way kids drink.*

more help ▸ D p. 116

*d)* **Extra** ● *Should soft drinks be sold in German schools? Why (not)? What do you think? Write a short text.*

## 10 //O Money is a problem (Definite article) ▸ D p. 116

*Add **the** where you need it.*

1 ? money really is a problem for my family because we aren't rich.
2 I've spent all ? money you gave me.
3 I love ? pizza. It's my favourite food.
4 ? pizza we had for lunch was delicious.
5 ? life of a farmer must be very hard.
6 Is ? life easier if you're rich?
7 All ? people at the party were very nice.
8 ? people will usually help you if you ask them nicely.
9 I'm interested in ? history of my hometown. I'm reading a book about the town in the 19th century.
10 Some people say ? history is boring. They are more interested in modern things.

## 11 WORDS Word building (Nouns from verbs and adjectives)

**a)** *Look at the nouns in the box. Which verb or adjective do they come from? Guess their meanings. Then check in a dictionary.*

A: I think 'cleverness' comes from 'clever'. It means *klug* or *schlau*. So it means *Klugheit*.
B: I think that's right. My turn. 'Collection' …

**b)** **Extra** ● *Write sentences with five nouns from a).*

cleverness • friendliness • happiness • illness • sadness • collection • humanity • imagination • reality • possibility

**Tip**

Nouns with **-ation**, **-ion**, **-ity**, **-ness** at the end: You can often understand the nouns because you know the first part of the word.

## 12 What a nice little party! (Past perfect)

*Complete the sentences. Use the **past perfect**.*

1 I went to Lea's birthday party with Tom. He was excited because he *had never met* (never/meet) her before.
2 When we arrived at the party Tom couldn't find his present. He … (leave) it on the bus.
3 Sam was late. She … (forget) Lea's address.
4 At the party I ate chicken curry. I … (never/try) Indian food before. It was delicious.
5 Lisa couldn't eat the chicken curry. She … (eat) too many biscuits.
6 Peter played Lea's guitar. It was awful. He … (never/play) before.

## 13 //O A morning at the Krugers' (Past perfect) ▸ D p. 117

*Which is correct – **simple past** or **past perfect**?*

1 When his father got up, Jake *had already gone* (went/had already gone) outside to feed his hog.
2 When Jake (came/had come) back, everything was ready. His mother … (prepared/had prepared) breakfast.
3 After breakfast Jake's father hurried to work. But he came back because he … (forgot/had forgotten) his cellphone.

**Tip**

Before you start, think: What happened first? Use the **past perfect** for that verb.

4 Jake ran for the bus. It wasn't there. It … (left/had left) when he got to the bus stop.
5 When he (arrived/had arrived) at school, there was nobody in the yard. The first period … (started/had already started).

## 14 STUDY SKILLS Summarizing texts

*a) Read this story about a rafting tour some 11th-graders from Hermann High School took. Find the main ideas.*

**A perfect day, by Carrie Langer**

I was a bit nervous. It was the first day of summer vacation and I was going on my first rafting tour. Cindy had tried to talk me out of it.

"Are you crazy, Carrie? You don't even like water. And the Castor River is pretty wild."

"I know," I said.

"So why are you doing this?"

I mumbled something about looking for adventure. Well, I couldn't tell her the real reason: Jim Nielson. Jim was a really sweet guy who did a lot of rafting. So when I heard he was going to be a guide on the school rafting tour, I put my name down on the list.

Sue sat next to me on the bus to the river and talked endlessly about Maifest. Jim was at the front talking to Nate, the other tour guide. At one point Jim walked down through the bus, so I got up and went towards the bathroom.

"Hi," he said as we met. "Carrie, right?"

"Right," I said. "And you're – er, Jim?"

"Right. – Well, enjoy the tour."

"Thanks," I said. "I'm sure I will."

At first the water was slow, so we talked and laughed as we paddled along. But after an hour it got faster. Suddenly Jim turned and shouted "Go left, left" but it was too late – the raft hit a rock and I fell into the water. "This is the end," I thought. But then I felt a hand on my arm. It pulled me back onto the raft. When I looked up, I saw Jim.

I was cold, so our group took a short break on shore, and Jim gave me some hot tea from his thermos. We drank out of the same cup!

For the rest of the trip I sat next to Jim, and he asked me every few minutes if I was all right. "Everything's perfect," I told him.

We're going out on Friday night!

*b) In groups of four, do a placemat activity. Each student writes which four of the ideas below he/she thinks are most important. Then agree on the most important four.*

- **A** Cindy tries to talk Carrie out of going rafting.
- **B** Carrie thinks the tour guide, Jim, is sweet.
- **C** The group takes a bus to the river.
- **D** On the bus Sue talks a lot about Maifest.
- **E** On the bus Jim and Carrie say hi.
- **F** When the raft hits a rock, Carrie falls into the water.
- **G** Carrie is afraid she'll die.
- **H** Jim saves her and gives her tea.
- **I** Jim is worried about Carrie.
- **J** In the end Jim and Carrie plan to go out together.

**STUDY SKILLS Summarizing texts**

If you summarize, you write or tell someone a shorter version of a text. You only give the most important information from the original.

- In the first one or two sentences tell the reader what the story or text is about.
- In the main part describe the main events.
- Explain **who** does **what** in the story, **where**, **when** and **why**.
- Use your own words.
- Leave out examples and direct speech.
- Use the simple present.

*c) Now summarize the story.*

*The story is about Carrie, a teenage girl who goes on a rafting tour because she wants to meet Jim, the tour guide.*

▸ SF Summarizing texts (p. 157) • WB 18 (p. 42)

## Angus Bethune's moment by Chris Crutcher (adapted)

*In an American high school, the popular kids always seem to have the most fun. The coolest boys get the prettiest girls. Angus Bethune is not one of the popular kids, but tonight he gets the chance to be with the girl of his dreams.*

I'm a big kid.

And my parents named me Angus.

"Angus is a cow," I said to my mother. "You named me after a cow."

"Your father's uncle was named Angus," she said.

"So my father's uncle was named after a cow too," I said. "What did *he* think of that?"

"Actually," Mom said, "I think he was kind of proud. Angus was a farmer, you know."

"Jesus help me," I said, and went to my room.

As Angus, the fat kid, I have my problems, although it isn't as bad as it sounds. I am very, very quick for a fat kid, and I have great reflexes. When I play football, no one can lose me. And I'm smart and get good grades. But I'd be happy to swap reflexes and good grades for a little beauty.

And that brings me to tonight. Tonight is a big night. See, I was elected Winter Ball King. That means I will be out on the dance floor of Lake Michigan High School with Melissa Lefevre, the girl of my dreams – and only my dreams. She was elected Winter Ball Queen. For a minute we'll be out there alone.

Alone with Melissa Lefevre.

Now I don't know how I was elected. I can't even imagine. I mean, it's a joke, I know that. And a good one. More than half the kids at my school voted for me and I don't know why.

The problem is that tonight I have to dance with Melissa. I can't dance.

I fell in love with Melissa in kindergarten. She was a tan, blond girl with long legs and brown eyes that made you ache.

I've never even talked to her. Until tonight. Tonight I'll *have* to talk to her.

All I want is my moment with her.

What can Melissa be thinking? She's probably telling herself that it's like a trip to the dentist. He's going to hurt you, but in an hour, you'll walk out of there. And you'll still be alive.

Of course, Melissa hasn't seen me dance.

Heads turn as I walk into the gym. I try to look cool and sit down at the nearest empty table. I see Melissa on the dance floor with her boyfriend – a real jerk, Rick Sanford – and I hear the announcement: the King and Queen have to be behind the stage in five minutes.

I'm sweating. I want my moment.

I get up and start walking to the stage when I see Melissa on her boyfriend's arm. They're walking toward me through the crowd on the

dance floor. As they get closer, I want to run. What am I doing here? What was I thinking?

They stand in front of me. "Angus, my man," Rick slurs, and I can see he's drunk. "I'm giving you this pretty thing for a few minutes. So she can compare."

Melissa drops his arm and smiles. "Don't listen to him. He's drunk. And rude."

Then she says, "Why don't we go?"

"Yeah," Rick says, "why don't you go, snowball king?"

Melissa whispers, "Shut up. I'm warning you, Rick. Shut up."

"Have fun," Rick says to me. "Your election cost me a lot of money. And don't put your big fat hands on my girl."

Melissa takes my arm and says, "Let's go."

At the side door to the stage I say, "By the way, there's something you should know."

She waits.

"I can't dance."

Melissa smiles. "We'll survive," she says.

We're almost ready to start. "What did he mean, my election cost him a lot of money?" I whisper.

"Never mind. He's rich, and he's rude," she says. "I'm embarrassed I'm with him." She pauses and puts her arm in mine. "I'm *not* with him."

The curtains open and the trumpets play. We get our crowns. I feel stupid. King Angus the Fat.

Melissa says, "I chose a slow song. We don't have to move much. Dance close to me. When you feel me move, you move. And don't listen to the music. Just follow."

She takes my arm and we go down the stairs to the dance floor. She smiles, then pulls me close. She says, "Be my shadow."

A part of me goes to heaven. In my wildest dreams I never imagined that Melissa Lefevre would be nice to me in my moment. She whispers, "Relax," into my ear, and I follow her.

"Angus?"

"Yeah?"

"Do you ever get tired of who you are?"

I pull back a second, then pull close again. "Do you know who you're talking to?"

I feel her smile. "Yeah," she says, "I thought so. I know it's not the same, but it's not always so great to look like I do. I pay too."

She's right. I think it's not the same.

"I'm bulimic. Do you know what that is?"

"Yes, I know what that is. It means when you eat too much, you throw up so you don't look like me."

"Close enough. Don't worry, I'm in therapy for it," she says. "A lot of pretty girls are."

"Actually," I say, "I even tried it once, but when I put my finger down my throat, I was still hungry and I almost ate my arm."

Melissa laughs and holds me tighter. "You're the only person I've ever told. I just wanted you to know things aren't always as they seem. Would you do me a favor?"

"Yes."

"Would you leave with me?"

"You mean leave this dance? Leave this dance with you?" I feel her nod.

The music ends; all dancers stop and clap politely. "I want to dance one more," Melissa says. "A fast one."

"I'll wait over by the table."

"No. I want to dance it with you."

"You don't understand," I say. "When I dance rock and roll, people across the country feel earthquakes."

She takes my hand. "Listen. Do what you do on the football field. Don't listen to the music; just follow me the way you follow the guy from the other team."

I try to protest, but then the band starts to play "Bad Moon Rising", and the dance floor is full. Melissa pushes me back, and I watch her body the way I would watch another player on the football field. I'm like a mirror and move with her, from top to bottom. Soon lots of kids are watching us; I'm in a circle of kids, and they're cheering. I'm Angus Bethune, Fat Man Extraordinaire, in the spotlight with Melissa Lefevre.

When the band finishes, everyone is clapping, even Melissa. I tell God he can take me now.

"You bitch!" Rick shouts. "You practiced with this fatty. You've been dancing together. You

bitch. You wanted to make me look stupid." He turns to me. "I'm gonna kill you, fat boy," he says. He's looking at my fist.

I say, "Don't even think it. After dancing, fighting is what I do best."

## Working with the text

### 1 Understanding the story

*Are these sentences true or false? Explain.*

1. Angus thinks it was a joke that he was elected Winter Ball King.
2. Angus is worried about the ball because he doesn't like Melissa.
3. Melissa understands Angus because she has problems too.
4. Angus is OK on the dance floor because he and Melissa had practised.

### 2 Extra What do they mean?

*Say who made each statement. What does it mean?*

1. "Angus is a cow." (p. 68, l. 6)
   *Angus says this to his mother. He means that the name ...*
2. "I'm giving you this pretty thing for a few minutes." (p. 69, ll. 63–64)
3. "Be my shadow." (p. 69, l. 97)

### 3 The story

***a)*** *What is the story about? Write one sentence about each of the following*

1. the characters (the people in the story)
   *The story is about Angus, a fat high school student; Melissa, a ...*
2. the scene (where the story takes place)
   *The story takes place in ...*
3. the time (when the story takes place)
4. the plot (what happens)

***b)*** *Look at the diagram. Explain in no more than three sentences how each character in the story feels towards each other character. Do their feelings change? How? Why?*

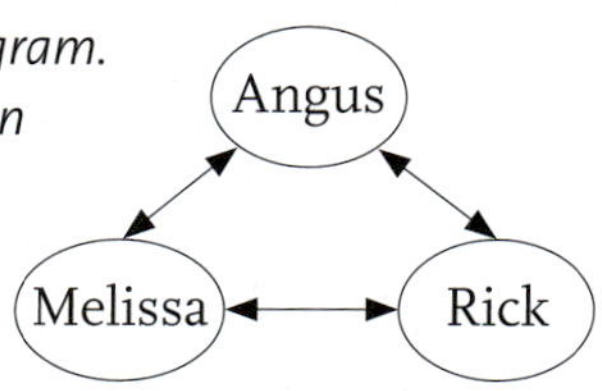


### 4 Melissa and Angus

***a)*** *Were you surprised by the way Melissa acted towards Angus? Why (not)?*

***b)*** *Why do you think Melissa told Angus that she's bulimic?*

### 5 Extra After the dance

*Think of the next day. What will things be like*
*– between Melissa and Angus?*
*– between Rick and Angus?*
*– between Melissa and Rick?*
*Write one dialogue.*

more help ▸ *D p. 118*

▸ *WB 20 (p. 44)* • **Checkpoint 3** *WB (p. 45)*

## How am I doing?

***a)*** *Find or choose the correct answers.*

### Hermann and Missouri

1 Missouri is a state in the ... of the US.
A south B east C west D middle

2 Wineries are an important ... in parts of Missouri.
A drink B industry C farm D food

3 'Missouri' is the name of a state, but also the name of a big ...
A national park. B forest. C river. D city.

### American schools

4 The school before the middle school is called ...

5 High school starts with the 9th ...

6 In the US sports and school clubs are called ...

7 The best grade in a test in US schools is ...

### Words

8 What are the British English words for the following American English words?
a) bulletin board b) schedule c) period

9 How do you say this?
a) 7.9 b) °C

10 In the US cola and lemonade are often called ...

11 To keep fit, eat the right food and do daily ...

12 Chicken and turkey are a kind of meat we call ...

### Summarizing texts

13 Which statement is *not* true? When you summarize a text you should write or say ...
A the most important information from the original text.
B as much as possible in your own words.
C lots of details from the original text.
D complete sentences, not just key words.

### Grammar

14 Add 'a/an' or 'some':
a) I need ... information.
b) Can I have ... glass of milk, please? – Of course, there's ... milk in the fridge.
c) Would you like ... fruit with your sandwich? – Yes, ... apple would be nice.

15 Add 'the' where necessary:
a) The students talked about ... food in their Health class. They agreed that ... food they eat isn't very healthy.
b) Is ... life in Hermann quiet? – Yes, usually, but ... life of the local newspaper reporter is quite busy.

16 Timo couldn't open the door. He ... his key.
A loses B lost C had lost D will lose

17 When I saw Jake at 11 o'clock, he ... his breakfast yet.
A didn't eat B doesn't eat C ate D hadn't eaten

***b)*** *Check your answers on p. 260 and add up your points – one for each correct answer.*

***c)*** *If you had 22 or more points, well done! Maybe you can help students with fewer points.*
*If you had 21 points or fewer, it's a good idea to do some more work before you go on to the next unit. Where did you make mistakes? The chart below will tell you what you can do to improve your English.*

| No. | Areas | Find out more | Exercises |
|---|---|---|---|
| 1– 3 | Hermann and Missouri | Unit 3 (pp. 54–55) | WB 1 (p. 34), 18 (p. 42), |
| 4– 8 | American schools | Unit 3 (pp. 56–57) | P 4–6 (pp. 63–64), WB 4–6 (pp. 36–37) |
| 9 | Words: Numbers | P 3 (p. 63) | WB 3 (p. 35) |
| 10–12 | Words: food | Unit 3 (p. 58) | WB 13 (p. 40) |
| 13 | Summarizing texts | SF (p. 157) | P 14 (p. 67), WB 18 (p. 42) |
| 14 | Countable/uncountable nouns | Unit 3 (p. 57), GF 3 (p. 165) | P 7–8 (p. 64), WB 7–9 (pp. 37–38) |
| 15 | Definite article | Unit 3 (p. 58), GF 4 (p. 166) | P 10 (p. 64), WB 10 (p. 38) |
| 16–17 | Past perfect | Unit 3 (p. 59), GF 5 (p. 167) | P 12–13 (p. 66), WB 15–16 (p. 41) |

## 1 WORDS Holidays

***a)*** *Collect ideas about holidays in four lists.*

| Getting there | Where to stay | Things to do | Describing things |
|---|---|---|---|
| fly / go by plane<br>go by ... | stay with friends<br>stay at a ... | see the sights<br>relax on the beach<br>visit a ... | It's fun / cool / ... here.<br>The beach is beautiful / lonely / ...<br>The weather is ... |

***b)*** *Write a short text for a brochure for an exciting holiday place. Use ideas from your lists.*

Come to ...!
It's easy to get here. You can ...
Stay at ... or ...
There's lots to do. You can ...
... has something for everyone!

## 2 WORDS Numbers

*Dates, times and prices are important on holidays.*
***a)*** *Practise these numbers.*

What's the time?
It's ...

| | | |
|---|---|---|
| 8:04 | 12:04 | 20:00 |
| 9:36 | 15:30 | 22:45 |
| 11:15 | 18:27 | 22:49 |

18th April • 12 May • 1 July • 2nd October • 23/8 • 3/1 • 25/12 • 30/11 • 29/2 • 21/9

| | | | | | |
|---|---|---|---|---|---|
| $1.50 | $8.30 | $15 | $17.56 | $44.99 | $71.65 |

***b)*** *Write down ...*
*– the times of three things you're doing next week*
*– three birthdays that are important to you*
*– the prices of three things you bought last week.*

*Read everything to your partner. He/she writes it down. Then compare.*

**Tip**

| | You see | You say |
|---|---|---|
| Times | 6:00 | six o'clock/six am |
| | 9:30 | nine thirty/half past nine |
| | 10:47 | ten forty-seven |
| | 17:00 | five o'clock/five pm |
| | 19:08 | nineteen o eight/ eight minutes past seven |
| | 22:15 | quarter past ten/ten fifteen/ twenty-two fifteen |
| Dates | 17 March | the seventeenth of March |
| | 14th June | the fourteenth of June |
| Prices | $1 | a/one dollar |
| | $1.20 | a/one dollar twenty |
| | $5 | five dollars |
| | $8.59 | eight dollars fifty-nine |

## 3 My school holidays start ... (Prepositions in time phrases)

*Complete the sentences with at, in or on.*

1. My school holidays start ... Thursday.
2. I want to relax ... the first day of the holidays.
3. Visit Las Vegas ... May – it's too hot ... July.
4. We often go to the beach ... the summer.
5. Hurry! The train leaves ... 8:04.
6. We arrived in London ... Monday morning.
7. We arrived in London ... the morning.
8. When's the concert? – It's ... 10 June.
9. We spent two weeks in the US ... 2006.
10. What do you want to do ... the weekend?

## 4 SPEAKING Let's go to the park

***a)*** *It's the summer vacation. Matt and Jon are talking about things to do today. Read their conversation with a partner.*

*Matt* Let's go to the park. We can skate there.
*Jon* No, I don't really want to do that again. We went to the park yesterday. What about going to the cinema today?
*Matt* Sorry, I can't. I haven't got any money. We could go back to my house. I've got a new computer game.
*Jon* That's a good idea. Let's do that.
*Matt* Cool. Come on then. Let's go.

**Tip**

When you talk about what you want to do, you usually make suggestions, disagree and agree.

**Making suggestions**
- Let's go/watch/...
- We could/go/watch/...
- What about going/watching/...?

**Disagreeing**
- I don't really want to do that.
- I'm not sure if I like that idea.

When you disagree, try and give a reason:
- We went there yesterday.
- I haven't got so much money.

**Agreeing**
- That's a good/great/... idea.
- Yes, let's do that.

***b)*** *Make a conversation like the one on the left. Here are some ideas for things to do.*

go shopping/swimming/... • go on a trip to ... • make a pizza • watch a film • play football/... • visit the photo museum/...

## 5 STUDY SKILLS Writing (Linking sentences)

*A good text needs* ***linking words*** *and* ***time phrases****. Use these words and phrases in the box to complete the text.*

and • At about one o'clock • before they went to bed • but (2x) • because • Last year • later in the afternoon • 90 minutes later • One morning in July • On their third day • so • when • where

(1) there was a competition in UK schools. It was organized by the German Tourist Information and the first prize was four days in Germany. (2) the 15 winners left London and just (3) they arrived at Cologne Bonn Airport. From there they took a train into Cologne and left their bags at their hotel.

(4) they had lunch in town and (5) they visited the cathedral and a sports museum. They had dinner at a restaurant with traditional Rhineland food and (6) they went for a short walk through the old town.

The next day they all went shopping. (They had to speak German (7) not all the shop assistants spoke English!) Later they went up the Rhine on a boat trip (8) visited a chocolate museum. Everyone ate lots of chocolate.

(9) they travelled to Bonn. There they saw the house (10) Beethoven was born, (11) there wasn't enough time to go to the city's other museums. In the evening they had tickets for a rock festival. It wasn't over until 1 am, (12) they all went to bed really late.

Everyone was very tired (13) they arrived back in London the next day, (14) they had all had a fantastic time in Germany. ► WB 1–4 (pp. 46–47)

## 1 Listening

*You will hear five travel announcements and mini-dialogues.*
*For each one choose the correct answer: A, B, or C. At the end you will hear the recordings again.*

1 Which gate at the airport must passengers for Denver go to?
A 8 B 18 C 8A

2 Where is the ticket office at this railway station?
A Platform 6 B Platform 9 C Ticket Office next to café →

3 How much does the man pay for his tickets?
A $8 B $10 C $25

4 Which platform must the woman go to?
A S3 Stadtmitte/City Centre 11:07 Gleis 16
B S3 Stadtmitte/City Centre 11:17 Gleis 6
C S3 Stadtmitte/City Centre 11:20 Gleis 2

5 When does the man want a hotel room?
A 8 May 12 May B 18 May 20 May C 18 March 20 March

## 2 Listening

*You will hear a radio programme from the US. Read the questions below. Then listen and choose the correct answer: A, B or C. You will hear the programme twice.*

1 You can hear the programme once a ...
A day. B week. C month.

2 Later in the show Annie will talk about ...
A school grades. B sport. C fashion.

3 Katie went on an interesting vacation last ...
A summer. B winter. C autumn.

4 She was a ... for a week.
A pop singer B circus clown C cowgirl

5 She went with her ...
A uncle and aunt. B parents. C sisters.

6 On the vacation, Katie ... every day.
A swam B ran 20 miles C rode horses

7 One day she helped Ben and Ted with a ...
A baby cow. B baby horse. C baby lion.

8 Once they had a ... in the mountains.
A camp fire B concert C picnic

9 On the vacation Katie slept in a ...
A hostel. B tent. C cabin.

10 Katie says the vacation would be great for ...
A everyone. B some people.
C kids only.

▸ *SF How to do well in a test (pp. 158–159)*

## 3 Speaking

*You're on holiday with your partner. You want to discuss things to do tomorrow.*
*– Look at the pictures below. Choose three things that you'd like to do.*
*– Tell your partner about your ideas. How many things can you find that you both want to do?*

*Give reasons why you want (or don't want) to do something.*
*Partner A begins:* *A:* Let's ... *B:* ...

1

2

3

4

5

6

7

8

9

## 4 Writing

Buddy *is a magazine for teenagers. They want to publish letters from their readers about 'The best holiday I've ever had'.*
*Write a short letter to the magazine. Say ...*
*– when the holiday was*
*– where you went*
*– who you went with*
*– some things you did*
*– why you liked the holiday so much.*

... (date)

Dear Buddy

You wanted to know about the best holiday I've ever had. It was ...

...

# Atlanta rising

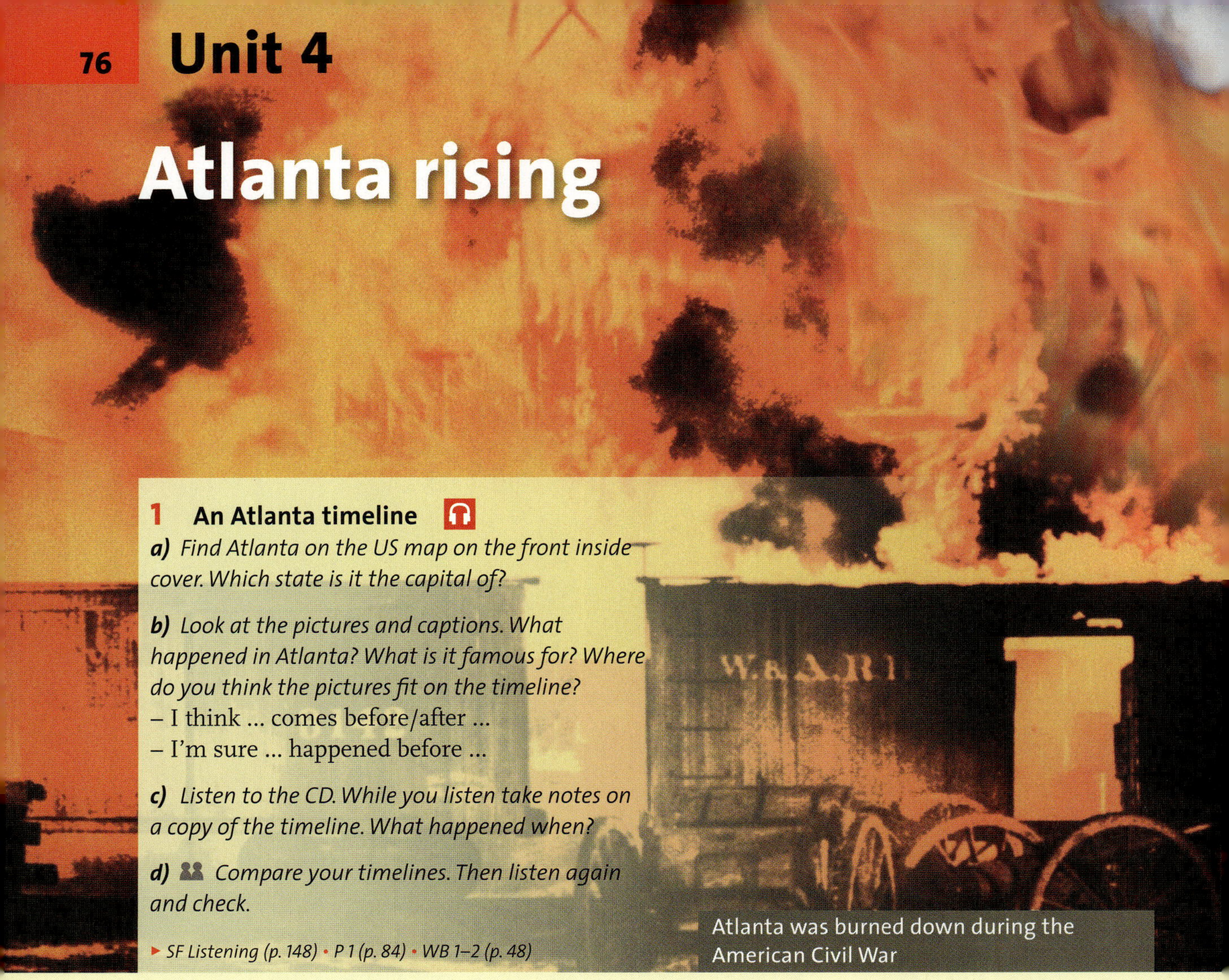

## 1 An Atlanta timeline

*a)* *Find Atlanta on the US map on the front inside cover. Which state is it the capital of?*

*b)* *Look at the pictures and captions. What happened in Atlanta? What is it famous for? Where do you think the pictures fit on the timeline?*
– I think ... comes before/after ...
– I'm sure ... happened before ...

*c)* *Listen to the CD. While you listen take notes on a copy of the timeline. What happened when?*

*d)* *Compare your timelines. Then listen again and check.*

▸ *SF Listening (p. 148) • P 1 (p. 84) • WB 1–2 (p. 48)*

Atlanta was burned down during the American Civil War

Black slaves on the cotton plantations around Atlanta had a terrible life of hard work and violence

The world's most famous soft drink was born

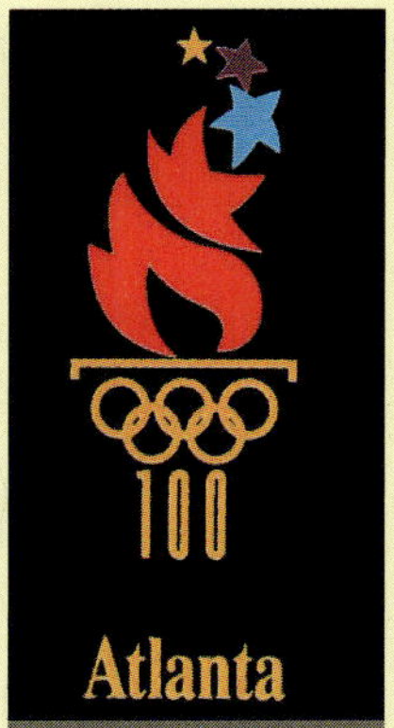


The 26th Olympic Games took place in Atlanta

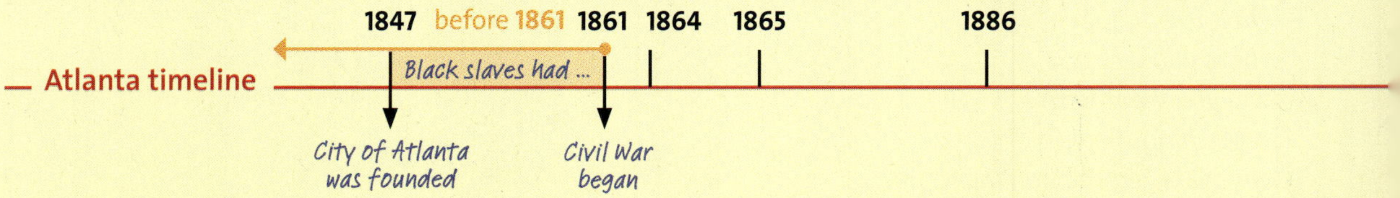

Shirley Franklin became the first African-American woman mayor of Atlanta

Dr Martin Luther King, Jr, leader of the Civil Rights Movement, was born in Atlanta

The famous news network CNN was founded in Atlanta

1929 | 1968 | 1980 | 1996 | 2002

▸ **Text File 11** *(pp 140–142)*

# All about ... television

## 1 TV listings

comedy series · cartoon · prime time: 8–10pm · drama series · crime series · reality show · news programme · documentary · competition · game show

**Atlanta, GA ★ cable**

**Wednesday, April 15**

| | | 7:00 pm | 7:30 pm | 8:00 pm | 8:30 pm | 9:00 p |
|---|---|---|---|---|---|---|
| 3 | ABC | World News Tonight | Entertainment Tonight | Grey's Anatomy | | Bostc |
| 4 | FOX | Access Hollywood | The Simpsons (Rerun) | Movie: Dodgeball | | |
| 5 | NBC | Evening News | Friends (Rerun) | Law & Order | | Las |
| 6 | CBS | News, Weather, Sports | The Price Is Right | Big Brother | | CSI |
| 34 | CNN | World News | World News | Business News | World News Europe | Worlc Asia |
| 50 | MTV | My Super Sweet 16 | America's Next Top Model | | Pimp My Ride | Nev |
| 61 | Animal Planet | Lions of Crocodile River | Animal C... | Serengheti | | AP |

*1 When can you watch 'Law & Order'? What channel is it on?*
*2 Can you watch 'America's Next Top Model' if you want to watch 'Dodgeball'?*
*3 What shows aren't on TV for the first time?*

## 2 TV words

***a)*** *Give examples of shows on German TV for each kind of programme in 1 above. Say more about these shows if you can, e.g.*
– 'Tatort' is a German crime series. It's about murders and the police.

***b)*** *Make a TV network. Collect words and phrases from this page. Add more words if you can.*

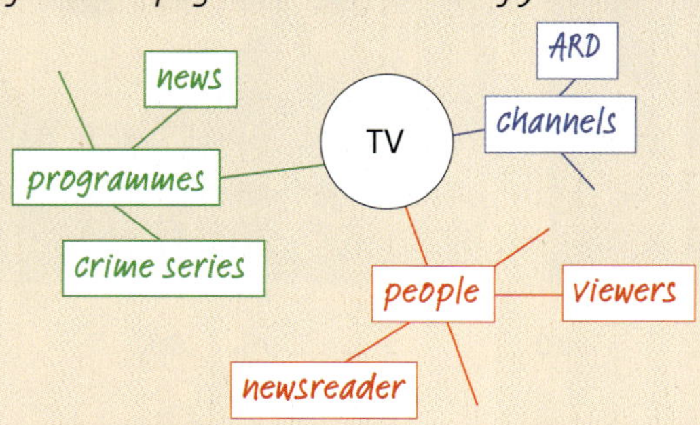


***c)*** *Compare your network with a partner's. Add words and phrases to your network.*

## 3 Now you

***a)*** *Write a text about the TV programmes you like. You can use these phrases:*

I watch TV about ... hours a day.
I like / don't like ... because ...
I usually / often / never watch ...
One of my favourite TV programmes is ...
You can watch it on ZDF / ...
It's on / It isn't on every week / day.
It lasts for ... minutes / hours.
My favourite actor / presenter / ... is ...

***b)*** *In small groups each student reads out his/her text. The others in the group give their opinion about the programmes he/she likes.*
– You watch more/less TV than me.
– I like/love/hate that programme too.
– I (don't) watch that programme because I think it's ...

▸ P 2–5 (pp. 84–85) • WB 3–6 (pp. 49–50)

## 4 It's 'Take Your Child to Work Day'

It was 'Take Your Child to Work Day' and Madison Young was going to spend the day at CNN with her mom. They were on their way to the studios.

'This is unbelievable, Mom,' said Madison. 'We've been in this traffic jam for 20 minutes. Is it always like this?'

'Well, it's been bad for two months now,' Mrs Young said. 'They're building a new bridge on Paces Ferry Road.'

Just then Mrs Young's cellphone rang. It was Dan, her boss at CNN.

'Josephine,' he said, 'I need you at the airport. There's been an explosion, and there have been no flights for over 50 minutes.'

'Terrorists?' she asked.

'We don't know anything yet, Josephine.'

'Cool,' said Madison after her mom's call. 'My day at CNN is going to be very exciting!'

'No, sorry, sweetheart. Your day at CNN has just ended. I can't take you with me. It might be dangerous. I'll drop you off at Dad's on the way.'

*Why isn't Madison in school? What kind of job does Mrs Young do?*

### Looking at language

***a)*** *Answer the questions:*
- How long have Madison and her mother been in the traffic jam?
  *They've been in the traffic jam for 20 minutes.*
- How long has the traffic been so bad?
  ...
- How long have there been no flights?
  ...

***b)*** *Translate the sentences you wrote for a) into German.*
*The English sentences use the* ***present perfect****.*
*What tense do you use in German?*

***c)*** **Extra** *Translate these sentences:*
- Ich bin seit drei Jahren an dieser Schule.
- Meine Eltern leben seit 15 Jahren hier.

► *P 6–9 (pp. 86–87) • WB 7–12 (pp. 51–54)*

### Americana ★ ★ ★

**Take Your Child to Work Day**
TYCTWD is a day when parents are allowed to take their children to their workplace. The kids can see what their mom or dad does there and get to know the world of work. TYCTWD takes place on the fourth Thursday in April.

Not all companies or schools take part in TYCTWD. But every year more than 25 million children visit their mother's or father's workplace on this special day.

*Is there something like TYCTWD in Germany? Do you think it's a good idea? Why (not)?*

## 5 Breaking news

Mr Young was surprised to see Madison at the King Center where he worked.

'Did you get bored with the TV studios?' he laughed.

'We never got to the studios,' said Madison angrily. 'There was a big explosion at the airport. So Mom dropped me off here.'

Mr Young looked worried. 'An explosion? That sounds dangerous!' He turned on the TV.

*What has happened at the airport? Is the problem over?*

## 6 At the King Center

Madison was happy that her mom was OK, but she was still disappointed that she couldn't spend her day at CNN.

'Well, I have to put away some of Dr King's letters,' said her dad. 'You could help me with that if you like. They've been on display for a few weeks – since April 4th.'

'Since the anniversary of his death,' Madison said.

Her dad was impressed. 'So you know when he died?'

'I've known that for years, Dad. And we started a school project on Dr King last Monday. So since Monday I've known even more about his life,' said Madison laughing. 'Dad, are the original letters he wrote really here?'

'They sure are! Follow me! By the way, when we're through with the letters, I have to work on a video for our website. Maybe you'd like to help.'

'That sounds great, Dad. Let's go.'

*How does Madison feel when she arrives? Does her mood change?*

The King Center has a library and archives on Martin Luther King.

### Looking at language

***a)*** *Collect all the phrases with* ***since*** *and* ***for*** *in* **5** *and* **6** *and add them to a copy of the table:*

| for | since |
|---|---|
| for a few weeks | since 8.30 this morning |
| for ... | since ... |

***b)*** *Which word –* ***since*** *or* ***for*** *– do you use for a period of time, which for a point in time?*

► GF 6: German 'seit' (pp.168–169) • P 10–12 (p. 88) • WB 13 (p. 54)

## 7 A timeline on Martin Luther King

*a) Fill in a copy of the timeline for Martin Luther King, Jr. Use information from this page. For three dates you have to do some research on the internet or in an encyclopedia.*

1929 1953 1955 1963 1964 1968

**Martin Luther King, Jr.**

Martin Luther King, Jr. (January 15, 1929 – April 4, 1968) became one of the most important leaders of the American Civil Rights Movement. As a young minister in the Baptist church, he saw that blacks were still segregated from whites and that they still didn't have many of the rights that whites had. King believed in non-violent protest and became famous through the March on Washington (1963).

It was in Washington, D.C., on August 28, 1963, that he made his most famous speech – 'I have a dream' in front of more than 250,000 people.

*This text is taken from a website. Why are some words in blue?*

*b) Read the Study Skills box on the right and discuss the questions below.*

- What sources could you use to find out more about Martin Luther King?
- What facts do you find if you use the 5 Ws on the website text on Martin Luther King in a)?
- What key words would you use to find out what Martin Luther King did in 1953?
- How would you search for more information on the March on Washington?

▸ SF Research (p. 146) • P 13 (p. 88) • WB 14–17 (pp. 55–56)

**STUDY SKILLS Research**

When you do research
- try to use English sources,
- always use more than one source,
- never copy whole sentences, use your own words.

Think of the 5 Ws (**Who**, **What**, **Where**, **When**, **Why**) to find useful facts in a text.

If you use the internet, you should choose **key words** carefully and put them into your search engine.

## 8 Extra Now you

*a) Make a timeline for another important person in the US Civil Rights Movement – Rosa Parks.*

*b) Compare timelines. Tell each other what you learned about Rosa Parks. Where did each of you get your information?*

# Extra Background File TOWARDS THE AFRICAN-AMERICAN DREAM

## A look at black America

*Look at the information below and discuss the question on the right. You can also use other information you already know, or you can do research on the internet, in books etc.*

Do you think Martin Luther King's dream has come true for black Americans? Think about:
- education
- the world of work
- sports
- politics
- music

### A Did you know ...?

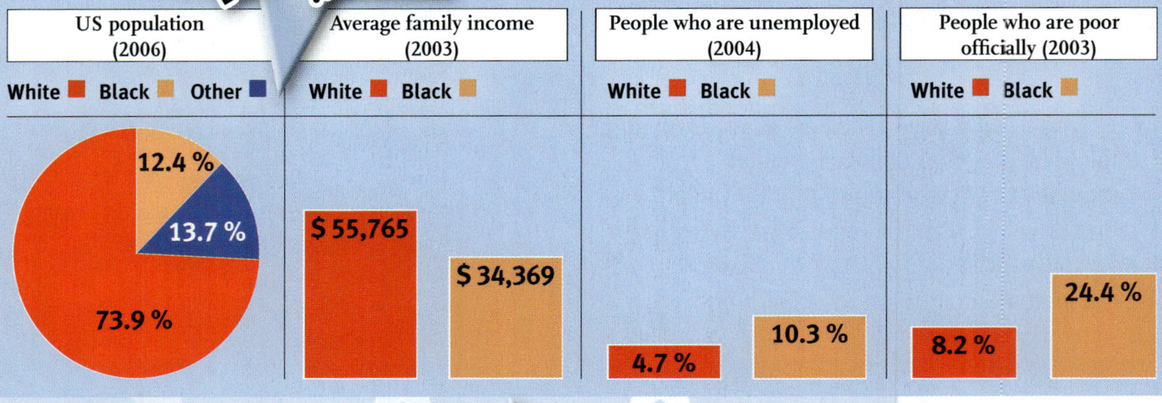


### B Education

In 2005, 6 % of white students left school without a high school diploma. For blacks the number was 10 %. 69 % of white students who finished high school in 2005 went on to college. The figure for black students was 57 %.

### C The Rodney King riots

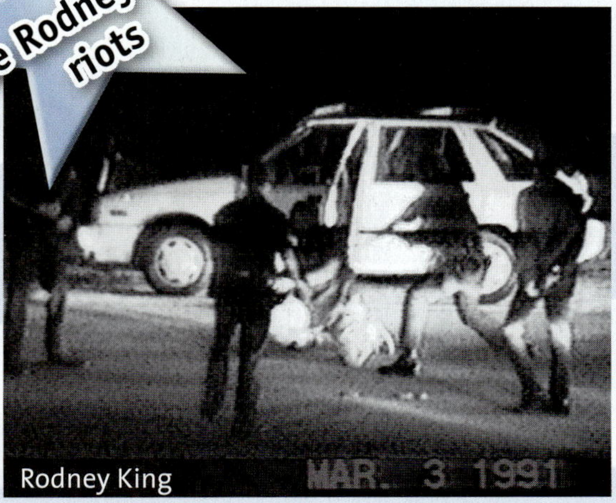

Rodney King

In 1991 ten Los Angeles policemen – all white – chased and stopped a car that was driven by Rodney King – a black man. Four of the policemen pulled King out of the car and beat him while the others watched.

What they didn't know: someone else was watching too, and he had a video camera. The film was shown on TV, and the policemen were arrested.

When a mostly white jury decided they had done nothing wrong, there were terrible riots in Los Angeles. The riots lasted six days and more than 50 people were killed.

## D Politics

Barack Obama

In 2004 Barack Obama was elected Senator for the state of Illinois. He was only the fifth African-American Senator in US history. In 2009 he became the 44th President of the United States and the first African American ever elected to that position.

## E Sports

LeBron James

Tiger Woods

In 1950, Earl Lloyd was the first black basketball player to play in the NBA. 55 years later, 73 % of NBA players were African Americans. Today, you can't imagine the NBA without black basketball stars like LeBron James or Stephon Marbury.

American football is another US sport with a lot of African-American players (65 %), but in baseball only 9 % of players are African Americans.

There are still very few black players in some other popular US sports, like hockey, golf or tennis. When Tiger Woods won the 2006 PGA championship he was the only black golf player out of 125 players in the competition.

## F Top Ten

Beyoncé

Black Eyed Peas

African-American musicians have become extremely popular, not only in the US but all over the world. They often set trends and are loved for their new sounds and lyrics.

On October 6, 2003, for the first time in the 50-year history of the Billboard music charts all Top Ten songs in the US were by black artists.

▸ *WB 18 (p. 57)* • **Text File 10** *(pp. 138–139)*

## 1 REVISION A bit of history (Passive)

*Which sentences would be better in the passive? Make changes if you need to.*

1 People brought African slaves to the US till 1808.
   *African slaves were brought to the US till 1808.*
2 Farmers in the South bought slaves to work on their cotton plantations.
   *No change.*
3 People founded the city of Atlanta in 1847.
4 People discovered gold in California in 1848.
5 John Pemberton first made Coca Cola in 1886.
6 Someone built the Hollywood sign in 1923.
7 They built the Empire State Building in only 13 1/2 months.
8 More than 12 million immigrants entered the US through Ellis Island.
9 Someone killed Martin Luther King in 1968.
10 They chose Atlanta for the 1996 Olympics.

**Remember**
You use the passive when you're more interested in what happened than in who did it. You need: a form of be + past participle.

## 2 WORDS Good programmes – bad programmes

**a)** *You can use these adjectives to describe TV programmes you like/don't like. Make two lists.*

awesome • awful • cool • excellent • exciting • fantastic • funny • stupid • terrible • uncool

**b)** *Here are some more words. Find the opposites.*

best • German • interesting • local • long • old-fashioned • recorded • same

boring • different • foreign • live • modern • national • short • worst

*best – worst* *German – ...*

**c)** *Use the words from a) and b) to write sentences about TV programmes you watch.*

*... is a fantastic music show. I'm not sure if it's live or recorded.*

*I'm not interested in soaps like ... because the stories are stupid. But I sometimes watch ...*

*I think reality shows like ... are a bit stupid sometimes. But I like ...*

*My favourite comedy show is ... It's excellent.*

*I love game shows like ... because they're exciting.*

## 3 WORDS More TV words

**a)** *Check the meaning of the words in the box. Then write sentences about yourself.*

+flat screen • +(to) hop channels • +(to) receive • +remote control • +satellite • +(to) turn up/down • +volume

1 We have cable TV/satellite TV/... *We have cable TV.*
2 We can receive 20/30/... channels. *We can ...*
3 We have a flat screen/a traditional TV.
4 I use the button on the TV/the remote control to turn the volume up or down.
5 I check/don't check the TV listings before I change channels.
6 I never/sometimes/... hop channels.
7 If I can't watch a programme I like, I record the programme/wait for a rerun.

**b)** *Compare with a partner.*

Do you look at the TV listings before you turn on the TV?

Do you have cable TV?

Do you ever record programmes?

Do your parents tell you to turn the volume down?

How many channels can you receive?

## 4 SPEAKING Talking about films or TV shows

***a)*** *Look at the dialogue between Emma and her friend Sally. What might go in the gaps? Write down the numbers 1 to 10 and possible words and phrases for each gap.*

*Emma* 1 the Simpsons last night?
*Sally* No, I didn't. What 2 ?
*Emma* Oh, Marge opened her own women-only fitness centre.
*Sally* And, 3 ?
*Emma* It wasn't bad. The 4 was really funny.
*Sally* Well, I was watching a documentary on tigers. I'm really 5 that kind of programme.
*Emma* I'm going to watch that Brad Pitt movie 6 tonight. Maybe we can watch together?
*Sally* I don't know. I 7 those big Hollywood movies.
*Emma* What 8 then?
*Sally* Well, I 9 documentaries on TV. And 10 music programmes.

***b)*** *Now listen to Emma and Sally. Take notes on the words and phrases they use in their dialogue. Compare them with your notes from a). If you have to, listen again.*

***c)*** *With your partner prepare a dialogue like the one between Emma and Sally. Don't write it out – just make notes. Then act out your dialogue for the class.*

more help ▸ D p. 118

## 5 MEDIATION TV in America

***a)*** *Todd, an American boy, is staying with the Kleins, a German family that you know. But Todd doesn't speak German and the family doesn't speak English. Help them in this conversation.*

*Frau K.* Kannst du bitte Todd fragen, wie er deutsches Fernsehen findet?
*You* She wants to know ...
*Todd* Well, my problem is that I don't understand very much. But I think it's funny when I hear American actors speaking German. I watched the Simpsons and Bart Simpson was speaking German. That was so funny.
*You* ...

***b)*** *Listen to the rest of the conversation and help Todd and the German family.*

**Remember**

You don't have to translate every word in a mediation situation. Just give the most important information.

▸ SF Mediation (p. 152)

## 6 READING The price of work for high school students (Drawing conclusions) ▸ SF p. 151

**1** Sometimes a text gives you the exact answers to your questions.

***a)*** ◻ ***What kind of things do students spend their money on? Find three things.***
*You can find the answer to this quite quickly in paragraph 1*

**2** For some questions you have to **look in different paragraphs** to find the information you need.

***b) Why do students work after school?***
*Here you need to look at paragraphs 1 and 6.*
*– want to buy what they want*
*– ...*

***c) What are the advantages of having a job?***
*Which paragraphs do you have to look at to answer this question?*
*Tip: The text talks about three advantages.*

**3** Sometimes the information you need is given indirectly. First find facts, then **draw conclusions.**

***d) Does the author think that students' school work suffers because they have a job?***
*The text doesn't give a direct answer. Find facts in the text and draw a conclusion to answer the question.*
*Facts:*
*– When I get home from my job at ...*
*– ...*
*Conclusion:*
*...*

***e)*** ◻ ***Does the author think it is a good or a bad thing for students to have a paid job?***
*Find facts in the text and draw a conclusion.*

***f)*** ◻ **Extra** *Do you think it's a good idea for students to have a job? Why (not)?*

# The price of work for high school students

(1) It's everywhere you look: Nike, GAP, and J-Lo are trying to sell you something. A lot of students want to wear the latest fashion, so they work after school to be able to buy cars, clothes or iPods without having to ask their parents for money.

(2) We talked to one hundred students from Watsonville High School in California and found that 30% work. Does their schoolwork suffer because they have a job?

(3) "A student who wants to be allowed to work has to have certain grades," Ms. Viotti, a counsellor at Watsonville High, said. But that doesn't mean you have to be a good student to be allowed to have a job. Average grades are enough to get the OK.

(4) "Having a job can have advantages for students' school career. Working often makes them more disciplined about doing schoolwork. And they learn how to organize their time," a chemistry teacher at Watsonville High said.

(5) But having a job isn't as great as it sounds. You have to do what others tell you to do and you often aren't paid well. Also, students go to school for seven hours, and many work for another four hours after school. That's an 11-hour work day.

(6) Having a paid job might be hard but many students have no choice. "Some students have to work to help their families in times of need," Ms. Viotti told us. "A lot of parents in Watsonville are poor or don't have jobs, so their kids have to help out."

(7) Watsonville High has a very high rate of students who don't finish their high school education. Their future usually suffers because of that. "When I get home from my job at 10 p.m. I'm often too tired to do my schoolwork," Kim, who works at a local supermarket, told us.

(8) In the US millions of teens like Kim work after school. For some it means getting work experience that will help them in their future jobs. But for many it means paying quite a high price: their education.

## 7 REVISION Madison's dreams (Present perfect)

*a)* ○ *Madison has a list of things she has always wanted to do. Write down which ones she has already done and which she hasn't done yet.*

1 *Madison has gone on the Grand Canyon skywalk.*
2 *She hasn't seen the Canyon ...*

*b) Make a list of 10 exciting things to do. Which have you (already) done? Which haven't you done (yet)? Mark them with a tick (✓) or a cross (×).*

*c) Tell your partner about the things on your list and if you've already done them or not.*

1 go on the Grand Canyon skywalk ✓
2 see the Canyon from a helicopter ×
3 fly to Washington with Mum and Dad ✓
4 visit the CNN studios ×
5 stay in a hotel in Las Vegas ✓
6 spend a holiday at Disney World in Florida ×
7 talk to people who knew Martin Luther King ✓
8 travel to Europe ×

## 8 WORDS believable/unbelievable (Word building)

**Tip**

Some adjectives are made by adding -able to a verb, e.g. *believe – believable*, *do – doable*. The new adjective means: You can do it or it can be done.
Adding un- often gives you the opposite, e.g. *believable – unbelievable*.

*a) Look at the adjectives in the box and try to say what they mean.*

breakable • doable • downloadable • drinkable • laughable • likeable • unbelievable • understandable • unreadable

*b) Choose adjectives from the box to complete the sentences.*

1 There are ... ringtones at this new website.
2 Ben is a really ... guy. Everyone wants to be his friend.
3 Be careful. Some of the things in the bag could be ...
4 Can you write your address again, please. I'm afraid it's ...
5 The water seems dirty. Are you sure it's ...?

*c)* ● **Extra** *With a partner make sentences with the four adjectives you didn't use in b).*

## 9 //○ I've known him for five years (Present perfect with 'for') ▸ D p. 118

*Answer the questions. Use the present perfect.*

1 Is Sam your best friend?
– *Sag ja, du kennst ihn seit fünf Jahren.*
*Yes, I ... (know) him for five years.*

2 Tim isn't at school today. Do you know why?
– *Sag, dass er seit einigen Tagen eine Erkältung hat.*
*He ... (have) a cold for a few days.*

3 How long has your mum been a waitress?
– *Sag, dass sie seit zwölf Jahren in einem Café arbeitet.*
*She ... (work) in a café for twelve years.*

4 How long has your Grandma lived in this town?
– Sag, dass sie seit Jahren hier wohnt.
*She ... (live) here for years.*

5 Is Rob ill? I haven't seen him for a while.
– *Sag ja, er liegt seit sechs Monaten im Krankenhaus.*
*Yes, he ... (be) in hospital for six months.*

6 How long have you had your skateboard? Is it new?
– *Sag nein, du hast es seit zwei Jahren.*
*No, I ... (have) it for two years.*

## 10 //○ Mr Young at the King Center (since/for)

▸ D p. 119

*Mr Young is telling Madison about his job. Add* **since** *or* **for** *to complete the sentences.*

1 I've been in my job ... 1999, Madison.
2 I've known my boss ... 2005.
3 I need a new computer. I've had this one ... almost six years.
4 Martin Luther King's wife started the Center, but she's been dead ... a few years.
5 We've had an online learning programme ... a number of years.
6 This place has been part of the National Park system ... the last 30 years.
7 Martin Luther King's birthday has been a holiday in the US ... 1986.

## 11 How long have you been here? (since/for)

**a)** *Copy the chart and fill it in for yourself.*

| How long ... | Me | Partner 1 |
|---|---|---|
| be / at this school | 4 years | last year |
| be / at school today | 8.05 | ... |
| know / your best friend | ... | |
| live / in this town | | |
| have / your mobile | | |

**b)** *Make appointments with three classmates. Ask and answer questions and fill in your chart.*
How long have you been at this school? ...

**c)** *Write sentences about you and your partners.*
*I've been at this school for four years. Malte and Tim have been here since last year. And Anne has ...*

## 12 ● The US has had 50 states ... (since/for)

The White House in Washington, D.C.

**a)** *Partner B: Look at p. 109. Partner A: Ask questions with* **How long ...** + **present perfect**. *Write down your partner's answers.*

1 US – have – 50 states?
A: How long has the US had 50 states?
B: The US ...
2 Washington – be – capital of the US?
3 the railway – link – the East Coast with the West Coast?
4 White House – be – home of US presidents?

**b)** *Answer your partner's questions. Use the* **present perfect** *with* **since** *or* **for**.

5 Georgia ... (be) a US state ... 1788.
6 Atlanta ... (be) the capital of Georgia ... almost 240 years.
7 Atlanta ... (have) black mayors ... 1974.
8 Martin Luther King ... (be) dead ... more than 40 years now

## 13 Extra ● LISTENING 'We shall overcome'

**a)** *As you listen to the radio programme, write down two key words for each question.*

1 What was the Civil Rights Movement trying to change?
2 Who were the Freedom Riders and what did they do?
3 What was happening at the restaurant?
4 What happened to Ellis Washington's uncle?
5 What's special about the song 'We shall overcome', and what did it mean to black people?

**b)** *Compare notes. Listen again. Then write some sentences to answer one of the five questions in a).*

# Melba's story

## Background

Slavery ended in the US in 1865. But for almost a century after that, blacks in many states, especially in the South, did not have the same rights as whites and were segregated from them.

'Segregation' meant that laws kept African Americans apart from white Americans – on buses and trains, in restaurants and hotels. There were cinemas, park benches, waiting rooms for 'white only' and for 'colored' people. There were separate schools for white children and schools for black children. And the schools for black children were almost always older and smaller.

*What was segregation? Collect as many examples as you can. What do you think about segregation?*

In 1954, the US Supreme Court ended school segregation: all schools now had to open their doors to both black and white children. But some states didn't want to do what the new law said.

In 1957, nine black students were chosen to move from the high school for black children in Little Rock, Arkansas, to the big high school for whites, Central High. Soon they would be known as the Little Rock Nine.

Classroom in a black school

Classroom in a white school

## The story

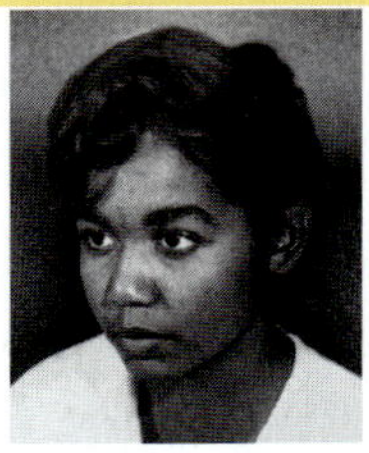

*One of the **Little Rock Nine** was Melba Pattillo, and this is her story.*

Melba Pattillo was born in Little Rock, the capital of Arkansas, on 7th December 1941. Arkansas was a segregated state.

When Melba was five years old, she saved five cents for a ride on the merry-go-round in the park. She wanted to ride the black and white horse and could see that it was empty.

"Could I have one ticket for the merry-go-round, please?" she asked.

"There's no space for you here," the ticket man said.

When she pointed to the empty horse, he shouted, "You don't belong here, you little nigger!"

In her book, *Warriors don't cry*, Melba wrote later: "Angry faces looked at me as if I had done something terribly wrong. As I ran past the people who were waiting I was terrified. I didn't even pick up my money. At the age of five I learned that – even if all the horses on the merry-go-round were empty – there would be no space for me."

In 1955, a year after the Supreme Court had said that segregation in schools was wrong, a teacher at Melba's all-black school asked if any students wanted to go to the white high school. Melba immediately volunteered. She was only thirteen years old.

Two years later, in 1957, at the start of the school year on 3rd September, the time had come for nine black students to join the 2,000 white students at Little Rock Central High School. Melba was now fifteen years old.

Lots of angry white people from all over the South came to the school. It was too dangerous for the nine black students: they had to stay home.

The next day they tried to get through all the angry white people to the steps of the school.

But the Governor of Arkansas supported the white people who didn't want blacks at their children's school. He sent the National Guard to the school to stop the black students. The white people became angrier and angrier so Melba and the others had to run and escape.

That night Melba wrote in her diary:

I was disappointed not to see what is inside Central High School. I don't understand why the governor sent soldiers to keep us out. I don't know if I should go back. But Grandma is right. If I don't go back, they will think they have won.

On 23rd September, the black students got into the school through a side door. Most of the white students were cruel to them – they shouted names at them and kicked them. And outside the people got angrier and angrier. In the end the police decided that they had to get the nine out or they might be killed.

> I feel specially cared about because the guard is there. If he wasn't there, I'd hear more of the voices of those people who say I'm a nigger ... that I'm not valuable, that I have no right to be alive. Thank you, Danny.

That night Melba wrote in her diary:

> There seems to be no space for me at Central High. I don't want integration to be like the merry-go-round. Please, God, make a space for me.

Two days later the US President sent soldiers to help the black students. The soldiers drove them to the school and protected them as they entered the school through the front door for the first time.

And each of the nine got a soldier as bodyguard for the school day. Melba's was a young soldier called Danny. That night she wrote:

But even Danny couldn't stop one attack on Melba. This is how she describes it in her book:

"I saw a boy – he was coming towards me. I tried to move aside, but he moved with me. The boy threw something in my face. The pain in my eyes was so terrible. I couldn't hear or see or feel anything except the fire in my eyes.

"Someone pulled me along very fast. Hands pulled my fingers from my eyes. Then cold, cold water was splashed in my eyes. The water felt so good."

The hands were the hands of Danny, Melba's bodyguard. He saved her eyes: the boy had thrown acid.

Melba spent a whole year at Central High. But the following year, the Governor of Arkansas closed all high schools in Little Rock because he didn't want black kids to go to school with white kids. Melba was offered a new home and the chance to finish her education by a family in California. They were white.

Melba went on to university and became a journalist. Today she lives in San Francisco.

## Working with the text

### 1 Headlines

*Which headline fits Melba's story best?*

Little Rock Nine welcomed at Central High School

☆ LITTLE ROCK NINE ENTER HIGH SCHOOL WITH HELP OF US SOLDIERS

President bans black students from Little Rock Central High

### 2 Headings for the parts of the story

***a)*** ○ *Put these eight headings for the different parts of the story in the right order.*

*1* Angry whites stop the Nine
*2* Schools closed in Little Rock, 1958
*3* Attack on Melba
*4* Governor sends National Guard
*5* Inside Central High for the first time
*6* Soldiers protect the Little Rock Nine
*7* Melba and the merry-go-round
*8* Melba volunteers to go to Central High

***b)*** ● *In one or two sentences say what each part is about.*

### 3 Who did what?

***a)*** //○ ▸ *D p. 119*

*Match the list of people and what they did.*

*1* The white people in Little Rock ...
*2* The Governor of Arkansas ...
*3* The National Guard ...
*4* The US President ...
*5* The soldiers ...
*6* Danny ...

- tried to stop attacks on Melba.
- didn't want blacks at their children's school.
- sent soldiers to help the black students.
- stopped the black students when they tried to enter the school.
- supported the white parents.
- drove the black students to school and protected them.

***b)*** ● *Did these people help Melba? Or did they make things more difficult for her?*

*The governor made things difficult for her. He ...*

▸ *WB 19 (pp. 58)* • **Checkpoint 4** *WB (p. 59)* • *Selbsteinschätzung 3–4 WB (pp. 60–61)*

### 4 //○ Melba's feelings ▸ *D p. 119*

*How do you think Melba felt when ...?*

*1* ... she couldn't go on the merry-go-round
*2* ... she volunteered to go to Central High
*3* ... she saw the angry white people
*4* ... she met her bodyguard, Danny
*5* ... a boy threw something in her face
*6* ... the governor closed Central High

*The words in the box can help you:*

amazed • angry • disappointed • excited • happy • glad • nervous • proud • sad • safe • scared • shy • terrified • unhappy • ...

### 5 Extra Your questions

*Think of three questions that you would like to ask Melba or the others about their experience.*

Melba Pattillo Beals in 2007

The Little Rock Nine in 2007

## How am I doing?

***a)*** *Find or choose the correct answers.*

### Atlanta and its history

1 The US Civil War was fought between ...
A black slaves and white farmers.
B states in the north and in the south.
C CNN and the BBC.
D Native Americans and European settlers.

2 Martin Luther King worked hard to stop ...
A the Civil Rights Movement.
B the selling of blacks as slaves.
C Shirley Franklin.
D discrimination against blacks.

3 Which of these is not at home in Atlanta?
A the White House B CNN
C Coca Cola D the King Center

### TV words

4 Write down the words that match these definitions:
a) a TV show that's on once a week
b) a show with real people, not actors, who do things naturally
c) a show with lots of jokes and funny scenes
d) the best time for TV, in the late evening
e) a film or TV show that tells you about things that really happened

5 Which is *not* a good way to find out about something that happened yesterday?
A newspaper B radio C TV D books

6 A good place to find out what's on TV is ...
A a TV show. B a news programme.
C the TV listings. D CNN.

### Research

7 When you do research, you should use ...
A only Wikipedia. B only one good source. C more than one source.
D only sources in your own language.

8 In your notes you should ...
A never use your own words.
B write down everything from an internet page. C always use complete sentences.
D never copy whole sentences, use your own words.

### Reading

9 You need special information from a text. When do you have to draw conclusions?
A All answers are directly in the text.
B The text is very long and gives lots of facts.
C There is nothing about it in the text.
D The information is given indirectly.

### Grammar

10 Put in the correct form of the verb:
a) We ... (live) in the same flat for six years.
b) I ... (have) English with Frau Marx since the beginning of last year.

11 Decide: 'since' or 'for'?
a) ... kindergarten b) ... an hour
c) ... 9/11 d) ... the accident
e) ... a long time

12 Say it in English.
a) Is Max your friend? – *Sag ja, du kennst ihn seit 2 Jahren.*
b) Is he ill? – *Sag ja, er ist seit Montag im Krankenhaus.*

***b)*** *Check your answers on p. 261 and add up your points.*

***c)*** *If you had 20 or more points, well done! Maybe you can help students who had fewer points. If you had 19 points or fewer, it's a good idea to do some more work before you go on to the next unit. Where did you make mistakes? The chart below will tell you what you can do to improve your English.*

| No. | Areas | Find out more | Exercises |
|---|---|---|---|
| 1– 3 | Atlanta and its history | Unit 4 (pp. 76–77, 81) | P 1 (p. 84), WB 1 (p. 48) |
| 4– 6 | TV words | Unit 4 (p. 78) | P 2–3 (p. 84), WB 3–4 (p. 49) |
| 7– 8 | Research | Unit 4 (p. 81), SF (p. 146) | WB 16 (p. 56) |
| 9 | Reading | P 6 (p. 86) | WB 9 (p. 52) |
| 10–12 | Grammar: since/for | GF 6 (pp. 168–169) | P 9–12 (pp. 87–88), WB 11–13 (pp. 53–54) |

## Extra Who did it? A mystery game[1]

### 1 The mystery

Mo, the reporter

Hi! I'm Mo. I write for the student newspaper at Westwood High. This week the big story is about a cheat[2] in Mr Bell's History class! On Thursday the class took a test. But after the test a student found a copy of the test paper[3] in the library ... So it seems that someone had the test paper *before* the test.
I've spoken to everyone in Mr Bell's class. And now I'm sure that one of the people in this room is the cheat. But who?
Let's meet the suspects[4].

1 Sam

2 Jacko

3 Flash

4 Nat

5 CJ

6 Scott

7 Cindy

8 Mr Bell

[1] mystery game ['mɪstri geɪm] *Detektivspiel* [2] cheat/(to) cheat [tʃiːt] *Betrüger/in, Schummler/in / betrügen, schummeln*
[3] test paper ['test peɪpə] *Klassenarbeit* [4] suspect ['sʌspekt] *Verdächtige(r)*

## 2 Who's who?

***a)*** *Match the photos (1–8) and the speech bubbles (A–H).*

***b)*** *What do you learn about the suspects?*
- ... works hard/doesn't work hard.
- ... gets/doesn't get good grades.
- ...

***c)*** *Choose one of the suspects. Read their part out loud to the class. Which of you is the best actor?*

**A** Mr Bell says I talk and joke too much in class. But his class is easy for me. If any student gets a better grade than me, I'll give them my MP3 player. I know I'm the best!

**B** I usually get A's. But now my family has money problems and I work at Mack's Burger Bar in the evenings and on the weekends to earn money. I'm always tired and I don't have much time to study. Cindy is my girlfriend.

**C** I usually get D's, sometimes C's or F's. I'm interested in photography[1]. I'm really excited about the school trip to Atlanta and the King Center with my class.

**D** I'm new to Westwood High. I don't have any friends here. I really don't like Jacko. He's really a big mouth and he thinks he's so smart.

**E** I'm popular. Everyone likes me. I would do anything for Scott. He's my boyfriend. I usually get C's in class.

**F** Study for tests? Not me! I'd rather play basketball. My family is rich, so I don't have to work hard. I like Cindy, but she's not interested in me. She's only interested in Scott.

**G** This is a very difficult job. The students give me a hard time. They always talk and laugh and they don't listen to me.

**H** I'm an average student. My parents always say I should do better. I study REALLY hard, but I usually get C's. I never fail[2], but I never get an A.

### Americana ★ ★ ★

In the US lots of schools have an honor code[3] to stop cheating. In some schools, students sign a promise at the start of the school year.

In other schools, students write the promise on every test and important piece of work. The teacher might not be in the room when a class takes a test. Students must tell the teacher if another student breaks the honor code.

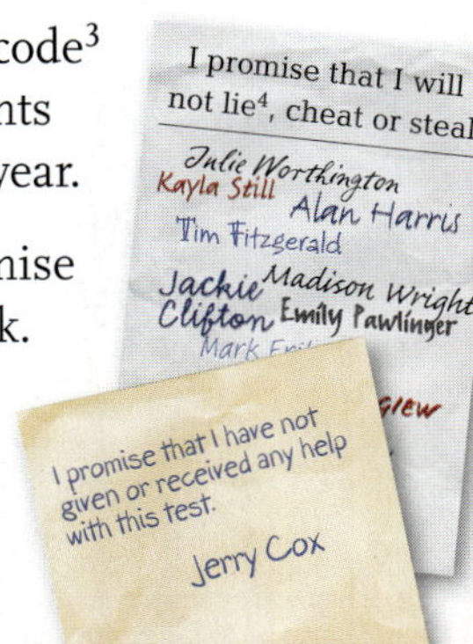


[1] photography [fəˈtɒgrəfi] *Fotografie* [2] (to) fail [feɪl] *durchfallen, nicht bestehen* [3] honor code [ˈɒnə kəʊd] *Ehrenkodex*
[4] (to) lie / the lie [laɪ] *lügen/die Lüge*

## 3 The scene of the crime

*Before the game starts, study Mo's notes.*

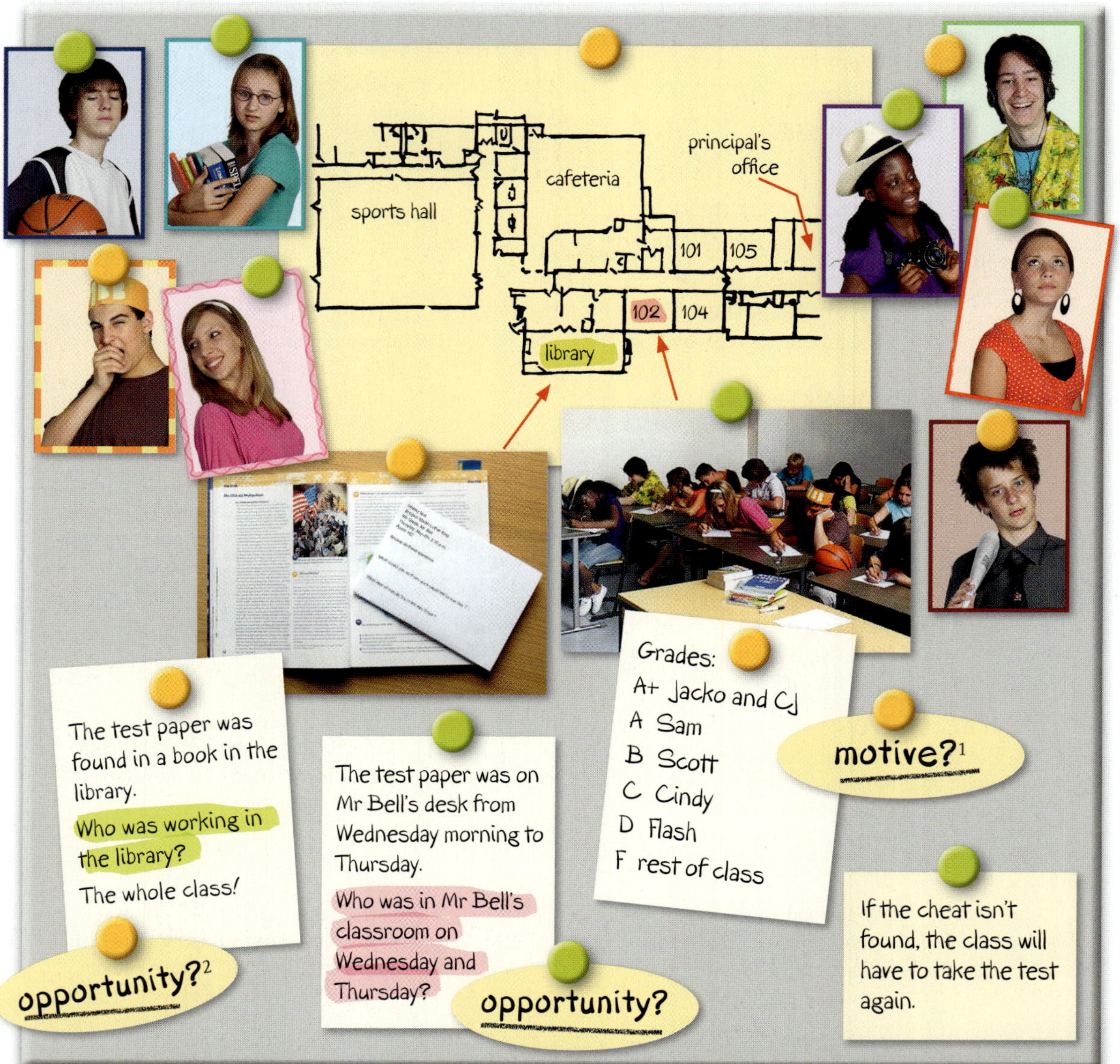


## 4 What do we know so far?

**a)** *Fill in the first two columns[3] (names of the suspects and grades) on a copy of this chart. Use the information from this page.*

**b)** *Add any other information that might be important from pp. 94–96.*

| Suspects | Got a good grade | Had a motive | Had an opportunity | Other comments |
|---|---|---|---|---|
| Sam | yes | | | |
| Jacko | yes | | | |

[1] motive ['məʊtɪf] *Motiv* [2] opportunity [ˌɒpətju:nəti] *Gelegenheit* [3] column ['kɒləm] *Spalte*

## 5 How the mystery game works

## Scene 1

*It's Friday, the day after the test. All the suspects are in Mr Bell's classroom.*

*Mr Bell* Maybe you could tell us where you found the test paper, Nat?

*Nat* Well, after the test I went to the library. I found the test paper inside a book about Martin Luther King. So someone had the questions before the test and was looking for the answers.

*Mr Bell* OK class, the person who did this is in a lot of trouble! Remember the school honor code! "I will not lie, steal or cheat." And if we don't find the cheat, the whole class will have to take the test again.

*Sam* *(worried)* Oh no, you can't make us do it again! I got an A! My grandmother will be really proud of me. Maybe I won't get an A on a second test.

*Mr Bell* Yes, Sam. Your A was a big surprise. Especially after that letter from the principal. Can I read it out?

*Sam* No problem.

*Mr Bell reads letter out loud.* →

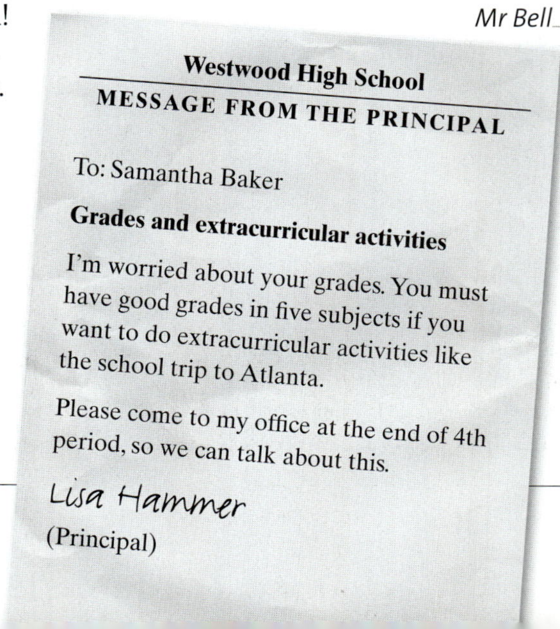

**Westwood High School**

**MESSAGE FROM THE PRINCIPAL**

To: Samantha Baker

**Grades and extracurricular activities**

I'm worried about your grades. You must have good grades in five subjects if you want to do extracurricular activities like the school trip to Atlanta.

Please come to my office at the end of 4th period, so we can talk about this.

Lisa Hammer
(Principal)

*Jacko* Hmm. I'm not sure if this is important, but err ... Sam was here in Mr Bell's room on Wednesday morning ... alone ... – Sorry Sam, but what were you doing in his room?

*Sam* *(not smiling)* I wanted to show a photo to Mr Bell. But you were in the room alone when I arrived, Jacko. And you got a better mark than me – A+!! Why were you here?

*Jacko* I had one of Mr Bell's books. I left it on his desk. I had to study extra hard for this test because of that stupid bet[1].

*Mr Bell* Bet? What bet?

*Cindy* Oh, don't you know, Mr Bell? Jacko said he'd give his MP3 player away if anyone got a better grade than him.

*Mr Bell* Hmm. So that's why the test was so important to you, Jacko!

[1] (to) bet / the bet [bet] *wetten/die Wette*

*Scott* (*laughing*) Hey, Jacko! Did you really do extra work? That doesn't sound like you!

*Nat* (*sadly*) You're lucky, Jacko. You always get good grades. You don't have to study hard. Not like me.

*Jacko* Listen. The person who took the test paper wanted to win my MP3 player. So who got good grades? CJ got A+ like me!

*CJ* (*angrily*) So what? I always got good grades at my old school.

*Flash* What about Scott? He got a good grade.

*Cindy* It wasn't Scott! Maybe it was you, Flash. Maybe the letter you gave me in class on Wednesday is a clue[1]?

*She reads the letter out loud.*

> Cindy
>
> I think you're amazing. We would look so good together. Everyone thinks Scott is a nice guy, but he's not as perfect as you think.
> Leave him. I can give you everything you need.
>
> Flash

*Flash* What has my letter got to do with it? I didn't get a good grade. I got a D. Anyway, I don't care about tests – the only thing that's important is basketball!

*Scott* You're so stupid, Flash!

*Flash* Listen! It was Scott! He came back to school after class on Wednesday. I saw him. Maybe he took the test paper then.

*Nat* I saw Flash and Scott on Wednesday after school. Flash wanted to fight with Scott. He pushed him. But Scott walked away.

*Scott* That's true. I was in a hurry. I wasn't going to fight Flash ... not in school anyway. That would be stupid! I could get into trouble for that.

*CJ* Hmm. I've just had an idea. Maybe the person who stole the test didn't do it to get a good grade.

*Nat* Err ... What do you mean?

*CJ* Well, maybe Flash's plan was to make Scott look bad[2]. He stole the paper so that we'd think it was Scott.

*Nat* (*excited*) Yes, yes and then he tried to start a fight with Scott. He wanted to get Scott into trouble.

*Cindy* But why did he want my darling Scotty to look bad?

*Nat* Oh Cindy, think about it! (*slowly*) That way you might think that Scott isn't perfect. And Ms Hammer might think he cheats and fights. And she might throw him out of school for breaking the honor code.

*Flash* Look, it's all lies! I didn't take the test paper.

[1] clue [klu:] *Hinweis* [2] (to) make sb. look bad *jn. schlecht dastehen lassen*

## 6 What do we know so far?

*a) Think about **scene 1**. Try to answer these questions.*

**If someone steals a test paper, they usually want to get a good grade**
- Who got a good grade?
- Whose grade was a surprise?
- Who needed a good grade? Why?

**Different people might have different motives to steal the paper**
- Who wanted to win Jacko's MP3 player?
- Who wanted people to think that someone else cheated?

**The cheat needs an opportunity to steal the paper**
- Who was in Mr Bell's room alone?
- Who was in school after class on Wednesday?

*b) Add to the chart you started in **4** (p. 96) like this:*

| Suspects | Got a good grade | Had a motive | Had an opportunity | Other comments |
|---|---|---|---|---|
| Sam | yes | yes | yes | her grade was a surprise |
| Jacko | yes | | | |

## 7 Questions and answers

*a) **Suspects**: Go to the **role cards** on pp. 254–255. You have to answer some questions. You'll find your answers on your role card.*

***Detectives**: Ask one or more of the suspects these questions:*

- Why do you think Sam got a good grade on the test?
- Did you want to win Jacko's MP3 player?
- Were you in school after class on Wednesday?

*b) Report back to the others. Do you think any of the suspects is lying?*

*c) Is there any important new information? Add it to your chart.*

## 8 What do we know so far?

*Listen to Mo and check your notes. Have you got everything?*

*Mo* OK. So what do we know so far? We know that Sam has to get good grades because she wants to go to Atlanta on the school trip. So she's lucky that her grandmother met Martin Luther King and told Sam all about him.

And then there's Jacko. He had to get the best grade in the class to keep his MP3 player. But who was interested? Everyone in the class has an MP3 player. But CJ likes the same music as Jacko. She'd like to have his playlist.

What about Flash? We know that he really likes Cindy. *(Other people laugh and whistle.)* And Flash usually gets what he wants. But Cindy has already got a boyfriend – Scott. Maybe Flash decided to try to get Scott out of the way? What do you think?

## Scene 2

*Nat has remembered something about CJ's old school.*

*Nat* Hey, CJ, what's the name of your old school? Is it South High? There was something in the news about that school.

*Mr Bell* That's right. A test paper was stolen, but they didn't find the thieves. I saw the story in this week's newspaper. I've got the paper here. *(He reads the article out loud.)*

> STOLEN TEST PAPER
> AT SOUTH HIGH SCHOOL
>
> Thieves stole an important test paper from the office at South High School. They tried to sell copies of the test to students on the internet. The thieves have not been caught yet.

*Jacko* So why did you leave your old school, CJ?

*CJ* *(angrily)* Oh Jacko, you've really got a big mouth! I left South High for a good reason ... and it had nothing to do with test papers! Sometimes I wish I could go back to my old school. I had some great friends there ...

*Jacko* OK, OK! Calm down!

*CJ* Right, Jacko. It's your turn now! Can you tell us what this is? It fell out of your pocket.

*Jacko* That's easy! It's a page out of an electronics magazine. I might buy something from that shop. Why?

*Sam* Wow. I need one of these! Look everyone. It's amazing! You put this in your ear and you can hear the answers to your test questions! Great!

*Nat* Hey! It's so small! I want one too!

*Mr Bell* Nat, Sam! That's not a good idea! It's wrong to cheat!

*Sam* Yeah yeah, Mr Bell. I'm joking! I would be too scared to use one of those. I'm not a cheat!

*CJ* But Jacko wants to buy one. He thinks cheating is a good idea.

*Jacko* No CJ, you're wrong! Look at the MP3 player! That's what I want to buy.

*Sam* Oh, yeah! Look at the MP3 player. That's cool! It's better than yours, Flash!

*Flash* Really? I don't know about that. But about the test. I've got something interesting here. *(He reads.)*

**$ 2000**
**Dunn Prize**
**for Best Student**
**at Westwood High School**

This prize is given at the end of the school year to the student with the best grades.

Last year's winner was Alex Davis.

*Sam* Do you think that the person who stole the paper wants to win the prize?

*Jacko* Exactly! And who could win the prize?

*Sam* *(laughs)* Not me!

*Nat* *(sadly)* Not me.

*Scott* Oh, go on Flash, say it. You think I did it for the prize money.

*Flash* That's right! We all know you need the money. Sorry Cindy, but your Mr Perfect isn't as perfect as he looks. He's a cheat.

*Cindy* But he doesn't have to cheat. He'll win the prize anyway. Scott's the best. Everyone knows that.

*Flash* Hah! But since he started working at Mack's Burger Bar he's too tired to study. So he needed a little extra help.

*Scott* You're wrong, Flash. Yes, I want to win the prize! Yes, I need the money! But I'm not a cheat.

*Nat* What about Cindy? She would do anything for Scott. Before the test she talked about stealing the paper for him. She was worried about his grades.

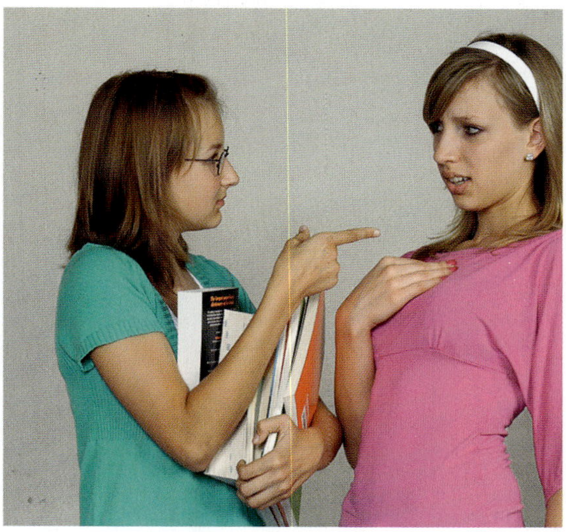

*Cindy* It's true. I said that. But, Nat, you know I was only joking.

*Nat* I thought you were joking, but maybe you were serious?

*Cindy* Thanks, Nat, I thought you were a friend. I felt sorry for you when you started to cry in the test.

*Nat* We are friends, but ...

*Cindy* You said that you would do anything to find out what was on the test paper. Maybe you were serious.

*Nat* But I got an F, remember. Sam got the A ... and the letter from the principal.

*Sam* I've just remembered something! When I was waiting to see Mr Bell, I saw that he had a letter from Ms Hammer too! I think it was about our grades. It might be important.

*Mr Bell* It's true, I got a letter from Ms Hammer. Here, you can read it if you want.

*Sam reads the letter out loud.*

**Westwood High School**

**MESSAGE FROM THE PRINCIPAL**

To: Mr. Bell

Please come to see me at 3:15 p.m. on Friday. I would like to talk to you about your classes. Please bring your grade book.

Lisa Hammer

(Principal)

*Mr Bell* But surely you don't think I stole my own test, Sam?

*Sam* Err ...No, maybe not ...

*Scott* Aha! But maybe it wasn't stolen. Maybe somebody wanted to do the test again so that we would get better grades.

*Nat* You don't think ...

*Scott* Yeah, we made you look really bad, Mr Bell.

*CJ* That's true! 21 students out of 26 got a grade below a C! What will the principal say?

## 9 What do we know so far?

*a) Who is it?*

1 She's stressed about her school work.

2 She'll do anything for Scott.

3 He's worried because his class got really bad grades.

4 He doesn't like Scott, but he likes Cindy a lot.

5 He's a bit crazy. He made a stupid bet.

6 He wants to win the Dunn Prize.

7 She needs good grades so that she can do extracurriculars.

8 She likes Jacko's music.

*b) Who did it? What do you think?*

*A:* I think Cindy did it because she ... *B:* I don't agree. I think Flash did it because he ...

... is crazy enough to cheat. After all he had that magazin.
... liked Jacko's music and wanted his MP3 player.
... really wanted to win the Dunn Prize.
... wanted the test paper for Scott.
... was so stressed by her bad grades.
... wants the class to do the test again.
... wants to make Scott look bad.
... needed good grades to go to Atlanta.

I agree. Or maybe ...
I don't agree. Maybe ...
I'm not sure ...
Maybe that's true. But I think ...
I think that's right. Or ...

*c) Go back to your chart in **6b** (p. 100). Can you add anything?*

## 10 Questions and answers

*a) **Suspects**: Go to the **role cards** on pp. 256–257. You have to answer some questions. You'll find your answers on your **role card**.*

***Detectives**: Ask one or more of the suspects these questions:*

Why did Nat start to cry in the test?

Do you want to take the test again?

Who do you think did it?

*b) When you've finished report back to the others. Add any important new information to your chart.*

## 11 What do we know so far?

*Listen and check your notes for the last time. Have you got everything?*

## 12 Who do you think did it?

**a)** *Say who you think did it and why. Your notes might help you.*

– I (don't) think it was ... because ...
– I think ... is lying when he/she says ...
– I believe ... when he/she says ...
– I think/don't think ... is a cheat.

**b)** *Listen to Mo and find out if you were right.*

[1] truth [tru:θ] *Wahrheit*

# Unit 1

## 1 The five boroughs of New York

▸ Unit 1 (p. 20)

***a)*** *Listen to your partner. Which of the five boroughs is he/she describing?*

***b)*** *Now read out the texts below. Your partner must say which boroughs you're describing.*

3 A famous ferry goes between this borough – also an island – and Manhattan. On the way it goes past the Statue of Liberty. This borough is south-west of Manhattan.

4 There's a river between this borough and the island of Manhattan. It's north of Manhattan. Lots of famous black singers and bands come from here.

3 The correct answer is 'Staten Island'. 4 The correct answer is 'The Bronx'.

EVERYDAY ENGLISH

## 14 SPEAKING Making plans together

▸ Unit 1 (p. 25)

*You and your partner are on holiday in New York. You want to spend the day together, but you have different ideas about what to do.*

***a)*** *Now listen to your partner's activities and take notes.* ▸ SF Taking notes (p. 149)

***b)*** *You want to go to the places below. Read the texts and tell your partner …*
- *where you want to go*
- *where the places are, what they cost, when you can go there*
- *one reason why you would like to go there*

**The World's Largest Department Store**

Macy's – New York's most famous department store! With 10 floors and half a million things for sale – you'll need lots of time!
Open 9 to 9!
Herald Square (6th Avenue and 34th Street)

**American Museum of Natural History**

Here you'll find the largest and probably one of the most awesome dinosaur collections in the world. You'll find the museum at Central Park West and 79th Street in New York City.
Open daily, 10:00 a.m. – 5:45 p.m.
Adults: $ 14.00
Children (2–12): $ 8.00

***c)*** *Now talk to her/him and decide where you'd like to go together – one place in the morning, one place in the afternoon. You each have $ 20. Check the prices and opening hours.*

## Unit 2

### 11 Which came first? (Passive – simple past) ▸ Unit 2 (p. 46)

***a)*** *Your partner is going to say what he/she thinks came first. Listen and correct his/her statements if they're wrong. Use these dates.*

1 Eiffel Tower: built in 1887 ◂▸ first car: made in 1885
2 America: discovered by Columbus in 1492 ◂▸ China: visited by Marco Polo in 1266
3 first plane: flown in 1903 ◂▸ first underground railway: opened in 1863
4 first Mickey Mouse film: shown in 1928 ◂▸ Ernie and Bert: first seen on TV in 1969

*A:* I think the Eiffel Tower was built before the first car was made.
*B:* That's right. / No, that's wrong. The first car was made in ..., the Eiffel Tower was ...

***b)*** *Look at these pairs of pictures. Guess which of the two came first. Tell your partner what you think.*

5

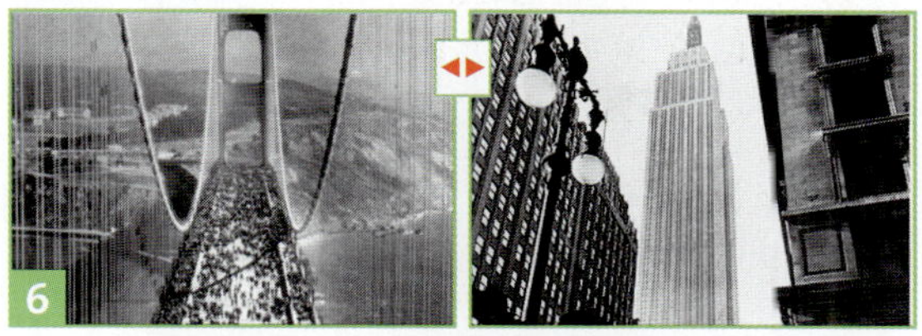
6

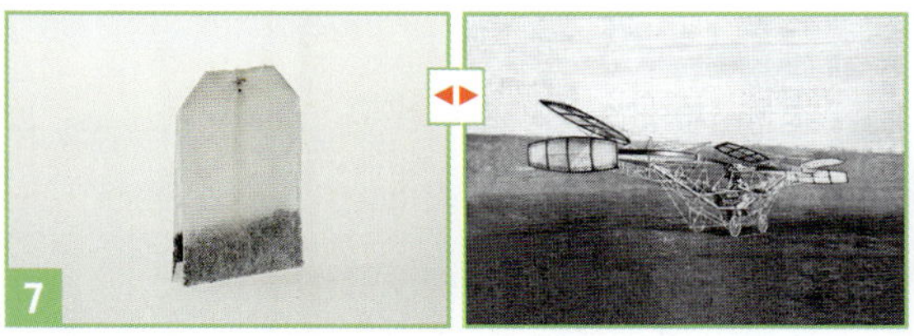
7

8

5 popcorn (eat) ◂▸ first pizza (sell)
6 Golden Gate Bridge (finish) ◂▸ Empire State Building (build)
7 first tea bags (sell) ◂▸ first helicopter (fly)
8 John F. Kennedy (kill) ◂▸ Berlin Wall (build)

## Unit 3

### 3 WORDS Using numbers Partner B ▸ Unit 3 (p. 63)

***a)*** *Listen to **partner A** and fill in the information about St. Louis in a copy of the chart. Then tell your partners about Los Angeles, the second largest city in the US. Then listen to **partner C** and fill in the information about New York.*

| | St. Louis | Los Angeles | New York |
|---|---|---|---|
| Founded in | | 1781 | |
| Population | | 3,844,000 | |
| Area | | 1290 sq km | |
| Average temperature | | 12°C (winter)<br>22°C (summer) | |
| Largest ethnic group | | Latino (46.5%) | |

*Partner B:* Los Angeles was founded in 1781. The population ...

Los Angeles, California

## Unit 2

### 14 SPEAKING A picture story ▸ Unit 2 (p. 47)

***a)*** *Partner B: Look at pictures* ***1–3****. Listen to your partner's story. Is it the same, or nearly the same, as the story in the green boxes?*

One day Tom and Debbie went into a new café. They sat down at a nice table in front of the pictures.

They ordered some drinks. After that they laughed and talked together. They had lots of fun.

Suddenly they saw a bright light. Then somebody shouted, 'Stop him!' Tom and Debbie were shocked.

***b)*** *Look at pictures* ***4–6****. Tell the story to your partner. You can use the ideas in the orange boxes.*

- saw – gun
- floor – near – table

- ran – towards them
- Debbie screamed
- didn't think – picked up gun

- shouted angrily – 'Cut!'
- film director
- felt – silly

## Unit 3

### 3 WORDS Using numbers Partner C

▸ *Unit 3 (p. 63)*

New York, New York

***a)*** *Listen to your **partners A** and **B** and fill in the information about St. Louis and Los Angeles in a copy of the chart. Then tell your partners about New York, the largest city in the US.*

| | St. Louis | Los Angeles | New York |
|---|---|---|---|
| Founded in | | | 1614 |
| Population | | | 8,215,000 |
| Area | | | 1214.4 sq km |
| Average temperature | | | 1°C (winter) 25°C (summer) |
| Largest ethnic group | | | White (44.5%) |

*Partner C:* New York was founded in 1614. The population ...

## Unit 4

### 12 The US has had 50 states (since/for)

▸ *Unit 4 (p. 88)*

***a)*** *Answer your partner's questions. Use the* ***present perfect*** *with* ***since*** *or* ***for***.

1 The US ... (have) 50 states ... over 50 years.
*A:* How long has the US had 50 states?
*B:* The US has had 50 states for over 50 years.
2 Washington ... (be) capital of the US ... 1800.
3 The railway ... (link) the East Coast with the West Coast ... 1869.
4 The White House ... (be) the home of US presidents ... more than 200 years.

***b)*** *Ask questions with* ***How long ...*** *+* ***present perfect***. *Write down your partner's answers.*

5 Georgia – be – US state?
6 Atlanta – be – capital of Georgia?
7 Atlanta – have – black mayors?
8 Martin Luther King – be – dead?

Georgia State Capitol, Atlanta

## Unit 1

### 4 //● Getting around New York (Gerund) ▸ Unit 1 (p. 21)

*a) Complete the sentences with the gerund of the verbs in the box.*

buy • cross • cycle • drive • go • spot • take • visit • walk

1 ... is a great way to get around New York – but wear good shoes.
2 ... the street in Manhattan's busy traffic is dangerous, so be careful.
3 ... can be dangerous too, so wear a helmet on your bike.
4 ... by bus is a good way to see lots of city sights.
5 ... can be expensive if you have to pay for parking.
6 ... the subway is cheap, but you don't see much of the city.
7 ... a subway ticket is easy if you've got the correct change.
8 ... a taxi is easy because they're all bright yellow.
9 ... New York's museums is fun, but it can be very expensive.

*1 Walking is a great way ...*

### 6 //● The life of a paramedic (Gerund) ▸ Unit 1 (p. 22)

*a) Complete this interview with a New York paramedic. Use gerunds of the verbs in the box.*

be • do • drive • get • meet • save • wait • work

**What do you like doing in your job?**
I like *saving* people's lives. That's number one. I love ... part of a great team. That's important. I like ... new people every day too. That's great. And I really enjoy ... different things every day.

**What don't you like so much?**
I hate ... up in the middle of the night. And I don't really enjoy ... long shifts. That's hard. I don't like ... for a call. That can be boring. And I hate ... fast through the city. It's no fun!

## TF 1

### US facts ▸ Text File 1 (p. 121)

#### 2 US quiz – Correct answers

1 13 stripes
2 United States of America
3 Washington, D.C.
4 two nickels in a dime
5 50 states
6 Kentucky, Kansas
7 27 times
8 Katrina
9 4th July
10 White House (Washington, D.C.)

## Unit 1

### 8 more help WRITING Taking a break in Central Park ▸ Unit 1 (p. 22)

*a) Here are some more questions. Try and answer them.*
- **Who** did you see in the park?
- **What** did you do there?
- **Where** did you eat?
- **When** did you leave?
- **Why** were you there?
- **How** did you feel?

*b) When you have some ideas, write your text. These phrases can help you.*

... and I went to Central Park to take a break from ...

It was getting dark, so ...

One day in June ... wanted to meet ...

When we got hungry, we ...

All around me I could see ...

We sat down / met / saw ...

In the background I could hear ...

Suddenly ...

... next to / in the middle of / under ...

Later ...

We took out our ... and started to ...

▸ SF The steps of writing (p. 154)

### 9 READING Fire safety (Working out the meaning of words) ▸ SF p. 150

Part 1 READING COURSE

*c)* more help ▸ Unit 1 (p. 23)

*Explain the highlighted words in the safety instructions.*
- You already know the words *hall* and *way*. What could *hallway* mean?
- Look at the picture. What could *wet cloth* mean?
- You already know one part of the word (*bath*). What could be the meaning of *bathtub*?
- Which part of your bed can you hang out of your window so that firefighters can see it?

**Fire safety in high-rise buildings**

FIRE DEPARTMENT CITY OF NEW YORK

**If the fire is NOT in your room**

- If the hallways are full of smoke, stay in your room.
- Place a wet cloth over your mouth and nose.
- Fill your bathtub with water. If your door gets hot, wet it down.
- If you are in great danger, hang a bedsheet out the window so that firefighters can spot you.

## Unit 2

### 5 //● A quiz (Passive – simple present) ▸ Unit 2 (p. 44)

**a)** *Write sentences. Use the correct form of the verb in brackets.*

1 Spanish ... (speak) in Portugal (I)/Mexico (H)/Italy (L).
*Spanish is spoken in ...*
2 California ... (call) the Yellow State (R)/Orange State (Q)/Golden State (Y).
3 Most US strawberries ... (grow) in Alaska (M)/California (W)/New York (N).
4 Computer software ... (make) in Napa Valley (K)/Silicon Valley (L)/Central Valley (M).
5 Californian wine ... (sell) in the US (S)/in Canada (T)/all over the world (O).
6 Park rangers ... (find) at all American beaches (H)/national parks (O)/stations (J).
7 Most of the big films ... (make) in Los Angeles (D)/San Francisco (T)/New York (N).
8 Oscars ... (give) to film stars (O)/good sportsmen or sportswomen (P)/governors (Q).
9 Millions of sausages (C)/burgers (L)/cookies (G) ... (eat) in Disneyland every year.

**b)** *The letters behind the correct answers form a word. Write down these letters and find this word.*

### 6 //● What else do you know about California? (Passive – simple present) ▸ Unit 2 (p. 44)

*Make passive sentences. Fill in the correct verb forms and match the sentence halves.*

1 Some of the best beaches in the US ... (find)
2 A lot of rubbish ... (pick up)
3 Software from California ... (use)
4 Every year lots of animals ... (kill)
5 California's Death Valley ... (visit)
6 Californian strawberries ... (sell)
7 Lots of workers ... (need)
8 Lots of Hollywood movies ... (show)

... in German cinemas.
... by thousands of tourists every year.
... along California's coast.
... on Californian farms every summer.
... from California's coast every year.
... in large forest fires.
... in computers all over the world.
... all over the US.

*1 Some of the best beaches in the US are found along ...*

Death Valley: one of the hottest places on earth

Forest fires in California

## Unit 2

### 8 WRITING More about 'Growing up in two cultures' (Writing letters) ► Unit 2 (p. 45)

more help *Write a (formal) letter to the editor about one of the e-mails on p. 37 – Kim's, Ashley's or Luis's. Say why you agree or disagree with it. Here are some phrases you can use.*

*Dear Sir or Madam* | *Dear Ms Winter* | *20 April …*

*I am writing about the letter from … about growing up in two cultures.*

*Kim / Luis / Ashley says …* | *I thought that was very interesting.* | *I understand / do not understand that.*

*I think that …* | *In my opinion …* | *there is / isn't a lot of prejudice in my country.*

*I agree / do not agree with Luis / Ashley / Kim when he / she says …*

*Kim / Luis / Ashley is right / wrong when he / she says …*

*growing up in two cultures helps you / is difficult* | *learning a language is difficult / important*

*Yours faithfully* | *Yours sincerely*

*…*

► SF Writing letters (p. 156)

### 10 //● California was discovered by … (Passive – simple past) ► Unit 2 (p. 45)

*Look at the pictures. Write down what happened when. Use* **by** *if you need it.*

1 California – discover – Spanish explorers – 1769

2 Golden Gate Bridge – build – Joseph Strauss – 1933–37

3 first film – make – in Hollywood – 1910

4 gold – find – near Sacramento – 1848

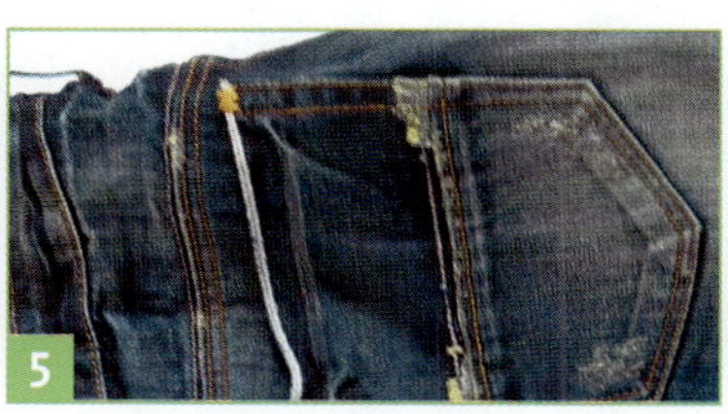

5 first jeans – sell – Levi Strauss – in the Gold Rush

6 fourteen people – kill – forest fires – last summer

## Unit 2

### 12 more help An accident – young man crashed into ... (Active and passive) ▸ Unit 2 (p. 46)

*Complete the report. Choose the correct verb form – active or passive.*

*An accident happened on Park Road yesterday morning.*

*1 A young man on a bike crashed into ...*
*2 The ...*

1 A young man on a bike (crashed/was crashed) into an old woman.
2 The old woman fell. She (hurt/was hurt) her head.
3 The man (left/was left) quickly.
4 He (didn't help/wasn't helped) the old woman.
5 The accident (saw/was seen) by a young woman.
6 She (called/was called) an ambulance.
7 The woman (took/was taken) to hospital.
8 The police (interviewed/was interviewed) the young woman.
9 Descriptions of the man (send/were sent) to all police stations.
10 The same man (saw/was seen) at the station a few minutes after the accident.
11 He (left/was left) his bike there.
12 The police (didn't find/weren't found) the man.

## Unit 3

EVERYDAY ENGLISH

### 2 WRITING A letter to an exchange student (Letter for information)

more help ▸ Unit 3 (p. 62)

*Here are some ideas for your letter. Complete the sentences and questions, find a good order, and write them with some more ideas in your letter.*

... (your address)
... (today's date)

*Dear ...*

*I hope you can write back.* | *How long – school day?* | *What time – school – start?*
*Can you answer some questions about your school?* | *My name is ... and I'm ... years old.*
*I'm writing to you because ...* | *How – get to school?* | *What – interested in?*
*I'm a student at ... School in the town of ... in Germany.* | *What – clubs / extracurricular activities?*
*I'm coming to your school as an exchange student soon.* | ...

*I'm looking forward to meeting you soon.*

*Best wishes*
... (your name)

▸ SF Writing letters (p. 156)

## Unit 3

### 4 //● WORDS School in the US and Britain ▸ Unit 3 (p. 63)

*Complete the sentences.*

1 When American students talk about what they do every day at school and when, they say *schedule*. British students say ___.
2 At Hermann High School there are seven of these in a school day and each one is 50 minutes long. They are called ___ in the US. In Britain they are called ___.
3 In every school you can find this on a wall. Teachers and students put information on it so that everyone can read it. In America they use the word ___. In Britain the word is ___.
4 In Britain and America teachers give you ___ to tell you how good or bad a piece of work is.
5 In HHS, they aren't so strict about what students wear to school. They only have a ___. In Britain, students must wear a ___ at school.
6 In the US they talk about the summer ___. In Britain they usually talk about the summer ___.

### 6 Now you

***a)*** more help ▸ Unit 3 (p. 57)
*You can make notes about your school in Germany and Hermann High School like this:*

IN HERMANN HIGH SCHOOL, MISSOURI

*The school year*
- *starts ...*
- *finishes ...*
- *summer holidays: ...*
- *other holidays?*

*The school day*
- *starts at ... am*
- *finishes at ... pm*
- *students get to school by ... or ...*
- *lessons are ... minutes long*
- *four lessons in the morning before lunch*
  *... lessons in the afternoon after lunch*
- *Lunch is from ... to ...*
  *Students eat in the school cafeteria.*
  *What they can eat: ...*

*Timetable*
*Some of the subjects that they have at Hermann High: ...*

*Activities in school*
*Students can do different activities / extracurriculars, e.g.*

IN OUR SCHOOL IN GERMANY

*The school year*
- *starts ...*
- *finishes ...*
- *summer holidays: ...*
- *other holidays?*

*The school day*
- *starts at ... am*
- *finishes at ... pm*
- *students get to school by ... or ...*
- *lessons are ...*
- *... lessons in ...*
  *... lessons in ...*
- *Lunch ...*

## Unit 3

### 6 Now you

***b)*** more help | Extra ▸ *Unit 3 (p. 57)*

*Here are some phrases you can use when you give your talk.*

▸ *SF Giving a presentation (p. 147)*

Part 3 READING COURSE

### 9 READING Soft drinks, hard facts (Finding the main ideas of a text) ▸ *SF p. 151*

***c)*** more help ▸ *Unit 3 (p. 65)*

*Here are three main ideas from the text. Write them down and add the ideas in the yellow boxes below to the main ideas.*

| Soft drinks are unhealthy | Soft drinks are one of the main reasons why kids are fat | Schools are trying to change the way kids drink |
|---|---|---|
| | | |

- kids drink less soda because it's not so easy to get it
- no soda machines are allowed in schools
- kids drink too many soft drinks
- kids can bring soft drinks to school, but can't buy them there
- there can be health problems later in life
- soft drinks contain too many calories (a cola: 400 calories)
- kids drink even more soda than ever before
- after drinking soft drinks kids are still hungry

### 10 //● Money is a problem (Definite article) ▸ *Unit 3 (p. 66)*

*Complete the sentences with words from the box. Add* **the** *where you need it.*

history • life • money • people • pizza

1. ... really is a problem for my family because we aren't rich.
2. I've spent all ... you gave me.
3. I love ... – it's my favourite food.
4. ... we had for lunch was delicious.
5. ... of a farmer must be very hard.
6. Is ... easier if you're rich?
7. All ... at the party were very nice.
8. ... will usually help you if you ask them nicely.
9. I'm interested in ... of my hometown. I'm reading a book about the town in the 19th century.
10. Some people say ... is boring. They are more interested in modern things.

## Unit 3

### 13 //● A morning at the Krugers' (Past perfect) ▸ Unit 3 (p. 66)

*Complete the sentences. Use the **simple past** or the **past perfect**.*

**Tip**
Before you start, think: What happened first? Use the **past perfect** for that verb.

1 When his father ... (get up), Jake ... (already/go) outside to feed his hog.
2 When Jake ... (come) back, everything was ready. His mother ... (prepare) breakfast.
3 After breakfast Jake's father ... (hurry) to work. But he came back because he ... (forget) his cellphone.
4 Jake ... (run) for the bus. It wasn't there. It ... (leave) when he got to the bus stop.
5 When he ... (arrive) at school, there was nobody in the yard. The first period ... (already/start).

## Extra Background File GOING WEST

### 2 Group puzzle (part 2)

**a)** more help ▸ Unit 3 (p. 61)
*In your group (A,B, C or D), compare your notes. Look at the questions for your text. They can help you to find the important points in your texts. Discuss them in your group.*

A **HERMANN**
- When and why did German immigrants found Hermann?
- Why did people in Hermann stop speaking German?

B **THE ROLE OF MISSOURI**
- When and why was Missouri called the 'Gateway to the West'?
- What did people do in St. Louis?

C **THE TRAILS TO THE WEST**
- What was the most famous trail? How long was it?
- How many people went west on the trails?
- Why was the journey to the West so hard?

D **THE NATIVE AMERICANS**
- Why did the arrival of the Europeans bring trouble for the Native Americans?
- How many Native Americans are there today? Where do many of them live?

## Unit 3

### Angus Bethune's moment by Chris Crutcher (adapted)

#### Working with the text ► Unit 3 (p. 70)

**5** more help **Extra** **After the dance**

*Choose two of the characters. What might they say to each other the next day? Here are some ideas. Use some of these and your own ideas and write a dialogue with your partner.*

*Angus*

*Melissa*

*Rick*

Hi, how are you today? | That was a brilliant/terrible/fantastic evening. | You must be crazy. | We have to talk. | Everyone is talking about last night. | I can't believe you like him/me. | I (don't) want to see you again. | You were awesome/great/unkind/rude/... | I felt really nervous/surprised/shocked/embarrassed/... when ... | I can't believe you did that!

## Unit 4

EVERYDAY ENGLISH

**4** **SPEAKING Talking about films or TV shows**

***c)*** more help ► Unit 4 (p. 85)

*Complete the dialogue with your partner. Then practise it and act it out for the class.*

*A:* Did you watch ... last night?
*B:* No, I didn't. What was it about?
*A:* Oh, ...
*B:* And, how was it?
*A:* It wasn't bad. The ending was really ... What about you? What did you watch?
*B:* Well, I watched ...
*A:* How was it?
*B:* It was ...
*A:* I'm going to watch ... on TV tonight. Maybe we can watch together?
*B:* Great idea. I love that kind of programme.

**9** //● **I've known him for five years** (Present perfect with 'for') ► Unit 4 (p. 87)

*Answer the questions. Use the present perfect.*

1. Is Sam your best friend?
   – *Sag ja, du kennst ihn seit fünf Jahren.*
   *Yes, I ... (know) him for ...*
2. Tim isn't at school today. Do you know why?
   – *Sag, dass er seit einigen Tagen eine Erkältung hat.*
   *He ... (have) a cold for ...*
3. How long has your mum been a waitress?
   – *Sag, dass sie seit zwölf Jahren in einem Café arbeitet.*
   *She ... (work) in a café ...*
4. How long has your Grandma lived in this town?
   – *Sag, dass sie seit Jahren hier wohnt.*
   *She ... (live) here ...*
5. Is Rob ill? I haven't seen him for a while.
   – *Sag ja, er liegt seit sechs Monaten im Krankenhaus.*
   *Yes, he ... (be) in hospital ...*
6. How long have you had your skateboard? Is it new?
   – *Sag nein, du hast es seit zwei Jahren.*
   *No, I ... (have) it ...*

## Unit 4

### 10 //● Mr Young at the King Center (since/for) ▸ Unit 4 (p. 88)

*Mr Young is telling Madison about his job.*
*Use the **present perfect** and add **since** or **for** to complete the sentences.*

1 I*'ve been* (be) in my job since 1999, Madison.
2 I ... (know) my boss ... 2005.
3 I need a new computer. I ... (have) this one ... almost six years.
4 Martin Luther King's wife started the Center, but she ... (be) dead ... a few years.
5 We ... (have) an online learning programme ... a number of years.
6 This place ... (be) part of the National Park system ... the last 30 years.
7 Martin Luther King's birthday ... (be) a holiday in the US ... 1986.

### Working with the text

### Melba's story ▸ Unit 4 (p. 92)

#### 3 Who did what?

***a)*** //● *Say in one sentence what the following people did.*

1 The white people in Little Rock ...
2 The Governor of Arkansas ...
3 The National Guard ...
4 The US President ...
5 The soldiers ...
6 Danny ...

#### 4 //● Melba's feelings

*How do you think Melba felt when ...?*

1 ... she couldn't go on the merry-go-round
2 ... she volunteered to go to Central High
3 ... she saw the angry white people
4 ... she met her bodyguard, Danny
5 ... a boy threw something in her face
6 ... the governor closed Central High

## Unit 1

### Working with the text

### You can tell me From *Kelly 'n' Me* by Myron Levoy (adapted) ▸ Unit 1 (p. 28)

#### 4 Extra What will happen next?

*This is the beginning of the next chapter of the story.*

It was getting dark. I sat in silence. Kelly – Kelsey? My world was upside down. That huge Fifth Avenue apartment was hers! But why couldn't she tell me? I bet she was laughing at me all the time! Yes, I was angry. But she looked so sad sitting there, like a kid who had stolen something and didn't know what would happen next. She was rich, so what!

She was just Kelly to me.

"Hey," I said and put my arm around her.

"Relax, okay? I'm not going to send you to the principal's office, okay?"

"Oh, Anthony ..." She started crying louder now, I held her close and said again and again, "It's okay. It's okay." I wished I could hold her forever.

## TF 1 US facts

### 1 Before you read

***a)*** *Name as many US states as you can. Then look at the US map on the front inside cover of this book. How many did you get right?*

***b)*** *Name other US places and people that you know.*

### ★ The US flag

The US flag has 50 stars – one for each of the 50 states today. It also has 13 stripes – that's one for each of the states in 1776.

**Fast facts**

**Country name:** United States of America
**Other names:** USA, US, US of A, America, The States
**Population**[1]**:** 305.8 million
**Capital:** Washington, D.C.
**Largest city:** New York City
**Area**[2]**:** 9.8 million square kilometres[3]
**Money:** 1 dollar ($ or USD) = 100 cents (¢)

**★ Did you know?**

- ★ Another name for the US flag is the Stars and Stripes.
- ★ The US is 27 times bigger than Germany.
- ★ 1 cent is also called a penny, 5 ¢ is a nickel, 10 ¢ is a dime[4] and 25 ¢ is a quarter.

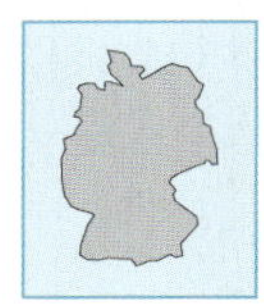


### ★ A big country

The US is the 3rd largest country in the world after Russia and Canada.

### ★ Extreme weather

The hottest place in the US is Death Valley in California. In 2001 the highest temperature there was 57.2 °C.

Three out of four of all the tornadoes in the world hit[5] the US.

In 2005 Hurricane Katrina was the worst hurricane in US history.

[1] population [ˌpɒpjuˈleɪʃn] *Bevölkerung, Einwohner(zahl)* [2] area [ˈeəriə] *Fläche* [3] square kilometres [skweə] *Quadratkilometer* [4] dime [daɪm] [5] (to) hit [hɪt] *hier: treffen*

## Some important dates

**About 30,000 BC or earlier**
The ancestors[1] of modern Native Americans came to Alaska from Russia by a land bridge.

**1492**
Christopher Columbus arrived in America.

**1607**
The British founded[2] Jamestown in Virginia.

**★ Did you know?**
Columbus thought that he was in India. That's why he called the people who lived there 'Indians'.

**1619**
The first slaves arrived from Africa.

**1776**
On 4th July, in the Declaration of Independence[3], thirteen states said that they wanted to be free from Britain. This was Independence Day – the birthday of the US!

**1776–1783**
The Americans fought a war[4] against Britain. America won in the end.

**1838**
Thousands of Native Americans died on the Trail of Tears.

**1848**
The Californian Gold Rush began.

**1861–1865**
The Northern states and the Southern states fought against each other in the Civil War[5].

Mount Rushmore, South Dakota

### ★ US Presidents
You can see the heads of four US Presidents at Mount Rushmore. They are George Washington, Thomas Jefferson, Theodore Roosevelt and Abraham Lincoln.

**★ Did you know?**
The US President lives in the White House in Washington, D. C.

### 2 US quiz
*Use the facts on these pages to answer the quiz questions. Check your answers on page 110.*
1 How many stripes are there on the US flag?
2 What do the letters 'USA' stand for?
3 What is the capital of the US?
4 How many nickels are in a dime?
5 How many states are there in the US?
6 Name a state that begins with the letter 'K'.
7 How much bigger than Germany is the US?
8 What is the name of the hurricane that hit the US in 2005?
9 When is the birthday of the US?
10 Where does the US President live?

[1] ancestor ['ænsestə] *Vorfahre* [2] (to) found [faʊnd] *gründen* [3] Declaration of Independence [ˌdekləˈreɪʃn_əv ˌɪndɪˈpendəns] *Unabhängigkeitserklärung* [4] war [wɔː] *Krieg* [5] civil war [ˌsɪvl ˈwɔː] *Bürgerkrieg*

## TF 2 The President and Mr Muir

> *What did both men like or find interesting? How were they different?*

Theodore Roosevelt at age 25

**Theodore Roosevelt (1858–1919, US President 1901–1909)**

As a boy, Theodore Roosevelt was weak and often ill. He had asthma and had to spend lots of time in bed. Because other boys bullied him, his father sent him to boxing lessons, which made him strong and fit. When he was at university, he boxed, and also rowed[1] for the university team.

Theodore not only loved sports – he loved nature[2] too. When he was only seven, he started his own natural history museum, and at age nine he wrote about insects. Later he published books about birds.

Theodore Roosevelt's other great love was books: he read one or more a day for most of his life. One day he discovered[3] the books of John Muir, who wrote about nature.

John Muir at age 23

**John Muir (1838–1914)**

John Muir was eleven years old when his family left Scotland to live in the US. As a boy John worked on his family's farm in Wisconsin, later he went to university, where he had his first botany[4] lesson. In 1863 he left university to spend time in the wilderness. In those days, the eastern US had more nature than cities and towns, and Muir walked from Indiana to Florida to enjoy the wilderness.

In 1868 Muir went to California. When he arrived in San Francisco, he found the big city – 149,000 people! – terrible. He wanted to be outdoors[5]. He read about Yosemite Valley almost 300 km east of San Francisco – so he walked there. Muir loved Yosemite and wanted to protect it. Over the next years he wrote books, articles and letters to tell people that they must protect not only Yosemite, but nature everywhere.

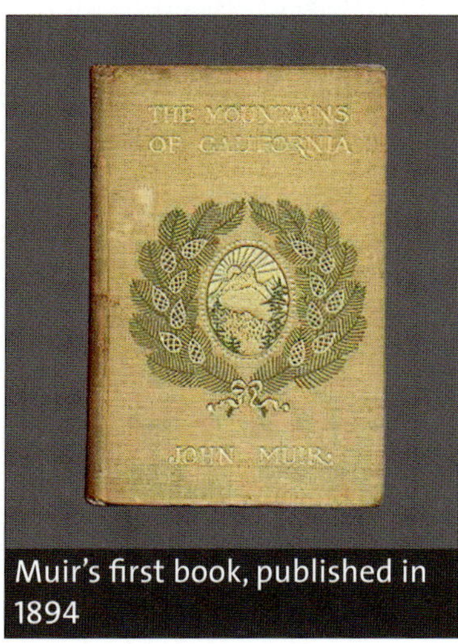


Muir's first book, published in 1894

Roosevelt and Muir at Glacier Point, Yosemite, in 1903

[1] (to) row [rəʊ] *rudern* [2] nature ['neɪtʃə] *Natur* [3] (to) discover [dɪ'skʌvə] *entdecken* [4] botany ['bɒtəni] *Botanik, Pflanzenkunde*
[5] outdoors [ˌaʊt'dɔːz] *draußen, im Freien*

### A famous camping trip

In 1903 President Roosevelt wrote Mr Muir and suggested that the two of them go camping. And that's what they did: President Roosevelt and Mr Muir spent four days and three nights in Yosemite. Under the stars, without a tent.

It was a camping trip the two men would never forget. Roosevelt called Yosemite 'the most beautiful place in the world'. One morning, when they woke up, they had snow on them.

Muir talked a lot while he was with the President. He talked about nature and how important it was to protect it. And the President listened.

When he got back to Washington, D.C., Roosevelt started the work that saved Yosemite, and other important natural places in the US.

There were national parks in the US before the famous camping trip, but Muir and Roosevelt did more to protect nature in the US than anyone before or after them. Thanks to these two men, land was protected and many new national parks and forests were created[3].

Today millions of people enjoy visiting America's national parks. The Grand Canyon and Yosemite are two of the most popular national parks, but visitors today can choose from almost 400 national parks, forests and nature reserves[4]. About 3.5 million people visit Yosemite National Park every year.

### 1 Fighting for nature

***a)*** *Why was the Roosevelt-Muir camping trip important? Could a trip like that happen today?*

***b)*** *Which organisations or people try to protect nature today? Do you support them? Why (not)?*

### 2 US national parks today

*Find out about a US national park. Where is it? How big is it? What can you see and do there?*

[1] with a bang [bæŋ] *etwa: mit einem Riesenknaller* [2] $ 400 worth of [wɜːθ] *im Wert von 400 Dollar* [3] created [kriːˈeɪtɪd] *geschaffen*
[4] nature reserve [ˈneɪtʃə rɪˈzɜːv] *Naturschutzgebiet*

## TF 3 New York – three poems, an essay and a song

### 1 Choose a word or a phrase

*Read the five texts about New York. Write down one word or phrase that you like or find interesting. Explain why.*

*I wrote down 'tickle the sun' because it's funny to imagine that a building tickles the sun and ...*

### A The city

If flowers[1] want to grow
right out of the concrete[2] sidewalk cracks[3]
I'm going to bend down[4] to smell them.

*Poem by David Ignatow*

### B Skyscraper

Skyscraper, skyscraper
Scrape[5] me some sky:
Tickle[6] the sun
While the stars go by.
Tickle the stars
While the sun's climbing high,
Then skyscraper, skyscraper
Scrape me some sky.

*Poem by Dennis Lee*

### C Subway rush hour

Mingled[7]
breath[8] and smell
so close
mingled
black and white
so near
no room for fear[9]

*Poem by Langston Hughes*

[1] flower [flaʊə] *Blume* [2] concrete [ˈkɒŋkriːt] *Beton* [3] crack [kræk] *Riss* [4] (to) bend down [bend] *sich hinunterbeugen*
[5] (to) scrape [skreɪp] *(ab)kratzen* [6] (to) tickle [tɪkl] *kitzeln* [7] mingled [ˈmɪŋgld] *vermischt* [8] breath [breθ] *Atem* [9] fear [fɪə] *Angst*

## D To the visitor

Visitors force[1] you to think. They arrive with that helpless do-with-me-what-you-will look and when you ask what they'd like to do or see they say, 'Oh, what's good?'

What's good? In New York?

You tell them – gently[2] – that this is New York where everything is good. Everything, baby.

A hot dog at Nathan's in Coney Island is good.

A westward walk on the Brooklyn Bridge when the sun is setting in New Jersey is good.

A ride on the Staten Island Ferry at sunset when the sky is a golden backdrop[3] to the Statue of Liberty and Ellis Island is very good.

Walk down Broadway. Watch people lining up for the ferry to Ellis Island and the Statue of Liberty. Just look at the people. Look. You're looking at the country's history. And listen to them in their various tongues. You're not eavesdropping[4]. You're listening to generations and yourself.

And all that is good.

*From an essay by Frank McCourt*

## E New York, New York

Start spreading[5] the news, I'm leaving today
I want to be a part of it – New York, New York

These vagabond shoes, are longing to stray[6]
Right through the very heart of it –
New York, New York

I want to wake up in a city that doesn't sleep
And find I'm king of the hill – top of the heap[7]

These little town blues[8] are melting away[9]
I'll make a brand new start of it –
in old New York
If I can make it there, I'll make it anywhere[10]
It's up to you – New York, New York

*Song by Fred Ebb*

## 2 A word picture of New York

*What picture of New York did the texts give you? Write down words or phrases that come to your head.*

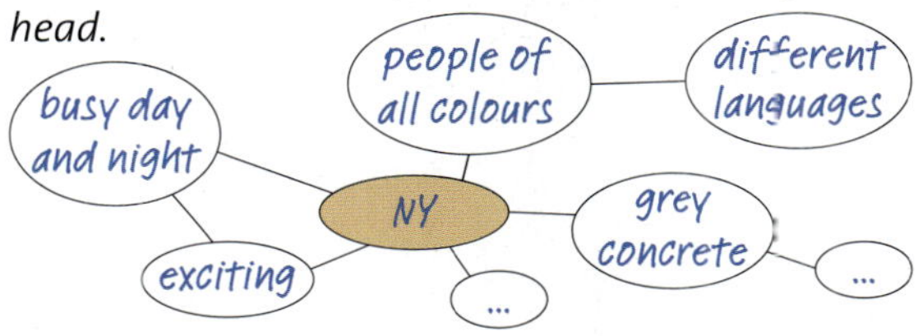


## 3 Three poems

***a)*** *Learn your favourite poem.*

***b)*** *Say it for your partner. Say why you like it.*

## 4 The song

*Where do you think the singer comes from? Why do you think he/she wants to go to New York? Would you like to live in New York? Why (not)?*

## 5 The essay

***a)*** *Would you like to do the things Frank McCourt describes? Why? If not, what would you like to do?*

***b)*** *Write a text like Frank McCourt's about your own city or town.*

---

[1] (to) force [fɔːs] *zwingen* [2] gently ['dʒentlɪ] *(adv) behutsam* [3] backdrop *Hintergrund* [4] (to) eavesdrop ['iːvzdrɒp] *lauschen* [5] (to) spread ['spred] *hier: verbreiten* [6] ... are longing to stray [lɒŋɪŋ], [streɪ] *etwa: ... wollen in die Welt hinaus* [7] top of the heap [hiːp] *ganz oben* [8] blues [bluːz] *pl etwa: Eintönigkeit* [9] (to) melt (away) [melt] *(weg)schmelzen* [10] I'll make it anywhere *ich schaffe es überall*

## TF 4 How about them Yankees? by Louie D'Agostino

*Look at the picture. Can you guess what sport this text is about?*

"'How about them Yankees?' That's all you need."

"I don't understand," I said to my old English teacher, Signor Bertanelli. I had come to visit him before leaving our little town in Sicily to go to the US – I was emigrating.

"Of course you don't understand, Luigi," he said. "You never were very good at English. Just remember this: 'How about them Yankees?'" He said it again slowly. "Then you will be fine when you get to New York."

I had no idea what the old man was talking about, but he had always been nice to me, although I was terrible at English. So I decided that I would remember the question: "How about them Yankees?" It didn't take long before I understood why it was a good sentence to know. And that was before I learned that the Yankees are a baseball team from the Bronx.

I made my way to Rome airport, and soon I was sitting on a plane between two American men from Brooklyn. They asked me lots of easy questions, but after a few minutes, my English was no longer enough. I almost panicked, but then I thought of what Signor Bertanelli had told me.

"How about them Yankees?" I asked. And just as my professore had promised, it was all I needed. The two men talked the rest of the way to New York – I didn't have to say anything. Yes, this one sentence was going to help me a lot.

When I got to New York, I used Signor Bertanelli's question with the Immigration man at JFK airport. I used it to get a room, and it worked when I went to get my first job in America. For three months I washed dishes in a restaurant. (Now I have my own restaurant.) I'll never forget the night when I went to my first bar in America. I was talking to a group of guys. When I couldn't think of anything to say, I asked them, "So, how about them Yankees?"

I became everybody's best friend! They bought me drinks. And they gave me my American name: Louie. As in "Hey, Joe. Meet Louie. Louie here's a big baseball fan." I had a great time, and I didn't have to pay for my beers: "Joe, Louie's drinks are on me."

Soon after that I learned that the question usually doesn't work with women. (My wife was different.) And that there are men who don't like baseball. (Not many though.) And that you have to be careful: Queens has its own baseball team, the Mets, and Mets fans aren't very friendly if you ask them the question. (This was especially true in 2000, when the Mets lost the World Series[1] to the Yankees.)

After a few months in the US, I was a big Yankees fan. I still am. And now I can talk with the best of them when somebody uses that great conversation opener, "How about them Yankees?"

Thank you, Signor Bertanelli.

### 1 Understanding the story

*Right or wrong? Correct the wrong statements.*

1. Louie has always spoken English well.
2. The question 'How about them Yankees?' works with everyone in New York.
3. Louie is a baseball fan today.
4. Louie has been successful in the US.

### 2 Conversation openers

***a)*** *How many 'conversation openers' can you think of? Write them down.*

*Have you been here before? / I like your shirt. / ...*

***b)*** *Vote in a group of four. Which is the best/worst conversation opener?*

[1] the World Series *die US Baseballmeisterschaft*

## 3 Baseball and hot dogs – an American tradition

For American baseball fans, summer means a sunny afternoon at the ballpark, the noise of the crowd ... and the smell of hot dogs. Ballparks sell lots of different food, like pizza, peanuts[1], popcorn, and chicken pieces, but hot dogs are still the favourite thing on the menu.

Yankee Stadium has room for about 53,000 fans.

Each ballpark has its own special hot dog. For example, Yankee Stadium has the world-famous Nathan's hot dogs.

A survey by the National Hot Dog and Sausage Council[2] (NHDSC) says that the best hot dogs are from Yankee Stadium and Wrigley Field (home to the Chicago Cubs).

A Yankees fan enjoying a Nathan's hot dog.

The NHDSC says that it is important to eat your ballpark hot dog the right way:

1. **Add extras in this order: Sauces like mustard[3] and chili sauce first, then onions and sauerkraut, then cheese.**
2. **Never take more than five bites[4] to finish a hot dog.**
3. **Don't use ketchup on your hot dogs after the age of 18. (Many adults don't take this rule too seriously!)**

*Is there a special smell that means summer/winter for you? Do you eat special food when you watch sport or go to the cinema?*

## 4 Crazy about sport

**BASEBALL FORUM** How baseball crazy are you?

**philliesphan** 11 minutes ago
I'm a huge fan. My room is full of Phillies newspaper stories, posters and pictures. I go to 10-15 games a year.

**Yankee4life** 14 minutes ago
I watch a baseball game every day of the season, even if my favorite team isn't playing that day. I know all the scores. I talk about baseball every day. I always watch Baseball Tonight. I'm a 100% baseball fan.

**Rizzo** 1 hour ago
I'm more interested in playing than watching ...

*People say that football (soccer) is Germany's national sport. How football crazy are you? Write a comment for a football forum.*

[1] peanut ['piːnʌt] *Erdnuss* [2] council ['kaʊnsl] *Rat* [3] mustard ['mʌstəd] *Senf* [4] bite [baɪt] *Biss*

## TF 5 Ryan Sheckler, skateboard phenom[1]

# RYAN

**When you walk around San Clemente, California, you just might run into a TV star. That's not unusual[2] for southern California, and Orange County is as good a place as any to find the rich and the beautiful.**

**But** this star is different: he's only 17, and he's not an actor. In the MTV reality show "Life of Ryan", Ryan Sheckler plays himself, 17-year-old skateboarding phenom Ryan Sheckler. The cameras follow him everywhere.

**Ryan** first got on a skateboard when he was 18 months old. By the time he was four, he was already doing tricks on the board. His parents built him a skateboard ramp when he was seven, and he soon moved on to skateparks. (He has his own now.) He became a professional skateboarder at age 13.

**Ryan** has won lots of competitions[3], but he earns more money from his sponsors. He gets money just for getting dressed in the morning! Lots of companies are happy to pay him money so he'll wear their clothes. Or, of course, use their sports gear. Ryan's talent takes him all over the world: he has skated in Europe, China, Australia and even Dubai.

**What** about school? Like lots of young celebrities[4], Ryan goes to Futures High School in Mission Viejo, California. Futures is a private high school where he meets alone with a teacher twice a week for an hour and a half at a time. He goes away "with a pile[5] of homework" after every meeting. But does he do it? You bet![6] Ryan is "really good" at Math, his favorite subject is Science, and he takes English very seriously: he wants to be prepared for having his own business, and communication skills are important for that.

**What** else does Ryan do? Well, at the top of his list of "likes" are skateboarding and girls. That golf is at number three will be a surprise for lots of fans. But no one will be surprised that "horrible music" and "broken bones[7]" are high on his list of dislikes!

**Ryan's advice for young skaters? "Don't ever give up. You've gotta keep trying and never give up."**

### 1 Ryan Sheckler's life

*What do you think is the most surprising thing about Ryan's life?*

---

[1] phenom [fə'nɒm] *Phänomen, Ausnahmeerscheinung* [2] unusual [ʌn'juːʒʊəl] *ungewöhnlich* [3] competition [ˌkɒmpə'tɪʃn] *Wettkampf* [4] celebrity [sɪ'lebrɪti] *Berühmtheit* [5] pile [paɪl] *Stapel* [6] you bet! [ˌjʊ 'bet] *und ob!* [7] bone ['bəʊn] *Knochen*

# Skateboard safety

**Skateboarding can be a lot of fun, but it can also be very dangerous. The Consumer Product Safety Commission (CPSC) says that every year more than 15,600 people go to emergency rooms[1] in the US because they are hurt in skateboarding accidents. These safety tips will help you to stay safe.**

**1 Wear safety gear.** Good shoes, helmets and pads are all important. Make sure that they fit well. Protect your ...

**... head**

**... knees**

**... elbows**

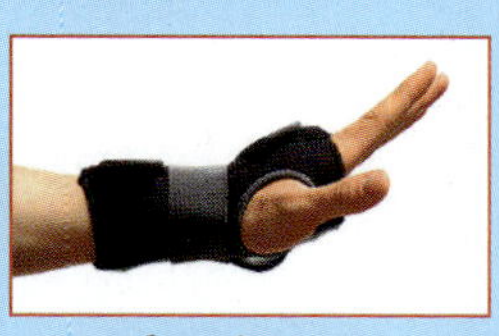

**... and wrists.**

**2 Learn how to fall.** Even the pros[2] fall, and you will too. Practise falling on grass or another soft place. Roll when you fall and try to relax your body.

**3 Don't suddenly try tricks** that are too far above your level. Learn new tricks step by step.

**4 NEVER ride in the street!**

> *Do you think skateboarders in Germany skate safely? Say why/why not.*

## 2 Reality TV

***a)*** *Do you watch reality shows? What do/don't you like about them?*

***b)*** *Imagine MTV wants to do a show about your life. Would you like that? Say why/why not.*

---

[1] emergency room [i'mɜːdʒənsi ruːm] *(US) Unfallstation* [2] pro [prəʊ] *(infml) Profi*

## TF 6 Child labour[1]

### 1 Child labour on the US-Mexican border

Many Californian farmers have large fruit and vegetable farms in northern Mexico. One of the main reasons is that labour is cheaper in Mexico. Farm workers are paid about US $ 9 an hour in California, but only US$ 11 a day in Mexico. Most of the fruit and vegetables that are grown on these farms in Mexico are exported back to the US.

#### A case study[2]: Adriana Salgado, Mexico

Adriana Salgado, 10, spends her days in a field in north-western Mexico, picking vegetables for US salad bowls.

Adriana goes to school for one hour a day (from 6 pm to 7 pm) and she doesn't know how to read. Her 15-year-old sister, who works with her, also can't read. Adriana had an 8-year-old brother too, but he was killed by a tractor while he was working in a tomato field last year.

Cruz Salgado, Adriana's father, says his family needs the extra $ 7 a day that Adriana earns. The $ 20 a day that he and his wife earn wouldn't be enough to live.

'I wish they didn't have to work,' said Adriana's father. 'But we need the money.'

Does Adriana enjoy working? 'Not much,' she said, 'I like school.'

*Source[3]: Chris Hawley, The Arizona Republic, May 8, 2008*

***a)*** *Compare the labour law information on the right to the information in the case study. What do you notice?*

#### Child labour laws in Mexico

Child labour is not legal in Mexico. Children must be over 14 to work. Children between 14 and 16 can only work 6 hours a day and they must have finished secondary school.

***b)*** *Look at the circle diagram[4] and complete the sentences.*

***c)*** *Describe the circle diagram.*

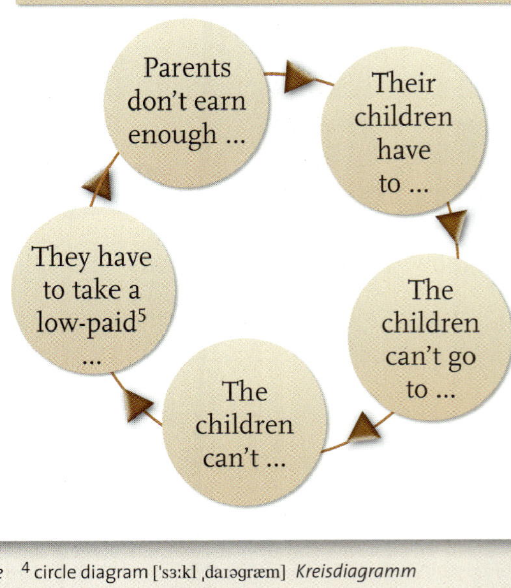


***Activate your English***
- The circle diagram shows ...
- Because parents ... their children have to ...
- And because of this the children can't ...
- The diagram is a circle because ...

[1] labour ['leɪbə] *Arbeit* [2] case study ['keɪs stʌdi] *Fallstudie* [3] source [sɔːs] *Quelle* [4] circle diagram ['sɜːkl ˌdaɪəgræm] *Kreisdiagramm*
[5] low-paid [ˌləʊ 'peɪd] *schlecht bezahlt*

## 2 Child labour around the world

*Describe what the map below shows. In which regions do children most often have to work?*

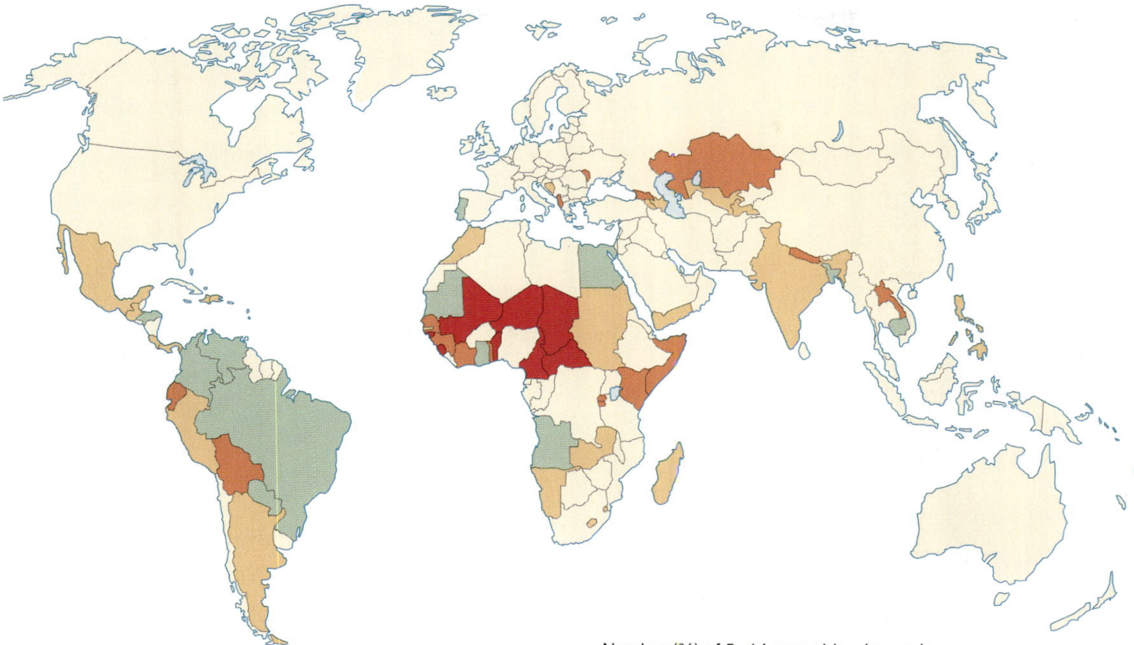


**GEOGRAPHY SKILLS** **Talking about maps**

When you talk about maps,
- look at the title and the key[1] and make sure you understand what the map is about
- start with a general statement about the map, then talk about details.

***Activate your English***

– The map shows/gives information about ...
– This is a map of ...
– It shows how many children ...
– You can see that the situation is ...

## 3 Now you

***a)*** *This is a UNICEF poster against child labour. Describe what it shows. What could be its message[2]?*

– The poster shows a jeans label[3]. On the label you can see ...
– I think the poster wants to tell us ...

***b)*** *What can you do to stop child labour? Think about the poster's message.*

[1] key [kiː] *Zeichenerklärung, Legende* [2] message ['mesɪdʒ] *hier: Botschaft, Aussage* [3] label ['leɪbl] *Etikett, Schild*

## TF 7 Earthquakes in California

### 1 An eyewitness account[1]

*Read what a teenager said after the Northridge earthquake in 1994.*

- How did the boy feel when the earthquake started?
- Where did he and his dad go during the earthquake?
- What happened inside their apartment?

"I was asleep when the earthquake came. I was so scared and I didn't know what to do. The house was shaking[2] so bad that I couldn't even walk. My dad came into my room and got me and we got under the table. We could see the refrigerator[3] sliding back and forth across the kitchen with its door opening and shutting and all of the stuff falling out onto the floor. Our TV went flying across the room and smashed into[4] the wall. All over we could hear things breaking. Then the lights went out. After it stopped we went outside. We could see all of the other people outside too. They were crying and looking around. Part of our apartment building fell down and now those people have to find another place to live. We might have to too."

### 2 After an earthquake

*Describe these photos of earthquakes in California.*

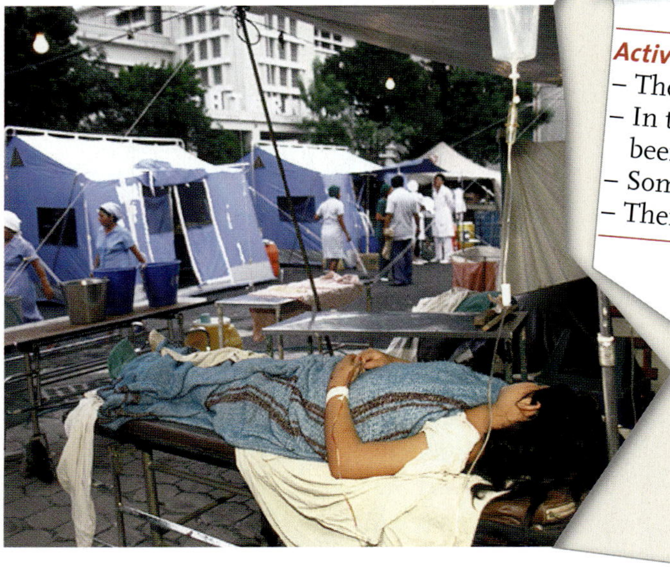

**Activate your English**
- The photos show different results of an ...
- In the first/second/... photo a road/ ... has been destroyed[5] and ...
- Some people are injured[6] ...
- There is a lot of rubble[7] everywhere ...

[1] eyewitness account ['aɪwɪtnəs‿ə'kaʊnt] *Augenzeugenbericht* [2] (to) shake [ʃeɪk] *wackeln, beben* [3] refrigerator [rɪ'frɪdʒəreɪtə] *Kühlschrank* [4] (to) smash into sth. [smæʃ] *gegen etwas krachen* [5] (to) destroy [dɪ'strɔɪ] zerstören [6] injured ['ɪndʒəd] *verletzt* [7] rubble [rʌbl] *Schutt, Trümmer*

## 3 Southern California earthquakes

**a)** *Read the text and find the most important facts about earthquakes in Southern California.*

Southern California has thousands of earthquakes every year. People don't feel most of them, only a few earthquakes cause great damage[1].

In California there are two tectonic plates, the Pacific Plate and the North American Plate. An earthquake happens when these plates move and scrape[2] against each other. The boundary[3] between these two plates is the San Andreas Fault. It is more than 1,000 km long and up to 15 km deep. The Pacific Plate moves north-west past the North American Plate at a rate of about 50 millimetres per year. That is about how fast your fingernails grow. As a result, Los Angeles City Hall is now 2.7 metres closer to San Francisco than when it was built in 1924.

The San Andreas Fault

**b)** *Look at the map and the diagram and answer these questions:*
- Which plates are San Francisco and Los Angeles on?
- What does the diagram show?

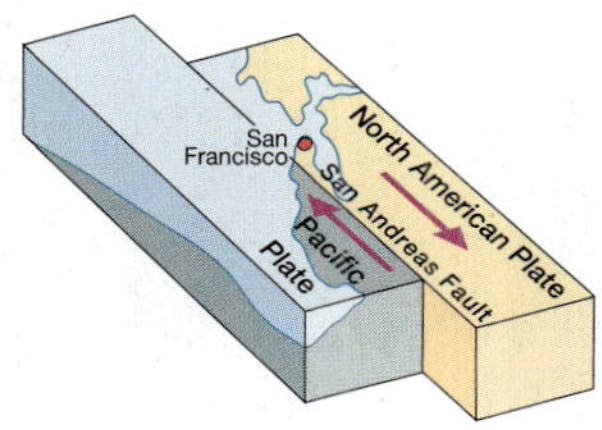


***Activate your English***
- The diagram shows ...
- One block moves from ... to ..., the other ... in the opposite direction.
- Part of the Pacific Ocean and Southern California is on ...

## 4 What to do before, during and after an earthquake

**a)** *Find more examples of things that you should ...*
- *fix[4] to the walls or the floor*
- *put in a disaster kit[5]*
- *do after an earthquake.*

**b)** *Discuss your results in class.*

**c)** *Design a poster to help people prepare for an earthquake. Add little drawings like this one.*

**Before an earthquake**

**1** Look around your home. Is there any heavy furniture and equipment that could fall and hurt you? Make sure they are fixed to the walls or the floor. Think about things like cupboards, TVs, ...

**2** Make disaster kits with food, water, ...

**During an earthquake**

Drop, cover, and hold on! Drop to the floor, take cover under a desk or table and hold on to it.

**After an earthquake**

**1** Check whether anyone is injured.

[1] (to) cause damage ['dæmidz] *Schaden verursachen* [2] (to) scrape [skreɪp] *scheuern, reiben* [3] boundary ['baʊndri] *Grenze*
[4] fix [fɪks] *hier: befestigen, sichern* [5] disaster kit [dɪ'zɑːstə kɪt] *Katastrophenausrüstung*

## TF 8 Building the Gateway Arch[1]

Since 1965, the Gateway Arch has been the symbol[2] of St. Louis, Missouri, and a monument to the men and women who settled[3] the western US. The Arch is the tallest monument in the US. It was designed by the architect Eero Saarinen, but a team of engineers was needed to find a way to build it.

**Climbing cranes**
The first 72 feet of the Arch were made with cranes on the ground. After that, special cranes rode up the sides with their heavy loads.

**Triangular[4] sections**
The sections were made in a factory far from the building site.

**Tracks[5]**
Two steel tracks took the cranes up the sides. The tracks were taken away when work was finished.

**South Entrance**

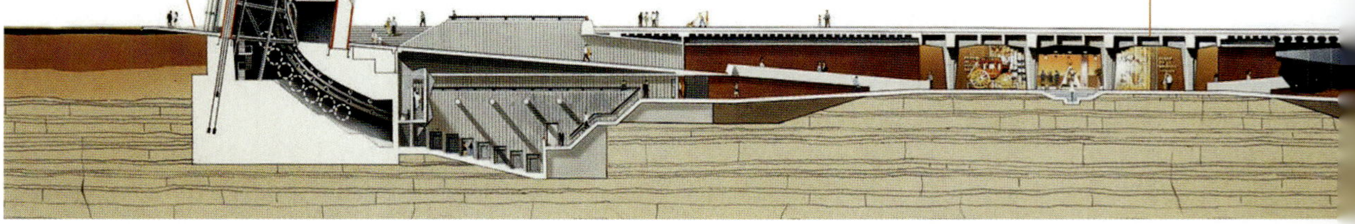

**Elevator**
A special elevator took workers up to do their jobs.

**Observation[6] Room**
There is an observation room at the top of the Arch at 630 feet (192 metres). From here you can see for miles to the east and west.

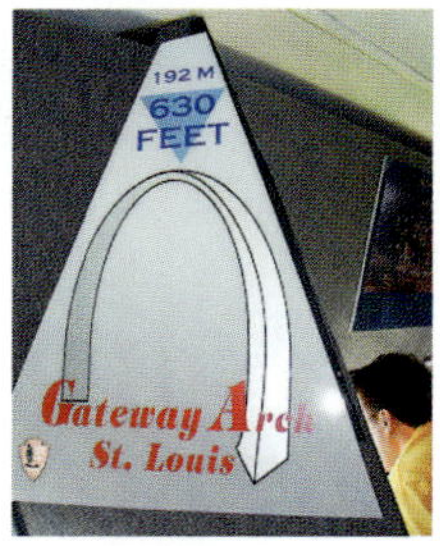

**Passenger trams**
Two trams, one in each leg, take visitors to the top of the Arch. The ride takes four minutes.

**Jefferson National Expansion Memorial[7]**
The Arch is in this beautiful park in downtown St. Louis.

**Museum of Westward Expansion**
A place to learn about how the Nation grew. You can see how the pioneers travelled and how they lived.

---

[1] gateway arch ['geɪtweɪ ˌɑːtʃ] *Torbogen* [2] symbol ['sɪmbl] *hier: Wahrzeichen* [3] (to) settle ['setl] *(be)siedeln*
[4] triangular [traɪ'æŋgjələr] *dreieckig* [5] track [træk] *Gleis* [6] observation [ˌɒbzə'veɪʃn] *Aussichts-* [7] memorial [me'mɔːriəl] *Denkmal, Mahnmal*

■ The skin[1]
The architect wanted it to be timeless, so he chose stainless steel[2].

■ Construction progress[3]

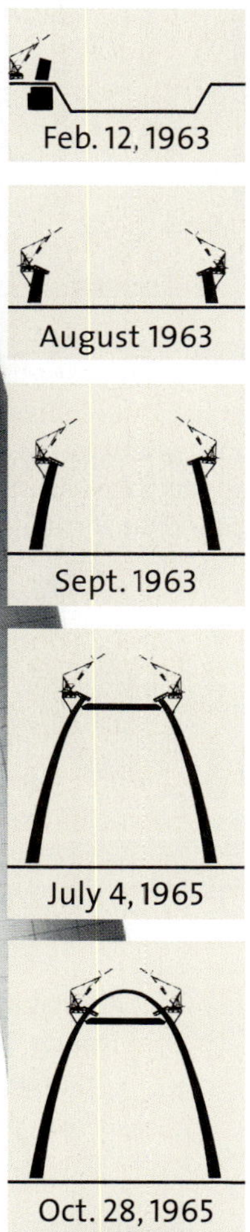


■ North Entrance

1 Tracks and climbing crane

2 A platform held the two legs in the last few months of construction.

3 A triangular section

4 The last piece of the Arch

## 1 Understanding the pictures and texts

*Look carefully at the drawings, photos and texts.*

1 Say how tall the Arch is in feet and in metres.
2 Describe how the work was done up to 72 feet and then above[4] that. Say how you think that influenced[5] the construction progress.
3 Work out how long it took to build the Arch.
4 Describe what you can see and do at the monument today.

## 2 Surprise!

*Do you think the Arch is taller than it is wide, or wider than it is tall? Use your ruler to check.*

## 3 Monuments

*Find out about a different monument: When was it built? How long did it take to build it? Why was it built?*

[1] skin [skɪn] *hier: (Außen-)Hülle* [2] stainless steel [ˌsteɪnləs 'stiːl] *rostfreier Stahl, Edelstahl*
[3] construction progress [kən'strʌkʃn ˌprəʊgres] *Baufortschritte* [4] above [ə'bʌv] *darüber* [5] (to) influence [ˌɪnfluəns] *beeinflussen*

## TF 9 The Trail of Tears[1] – Georgia to Oklahoma

The darkest time in the history of the Cherokee people was the 'Trail of Tears', when in 1838 16,000 of them were removed[2] from the south-eastern US. In their language this journey of nearly 2000 kilometres is called 'the trail where they cried'.

[1] trail of tears [ˌtreɪl‿əv 'tɪəz] *etwa: Pfad der Tränen* [2] (to) remove *umsiedeln* [3] law [lɔː] *Gesetz* [4] Indian Removal Act ['ɪndiən rɪ'muːvl ækt] *Gesetz zur Umsiedlung der Indianer* [5] territory ['terɪtərɪ] *Gebiet* [6] Supreme Court [sʊ'priːm ˌkɔːt] *Oberster Gerichtshof (US)* [7] (to) leave sb. alone *jn in Ruhe lassen*

## 1 What happened?

*Match these headings to the pictures.*

*A* The Cherokee were cold and hungry.
*B* The President sent the army to move the Cherokee.
*C* A law said that the Cherokee had to move away.
*D* People come to New Echota today to remember what happened.
*E* Many Cherokee died on the journey.
*F* Gold was found in Georgia.
*G* The US Supreme Court said that the new law was wrong.
*H* The Cherokee were good farmers.

---

[1] make sure (that) *dafür sorgen, dass* [2] cholera ['kɒlərə] *Cholera (Krankheit, die von starkem Durchfall und Erbrechen begleitet wird)*
[3] hunger ['hʌŋgə] [4] historic site [hɪ'stɒrɪk ˌsaɪt] *historische Gedenkstätte* [5] (to) do sth. to sb. *jm. etwas antun*

## TF 10 Black music

For 400 years, since the first black slaves arrived in America in 1619, black music has changed the look[1] and sound of music in the US. From spirituals to contemporary[2] R&B, here are ten important black music styles.

**1 SPIRITUALS** The earliest black songs in the US were the work songs and spirituals that the slaves sang in the fields. Spirituals were religious songs that gave hope of a better future to the slaves. One very famous spiritual is 'Swing low, sweet chariot'[3]. Gospel music, which started in the African American churches in the early 1900s, comes from the spirituals sung by southern slaves.

Slaves in the fields

**2 BLUES** Slavery was abolished[4] in 1865. As blacks moved north to the towns, a new type of black music was born – the blues. Robert Johnson was one of the most famous blues musicians[5], and there were many more great blues singers, like Ma Rainey and Bessie Smith.

Bessie Smith

Robert Johnson

Louis Armstrong

**3 JAZZ** In the 1920s jazz music was very popular in the US. Buddy Bolden, Jelly Roll Morton and Louis Armstrong were some of the first stars of this amazing new music style.

Bo Diddley

**4 R&B** Rhythm and blues was a music style that started in the 1930s and 1940s. It was a mix of jazz, gospel and blues music. Ruth Brown, Bo Diddley and Fats Domino were popular R&B artists at that time.

**5 ROCK 'N' ROLL** In the 1950s, the first rock 'n' roll songs were played by black artists. 'Tutti Frutti' by Little Richard and 'Johnny B. Goode' by Chuck Berry were two of the first rock 'n' roll songs.

Chuck Berry

[1] look [lʊk] *Aussehen* [2] contemporary [kən'temprəri] *zeitgenössisch, modern* [3] Swing low, sweet chariot [ləʊ], ['tʃæriət] *etwa: Schwing dich herab, du himmlischer Wagen* [4] (to) abolish [ə'bɒlɪʃ] *abschaffen* [5] musician [mju:'zɪʃn] *Musiker(in)*

Aretha Franklin

## 6 SOUL

**SOUL** Soul came from R&B and gospel. It was started in the late 1950s by black artists like Sam Cooke, Ray Charles and James Brown. In the 1960s one of the most popular soul stars was Aretha Franklin. People call her 'The Queen of Soul'.

Kool and the Gang

## 7 DISCO

**DISCO** In the 1970s, black disco stars, like B.T. Express, Kool and the Gang, Sister Sledge and Donna Summer, were popular.

## 8 RAP AND HIP HOP

**RAP AND HIP HOP** In 1979, The Sugar Hill Gang produced the first rap hit, 'Rapper's Delight'. This was the start of a new sound in the music world.

Alicia Keys

## 9 NEO SOUL

**NEO SOUL** In the late 1990s there was a new mix of sounds which people called neo soul. It was made up of hip hop, reggae, jazz, soul and Latin music. Lauryn Hill, Erykah Badu and Alicia Keys are famous neo soul artists of the 1990s and 2000s.

Usher

LeToya

## 10 CONTEMPORARY R&B

**CONTEMPORARY R&B** Contemporary R&B is a style of music that comes from soul, funk and disco. Today, black R&B singers like Beyoncé, LeToya, Usher and Ne-Yo are continuing[1] the black music tradition in the US.

### 1 Black music quiz

*Answer the quiz questions.*

1 What were the religious slave songs called?
2 What came first? The blues, soul or jazz?
3 What music came from jazz, gospel and the blues and was popular in the 1930s and 1940s?
4 Who first sang the rock 'n' roll song 'Johnny B. Goode'?
5 She was born on March 25, 1942 and they call her 'The Queen of Soul'. What's her name?
6 Which trio[2] had the first rap hit?

### 2 Radio quiz show

*Listen to the quiz show. Check your answers and correct any wrong answers.*

[1] (to) continue [kən'tɪnjuː] *fortführen* [2] trio [triːˈəʊ] *Trio (Gruppe, die aus drei Mitgliedern besteht)*

# TF 11 The American Civil War[1] (1861–1865)

## 1 Causes[2] of the Civil War

The Civil War (1861–1865) was a conflict between the North and the South in the US. At that time, the Northern states and the Southern states were very different. In the South, farming was very important and there were big plantations that used slaves to do the work. In the North, industry was more important than farming and most of the Northern states did not use slaves. A lot of people in the North thought that slavery was wrong and that it should stop.

In 1860 Abraham Lincoln became president. He was against slavery. The South thought that the new president would try to end slavery. Between 1860 and 1861, 11 Southern states left the Union[3] to form the Confederate States[4] of America.

Saving the Union was important to President Lincoln. He sent soldiers[5] to the South to try to bring the Confederate States back into the Union. The fighting between 'the Union' and 'the Confederacy' started in April 1861 and went on for four years.

In April 1865, the Union won the war and North and South were united again. 620,000 American soldiers died in the Civil War. That is more than in any war in the history of the US. In the South, many farms and cities were destroyed[6]. In December 1865, slavery was abolished[7] in the US.

## 2 The United States – divided[8] by war

**a)** *Describe what the map shows.*

**b)** *Find the following states on the map: California, Missouri, New York, Georgia. Which side were they on in the Civil War? Were they for or against slavery?*

***Activate your English***

- The map shows ...
- The US was divided into two main parts: ...
- The blue states were in the ...
- The grey states ...

A divided nation 1861–1865

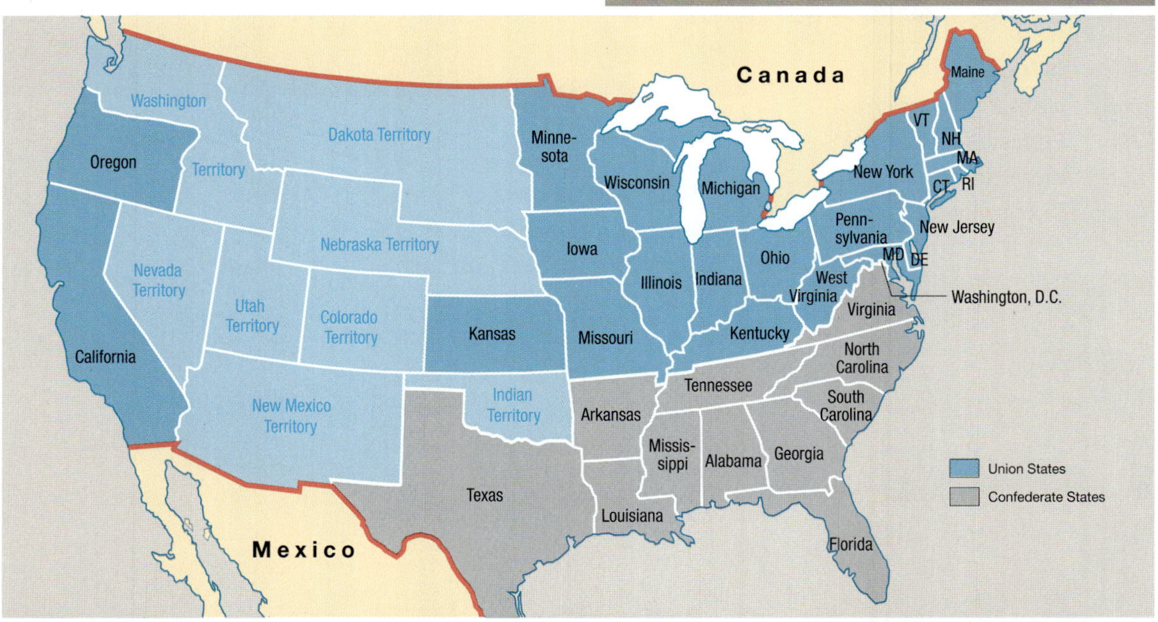


Before 1861, the US was made up of 19 free states, 15 slave states and some territories. Then 11 slave states left the Union to form the Confederate States of America.

[1] civil war [ˌsɪvl 'wɔ:] *Bürgerkrieg* [2] cause [kɔ:z] *Ursache* [3] the Union ['ju:njən] *die Vereinigten Staaten; (civil war) die Unionsstaaten* [4] Confederate States [kən'fedərɪt steɪts] *Konföderierte (d.h. verbündete) Staaten* [5] soldier ['səʊldʒə] *Soldat* [6] (to) destroy [dɪ'strɔɪ] *zerstören* [7] (to) abolish [ə'bɒlɪʃ] abschaffen [8] (to) divide [dɪ'vaɪd] *teilen*

## 3 Causes and effects[1]

*Copy and complete the diagram. Use the information from page 140.*

| main causes | | | main effects |
|---|---|---|---|
| **Slavery:** ... used slaves. ... thought slavery was wrong. | → Civil War (1861–1865) → | ... abolished. | |
| **The Union:** 11 Southern states ... the Union. | | ... united again. | |

## 4 Sullivan Ballou, a major[2] in the Civil War

***a)*** *Read the text and the letter.*

Sullivan Ballou was a major in the Northern army. He died in the Battle[3] of Bull Run (Virginia) in July 1861. Shortly before the battle he wrote this letter to his wife.

July 14th, 1861
Washington, D.C.

My dear Sarah,

If it is necessary that I should fall on the battlefield for my country, I am ready. [...] And I am willing[4] – perfectly willing – to lay down all my joys[5] in this life, to help maintain[6] this Government [...].

***b)*** *Choose the right answers.*

1 Sullivan Ballou ... in the battle.
A was afraid to die B was willing to die
C expected to be hurt D lost his friend

2 He went to war because he wanted to save ...
A his fields. B his life.
C his government. D his family.

***c)*** *Look at the box on the right and try to answer the questions on Sullivan Ballou's letter:*
*The letter was written in ... by ...*

***d)*** *Would you do for your country what Sullivan Ballou did for his?*

**HISTORY SKILLS Primary sources[7]**

Primary sources are texts or materials (letters, poems, diaries, photographs or newspaper articles) that were written or produced at the time of a historical event[8]. When you look at a primary source, like a letter, it is important to know the answers to these questions:
– When and where was it written?
– Who wrote it?
– Why was it written?

[1] effect [ɪ'fekt] *Wirkung* [2] major ['meɪdʒə] Major [3] battle ['bætl] *Schlacht* [4] (to) be willing ['wɪlɪŋ] *bereit sein* [5] joy [dʒɔɪ] *Freude* [6] (to) maintain [meɪn'teɪn] *bewahren* [7] primary source ['praɪməri ˌsɔːs] *Primärquelle* [8] event [ɪ'vent] *Ereignis*

## 6 A photo from 1865

**a)** *Look at the photo. Try to answer the questions. Make notes.*
- Who are the men in the photo?
- How do they feel?
- Which army do they belong to?
- When was the photo taken? What was the situation like?
- If you saw a photo of soldiers in the US army today, what would be different?

**b)** *Read the text on the right to find out more about the photo. Take notes.*

**c)** *In groups of three, compare your notes. Try to agree on answers to all the questions in a).*

The photo shows soldiers of Company E, 4th Colored Infantry Regiment[1] at Fort[2] Lincoln. It was taken in 1865, after the end of the Civil War.

About 200,000 black soldiers, many of them former[3] slaves, volunteered for the Northern army. They made up about 10% of the Northern soldiers.

Black soldiers were often discriminated against by their white officers. But they still were proud to fight for the North. Many hoped that fighting in the war would help them to become respected citizens.

### *Activate your English*
- I think the photo was taken in/between ...
- At that time the Civil War ... These men belonged to ...
- The men seem to be/feel ...
- The main thing that would be different today is ...

### HISTORY SKILLS Historical photos

Historical photos can tell you a lot about past events. To understand historical photos you have to know about the context in which they were taken. Think about:
- when the photo was taken
- where the photo was taken
- who took the photo and for what reason.

[1] infantry regiment ['ɪnfəntrɪ ˌredʒɪmənt] *Infanterieregiment (Fußtruppe)* [2] fort [fɔːt] *Fort (kleine Befestigungsanlage)* [3] former ['fɔːmə] *ehemalig*

## Skills File – Inhalt



Im **Skills File** findest du Hinweise zu Arbeits- und Lerntechniken. Was du in den Skills-Kästen der Units gelernt hast, wird hier näher erläutert.

Was du bereits aus Band 3 von English G 21 kennst, ist mit **REVISION** gekennzeichnet,
z. B.
– **REVISION Describing pictures**, Seite 147
– **REVISION Giving a presentation**, Seite 147.

Viele neue Hinweise helfen dir bei der Arbeit mit Hör- und Lesetexten, beim Sprechen, beim Schreiben von eigenen Texten, bei der Sprachmittlung und beim Lernen von Methoden.

Manchmal gibt es auch Aufgaben dazu.

# STUDY AND LANGUAGE SKILLS

## SF REVISION Learning words

### Worauf solltest du beim Lernen und Wiederholen von Vokabeln achten?

- Lerne immer 7–10 Vokabeln auf einmal.
- Lerne neue und wiederhole alte Vokabeln regelmäßig – am besten jeden Tag 5–10 Minuten.
- Lerne mit jemandem zusammen. Fragt euch gegenseitig ab.
- Schreib die neuen Wörter immer auch auf und überprüfe die Schreibweise mithilfe des *Dictionary* oder *Vocabulary*.

### Wie kannst du Wörter besser behalten?

Wörter kannst du besser behalten, wenn du sie in Wortgruppen sammelst und ordnest:

- **Gegensatzpaare** sammeln, z. B. alive ◂▸ dead, majority ◂▸ minority, forget ◂▸ remember
- Wörter mit **gleicher Bedeutung** sammeln, z. B. (to) train – (to) practise
- Wörter in **Wortfamilien** sammeln, z. B. (to) dance, dance, dancer, dancing lessons; friend, boyfriend, girlfriend, friendly, unfriendly, ...
- Wörter in **Wortnetzen** *(networks)* sammeln und ordnen.

## SF Check yourself ▸ *Unit 1, p. 29*

### How am I doing?

Damit du weißt, in welchen Bereichen des Englischen du noch Schwächen hast und welche du schon beherrschst, solltest du dich immer wieder selbst überprüfen. Das kannst du auf unterschiedlichen Wegen tun. Eine Reihe von Tipps kennst du schon vom **Stop-Check-Go** aus Band 1–2.
Du kannst dich auch nach jeder Unit mithilfe der *How am I doing*-Seiten selbst überprüfen, die du schon aus Band 3 kennst. Dabei gehst du wie folgt vor:

1. Du machst die einzelnen Aufgaben und überprüfst deine Ergebnisse.
2. Dann schaust du dir die Bereiche, in denen du Fehler gemacht hast, nochmal an. Halte dich dabei an die Hinweise in der Spalte *Find out more*.
3. Nun übst du gezielt diese Bereiche. Dazu schaust du in der Spalte *Exercises* nach, wo du im Englischbuch und *Workbook* Übungen dazu findest.
4. Nach einiger Zeit machst du die Aufgaben in *How am I doing?* noch einmal und vergleichst die Lösungen mit deinen Ergebnissen vom ersten Mal.

### Die Arbeit mit einer persönlichen Fehlerliste

Führe eine Liste der Fehler, die du oft machst, und nutze sie beim Schreiben von Texten als persönliche Checkliste. Hefte diese Listen in deinem Englischordner ab oder lege dir dafür ein extra Heft an (z.B. in DIN-A5).
Das Heft kannst du z.B. nach folgenden Schwerpunkten unterteilen:

1. Drittel: *Words* 2. Drittel: *Grammar* 3. Drittel: *Spelling*

Dann untersuchst du deine Klassenarbeiten und andere schriftliche Arbeiten auf deine Fehlerquellen hin. Dein/e Englischlehrer/in zeigt durch Abkürzungen am Rand, was für eine Art Fehler du gemacht hast.

*WORDS*

| *Wrong* | *Correct* | *REMEMBER* |
|---|---|---|
| *He goes to school ~~with the~~ bus.* | *He goes to school by bus.* | *mit dem Bus fahren – go by bus* |
| *We've got a ~~strong~~ teacher.* | *We've got a strict teacher.* | *Nicht verwechseln!* *streng – strict / strong – stark* |
| *I climbed ~~on~~ a tree.* | *I climbed a tree.* | *auf einen Baum klettern – climb a tree* |

**Tipp**

- Ergänze das Heft jedes Mal, wenn du eine Klassenarbeit oder einen Text von deinem Lehrer/deiner Lehrerin zurückbekommen oder wenn du eine *How am I doing*-Seite bearbeitet hast.
- Überprüfe, ob du bestimmte Fehler immer wieder machst. Wenn ja, such dafür Übungen in deinem Englischbuch, deinem *Workbook*, deinem *e-Workbook* oder frag deinen Lehrer/deine Lehrerin nach Übungen.
- Schau dir vor jeder Klassenarbeit die Fehler an, die du oft machst.
- Mach dir mithilfe des Grammatikteils die Regeln, die dir besonders schwerfallen, noch einmal bewusst.

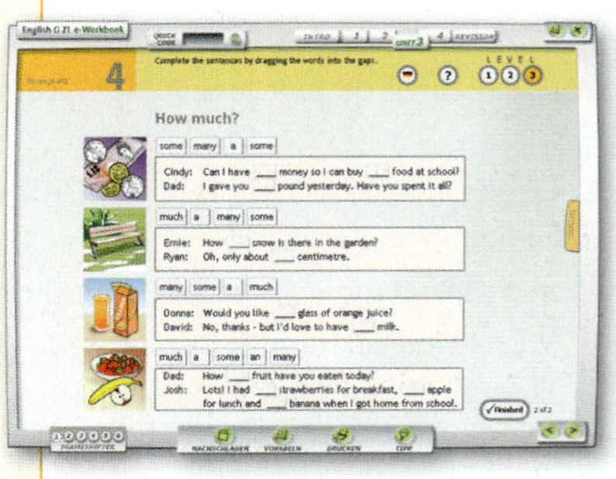

# SF REVISION Using a bilingual dictionary

## Wann brauche ich ein zweisprachiges Wörterbuch?

Du verstehst einen Text nicht, weil er zu viele Wörter enthält, die dir unbekannt sind, und die Worterschließungstechniken (► *SF Working out the meaning of words, p. 150*) helfen dir nicht weiter?
Du sollst einen Text auf Englisch schreiben, und dir fehlt das eine oder andere Wort, um deine Ideen auszudrücken? Du willst z.B. über die Ankunft eines Einwanderers in einem neuen Land schreiben (vgl. S.19) und kennst das englische Wort für „Grenze“ nicht?
In jedem Fall hilft dir ein zweisprachiges Wörterbuch.

## Wie benutze ich ein zweisprachiges Wörterbuch?

- Die **Leitwörter** oben auf der Seite helfen dir, schneller zu finden, was du suchst. Auf der linken Seite steht das erste Stichwort, auf der rechten Seite das letzte Stichwort der Doppelseite.
- Grenze ist das **Stichwort**. Alle Stichwörter sind alphabetisch geordnet: g vor h, ga vor ge und gre vor gri usw.
- Die **kursiv gedruckten** Hinweise helfen dir, die für deinen Text passende Bedeutung zu finden.
- Die **Ziffern** 1, 2 usw. zeigen, dass ein Stichwort mehrere ganz verschiedene Bedeutungen hat.
- **Beispielsätze** und **Redewendungen** sind dem Stichwort zugeordnet. In den Beispielsätzen und Redewendungen ersetzt eine **Tilde** (~) das Stichwort.
- Im englisch-deutschen Teil der meisten Wörterbücher findest du außerdem Hinweise auf **unregelmäßige Verbformen**, auf die **Steigerungsformen der Adjektive** und Ähnliches.
- Die **Lautschrift** gibt Auskunft darüber, wie das Wort ausgesprochen und betont wird. (→ *English sounds, p. 224*)

**gottlos**

divinely
**gottlos** godless, wicked
**gottverlassen** *umg.* godforsaken
**Götze**, **Götzenbild** idol ['aɪdl]
**Gouverneur** governor

**Grazie** grace
**graziös** **1** *Adj* graceful (⚠ *nicht* gracious) **2** *Adv* gracefully; **~ *tanzen*** dance gracefully
**greifen** **1** *Verb mit Obj* seize, take* hold of **2** *Verb ohne Obj; übertragen: von Maßnahmen* take* effect; **~ *nach*** reach for; *fest* grab at; ***sie griff in ihre Handtasche*** she reached into her handbag
**Greis** old man
**greisenhaft** senile (*auch* MED)
**Greisin** old woman
**grell** *Licht* glaring, harsh; *Farbe* garish; *Ton* shrill
**Grenze** border; *Linie* boundary; *übertragen* limit; ***es hält sich in Grenzen*** it's not too bad
**grenzen**: **~ *an*** border on (*auch übertragen*)
**grenzenlos** **1** *Adj* boundless **2** *Adv; sehr*

Bei kniffligen Wörtern gibt es in vielen Wörterbüchern **Info-Boxes**, in denen dir mehr Hilfen und Hinweise gegeben werden, hier z.B. für das deutsche Wort „schwer“.

**schwer krank**

**schwer**

Das deutsche **schwer** hat drei Hauptbedeutungen:
1) *schwer von Gewicht*: **heavy**;
2) *schwerwiegend, ernst*: **serious**, **bad**;
3) *schwierig*: **difficult**, **hard**, **tough**.

Welche englische Entsprechung von **Grenze** brauchst du in diesen Sätzen?
1. The ... between the US and Mexico is over 3000 km long.
2. In yesterday's run he pushed himself to his ...

**Tipp**

Nimm nicht einfach die erste Übersetzung, die dir angeboten wird! Lies den Wörterbucheintrag, bis du die richtige Übersetzung gefunden hast.

## SF Research ▸ *Unit 4, p. 81*

### Wo kann ich Informationen finden?

*Find some information about African Americans in the 1960s* – so oder so ähnlich lauten Aufgaben, die dir oft als Hausaufgabe gestellt werden.
Wenn du nach Informationen suchst, solltest du immer **mehrere Quellen** verwenden. Du kannst im Internet, in einem Lexikon, Atlas, Wörterbuch, Schulbuch oder in anderen Quellen suchen. Auch CDs und DVDs sind mögliche Quellen. Benutze auch einige englische Quellen, das kann dir beim Ausformulieren deines englischen Textes helfen.

- Internet/Lexikon: alle Wissensgebiete, wichtige Personen und Ereignisse
- Atlas: geografische und politische Übersichten, Städte, Flüsse
- Wörterbücher: Rechtschreibung und Bedeutung von Wörtern
- Schulbücher: verschiedene Wissensgebiete
- Zeitungen/Zeitschriften: aktuelle Informationen zu allen Themenbereichen

### Wie kann ich das Internet zur Recherche nutzen?

Eine wichtige Informationsquelle ist das Internet. Aber manchmal findest du dort so viele Informationen, dass du schnell den Überblick verlierst. Diese Tipps sollen dir helfen, damit du nicht im *world wide web* verloren gehst.

- Fertige eine Liste mit Schlüsselwörtern (**key words**) zu deinem Thema an: *African American, history, USA, discrimination, ...*
- Überlege, welches Schlüsselwort oder welche Kombination von Schlüsselwörtern am besten sein könnten:
  **„African Americans" history** oder **African+Americans+history**
- Wenn du dir zunächst einen Überblick verschaffen willst, kannst du auch ein Nachschlagewerk im Internet anklicken wie z.B.:
  www.infoplease.com www.en.wikipedia.org
  Manchmal gibt es dort auch Links, die dir weiterhelfen können.
- Suchmaschinen (wie z.B. *Google, Altavista* oder *Yahoo*) helfen dir, Websites zu deinem Thema zu finden. Verwende eine Suchmaschine und gib deine Schlüsselwörter in das Suchfenster ein.
- Wenn die angezeigten Websites dir nicht helfen oder du zu viele Websites angezeigt bekommst, versuch es noch einmal, indem du deine Schlüsselwörter präzisierst.

| | | |
|---|---|---|
| mit **allen** Wörtern | "African Americans"+history | 10 Ergebnisse |
| mit der **genauen Wortgruppe** | discrimination in the 1960s | |
| mit **irgendeinem** der Wörter | | |
| **ohne** die Wörter | | |

#### Tipp

- Verwende immer mehrere Internet-Quellen, um sicherzugehen, dass die Informationen stimmen.
- Suche Antworten auf die **5 Ws** (**who**, **what**, **where**, **when**, **why**).
- Bei englischen Quellen brauchst du nicht alles zu verstehen. Konzentrier dich auf das Wesentliche.
- Schreib die Quellen nicht wortwörtlich ab, sondern mach dir Notizen in deinen eigenen Worten (▸ *Reading Course S. 150*).

## SF REVISION Describing pictures

### Wie kann ich Bilder beschreiben?

- Um zu sagen, wo genau etwas abgebildet ist, benutze:
  at the top/bottom • in the foreground/background • in the middle • on the left/right
- Diese Präpositionen sind auch hilfreich:
  behind • between • in front of • next to • under
- Um zu beschreiben, was die Personen auf dem Bild tun, benutze das **present progressive**.
  The girl is looking down into the Grand Canyon.

### Wie kann ich beschreiben, was die Personen fühlen?

Oft sollst du dich in eine Person auf einem Foto hineinversetzen und beschreiben, was sie fühlt oder denkt. Schau dir das Foto genau an und nimm dir Zeit, dir die Situation vorzustellen. Beim Formulieren helfen dir *phrases* wie:
Maybe the woman/man in the photo feels ... /is thinking about ... •
I think he/she feels/wants to/...

## SF REVISION Giving a presentation

### Wie mache ich eine gute Präsentation?

**Vorbereitung**
- Schreib die wichtigsten Gedanken als Notizen auf, z. B. auf nummerierte Karteikarten oder als Mindmaps.
- Übe deine Präsentation zu Hause vor einem Spiegel. Sprich laut, deutlich und langsam.

**Folien oder Poster**
- Overhead-Folien oder Poster sind gut, um
  - zu zeigen, wie dein Vortrag aufgebaut ist
  - Tabellen, Diagramme usw. für alle lesbar zu präsentieren
  - die wichtigsten Punkte zusammenzufassen.
- Schreib groß und für alle gut lesbar.

**Durchführung**
- Bevor du beginnst, leg deine Folie auf den ausgeschalteten Projektor bzw. häng das Poster auf und sortiere deine Vortragskarten.
- Warte, bis es ruhig ist. Schau die Zuhörer an.
- Erkläre zu Anfang, worüber du sprechen wirst. Lies nicht von deinen Karten ab, sondern sprich frei, nutze deine Karten nur als Gedankenstütze.

My presentation is about ... First, I'd like to talk about ... Second, ...

This picture/photo/ ... shows ...

**Schluss**
- Sag, dass du fertig bist.
- Frag die Zuhörenden, ob sie Fragen haben. Bedanke dich fürs Zuhören.

That's the end of my presentation. Have you got any questions?

# LISTENING AND READING SKILLS

## SF REVISION Listening

### Was muss ich allgemein beim *Listening* beachten?

**Vor dem Hören:**

– Überlege, worum es in dem Hörtext gehen wird. Frag dich, was du schon über das Thema weißt.
– Lies die Aufgabe gut durch, damit du weißt, worauf du achten sollst:
  • auf die Hauptgedanken oder
  • auf bestimmte Informationen, wie z.B. Namen, Uhrzeiten, Jahreszahlen.
– Bereite dich darauf vor, Notizen zu machen. Leg z.B. eine Tabelle oder Liste an.

**Beim Hören:**

– Keine Panik! Du musst nicht alles verstehen. Konzentriere dich auf das Wesentliche. Oft werden wichtige Informationen auch wiederholt.

– Achte auf Geräusche und unterschiedliche Stimmen. Was ein Sprecher/eine Sprecherin besonders betont, das ist wichtig!

– Wenn du gezielt nach Informationen suchst, denk an die Aufgabe und lass dich von anderen Einzelheiten nicht ablenken.
  Aufgepasst! Die Informationen, die du suchst, kommen vielleicht in einer anderen Reihenfolge vor, als du sie erwartest.

– Manche Signalwörter machen es dir leichter, den Hörtext zu verstehen:
  • Aufzählung: **and**, **another**, **too**
  • Gegensatz: **although**, **but**
  • Grund, Folge: **because, so**, **so that**
  • Vergleich: **larger/older/... than**, **more**, **most**
  • Reihenfolge: **before**, **after**, **then**, **next**, **later**, **when**, **at last**, **at the same time**

– Mach nur kurze Notizen, z.B. Anfangsbuchstaben, Symbole oder Stichworte, schreib keine ganzen Sätze.
  Unterteile Telefonnummern beim Aufschreiben: 0171 572 42 589.

**Nach dem Hören:**

– Vervollständige deine Notizen sofort.
– Konzentriere dich beim zweiten Hören auf das, was du zuerst nicht gut verstanden hast.

### Worauf sollte ich bei automatischen Telefonansagen achten?

Wenn du eine telefonische Auskunft einholen willst, hörst du manchmal eine automatische Telefonansage.

– Keine Panik! Du kannst eine automatische Telefonansage mehrmals hören.
– Achte besonders auf Zahlen! Meist wirst du aufgefordert, bestimmte Tasten auf deinem Telefon zu drücken, um die gewünschte Information zu erhalten. Oft werden diese Zahlen wiederholt.
– Überlege dir vorher, welche Informationen du suchst und auf welche Schlüsselwörter du dafür achten solltest. Schreib sie auf.
– Höre dann besonders genau zu, wenn deine Schlüsselwörter genannt werden, und mach dir Notizen zu ihnen. ▸ *Unit 2, p. 48*

# SF REVISION Taking notes

## Worum geht es beim Notizenmachen?

Wenn du beim Lesen oder Zuhören Notizen machst, kannst du dich später besser an das Gehörte oder Gelesene erinnern, wenn du etwas vortragen, nacherzählen oder einen Bericht schreiben sollst.

## Wie mache ich Notizen?

In Texten oder Gesprächen gibt es immer wichtige und unwichtige Wörter. Die wichtigen Wörter werden Schlüsselwörter (**key words**) genannt und nur die solltest du notieren. Meist sind das Substantive und Verben, manchmal auch Adjektive oder Zahlen.

**Tipp**

- Verwende Ziffern (z.B. „7“ statt „seven“).
- Verwende Symbole und Abkürzungen, z.B. ✔ (für „ja“) und + (für „und“) oder US für United States, C. für Caitlin.
  Du kannst auch eigene Symbole erfinden.
- Verwende **not** oder ✗ statt „doesn't“ oder „don't“.

# SF REVISION Marking up a text

## Wann sollte ich einen Text markieren?

Du hast einen Text mit vielen Fakten vor dir liegen und sollst später über bestimmte Dinge berichten. Dann wird es dir helfen, die für die Aufgabenstellung wichtigen Informationen im Text zu markieren.

## Wie gehe ich am besten vor?

Lies den Text und markiere nur die für dein Thema wichtigen Informationen. Nicht jeder Satz enthält für deine Aufgabe wichtige Wörter, und oft reicht es aus, nur ein oder zwei Wörter in einem Satz zu markieren.

- Du kannst wichtige Wörter einkreisen.
- Du kannst sie unterstreichen.
- Du kannst sie mit einem Textmarker hervorheben.

**ABER:**
Markiere nur auf Fotokopien von Texten oder in Büchern, die dir gehören, oder verwende eine Folie und einen wasserlöslichen Folienstift.

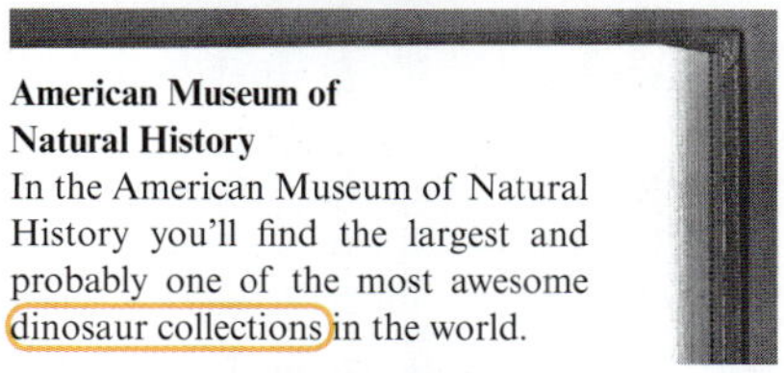
**American Museum of Natural History**
In the American Museum of Natural History you'll find the largest and probably one of the most awesome dinosaur collections in the world.

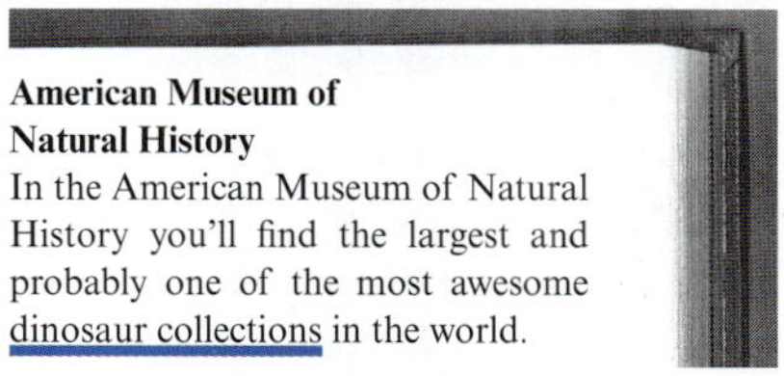
**American Museum of Natural History**
In the American Museum of Natural History you'll find the largest and probably one of the most awesome dinosaur collections in the world.

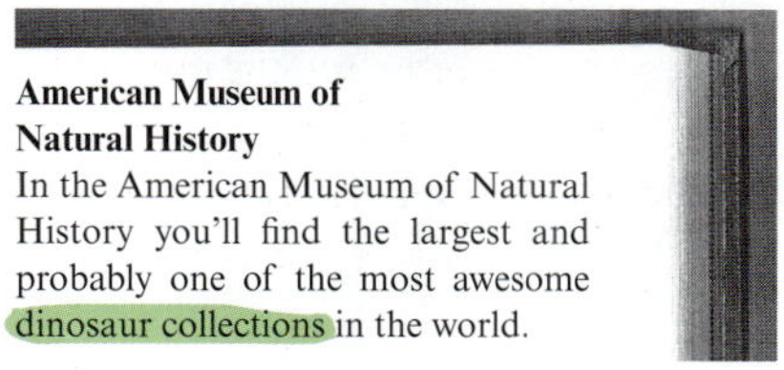
**American Museum of Natural History**
In the American Museum of Natural History you'll find the largest and probably one of the most awesome dinosaur collections in the world.

# READING COURSE – Zusammenfassung

## REVISION Working out the meaning of words ▸ *Unit 1, p. 23*

Das Nachschlagen unbekannter Wörter im Wörterbuch kostet Zeit und nimmt auf Dauer den Spaß am Lesen. Oft geht es auch ohne Wörterbuch!

### Was hilft dir, unbekannte Wörter zu verstehen?

1. **Bilder** zeigen oft die Dinge, die du im Text nicht verstehst. Wenn es Bilder zum Text gibt, dann schau sie dir vor dem Lesen genau an.
2. Oft hilft dir der **Textzusammenhang**, z.B. *When we* ***reached*** *the station, Judy went to the ticket machine to buy our tickets.*
3. Manche englischen Wörter werden **ähnlich wie im Deutschen** geschrieben oder ausgesprochen, z.B. **excellent**, **millionaire**, **nation**, **reality**.
4. Manchmal stecken in unbekannten Wörtern **bekannte Teile**, z.B. **friendliness**, **helpless**, **understandable**, **gardener**, **tea bag**, **waiting room**.

## REVISION Skimming and Scanning ▸ *Unit 2, p. 43*

### *Skimming:* Lesen, um sich einen Überblick zu verschaffen

Beim **Skimming** überfliegst du einen Text schnell, um dir einen ersten **Überblick** zu verschaffen, worum es geht. Du willst herausfinden, ob ein Text, den du im Internet oder in einem Buch gefunden hast, überhaupt nützliche Informationen zu deinem Thema (z.B. für ein Referat) enthält. Achte beim Skimming auf:

- die **Überschrift**
- die **Zwischenüberschriften** und **hervorgehobene** Wörter oder Sätze
- die **Bilder** und **Bildunterschriften**
- den **ersten** und **letzten Satz** jedes Absatzes
- **Grafiken**, **Statistiken** und die **Quelle** des Textes.

### *Scanning:* Lesen, um nach bestimmten Informationen zu suchen

Beim **Scanning** suchst du in einem Text nach **bestimmten Informationen**, die z.B. für ein Referat wichtig sind. Dazu brauchst du nicht den gesamten Text zu lesen, sondern du suchst nach Schlüsselwörtern (**key words**) und liest nur dort genauer, wo du sie findest. Geh dabei so vor:

**Schritt 1:** Denk an das Schlüsselwort, nach dem du suchst, oder schreib es auf.

**Schritt 2:** Geh mit den Augen und dem Finger schnell durch den Text, in breiten Schlingen wie bei einem „S" oder „Z" oder von oben nach unten wie bei einem „U". Dabei hast du das Schriftbild oder das Bild des Wortes, nach dem du suchst, vor Augen. Das gesuchte Wort wird dir sofort „ins Auge springen". Lies nur dort weiter, um Näheres zu erfahren.

**Schritt 3:** Wenn das Schlüsselwort, nach dem du suchst, im Text nicht vorkommt, überleg dir, welche anderen Wörter mit den benötigten Informationen zu tun haben, und such nach diesen.

## Finding the main ideas of a text ▸ *Unit 3, p. 65*

Wenn du Texte wie Zeitungsartikel, Berichte oder Kommentare richtig verstehen willst, ist es gut, wenn du ihre Hauptaussagen erkennst und nachvollziehst, wie sie zusammenhängen. Dabei hilft dir ein Blick auf die Struktur dieser Texte.

### Wie finde ich die Hauptaussagen eines Textes?

1. Jeder Text dreht sich um ein Thema oder hat eine Hauptaussage, z. B.
   *Drinking soda is one of the worst things you can do to your health.*
   Diese Hauptaussage findest du oft im **ersten Absatz**. Lies ihn deshalb besonders gründlich durch.
2. Die Hauptaussage wird in der Regel durch weitere Aussagen bzw. Gedanken unterstützt, z. B.
   *Experts agree that sugary soft drinks and fast food are the main reasons why so many American teenagers are fat.*
   Du findest sie oft im ersten oder letzten Satz der nachfolgenden Absätze.
3. Diese weiteren Aussagen bzw. Gedanken werden meist durch Beispiele und Begründungen ergänzt, z. B.
   *About 7% of the calories that they take in come from soft drinks alone.*

**Tipp**

Die folgenden Wörter oder Wendungen werden oft im Zusammenhang mit Begründungen oder Beispielen verwendet:
**... % of ... are ... • and so • because • e.g. / for example • etc. • for lots of reasons • this shows that • that's why**

## Drawing conclusions ▸ *Unit 4, p. 86*

Wenn du bei einer Arbeit Fragen zu einem Text beantworten sollst oder bei einer Recherche Informationen zu einer bestimmten Frage in einem Text suchst, kann es gut sein, dass du an mehreren Stellen schauen musst oder dass die Antwort nicht 1:1 im Text steht.

### Wie funktioniert schlussfolgerndes Lesen?

1. Die einfachste Form des schlussfolgernden Lesens besteht darin, die Informationen aus verschiedenen Textstellen zusammenzuführen. Im Text auf S. 86 z. B. musst du mehrere Textstellen anschauen, wenn du alle Gründe finden willst, warum Schüler/innen in den USA arbeiten gehen.
2. Manchmal steht die Antwort auf eine Frage nicht direkt im Text. Dann musst du sie dir erschließen. Im Text auf S. 86 geht es um die Frage, welche Auswirkungen das Arbeiten auf die schulischen Leistungen hat. Dafür musst du Fakten im Text finden, die etwas mit dieser Frage zu tun haben:

*FACTS: students have an 11-hour work day; after work they're often too tired to do their homework = negative effects*
*working makes students more disciplined; they learn to organize their time = positive effects*
*CONCLUSION: for some students it's good, but for many it means bad grades*

# MEDIATION SKILLS

## SF REVISION Mediation

### Wann muss ich zwischen zwei Sprachen vermitteln?

Manchmal musst du zwischen zwei Sprachen vermitteln. Das nennt man mediation.

1. Du gibst englische Informationen auf Deutsch weiter:
   Du fährst z. B. mit deiner Familie in die USA und deine Eltern oder Geschwister wollen wissen, was jemand in einem Café gesagt hat oder was an einer Informationstafel steht.
2. Du gibst deutsche Informationen auf Englisch weiter:
   Vielleicht ist bei dir zu Hause eine Austauschschülerin aus den USA oder Dänemark zu Gast, die kein Deutsch spricht und Hilfe braucht.
3. In schriftlichen Prüfungen musst du manchmal in einem englischen Text gezielt nach Informationen suchen und diese auf Deutsch wiedergeben. Oder du sollst Informationen aus einem deutschen Text auf Englisch wiedergeben.

### Worauf muss ich bei *mediation* achten?

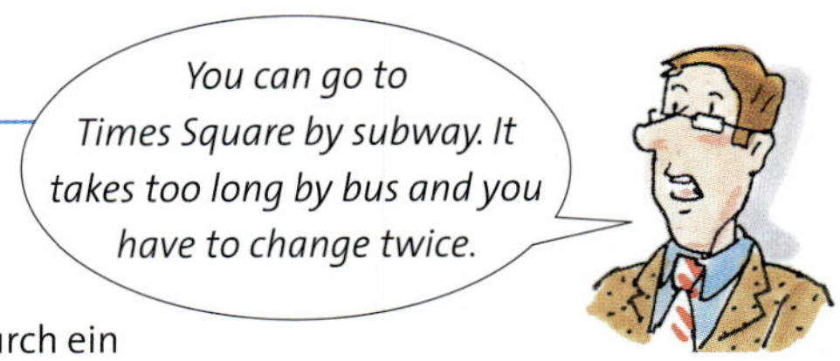


- Übersetze nicht alles wörtlich.
- Gib nur das Wesentliche weiter, lass Unwichtiges weg.
- Verwende kurze und einfache Sätze.
- Wenn du ein Wort nicht kennst, umschreibe es oder ersetze es durch ein anderes Wort.

### Was kann ich tun, wenn ich ein wichtiges Wort nicht kenne?

Vielleicht findest du es manchmal schwer, mündliche Aussagen oder schriftliche Textvorlagen in die andere Sprache zu übertragen, z. B. weil:
- dein Wortschatz nicht ausreicht
- dir bekannte Wörter „im Stress" nicht einfallen
- spezielle Fachbegriffe auftauchen.

Manche Wörter kannst du umschreiben, z. B. mithilfe von Relativsätzen wie:
**It's somebody/a person who ...**
**It's something that you use to ...**
**It's an animal that ...**
**It's a place where ...**

▸ *SF Paraphrasing, p. 153*

# SPEAKING AND WRITING SKILLS

## SF REVISION Paraphrasing

### Worum geht es beim Paraphrasing?

Paraphrasing bedeutet, etwas mit anderen Worten zu erklären. Das ist hilfreich, wenn dir ein bestimmtes Wort nicht einfällt oder wenn dein Gegenüber dich nicht verstanden hat (siehe auch ▸ *SF Mediation, p. 152*).

### Wie gehe ich beim Paraphrasing vor?

- Man kann mit einem Wort umschreiben, das dieselbe Bedeutung hat:
  **to train is the same as to practise**
  Oder man sagt das Gegenteil: **alive is the opposite of dead**
- Manchmal braucht man mehrere Wörter, z. B. wenn man etwas beschreibt oder erklärt. Dabei benutzt man ein allgemeines Wort (**general word**) und nennt weitere Eigenschaften.
  **A skyscraper is a very tall building.**
- Oder du umschreibst das Wort mit **... is/are like ...**
  **A cabin is like a small house, it's in the country.**
- Du kannst zum Umschreiben auch ein allgemeines Wort nehmen (z.B. **person**, **something**) und dieses mit einem durch **who**, **that** oder **where** eingeleiteten Satz näher erklären: **A ranger is a person who works in national parks and protects the parks and helps visitors.**
  **A ticket office is a shop where you can buy tickets for shows and concerts.**

## SF REVISION Brainstorming

### Wofür ist Brainstorming gut?

Bei vielen Aufgaben ist es nützlich, wenn du im ersten Schritt möglichst viele Ideen zum Thema sammelst. Dabei hilft dir das Brainstorming.

### Wie gehe ich beim Brainstorming vor?

**Schritt 1:**
Schreib alle Ideen so auf, wie sie dir einfallen. Es ist zunächst völlig egal, ob sie gut sind oder nicht. Du kannst die Ideen durcheinander auf einen Zettel schreiben oder schon etwas geordnet, z.B. für jede eine neue Zeile.

**Schritt 2:**
Lies alle deine Ideen durch und wähle die besten aus. Dann sortiere sie und fasse sie sinnvoll zusammen. Dabei kannst du folgende **Techniken** anwenden:

1. Leg eine **Mindmap** an. Schreib das Thema in die Mitte eines Blattes Papier. Überlege, welche Oberbegriffe zu deiner Sammlung von Ideen passen. Verwende unterschiedliche Farben. Ergänze jede Idee, die zu einem Oberbegriff passt, auf einem Nebenast. Nimm dafür nur wichtige Schlüsselwörter. Du kannst statt Wörtern auch Symbole verwenden und Bilder ergänzen.
2. **The 5 Ws**: Schreib die **5** W-Fragen **Who? What? When? Where? Why?** in eine Tabelle. Die Ideen, die dir zu jeder Frage kommen, kannst du darunter schreiben.

# REVISION WRITING COURSE – Zusammenfassung

**The steps of writing**

1. Brainstorming – Ideen sammeln, dann sortieren (▸ *SF Brainstorming, p. 153*).
2. Schreiben. Dabei achte darauf,
   - deine Sätze zu verbinden und auszubauen (*Writing better sentences*)
   - deinen Text gut zu strukturieren (*Using paragraphs*)
   - bei einem Bericht die 5 Ws abzudecken (*Writing a report*)
3. Deinen Text inhaltlich und sprachlich überprüfen (*Correcting your text*)

## Writing better sentences

### Linking words

Eine Geschichte klingt interessanter, wenn du die Sätze mit **linking words** miteinander verbindest. Dabei gibt es mehrere Möglichkeiten:

- **Time phrases** wie **at 7 o'clock**, **every morning**, **a few minutes later**, **then**, **next** ...
- **Konjunktionen** wie **although**, **because**, **but**, **so** ... **that**, **that**, **when**, **while**
- **Relativpronomen** wie **that** und **who**

### Adjektive und Adverbien

- Mit Adjektiven kannst du Personen, Orte oder Erlebnisse genauer und interessanter beschreiben. Vergleiche: **The man looked into the room.**
  ▸ **The young man looked into the empty room.**
- Mit Adverbien kannst du beschreiben, **wie** jemand etwas macht:
  **The young man looked nervously into the empty room.**

## Using paragraphs

### Structuring a text

Ein längerer Text ist besser zu verstehen, wenn er in mehrere Absätze unterteilt ist:

- eine Einleitung (**beginning**) – hier schreibst du, worum es geht
- einen Hauptteil (**middle**) – hier schreibst du mehr über dein Thema
- einen Schluss (**end**) – hier bringst du den Text zu einem interessanten Ende.

### Topic sentences

Am Anfang eines Absatzes sind kurze, einleitende Sätze (**topic sentences**) gut, weil sie den Lesern sofort sagen, worum es geht, z. B.

1. Orte: **My trip to ... was fantastic. / ... is famous for ... / ... is a great place.**
2. Personen: **... is great/funny/interesting/clever ...**
3. Aktivitäten: **... is great fun. / Lots of people ... every day.**

### Wie kann ich meine Absätze interessant gestalten?

- Beginne mit einem interessanten Einstiegssatz:
  **You'll never guess what happened to me today! / Did I tell you that ...?**
- Fang für jeden neuen Aspekt einen neuen Absatz an.
- Beende deinen Text mit einer Zusammenfassung oder etwas Persönlichem.

## Writing a report – collecting and organizing ideas

### Worauf kommt es bei einem Bericht an?

- Gib dem Leser **eine schnelle Orientierung**, was passiert ist.
- Beginne mit **wichtigen Informationen** und gib erst dann Detailinformationen.
- Ein Bericht gibt immer Antworten auf die **5 Ws**:
  **Who? What? When? Where? Why?** und manchmal auch auf **How?**
- Verwende das **simple past**.

## Correcting your text

Ein Text ist noch nicht „fertig", wenn du ihn zu Ende geschrieben hast. Du solltest ihn immer mehr als einmal durchlesen:
- einmal, um zu sehen, ob er vollständig und gut verständlich ist
- noch einmal, um ihn auf Fehler zu überprüfen, z. B. **Rechtschreibfehler *(spelling mistakes)*** oder **Grammatikfehler *(grammar mistakes)***.

**tomato** [tə'mɑːtəʊ], *pl* **tomatoes** Tomate II

**wife** [waɪf], *pl* **wives** [waɪvz] Ehefrau II

**drop (-pp-)** [drɒp] fallen lassen I

**forget (-tt-)** [fə'get] vergessen I

### Spelling mistakes

Lies deinen Text langsam, Wort für Wort, Buchstabe für Buchstabe. Wenn du unsicher bist, hilft dir ein Wörterbuch. Beachte folgende Regeln:

**Tipp**

- Manche Wörter haben Buchstaben, die man nicht spricht, aber schreibt, z. B. **knife**, **climb**.
- Manchmal ändert sich die Schreibweise, wenn ein Wort eine Endung erhält,
  z. B. **take** → **taking**, **terrible** → **terribly**, **lucky** → **luckily**,
  **try** → **tries** (**aber** **stay** → **stays**), **run** → **running**, **drop** → **dropped**.
- Beim Plural tritt manchmal noch ein **-e** zum **-s**, z. B. **church** → **churches**.

### Grammar mistakes

Diese Tipps helfen dir, typische Fehler zu vermeiden:

**Tipp**

- Im **simple present** wird in der 3. Person Singular **-s** angehängt: **she knows**
- **Unregelmäßige Verben:** Manche Verben bilden die Formen des *simple past* und des Partizip Perfekt *(past participle)* unregelmäßig. Die unregelmäßigen Formen musst du lernen. Die Liste steht auf S. 258–259.
  **go – went – gone; buy – bought – bought**
- **Verneinung bei Vollverben:** Im *simple present* mit ***don't/doesn't***, im *simple past* mit **didn't**, z. B. **He doesn't speak French**, **he didn't learn it at school**.
- **Satzstellung**: Im Englischen gilt immer (auch im Nebensatz):
  a) subject – verb – object (SVO) **... when I saw my brother.**
  **... als ich meinen Bruder sah.**
  b) Orts- vor Zeitangabe **I bought a nice book in the city yesterday.**

## SF Writing formal and informal letters ▸ *Unit 2, p. 45*

Beim Schreiben von Briefen und E-Mails musst du unterschiedliche Regeln beachten, je nachdem, ob du einen förmlichen Brief (*formal letter*) an unbekannte Personen, Behörden, Zeitschriften usw. schreibst oder einen persönlichen, informellen Brief (*informal letter*) an Freunde oder Verwandte.

### Worauf kommt es bei förmlichen Briefen an? (Formal letters)

① Schreibe deine Adresse (ohne Namen) und das Datum in die rechte obere Ecke. Verwende keine typisch deutschen Buchstaben wie z.B. ß, ä, ö, oder ü.
② Die Anschrift steht links.
③ Die Anrede lautet *Dear Sir or Madam*. Wenn du den Namen des Adressaten kennst, beginne deinen Brief mit *Dear Mr/Mrs/Ms ...*
④ Nenne zu Beginn den Grund deines Briefes.
⑤ Bedanke dich bei Bitten und Anfragen im Voraus (*I look forward to hearing from you. Thank you.*).
⑥ Beende den Brief mit *Yours faithfully*, wenn du den Adressaten nicht kennst. Hast du den Adressaten am Anfang des Briefes mit Namen angeredet, dann schreibe *Yours sincerely*.
⑦ Unterschreibe den Brief und tippe zusätzlich deinen Namen.

**Tipp**

Beachte, was du zum Schreiben von Texten gelernt hast:
- Vor dem Schreiben: Ideen sammeln, dann sortieren.
- Während des Schreibens: Sätze verbinden und ausbauen; strukturieren.
- Nach dem Schreiben: Überprüfe deinen Brief inhaltlich und sprachlich. ▸ *SF Writing course, pp. 154–155*

① Waldstr. 5
50933 Koeln
Germany

② 1532 Beachview Place
Los Angeles, CA
94832 - 1384
USA

20 May 2009

③ Dear Sir or Madam

I am writing to you because I am really interested in ④ an article I read in your newspaper (May 2009). The title of the article is "New World, New Hopes, and New Problems" and it is about three immigrant families living in America. I have some questions and I hope that you can answer them.

I know that a lot of Americans are proud of their country. What about people who live in America but were not born there? Are they proud of America? Have you asked the families from the article how they feel about America? I would really like to know what they think.

I look forward to hearing from you soon. Thank you ⑤ very much.

⑥ Yours faithfully

⑦ *Tom Winter*
Tom Winter

### Was ist bei persönlichen Briefen anders? (Informal letters)

Hier sind die Regeln nicht ganz so streng. Aber beachte Folgendes:
- Schreibe deine Adresse (ohne Namen) und das Datum in die rechte obere Ecke.
- Verwende keine typisch deutschen Buchstaben wie z.B. ß, ä, ö, oder ü.
- Du benötigst keine Anschrift.
- Du kannst deinen Brief mit *Dear/Hello/Hi* ... beginnen.
- Nenne zu Beginn den Grund deines Briefes, stelle auch Fragen.
- Beende den Brief mit einem freundlichen Gruß/Ausblick/Erwartungen/...
- Schließe deinen Brief mit *Yours/Best wishes/Love/...* ab.

Alles klar? Wohin gehören die Wendungen im blauen Kasten?

| | Formal letter | Informal letter |
|---|---|---|
| opening | Dear Mr Smith, ... | Dear Pete, ... |
| closing | ... | ... |

Best wishes • Dear Pete •
I look forward to hearing from you •
Yours faithfully • Dear Mr Smith •
Yours sincerely • Lots of love •
I look forward to meeting you. • Love •
Dear Sir or Madam • See you soon! •
Hello Sarah • Thank you very much. •
Happy birthday! I've just heard ...

## SF Summarizing texts ▸ Unit 3, p. 67

Wenn du einen Text (mündlich oder schriftlich) zusammenfasst, gibst du die wichtigen Informationen oder Ereignisse in kürzerer Form wieder.

### Wie gehe ich beim summarizing vor?

1. Lies den Text mindestens einmal genau durch, damit du verstehst, worum es geht. Mach dir noch keine Notizen.
2. Lies den Text erneut, Satz für Satz, durch und mach dir Notizen zu den 5 Ws:

| | |
|---|---|
| **Who?** | Who is the text about? |
| **What?** | What happens?/What does he/she do? |
| **Where?** | Where does it happen? |
| **When?** | When does it happen? |
| **Why?** | Why does it happen? / Why does he/she do this? |

Was auf diese Fragen Antwort gibt, ist wichtig. Auslassen solltest du dagegen Beispiele, Vergleiche, Zitate, direkte Rede, ausschmückende Adjektive und andere Textteile, die der Beschreibung dienen.

3. Leg den Text nun beiseite und schreib mithilfe deiner Notizen eine Zusammenfassung des Texts in deinen eigenen Worten.

– Erklär in den ersten ein oder zwei Sätzen, worum es in dem Text geht.

• Vergleiche diese drei Anfänge einer Zusammenfassung von *You can tell me* (S. 26–28). Welcher gibt am besten das Thema der Geschichte wieder?

*YOU CAN TELL ME is a story about New York.*

*YOU CAN TELL ME is a story about Anthony and Kelly, two teenagers from New York.*

*Anthony and Kelly play music together. They have a nice picnic in the park.*

Du kannst für deine einleitenden Sätze die folgenden phrases verwenden:
**The story is about ...** • **The text describes ...** • **The article shows ...** • **In the story we get to know ...**

– Im Hauptteil solltest du die wichtigen Ereignisse (z.B. einer Geschichte) oder die Hauptpunkte eines Textes (z.B. eines Zeitungsartikels) wiedergeben. Bring die Informationen in eine logische Reihenfolge.
  - Verwende dafür deine Notizen zu den **5 Ws**.
  - Schreib den Text nicht ab, sondern benutze deine eigenen Worte.

Well, I couldn't tell her the real reason: Jim Nielson. Jim was a really sweet guy. → *Carrie thinks Jim is sweet.*

– Schreib im **simple present**, auch wenn die Geschichte oder der Artikel in der Vergangenheit spielt. Nicht vergessen: im **simple present** wird in der 3. Person Singular **-s** angehängt: **Carrie thinks**.

# EXAM SKILLS

## SF How to do well in a test

▸ *Getting ready for a test (p. 31)*

### Countdown zum Testerfolg

Ein Test ist angekündigt? Kein Grund zur Panik. Wichtig ist, dass du weißt, worauf du dich vorbereiten musst. Im Zweifelsfall frag deine Lehrerin oder deinen Lehrer. Der Countdown kann beginnen!

**Eine Woche vor dem Test**

1. Lies noch einmal die **Texte** der zuletzt durchgenommenen Unit (vor allem *Lead-in*, *A-Section* und *Text*, eventuell auch das *Background File*). Fasse mündlich oder schriftlich zusammen, worum es ging.

2. Wiederhole den **Wortschatz** der Unit mithilfe des *Vocabulary*, des *Wordmaster* oder des *English Coach*. Schreibe dir die Wörter und Wortverbindungen, die du immer wieder vergisst, auf ein Blatt Papier. Eine Mindmap oder ein Wortfeld helfen beim Behalten.

3. Geh noch einmal die neue **Grammatik** durch. Aufgaben zur Selbstüberprüfung und zum Üben findest du im *Practice*-Teil, auf der *How am I doing?*-Seite, im *Grammar File*, in deinem *Workbook* und im e-*Workbook*. (▸ *SF Check yourself, p. 144*)

**Zwei oder drei Tage vor dem Test**

1. Wiederhole den **Wortschatz**. Manche Wörter sitzen noch nicht? Schreibe einen kurzen Text, in dem du sie verwendest.

2. Lies die **Schülerbuch-Texte** ein weiteres Mal.

3. Erkläre einem Freund oder einer Freundin die neue **Grammatik**. Klappt nicht richtig? Dann lies nochmal im *Grammar File* nach.

**Am Abend vor dem Test**

1. Entspanne dich. Du kannst lesen, dich in die Badewanne legen, Musik hören, fernsehen, ...

2. Geh zur gewohnten Zeit ins Bett.

**Am Morgen des Tests**

1. Steh rechtzeitig auf, damit du dich nicht hetzen musst.

2. Lies etwas „zum Aufwärmen", aber schau nicht mehr in dein Schülerbuch.

**Während des Tests**

1. Denk daran: Du hast dich gut vorbereitet. Es gibt keinen Grund, nervös zu sein.

2. Konzentriere dich auf den Test, lass dich nicht ablenken.

3. Lies dir die Aufgaben genau durch. Dann löse zuerst die Aufgaben, die dir einfach scheinen. Wende dich erst danach den schwereren Aufgaben zu.

4. Aufgaben, die du bearbeitet hast, hakst du ab. So siehst du, wie du voran- kommst, und behältst den Überblick.

5. Schau ab und zu auf die Uhr. Du solltest dir für den Schluss noch Zeit einplanen, um deine Antworten noch einmal durchzulesen und zu korrigieren.

Good luck!

## Aufgabenstellungen verstehen

Bevor du damit anfängst, die Aufgaben zu bearbeiten, stell sicher, dass du genau weißt, was du machen sollst. Lies die Aufgabenstellung Wort für Wort langsam und gründlich und von Anfang bis Ende durch. Du kannst besonders wichtige Dinge der Aufgabenstellung unterstreichen und die Aufgabe, wenn nötig, für dich in einzelne Schritte unterteilen.

## Worauf sollte ich bei Multiple-Choice-Aufgaben achten?

- Lies die Frage oder den Satz sehr genau durch.
- Bevor du dir die Lösungsangebote anschaust, deck sie mit Papier ab. Überleg dir, was die richtige Antwort sein könnte. Wenn das dann auch als eine Lösungsmöglichkeit angeboten wird, ist es meistens richtig.
- Lies immer alle vorgegebenen Lösungen, bevor du dich entscheidest.
- Achte darauf, dass du nur **eine** der Antworten ankreuzt – es sei denn, dass in der Aufgabenstellung ausdrücklich gesagt wird, dass mehrere Antworten richtig sein können.
- Mach erst alle Aufgaben so gut du kannst. Lass keine Aufgabe aus, aber geh zum Schluss zu den Fragen zurück, bei denen du unsicher bist.
- Wenn das alles nicht hilft, such nicht mehr nach der richtigen Antwort, sondern nach den falschen Antworten. Weil drei Antwortmöglichkeiten falsch sein müssen, kannst du erschließen, dass die vierte Antwort richtig ist. Hier ist ein Beispiel. Stell dir vor, du hörst folgenden Dialog.

  Boy *Wow, that was great, Dad. Thanks. Can we do it again next weekend?*

  Dad *Sure, Greg – if the weather's nice. But let's find an easier tour then – I'm a bit tired.*

Dazu wird dir die Multiple-Choice-Frage hier unten gestellt.
Greg und sein Vater müssen etwas im Freien gemacht haben, denn Gregs Dad spricht über das Wetter. Also sind die Antworten **B** und **C** falsch. Man schwimmt keine Touren, also ist **A** auch falsch. Daher muss **D** die richtige Antwort sein.

**1.** Greg and his dad have just
- A been swimming.
- B been to a fitness club.
- C seen a movie.
- D been on a bike ride.

# Grammar File – Inhalt



Im **Grammar File** (S. 160–171) wird zusammengefasst, was du in diesem Band **über die englische Sprache** lernst.

In der **linken Spalte** findest du **Beispielsätze** und **Übersichten**.

In der **rechten Spalte** stehen **Erklärungen** und nützliche **Hinweise**. Das **rote Ausrufezeichen** (**!**) macht dich auf besondere Fehlerquellen aufmerksam.

Hinweise wie ▸ *Unit 1 (p. 15)* • *P 4, 6–7 (pp. 21–22)* zeigen dir, zu welcher Unit und welcher Seite ein **Grammar-File-Abschnitt** gehört und welche Übungen du dazu im *Practice*-Teil findest.

**Grammatische Fachbegriffe** (*grammatical terms*) kannst du auf den Seiten 170–171 nachschlagen.

**Additional information**

So gekennzeichnete Abschnitte enthalten Grammatik, die du nicht selbst zu verwenden brauchst. Du solltest aber verstehen, was dort erklärt wird, damit du keine Schwierigkeiten mit Texten hast, in denen diese Grammatik vorkommt.

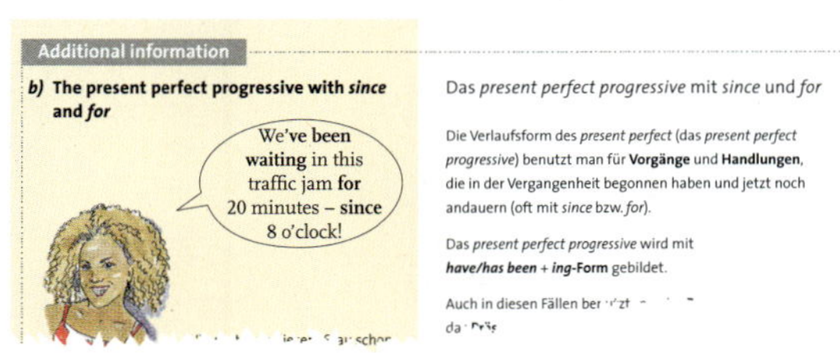

Am Ende der Abschnitte stehen kleine Aufgaben zur Selbstkontrolle. Schreib die Lösungen in dein Heft. Überprüfe sie dann auf Seite 171.

## Unit 1

## GF 1 The gerund Das Gerundium

### a) Use and form

Flying is exciting.
**Fliegen** ist aufregend.

Travelling makes me tired.
**Reisen** macht mich müde.

Taking **a taxi** is quite expensive.
**Mit dem Taxi zu fahren / Taxifahren** ist ziemlich teuer.

Cycling **in New York** can be dangerous.
**In New York Rad zu fahren / Radfahren in New York** kann gefährlich sein.

### Gebrauch und Form

Als **Gerundium** *(gerund)* bezeichnet man die *-ing*-Form eines Verbs, wenn sie als **Nomen** verwendet wird.

Das Gerundium kann wie ein Verb erweitert werden, z.B. durch ein Objekt *(a taxi)* oder eine Orts- oder Zeitangabe *(in New York)*.

Im Deutschen wird das Gerundium oft durch einen Infinitiv mit „zu" oder durch ein Nomen wiedergegeben.

### b) The gerund as subject and object

### Das Gerundium als Subjekt und als Objekt

Das Gerundium (und seine Erweiterung) kann im Satz **Subjekt** oder **Objekt** sein:

| Subjekt | |
|---|---|
| ***Flying*** | *is exciting.* |
| ***Cycling in a big city*** | *isn't very healthy.* |

| | Objekt |
|---|---|
| *My sister likes* | ***skating.*** |
| *I like* | ***riding my bike in Central Park.*** |

Ich wohne gern in einer Großstadt. / Ich genieße es, in einer Großstadt zu wohnen.
Ich kann mir nicht vorstellen, auf dem Land zu leben.

**!** Beachte:

◄ **1** Folgt bestimmten Verben – z.B. ***enjoy, finish, imagine, miss, practise*** – ein weiteres Verb, so steht es als Gerundium:

*I **enjoy** living ..., I can't **imagine** living ...*

Anders als im Deutschen darf nach diesen Verben **kein Infinitiv** stehen!
Also nicht: *I ~~enjoy to live~~ ..., I can't ~~imagine to live~~ ...*

When I got to Times Square, it **started** raining. / to rain.

I **like/love** riding / to ride my bike in the rain.

◄ **2** Nach ***begin/start, continue, hate, like, love*** kann ein Gerundium oder ein *to*-Infinitiv stehen.

I'**d like/love** to ride in a New York taxi too.
I **would hate** to live in the country.

◄ **3** Nach ***would** like, **would** love, **would** hate* kann nur der *to*-Infinitiv stehen.

▸ *Unit 1 (p. 15) • P 4, 6–7 (pp. 21–22)*

### c) The gerund after prepositions

After so much walking, we were tired.
Nach all der Herumlauferei ... /
Nachdem wir so viel herumgelaufen waren, ...

Never cross a street without looking.
Überquere nie eine Straße, ohne zu schauen.

Ryan is **scared** of going in lifts.
Ryan hat Angst davor, mit dem Lift zu fahren.

Ryan was **excited** about going to the fire station.
Ryan freute sich darauf, die Feuerwache zu besuchen.

### Das Gerundium nach Präpositionen

Nach einer Präposition *(after, without, for, of, ...)* steht ein Verb immer als Gerundium.

Beachte die verschiedenen deutschen Entsprechungen:

| englisch | deutsch |
|---|---|
| – ***after walking*** | → „nach der Herumlauferei" *oder* „nachdem wir herumgelaufen waren" |
| – ***without looking*** | → „ohne zu schauen" |
| – *scared* ***of going ...*** | → „Angst, ... zu fahren" |

Nützliche Wendungen mit Präposition + Gerundium sind:

Ryan is **interested** in learning about New York firefighters.
Ryan ist daran interessiert, etwas über ... zu erfahren.
They were **tired** of looking down at New York.
Sie hatten genug davon, auf New York hinabzuschauen.

| | | |
|---|---|---|
| – *(to) be* | ***interested in*** <br> ***excited about*** <br> ***afraid of*** <br> ***good/bad at*** <br> ***tired of*** | ***doing*** *sth.* |

Ryan's **reason** for going to New York was to visit family. Sein Grund, dort hinzufahren, war ...
Caitlin had the **idea** of visiting the fire station.
Caitlin hatte die Idee, die Feuerwache zu besuchen.

| | | |
|---|---|---|
| – *the* | ***reason for*** <br> ***idea of*** <br> ***hope of*** <br> ***danger of*** | ***doing*** *sth.* |

Caitlin **was** against going to Brooklyn Bridge.
Caitlin war dagegen, zur Brooklyn Bridge zu gehen.
Ryan and Caitlin **talked** about meeting Ruth.
Ryan und Caitlin sprachen darüber, Ruth zu treffen.

| | | |
|---|---|---|
| – *(to)* | ***be against*** <br> ***dream of*** <br> ***talk about*** <br> ***think of*** | ***doing*** *sth.* |

▸ *Unit 1 (p. 16) • P 10 (p. 24)*

*Vervollständige die Sätze in deinem Heft. Wähle ein Verb aus dem Kästchen. Achte auf die richtige Form.*

1 ... alone to New York was very exciting for Ryan.
2 He didn't enjoy ... in the queues at the airport.
3 At first he was a bit afraid of ... up the ESB in a fast lift.
4 He was very interested in ... all the sights.
5 Later he talked about ... down from the ESB for hours.

(to) fly • (to) go • (to) look • (to) see • (to) wait

# Unit 2

## GF 2 The passive Das Passiv

### *a)* Active and passive

**Active:** **Farmers in California** grow strawberries on huge farms.
Landwirte in Kalifornien bauen Erdbeeren auf großen Farmen an.

**Passive:** **Strawberries** are grown on huge farms.
Erdbeeren werden auf großen Farmen angebaut.

### Aktiv und Passiv

◄ Mit einem **Aktivsatz** drückst du aus, **wer oder was etwas tut**:

| **Subjekt** | **Verb** | **Objekt** |
|---|---|---|
| *Farmers in California* | *grow* | *strawberries ...* |

◄ Mit einem **Passivsatz** drückst du aus, **mit wem oder womit etwas geschieht**. Das Objekt des Aktivsatzes *(strawberries)* ist Subjekt des Passivsatzes geworden:

| **Subjekt** | **Verb** | |
|---|---|---|
| *Strawberries* | *are grown* | *on huge farms.* |

### *b)* Form

... wird produziert ...
... wird verkauft ...
... wurden angebaut ...

### Form

Das Passiv bildest du mit einer **Form von *be*** und der 3. Form des Verbs*.

**Simple present:** *am/are/is* + **3. Form des Verbs**
*A lot of wine is **produced** ...*

**Simple past:** *was/were* + **3. Form des Verbs**
*700,000 tons were **grown** ...*

*Die 3. Form des Verbs heißt **Partizip Perfekt** *(past participle)*. Sie wird bei regelmäßigen Verben mit ***-ed*** gebildet: *(to) produce, produced, produced*. Unregelmäßige Verben haben eigene Formen: *(to) grow, grew, grown*.

► *Unregelmäßige Verben (pp. 258–259)*

### *c)* Use

At 8.45 yesterday morning a 12-year-old boy was hurt in a car accident on Duke Street. The police were called and the boy was taken to hospital.

► *Unit 2 (p. 36)* • *P 5–6 (p. 44)*

### Gebrauch

In einem Passivsatz steht nicht, wer die Handlung ausführt. Oft ist das unwichtig oder gar nicht bekannt. Du findest daher das Passiv oft in Nachrichten und in Zeitungsberichten (z. B. über Unfälle, Verbrechen) oder auf Schildern.

Ein englischer Passivsatz wird im Deutschen oft durch einen Aktivsatz mit „man“ wiedergegeben:

*The boy **was taken** to hospital.*
***Man brachte** den Jungen ins Krankenhaus.*

**d) Passive sentences with *by* ...**

The gardener **was attacked** by a dog.
... wurde von einem Hund angefallen.

The Golden Gate Bridge **was built** by Joseph Strauss.
... wurde von Joseph Strauss erbaut.

My parents' house **was destroyed** by fire.
... wurde durch ein Feuer zerstört.

▸ *Unit 2 (p. 38) • P 10–12 (pp. 45–46)*

Passivsätze mit *by* ...

Wenn du in einem Passivsatz den „Täter" oder „Verursacher" nennen willst, verwendest du ***by*** („von", „durch").

*Sieh dir die Bilder und den Kasten mit den Verben und den Namen an. Schreib die richtigen Passivsätze in dein Heft.*

1

2

3

1 The telephone was ... by ...
2 'We will rock you!' was ...
3 Clifton Suspension Bridge ...

**build • invent • sing**
**Alexander Bell • Brunel • Queen**

**e) Extra The passive: *will*-future and modal auxiliaries**

Our new attractions will be opened soon.
... werden bald eröffnet (werden).

Coloma can be visited at any time of the year.
... kann das ganze Jahr über besucht werden.

The fire couldn't be put out.
... konnte nicht gelöscht werden.

▸ *Unit 2 (p. 39) • P 16 (p. 48)*

Das Passiv:
*will-future* und modale Hilfsverben

Passivsätze mit Hilfsverben (z.B. *will, can, could, must, should, may*) bildest du mit *be* + Partizip Perfekt:

| | | |
|---|---|---|
| ***will*** | ***be*** | ***opened*** |
| ***can*** | ***be*** | ***visited*** |
| ***could*** | ***be*** | ***put out*** |
| ***must*** | ***be*** | ... |
| ***should*** | ***be*** | ... |
| ***may*** | ***be*** | ... |

# Unit 3

## GF 3 Countable and uncountable nouns — Zählbare und nicht zählbare Nomen

### a) Countable nouns — Zählbare Nomen

a friend – two friends
a CD – lots of CDs
one hour – many hours

◂ Die meisten Nomen sind **zählbar**, d.h., sie kommen im Singular und im Plural vor.

### b) Uncountable nouns — Nicht zählbare Nomen

| | | | |
|---|---|---|---|
| **bread** | Brot | **money** | Geld |
| **butter** | Butter | **music** | Musik |
| **equipment** | Ausrüstung | **news** | Nachricht(en) |
| **health** | Gesundheit | **sugar** | Zucker |
| **homework** | Hausaufgabe(n) | **traffic** | Verkehr |
| **information** | Information(en) | **water** | Wasser |
| **milk** | Milch | **work** | Arbeit |

◂ **Nicht zählbare** Nomen stehen **nie** im Plural.
Zu den nicht zählbaren Nomen gehören viele Bezeichnungen für Lebensmittel und viele abstrakte Begriffe, z.B. *health*.

! Auch die Nomen ***homework, information*** und ***news*** sind nicht zählbar – anders als ihre deutschen Entsprechungen.

! Beachte:

***not:*** ~~a bread; breads~~
~~an information; many informations~~
~~a homework; two homeworks~~

◂ Nicht zählbare Nomen haben **keinen Plural** und stehen **nie mit *a/an* oder mit *one/two/three/...***

That's too much **homework**. I can't do it.
Das sind zu viele **Hausaufgaben**. Ich kann sie nicht machen.

Where did you get this **information**?
Wo hast du diese **Information(en)** her?

◂ Auch die zugehörigen **Begleiter, Verben und Pronomen** stehen immer **im Singular**.

Would you like a glass of **milk**.
Möchtest du **ein Glas Milch**?

That's a useful piece of **information**.
Das ist **eine** nützliche **Information**.

◂ Wenn du **bestimmte Mengen** oder eine **bestimmte Anzahl** nennen willst, musst du passende Wendungen wie ***a glass of ..., a kilo of ..., a piece of ...*** verwenden.

### c) Quantifiers: *some, lots of, many, much* — Mengenangaben: *some, lots of, many, much*

| Countable nouns | Uncountable nouns |
|---|---|
| some **students**<br>einige/ein paar ... | some **bread/information**<br>etwas Brot/einige Informationen |
| lots of **students**<br>viele ... | lots of **bread/information**<br>viel Brot/viele Informationen |
| **how** many **students?**<br>wie viele ...? | **how** much **bread/information?**<br>wie viel Brot? / wie viele Informationen? |

Die Mengenangaben *some* und *lots of* (oder *a lot of*) verwendest du mit **zählbaren Nomen** und **nicht zählbaren Nomen**.

! – *many* heißt „**viele**" und steht nur mit **Nomen im Plural**.
– *much* heißt „**viel**" und steht nur mit **nicht zählbaren Nomen**.

▸ *Unit 3 (p.57) • P 7–8 (p.64)*

*Sieh dir die Bilder an und vervollständige die Sätze mit* a *(1x)*, an *(1x)*, some *(2x)*, many *(1x)*, much *(3x)*.

1 There's ... milk but there isn't ... bread.

2 Here's ... information about the Grand Canyon. I'm doing ... project on it.

3 We haven't got ... eggs, and we haven't got ... butter.

4 I haven't got ... homework, just ... exercise for French.

## GF 4 The definite article *the* Der bestimmte Artikel *the*

Wenn ein Nomen **ganz allgemein** gebraucht wird, steht es **ohne den bestimmten Artikel**.

Das gilt insbesondere für

**1** For Timo and his family, life is exciting at the moment.
... ist das Leben im Moment aufregend.

**1** **abstrakte Begriffe** wie *life, history, health, traffic*

**2** Clean air is important to health.
Saubere Luft ist wichtig für die Gesundheit.

**2** **Stoffbezeichnungen** wie *air, oil, gold, coffee, bread*

**3** American students do lots of extracurricular activities.

**3** **Nomen im Plural** (hier: *students*).

**1a** At the FFA meeting Timo learned a lot about the life **of Missouri farmers.**
... über das Leben der Farmer in Missouri.

**2a** The Schmidts are happy that the air **in Hermann** is clean.
... die Luft in Hermann ...

**3a** The students **who went to the FFA meeting** were very interested in hogs.

◀ Wenn diese Nomen aber **näher bestimmt** sind, stehen sie **mit bestimmtem Artikel**.
Die nähere Bestimmung erfolgt z.B. in Satz 1a durch eine *of*-Fügung *(of Missouri farmers)* und in Satz 3a durch einen Relativsatz *(who went to the FFA meeting)*.

Vergleiche die Sätze 1a–3a mit den Sätzen 1–3.

▸ *Unit 3 (p. 58)* • *P 10 (p. 66)*

*Mit oder ohne* the? *Schreib die Sätze in dein Heft.*

1 We can learn a lot from ... history.
2 What do you know about ... history of England?
3 Is ... food that you like best healthy?
4 In Jake's health class they're talking about ... food.
5 ... tourists like to visit Hermann's Festhalle.
6 ... tourists who asked us the way were from Germany.

## GF 5 The past perfect Das *past perfect*

### *a)* Use

Gebrauch

Andreas Schmidt first **visited** Hermann over 20 years ago. ... besuchte ...
He **stayed** with the Kruger family. ... wohnte ...

◀ Du benutzt das *simple past* für abgeschlossene **Handlungen, Ereignisse und Zustände in der Vergangenheit**.

Andreas Schmidt had never heard of Missouri wine when he **discovered** that Hermann had a lot of wineries.
... hatte noch nie von Wein aus Missouri gehört, ...

They had already sold their house in Germany when Karla Schmidt **got** worried.
Sie hatten ihr Haus in Deutschland bereits verkauft, ...

◀ Mit dem *past perfect* (Plusquamperfekt, Vorvergangenheit) drückst du aus, dass etwas noch **vor etwas anderem in der Vergangenheit** stattgefunden hatte.
Die Handlung/das Ereignis im *past perfect* geschah zuerst:

| **1.** | **2.** |
|---|---|
| *They had already sold ...* | *when she **got worried**.* |

| Simple past | Past perfect |
|---|---|
| **1 The concert began when they arrived.** | **2 The concert had begun when they arrived.** |
| *Das Konzert begann, als sie ankamen.* | *Das Konzert hatte begonnen, als sie ankamen.* |

**!** Beachte die Bedeutungsunterschiede zwischen *simple past* und *past perfect*:
In **Satz 1** begann die Band erst zu spielen, als sie ankamen.
In **Satz 2** hatte die Band bereits angefangen zu spielen, als sie ankamen.

### *b)* Form

Form

We had sold our house, so there was no way back.
They hadn't played soccer before.

Das *past perfect* bildest du mit ***had*** und der 3. Form des Verbs (Partizip Perfekt, *past participle*).
(Zur Bildung der 3. Form des Verbs siehe S. 163, GF 2b.)
▸ *Unregelmäßige Verben (pp. 258–259)*

Had the Schmidts already moved to Hermann when Timo was 12?
Waren die Schmidts schon nach Hermann gezogen, ...?

**!** Beim *past perfect* must du immer ***had*** verwenden, egal ob im Deutschen „hatte" oder „war" steht.

▸ *Unit 3 (p. 59)* • *P 12–13 (p. 66)*

Simple past *oder* past perfect? *Sieh dir die Bilder an und vervollständige die Sätze.*

1 The band (start) to play when I arrived.

2 The band (start) to play when I arrived.

3 When his mum came home from work, Jason ... (make) tea.

4 When his mum came home from work, Jason ... (make) tea.

# Unit 4

## GF 6 *since* and *for* (German 'seit') *since* und *for* (Deutsch „seit")

### *a)* The present perfect with *since* and *for*

1 Dad **has been** at the King Center since 1999.

2 He's **known** his boss for years.

Dad ist **seit** 1999 beim King Center.
Er kennt seinen Chef **seit** Jahren.

### Das *present perfect* mit *since* und *for*

Du kannst das *present perfect* verwenden, um über einen **Zustand** zu sprechen, der in der Vergangenheit begonnen hat und jetzt noch andauert.

**!** Wenn du sagen willst, **seit wann** oder **wie lange** der Zustand bereits andauert, musst du aufpassen – es gibt zwei englische Wörter für das deutsche „seit":

◂ 1 Mit *since* gibst du einen **Zeit**punkt an *(since 1999; since May; since 12 o'clock).* ***since*** + **Zeit<u>punkt</u>** drückt also aus, **<u>seit wann</u>** ein Zustand andauert.

◂ 2 Mit *for* gibst du einen **Zeit**raum an *(for years; for a month; for a long time).* ***for*** + **Zeit<u>raum</u>** drückt also aus, **<u>wie lange</u>** ein Zustand bereits andauert.

***since*** **+ Zeitpunkt** | ***for*** **+ Zeitraum**

Madison and her mom are in the car on the way to the CNN studios. **It's 8.20.**

They**'ve been** in the traffic jam since 8 o'clock. ... seit 8 Uhr.

They**'ve been** in the traffic jam for 20 minutes. ... seit 20 Minuten.

We**'ve lived** in this house since 2004.
Wir wohnen seit 2004 in diesem Haus.

I**'ve had** my computer for three years.
Ich habe meinen Computer schon seit drei Jahren.

**!** Achtung:
Im **Deutschen** benutzt man meist das **Präsens**:
*Wir **wohnen** seit ... / Ich **habe** ... seit ...*

Im **Englischen** <u>muss</u> das ***present perfect*** stehen:
*We**'ve lived** ... since ... / I**'ve had** ... for ...*

How long **have** you **lived** in Atlanta?
– Since 2005. / For a few years.
Wie lange **wohnt** ihr in Atlanta?
– Seit 2005. / Seit ein paar Jahren.

Mit ***How long ...?*** + *present perfect* fragst du, seit wann oder wie lange ein Zustand schon andauert.

▸ *Unit 4 (pp. 79–80) • P 9–12 (pp. 87–88)*

Since *oder* for? *Schreib die vollständigen Sätze in dein Heft.*

1 We've lived here ... four years.
2 Madison has been in the car ... over 20 minutes now.
3 She's been at her school ... 2005.
4 I've known my best friend ... five years.
5 The weather has been bad ... over a week.

*Beantworte die folgenden Fragen – auf Englisch.*

6 How long have you known Emily? *(du kennst sie seit 2004)*
7 That bike looks great. Is it new? *(ja; du hast es seit zwei Wochen)*
8 Is Mum in the garden? *(ja; sie ist seit 9 Uhr dort)*

## Additional information

### *b)* The present perfect progressive with *since* and *for*

**We've been waiting** in this traffic jam **for** 20 minutes – **since** 8 o'clock!

Wir warten in diesem Stau schon seit 20 Minuten – seit 8 Uhr!

### Das *present perfect progressive* mit *since* und *for*

Die Verlaufsform des *present perfect* (das *present perfect progressive*) benutzt man für **Vorgänge** und **Handlungen**, die in der Vergangenheit begonnen haben und jetzt noch andauern (oft mit *since* bzw. *for*). Dabei wird die Dauer des Geschehens betont.

Das *present perfect progressive* wird mit ***have/has been*** + ***ing*-Form** gebildet.

Auch in diesen Fällen benutzt man im **Deutschen** meist das **Präsens**:

*Wir **warten** seit ...*

Im **Englischen** steht das ***present perfect progressive***:

*We**'ve been waiting** since/for ...*

## Grammatical terms (Grammatische Fachbegriffe)

| | | |
|---|---|---|
| **active** ['æktɪv] | Aktiv | *Shakira* ***sang*** *that song.* |
| **adjective** ['ædʒɪktɪv] | Adjektiv | *good, red, new, boring, ...* |
| **adverb** ['ædvɜːb] | Adverb | *always, badly, here, really, today* |
| **adverb of frequency** ['friːkwənsi] | Häufigkeitsadverb | *always, often, never, ...* |
| **adverb of indefinite time** [ɪnˌdefɪnət 'taɪm] | Adverb der unbestimmten Zeit | *already, ever, just, never, ...* |
| **adverb of manner** ['mænə] | Adverb der Art und Weise | *badly, happily, quietly, well, ...* |
| **article** ['ɑːtɪkl] | Artikel | *the, a/an* |
| **auxiliary** [ɔːg'zɪliəri] | Hilfsverb | *be, have, do; will, can, must, ...* |
| **comparison** [kəm'pærɪsn] | Steigerung | *old – older – oldest* |
| **conditional sentence** [kənˌdɪʃənl 'sentəns] | Bedingungssatz | *I'd call him if I knew his number.* |
| **conjunction** [kən'dʒʌŋkʃn] | Konjunktion | *and, or, but; because, before, ...* |
| **contact clause** ['kɒntækt klɔːz] | Relativsatz ohne Relativpronomen | *She's the girl* ***I love****.* |
| **countable noun** ['kaʊntəbl] | zählbares Nomen | *girl – girls, pound – pounds, ...* |
| **definite article** ['defɪnət] | bestimmter Artikel | *the* |
| **future** ['fjuːtʃə] | Zukunft, Futur | |
| **gerund** ['dʒerənd] | Gerundium | *I like* ***dancing****.* ***Dancing*** *is fun.* |
| ***going to*****-future** | Futur mit *going to* | ***I'm going to watch*** *TV tonight.* |
| ***if*****-clause** ['ɪf klɔːz] | *if*-Satz, Nebensatz mit *if* | ***If I see Jack****, I'll tell him.* |
| **imperative** [ɪm'perətɪv] | Imperativ (Befehlsform) | *Open your books. Don't talk.* |
| **infinitive** [ɪn'fɪnətɪv] | Infinitiv (Grundform des Verbs) | *(to) open, (to) see, (to) read, ...* |
| **irregular verb** [ɪˌregjələ 'vɜːb] | unregelmäßiges Verb | *(to) go – went – gone* |
| **main clause** | Hauptsatz | ***I like Scruffy*** *because I like dogs.* |
| **modal, modal auxiliary** [ˌməʊdl‿ɔːg'zɪliəri] | modales Hilfsverb, Modalverb | *can, could, may, must, ...* |
| **negative statement** [ˌnegətɪv 'steɪtmənt] | verneinter Aussagesatz | *I don't like bananas.* |
| **noun** [naʊn] | Nomen, Substantiv | *Sophie, girl, brother, time, ...* |
| **object** ['ɒbdʒɪkt] | Objekt | *My sister is writing* ***a letter****.* |
| **object form** ['ɒbdʒɪkt fɔːm] | Objektform (der Personalpronomen) | *me, you, him, her, it, us, them* |
| **passive** ['pæsɪv] | Passiv | *That song* ***was sung*** *by Shakira.* |
| **past** [pɑːst] | Vergangenheit | |
| **past participle** [ˌpɑːst 'pɑːtɪsɪpl] | Partizip Perfekt | *cleaned, planned, gone, seen, ...* |
| **past perfect** [ˌpɑːst 'pɜːfɪkt] | Plusquamperfekt, Vorvergangenheit | *He was late because he* ***had missed*** *the bus.* |
| **past progressive** [ˌpɑːst prə'gresɪv] | Verlaufsform der Vergangenheit | *At 7.30 I* ***was having*** *dinner.* |
| **personal pronoun** [ˌpɜːsənl 'prəʊnaʊn] | Personalpronomen (persönliches Fürwort) | *I, you, he, she, it, we, they; me, you, him, her, it, us, them* |
| **plural** ['plʊərəl] | Plural, Mehrzahl | |
| **positive statement** [ˌpɒzətɪv 'steɪtmənt] | bejahter Aussagesatz | *I like oranges.* |
| **possessive determiner** [pəˌzesɪv dɪ'tɜːmɪnə] | Possessivbegleiter (besitzanzeigender Begleiter) | *my, your, his, her, its, our, their* |
| **possessive form** [pəˌzesɪv fɔːm] | *s*-Genitiv | *Jo's brother; my sister's room* |
| **possessive pronoun** [pəˌzesɪv 'prəʊnaʊn] | Possessivpronomen | *mine, yours, his, hers, ours, theirs* |
| **preposition** [ˌprepə'zɪʃn] | Präposition | *after, at, in, next to, under, ...* |
| **present** ['preznt] | Gegenwart | |
| **present perfect** [ˌpreznt 'pɜːfɪkt] | *present perfect* | *We****'ve made*** *a cake for you.* |
| **present perfect progressive** [ˌpreznt ˌpɜːfɪkt prə'gresɪv] | Verlaufsform des *present perfect* | *We****'ve been waiting*** *for an hour.* |
| **present progressive** [ˌpreznt prə'gresɪv] | Verlaufsform der Gegenwart | *The Hansons* ***are having*** *lunch.* |
| **pronoun** ['prəʊnaʊn] | Pronomen, Fürwort | |
| **quantifier** ['kwɒntɪfaɪə] | Mengenangaben | *some, a lot of, many, much, ...* |
| **question tag** ['kwestʃən tæg] | Frageanhängsel | *This place is great,* ***isn't it?*** |

| | | |
|---|---|---|
| **question word** ['kwestʃən wɜːd] | Fragewort | *what?, when?, where?, how?, …* |
| **reflexive pronoun** [rɪ,fleksɪv 'prəʊnaʊn] | Reflexivpronomen | *myself, yourself, themselves, …* |
| **regular verb** [,regjələ 'vɜːb] | regelmäßiges Verb | *(to) help – helped – helped* |
| **relative clause** [,relətɪv 'klɔːz] | Relativsatz | *There's the girl* ***who helped me****.* |
| **relative pronoun** [,relətɪv 'prəʊnaʊn] | Relativpronomen | *who, that, which* |
| **short answer** [,ʃɔːt‿'ɑːnsə] | Kurzantwort | *Yes, I am. / No, I don't. / …* |
| **simple past** [,sɪmpl 'pɑːst] | einfache Form der Vergangenheit | *Jo* ***wrote*** *two letters yesterday.* |
| **simple present** [,sɪmpl 'preznt] | einfache Form der Gegenwart | *I always* ***go*** *to school by bike.* |
| **singular** ['sɪŋgjələ] | Singular, Einzahl | |
| **subject** ['sʌbdʒɪkt] | Subjekt | ***My sister*** *is writing a letter.* |
| **subject form** ['sʌbdʒɪkt fɔːm] | Subjektform (der Personalpronomen) | *I, you, he, she, it, we, they* |
| **subordinate clause** [sə,bɔːdɪnət 'klɔːz] | Nebensatz | *I like Scruffy* ***because I like dogs****.* |
| **uncountable noun** [ʌn'kaʊntəbl] | nicht zählbares Nomen | *bread, milk, money, news, work, …* |
| **verb** [vɜːb] | Verb | *hear, open, help, go, …* |
| ***will*-future** | Futur mit *will* | *I think it* ***will be*** *cold tonight.* |
| **word order** ['wɜːd‿ɔːdə] | Wortstellung | |
| **yes/no question** | Entscheidungsfrage | *Are you 13? Do you like comics?* |

## Lösungen der Grammar-File-Aufgaben

p.162
1 **Flying** alone to New York was very exciting for Ryan.
2 He didn't enjoy **waiting** in the queues at the airport.
3 At first he was a bit afraid of **going** up the ESB in a fast lift.
4 He was very interested in **seeing** all the sights.
5 Later he talked about **looking** down from the ESB for hours.

p.164
1 The telephone **was invented by Alexander Bell.**
2 'We will rock you!' **was sung by Queen.**
3 Clifton Suspension Bridge **was built by Brunel.**

p.166/1
1 There's **some** milk but there isn't **much** bread.
2 Here's **some** information about the Grand Canyon. I'm doing **a** project on it.
3 We haven't got **many** eggs, and we haven't got **much** butter.
4 I haven't got **much** homework, just **an** exercise for French.

p.166/2
1 We can learn a lot from history.
2 What do you know about **the** history of England?
3 Is **the** food that you like best healthy?
4 In Jake's health class they're talking about food.
5 Tourists like to visit Hermann's Festhalle.
6 **The** tourists who asked us the way were from Germany.

p.167
1 The band **started** to play when I arrived.
2 The band **had started** to play when I arrived.
3 When his mum came home from work, Jason **had made** tea.
4 When his mum came home from work, Jason **made** tea.

p.169
1 We've lived here **for** four years.
2 Madison has been in the car **for** over 20 minutes now.
3 She's been at her school **since** 2005.
4 I've known my best friend **for** five years.
5 The weather has been bad **for** over a week.
6 I've known her **since** 2004.
7 Yes, it is. I've had it **for** two weeks.
8 Yes, she is. She's been there/in the garden **since** 9 o'clock.

**Diese Wörterverzeichnisse findest du in deinem Englischbuch:**

- Das **Vocabulary** (Vokabelverzeichnis – S. 172–193) enthält alle Wörter und Wendungen, die du lernen musst. Sie stehen in der Reihenfolge, in der sie in den Units vorkommen.
- Das **Dictionary** besteht aus zwei alphabetischen Wörterlisten zum Nachschlagen:
  Englisch – Deutsch: S. 194–224
  Deutsch – Englisch: S. 225–251.

## So ist das Vocabulary aufgebaut:

- Hier siehst du, wo die Wörter vorkommen:
  p. 16/A 6 = Seite 16, Abschnitt 6
  p. 23/P 9 = Seite 23, Übung 9
- Die Lautschrift zeigt dir, wie ein Wort ausgesprochen und betont wird. (→ Englische Laute: S. 224)
- Eingerückte Wörter lernst du am besten zusammen mit dem vorausgehenden Wort, weil die beiden zusammengehören.
- Die blauen Kästen solltest du dir besonders gut ansehen.

Tipps zum Wörterlernen findest du im Skills File auf Seite 143.

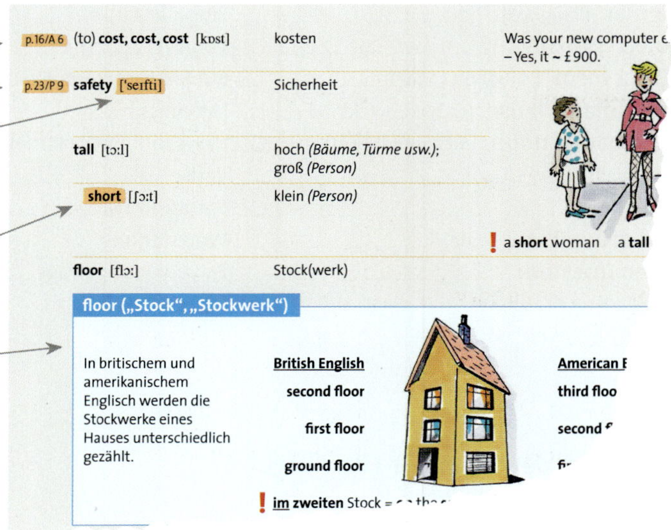


## Abkürzungen:

| | | | |
|---|---|---|---|
| *n* | = *noun* | *v* | = *verb* |
| *adj* | = *adjective* | *adv* | = *adverb* |
| *prep* | = *preposition* | *conj* | = *conjunction* |
| *pl* | = *plural* | *no pl* | = *no plural* |
| p. | = page | pp. | = pages |
| sb. | = somebody | sth. | = something |
| jn. | = jemanden | jm. | = jemandem |
| *AE* | = *American English* | *BE* | = *British English* |
| *infml* | = *informal* (umgangssprachlich, informell) | | |

## Symbole:

**!** Hier stehen Hinweise auf Besonderheiten, bei denen man leicht Fehler machen kann.

◄► ist das „Gegenteil"-Zeichen: **slow** ◄► **fast** (**slow** ist das Gegenteil von **fast**)

~ Die **Tilde** in den Beispielsätzen steht für das neue Wort. Beispiel:
**shocked** – Mr Brown was ~ when he saw his daughter's green hair.

# Introduction – Welcome to the United States of America

| | | | |
|---|---|---|---|
| p. 6 | **Guess what!** [ˌges 'wɒt] | Stell dir vor! / Stellt euch vor! | **Guess** ~! Mum is going to have a baby. |
| p. 8 | **canyon** ['kænjən] | Schlucht | |
| | **deep** [diːp] | tief | How long and how ~ is your swimming pool? |
| | **wide** [waɪd] | weit, breit | And how ~ is it? |
| | **in** 1919 | 1919, im Jahre 1919 | Charlie Chaplin was born ~ 1889. |
| | **awesome** ['ɔːsəm] *(AE, infml)* | klasse, großartig | very good, great |
| | **hometown** ['həʊmtaʊn] | Heimatstadt | |
| | (to) **look forward to** sth. ['fɔːwəd] | sich auf etwas freuen | I'm really **looking ~ to** the weekend. We're going to drive to the Grand Canyon. |

| | | |
|---|---|---|
| **daily** ['deɪli] | täglich, Tages- | Do your parents get a ~ newspaper? |
| **gear** *(no pl)* [gɪə] | Ausrüstung | Where is our camping ~? |
| (to) **cross** [krɒs] | *(Zeitzone)* passieren | |
| **zone** [zəʊn] | Zone, Gebiet | You cross six time **~s** between Berlin and New York. |
| **three and a half days** | dreieinhalb Tage | ! with **and**: **three <u>and</u> a half days** |
| **rim** [rɪm] | Rand, Kante | |
| (to) **hike** [haɪk] | wandern | (to) go for long walks in the country |
| **hike** | Wanderung, Marsch | (to) go on a **hike** = wandern gehen |
| **comment (on, about)** ['kɒment] | Kommentar, Bemerkung (zu, über) | ! stress: **<u>com</u>ment** ['kɒment] |
| **Good to have you back.** | Schön, dass du wieder da bist. | |
| p. 9 **middle school** | *(USA) Schule für 11- bis 14-Jährige* | |
| **grade** [greɪd] *(AE)* | Jahrgangsstufe, Klasse | = *BE* year |
| (to) **raise money (for)** [reɪz] | Geld sammeln (für) | |

| | | |
|---|---|---|
| (to) **cut the grass** [grɑːs] | Rasen mähen | |
| **grass** | Gras; Rasen | |

| | | |
|---|---|---|
| **sale** [seɪl] | (Aus-, Schluss-)Verkauf | |
| **tent** [tent] | Zelt | |
| **how to do** sth. | wie man etwas tut / tun kann / tun soll | |

### Question words + *to* + infinitive: *how to … / what to … / where to … / …*

Nach **Fragewörtern** kannst du einen **Infinitiv mit *to*** verwenden.
Im Deutschen steht meist ein Nebensatz mit „können" oder „sollen".

| | |
|---|---|
| Can you tell me **how to get** to the station? | Können Sie mir sagen, wie ich zum Bahnhof komme / kommen kann? |
| I don't know **what to do**. | Ich weiß nicht, was ich machen soll. |
| He had no idea **where to go** or **who to ask**. | Er hatte keine Ahnung, wohin er gehen sollte oder wen er fragen könnte. |

| | | |
|---|---|---|
| **tool** [tuːl] | Werkzeug | |
| **Native American** [ˌneɪtɪv‿ə'merɪkən] | amerikanische(r) Ureinwohner/in, Indianer/in | ! Der Begriff **Native American** wird heute von vielen dem älteren Begriff **Indian** vorgezogen. |
| **monument** ['mɒnjumənt] | Denkmal, Monument | ! stress: **<u>mon</u>ument** ['mɒnjumənt] |

| | | | |
|---|---|---|---|
| | **natural** ['nætʃrəl] | Natur-, natürlich | |
| | **human** ['hjuːmən] | Menschen-, menschlich | When did ~ life on earth begin? Do you know? |
| p.10 | **high school** ['haɪ skuːl] | *(USA) Schule für 14- bis 18-Jährige* | |
| | **highway** ['haɪweɪ] | *(USA)* Fernstraße *(oft mit vier oder mehr Spuren)* | |
| | **route** [ruːt] | Strecke, Route | ! In den USA werden wichtige Fernstraßen mit **Route** + Nummer bezeichnet: **Route 66**. |

| | | | |
|---|---|---|---|
| | **gas** [gæs] *(AE)*, **petrol** ['petrəl] *(BE)* | Benzin | |
| | **gas station** *(AE)*, **petrol station** *(BE)* | Tankstelle | |
| | **souvenir** [ˌsuːvə'nɪə] | Souvenir, Mitbringsel | |
| | **license plate** ['laɪsns pleɪt] *(AE)*, **number plate** ['nʌmbə pleɪt] *(BE)* | Nummernschild | |
| | **auto** ['ɔːtəʊ] *(AE)* | Auto, PKW | |

| | | | |
|---|---|---|---|
| | **grand** [grænd] | eindrucksvoll, beeindruckend | The hotel looked ~ from outside, but our room was small and dark. |
| | **multi-** ['mʌlti] | viel-, mehr-; multi-, Multi- | **multi**-coloured; a **multi-millionaire** |
| | **foot** [fʊt], *pl* **feet** [fiːt] | Fuß *(Längenmaß; 1 Fuß = 30,48 cm)* | The cabin was quite small, only about 6 **feet** high. |
| | **wing** [wɪŋ] | Flügel | |
| | **tip** [tɪp] | Spitze | |

| | | | |
|---|---|---|---|
| | (to) **forgive** [fə'gɪv], **forgave** [fə'geɪv], **forgiven** [fə'gɪvn] | vergeben, verzeihen | I know that she has hurt you, but try and ~ her. |
| p.11 | **adventure** [əd'ventʃə] | Abenteuer | Our fishing trip in Canada was a great ~. We even saw some bears. |

## Unit 1: New York, New York

| | | | |
|---|---|---|---|
| p.12 | **avenue** ['ævənjuː] | Allee | We moved to a new house in Park **Avenue**. |
| | **deli** ['deli] | Deli *(Lebensmittelgeschäft mit Fastfoodrestaurant)* | If you're hungry, we can get some sandwiches at the ~ on the way home. |
| | **stop** [stɒp] | Halt; *hier:* Anlaufstelle | noun: **stop** – verb: (to) **stop** |
| | **immigrant** ['ɪmɪgrənt] | Einwanderer/Einwanderin | ! stress: **immigrant** ['ɪmɪgrənt] |
| p.13 | (to) **lie** [laɪ], **lay** [leɪ], **lain** [leɪn] | liegen | ! ing-form: **lying**<br>I love **lying** in bed on a rainy Sunday afternoon. |

| | | | |
|---|---|---|---|
| | **borough** ['bʌrə, *AE:* 'bɜːrəʊ] | (Stadt-)Bezirk | |

## New York: the five boroughs

| | | |
|---|---|---|
| **the Bronx** | [brɒŋks] | der nördlichste Bezirk; liegt als einziger auf dem Festland |
| **Manhattan** | [mæn'hætn] | Insel zwischen dem Hudson und dem East River, berühmt für ihre Wolkenkratzer |
| **Queens** | [kwiːnz] | der größte Bezirk; im Südwesten der Insel Long Island gelegen; vor allem Wohngebiet |
| **Brooklyn** | ['brʊklɪn] | wie Queens auf Long Island gelegen; die berühmte Brooklyn Bridge verbindet Brooklyn mit Manhattan |
| **Staten Island** | [ˌstætn_'aɪlənd] | Insel an der Einfahrt zum Hafen von New York, mit Manhattan durch Fährbetrieb verbunden *(→ Karte auf S. 20)* |

| | | | |
|---|---|---|---|
| p.14/A 1 | **directions** *(pl)* [də'rekʃnz] | Wegbeschreibung | I didn't know the way so I asked for ~. |
| | **downtown** [ˌdaʊn'taʊn] *(AE)* | (im/in das) Stadtzentrum | Dad works at a bank ~. |
| | **block** [blɒk] | (Häuser-, Wohn-)Block | |
| p.14/A 2 | **sidewalk** ['saɪdwɔːk] *(AE)*, **pavement** ['peɪvmənt] *(BE)* | Gehweg, Bürgersteig | **sidewalk** *(AE)*, **pavement** *(BE)* |
| | **line** [laɪn] *(AE)*, **queue** [kjuː] *(BE)* | Schlange, Reihe *(wartender Menschen)* | a **line** *(AE)*, a **queue** *(BE)* |

## British English – American English (I)

### Different words

| British English | American English | |
|---|---|---|
| **mobile (phone)** | **cellphone** | Handy |
| **city centre** | **downtown** | Stadtzentrum, Innenstadt |
| **lift** | **elevator** | Fahrstuhl, Aufzug |
| **petrol** | **gas** | Benzin |
| **year** | **grade** | Jahrgangsstufe |
| **queue** | **line** | Schlange, Reihe |
| **pavement** | **sidewalk** | Gehweg, Bürgersteig |
| **underground** | **subway** | U-Bahn |
| **holiday(s)** | **vacation** | Ferien, Urlaub |

### Different spelling

| British English *-tre* | American English: *-ter* |
|---|---|
| cent**re** | cent**er** |
| met**re** | met**er** |
| theat**re** | theat**er** |

| British English: *-our* | American English: *-or* |
|---|---|
| col**our** | col**or** |
| fav**our**ite | fav**or**ite |
| harb**our** | harb**or** |
| neighb**our** | neighb**or** |

| British English: | American English: |
|---|---|
| trave**ll**ed, trave**ll**ing | trave**l**ed, trave**l**ing |

| | | | |
|---|---|---|---|
| p.15/A 4 | **difference** ['dɪfrəns] | Unterschied | |
| | **fire station** ['faɪə steɪʃn] | Feuerwache | |
| | **firefighter** ['faɪəfaɪtə] | Feuerwehrmann, -frau | |
| | **as** a firefighter | als Feuerwehrmann, -frau | He works ~ a firefighter. |

| | | | |
|---|---|---|---|
| p.15/A 5 | **anything else** [els] | (irgend)etwas anderes | |

**... else**

**1.** *(anders, unterschiedlich)*

| | |
|---|---|
| I don't like apple juice. Have you got **anything else**? | ... Hast du **irgendetwas anderes**? |
| I'm tired. **Somebody else** will have to tidy up. | ... **Jemand anders** muss aufräumen. |
| Oh no, not France again! Let's go **somewhere else** this year. | ... Lass uns dieses Jahr **woanders** hinfahren. |

**2.** *(außerdem, zusätzlich)*

| | |
|---|---|
| Do you need **anything else**? | Brauchst du **sonst noch etwas**? |
| **What else** do you know about New York? | **Was** weißt du **(sonst) noch** über New York? |
| I met Susan at the party.<br>– **Who else** did you meet? /<br>Did you meet **anybody else**? | **Wen** hast du **(sonst) noch** getroffen? /<br>Hast du **sonst noch jemanden** getroffen? |

| | | | |
|---|---|---|---|
| | **sure** [ʃʊə, ʃɔː] | klar, sicher | Can I have your pencil? – **Sure**, here you are. |
| | (to) **put out a fire** | ein Feuer löschen | |
| | **shift** [ʃɪft] | Schicht *(bei der Arbeit)* | My dad works 12-hour **~s**. There are eight men and women on his **~**.<br>❗ **on my shift** = in meiner Schicht |
| | **guy** [gaɪ] *(infml)* | Typ, Kerl | an informal word for 'man' or 'boy' |
| | **hijacker** ['haɪdʒækə] | (Flugzeug-)Entführer/in | |
| | (to) **take** sth. **over** | etwas übernehmen;<br>etwas in seine Gewalt bringen | |
| | **skyscraper** ['skaɪskreɪpə] | Wolkenkratzer |  |
| | (to) **burn** [bɜːn] | brennen; verbrennen | The light in the bedroom was still **~ing** at 4 am.<br>Don't ~ those newspapers! Recycle them! |
| | (to) **take place** | stattfinden | Our next school trip will **take ~** in two months. |
| p.16/A 6 | a **must** [mʌst] | ein Muss | Have you been to Brooklyn Bridge yet? It's a ~.<br>noun: **must** – verb: **must** |
| | **floor** [flɔː] | Stock(werk) | |

**floor („Stock", „Stockwerk")**

In britischem und amerikanischem Englisch werden die Stockwerke eines Hauses unterschiedlich gezählt.

| British English | American English | |
|---|---|---|
| **second floor** | **third floor** | zweiter Stock |
| **first floor** | **second floor** | erster Stock |
| **ground floor** | **first floor** | Erdgeschoss |

❗ **im zweiten** Stock = **on** the **second** floor *(BE)* / **on** the **third** floor *(AE)*

| | | |
|---|---|---|
| (to) **cost, cost, cost** [kɒst] | kosten | Was your new computer expensive? – Yes, it ~ £ 900. |
| **dollar ($)** ['dɒlə] | Dollar | How much is £ 900 in **~s**? |
| **tall** [tɔ:l] | hoch *(Bäume, Türme usw.)*; groß *(Person)* | |
| **short** [ʃɔ:t] | klein *(Person)* | |

a **short** woman a **tall** woman

| | | |
|---|---|---|
| **(opening) hours** | Öffnungszeiten | |
| **admission** [əd'mɪʃn] | Eintritt, Eintrittspreis | Tickets cost $ 5, but ~ is free for kids under 14. |
| **perfect** ['pɜ:fɪkt] | perfekt; ideal; vollkommen | ! stress: **perfect** ['pɜ:fɪkt] |
| **ticket office** ['tɪkɪt‿ˌɒfɪs] | Kasse *(für den Verkauf von Eintrittskarten)*; Fahrkartenschalter | |
| **I'll/You'll/She'll/ ... be OK.** | Mir/Dir/Ihr/ ... wird nichts passieren. | Be careful when you climb that tree. – Don't worry. **I'll be ~.** |
| (to) **be tired of** sth. | genug von etwas haben, etwas satt haben | I'm really **~ of** that CD. / I'm really **~ of** listening to that CD. Can't you play something else? |
| p.17/A 8 **crowded** ['kraʊdɪd] | überfüllt, voll | We couldn't find a table at the deli because it was so **~**. |
| **crowd** [kraʊd] | (Menschen-)Menge, Masse; *(infml auch: )* Clique, Gruppe | |
| **bagel** ['beɪgl] | Bagel *(ringförmiges Brötchen)* | |
| **cream cheese** [ˌkri:m 'tʃi:z] | Frischkäse | |
| **cream** [kri:m] | Sahne; Creme | |
| **coffee** ['kɒfi] | Kaffee | |

| | | |
|---|---|---|
| **counter** ['kaʊntə] | Theke, Ladentisch | |
| (to) **order** ['ɔ:də] | bestellen | |
| **regular** ['regjələ] | normal *(Größenangabe bei Getränken und Fastfood)* | |

**coffee to go: large regular**

| | | |
|---|---|---|
| **sparkling water** ['spɑ:klɪŋ] | Mineralwasser mit Kohlensäure, Sprudel | |
| (to) **grab** sth. **(-bb-)** [græb] | sich etwas schnappen | He said goodbye, **~bed** his bag and hurried out. |
| **Jewish** ['dʒu:ɪʃ] | jüdisch | |

## British English – American English (II)

p.20/P 2

### Different words

| **British English** | **American English** | |
|---|---|---|
| **rucksack** | **backpack** ['bækpæk] | Rucksack |
| **biscuit** | **cookie** ['kʊki] | Keks |
| **rubber** | **eraser** [ɪ'reɪsər] | Radiergummi |
| **chips** | **French fries** [fraɪz] | Pommes frites |
| **rubbish** | **garbage** ['gɑːrbɪdʒ] | Müll, Abfall |
| **trousers** | **pants** [pænts] | Hose |
| **crisps** | **potato chips** | Kartoffelchips |
| **timetable** | **schedule** ['skedʒuːl] [*BE:* 'ʃedjuːl] | Stundenplan; Fahrplan |

### Different pronunciation

| | **BE:** [ɑː] | **AE:** [æ] |
|---|---|---|
| **ask, last** | [ɑːsk], [lɑːst] | [æsk], [læst] |
| | **BE:** [juː] | **AE:** [uː] |
| **new, Tuesday** | [njuː], ['tjuːzdeɪ] | [nuː], ['tuːzdeɪ] |
| | **BE:** [ɒ] | **AE:** [ɑː] |
| **clock, hot** | [klɒk], [hɒt] | [klɑːk], [hɑːt] |

- In American English, you can usually hear the **'r'** in words like **here, more, shirt, farm**.
- In AE a **'t'** between two vowels often sounds more like a **'d'**, for example in **city, better, writer**.

| | | | |
|---|---|---|---|
| p.22/P 8 | (to) **take a break** | eine Pause machen | We've worked long enough now. Let's **take a ~**. |
| p.23/P 9 | **safety** ['seɪfti] | Sicherheit | |
| | (to) **work** sth. **out** | etwas herausarbeiten, herausfinden | |
| | **context** ['kɒntekst] | Kontext, Zusammenhang | |
| p.25/P 14 | **zoo** [zuː] | Zoo | |
| | **dinosaur** ['daɪnəsɔː] | Dinosaurier | **!** stress and pronunciation: **dinosaur** ['daɪnəsɔː] |
| | **collection** [kə'lekʃn] | Sammlung | verb: (to) **collect** – noun: **collection** |
| | **in the world** | (auf) der Welt | |

## You can tell me

| | | | |
|---|---|---|---|
| p.26 | (to) **earn** [ɜːn] | verdienen | |
| | **apartment** [ə'pɑːtmənt] *(AE)* | Wohnung | *(BE)* flat |
| | (to) **decide (on)** [dɪ'saɪd] | beschließen; sich entscheiden (für) | Have you **~d** what project you would like to do? We've **~d on** a project about New York. (= We've **~d** to do a project about New York.) |
| | (to) **seem (to be / to do)** [siːm] | (zu sein / zu tun) scheinen | You **~ (to be)** tired. Did you sleep long enough? |
| | (to) **be on drugs** [drʌgz] | Drogen/Rauschgift nehmen | His eyes look strange. He seems to **be on ~**. |
| | **I feel sick.** [sɪk] | Mir ist schlecht. | |
| p.27 | **kiss** [kɪs] | Kuss | |
| | (to) **kiss** | küssen | |

| | | |
|---|---|---|
| **tear** [tɪə] | Träne | **tears** |
| (to) **cry** [kraɪ] | weinen | She's **crying**. |

## any/anything/anybody ... in positive statements

Du kennst **any** bereits in Fragen und verneinten Aussagesätzen:

| | |
|---|---|
| Have we got **any** orange juice? | Haben wir Orangensaft? |
| We haven't got **any** biscuits. | Wir haben keine Kekse. |

Man verwendet **any** auch, wenn „irgendein", „jeder beliebige" gemeint ist.
In dieser Bedeutung kann **any** auch in bejahten Aussagesätzen stehen.

| | |
|---|---|
| You can have **any** bagel with tomato, bacon, ... | ... **jeden (beliebigen)** Bagel ... |
| It's easy to dance – **anybody** can do it. | ... **jeder (Beliebige)** ... |
| You can tell me **anything**. | ... **alles (, was es auch sei / egal, was es ist)**. |
| I was too tired to say **anything.** | ... **irgendetwas** zu sagen |
| California has more people than **any** other state. | ... als **jeder** andere Staat/ ... als **irgendein (beliebiger)** anderer Staat |
| You can come and visit us **any time**. | ... **jederzeit** ... |

**any/anybody** wird oft nach **if** verwendet: If **anybody** has **any** questions, I'll try to answer them.

| | | | |
|---|---|---|---|
| | (to) **notice** ['nəʊtɪs] | bemerken | Sue was at the party too, but I didn't ~ her.<br>**!** (to) **notice** = bemerken – **note** = Notiz |
| | **beard** [bɪəd] | Bart | |
| | **blond** [blɒnd] | blond, hell | |
| | (to) **kick** [kɪk] | treten | |
| | **gun** [gʌn] | Gewehr, Schusswaffe | |
| | **below** [bɪ'ləʊ] | unten; unter, unterhalb (von) | First look at the pictures ~. ↓<br>I don't like the subway. I feel scared ~ ground. |
| | **above** [ə'bʌv] | oben; über, oberhalb (von) | Then look at the chart ~. ↑<br>We live on a hill ~ the city. |
| | **blood** [blʌd] | Blut | |
| | (to) **tear** sth. **off** [teə], **tore** [tɔː], **torn** [tɔːn] | etwas abreißen | She **tore** ~ a piece of paper and wrote down my phone number. |
| | **cheek** [tʃiːk] | Wange | Sam leaned over to Sally and gave her a kiss on the ~. |
| | (to) **get a cab** [kæb] | ein Taxi nehmen |  |
| p.28 | **bench** [bentʃ] | Bank *(zum Sitzen)* | **!** **bench** = Bank *(zum Sitzen)*<br>**bank** = Bank *(Geldinstitut)* |
| | **a couple of** ['kʌpl] | ein paar | I met her **a ~ of** weeks ago. |
| | **conversation** [ˌkɒnvə'seɪʃn] | Gespräch, Unterhaltung | |
| | **false** [fɔːls] | falsch, unwahr | What do you think – is this statement true or ~? |
| p.29 | (to) **improve** [ɪm'pruːv] | verbessern | |

## Unit 2: California, the 'Golden State'?

| | | | |
|---|---|---|---|
| p.34 | **golden** ['gəʊldən] | goldene(r,s) | |
| | **gold** [gəʊld] | Gold | |
| | **earthquake** ['ɜːθkweɪk] | Erdbeben | |
| | **earth** [ɜːθ] | Erde | What's the hottest country on ~? (= auf der Erde) |

### everybody/everyone, anybody/anyone, ...

Neben den Zusammensetzungen **anybody, everybody, somebody, nobody** gibt es auch – bei gleicher Bedeutung – die Zusammensetzungen auf **-one:**

**anyone, everyone, someone,** ! *(two words:)* **no one**

| | | |
|---|---|---|
| **anybody / anyone** | ['eniwʌn] | (irgend)jemand |
| **everybody / everyone** | ['evriwʌn] | jeder, alle |
| **somebody / someone** | ['sʌmwʌn] | jemand |
| **nobody / no one** | ['nəʊ‿wʌn] | niemand |

| | | | |
|---|---|---|---|
| | **homeless** ['həʊmləs] | obdachlos | |
| p.35 | **governor** ['gʌvənə] | Gouverneur/in | ! stress: **governor** ['gʌvənə] |
| | **border** ['bɔːdə] | Grenze | The US only has a ~ with Canada and Mexico. |
| p.36/A 1 | **business** ['bɪznəs] | Geschäft; Handel | Tina has got a new ~ – a party service. |
| | **farming** ['fɑːmɪŋ] | Landwirtschaft | |
| | **industrial** [ɪn'dʌstriəl] | industriell, Industrie- | |
| | **industry** ['ɪndəstri] | Industrie | There's no ~ in our area, but a lot of farming.<br>! noun: **industry** – adjective: **industrial** |
| | **wine** [waɪn] | Wein | |
| | (to) **have a look at** sth. | sich etwas ansehen, einen Blick werfen auf etwas | |
| | **product** ['prɒdʌkt] | Produkt | |
| | **production** [prə'dʌkʃn] | Produktion, Herstellung | ! stress: **production** [prə'dʌkʃn] |
| | **attraction** [ə'trækʃən] | Attraktion | Golden Gate Bridge is one of the main tourist **~s** in San Francisco. |
| | **grape** [greɪp] | Weintraube | some **grapes** |
| p.37/A 2 | **culture** ['kʌltʃə] | Kultur | ! stress: **culture** ['kʌltʃə] |
| | **attitude (to/towards)** ['ætɪtjuːd] | Haltung (gegenüber), Einstellung (zu) | What's your ~ **to/towards** clothes? Do you always buy the latest fashion? |
| | **minority** [maɪ'nɒrəti] | Minderheit | There are 16 girls and 11 boys in my class. The boys are in the ~. |
| | **majority** [mə'dʒɒrəti] | Mehrheit | The girls are in the ~.<br>**majority ◄► minority** |
| | (to) **fit in** **(-tt-)** [ˌfɪt‿'ɪn] | hineinpassen; sich einfügen, sich anpassen | You won't ~ **in** if you don't like team work.<br>He didn't like the others, but he tried to ~ **in**. |
| | **member (of)** ['membə] | Mitglied (von, in) | I'm a ~ **of** the German club at school. |
| | (to) **laugh at** sb. | jn. auslachen, über jn. lachen | |
| | **experience** [ɪk'spɪəriəns] | Erlebnis, Erfahrung | How was your trip to Canada? – It was a great ~.<br>He didn't get the job. He hasn't got enough ~. |
| | (to) **experience** [ɪk'spɪəriəns] | erleben, erfahren | Have you ever **~d** bullying at school? |

| | | |
|---|---|---|
| (to) **belong (to)** ['bɪlɒŋ] | gehören (zu) | This book **~s to** me. I bought it yesterday.<br>Kim **~s to** the Chinese minority in San Francisco. |
| **ethnic** ['eθnɪk] | ethnisch | |
| **citizen** ['sɪtɪzn] | (Staats-)Bürger/in,<br>Staatsangehörige(r) |  |
| **disadvantage** [ˌdɪsəd'vɑːntɪdʒ] | Nachteil | |
| **advantage (over** sb./sth.**)** [əd'vɑːntɪdʒ] | Vorteil (gegenüber jm./etwas) | Cats have an **~ over** dogs: they can climb trees.<br>**advantage ◄► disadvantage** |
| (to) **get on well/badly (with** sb.**)** | sich gut/schlecht verstehen (mit jm.), gut/schlecht aus-kommen (mit jm.) | They **~ on well with** each other. They're good friends. |
| **discrimination (against)** [dɪˌskrɪmɪ'neɪʃn] | Diskriminierung (von),<br>Benachteiligung (von) | Men often get more money than women for the same job. That's **~ against** women. |
| (to) **discriminate against** sb. [dɪ'skrɪmɪneɪt] | jn. diskriminieren,<br>jn. benachteiligen | I think it's wrong to **~ against** minorities.<br>! **jn. diskriminieren** = (to) **discriminate against sb.** |
| **prejudice (against)** ['predʒudɪs] | Voreingenommenheit (gegen),<br>Vorurteil (gegenüber) | |
| (to) **be prejudiced (against)** ['predʒədɪst] | voreingenommen sein (gegen),<br>Vorurteile haben (gegenüber) | I can't understand why some people **are ~ against** minorities. |
| (to) **succeed (in** sth.**)** [sək'siːd] | Erfolg haben, erfolgreich sein (mit etwas, bei etwas) | (to) be successful |
| (to) **act** [ækt] | handeln, sich verhalten | Jane is 15 now, but she still **~s** like a child. |
| **population** [ˌpɒpju'leɪʃn] | Bevölkerung, Einwohner(zahl) | |
| p.38/A 4 **gardener** ['gɑːdnə] | Gärtner/in | |
| (to) **beg (for) (-gg-)** [beg] | betteln (um);<br>(eindringlich) bitten (um) | <br>The old man sat on the street and **~ged for** money.<br>She **~ged** her mum to let her go to the party. |
| **government** ['gʌvənmənt] | Regierung | |
| **fence** [fens] | Zaun | a **fence**  |
| **illegal** [ɪ'liːgl] | illegal, ungesetzlich | |
| **legal** ['liːgl] | legal | ! stress: **legal** ['liːgl]<br>**legal ◄► illegal** |

| | | | |
|---|---|---|---|
| | **half of ...** | die Hälfte der/des ... | **Half ~** the students in my class belong to a minority. |
| | **little** ['lɪtl] | wenig | This plant needs very ~ water. (= not much) |

### little („wenig") – few („wenige")

- **little** + uncountable nouns: <u>wenig</u> + nicht zählbare Nomen: — **a <u>little</u> time, money, water, bread, ...** ein <u>wenig</u> / ein <u>bisschen</u> Zeit, Geld, Wasser, Brot, ...
- **few** + plural of countable nouns: <u>wenige</u> + Plural von zählbaren Nomen: — **a <u>few</u> hours, dollars, bottles, sandwiches, ...** <u>wenige</u> / ein <u>paar</u> Stunden, Dollar, Flaschen, Sandwiches, ...

Are you hungry? We've got **<u>a little</u> bacon** and **<u>a few</u> eggs**. ... ein wenig / ein bisschen Schinken und ein paar Eier

**Comparison** (Steigerung)**:**
**little – less – (the) least**

I've got so **little** hair.
... so wenig Haare

I've got **less** hair.
... weniger Haare

I've got **the least** hair.
... die wenigsten Haare

| | | | |
|---|---|---|---|
| p.38/A 5 | **amnesty** ['æmnəsti] | Amnestie, Begnadigung | |
| p.42/P 2 | **synonym** ['sɪnənɪm] | Synonym *(Wort mit gleicher oder ähnlicher Bedeutung)* | Words with the same meaning are called **~s**, for example cab – taxi. |
| p.43/P 4 | **camp** [kæmp] | Camp, (Ferien-)Lager | |
| | **specific** [spə'sɪfɪk] | bestimmte(r, s), spezifische(r, s) | Let's meet between three and six. – No. Let's agree on a ~ time. |
| | **vegetarian** [ˌvedʒə'teəriən] | vegetarisch; Vegetarier/in | We only eat ~ food (= meals without meat). We're **~s**. |
| p.44/P 5 | **sportsman, sportswoman** | Sportler, Sportlerin | |
| p.45/P 8 | **rule** [ruːl] | Regel, Vorschrift | |
| | **Dear Sir or Madam** [sɜː, sə]; ['mædəm] | Sehr geehrte Damen und Herren *(Anrede in Briefen)* | |
| | **Yours faithfully** ['feɪθfəli] | Mit freundlichen Grüßen *(man kennt den Namen nicht)* | |
| | **Yours sincerely** [sɪn'sɪəli] | Mit freundlichen/herzlichen Grüßen *(man kennt den Namen)* | |

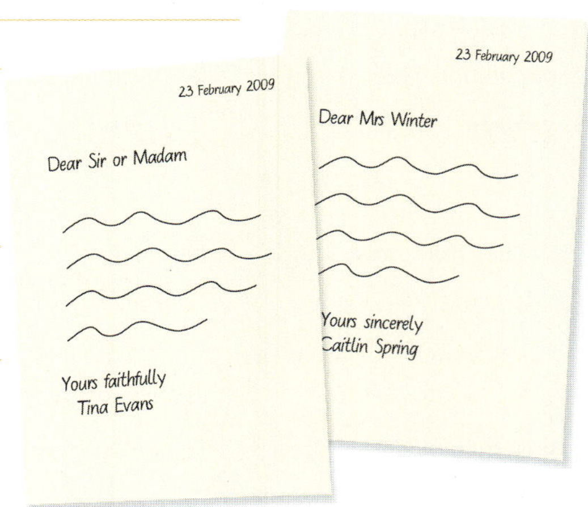


| | | | |
|---|---|---|---|
| p.45/P 10 | (to) **discover** [dɪ'skʌvə] | entdecken; herausfinden | |
| p.46/P 12 | (to) **crash (into)** [kræʃ] | zusammenstoßen (mit) / hineinfahren (in) | |
| p.47/P 14 | **shocked** [ʃɒkt] | schockiert | Mr Brown was ~ when he saw his daughter's green hair. |
| | **film director** ['fɪlm dəˌrektə] | Regisseur/in | |
| p.48/P 15 | **Don't panic.** ['pænɪk] | Keine Panik. / Bleib ruhig. | |

## Santa Monica – Episode 1 of a TV series

| | | | |
|---|---|---|---|
| p.49 | **the Pacific (Ocean)** [pəˌsɪfɪk‿ˈəʊʃn] | der Pazifische Ozean, der Pazifik | |
| | **the Atlantic (Ocean)** [ətˌlæntɪk‿ˈəʊʃn] | der Atlantische Ozean, der Atlantik | |
| | (to) **appear** [əˈpɪə] | erscheinen | (to) **appear** ◄► (to) **disappear** |
| | **cold** [kəʊld] | Kälte | adjective: **cold** – noun: **cold** |
| | **comfortable** [ˈkʌmftəbl] | bequem, behaglich | a **comfortable** sofa  Come in and make yourself ~. (= ... und machen Sie es sich bequem.) ! stress: **comfortable** [ˈkʌmftəbl] |
| | **uncomfortable** [ʌnˈkʌmftəbl] | unbequem, unbehaglich | |
| | **engine** [ˈendʒɪn] | Motor | |
| | (to) **make sure** that ... | sich vergewissern, dass ...; dafür sorgen dass ... | Please ~ **sure** that the windows are closed when you leave the house. |
| | **whatever** [wɒtˈevə] | was (auch) immer | It's *your* money; you can buy ~ you like. |

### whatever, whoever, whenever, wherever

| | |
|---|---|
| I'll help you **whatever** happens. | Ich werde dir helfen, **was immer auch** geschieht. |
| **Whoever** told you that was wrong. | **Wer immer** dir das **(auch)** erzählt hat, hatte Unrecht. |
| Visit us **whenever** you like. | Besuch uns, **wann immer** du magst. |
| **Wherever** you go, I'll come with you. | Ich komme mit, **wo auch immer** du hingehst. |

| | | | |
|---|---|---|---|
| | **except** | außer |   |
| p.50 | **depressed** [dɪˈprest] | deprimiert, niedergeschlagen | |
| | **depressing** [dɪˈpresɪŋ] | deprimierend, trostlos | |
| | **guilty** [ˈgɪlti] | schuldbewusst; schuldig | I felt so ~ because I forgot my mum's birthday. He would never steal anything. He can't be ~. |
| | **jail** [dʒeɪl] | Gefängnis |  |
| | **fight** [faɪt] | Kampf; Schlägerei | verb: (to) **fight** – noun: **fight** |
| | (to) **change** [tʃeɪndʒ] | (sich) ändern; (sich) verändern | We've **~d** our plans. We're having lunch here, not at the café. Water **~s** into ice when it's very cold. |
| | (to) **give up** | aufgeben | Good footballers never **~ up** – they fight till the last minute. |

| | | | |
|---|---|---|---|
| | **boyfriend** ['bɔɪfrend] | (fester) Freund | |
| | **girlfriend** ['gɜːlfrend] | (feste) Freundin | |
| | (to) **get to know** sb. | jn. kennenlernen | ! • I **got to know** her better during summer camp. (jn. ***im Lauf der Zeit*** kennenlernen)<br>• You don't know him, but you'll **meet** him on Sunday. (jn. ***erstmals*** kennenlernen) |
| | **serious** ['sɪəriəs] | ernst, ernsthaft | We've got a ~ problem. I've lost the car keys. We could walk home. – **Seriously**? You can't mean that. It's over five miles! („Im Ernst? ...") |
| p.51 | **bored** [bɔːd] | gelangweilt | Some children are ~ in the long holidays. |
| | **drunk** [drʌŋk] | betrunken | |
| | (to) **work out** [ˌwɜːk‿'aʊt] | gut ausgehen | Don't worry. Things will **work** ~ in the end. |
| | **since** [sɪns] | da, weil | **Since** it was raining, we decided to stay at home and watch TV. |
| | **niece** [niːs] | Nichte | a daughter of your brother or sister |
| | **nephew** ['nefjuː, 'nevjuː] | Neffe | |
| | **fat** [fæt] | fett | |
| | **skinny** ['skɪni] | mager | |

| | | | |
|---|---|---|---|
| p.52 | (to) **offer** ['ɒfə] | anbieten | |
| | **offer** ['ɒfə] | Angebot | ! verb: (to) **offer** – noun: **offer** |
| | **towel** ['taʊəl] | Handtuch | |
| | **mystery** ['mɪstri] | Geheimnis, Rätsel | I don't know how I lost my book – it's a ~ to me. |
| | **character** ['kærəktə] | Person, Figur *(in Roman, Film);* Charakter, Wesen | ! stress: **<u>cha</u>racter** ['kærəktə] |
| | **romance** [rəʊ'mæns] | Romanze; Romantik | |

| | | | |
|---|---|---|---|
| | **jealousy** ['dʒeləsi] | Eifersucht | noun: **jealousy** – adjective: **jealous** |
| | **social** ['səʊʃl] | sozial, Sozial- | Homelessness is a serious ~ problem in big cities. |

## Unit 3: Hermann says 'Willkommen'

| | | | |
|---|---|---|---|
| p.54 | **traffic light** ['træfɪk laɪt] | (Verkehrs-)Ampel | |
| | (to) **found** [faʊnd] | gründen | (to) **found** a new club = (to) start a new club<br>! Nicht verwechseln:<br>(to) **find, found, found** = finden<br>(to) **found, founded, founded** = gründen |
| | **tradition** [trə'dɪʃn] | Tradition | ! stress: **tra<u>di</u>tion** [trə'dɪʃn] |

| | | | |
|---|---|---|---|
| | **alive** [ə'laɪv] | am Leben, lebendig | Both my grandparents are still ~.<br>**alive ◄► dead** |
| p.55 | **countryside** ['kʌntrisaɪd] | Land(schaft), Natur | |
| | **event** [ɪ'vent] | Ereignis; Veranstaltung | The first day at school is a big ~ in a child's life. |
| | **at first** | zuerst, am Anfang | ! • I didn't like him **at first**, but later we became friends. (= **zuerst, am Anfang**)<br>• I'd like to go out, but I have to finish my homework **first**. (= **zuerst, als Erstes**) |
| p.56/A 1 | **system** ['sɪstəm] | System | ! stress: **sy̲stem** ['sɪstəm] |
| | **elementary school** [ˌelɪ'mentri sku:l] | *(USA)* Grundschule *(für 6- bis 11-Jährige)* | |
| | **kindergarten** ['kɪndəgɑ:tn] | Kindergarten; *(USA)* Vorschule *(für 5- bis 6-Jährige)* | |
| | **semester** [sɪ'mestə] | Semester *(Schulhalbjahr in den USA)* | ! In Großbritannien ist das Schuljahr in drei **terms** unterteilt, in den USA in zwei **semesters**. |
| | a week/day/month ... **off** | eine Woche / einen Tag / einen Monat / ... frei | |
| | **Easter** ['i:stə] | Ostern; Oster- |  an **Easter** egg |
| | **cafeteria** [ˌkæfə'tɪəriə] | Cafeteria; *(USA)* Schulmensa | |
| | **grade** [greɪd]<br>(*BE auch:* **mark** [mɑ:k]) | (Schul-)Note, Zensur | |

## US school grades

| | | | |
|---|---|---|---|
| + | A | **excellent** ['eksələnt] | ausgezeichnet, hervorragend |
| ↑ | B | **good** | gut |
| | C | **average** *(n; adj)* ['ævərɪdʒ] | Durchschnitt; durchschnittlich |
| ↓ | D | **below average** | unter Durchschnitt; unterdurchschnittlich |
| – | F | **failure** *(n)* ['feɪljə] | ungenügend |

| | | | |
|---|---|---|---|
| | **extracurricular activities** (*or:* **extracurriculars**) [ˌekstrəkə'rɪkjələz] | *schulische Angebote außerhalb des regulären Unterrichts, oft als Arbeitsgemeinschaften* | |
| p.56/A 2 | **period** ['pɪəriəd] | (Unterrichts-/Schul-)Stunde | = *BE* lesson |
| | **health** [helθ] | Gesundheit; Gesundheitslehre | noun: **health** – adjectives: **healthy, unhealthy** |
| | **study hall** ['stʌdi hɔ:l] | *Zeit zum selbstständigen Arbeiten/Lernen in der Schule* | At Hermann High students have ~ **hall** every day after lunch. |
| | (to) **study** ['stʌdi] | studieren;<br>sorgfältig durchlesen;<br>lernen | When I finish school, I'm going to ~ history.<br>My dad **studies** the sports page every morning.<br>There's a test tomorrow, so I have to ~ tonight. |
| | **gym** [dʒɪm] | Sporthalle, Turnhalle; Fitnessstudio | ! **gym** = Sport-, Turnhalle (*nicht:* ~~Gymnasium~~) |
| p.56/A 3 | **bulletin board** ['bʊlətɪn bɔ:d] *(AE)* | schwarzes Brett, Anschlagtafel | = *BE* notice board |
| | **dress code** ['dres kəʊd] | Kleiderordnung | |
| | **hole** [həʊl] | Loch | |

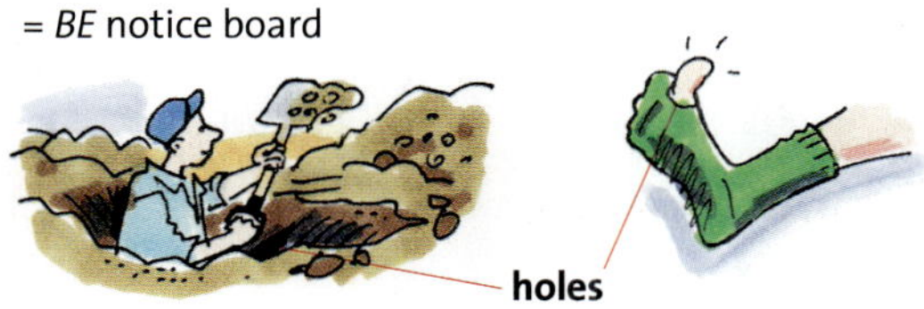
holes

| | | | |
|---|---|---|---|
| | (to) **be allowed** | erlaubt sein | ! • Hats or caps **are not allowed** here. = ... **sind** hier **nicht erlaubt**. • **I'm not allowed to** go out late. = Ich **darf nicht** ... |
| | (to) **break** [breɪk], **broke** [brəʊk], **broken** ['brəʊkən] | (zer)brechen; kaputt gehen | She **broke** the school rules and was sent home. Please be careful with my MP3 player. Don't ~ it. All the plates fell to the floor and **broke**. |
| | (to) **change** [tʃeɪndʒ] | sich umziehen; wechseln | |

**(to) change – change**

| | |
|---|---|
| **(sich) ändern, (sich) verändern** | We had to **change** our holiday plans. The weather was **changing**, so we hurried home. |
| **wechseln** | We **changed** some money at the airport. We were late and didn't have time to **change** clothes. At US schools students **change** rooms for each lesson. |
| **sich umziehen** | I was still wearing my working clothes, so I went upstairs and **changed**. |
| **umsteigen** | Can we go directly to Berlin or do we have to **change** at Hanover? |
| **(Ver-)Änderung, Wechsel** | It will be a big **change** when you move from London to the country. The **change** from one school to another can be hard for some students. |
| **Wechselgeld; Kleingeld** | Always count your **change**! Shop assistants can make mistakes. Have you got enough **change** for the ticket machine? |

| | | | |
|---|---|---|---|
| p.57/A 5 | **meeting** ['mi:tɪŋ] | Versammlung, Besprechung | The photo club **~s** are on Fridays. verb: (to) **meet** – noun: **meeting** |
| | **and so on** (*short:* **etc.** [et'setərə]) | und so weiter (usw.) | We need stuff for sandwiches: bread, lettuce, ham, cheese, **and so ~**. (... ham, cheese, **etc.**) |
| | (to) **get involved (in)** [ɪn'vɒlvd] | sich engagieren (für, bei); sich beteiligen (an) | Alex **got ~ in** the drama club soon after he started school. |
| | **foreign** ['fɒrən] | ausländisch, fremd | That car must be ~. Look at the number plate. (to) learn ~ languages = Fremdsprachen lernen |
| | (to) **debate** [dɪ'beɪt] | debattieren | verb: (to) **debate** – noun: **debate** |
| p.58/A 7 | **class** | Unterricht; Kurs | What did you learn in French ~ today? I do an evening ~ in painting on Fridays. |
| | **pyramid** ['pɪrəmɪd] | Pyramide | ! stress: **py̲ramid** ['pɪrəmɪd] |
| | **soda** ['səʊdə] *(AE)* | Limonade | |
| | **poultry** ['pəʊltri] | Geflügel | Can you buy a chicken at the ~ shop, please? |
| | **nut** [nʌt] | Nuss | |
| | **bean** [bi:n] | Bohne | |
| | **whole-grain** ['həʊlgreɪn] | Vollkorn- | |

| | | | |
|---|---|---|---|
| | **exercise** *(no pl)* | (körperliche) Bewegung, Training | ! • **exercise(s)** = Übung(en): Which **exercises** have we got for homework? • **exercise** *(no pl, no article)* = Bewegung: The doctors say I need more **exercise**. |
| p.58/A 8 | **muesli** ['mju:zli] | Müsli | |
| p.58/A 9 | **fresh** [freʃ] | frisch | |

| | | | |
|---|---|---|---|
| p.59/A 10 | **local** ['ləʊkl] | Lokal-, örtlich; am/vom Ort | Find out what's going on in your hometown! Read your ~ paper and listen to your ~ radio station! |
| | **sister city** *(AE)* | Partnerstadt | = *BE* **twin town** |
| | **worried (about)** ['wʌrid] | beunruhigt, besorgt (wegen/um) | Sandra is ~ **about** her grandfather. He's very ill. verb: (to) **worry** – adjective: **worried** |
| | **soccer** ['sɒkə] | Fußball | ! In Amerika wird „Fußball" als **soccer** bezeichnet (**football** steht dort für **American football**). In Großbritannien wird meist **football** verwendet; **soccer** klingt dort eher förmlich. |
| | **active** ['æktɪv] | aktiv, tätig | ! stress: **active** ['æktɪv] |
| p.62/P 2 | **Best wishes** ['wɪʃɪz] | *etwa:* Alles Gute / Mit besten Grüßen *(als Briefschluss)* | |
| | (to) **sign** [saɪn] | unterschreiben | Would you like to ~ this birthday card for Kim? |
| p.63/P 3 | **average** *(n; adj)* ['ævərɪdʒ] | Durchschnitt, durchschnittlich, Durchschnitts- | **On** ~ German teenagers get about 35 Euros pocket money a month. ! **on** average = **im** Durchschnitt. |
| | **square** km **(sq** km**)** [skweə] | Quadratkilometer | |
| | **minus** ['maɪnəs] | minus | ! pronunciation: **minus** ['maɪnəs] |
| | **plus** [plʌs] | plus | |
| | **Celsius (C)** ['selsiəs] | Celsius | 22 °**C** = 22 degrees **Celsius** |

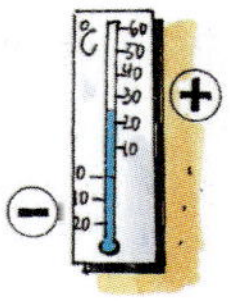


### REVISION: Numbers

| You write: | You say: | In German: |
|---|---|---|
| **10.35** | ten **point** three five | **10,35** (zehn **Komma** drei fünf) |
| **5.6 %** | five **point** six **per cent** | **5,6 %** (fünf **Komma** sechs **Prozent**) |
| **10,000** | ten thousand | **10 000** |

**German 'null':**

- phone numbers and dates: **o** [əʊ]
  **340926** = three four **o** nine two six
  **1907** = nineteen **o** seven
- temperatures: **zero**
  **- 3°** = three degrees below **zero**
- in most sports: **nil**
  What's the score? – **2–0.** = two **nil**

| | | | |
|---|---|---|---|
| p.64/P 6 | **thought** [θɔːt] | Gedanke | verb: (to) **think, thought, thought** – noun: **thought** |
| p.64/P 7 | **on the internet** | im Internet | **on the internet** = **im** Internet |
| p.65/P 9 | **soft** [sɒft] | weich | **soft** ◄► **hard** |
| | **soft drink** | alkoholfreies Getränk *(enthält meist Zucker und Kohlensäure)* | Everybody at the party was under 16, so they only had ~ **drinks**. |
| | **helpful** ['helpfl] | hilfreich, nützlich | |
| | **calorie** ['kæləri] | Kalorie | |
| | (to) **contain** [kən'teɪn] | enthalten | Soda **~s** a lot of sugar. |
| p.67/P 14 | (to) **summarize** sth. ['sʌməraɪz] | etwas zusammenfassen | Try and ~ the story in about 50 words. |
| | **summary** ['sʌməri] | Zusammenfassung | |

Going rafting.

| | | |
|---|---|---|
| **guide** [gaɪd] | (Fremden-)Führer/in, Reiseleiter/in | |
| **raft** [rɑːft] | Schlauchboot *(wildwassertauglich)* | |
| **version** ['vɜːʃn] | Version, Fassung | **!** stress and pronunciation: **version** ['vɜːʃn] |
| **original** *(n; adj)* [ə'rɪdʒənl] | Original; Original- | |
| (to) **leave** sth. **out** [ˌliːv‿'aʊt] | etwas weglassen/auslassen | If a test question is difficult, ~ it **out** and go back to it later.<br>If you don't like onions, ~ them **out**. |

## Angus Bethune's moment

| | | |
|---|---|---|
| p.68 **chance** [tʃɑːns] | Möglichkeit, Chance | I'd go on holiday to New York if I had the ~. |
| (to) **swap** sth. **(for** sth.**)** **(-pp-)** [swɒp] | etwas (ein)tauschen (für etwas / gegen etwas) | Jake **~ped** his old bike **for** a new skateboard. |
| (to) **elect** sb. sth. [ɪ'lekt] | jn. zu etwas wählen | They **~ed** her leader of the youth club.<br>**!** ... **elected her leader** = ... wählten sie **zur** Leiterin |
| **election** [ɪ'lekʃn] | Wahl *(von Kandidaten bei einer Abstimmung)* | |
| (to) **vote for** sb. [vəʊt] | für jn. stimmen | **!** Nicht verwechseln:<br>• 14 members **voted for** Fay, but 19 members **voted for** Kate. ... stimmten für Kate<br>• Kate **was elected** leader of the club. Kate wurde zur Leiterin des Klubs gewählt. |
| (to) **fall in love (with** sb.**)** | sich verlieben (in jn.) | My best friend **has fallen in ~ with** my sister. |
| (to) **ache** [eɪk] | wehtun | **!** pronunciation: (to) **ache** [eɪk] |
| **dentist** ['dentɪst] | Zahnarzt, -ärztin | |
| (to) **sweat** [swet] | schwitzen | **!** pronunciation: (to) **sweat** [swet], **sweatshirt** ['swetʃɜːt]<br>verb: (to) **sweat** – noun: **sweat** („Schweiß“) |
| p.69 (to) **compare** [kəm'peə] | vergleichen | |
| **Never mind.** [ˌnevə 'maɪnd] | *etwa:* Nicht so wichtig. / Ist (doch) egal. / Das willst du gar nicht wissen. | |

| | | |
|---|---|---|
| **I'm embarrassed.** [ɪm'bærəst] | Es ist mir peinlich. | |
| **curtain** ['kɜːtn] | Vorhang | |
| **shadow** ['ʃædəʊ] | Schatten | |

| | | |
|---|---|---|
| **heaven** ['hevn] | Himmel *(im religiösen Sinn)* | ! • (clouds/planes) in the **sky** = (Wolken/Flugzeuge) am Himmel<br>• (to) be in **heaven** / (to) go to **heaven** = im Himmel sein / in den Himmel kommen |
| (to) **throw up** [ˌθrəʊ_'ʌp], **threw up** [θruː], **thrown up** [θrəʊn] | sich übergeben | The man was so drunk that he **threw ~** all over the taxi. |
| **actually** ['æktʃuəli] | nebenbei bemerkt; übrigens | I love Katie Melua. She's a great singer! – And she's a good songwriter, **~**. |
| **tight** [taɪt] | fest | |
| (to) **do** sb. **a favour** ['feɪvə] | jm. einen Gefallen tun | Could you **do** me **a ~** and post this letter for me? |
| (to) **clap (-pp-)** [klæp] | (Beifall) klatschen | |
| **polite** [pə'laɪt] | höflich | She told me to mind my own business. – That wasn't very **~**. Actually, it was quite rude. |
| p.70 (to) **protest** [prə'test] | protestieren | Hundreds of people came out to ~ against the new road through the forest. |
| **circle** ['sɜːkl] | Kreis | a **circle** 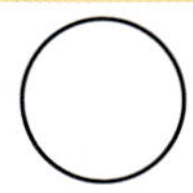 |
| **fist** [fɪst] | Faust |  a **fist** |
| **plot** [plɒt] | Handlung *(eines Romans, Films)* | |

## Unit 4: Atlanta rising

| | | |
|---|---|---|
| p.76 (to) **rise** [raɪz], **rose** [rəʊz], **risen** ['rɪzn] | (auf)steigen | The helicopter **rose** and disappeared into the sky. Black smoke was **rising** from the building. |
| **during** ['djʊərɪŋ] | während | |

**German 'während'**

- before a <u>noun</u>: **during** *(prep)*

  John phoned **during** <u>the football match</u>. ... **während** <u>des Fußballspiels</u>

- before a <u>clause</u>: **as** *or* **while** *(conj)*

  John phoned **as/while** <u>we were watching the football match</u>. ... **während** <u>wir das Fußballspiel schauten</u>

| | | |
|---|---|---|
| **civil war** [ˌsɪvl 'wɔː] | Bürgerkrieg | |
| **war** [wɔː] | Krieg |  |
| **cotton** ['kɒtn] | Baumwolle | |
| **plantation** [plɑːn'teɪʃn] | Plantage | |
| **violence** ['vaɪələns] | Gewalt, Gewalttätigkeit | My dad says there's too much sex and ~ on TV. |
| **violent** ['vaɪələnt] | gewalttätig; gewaltsam | noun: **violence** – adjective: **violent** |
| **non-violent** [nɒn] | gewaltlos, gewaltfrei | **violent** ◄► **non-violent** |
| **Olympic Games** [əˌlɪmpɪk 'geɪmz] (*or*: **Olympics** [ə'lɪmpɪks]) | Olympische Spiele |  |

| | | | |
|---|---|---|---|
| p.77 | **African American** [ˌæfrɪkən_ə'merɪkən] | afro-amerikanisch; Afro-Amerikaner/in | If you're in Detroit, try and visit the Museum of **~-American** History. |
| | **mayor** [meə] | Bürgermeister/in | ! pronunciation: **mayor** [meə] |
| | **civil rights** *(pl)* [ˌsɪvl 'raɪts] | Bürgerrechte | |
| | **right** [raɪt] | Recht | ! (to) **be right** = Recht haben, im Recht sein |
| | **network** ['netwɜːk] | *(Radio-, Fernseh-)*Sendernetz | |
| p.78/A 1 | **TV listings** *(pl)* ['lɪstɪŋz] | das Fernsehprogramm | |
| | **prime time** ['praɪm taɪm] | Hauptsendezeit | What kind of programmes can you see at **~ time**? |
| | **cable** ['keɪbl] | Kabel (*auch kurz für* Kabelfernsehen) | a piece of **cable**  |
| | **rerun** ['riːrʌn] *(AE)*, **repeat** [rɪ'piːt] *(BE)* | Wiederholung *(einer Fernsehsendung)* | |
| | **comedy** ['kɒmədi] | Komödie; Comedy | |
| | **documentary** [ˌdɒkju'mentri] | Dokumentarfilm, -beitrag | |
| | **drama** ['drɑːmə] | Fernsehspiel; Drama | |
| | **crime series** ['kraɪm ˌsɪəriːz] | Krimiserie | |
| | **crime** | Kriminalität; Verbrechen | ! *German* **Krimi** = *English* **crime film, crime story** |
| | **competition** [ˌkɒmpə'tɪʃn] | Wettbewerb, Wettkampf | |
| p.78/A 2 | **murder** ['mɜːdə] | Mord | the crime of killing somebody |
| | **programme** ['prəʊgræm] | (Fernseh-)Sendung; Programm |   |
| | **channel** ['tʃænl] | (Radio-, Fernseh-)Kanal, (Radio-, Fernseh-)Programm | |
| | **newsreader** ['njuːzˌriːdə] | Nachrichtensprecher/in | |
| | **viewer** ['vjuːə] | Zuschauer/in | |
| p.78/A 3 | (to) **be on** | gezeigt werden, laufen *(im Fernsehen/im Kino)* | Please be quiet while the news **is ~**. |
| | (to) **last (for)** [lɑːst] | dauern | The meeting **~ed (for)** over an hour. |
| p.79/A 4 | **unbelievable** [ˌʌnbɪ'liːvəbl] | unglaublich | This is **~**! (= It's hard to believe.) |
| | **traffic jam** ['træfɪk dʒæm] | (Verkehrs-)Stau |  |
| | **for** 20 minutes | seit 20 Minuten; 20 Minuten lang | We've lived here **for** five years now. (Wir wohnen jetzt seit fünf Jahren hier.) ! *Nicht:* We ~~live~~ here **for** five years now. |
| | **like this** | so | You have no right to talk to me **~ this**. |
| | **explosion** [ɪk'spləʊʒn] | Explosion | ! stress: **explosion** [ɪk'spləʊʒn] |

| | | | |
|---|---|---|---|
| | **terrorist** ['terərɪst] | Terrorist/in; Terror-, terroristisch | ! stress: **terrorist** ['terərɪst] |
| | (to) **drop** sb. **off** **(-pp-)** [drɒp] | jn. absetzen *(aussteigen lassen)* | He **~ped** her **off** at the station. |

| | | | |
|---|---|---|---|
| | **How long ...?** | Seit wann ...? / Wie lange ...? | ~ ~ have Grandma and Grandpa been married? |
| p. 80/A 5 | **because of** [bɪ'kɒz‿əv] | wegen | We stayed at home **because** ~ the bad weather.<br>! **because of** the bad weather = **wegen** ...<br>**because** the weather was bad = **weil** ... |
| | **fortunately** ['fɔːtʃənətli] | zum Glück | I arrived late, but ~ nobody noticed.<br>**fortunately** ◄► **unfortunately** [ʌn'fɔːtʃənətli] (= leider) |
| | **cause (of** sth.**)** [kɔːz] | Grund, Ursache (für etwas) | Doctors still don't understand the ~ of the problem. |
| | (to) **cause** sth. [kɔːz] | etwas verursachen | The police think the fire was **~d** by a cigarette. |
| | **since** 8:30 [sɪns] | seit 8:30 | We've lived here **since** 2003.<br>(Wir wohnen seit 2003 hier.)<br>! *Nicht:* We ~~live~~ here **since** 2003. |

### German 'seit'

- **since** mit Zeit**punkt** ● ——► I (wann etwas begonnen hat) — We've been here **since** last Sunday / April / 1998. Wir sind **seit** letztem Sonntag / April / 1998 hier.
- **for** mit Zeit**raum** ⌒ I (wie lange etwas bereits der Fall ist) — We've been here **for** three days / a long time / years. Wir sind **seit** drei Tagen / langem / Jahren hier.

| | | | |
|---|---|---|---|
| | **so far** | bisher, bis jetzt | Is the film good? – **So** ~ it has been OK. |
| p. 80/A 6 | **disappointed (about)** [ˌdɪsə'pɔɪntɪd] | enttäuscht (von/über) | I was really ~ that she couldn't come to my party. |
| | (to) **disappoint** [ˌdɪsə'pɔɪnt] | enttäuschen | |
| | (to) **be on display** [dɪ'spleɪ] | ausgestellt sein/werden | Her photos **are on** ~ at the local museum. |
| | **anniversary** [ˌænɪ'vɜːsəri] | Jahrestag | May 8th is the **anniversary** of John's **death**. (Johns **Todestag**) |
| | **death** [deθ] | Tod | |

| | | | |
|---|---|---|---|
| | **impressed** [ɪm'prest] | beeindruckt | Jo wrote a great essay. His teacher was really ~. |
| | **archive** ['ɑːkaɪv] | Archiv | ! stress and pronunciation: **archive** ['ɑːkaɪv] |
| p. 81/A 7 | **minister** ['mɪnɪstə] | Pfarrer/in, Pastor/in | ! stress: **minister** ['mɪnɪstə] |
| | (to) **segregate** ['segrɪgeɪt] | trennen *(nach Rasse, Religion, Geschlecht)* | Some people say that boys and girls learn better if they're **~d** at school. |
| | **segregation** [ˌsegrɪ'geɪʃn] | (Rassen-)Trennung | |

| | | | |
|---|---|---|---|
| | **protest** ['prəʊtest] | Protest | ! noun: **protest** ['prəʊtest] Protest<br>verb: (to) **protest** [prə'test] protestieren |
| | **march** [mɑːtʃ] | Marsch, Demonstration | a **protest march**   |
| | **nation** ['neɪʃn] | Nation | noun: **nation** – adjective: **national** |
| | (to) **judge** sb. **(by)** [dʒʌdʒ] | jn. beurteilen, einschätzen (nach) | You shouldn't ~ people **by** their clothes. |
| | **skin** [skɪn] | Haut | And you shouldn't judge people by the colour of their ~. |
| | **but** | sondern | He isn't just good at athletics, ~ at swimming too. |
| | (to) **make a speech** [spiːtʃ] | eine Rede halten | |
| | **research (on)** *(no pl)* [rɪ'sɜːtʃ, 'riːsɜːtʃ] | Recherche; Nachforschung(en) (zu, über) | I have to do some ~ **on** Atlanta for homework.<br>! (to) **do research** = recherchieren |
| | **source** [sɔːs] | Quelle *(von Information, Energie usw.)* | The internet is a good ~ of information if you have to do research. |
| | **search engine** ['sɜːtʃ‿ˌendʒɪn] | Suchmaschine | |
| | (to) **search (for)** [sɜːtʃ] | suchen (nach), durchsuchen | |
| p.84/P 3 | **flat screen** ['flæt skriːn] | Flachbildschirm | a **remote control** a **flat screen**  |
| | **remote control** [rɪˌməʊt kən'trəʊl] | Fernbedienung | |
| | (to) **hop channels (-pp-)** [hɒp] | zappen | |
| | (to) **receive** [rɪ'siːv] | empfangen | We can ~ 30 channels. |
| | **satellite** ['sætəlaɪt] | Satellit; Satelliten- | |
| | (to) **turn** sth. **down/up** [tɜːn] | etwas leiser/lauter stellen | Can you ~ **down** that music? It's too loud. |
| | **volume** ['vɒljuːm] | Lautstärke | I can't hear anything. Can you turn up the ~? |
| p.86/P 6 | (to) **draw conclusions** [ˌdrɔː kən'kluːʒnz] | Schlüsse ziehen, schlussfolgern | Don't ~ **conclusions** before you know all the facts. |
| | **exact** [ɪg'zækt] | exakt, genau | What's the ~ size of Germany? Do you know? |
| | (to) **suffer (from** sth.**)** ['sʌfə] | (an/unter etwas) leiden | Mary often ~ **from** bad headaches. |
| p.88/P 10 | **holiday** ['hɒlədeɪ] | Feiertag | Christmas is a ~ in most countries. |
| p.88/P 12 | **president** ['prezɪdənt] | Präsident/in | ! stress: **president** ['prezɪdənt] |

## Melba's story

| | | | |
|---|---|---|---|
| p.89 | **especially** [ɪ'speʃəli] | besonders | I love sports, ~ hockey and rugby. |
| | **law** [lɔː] | Gesetz | It's against the ~ to drive a car when you're drunk. |
| | **apart** [ə'pɑːt] | auseinander, getrennt | My parents live ~, but they aren't divorced yet. |
| | **court** [kɔːt] | Gericht(shof) | Do you have to appear in ~ if you break traffic rules? |
| p.90 | **space** [speɪs] | Platz (*Raum*) | |
| | **as if** [əz‿'ɪf] | als ob | Those flowers look ~ **if** they need water |
| | (to) **be terrified (of)** ['terɪfaɪd] | schreckliche Angst haben (vor) | Everyone **was** ~ when the bank robber pulled out a gun. |
| | **immediately** [ɪ'miːdiətli] | sofort | My dog usually comes ~ when I call him. |
| | (to) **volunteer** [ˌvɒlən'tɪə] | sich freiwillig melden, sich bereit erklären | Hundreds of doctors **~ed** to help the earthquake victims. |
| | **volunteer** [ˌvɒlən'tɪə] | Freiwillige(r) | |
| | **step** [step] | Stufe | |
| p.91 | **soldier** ['səʊldʒə] | Soldat/in | |
| | **cruel** [kruːəl] | grausam | Don't you think it's ~ to keep animals in cages? |
| | (to) **want** sth./sb. **to do** sth. | wollen, dass etwas/jd. etwas tut | I **want <u>you to help</u>** your sister. = Ich **möchte, <u>dass du</u>** deiner Schwester **<u>hilfst</u>**. *Nie:* I want ~~that you help~~ ... |
| | **for the first time** | zum ersten Mal | Some people are nervous when they fly ~ **the first** ~. |
| | **voice** [vɔɪs] | Stimme | |
| | **valuable** ['væljuəbl] | wertvoll; nützlich | She keeps her earrings in the bank because they're so ~. |
| | **pain** [peɪn] | Schmerz(en) | |
| | **painful** ['peɪnfl] | schmerzhaft | |
| | (to) **splash** [splæʃ] | spritzen | He's **~ing** water on his face. |
| | **education** [ˌedʒu'keɪʃn] | (Schul-)Bildung, Ausbildung; Erziehung | You need a good ~ if you want to get a good job. |
| | **university** [ˌjuːnɪ'vɜːsəti] | Universität | |
| | **journalist** ['dʒɜːnəlɪst] | Journalist/in | **!** stress: **<u>jour</u>nalist** ['dʒɜːnəlɪst] |
| p.92 | **headline** ['hedlaɪn] | Schlagzeile | |
| | **heading** ['hedɪŋ] | Überschrift, Titel | |

**Das Dictionary besteht aus zwei alphabetischen Wörterlisten:**

**Englisch – Deutsch** (S. 194–224)
**Deutsch – Englisch** (S. 225–251).

Das **English – German Dictionary** enthält den Wortschatz der Bände 1 bis 4 von *English G 21*.
Wenn du wissen möchtest, was ein Wort bedeutet, wie man es ausspricht oder wie es genau geschrieben wird, kannst du hier nachschlagen.

Im **English – German Dictionary** werden folgende **Abkürzungen** und **Symbole** verwendet:

| | | | |
|---|---|---|---|
| jm. = jemandem | sb. = somebody | *pl = plural* | *AE = American English* |
| jn. = jemanden | sth. = something | *no pl = no plural* | *infml = informal* |

° Mit diesem Kringel sind Wörter markiert, die nicht zum Lernwortschatz gehören.
► Der Pfeil verweist auf Kästchen im Vocabulary (S. 172–193), in denen du weitere Informationen zu diesem Wort findest.

Die **Fundstellenangaben** zeigen, wo ein Wort zum ersten Mal vorkommt.
Die Ziffern in Klammern bezeichnen Seitenzahlen:

I = Band 1 • II = Band 2 • III = Band 3 • IV = Band 4
IV Intro (6) = Band 4, Introduction, Seite 6
IV Intro (6/173) = Band 4, Introduction, Seite 173 (im Vocabulary, zu Seite 6)
IV 1 (12) = Band 4, Unit 1, Seite 12
IV 1 (16/177) = Band 4, Unit 1, Seite 177 (im Vocabulary, zu Seite 16)

**Tipps zur Arbeit mit dem Dictionary** findest du im Skills File auf Seite 145.

## A

**a** [ə]
**1.** ein, eine I
**2. once/twice a week** einmal/zweimal pro Woche III • **a bit** ein bisschen, etwas II • **a few** ein paar, einige II • **a little** ein bisschen, wenig IV 2 (38) • **a lot (of)** eine Menge, viel, viele II • **He likes her a lot.** Er mag sie sehr. I
► S.182 little („wenig") – few („wenige")

**able** ['eɪbl]: **be able to do sth.** etwas tun können; fähig sein / in der Lage sein, etwas zu tun III

**about** [ə'baʊt]
**1.** über I
**2.** ungefähr II
**about yourself** [jə'self, jɔ:'self] über dich (selbst) III • **ask about sth.** nach etwas fragen I • **How about ...?** Wie wär's mit ...? III
**This is about Mr Green.** Es geht um Mr Green. I • **What about ...? 1.** Was ist mit ...? / Und ...? I; **2.** Wie wär's mit ...? I • **What are you talking about?** Wovon redest du? I • **What was the best thing about ...?** Was war das Beste an ...? II

**above** [ə'bʌv] oben; über, oberhalb (von) IV 1 (27/179)

**accent** ['æksənt] Akzent II

**accident** ['æksɪdənt] Unfall II

**ache** [eɪk] wehtun IV 3 (68)

°**acid** ['æsɪd] Säure

**across** [ə'krɒs]
**1.** (quer) über III
**2.** hinüber, herüber III

**act** [ækt]
**1.** sich verhalten IV 2 (37
**2.** aufführen, spielen I
°**Act out** ... Spiele/Spielt ... vor.

**active** ['æktɪv] aktiv, tätig IV 3 (59)

**activity** [æk'tɪvəti] Aktivität, Tätigkeit I

**actor** ['æktə] Schauspieler/in II

**actually** ['æktʃuəli]
**1.** eigentlich; in Wirklichkeit III
**2.** nebenbei bemerkt; übrigens IV 3 (69)

°**adapted** [ə'deptɪd] basierend auf

**add (to)** [æd] hinzufügen, ergänzen, addieren (zu) I

**address** [ə'dres] Adresse, Anschrift II

**admission** [əd'mɪʃn] Eintritt, Eintrittspreis IV 1 (16)

**adult** ['ædʌlt] Erwachsene(r) III

**advantage (over sb./sth.)** [əd'vɑ:ntɪdʒ] Vorteil (gegenüber jm./etwas) IV 2 (37)

**adventure** [əd'ventʃə] Abenteuer IV Intro (11)

°**advertiser-courier** [,ædvətaɪzə 'kʊriə] Anzeigenblatt

**afraid** [ə'freɪd]
**1. be afraid (of)** Angst haben (vor) I
**2. I'm afraid** leider II

**African American** [,æfrɪkən‿ə'merɪkən] afro-amerikanisch; Afro-Amerikaner/in IV 4 (77)

**after** ['ɑ:ftə] nach *(zeitlich)* I
°**after dark** [dɑ:k] nach Einbruch der Dunkelheit • **after that** danach I

**after** ['ɑ:ftə] nachdem II

**afternoon** [,ɑ:ftə'nu:n] Nachmittag I • **in the afternoon** nachmittags, am Nachmittag I • **on Friday afternoon** freitagnachmittags, am Freitagnachmittag I

**again** [ə'gen] wieder; noch einmal I

**against** [ə'genst] gegen III

**age** [eɪdʒ] Alter III

°**ages** ['eɪdʒəz] Altersstufen, Altersgruppen

**ago** [ə'gəʊ]: **a minute ago** vor einer Minute I

**agree (on)** [ə'gri:] sich einigen (auf) I • **agree with sb./sth.** jm./etwas zustimmen; mit jm./etwas übereinstimmen II

**air** [eə] Luft III

**airport** ['eəpɔ:t] Flughafen III

**album** ['ælbəm] Album III

°**algebra** ['ældʒɪbrə] Algebra

**alive** [ə'laɪv] am Leben, lebendig IV 3 (55)
**all** [ɔ:l] alle; alles I • **2 all** [ˌtu:‿'ɔ:l] 2 beide (2:2 unentschieden) III **all day** den ganzen Tag (lang) I **°all of a sudden** ['sʌdn] plötzlich • **all over the world** auf der ganzen Welt III • **all right** gut, in Ordnung II • **all the time** die ganze Zeit I • **all the way** den ganzen Weg IV Intro (10) • **from all over the UK/the world/England** aus dem gesamten Vereinigten Königreich / aus der ganzen Welt / aus ganz England III • **°She was all right** Es ging ihr gut • **This is all wrong.** Das ist ganz falsch. I
**°all-black school** *Schule, die ausschließlich von Schwarzen besucht wird*
**allowed** [ə'laʊd]**: be allowed** erlaubt sein IV 3 (56) • **be allowed to do sth.** etwas tun dürfen III
**almost** ['ɔ:lməʊst] fast, beinahe III
**alone** [ə'ləʊn] allein I • **°leave sb. alone** jd. in Ruhe lassen
**along** [ə'lɒŋ]**: along the street** entlang der Straße / die Straße entlang II • **°And now you've come along.** Und jetzt bist du plötzlich aufgetaucht.
**alphabet** ['ælfəbet] Alphabet I
**°alphabetical** [ˌælfə'betɪkl] alphabetisch
**already** [ɔ:l'redi] schon, bereits II
**also** ['ɔ:lsəʊ] auch II
**although** [ɔ:l'ðəʊ] obwohl III
**always** ['ɔ:lweɪz] immer I
**am** [ˌeɪ‿'em]**: 7 am** 7 Uhr morgens/vormittags I
**°amaze sb.** [ə'meɪz] jd. erstaunen, jn. in Erstaunen versetzen
**amazing** [ə'meɪzɪŋ] erstaunlich, unglaublich II
**ambulance** ['æmbjələns] Krankenwagen III
**American football** [əˌmerɪkən 'fʊtbɔ:l] Football I
**°Americana** [əˌmerɪ'kɑ:nə] *Sammelbegriff für alles, was als „typisch amerikanisch" empfunden wird*
**amnesty** ['æmnəsti] Amnestie, Begnadigung IV 2 (38)
**an** [ən] ein, eine I
**°analysis** [ə'næləsɪs] Analyse
**and** [ənd, ænd] und I • **and so on** und so weiter (usw.) IV 3 (57)
**angel** ['eɪndʒl] Engel II
**angry (about sth. / with sb.)** ['æŋgri] wütend, böse (über etwas / auf jn.) II
**animal** ['ænɪml] Tier II

**anniversary** [ˌænɪ'vɜ:səri] Jahrestag IV 4 (80) • **anniversary of sb.'s death** jemandes Todestag IV 4 (80)
**announce** [ə'naʊns] ankündigen, bekanntgeben III
**announcement** [ə'naʊnsmənt] Durchsage, Ansage; Ankündigung, Bekanntgabe III
**annoy sb.** [ə'nɔɪ ] jn. ärgern, belästigen III
**annoying** [ə'nɔɪɪŋ]**: My dad is annoying.** Mein Vater geht mir auf die Nerven. III
**anorak** ['ænəræk] Anorak, Windjacke III
**another** [ə'nʌðə] ein(e) andere(r, s); noch ein(e) I • **another 45 p** weitere 45 Pence, noch 45 Pence II
**answer** ['ɑ:nsə] antworten; beantworten I
**answer (to)** ['ɑ:nsə] Antwort (auf) I
**any** ['eni] jede(r,s) (beliebige); irgendein(e) IV 1 (27/183) • **any ...?** (irgend)welche ...? I • **any time** jederzeit IV 1 (27/179) • **not (...) any** kein, keine I • **not (...) any more** nicht mehr III
► S.179 any
**anybody** ['enibɒdi] (irgend)jemand II; jede(r) IV 1 (27/179) • **anybody else?** sonst noch jemand? IV 1 (15/176) • **not (...) anybody** niemand II
► S.179 any
► S.176 ... else
**anyone** ['eniwʌn] (irgend)jemand; jede(r) IV 2 (34/180)
► S.179 any
**anything** ['eniθɪŋ] (irgend)etwas II alles, was es auch sei / egal was IV 1 (27) • **anything else** irgendetwas anderes IV 1 (15) • **anything else?** sonst noch etwas? IV 1 (15/176) **not (...) anything** nichts II
► S.176 ... else
**anyway** ['eniweɪ]
**1.** sowieso I
**2.** trotzdem II
**3.** aber egal, ...; wie auch immer, ...; wie dem auch sei, ... III
**anywhere** ['eniweə] irgendwo(hin) II • **°anywhere else** irgendwo sonst • **not (...) anywhere** nirgendwo(hin) II
**apart** [ə'pɑ:t] auseinander, getrennt IV 4 (89)
**apartment** [ə'pɑ:tmənt] Wohnung IV 1 (26)
**appear** [ə'pɪə] erscheinen IV 2 (49)
**appetite** ['æpɪtaɪt] Appetit III
**apple** ['æpl] Apfel I

**appointment** [ə'pɔɪntmənt] Termin, Verabredung I • **°make appointments** einen Termin machen, eine Verabredung treffen
**April** ['eɪprəl] April I
**°arch** [ɑ:tʃ, ɑ:k] Bogen
**archive** ['ɑ:kaɪv] Archiv IV 4 (80)
**are** [ɑ:] bist; sind; seid I • **How are you?** Wie geht es dir/Ihnen/euch? II • **The pencils are 35 p.** Die Bleistifte kosten 35 Pence. I • **You're joking, aren't you?** Du machst Witze, nicht wahr? / Das ist nicht dein Ernst, oder? II
**area** ['eəriə] Bereich; Gebiet, Gegend III
**argue** ['ɑ:gju:] sich streiten, sich zanken I
**argument** ['ɑ:gjumənt]
**1.** Argument, Begründung III
**2.** Streit III
**arm** [ɑ:m] Arm I
**armchair** ['ɑ:mtʃeə] Sessel I
**around** [ə'raʊnd] um ... (herum); in ... umher, durch III • **around six** um sechs herum, gegen sechs III • **around the lake** um den See (herum) III • **around the town** in der Stadt umher, durch die Stadt **jump/run/walk around** herumspringen/-rennen / umherspazieren III
**°arrest** [ə'rest] verhaften
**arrival (arr)** [ə'raɪvl] Ankunft III
**arrive** [ə'raɪv] ankommen, eintreffen II
**art** [ɑ:t] Kunst I
**article** ['ɑ:tɪkl] (Zeitungs-)Artikel III
**artificial** [ˌɑ:tɪ'fɪʃl] künstlich, Kunst- III
**artist** ['ɑ:tɪst] Künstler/in III
**as** *(prep)* [əz, æz] als IV 1 (15) • **as a firefighter** als Feuerwehrmann, -frau IV 1 (15)
**as** *(conj)* [əz, æz]
**1.** als, während II
**°2.** da, weil
**as you can see** wie du sehen kannst II • **as if** als ob IV 4 (90)
► S.189 German 'während'
**as ... as** [əz, æz] so ... wie II • **as big/exciting as** so groß/aufregend wie II
**°aside** [ə'saɪd] beiseite
**ask** [ɑ:sk]
**1.** fragen I • **ask about sth.** nach etwas fragen I • **ask questions** Fragen stellen I • **ask sb. the way** jn. nach dem Weg fragen II • **ask sb. for directions** jn. nach dem Weg fragen; jn. um eine Wegbeschreibung bitten IV 1 (14/175)

°**2. ask sb. for help**. jn. um Hilfe bitten
**asleep** [ə'sli:p]: **be asleep** schlafen I
°**ass** [æs] *(AE, infml)* Arsch
**Assembly** [ə'sembli] Versammlung *(morgendliche Schulversammlung, oft mit Andacht)* III
**at** [ət, æt]: **at 7 Hamilton Street** in der Hamiltonstraße 7 I • **at 8.45** um 8.45 I • **at break** in der Pause *(zwischen Schulstunden)* II • **at first** zuerst, am Anfang IV 3 (55)
**at home** daheim, zu Hause I • **at last** endlich, schließlich I • **at least** zumindest, wenigstens I
**at night** nachts, in der Nacht I
**at school** in der Schule I • **at that table** an dem Tisch (dort) / an den Tisch (dort) I • **at the bottom (of)** unten, am unteren Ende (von) II • **at the butcher's** beim Metzger/Fleischer III • **at the chemist's** beim Apotheker III
**at the end (of)** am Ende (von) I
**at the Shaws' house** im Haus der Shaws / bei den Shaws zu Hause I
**at the station** am Bahnhof I • **at the top (of)** oben, am oberen Ende, an der Spitze (von) I • **at the weekend** am Wochenende I • **at work** bei der Arbeit / am Arbeitsplatz I
**ate** [et, eɪt] *siehe* **eat**
**athletics** [æθ'letɪks] Leichtathletik III
**Atlantic: the Atlantic (Ocean)** [ət,læntɪk_'əʊʃn] der Atlantische Ozean, der Atlantik IV 2 (49/183)
**attack** [ə'tæk] angreifen III
**attack** [ə'tæk] Angriff III
**attitude (to, towards)** ['ætɪtju:d] Haltung (gegenüber), Einstellung (zu, gegenüber) IV 2 (37)
**attraction** [ə'trækʃən] Attraktion IV 2 (36)
°**attractive** [ə'træktɪv] attraktiv, anziehend, reizvoll
**audience** ['ɔ:dɪəns] Publikum; Zuschauer/innen, Zuhörer/innen II
**August** ['ɔ:gəst] August I
**aunt** [ɑ:nt] Tante I • **auntie** ['ɑ:nti] Tante II
°**author** ['ɔ:θə] Autor/in, Schriftsteller/in
**auto** ['ɔ:təʊ] *(AE)* Auto, PKW IV Intro (10)
**autumn** ['ɔ:təm] Herbst I
**avenue** ['ævənju:] Allee IV 1 (12)
**average** ['ævərɪdʒ] Durchschnitt, durchschnittlich, Durchschnitts- IV 3 (63)
▸ S.185 US school grades
**away** [ə'weɪ] weg, fort I
**awesome** ['ɔ:səm] *(AE, infml)* klasse, großartig IV Intro (8)
**awful** ['ɔ:fl] furchtbar, schrecklich II

# B

**baby** ['beɪbi] Baby I • **have a baby** ein Baby/Kind bekommen II
**back (to)** [bæk] zurück (nach) I
**Good to have you back**. Schön, dass du wieder da bist. IV Intro (8)
**back door** [,bæk 'dɔ:] Hintertür II
**background** ['bækgraʊnd] Hintergrund II • **background file** *etwa:* Hintergrundinformation(en) II
**backpack** ['bækpæk] *(AE)* Rucksack IV 1 (20)
**bacon** ['beɪkən] Schinkenspeck II
**bad** [bæd] schlecht, schlimm • **bad timing** schlechtes Timing III • **be bad at sth.** in etwas schlecht sein, etwas schlecht können III
**badly** ['bædli]: **do badly (in)** schlecht abschneiden (in) III
**badminton** ['bædmɪntən] Badminton, Federball I • **badminton racket** Badmintonschläger III
**bag** [bæg] Tasche, Beutel, Tüte I
**bagel** ['beɪgl] Bagel *(ringförmiges Gebäck)* IV 1 (17)
**bagpipes** *(pl)* ['bægpaɪps] Dudelsack III
**bakery** ['beɪkəri] Bäckerei III
°**bake sale** ['beɪk ,seɪl] Verkauf von Backwaren um Geld zu sammeln
**ball** [bɔ:l]
**1.** Ball I
**2.** Ball *(Tanzveranstaltung)* IV 3 (68)
**banana** [bə'nɑ:nə] Banane I
**band** [bænd] Band, (Musik-)Gruppe I
**bank** [bæŋk] Bank, Sparkasse I
**bank robber** ['bæŋk ,rɒbə] Bankräuber/in I
°**Baptist** ['bæptɪst] Baptist/in, baptistisch
**bar** [bɑ:] Bar II
**baseball** ['beɪsbɔ:l] Baseball I
**baseball cap** Baseballmütze II
°**basil** ['bæzl] Basilikum
**basket** ['bɑ:skɪt] Korb I • **a basket of apples** ein Korb Äpfel I
**basketball** ['bɑ:skɪtbɔ:l] Basketball I
**bath** [bɑ:θ] Bad, Badewanne II
**have a bath** baden, ein Bad nehmen II
**bathroom** ['bɑ:θru:m] Badezimmer I
**bay** [beɪ] Bucht III
**be** [bi:], **was/were, been** sein I
**be with sb.** mit jemandem zusammen sein IV 3 (69)
**beach** [bi:tʃ] Strand II • **on the beach** am Strand II
**bean** [bi:n] Bohne IV 3 (58)
**bear** [beə] Bär II
**beard** [bɪəd] Bart IV 1 (27)
**beat** [bi:t], **beat, beaten** schlagen; besiegen III
**beaten** ['bi:tn] *siehe* **beat**
**beautiful** ['bju:tɪfl] schön I
**beauty** ['bju:ti] Schönheit III
**became** [bɪ'keɪm] *siehe* **become**
**because** [bɪ'kɒz] weil I • **because of** [bɪ'kɒz_əv] wegen IV 4 (80)
**become** [bɪ'kʌm], **became, become** werden II
**bed** [bed] Bett I • **Bed and Breakfast (B&B)** [,bed_ən 'brekfəst] Frühstückspension I • **go to bed** ins Bett gehen I
**bedroom** ['bedru:m] Schlafzimmer I
**beef** [bi:f] Rindfleisch III
**been** [bi:n] *siehe* **be**
**before** [bɪ'fɔ:] vor *(zeitlich)* I
**before** [bɪ'fɔ:] bevor II
**beg (for)** **(-gg-)** [beg] betteln (um); (eindringlich) bitten (um) IV 2 (38)
**began** [bɪ'gæn] *siehe* **begin**
**begin** **(-nn-)** [bɪ'gɪn], **began, begun** beginnen, anfangen (mit) III
**beginning** [bɪ'gɪnɪŋ] Beginn, Anfang; Einleitung II
**begun** [bɪ'gʌn] *siehe* **begin**
**behind** [bɪ'haɪnd] hinter II
**believe** [bɪ'li:v] glauben III
**bell** [bel] Klingel, Glocke III
**belong to** [bɪ'lɒŋ] gehören (zu) IV 2 (37)
**below** [bɪ'ləʊ] unten; unter, unterhalb (von) IV 1 (27)
**bench** [bentʃ] (Sitz-)Bank IV 1 (28)
**best** [best] am besten II • **the best ...** der/die/das beste ...; die besten I • **What was the best thing about ...?** Was war das Beste an ...? II • **Best wishes** *etwa:* Alles Gute / Mit besten Grüßen *(als Briefschluss)* IV 3 (62)
°**bet** [bet] wetten
**better** ['betə] besser I • **like sth. better** etwas lieber mögen II
**between** [bɪ'twi:n] zwischen II
**big** [bɪg] groß I • **big wheel** [,bɪg 'wi:l] Riesenrad III
**bike** [baɪk] Fahrrad I • **bike ride** (Rad-)Fahrt II • **ride a bike** Rad fahren I

°**bilingual** [baɪˈlɪŋgwəl] bilingual, zweisprachig
**bill** [bɪl] Rechnung III
**bin** [bɪn] Mülltonne II
°**binoculars** *(pl)* [bɪˈnɒkjuləz] Fernglas
**biography** [baɪˈɒgrəfi] Biografie III
**biology** [baɪˈɒlədʒi] Biologie I
**bird** [bɜːd] Vogel I
**birthday** [ˈbɜːθdeɪ] Geburtstag I
**Happy birthday.** Herzlichen Glückwunsch zum Geburtstag. I • **My birthday is in May.** Ich habe im Mai Geburtstag. I • **My birthday is on 13th June.** Ich habe am 13. Juni Geburtstag. I • **When's your birthday?** Wann hast du Geburtstag? I
**biscuit** [ˈbɪskɪt] Keks, Plätzchen I
**bit: a bit** [ə ˈbɪt] ein bisschen, etwas II
°**bitch** [bɪtʃ] *(infml)* Miststück, Schlampe
**black** [blæk] schwarz I
**blame sb. (for)** [bleɪm] jm. die Schuld geben (an); jm. Vorwürfe machen (wegen) III
**bleep** [bliːp] piepsen II
**bleep** [bliːp] Piepton II
**blew** [bluː] *siehe* **blow**
**block** [blɒk] (Häuser-, Wohn-)Block IV 1 (14)
**blog** [blɒg] *(von web log)* Blog *(Internet-Tagebuch)* IV Intro (8)
**blond** [blɒnd] blond, hell IV 1 (27)
°**blondie** [ˈblɒndɪ] Blondkopf
**blood** [blʌd] Blut IV 1 (27)
**blow** [bləʊ], **blew, blown** wehen, blasen III
**blown** [bləʊn] *siehe* **blow**
**blue** [bluː] blau I
**board** [bɔːd] (Wand-)Tafel I • **on the board** an der/die Tafel I
**bulletin board** *(AE)* schwarzes Brett, Anschlagtafel IV 3 (56)
**notice board** *(BE)* Anschlagtafel, schwarzes Brett I
**boat** [bəʊt] Boot, Schiff I
°**bod** [bɒd] *(infml) kurz für* **body**
**body** [ˈbɒdi] Körper I
**bodyguard** [ˈbɒdigɑːd] Bodyguard, Leibwächter/in IV 4 (91)
**bold print** [ˌbəʊld ˈprɪnt] Fettdruck III
**book** [bʊk] Buch I
**boot** [buːt] Stiefel I
**border** [ˈbɔːdə] Grenze IV 2 (35)
°**border patrol** Grenzschutz
**bored** [bɔːd] gelangweilt IV 2 (51)
**boring** [ˈbɔːrɪŋ] langweilig I
**born** [bɔːn]: **be born** geboren sein/werden II
**borough** [ˈbʌrə, *AE:* ˈbɜːrəʊ] (Stadt-)Bezirk IV 1 (13)
► S.175 New York: the five boroughs
**boss** [bɒs] Chef/in, Boss III
**both** [bəʊθ] beide I
**bottle** [ˈbɒtl] Flasche I • **a bottle of milk** eine Flasche Milch I
**bottom** [ˈbɒtəm] unteres Ende II
**at the bottom (of)** unten, am unteren Ende (von) II
**bought** [bɔːt] *siehe* **buy**
**bowl** [bəʊl] Schüssel I • **a bowl of cornflakes** eine Schale Cornflakes I
**box** [bɒks] Kasten, Kästchen, Kiste I • **sandwich box** Brotdose I
**boy** [bɔɪ] Junge I
**boyfriend** [ˈbɔɪfrend] (fester) Freund IV 2 (50)
°**bracket** [ˈbrækɪt] Klammer *(in Texten)*
**brainstorm** [ˈbreɪnstɔːm] brainstormen *(so viele Ideen wie möglich sammeln)* III
**brave** [breɪv] tapfer, mutig III
**bread** *(no pl)* [bred] Brot I
**break** [breɪk] Pause I • **at break** in der Pause *(zwischen Schulstunden)* II • **take a break** eine Pause machen IV 1 (22)
**break** [breɪk], **broke, broken** (zer-)brechen; kaputt gehen IV 3 (56) **break a journey** eine Reise unterbrechen III
**breakable** [ˈbreɪkəbl] zerbrechlich IV 4 (87)
**breakdance** [ˈbreɪkdɑːns] Breakdance IV 1 (13)
**breakfast** [ˈbrekfəst] Frühstück I
**have breakfast** frühstücken I
°**breaking news** aktuelle Nachrichten
**bridge** [brɪdʒ] Brücke I
**bridle path** [ˈbraɪdl pɑːθ] Reitweg III
**bright** [braɪt] hell, leuchtend II
**brilliant** [ˈbrɪliənt] genial, toll III
**bring** [brɪŋ], **brought, brought** (mit-, her)bringen I
**British** [ˈbrɪtɪʃ] britisch; Brite, Britin II
**brochure** [ˈbrəʊʃə] Prospekt, Broschüre II
**broke** [brəʊk] *siehe* **break**
**broken** [ˈbrəʊkən] *siehe* **break**
**broken** [ˈbrəʊkən] gebrochen; zerbrochen, kaputt II
**brother** [ˈbrʌðə] Bruder I
**brought** [brɔːt] *siehe* **bring**
**brown** [braʊn] braun I
**budgie** [ˈbʌdʒi] Wellensittich I
**build** [bɪld], **built, built** bauen II
**building** [ˈbɪldɪŋ] Gebäude II
**built** [bɪlt] *siehe* **build**
°**bulimic** [buˈlɪmɪk] bulimisch, ess-brechsüchtig
**bulletin board** [ˈbʊlətɪn bɔːd] *(AE)* schwarzes Brett, Anschlagtafel IV 3 (56)
**bully** [ˈbʊli] einschüchtern, tyrannisieren II
**bully** [ˈbʊli] (Schul-)Tyrann III
**bunk (bed)** [bʌŋk] Etagenbett, Koje II
**burger** [ˈbɜːgə] Burger IV 2 (36)
**burn** [bɜːn] brennen; verbrennen IV 1 (15)
**bus** [bʌs] Bus I • **bus stop** [ˈbʌs stɒp] Bushaltestelle III
**business** [ˈbɪznəs] Geschäft; Handel IV 2 (36) • **Mind your own business.** Das geht dich nichts an! / Kümmere dich um deine eigenen Angelegenheiten! II
**busy** [ˈbɪzi] belebt, verkehrsreich; hektisch III
**but** [bət, bʌt]
**1.** aber I
**2.** sondern IV 4 (81)
**butcher** [ˈbʊtʃə] Fleischer/in, Metzger/in III • **at the butcher's** beim Fleischer/Metzger III
**butter** [ˈbʌtə] Butter III
**button** [ˈbʌtn] Knopf III
**buy** [baɪ], **bought, bought** kaufen I
**by** [baɪ]
**1.** von I
**2.** an; (nahe) bei II
**3. by car/train/bike/...** mit dem Auto/Zug/Rad/... II
**4.** bis spätestens; nicht später als **by ten o'clock** bis (spätestens) zehn Uhr III
**5. by the way** übrigens I
**Bye.** [baɪ] Tschüs! I

## C

**cab** [kæb] Taxi IV 1 (27) • **get a cab** ein Taxi nehmen IV 1 (27)
**cabin** [ˈkæbɪn] Hütte III
**cable** [ˈkeɪbl] Kabel *(auch kurz für Kabelfernsehen)* IV 4 (78) • °**cable car** *(USA)* Kabelbahn *(von Drahtseilen gezogene Straßenbahn)*
**café** [ˈkæfeɪ] *(kleines)* Restaurant, Imbissstube, Café II
**cafeteria** [ˌkæfəˈtɪəriə] Cafeteria IV 3 (56), *(USA)* Schulmensa IV 3 (56)
**cage** [keɪdʒ] Käfig I
**cake** [keɪk] Kuchen, Torte I
**calendar** [ˈkælɪndə] Kalender I

**call** [kɔːl]
**1.** rufen; anrufen I
**2.** nennen I
**call sb. names** jn. mit Schimpfwörtern hänseln, jm. Schimpfwörter nachrufen III • **°call out** herausrufen
**call** [kɔːl] Anruf, Telefongespräch I
**called** [kɔːld]**: be called** heißen, genannt werden III
**calm down** [ˌkɑːm ˈdaʊn] sich beruhigen II
**calorie** [ˈkæləri] Kalorie IV 3 (65)
**came** [keɪm] *siehe* **come**
**camel** [ˈkæml] Kamel II
**camera** [ˈkæmərə] Kamera, Fotoapparat I
**camp** [kæmp] zelten III
**camp** [kæmp] Camp, (Ferien-)Lager IV 2 (43)
**can** [kən, kæn]
**1.** können I
**2.** dürfen I
**Can I help you?** Kann ich Ihnen helfen? / Was kann ich für Sie tun? *(im Geschäft)* I
**canal** [kəˈnæl] Kanal III
**canoe** [kəˈnuː] Kanu III
**canoe** [kəˈnuː] paddeln, Kanu fahren III
**canteen** [kænˈtiːn] Kantine, Schulmensa II
**canyon** [ˈkænjən] Schlucht IV Intro (8)
**cap** [kæp] Mütze, Kappe II
**capital** [ˈkæpɪtl] Hauptstadt III
**capital letter** [ˌkæpɪtl ˈletə] Großbuchstabe III
**caption** [ˈkæpʃn] Bildunterschrift III
**car** [kɑː] Auto I • **car park** Parkplatz III
**caravan** [ˈkærəvæn] Wohnwagen II
**card** [kɑːd] (Spiel-, Post-)Karte I
**°care** [keə]**: °feel cared about** sich behütet/beschützt fühlen
**°I don't care.** Es ist mir egal.
**career** [kəˈrɪə] Karriere III
**careful** [ˈkeəfl]
**1.** vorsichtig II
**2.** sorgfältig II
**caretaker** [ˈkeəteɪkə] Hausmeister/in II
**carrot** [ˈkærət] Möhre, Karotte I
**cartoon** [kɑːˈtuːn] Cartoon (Zeichentrickfilm; Bilderwitz) II
**case** [keɪs] Fall II
**castle** [ˈkɑːsl] Burg, Schloss II
**cat** [kæt] Katze I
**catch** [kætʃ]**, caught, caught** fangen; erwischen II
**cathedral** [kəˈθiːdrəl] Kathedrale, Dom III
**caught** [kɔːt] *siehe* **catch**
**cause** [kɔːz] verursachen IV 4 (80/191)
**cause (of sth.)** [kɔːz] Grund, Ursache (für etwas) IV 4 (80)
**°caution** [ˈkɔːʃn] Warnung
**CD** [ˌsiːˈdiː] CD I • **CD player** CD-Spieler I
**ceilidh** [ˈkeɪli] *Musik- und Tanzveranstaltung, vor allem in Schottland und Irland* III
**cellphone** [ˈselfəʊn] *(AE)* Handy, Mobiltelefon IV 1 (14)
**Celsius (C)** [ˈselsiəs] Celsius IV 3 (63)
**cent (c)** [sent] Cent I • **per cent (%)** [pə ˈsent] Prozent III
**centimetre (cm)** [ˈsentɪmiːtə] Zentimeter III
**central** [ˈsentrəl] Zentral-, Mittel- III
**centre** [ˈsentə] Zentrum, Mitte I
**city centre** Stadtzentrum, Innenstadt I • **sports centre** Sportzentrum I
**century** [ˈsentʃəri] Jahrhundert II
**°ceremony** [ˈserɪməni] Feier, Zeremonie
**chair** [tʃeə] Stuhl I
**champion** [ˈtʃæmpiən] Meister/in, Champion I
**championship** [ˈtʃæmpiənʃɪp] Meisterschaft III
**chance** [tʃɑːns] Chance, Möglichkeit IV 3 (68)
**change** [tʃeɪndʒ]
**1.** (sich) ändern; (sich) verändern IV 2 (50)
**2.** wechseln IV 3 (56)
**3.** umsteigen III
**4.** sich umziehen IV 3 (56)
► S.186 (to) change – change
**change** [tʃeɪndʒ]
**1.** (Ver-)Änderung, Wechsel IV 3 (56/186)
**2.** Wechselgeld I; Kleingeld IV 3 (56/186)
► S.186 (to) change – change
**channel** [ˈtʃænl] Kanal, Sender IV 4 (78) • **hop channels** [ˌhɒp ˈtʃænəlz] zappen IV 4 (84)
**character** [ˈkærəktə]
**1.** Charakter, Wesen IV 2 (52)
**2.** Person, Figur *(in Roman, Film, Theaterstück)* IV 2 (52)
**°chart** [tʃɑːt] Schaubild, Diagramm, Tabelle, Grafik
**charts** [tʃɑːts] Charts, Hitliste III
**°chase** [tʃeɪs] jagen
**chat (-tt-)** [tʃæt] plaudern; chatten II
**chat room** [ˈtʃæt ruːm] Chatroom III
**cheap** [tʃiːp] billig I
**check** [tʃek] (über)prüfen, kontrollieren I
**°checklist** [ˈtʃeklɪst] Checkliste
**checkpoint** [ˈtʃekpɔɪnt] Kontrollpunkt *(hier: zur Selbstüberprüfung)* I
**°cheddar** [ˈtʃedə] Cheddar(käse)
**cheek** [tʃiːk] Wange IV 1 (27)
**cheer** [tʃɪə] jubeln, Beifall klatschen II
**cheerleader** [ˈtʃɪəliːdə] Cheerleader *(Stimmungsanheizer/in bei Sportereignissen* IV 3 (57)
**cheese** [tʃiːz] Käse I • **cream cheese** Frischkäse IV 1 (17)
**chemist** [ˈkemɪst] Drogerie, Apotheke II • **at the chemist's** beim Apotheker III
**cherry** [ˈtʃeri] Kirsche II
**chicken** [ˈtʃɪkɪn] Huhn; (Brat-)Hähnchen I
**child** [tʃaɪld]**,** *pl* **children** [ˈtʃɪldrən] Kind I
**°chili con carne** [ˌtʃɪli kɒn ˈkɑːni] Chili con Carne *(scharfes Gericht aus Fleisch, Chilischoten und anderen Zutaten)*
**chips** *(pl)* [tʃɪps]
**1.** *(BE)* Pommes frites I
**2. (potato) chips** *(AE)* Kartoffelchips IV 1 (20)
**chocolate** [ˈtʃɒklət] Schokolade I
**°chocolate milk** [ˈtʃɒklət mɪlk] Kakao
**choir** [ˈkwaɪə] Chor I
**choose** [tʃuːz]**, chose, chosen** (sich) aussuchen, (aus)wählen I
**chorus** [ˈkɔːrəs] Refrain III
**chose** [tʃəʊz] *siehe* **choose**
**chosen** [ˈtʃəʊzn] *siehe* **choose**
**Christmas** [ˈkrɪsməs] Weihnachten I
**church** [tʃɜːtʃ] Kirche I
**cinema** [ˈsɪnəmə] Kino I • **go to the cinema** ins Kino gehen II
**circle** [ˈsɜːkl] Kreis IV 3 (69)
**circus** [ˈsɜːkəs] (runder) Platz III
**citizen** [ˈsɪtɪzn] (Staats-)Bürger/in, Staatsangehörige(r) IV 2 (37)
**city** [ˈsɪti] (Groß-)Stadt I • **city centre** Stadtzentrum, Innenstadt I
**civil** [ˈsɪvl]**: civil rights** *(pl)* Bürgerrechte IV 4 (77) • **civil war** Bürgerkrieg IV 4 (76)
**clap (-pp-)** [klæp] (Beifall) klatschen IV 3 (69)
**class** [klɑːs]
**1.** (Schul-)Klasse I • **class teacher** Klassenlehrer/in I
**2.** Unterricht; Kurs IV 3 (58)

**classical** ['klæsɪkl] klassisch III
**classmate** ['klɑːsmeɪt] Klassenkamerad/in, Mitschüler/in I
**classroom** ['klɑːsruːm] Klassenzimmer I
**clean** [kliːn] sauber II
**clean** [kliːn] sauber machen, putzen I • **I clean my teeth.** Ich putze mir die Zähne. I
**cleaner** ['kliːnə] Putzfrau, -mann II
**clear** [klɪə] klar, deutlich I
**clever** ['klevə] schlau, klug I
**cleverness** ['klevənəs] Klugheit, Schlauheit IV 3 (66)
**click on sth.** [klɪk] etwas anklicken II
**cliff** [klɪf] Klippe, Felsen III
**climb** [klaɪm] klettern; hinaufklettern (auf) I • **Climb a tree.** Klettere auf einen Baum. I
**clinic** ['klɪnɪk] Klinik II
**clock** [klɒk] (Wand-, Stand-, Turm-) Uhr I
**clone** [kləʊn] Klon III
**close (to)** [kləʊs] nahe (bei, an) III **That was close.** Das war knapp. II
**close** [kləʊz] schließen, zumachen I
**closed** [kləʊzd] geschlossen II
°**closing phrase** ['kləʊzɪŋ freɪz] Grußformel *(am Briefende)*
**clothes** *(pl)* [kləʊðz, kləʊz] Kleider, Kleidung(sstücke) II
**cloud** [klaʊd] Wolke II
**cloudless** ['klaʊdləs] wolkenlos IV 2 (42)
**cloudy** ['klaʊdi] bewölkt II
**clown** [klaʊn] Clown/in II
**club** [klʌb] Klub; Verein I
°**clue** [kluː] Hinweis
**coach** [kəʊtʃ] Trainer/in III
**coast** [kəʊst] Küste III
**code: dress code** ['dres kəʊd] Kleiderordnung IV 3 (56)
**coffee** ['kɒfi] Kaffee IV 1 (17) **coffee to go** Kaffee zum Mitnehmen IV 1 (17/177)
**cola** ['kəʊlə] Cola I
**cold** [kəʊld] kalt I • **be cold** frieren I
**cold** [kəʊld]
1. Kälte IV 2 (49)
2. Erkältung II • **have a cold** erkältet sein, eine Erkältung haben II
°**collapse** [kə'læps] zusammenbrechen; einstürzen
**collect** [kə'lekt] sammeln I
**collection** [kə'lekʃn] Sammlung IV 1 (25)
**collector** [kə'lektə] Sammler/in II
°**colony** ['kɒləni] Kolonie

**colour** ['kʌlə] kolorieren, färben, bunt an-, ausmalen III
**colour** ['kʌlə] Farbe I • **What colour is ...?** Welche Farbe hat ...? I
**column** ['kɒləm] Säule III
°**combine** [kəm'baɪn] kombinieren, verbinden
**come** [kʌm], **came, come** kommen I • **come home** nach Hause kommen I • **come in** hereinkommen I • **Come on. 1.** Na los, komm. II; **2.** Ach komm! / Na hör mal! II °**come true** [ˌkʌm 'truː] wahr werden, in Erfüllung gehen • °**come with** erhältlich sein °**And now you've come along.** Und jetzt bist du plötzlich aufgetaucht.
**comedy** ['kɒmədi] Komödie IV 4 (78)
**comfortable** ['kʌmftəbl] bequem, behaglich IV 2 (49) • **Make yourself comfortable.** Machs dir bequem. IV 2 (49)
**comic** ['kɒmɪk] Comic-Heft I
**comment** ['kɒment] Kommentar, Bemerkung IV Intro (8)
**Commonwealth** ['kɒmənwelθ]**: the Commonwealth** *Gemeinschaft der Länder des ehemaligen Britischen Weltreichs* III
°**communication** [kəˌmjuːnɪ'keɪʃn] Kommunikation
**community hall** [kə'mjuːnəti hɔːl] Gemeinschaftshalle, -saal, Gemeindehalle, -saal III
**company** ['kʌmpəni] Firma, Gesellschaft III
**compare** [kəm'peə] vergleichen IV 3 (68)
**comparison** [kəm'pærɪsn] Steigerung; Vergleich II
**competition** [ˌkɒmpə'tɪʃn] Wettbewerb, Wettkampf IV 4 (78)
**complain (about sth.)** [kəm'pleɪn] sich (über etwas) beschweren, beklagen III
°**complete** [kəm'pliːt] vervollständigen, ergänzen
**computer** [kəm'pjuːtə] Computer I
**concert** ['kɒnsət] Konzert III
**conclusion** [kən'kluːʒn] Schluss(folgerung) IV 4 (86) • **draw conclusions** Schlüsse ziehen, schlussfolgern IV 4 (86)
°**condor** ['kɒndɔː] Kondor
°**confused** [kən'fjuːzd] verwirrt, durcheinander
**contain** [kən'teɪn] enthalten IV 3 (65)
°**content** ['kɒntent] Gehalt, Inhalt
**context** ['kɒntekst] Zusammenhang, Kontext IV 1 (23) • °**from the context** aus dem Zusammenhang, aus dem Kontext

°**continent** ['kɒntɪnənt] Kontinent
°**continue** [kən'tɪnjuː] fortführen, fortsetzen
**control: remote control** [rɪˌməʊt kən'trəʊl] Fernbedienung IV 4 (84)
**conversation** [ˌkɒnvə'seɪʃn] Gespräch, Unterhaltung IV 1 (28)
**cook** [kʊk] kochen, zubereiten II
**cook** [kʊk] Koch/Köchin III
**cooker** ['kʊkə] Herd I
**cookie** ['kʊkɪ] *(AE)* Keks IV 1 (20)
**cool** [kuːl]
1. kühl II
2. cool I
**copy** ['kɒpi] kopieren; abschreiben II
**copy** ['kɒpi]
1. Kopie, Abschrift II
2. Exemplar III
**corner** ['kɔːnə] Ecke I • **on the corner of Green Street and London Road** Green Street, Ecke London Road II
**cornflakes** ['kɔːnfleɪks] Cornflakes I
**correct** [kə'rekt] berichtigen, korrigieren II
**correct** [kə'rekt] richtig III
**cost** [kɒst], **cost, cost** kosten IV 1 (16)
**cotton** ['kɒtn] Baumwolle IV 4 (76)
**could** [kəd, kʊd]
**1. he could ...** er konnte ... II
**2. he could ...** er könnte ... III
**count** [kaʊnt] zählen II
**countable** ['kaʊntəbl] zählbar IV 3 (64)
**countdown** ['kaʊntdaʊn] Countdown III
**counter** ['kaʊntə] Theke, Ladentisch IV 1 (17)
**country** ['kʌntri] Land *(auch als Gegensatz zur Stadt)* II • **in the country** auf dem Land II
**countryside** ['kʌntrisaɪd] Land(schaft), Natur IV 3 (55)
°**county fair** ['kaʊnti feə] Landwirtschaftsschau
**couple** ['kʌpl]**: a couple of weeks** ein paar Wochen IV 1 (28)
**course** [kɔːs] Kurs, Lehrgang III
**course: of course** [əv 'kɔːs] natürlich, selbstverständlich I
**court** [kɔːt]
1. Platz, Court *(für Squash, Badminton, Tennis)* III
2. Gericht(shof) IV 4 (89) • °**the Supreme Court** [suːˌpriːm 'kɔːt] der Oberste Gerichtshof
**cousin** ['kʌzn] Cousin, Cousine I
**cover** ['kʌvə] (CD-)Hülle I • °**inside cover** [ˌɪnsaɪd 'kʌvə] Buchumschlaginnenseite

°**cover** ['kʌvə] sich/etwas zudecken, bedecken
**cow** [kaʊ] Kuh II
**crash (into)** [kræʃ] zusammenstoßen (mit); hineinfahren (in) IV 2 (46)
**crazy** ['kreɪzi] verrückt III
**cream** [kriːm] Sahne; Creme IV 1 (17)
**cream cheese** Frischkäse IV 1 (17)
**crime** [kraɪm] Kriminalität; Verbrechen IV 4 (78) • **crime film** Krimi IV 4 (78/190) • **crime series** Krimiserie IV 4 (78) • **crime story** Krimi IV 4 (78/190)
**crisps** *(pl)* [krɪsps] Kartoffelchips I
**crocodile** ['krɒkədaɪl] Krokodil II
**cross** [krɒs] überqueren II • **cross a time zone** eine Zeitzone passieren/durchqueren IV Intro (8)
**cross** [krɒs]**: be cross (with)** böse, sauer sein (auf) I
**crowd** [kraʊd] (Menschen-)Menge, Masse; *(infml auch:)* Clique, Gruppe IV 1 (17/177)
**crowded** ['kraʊdɪd] überfüllt, voll IV 1 (17)
°**crown** [kraʊn] Krone
**cruel** ['kruːəl] grausam IV 4 (91)
**crush** [krʌʃ]**: have a crush on sb.** in jn. verknallt sein III
**cry** [kraɪ] weinen IV 1 (27)
**culture** ['kʌltʃə] Kultur IV 2 (37)
**cup** [kʌp]
1. Tasse • **a cup of tea** eine Tasse Tee III
2. Pokal III
**cupboard** ['kʌbəd] Schrank I
**curry** ['kʌri] Curry(gericht) III
**curtain** ['kɜːtn] Vorhang IV 3 (69)
**customer** ['kʌstəmə] Kunde, Kundin II
**cut (-tt-)** [kʌt]**, cut, cut** schneiden III • **cut sth. off** etwas abtrennen, abschneiden III • **cut the grass** Rasen mähen IV Intro (9) • °**cut into** einschneiden, eingraben
°**cut** [kʌt] Schnitt
**cycle** ['saɪkl] (mit dem) Rad fahren II • **cycle path** Radweg II

# D

**dad** [dæd] Papa, Vati; Vater I
**daily** ['deɪli] täglich IV Intro (8)
°**damage** ['dæmɪdʒ] Schaden
**dance** [dɑːns] tanzen I
**dance** [dɑːns] Tanz I • **dance floor** ['dɑːns flɔː] Dancefloor, Tanzfläche IV 3 (68)
**dancer** ['dɑːnsə] Tänzer/in II
**dancing** ['dɑːnsɪŋ] Tanzen I
**dancing lessons** Tanzstunden, Tanzunterricht I
**danger** ['deɪndʒə] Gefahr III
**dangerous** ['deɪndʒərəs] gefährlich II
**dark** [dɑːk] dunkel I • °**after dark** nach Einbruch der Dunkelheit
**date** [deɪt] Datum I
**daughter** ['dɔːtə] Tochter I
**day** [deɪ] Tag I • **one day** eines Tages I • **days of the week** Wochentage I • **day out** Tagesausflug III
**dead** [ded] tot I
°**deal** [diːl] Angebot • **It's a deal.** Abgemacht! III • **make a deal** ein Abkommen / eine Abmachung treffen III
**dear** [dɪə] Schatz, Liebling I • **Oh dear!** Oje! II
**dear** [dɪə]**: Dear Jay ...** Lieber Jay, ... I • **Dear Sir or Madam** Sehr geehrte Damen und Herren *(Anrede in Briefen)* IV 2 (45)
**death** [deθ] Tod IV 4 (80)
**debate** [dɪ'beɪt] debattieren IV 3 (57)
**debate** [dɪ'beɪt] Debatte IV 3 (56/186)
**December** [dɪ'sembə] Dezember I
**decide (on)** [dɪ'saɪd] beschließen; sich entscheiden (für) IV 1 (26)
**deep** [diːp] tief IV Intro (8)
**deer**, *pl* **deer** [dɪə] Reh, Hirsch II
°**defeat** [dɪ'fiːt] besiegen
°**definition** [ˌdefɪ'nɪʃn] Definition
**degree** [dɪ'griː] Grad II
**deli** ['deli] Deli *(Lebensmittelgeschäft und Fastfoodrestaurant)* IV 1 (13)
**delicious** [dɪ'lɪʃəs] köstlich, lecker II
**dentist** ['dentɪst] Zahnarzt, -ärztin IV 3 (68)
**department store** [dɪ'pɑːtmənt stɔː] Kaufhaus II
**departure (dep)** [dɪ'pɑːtʃə] Abfahrt, Abflug; Abreise III
**depressed** [dɪ'prest] deprimiert, niedergeschlagen IV 2 (50)
**depressing** [dɪ'presɪŋ] deprimierend, trostlos IV 2 (50)
**describe sth. (to sb.)** [dɪ'skraɪb] (jm.) etwas beschreiben II
**description** [dɪ'skrɪpʃn] Beschreibung II
°**desert** ['dezət] Wüste
**design** [dɪ'zaɪn] entwerfen, gestalten II
**desk** [desk] Schreibtisch I
**destroy** [dɪ'strɔɪ] zerstören III
**detail** ['diːteɪl] Detail, Einzelheit II
**detective** [dɪ'tektɪv] Detektiv/in I
°**dialogue** ['daɪəlɒg] Dialog
**diary** ['daɪəri] Tagebuch; Terminkalender I
**dice**, *pl* **dice** [daɪs] Würfel II
°**dictate** [dɪk'teɪt] diktieren
**dictionary** ['dɪkʃənri] Wörterbuch, *(alphabetisches)* Wörterverzeichnis I
**did** [dɪd] *siehe* **do** • **Did you go ...?** Bist du ... gegangen? / Seid ihr ... gegangen? I • **we didn't sing** wir sangen nicht / wir haben nicht gesungen I
**die (of)** *(-ing form:* **dying***)* [daɪ] sterben (an) II
**difference** ['dɪfrəns] Unterschied IV 1 (15)
**different (from)** ['dɪfrənt] verschieden, unterschiedlich; anders (als) I
**difficult** ['dɪfɪkəlt] schwierig, schwer I
**dining room** ['daɪnɪŋ ruːm] Esszimmer I
**dinner** ['dɪnə] Abendessen, Abendbrot I • **have dinner** Abendbrot essen I
**dinosaur** ['daɪnəsɔː] Dinosaurier IV 1 (25)
**directions** *(pl)* [də'rekʃnz] Wegbeschreibung IV 1 (14)
**director: film director** ['fɪlm dəˌrektə] Regisseur/in IV 2 (47)
**dirty** ['dɜːti] schmutzig II
**disabled** [dɪs'eɪbld] (körper)behindert III
**disadvantage** [ˌdɪsəd'vɑːntɪdʒ] Nachteil IV 2 (37)
**disagree (with)** [ˌdɪsə'griː] nicht übereinstimmen (mit); anderer Meinung sein (als) III
**disappear** [ˌdɪsə'pɪə] verschwinden II
**disappoint** [ˌdɪsə'pɔɪnt] enttäuschen IV 4 (80/191)
**disappointed (about)** [ˌdɪsə'pɔɪntɪd] enttäuscht (von/über) IV 4 (80)
**disc jockey (DJ)** ['dɪsk dʒɒki, 'diː dʒeɪ] Diskjockey (DJ)
**disco** ['dɪskəʊ] Disko I
**discover** [dɪ'skʌvə] entdecken; herausfinden IV 2 (45)
**discriminate against sb.** [dɪ'skrɪmɪneɪt] jn. diskriminieren, jn. benachteiligen IV 2 (37/181)
**discrimination (against)** [dɪˌskrɪmɪ'neɪʃn] Diskriminierung (von), Benachteiligung (von) IV 2 (37)
°**discuss** [dɪ'skʌs] besprechen; diskutieren (über)
**discussion** [dɪ'skʌʃn] Diskussion II
**dish** [dɪʃ] Gericht *(Speise)* III

**dishwasher** ['dɪʃwɒʃə] Geschirrspülmaschine I
**display** [dɪ'spleɪ]: **be on display** ausgestellt sein/werden IV 4 (80)
°**divide (into)** [dɪ'vaɪd] auf-, einteilen (in)
**divorced** [dɪ'vɔːst] geschieden I
**DJ** ['diː dʒeɪ] Diskjockey III
**DJ** ['diː dʒeɪ] (Musik/CDs/Platten) auflegen *(in der Disko)* III
**do** [duː], **did, done** tun, machen I
**Do you like ...?** Magst du ...? I
**do a gig** einen Auftritt haben, ein Konzert geben III • **do a good job** gute Arbeit leisten II • **do a project** ein Projekt machen, durchführen II • **do an exercise** eine Übung machen II • **do badly/well (in)** schlecht/gut abschneiden (in) III • **do research** recherchieren IV 4 (81) • **do sport** Sport treiben I
**doable** ['duːəbl] machbar IV 4 (87)
**doctor** ['dɒktə] Doktor; Arzt/Ärztin II • **to the doctor's** zum Arzt III
**documentary** [ˌdɒkju'mentri] Dokumentarfilm, -beitrag IV 4 (78)
**dog** [dɒg] Hund I
**dollar ($)** ['dɒlə] Dollar IV 1 (16)
°**dominate** ['dɒmɪneɪt] dominieren, beherrschen
**done** [dʌn] *siehe* **do**
**don't** [dəʊnt]: **Don't listen to Dan.** Hör/Hört nicht auf Dan. I • **I don't like ...** Ich mag ... nicht. / Ich mag kein(e) ... I
**door** [dɔː] Tür I
**doorbell** ['dɔːbel] Türklingel I
**dossier** ['dɒsieɪ] Mappe, Dossier *(des Sprachenportfolios)* I
**double** ['dʌbl] zweimal, doppelt, Doppel- I • °**double circle** Doppelkreis, „Kugellager" *(als Gesprächskreis)*
**down** [daʊn] hinunter, herunter, nach unten I • **down there** dort unten II • **fall down** hinfallen II **turn sth. down** etwas leiser stellen IV 4 (84)
**download** [ˌdaʊn'ləʊd] runterladen, downloaden III
**downloadable** [ˌdaʊn'ləʊdəbl] herunterladbar, zum Herunterladen IV 4 (87)
**downstairs** [ˌdaʊn'steəz] unten; nach unten I
**downtown** [ˌdaʊn'taʊn] (im/in das) Stadtzentrum IV 1 (14) • **the downtown bus** der Bus Richtung Stadtzentrum IV 1 (14/175)
**drama** ['drɑːmə]
**1.** Schauspiel, darstellende Kunst I
**2.** Fernsehspiel; Drama IV 4 (78)

**drank** [dræŋk] *siehe* **drink**
**draw** [drɔː], **drew, drawn**
**1.** zeichnen III
**2. draw conclusions** Schlüsse ziehen, schlussfolgern IV 4 (86)
**draw** [drɔː] Unentschieden III
**Our last match was a draw, 2–2.** *(you say: two all)* Unser letztes Spiel war ein Unentschieden, 2:2. III
**drawing** ['drɔːɪŋ] Zeichnung III
**drawn** [drɔːn] *siehe* **draw**
**dream (of, about)** [driːm] träumen (von) III
**dream** [driːm] Traum I • **dream house** Traumhaus I
**dress** [dres] Kleid I
**dress code** ['dres kəʊd] Kleiderordnung IV 3 (56)
**dressed** [drest]: **get dressed** sich anziehen I
**drew** [druː] *siehe* **draw**
**drink** [drɪŋk] Getränk I
**drink** [drɪŋk], **drank, drunk** trinken I
**drinkable** ['drɪŋkəbl] trinkbar, Trink- IV 4 (87)
**drive** [draɪv], **drove, driven** *(ein Auto / mit dem Auto)* fahren II
**drive** [draɪv] (Auto-)Fahrt III
**driven** ['drɪvn] *siehe* **drive**
**driver** ['draɪvə] Fahrer/in II
**drop (-pp-)** [drɒp]
**1.** fallen lassen I
°**2.** sich fallen lassen
**3. drop sb. off** jn. absetzen *(aussteigen lassen)* IV 4 (79)
**drove** [drəʊv] *siehe* **drive**
**drug** [drʌg] Droge, Rauschgift; Medikament IV 1 (26) • **be on drugs** Drogen nehmen IV 1 (26)
**drum** [drʌm] Trommel III • **drums** *(pl)* [drʌmz] Schlagzeug III • **play the drums** Schlagzeug spielen III
**drunk** [drʌŋk] *siehe* **drink**
**drunk** [drʌŋk] betrunken IV 2 (51)
°**dumb** [dʌm] dumm
**during** *(prep)* ['djuərɪŋ] während IV 4 (76)
► S.191 German 'während'
**dustbin** ['dʌstbɪn] Mülltonne II
**DVD** [ˌdiː viː' diː] DVD I

## E

**each** [iːtʃ] jeder, jede, jedes (einzelne) I • **each other** [iːtʃ_'ʌðə] einander, sich (gegenseitig) III
**ear** [ɪə] Ohr I
**earache** ['ɪəreɪk] Ohrenschmerzen II

**early** ['ɜːli] früh I
**earn** [ɜːn] verdienen IV 1 (26)
**earring** ['ɪərɪŋ] Ohrring I
**earth** [ɜːθ] Erde IV 2 (34/180) • **on earth** auf der Erde IV 2 (34/180)
**earthquake** ['ɜːθkweɪk] Erdbeben IV 2 (34)
**east** [iːst] Osten; nach Osten; östlich III
**eastbound** ['iːstbaʊnd] Richtung Osten III
**Easter** ['iːstə] Ostern; Oster- IV 3 (56)
**easy** ['iːzi] leicht, einfach I
**easy-going** [ˌiːzi'gəʊɪŋ] gelassen, locker III
**eat** [iːt], **ate, eaten** essen I
**eaten** ['iːtn] *siehe* **eat**
**editor** ['edɪtə] Redakteur/in III
°**letter to the editor** Leserbrief
**education** [ˌedʒʊ'keɪʃn] Bildung IV 4 (91)
**egg** [eg] Ei II
**elect sb. sth.** [ɪ'lekt] jn. zu etwas wählen IV 3 (68)
**election** [ɪ'lekʃn] Wahl *(von Kandidaten bei einer Abstimmung)* IV 3 (68/188)
**electric** [ɪ'lektrɪk] elektrisch, Elektro- III
**electricity** [ɪˌlek'trɪsəti] Strom, Elektrizität III
**electronic** [ɪˌlek'trɒnɪk] elektronisch III
**elementary school** [ˌelɪ'mentri skuːl] *(USA) Grundschule für 6- bis 11-Jährige* IV 3 (56)
**elephant** ['elɪfənt] Elefant I
°**elevated train** ['elɪveɪtɪd] Hochbahn
**elevator** ['elɪveɪtə] *(AE)* Fahrstuhl, Aufzug II
**else** [els]: **anything else** irgendetwas anderes IV 1 (15) • **anything else?** sonst noch etwas? IV 1 (15/176) **anybody else?** ... sonst noch jemand? IV 1 (15/176) • °**anywhere else** irgendwo sonst • **somebody else** jemand anders IV 1 (15/176) **somewhere else** woanders IV 1 (15/176) • **what else?** was (sonst) noch? IV 1 (15/176) • **who else?** wen (sonst) noch? IV 1 (15/176)
► S.176 ... else
**e-mail** ['iːmeɪl] E-Mail I
**embarrassed** [ɪm'bærəst]: **I'm embarrassed.** Es ist mir peinlich. IV 3 (69)
°**empanadas** *(pl)* [empə'nɑːdəz] gefüllte Teigtaschen
**empty** ['empti] leer I
°**encyclopedia** [ɪnˌsaɪklə'piːdiə] Enzyklopädie, Lexikon

**end** [end] enden; beenden III
**°end up** enden
**end** [end] Ende, Schluss I • **at the end (of)** am Ende (von) I • **in the end** schließlich, zum Schluss III
**ending** ['endɪŋ] Ende, (Ab-)Schluss *(einer Geschichte, eines Films usw.)* III
**endless** ['endləs] endlos IV 2 (42)
**enemy** ['enəmi] Feind/in II
**engine** ['endʒɪn] Motor IV 2 (49)
**search engine** Suchmaschine *(im Internet)* IV 4 (81)
**engineer** [ˌendʒɪ'nɪə] Ingenieur/in II
**English** ['ɪŋglɪʃ] Englisch; englisch I
**enjoy** [ɪn'dʒɔɪ] genießen II • **Enjoy yourself.** Viel Spaß / Amüsier dich gut! III
**enough** [ɪ'nʌf] genug I
**°Enough's enough.** Jetzt reicht es!
**enter** ['entə]
**1.** betreten; eintreten (in) III
**°2.** einreisen
**°entertainment** [ˌentə'teɪnmənt] Unterhaltung
**entry** ['entri] Eintrag, Eintragung *(im Wörterbuch/Tagebuch)* III
**°episode** ['epɪsəʊd] Episode
**equipment** [ɪ'kwɪpmənt] Ausrüstung III
**eraser** [ɪ'reɪsər] *(AE)* Radiergummi IV 1 (20)
**escape (from sb./sth.)** [ɪ'skeɪp] fliehen (vor jm./aus etwas); entkommen III
**especially** [ɪ'speʃəli] besonders IV 4 (89)
**essay (about, on)** ['eseɪ] Aufsatz (über) I
**etc.** [et'setərə] und so weiter (usw.) IV 3 (56/186)
**ethnic** ['eθnɪk] ethnisch, Volks- IV 2 (37)
**euro (€)** ['jʊərəʊ] Euro I
**even** ['i:vn]
**1.** sogar II • **even if** sogar wenn IV 4 (90)
**2. not even** (noch) nicht einmal III
**He didn't even open the letter.** Er hat den Brief nicht einmal geöffnet. III
**evening** ['i:vnɪŋ] Abend I • **in the evening** abends, am Abend I
**on Friday evening** freitagabends, am Freitagabend I
**event** [ɪ'vent] Ereignis; Veranstaltung IV 3 (55)
**ever?** ['evə] je? / jemals? / schon mal? II
**every** ['evri] jeder, jede, jedes I
**everybody** ['evribɒdi] jeder, alle II
**everyday** *(adj)* ['evrideɪ] Alltags-; alltägliche(r, s) III
**everyone** ['evrɪwʌn] jeder, alle IV 2 (34/180)
**everything** ['evriθɪŋ] alles I
**everywhere** ['evriweə] überall III
**exact** [ɪg'zækt] exakt, genau IV 4 (86)
**exactly** [ɪg'zæktli] genau III
**example** [ɪg'zɑ:mpl] Beispiel III
**for example** zum Beispiel III
**excellent** ['eksələnt] ausgezeichnet, hervorragend IV 3 (56)
► S.185 US school grades
**except** [ɪk'sept] außer IV 4 (49)
**°exchange ideas** [ɪks'tʃeɪndʒ] Ideen austauschen
**exchange student** [ɪks'tʃeɪndʒ ˌstju:dnt] Austauschschüler/in III
**excited** [ɪk'saɪtɪd] begeistert, aufgeregt III
**exciting** [ɪk'saɪtɪŋ] aufregend, spannend I
**Excuse me, ...** [ɪk'skju:z mi:] Entschuldigung, ... / Entschuldigen Sie, ... I
**exercise** ['eksəsaɪz]
**1.** Übung, Aufgabe I
**2.** *(no pl)* (körperliche) Bewegung, Training IV 3 (58)
**exercise book** ['eksəsaɪz bʊk] Schulheft, Übungsheft I
**°exist** [ɪg'zɪst] existieren
**expect** [ɪk'spekt] erwarten III
**expensive** [ɪk'spensɪv] teuer I
**experience** [ɪk'spɪəriəns] Erfahrung(en), Erlebnis IV 2 (37) • **in my experience** meiner Erfahrung nach IV 2 (37)
**experience** [ɪk'spɪəriəns] erfahren, erleben IV 2 (37)
**explain sth. to sb.** [ɪk'spleɪn] jm. etwas erklären, erläutern II
**explanation** [ˌeksplə'neɪʃn] Erklärung II
**explore** [ɪk'splɔ:] erkunden, erforschen I
**explorer** [ɪk'splɔ:rə] Entdecker/in, Forscher/in II
**explosion** [ɪk'spləʊʒn] Explosion IV 4 (79)
**extra** ['ekstrə] zusätzlich I
**extracurricular activities** (*kurz:* **extracurriculars)** [ˌekstrəkə'rɪkjələz] *schulische Angebote außerhalb des regulären Unterrichts, oft als Arbeitsgemeinschaften* IV 3 (56)
**°extraordinaire** [ɪkˌstrɔ:dɪ'neə] unvergleichlich
**°extreme** [ɪk'stri:m] extrem, äußerst
**eye** [aɪ] Auge I
**°eyed** [aɪd]**: black eyed** mit schwarzen Augen

## F

**face** [feɪs] Gesicht I
**fact** [fækt] Tatsache, Fakt III
**factory** ['fæktri] Fabrik II
**failure** *(n)* ['feɪljə] ungenügend *(USA, Schulnote)* IV 3 (56)
► S.185 US school grades
**fair** [feə] fair, gerecht II
**°fair: °county fair** ['kaʊnti feə] Landwirtschaftsschau
**faithfully** ['feɪθfəli]**: Yours faithfully** Mit freundlichen Grüßen *(Briefschluss bei namentlich unbekanntem Empfänger)* IV 2 (45)
**fall** [fɔ:l]**, fell, fallen** fallen, stürzen; hinfallen II • **fall down** hinfallen II • **fall in love (with sb.)** sich verlieben (in jn.) IV 3 (68) • **fall off** herunterfallen (von) II
**fallen** ['fɔ:lən] *siehe* **fall**
**false** [fɔ:ls] falsch IV 1 (28)
**family** ['fæməli] Familie I • **family tree** (Familien-)Stammbaum I
**famous (for)** ['feɪməs] berühmt (für, wegen) II
**fan** [fæn] Fan I
**fantastic** [fæn'tæstɪk] fantastisch, toll I
**far** [fɑ:] weit (entfernt) II • **so far** bisher, bis jetzt IV 4 (80)
**farm** [fɑ:m] Bauernhof, Farm II
**farmer** ['fɑ:mə] Bauer/Bäuerin, Landwirt/in; (Fisch-)Züchter/in III
**farmhouse** ['fɑ:mhaʊs] Farmhaus, Bauernhaus IV 3 (55)
**farming** ['fɑ:mɪŋ] Landwirtschaft IV 2 (36)
**fashion** ['fæʃn] Mode II
**fast** [fɑ:st] schnell II • **fast food** [ˌfɑ:st 'fu:d] Fastfood III
**fat** [fæt] fett IV 2 (51)
**father** ['fɑ:ðə] Vater I
**°fatty** ['fæti] *(infml)* Dickerchen
**fault** [fɔ:lt]**: It's not my fault.** Es ist nicht meine Schuld. III
**favour** ['feɪvə]**: Would you do me a favour?** Würdest du mir einen Gefallen tun? IV 3 (69)
**favourite** ['feɪvərɪt] Lieblings- I
**my favourite colour** meine Lieblingsfarbe I
**February** ['februəri] Februar I
**fed** [fed] *siehe* **feed** • **be fed up (with sth.)** [ˌfed_'ʌp] die Nase voll haben (von etwas) II
**feed** [fi:d]**, fed, fed** füttern I
**feel** [fi:l]**, felt, felt** sich fühlen; fühlen; sich anfühlen II • **I feel sick.** Mir ist schlecht. IV 1 (26)
**°feel cared about** sich behütet/be-

schützt fühlen • °**feel sth. towards sb.** etwas für jn. empfinden
**feeling** ['fi:lɪŋ] Gefühl III
**feet** [fi:t] *Plural von „foot"*
**fell** [fel] *siehe* **fall**
**felt** [felt] *siehe* **feel**
**felt tip** ['felt tɪp] Filzstift I
**female** ['fi:meɪl] weiblich III
**fence** [fens] Zaun IV 2 (38)
**ferry** ['feri] Fähre III
**festival** ['festɪvl] Fest, Festival, Festspiele III
**few** [fju:]: **a few** ein paar, einige II
► S.182 little („wenig") – few („wenige")
**fiddle** ['fɪdl] *(infml)* Fiedel, Geige III • **play the fiddle** Geige spielen III
**field** [fi:ld] Feld, Acker, Weide II
**in the field** auf dem Feld II
**fight (for)** [faɪt], **fought, fought** kämpfen (für, um) III
**fight** [faɪt] Kampf; Schlägerei IV 2 (50)
**file** [faɪl]
°**1.** (Akten-)Ordner, Hefter
**2. background file** *etwa:* Hintergrundinformation(en) II • **grammar file** *Grammatikanhang* I
**skills file** *Anhang mit Lern- und Arbeitstechniken* I • **sound file** Tondatei, Soundfile III
°**fill in** [ˌfɪl_'ɪn]
**1.** einsetzen
**2.** ausfüllen
°**filling** ['fɪlɪŋ] (Brot-)Belag
**film** [fɪlm] Film I • **film director** Regisseur/in IV 2 (47) • **film star** Filmstar I • **film studio** Filmstudio III
**film** [fɪlm] filmen III
**film-maker** ['fɪlm meɪkə] Filmemacher/in III
**final** ['faɪnl] letzte(r, s); End- III
**final score** Endstand III
**final** ['faɪnl] Finale, Endspiel III
°**finally** ['faɪnəli] schließlich
°**financial** [faɪ'nænʃl] finanziell, Finanz-
**find** [faɪnd], **found, found** finden I
**find out (about)** herausfinden (über) I
**finder** ['faɪndə] Finder I
**fine** [faɪn]
**1.** gut, schön; in Ordnung II
**2.** *(gesundheitlich)* gut II
**I'm/He's fine.** Es geht mir/ihm gut. II
**finger** ['fɪŋgə] Finger I
**finish** ['fɪnɪʃ] beenden, zu Ende machen; enden I
**fire** ['faɪə] Feuer, Brand II • **fire safety** Verhalten im Brandfall IV 1 (23) • **fire station** Feuerwache IV 1 (15) **put out a fire** ein Feuer löschen IV 1 (15)
**firefighter** ['faɪəfaɪtə] Feuerwehrfrau, -mann IV 1 (15)
**fireman/-woman** ['faɪəmən, 'faɪəˌwʊmən] Feuerwehrmann/-frau II
**first** [fɜ:st]
**1.** erste(r, s) I
**2.** zuerst, als Erstes I
**at first** zuerst, am Anfang IV 3 (55)
**be first** der/die Erste sein I • **first floor** erster Stock *(BE)* / Erdgeschoss *(AE)* IV 1 (16/176) • **first half** erste Halbzeit III
► S.176 floor
**fish** [fɪʃ] fischen, angeln III
**fish**, *pl* **fish** [fɪʃ] Fisch I
**fist** [fɪst] Faust IV 3 (70)
**fit (-tt-)** [fɪt] passen I • **fit in** hineinpassen; sich einfügen, sich anpassen IV 2 (37)
**fitness** ['fɪtnəs] Fitness IV 3 (58)
**flash** [flæʃ] Lichtblitz III
**flat** [flæt] Wohnung I
**flat screen** ['flæt skri:n] Flachbildschirm IV 4 (84)
**flew** [flu:] *siehe* **fly**
**flight** [flaɪt] Flug II • **a 14-hour flight** ein 14-stündiger Flug, ein 14-Stunden-Flug III
**floor** [flɔ:]
**1.** Fußboden I
**2.** Stock(werk) IV 1 (16) • **first floor** erster Stock *(BE)* / Erdgeschoss *(AE)* IV 1 (16/176) • **ground floor** *(BE)* Erdgeschoss IV 1 (16/176) • **on the second floor** im zweiten Stock *(BE)* / im ersten Stock *(AE)* IV 1 (16/176)
► S.176 floor
°**flow chart** ['fləʊ tʃɑ:t] Flussdiagramm
**flown** [fləʊn] *siehe* **fly**
**flute** [flu:t] Querflöte III
**fly** [flaɪ], **flew, flown** fliegen II
**fog** [fɒg] Nebel II
**foggy** ['fɒgi] neblig II
**folk (music)** ['fəʊk ˌmju:zɪk] Folk *(englische, schottische, irische oder nordamerikanische Volksmusik des 20. Jahrhunderts)* III
**follow** ['fɒləʊ] folgen; verfolgen I
°**following** ['fɒləʊɪŋ]: **the following ...** die folgenden ...
**food** [fu:d]
**1.** Essen; Lebensmittel I
**2.** Futter I
**foot** [fʊt], *pl* **feet** [fi:t] Fuß I; Fuß *(Längenmaß: 30, 48 cm)* IV Intro (10) • °**on foot** zu Fuß
**football** ['fʊtbɔ:l] Fußball I • **football boots** Fußballschuhe, -stiefel I
**for** [fə, fɔ:] für I • **for breakfast/lunch/dinner** zum Frühstück/Mittagessen/Abendbrot I • **for example** zum Beispiel III • **for lots of reasons** aus vielen Gründen I • **for miles** meilenweit II
**for sale** *(auf Schild)* zu verkaufen IV Intro (9/173) • **for the first time** zum ersten Mal IV 4 (91) • **for 20 minutes** seit 20 Minuten; 20 Minuten lang IV 4 (79) • **for three days** drei Tage (lang) I • **just for fun** nur zum Spaß I • **What for?** Wofür? II • **What's for homework?** Was haben wir als Hausaufgabe auf? I
► S.191 German 'seit'
°**force** [fɔ:s] zwingen
**foreground** ['fɔ:graʊnd] Vordergrund II
**foreign** ['fɒrən] ausländisch, fremd IV 3 (57) • **foreign language** Fremdsprache IV 3 (57)
**forest** ['fɒrɪst] Wald II
°**forever** [fə'revə] für immer
**forgave** [fə'geɪv] *siehe* **forgive**
**forget (-tt-)** [fə'get], **forgot, forgotten** vergessen I
**forgive** [fə'gɪv], **forgave, forgiven** vergeben, verzeihen IV Intro (10)
**forgiven** [fə'gɪvn] *siehe* **forgive**
**forgot** [fə'gɒt] *siehe* **forget**
**forgotten** [fə'gɒtn] *siehe* **forget**
**fork** [fɔ:k] Gabel III
**form** [fɔ:m]
**1.** (Schul-)Klasse I • **form teacher** Klassenlehrer/in I
°**2.** Form
°**form** [fɔ:m] bilden
°**formal letter** ['fɔ:ml] förmlicher Brief
**fortunately** ['fɔ:tʃənətli] zum Glück IV 4 (80)
**forward** ['fɔ:wəd]: **look forward to sth.** sich auf etwas freuen IV Intro (8)
**fought** [fɔ:t] *siehe* **fight**
**found** [faʊnd] *siehe* **find**
**found** [faʊnd] gründen IV 3 (54)
**fox** [fɒks] Fuchs II
**free** [fri:]
**1.** frei I • **free time** Freizeit, freie Zeit I
**2.** kostenlos I
°**freedom** ['fri:dəm] Freiheit
**French** [frentʃ] Französisch I
**French fries** *(AE)* [fraɪz] Pommes Frites IV 1 (20)
**fresh** [freʃ] frisch IV 3 (58)

**Friday** ['fraɪdeɪ, 'fraɪdi] Freitag I
**fridge** [frɪdʒ] Kühlschrank I
**friend** [frend] Freund/in I
**friendliness** ['frendlinəs] Freundlichkeit IV 3 (66)
**friendly** ['frendli] freundlich III
**fries** [fraɪz]: **French fries** *(AE)* Pommes Frites IV 1 (20)
**frog** [frɒg] Frosch II
**from** [frəm, frɒm]
**1.** aus I
**2.** von I
**from all over the UK/the world/England** aus dem gesamten Vereinigten Königreich / aus der ganzen Welt / aus ganz England III
**from Monday to Friday** von Montag bis Freitag III • **I'm from ...** Ich komme aus ... / Ich bin aus ... I
**Where are you from?** Wo kommst du her?
**front** [frʌnt]: **in front of** vor *(räumlich)* I • **front door** [ˌfrʌnt 'dɔː] Wohnungstür, Haustür I • °**front inside cover** [ˌfrʌnt‿ɪnsaɪd 'kʌvə] Buchumschlaginnenseite
**fruit** [fruːt] Obst, Früchte; Frucht I
**fruit salad** ['fruːt ˌsæləd] Obstsalat I
**full** [fʊl] voll I
**fun** [fʌn] Spaß I • **have fun** Spaß haben, sich amüsieren I • **Have fun!** Viel Spaß! I • **just for fun** nur zum Spaß I • **Riding is fun.** Reiten macht Spaß. I
**funny** ['fʌni] witzig, komisch I

## G

**game** [geɪm] Spiel I
°**gap** [gæp] Lücke
**garage** ['gærɑːʒ] Garage II
**garbage** ['gɑːrbɪdʒ] *(AE)* Müll, Abfall IV 1 (20)
**garden** ['gɑːdn] Garten I
**gardener** ['gɑːdnə] Gärtner/in IV 2 (38)
**gas** [gæs]
**1.** Gas IV 4 (80)
**2.** *(AE)* Benzin IV Intro (10) • **gas station** *(AE)* Tankstelle IV Intro (10)
**gate** [geɪt]
**1.** Tor III
**2.** Flugsteig III
°**gateway (to)** ['geɪtweɪ] Tor (zu), Zugang (zu)
**gave** [geɪv] *siehe* **give**
**gear** [gɪə] Ausrüstung IV Intro (8)
**general** ['dʒenrəl] allgemeine(r,s) III
**geography** [dʒi'ɒgrəfi] Geografie, Erdkunde I
**German** ['dʒɜːmən] Deutsch; deutsch; Deutsche(r) I
**Germany** ['dʒɜːməni] Deutschland I
**get (-tt-)** [get], **got, got**
**1.** bekommen, kriegen II
**2.** holen, besorgen II
**3.** gelangen, (hin)kommen I
**4. get angry/hot/...** wütend/heiß/... werden II
**5. get off (the train/bus)** (aus dem Zug/Bus) aussteigen I • **get on (the train/bus)** (in den Zug/Bus) einsteigen I
**6. get up** aufstehen I
**get a cab** ein Taxi nehmen IV 1 (27)
**get dressed** sich anziehen I • **get involved** sich engagieren (für, bei); sich beteiligen (an) IV 3 (57) • **get on well/badly with sb.** sich gut/schlecht mit jm. verstehen IV 2 (37)
**get ready (for)** sich fertig machen (für), sich vorbereiten (auf) I • **get sth. off the ground** etwas auf den Weg bringen; etwas auf die Beine stellen III • **get things ready** Dinge fertig machen, vorbereiten I • **get to know sb.** jn. kennenlernen IV 2 (50) • °**Let's get out of here.** Lass uns abhauen.
**getting by in English** [ˌgetɪŋ 'baɪ] *etwa:* auf Englisch zurechtkommen I
**ghost** [gəʊst] Geist, Gespenst II
°**giant** ['dʒaɪənt] riesig, Riesen-
**gig** [gɪg] *(infml)* Gig, Auftritt III
**do a gig** einen Auftritt haben, ein Konzert geben III
**giraffe** [dʒə'rɑːf] Giraffe II
**girl** [gɜːl] Mädchen I
**girlfriend** ['gɜːlfrend] (feste) Freundin IV 2 (50/184)
**give** [gɪv], **gave, given** geben I
**give up** aufgeben, resignieren IV 2 (50) • °**give a talk** einen Vortrag halten • °**give sb. problems** Probleme/ Schwierigkeiten bereiten
**given** ['gɪvn] *siehe* **give**
**glad** [glæd] froh, dankbar III
**glass** [glɑːs] Glas I • **a glass of water** ein Glas Wasser I
**glasses** *(pl)* ['glɑːsɪz] (eine) Brille I
**glue** [gluː] (auf-, ein)kleben II
**glue** [gluː] Klebstoff I • **glue stick** Klebestift I
**go** [gəʊ], **went, gone** gehen I; fahren II • **go by car/train/bike/...** mit dem Auto/Zug/Rad/... fahren II • **go for a walk** spazieren gehen, einen Spaziergang machen II
**go home** nach Hause gehen I
°**go in** hineingehören • **go on**
**1.** weitermachen I, **2.** weiterreden III • **Go on.** Mach/Erzähl weiter. I
**go on a trip** einen Ausflug machen II • **go on holiday** in Urlaub fahren II • **go riding** reiten gehen I
**go shopping** einkaufen gehen I
**go surfing** wellenreiten gehen, surfen gehen II • **go swimming** schwimmen gehen I • **go to bed** ins Bett gehen I • **go to the cinema** ins Kino gehen II • **go together** zusammenpassen, -gehören II • °**go out** ausgehen, eine Verabredung haben • **go well** gut (ver)laufen, gutgehen III • **go with** gehören zu, passen zu III
**coffee to go** Kaffee zum Mitnehmen IV 1 (17/177) • °**I just go for it.** Ich handle/reagiere einfach nur.
**Let's go.** Auf geht's! I • °**There you go.** *(infml) etwa:* So, das hätten wir.
**goal** [gəʊl] Tor *(im Sport)* III • **score a goal** ein Tor schießen, einen Treffer erzielen III
**goalkeeper** ['gəʊlkiːpə] Torwart, Torfrau III
°**going west** *Besiedlung des Westens der USA im 19. Jahrhundert*
**gold** [gəʊld] Gold IV 2 (34/180)
**golden** ['gəʊldən] goldene(r,s) IV 2 (34)
°**gold rush** ['gəʊld rʌʃ] Goldrausch
**golf** [gɒlf] Golf III
**gone** [gɒn] *siehe* **go**
°**gonna** ['gɒnə] *(infml) going to*
**good** [gʊd]
**1.** gut I
**2.** brav II
**Good afternoon.** Guten Tag. *(nachmittags)* I • **Good luck (with ...)!** Viel Glück (bei/mit ...)! I
**Good morning.** Guten Morgen. I
**Good to have you back.** Schön, dass du wieder da bist. IV Intro (8)
**be good at sth.** gut in etwas sein; etwas gut können III • °**The money was good.** Wir haben gut verdient.
► S.185 US school grades
**Goodbye.** [ˌgʊd'baɪ] Auf Wiedersehen. I • **say goodbye** sich verabschieden I
**got** [gɒt] *siehe* **get**
**got** [gɒt]: **I've got ...** Ich habe ... I
**I haven't got a chair.** Ich habe keinen Stuhl. I
**government** ['gʌvənmənt]
**1.** Regierung IV 2 (38)
°**2.** *als Schulfach in den USA etwa:* Staatskunde

**governor** ['gʌvənə] Gouverneur/in *(Oberhaupt eines US-Bundesstaates)* IV 2 (34)
**grab sth. (-bb-)** [græb] schnappen IV 1 (17)
**grade** [greɪd]
**1.** Klasse, Jahrgangsstufe IV Intro (9)
**2.** (Schul-)Note, Zensur IV 3 (56)
► S.185 US school grades
°**grader** ['greɪdə]**: 11th-graders** 11-Klässler
**grammar** ['græmə] Grammatik I
**grammar file** *Grammatikanhang* I
**grand** [grænd] eindrucksvoll, beeindruckend IV Intro (10)
**grandad** ['grændæd] Opa III
**grandchild** ['græntʃaɪld], *pl* **grandchildren** Enkel/in I
**grandfather** ['grænfɑ:ðə] Großvater I
**grandma** ['grænmɑ:] Oma I
**grandmother** ['grænmʌðə] Großmutter I
**grandpa** ['grænpɑ:] Opa I
**grandparents** ['grænpeərənts] Großeltern I
**granny** ['græni] Oma II
**grape** [greɪp] Weintraube IV 2 (36)
**grass** [grɑ:s] Gras, Rasen IV Intro (9)
**cut the grass** Rasen mähen IV Intro (9)
**great** [greɪt] großartig, toll I
**great-grandfather** [ˌgreɪt 'grænfɑ:ðə] Urgroßvater III
**great-grandmother** [ˌgreɪt 'grænmʌðə] Urgroßmutter III
**green** [gri:n] grün I
°**greeting** ['gri:tɪŋ] Gruß, Begrüßung
**grew** [gru:] *siehe* **grow**
**grey** [greɪ] grau II
**ground** [graʊnd] (Erd-)Boden III
**ground floor** *(BE)* Erdgeschoss IV 1 (16/176) • °**Ground Zero** [ˌgraʊnd 'zɪərəʊ] Bodennullpunkt *(Bezeichnung für das zerstörte World Trade Center; ursprünglich: Explosionsstelle einer Bombe oder Rakete über dem Boden)* • **get sth. off the ground** etwas auf den Weg bringen; etwas auf die Beine stellen III
► S.176 floor
**grounded** ['graʊndɪd]**: be grounded** Ausgehverbot/Hausarrest haben III
**group** [gru:p] Gruppe I • **group word** Oberbegriff II
°**group** gruppieren
**grow** [grəʊ], **grew, grown**
**1.** *(Getreide usw.)* anbauen, anpflanzen II
**2. grow up** [ˌgrəʊ‿'ʌp] erwachsen werden; aufwachsen III
**grown** [grəʊn] *siehe* **grow**
**grumble** ['grʌmbl] murren, nörgeln I
°**guard** [gɑ:d]**: National Guard** Nationalgarde
**guess** [ges] raten, erraten, schätzen III • **Guess what!** [ˌges 'wɒt] Stell dir vor! / Stellt euch vor! IV Intro (6)
**guest** [gest] Gast I
**guide** [gaɪd]**: (tour) guide** (Fremden-)Führer/in, Reiseleiter/in IV 3 (67)
**guilty** ['gɪlti] schuldbewusst; schuldig IV 2 (50)
**guinea pig** ['gɪni pɪg] Meerschweinchen I
**guitar** [gɪ'tɑ:] Gitarre I • **play the guitar** Gitarre spielen I
**gun** [gʌn] Gewehr IV 1 (27)
**guy** [gaɪ] *(infml)* Typ, Kerl IV 1 (15)
**guys** *(pl)* [gaɪz] *(AE, infml)* Leute III
**gym** [dʒɪm] Sporthalle, Turnhalle; Fitnessstudio IV 3 (56)

## H

**had** [hæd] *siehe* **have** *und* **have got**
**hair** *(no pl)* [heə] Haar, Haare I
**hairdresser** ['heədresə] Friseur/in III
**half** [hɑ:f], *pl* **halves** [hɑ:vz] Hälfte III • **first half** erste Halbzeit III
**half of** die Hälfte der/des IV 2 (38)
**half** [hɑ:f]**: half an hour** eine halbe Stunde III • **half past 11** halb zwölf (11.30/23.30) I • **three and a half days** dreieinhalb Tage IV Intro (8)
**half-pipe** ['hɑ:fpaɪp] Halfpipe III
**half-time** [ˌhɑ:f 'taɪm] Halbzeit(pause) III
**hall** [hɔ:l] Flur, Diele I • **study hall** ['stʌdɪ hɔ:l] *Zeit zum selbstständigen Arbeiten/Lernen in der Schule* IV 3 (56)
**halves** [hɑ:vz] *Plural von „half"*
**hamburger** ['hæmbɜ:gə] Hamburger I
**hamster** ['hæmstə] Hamster I
**hand** [hænd] Hand I
**handball** ['hændbɔ:l] Handball III
**hang** [hæŋ], **hung, hung: hang out (with friends)** *(infml)* rumhängen, abhängen (mit Freunden/Freundinnen) III
**happen (to)** ['hæpən] geschehen, passieren (mit) I
**happiness** ['hæpinəs] Glück IV 3 (66)
**happy** ['hæpi] glücklich, froh I
**Happy birthday.** Herzlichen Glückwunsch zum Geburtstag. I
**happy ending** Happyend II
**harbour** ['hɑ:bə] Hafen II
**hard** [hɑ:d] hart; schwer, schwierig II • **work hard** hart arbeiten II
**hard-working** [ˌhɑ:d 'wɜ:kɪŋ] fleißig, tüchtig III
**hat** [hæt] Hut II
**hate** [heɪt] hassen, gar nicht mögen I
**have** [həv, hæv], **had, had** haben, besitzen II • **have a baby** ein Baby/Kind bekommen II • **have a bath** baden, ein Bad nehmen II
**have a cold** erkältet sein, eine Erkältung haben II • **have a crush on sb.** in jn. verknallt sein III
**have a look at sth.** sich etwas ansehen, einen Blick werfen auf etwas IV 2 (36) • **have a picnic** ein Picknick machen I • **have a sauna** in die Sauna gehen II • **have a shower** (sich) duschen I • **have a sore throat** Halsschmerzen haben II • **have a temperature** Fieber haben II • **have breakfast/dinner** frühstücken / Abendbrot essen I
**have ... for breakfast** ... zum Frühstück essen/trinken I • **have fun** Spaß haben, sich amüsieren I
**have sleepovers** Schlafpartys veranstalten III • **have to do** tun müssen I • **Good to have you back.** Schön, dass du wieder da bist. IV Intro (8)
**have got: I've got ...** [aɪv 'gɒt] Ich habe ... I • **I haven't got a chair.** Ich habe keinen Stuhl. I
**he** [hi:] er I
**head** [hed] Kopf I • **head teacher** Schulleiter/in III
**headache** ['hedeɪk] Kopfschmerzen II
**heading** ['hedɪŋ] Überschrift, Titel IV 4 (92)
**headless** ['hedləs] kopflos IV 2 (42)
**headline** ['hedlaɪn] Schlagzeile IV 4 (92)
**headphones** *(pl)* ['hedfəʊnz] Kopfhörer III
**health** [helθ] Gesundheit; Gesundheitslehre IV 3 (56)
**healthy** ['helθi] gesund II
**hear** [hɪə], **heard, heard** hören I
**heard** [hɜ:d] *siehe* **hear**
**heart** [hɑ:t] Herz II
**heaven** ['hevn] Himmel *(im religiösen Sinn)* IV 3 (69)
**hedgehog** ['hedʒhɒg] Igel II
**held** [held] *siehe* **hold**
**helicopter** ['helɪkɒptə] Hubschrauber, Helikopter II
**Hello.** [hə'ləʊ] Hallo. / Guten Tag. I

**helmet** ['helmɪt] Helm III
**help** [help] helfen I • **Can I help you?** Kann ich Ihnen helfen? / Was kann ich für Sie tun? *(im Geschäft)* I
**help** [help] Hilfe I
**helpful** ['helpfl] nützlich, hilfreich IV 3 (65)
**helpless** ['helpləs] hilflos IV 2 (42)
**her** [hə, hɜː]
1. ihr, ihre I
2. sie; ihr I
**here** [hɪə]
1. hier I
2. hierher I
**Here you are.** Bitte sehr. / Hier bitte. I
**hers** [hɜːz] ihrer, ihre, ihrs II
**herself** [hə'self, hɜː'self] sich (selbst) III
**Hey!** [heɪ] Hallo! III
**Hi!** [haɪ] Hallo! I • **Say hi to Dilip for me.** Grüß Dilip von mir. I
**hid** [hɪd] *siehe* **hide**
**hidden** ['hɪdn] *siehe* **hide**
**hide** [haɪd], **hid, hidden** sich verstecken; *(etwas)* verstecken I
**high** [haɪ] hoch III • **high school** ['haɪ skuːl] *(USA) Schule für 14-18-Jährige* IV Intro (10)
°**highlighted** ['haɪlaɪtɪd] hervorgehoben
**highway** ['haɪweɪ] *(USA) Fernstraße (oft mit vier oder mehr Spuren)* IV 4 (10)
**hijacker** ['haɪdʒækə] (Flugzeug-)Entführer/in IV 1 (15)
**hike** [haɪk] wandern IV Intro (8)
**hike** [haɪk] Wanderung, Marsch IV Intro (8/173) • **go on a hike** wandern gehen IV Intro (8/173)
**hill** [hɪl] Hügel II
**hilly** ['hɪli] hügelig III
**him** [hɪm] ihn; ihm I
**himself** [hɪm'self] sich (selbst) III
**hip hop** ['hɪp hɒp] Hip Hop III
**hippo** ['hɪpəʊ] Flusspferd II
**his** [hɪz]
1. sein, seine I
2. seiner, seine, seins II
°**Hispanic** [hɪs'pænɪk] *(AE) Bezeichnung für Menschen mit Wurzeln in spanischsprachigen Ländern, besonders in Mittelamerika*
°**historic** [hɪ'stɒrɪk] historisch
**history** ['hɪstri] Geschichte I
°**natural history** Naturkunde
**hit (-tt-)** [hɪt] **hit, hit, hit**
1. schlagen II • °**hit your head** sich den Kopf anschlagen
°2. treffen
**hit** [hɪt] Hit III
°**hi-tech** [ˌhaɪ'tek] Hightech-
**hobby** ['hɒbi] Hobby I
**hockey** ['hɒki] Hockey I • **hockey shoes** Hockeyschuhe I
°**hog** [hɒg] (männliches) Mastschwein
**hold** [həʊld], **held, held** halten II
°**hold on to sth.** sich an etwas festhalten
**hole** [həʊl] Loch IV 3 (56)
**holiday** ['hɒlədeɪ]
1. Feiertag IV 4 (88)
2. **holiday(s)** Ferien I
**holiday flat** Ferienwohnung II
**be on holiday** in Urlaub sein; Ferien haben/machen II • **go on holiday** in Urlaub fahren II • **a two-week holiday** ein zweiwöchiger Urlaub III
**home** [həʊm] Heim, Zuhause I
**at home** daheim, zu Hause I
**come home** nach Hause kommen I • **get home** nach Hause kommen I • **go home** nach Hause gehen I
**homeless** ['həʊmləs] obdachlos IV 2 (34)
**hometown** ['həʊmtaʊn] Heimatstadt, -ort IV Intro (8)
**homework** *(no pl)* ['həʊmwɜːk] Hausaufgabe(n) I • **do homework** die Hausaufgabe(n) machen I
**What's for homework?** Was haben wir als Hausaufgabe auf? I
**Hooray!** [hu'reɪ] Hurra! II
**hop channels** [ˌhɒp 'tʃænəlz] zappen IV 4 (84)
**hope** [həʊp] hoffen II
**hope** [həʊp] Hoffnung III
**horrible** ['hɒrəbl] scheußlich, grauenhaft II
**horse** [hɔːs] Pferd I
**hospital** ['hɒspɪtl] Krankenhaus II
**hostel** ['hɒstl] Herberge, Wohnheim III
°**hostess** ['həʊstes] Gastgeberin *(in USA auch: Frau, die im Restaurant die Gäste empfängt und an ihren Platz führt)*
**hot** [hɒt] heiß I • **hot chocolate** heiße Schokolade I
**hotel** [həʊ'tel] Hotel II
**hotline** ['hɒtlaɪn] Hotline II
**hour** ['aʊə] Stunde II • **half an hour** eine halbe Stunde III • **a 14-hour flight** ein 14-stündiger Flug, ein 14-Stunden-Flug III • **a 24-hour supermarket** ein Supermarkt, der 24 Stunden geöffnet ist III
**hours** *(pl)* ['aʊəz] Öffnungszeiten IV 1 (16)
**house** [haʊs] Haus I • **at the Shaws' house** im Haus der Shaws / bei den Shaws zu Hause I
**how** [haʊ] wie I • **How about ...?** Wie wär's mit ...? III • **How am I doing?** Wie komme ich voran? *(Wie sind meine Fortschritte?)* III
**How are you?** Wie geht es dir/Ihnen/euch? II • **How do you know ...?** Woher weißt/kennst du ...? I • **how long?** Seit wann? / Wie lange? IV 4 (79) • **how many?** wie viele? I • **how much?** wie viel? I • **How much is/are ...?** Was kostet/kosten ...? / Wie viel kostet/kosten ...? I • **How old are you?** Wie alt bist du? I • **how to do sth.** wie man etwas tut / tun kann / tun soll IV Intro (9) • **How was ...?** Wie war ...? I
▶ S.173 Question words + to-infinitive: how to ... / what to ... / ...
°**however** [haʊ'evə] jedoch, aber
°**Hualapai** ['wæləpaɪ] *Indianerstamm im Nordwesten Arizonas, auf der Südseite des Grand Canyon (wörtliche Bedeutung: Volk des hohen Pinienbaums)*
**huge** [hjuːdʒ] riesig, sehr groß III
**human** ['hjuːmən] Menschen-, menschlich IV Intro (9) • °**human history** Menschheitsgeschichte
**hundred** ['hʌndrəd] hundert I
**hung** [hʌŋ] *siehe* **hang**
**hungry** ['hʌŋgri] hungrig III
**I'm hungry.** Ich habe Hunger III
**hunt** [hʌnt] jagen III
**hunt** [hʌnt] Jagd III
**hurry** ['hʌri] eilen; sich beeilen II
**hurry up** sich beeilen I
**hurry** ['hʌri]: **be in a hurry** in Eile sein, es eilig haben I
**hurt** [hɜːt], **hurt, hurt** wehtun; verletzen I
**hurt** [hɜːt] verletzt II
**husband** ['hʌzbənd] Ehemann II
**hutch** [hʌtʃ] (Kaninchen-)Stall I

## I

**I** [aɪ] ich I • **I'm** [aɪm] ich bin I
**I'm from ...** Ich komme aus ... / Ich bin aus ... I • **I'm sorry.** Tut mir leid. / Entschuldigung. I
**ice** [aɪs]: **ice cream** (Speise-)Eis I
**ice hockey** Eishockey III • **ice rink** Schlittschuhbahn II
**idea** [aɪ'dɪə] Idee, Einfall I
**if** [ɪf]
1. falls, wenn II

2. ob II
**as if** als ob IV 4 (90) • **even if** sogar wenn IV 4 (90)
ill [ɪl] krank II
illegal [ɪ'li:gl] illegal, ungesetzlich IV 2 (38)
illness ['ɪlnəs] Krankheit IV 3 (66)
°imaginary [ɪ'mædʒɪnəri] imaginär (*nur in der Vorstellung vorhanden*)
imagination [ɪˌmædʒɪ'neɪʃn] Fantasie, Vorstellung IV 3 (66)
imagine sth. [ɪ'mædʒɪn] sich etwas vorstellen III
immediately [ɪ'mi:diətli] sofort IV 4 (90)
immigrant ['ɪmɪgrənt] Einwanderer/Einwanderin IV 1 (12)
°immigration [ˌɪmɪ'greɪʃn] Einwanderung • **°immigration station** [ˌɪmɪ'greɪʃn steɪʃn] Einwanderungsstation
important [ɪm'pɔ:tnt] wichtig II
impossible [ɪm'pɒsəbl] unmöglich II
impressed [ɪm'prest] beeindruckt IV 4 (80)
improve [ɪm'pru:v] verbessern IV 1 (29)
in [ɪn] in I • **in ... Street** in der ...straße I • **in English** auf Englisch I • **in front of** vor (*räumlich*) I
**in here** hier drinnen I • **in the afternoon** nachmittags, am Nachmittag I • **in the country** auf dem Land II • **in the end** schließlich, zum Schluss III • **in the evening** abends, am Abend I • **in the field** auf dem Feld II • **in the morning** am Morgen, morgens I
**in the photo** auf dem Foto I • **in the picture** auf dem Bild I • **in the world** (auf) der Welt IV 1 (25)
**in the yard** auf dem Hof II • **in time** rechtzeitig II • **in 1919** 1919, im Jahre 1919 IV Intro (8)
°income ['ɪnkʌm] Einkommen
°independence [ˌɪndɪ'pendəns] Unabhängigkeit
°indirectly [ˌɪndə'rektli] indirekt
industrial [ɪn'dʌstriəl] industriell, Industrie- IV 2 (36)
industry ['ɪndəstri] Industrie IV 2 (36)
infinitive [ɪn'fɪnətɪv] Infinitiv (*Grundform des Verbs*) I
°informal letter [ɪn'fɔ:ml] informeller, nicht förmlicher Brief
information (about/on) (*no pl*) [ˌɪnfə'meɪʃn] Information(en) (über) II
inside [ˌɪn'saɪd]
1. innen (drin), drinnen I
2. nach drinnen II
3. innerhalb IV 3 (56)
**4. inside the car** ins Auto (hinein), ins Innere des Autos II
**°inside cover** [ˌɪnsaɪd 'kʌvə] Buchumschlaginnenseite
install [ɪn'stɔ:l] installieren, einrichten II
instant messages (*pl*) [ˌɪnstənt 'mesɪdʒɪz] *Nachrichten, die man im Internet austauscht (in Echtzeit)* III
instructions (*pl*) [ɪn'strʌkʃnz] (Gebrauchs-)Anweisung(en), Anleitung(en) II
instrument ['ɪnstrəmənt] Instrument III
°integration [ɪntəgreɪʃn] *hier:* Integrationspolitik gegen Rassentrennung *(USA, 1960er Jahre)*
interested ['ɪntrəstɪd]: **be interested (in)** interessiert sein (an), sich interessieren (für) III
interesting ['ɪntrəstɪŋ] interessant I
international [ˌɪntə'næʃnəl] international III
internet ['ɪntənet] Internet III
**on the internet** im Internet IV 3 (64) • **surf the internet** im Internet surfen III
°interstate [ˌɪntə'steɪt] *(AE)* Autobahn
interview ['ɪntəvju:] Interview I
interview ['ɪntəvju:] interviewen, befragen II
into ['ɪntə, 'ɪntʊ] in ... (hinein) I
°introduce [ˌɪntrə'dju:s] vorstellen
introduction (to) [ˌɪntrə'dʌkʃn] Einführung (in) III
invitation (to) [ˌɪnvɪ'teɪʃn] Einladung (zu) I
invite (to) [ɪn'vaɪt] einladen (zu) I
involved [ɪn'vɒlvd]: **get involved** sich engagieren (für, bei); sich beteiligen (an) IV 3 (57)
°irregular [ɪ'regjələ] unregelmäßig
is [ɪz] ist I
island ['aɪlənd] Insel II
°issue ['ɪʃu:] (Streit-)Frage, Thema, Angelegenheit
it [ɪt] er/sie/es I • **It's £1.** Er/Sie/Es kostet 1 Pfund. I • **It says here: ...** Hier steht: ... / Es heißt hier: ... II
its [ɪts] sein/seine; ihr/ihre I
itself [ɪt'self] sich (selbst) III

## J

jacket ['dʒækɪt] Jacke, Jackett II
jail [dʒeɪl] Gefängnis IV (50)
jam: **traffic jam** ['træfɪk dʒæm] (Verkehrs-)Stau IV 4 (79)
January ['dʒænjuəri] Januar I
jazz [dʒæz] Jazz III
jealous (of) ['dʒeləs] neidisch (auf); eifersüchtig (auf) III
jealousy ['dʒeləsi] Eifersucht IV 2 (52)
jeans (*pl*) [dʒi:nz] Jeans I
°jerk [dʒɜ:k] Dummkopf
Jewish ['dʒu:ɪʃ] jüdisch IV 1 (17)
job [dʒɒb] Aufgabe, Job I
jobless ['dʒɒbləs] arbeitslos IV 2 (42)
join sb. [dʒɔɪn] sich jm. anschließen; bei jm. mitmachen II
joke [dʒəʊk] Witz I
joke [dʒəʊk] scherzen, Witze machen II
journalist ['dʒɜ:nəlɪst] Journalist/in IV 4 (91)
journey ['dʒɜ:ni] Fahrt, Reise III
°Jr. (junior) ['dʒu:niə] der Jüngere (*bes. in den USA: unterscheidet den Sohn vom gleichnamigen Vater*)
judge (by) [dʒʌdʒ] beurteilen, einschätzen (nach) IV 4 (81)
judo ['dʒu:dəʊ] Judo I • **do judo** Judo machen I
jug [dʒʌg] Krug I • **a jug of milk** ein Krug Milch I
juice [dʒu:s] Saft I
July [dʒu'laɪ] Juli I
jumble sale ['dʒʌmbl seɪl] Wohltätigkeitsbasar I
jump [dʒʌmp] springen II • **jump around** herumspringen III
June [dʒu:n] Juni I
junior ['dʒu:niə] Junioren-, Jugend- I
°jury ['dʒʊəri] Jury
just [dʒʌst]
1. (einfach) nur, bloß I • **It's just a game.** Es ist nur/bloß ein Spiel. III
2. einfach III • **I just can't find my keys.** Ich kann einfach meine Schlüssel nicht finden. III • **Just don't listen to them.** Hör einfach nicht hin. III
3. gerade (eben), soeben II • **just then** genau in dem Moment / gerade dann III
**4. just like your mother** genau wie deine Mutter III
**°5. just off** ... in der Nähe von ...

## K

kangaroo [ˌkæŋgə'ru:] Känguru II
keep [ki:p], **kept, kept** (be)halten; aufbewahren III • **keep in touch** in Verbindung bleiben, Kontakt

halten III • **keep sth. warm/cool/open/...** etwas warm/kühl/offen/... halten II
kept [kept] *siehe* keep
key [ki:] Schlüssel II • **key ring** Schlüsselring II • **key word** Stichwort, Schlüsselwort I
keyboard ['ki:bɔ:d] Keyboard *(elektronisches Tasteninstrument)* III
kick [kɪk] treten IV 1 (27)
kid [kɪd] Kind, Jugendliche(r) I
kill [kɪl] töten I
kilogram (kg) ['kɪləgræm], **kilo** ['ki:ləʊ] Kilogramm, Kilo (kg) III **a 150-kilogram bear** ein 150 Kilogramm schwerer Bär III
kilometre (km) ['kɪləmi:tə] Kilometer III • **a ten-kilometre walk** eine Zehn-Kilometer-Wanderung III
kind (of) [kaɪnd] Art III • **What kind of car ...?** Was für ein Auto ...? III • **°the only museum of its kind** das einzige Museum seiner Art
kindergarten ['kɪndəgɑ:tn] Kindergarten; *(USA)* Vorschule *(für 5- bis 6-Jährige)* IV 3 (56)
king [kɪŋ] König I
kingdom: **the United Kingdom (UK)** [ju,naɪtɪd 'kɪŋdəm, ,ju:'keɪ] das Vereinigte Königreich III
kiss [kɪs] Kuss IV 1 (27)
kiss [kɪs] küssen IV 1 (27/178)
kitchen ['kɪtʃɪn] Küche I
kite [kaɪt] Drachen I
kiwi ['ki:wi:] Kiwi II
knee [ni:] Knie I
knew [nju:] *siehe* know
knife [naɪf], *pl* **knives** [naɪvz] Messer III
know [nəʊ], **knew, known**
**1.** wissen I
**2.** kennen I
**know about sth.** von etwas wissen; über etwas Bescheid wissen II • **get to know** kennenlernen IV 2 (50) • **How do you know ...?** Woher weißt du ...? / Woher kennst du ...? I • **I don't know.** Ich weiß es nicht. I • **..., you know.** ..., wissen Sie. / ..., weißt du. I • **You know what, Sophie?** Weißt du was, Sophie? I
known [nəʊn]
**1.** *siehe* know
**2.** bekannt IV 4 (89)
°known: **°be known as** bekannt sein als

## L

°label ['leɪbl] beschriften, etikettieren
laid [leɪd] *siehe* lay the table
lain [leɪn] *siehe* lie
lake [leɪk] (Binnen-)See II
lamb [læm] Lamm(fleisch) III
lamp [læmp] Lampe I
land [lænd] landen II
land [lænd] Land, Grund und Boden II
lane [leɪn] Gasse, Weg III
language ['læŋgwɪdʒ] Sprache I **foreign language** Fremdsprache IV 3 (57)
large [lɑ:dʒ] groß II
lasagne [lə'zænjə] Lasagne I
last [lɑ:st] letzte(r, s) I • **the last day** der letzte Tag I • **at last** endlich, schließlich I
last (for) [lɑ:st] dauern IV 4 (78)
late [leɪt] spät; zu spät I • **be late** zu spät sein/kommen I • **Sorry, I'm late.** Entschuldigung, dass ich zu spät bin/komme. I
later ['leɪtə] später I
latest ['leɪtɪst] neueste(r, s) III
°Latino [læ'ti:nəʊ] *Amerikaner/in lateinamerikanischer Herkunft*
laugh [lɑ:f] lachen I • **laugh at sb.** jn. auslachen IV 2 (37)
laughable ['lɑ:fəbl] lächerlich IV 4 (87)
laughter ['lɑ:ftə] Gelächter II
law [lɔ:] Gesetz IV 4 (89)
lay [leɪ] *siehe* lie
lay the table [leɪ], **laid, laid** den Tisch decken I
leader ['li:də] Leiter/in, (An-)Führer/in III
°lean over [,li:n_'əʊvə] sich herüberbeugen, herüberlehnen
learn [lɜ:n] lernen I • **learn sth. about sth.** etwas über etwas erfahren, herausfinden II
least [li:st] am wenigsten III • **at least** zumindest, wenigstens I
leather ['leðə] Leder III
leave [li:v], **left, left**
**1.** (weg)gehen; abfahren II
**2.** verlassen II
**3.** zurücklassen II
**°leave sb. alone** jd. in Ruhe lassen • **leave sth. out** etwas weglassen/auslassen IV 3 (67)
left [left] *siehe* leave
left [left] linke(r, s) II • **look left** nach links schauen II • **on the left** links, auf der linken Seite II • **turn left** (nach) links abbiegen II
leg [leg] Bein I
legal ['li:gl] legal, gesetzlich IV 2 (38/181)
°legend ['ledʒənd] Legende
leisure centre ['leʒə sentə] Freizeitzentrum, -park II
lemon ['lemən] Zitrone III
lemonade [,lemə'neɪd] Limonade I
less [les] weniger IV 2 (38/182)
lesson ['lesn] (Unterrichts-)Stunde I • **lessons** *(pl)* Unterricht I
let [let], **let, let** lassen II • **Let's ...** Lass uns ... / Lasst uns ... I • **° Let's get out of here.** Lass uns abhauen. **Let's go.** Auf geht's! I • **Let's look at the list.** Sehen wir uns die Liste an. / Lasst uns die Liste ansehen. I **let sb. do sth.** jm. erlauben, etwas zu tun; zulassen, dass jd. etwas tut III
letter ['letə]
**1.** Buchstabe I • **capital letter** [,kæpɪtl 'letə] Großbuchstabe III
**2. letter (to)** Brief (an) II
**°informal letter** [ɪn'fɔ:ml] informeller, nicht förmlicher Brief
**°letter to the editor** ['edɪtə] Leserbrief
lettuce ['letɪs] (Kopf-)Salat II
°liberty ['lɪbəti] Freiheit
library ['laɪbrəri] Bibliothek, Bücherei I
license plate ['laɪsns pleɪt] *(AE)* Nummernschild IV Intro (10)
lie [laɪ], **lay, lain** liegen IV 1 (13)
life [laɪf], *pl* **lives** [laɪvz] Leben I
lift [lɪft] Fahrstuhl, Aufzug II
light [laɪt] Licht III • **traffic light** (Verkehrs-)Ampel IV 3 (54)
like [laɪk] wie I • **What was the weather like?** Wie war das Wetter? II • **like that / like this** so IV 4 (79)
like [laɪk] mögen, gernhaben I **like sth. better** etwas lieber mögen II • **I like swimming/dancing.** Ich schwimme/tanze gern. I • **I'd like ... (= I would like ...)** Ich hätte gern ... / Ich möchte gern ... I • **I'd like to talk about ... (= I would like to talk about ...)** Ich möchte/würde gern über ... reden I • **Would you like ...?** Möchtest du ...? / Möchten Sie ...? I • **Would you like some?** Möchtest du etwas/ein paar? / Möchten Sie etwas/ein paar? I
likeable ['laɪkəbl] liebenswert, nett, sympathisch IV 4 (87)
line [laɪn]
**1.** Zeile II
**°2.** Linie
**3.** (U-Bahn-)Linie III

**4.** *(AE)* Schlange, Reihe *(wartender Menschen)* IV 1 (14)
link [lɪŋk] verbinden, verknüpfen I
link [lɪŋk] Verbindung, Verknüpfung III
linking word ['lɪŋkɪŋ wɜːd] Bindewort II
lion ['laɪən] Löwe II
°lip [lɪp] Lippe • **°be on everyone's lips** in aller Munde sein
list [lɪst] Liste I
list [lɪst] auflisten, aufzählen II
listen (to) ['lɪsn] zuhören; sich etwas anhören I • **listen for sth.** auf etwas horchen, achten III
listener ['lɪsənə] Zuhörer/in II
listing ['lɪstɪŋ]: **TV listings** *(pl)* das Fernsehprogramm IV 4 (78)
°lite [laɪt] *(AE)* kalorienarm
little ['lɪtl]
**1.** klein I
**2.** wenig IV 2 (38)
▶ S.182 little („wenig") – few („wenige")
live [lɪv] leben, wohnen I
°lively ['laɪvli] *hier:* peppig
live music [laɪv] Livemusik II
lives [laɪvz] *Plural von „life"*
living room ['lɪvɪŋ ruːm] Wohnzimmer I
local ['ləʊkl] Orts-, örtlich II; Lokal-, IV 3 (59) • **local paper** Lokalzeitung IV 3 (59)
location [ləʊ'keɪʃn]
**1.** (Wohn-)Ort III
**2.** (Veranstaltungs-)Ort III
**3.** Drehort
lock [lɒk] abschließen; sperren III
lock [lɒk] Schleuse III
logo ['ləʊgəʊ] Logo III
lonely ['ləʊnli] einsam III
long [lɒŋ] lang I • **°no longer** nicht länger, nicht mehr
look [lʊk]
**1.** schauen, gucken I
**2. look different/great/old** anders/toll/alt aussehen I
**look after sth./sb.** auf etwas/jn. aufpassen; sich um etwas/jn. kümmern II • **look at** ansehen, anschauen I • **look for** suchen II
**look forward to** sich auf etwas freuen IV Intro (8) • **look left/right** nach links/rechts schauen II
**look round** sich umsehen I
**look sth. up** etwas nachschlagen III • **look up (from)** hochsehen, aufschauen (von) II
look [lʊk] Blick IV 2 (36) • **have a look at sth.** einen Blick auf etwas werfen, sich etwas ansehen IV 2 (36)
lorry ['lɒri] Lastkraftwagen III
lose [luːz], **lost, lost** verlieren II
lost [lɒst] *siehe* **lose**
lot [lɒt]: **a lot (of) / lots (of)** eine Menge, viel, viele II • **Thanks a lot!** Vielen Dank! I • **He likes her a lot.** Er mag sie sehr. I • **lots more** viel mehr I
loud [laʊd] laut I
love [lʌv] lieben, sehr mögen II
love [lʌv] Liebe II • **Love ...** Liebe Grüße, ... *(Briefschluss)* I • **fall in love (with sb.)** sich verlieben (in jn.) IV 3 (68)
°lox [lɑːks] *Jiddisch:* (gepökelter) Lachs
luck [lʌk]: **Good luck (with ...)!** Viel Glück (bei/mit ...)! I
luckily ['lʌkɪli] zum Glück, glücklicherweise II
lucky ['lʌki]: **be lucky (with)** Glück haben (mit) III
lunch [lʌntʃ] Mittagessen I
**lunch break** Mittagspause I
lyrics *(pl)* ['lɪrɪks] Liedtext(e), Songtext(e) III

## M

machine [mə'ʃiːn] Maschine, Gerät; *hier:* Automat III • **ticket machine** Fahrkartenautomat III
mad [mæd] verrückt I • **be mad about sth.** verrückt nach/auf etwas sein III
madam: **Dear Sir or Madam** [sɜː, sə; 'mædəm] Sehr geehrte Damen und Herren *(Anrede in Briefen)* IV 2 (45)
made [meɪd] *siehe* **make**
magazine [ˌmægə'ziːn] Zeitschrift, Magazin I
mail [meɪl] schicken, senden *(per Post oder E-mail)*; mailen III • **mail sb.** jn. anmailen II
main [meɪn] Haupt- III
majority [mə'dʒɒrəti] Mehrheit IV 2 (37/180)
make [meɪk], **made, made** machen; bauen I • **make a deal** ein Abkommen / eine Abmachung treffen III • **make a mess** alles durcheinanderbringen, alles in Unordnung bringen I • **make a point** ein Argument vorbringen III
**make a speech** eine Rede halten IV 4 (81) • **°make notes** sich Notizen machen • **°make sth. up** sich etwas ausdenken • **make sure that** sich vergewissern, dass ...; dafür sorgen, dass ... IV 2 (49)
**Make yourself comfortable.** Machs dir bequem. IV 2 (49)
make-up ['meɪkʌp] Make-up II
male [meɪl] männlich III
man [mæn], *pl* **men** [men] Mann I
manager ['mænədʒə] Manager/in III
many ['meni] viele I • **how many?** wie viele? I
map [mæp] Landkarte, Stadtplan II
March [mɑːtʃ] März I
march [mɑːtʃ] Marsch, Demonstration IV 4 (81)
mark [mɑːk] *(BE)* (Schul-)Note, Zensur IV 3 (56/185)
mark sth. up [ˌmɑːk_'ʌp] etwas markieren, kennzeichnen II
market ['mɑːkɪt] Markt II
marmalade ['mɑːməleɪd] (Orangen-)Marmelade I
married (to) ['mærɪd] verheiratet (mit) I
match [mætʃ] Spiel, Wettkampf I
°match [mætʃ]
**1.** passen zu
**2.** zuordnen
**°Match the letters and numbers.** Ordne die Buchstaben den Zahlen zu.
mate [meɪt] *(infml)* Freund/in, Kumpel III
°material [mə'tɪəriəl] Material
maths [mæθs] Mathematik I
matter ['mætə]: **What's the matter?** Was ist los? / Was ist denn? II
May [meɪ] Mai I
may [meɪ] dürfen III
maybe ['meɪbi] vielleicht I
mayor ['meə] Bürgermeister/in IV 4 (77)
me [miː] mir; mich I • **Me too.** Ich auch. I • **more than me** mehr als ich II • **That's me.** Das bin ich. I
**Why me?** Warum ich? I
meal [miːl] Mahlzeit, Essen III
mean [miːn], **meant, meant**
**1.** bedeuten III
**2.** meinen *(sagen wollen)* II
meaning ['miːnɪŋ] Bedeutung III
meant [ment] *siehe* **mean**
meat [miːt] Fleisch I
medal ['medl] Medaille III
media *(pl)* ['miːdiə] Medien III
mediation [ˌmiːdi'eɪʃn] Vermittlung, Sprachmittlung, Mediation II
medium ['miːdiəm] mittel(groß) II
meet [miːt], **met, met**
**1.** treffen; kennenlernen I
**2.** sich treffen I
**Nice to meet you.** Nett, dich kennenzulernen. III
meeting ['miːtɪŋ] Versammlung, Besprechung IV 3 (57)

**member (of)** ['membə] Mitglied (von, in) IV 2 (37)
**men** [men] *Plural von „man"*
°**mention** ['menʃn] erwähnen
**menu** ['menju:] Speisekarte II
°**merry-go-round** ['merɪgəʊraʊnd] Karussel
**mess** [mes]**: be a mess** sehr unordentlich sein; fürchterlich aussehen II • **make a mess** alles durcheinanderbringen, alles in Unordnung bringen I
**message** ['mesɪdʒ] Nachricht III °**recorded message** [rɪkɔ:dɪd] aufgezeichnete Nachricht • **text message** SMS III • **instant messages** [,ɪnstənt 'mesɪdʒɪz] *Nachrichten, die man im Internet austauscht (in Echtzeit)* III
**met** [met] *siehe* **meet**
°**method** ['meθəd] Methode
**metre** ['mi:tə] Meter II
**mice** [maɪs] *Plural von „mouse"*
**microphone** ['maɪkrəfəʊn] Mikrofon III
**middle (of)** ['mɪdl] Mitte I; Mittelteil II • **middle school** *(USA) Schule für 11- bis 14-Jährige* IV Intro (9)
**midnight** ['mɪdnaɪt] Mitternacht III
°**midtown** ['mɪdtaʊn] *Teil Manhattans, New York City, Geschäftsviertel, bekannt für das Empire State Building und das Chrysler Building*
°**Midwest** [,mɪd'west] mittler Westen *(in den USA)*
**might** [maɪt]**: you might need help** du könntest (vielleicht) Hilfe brauchen III
**mild** [maɪld] mild III
**mile** [maɪl] Meile *(= ca. 1,6 km)* II **for miles** meilenweit II
**milk** [mɪlk] Milch I
**million** ['mɪljən] Million III
**millionaire** [,mɪljə'neə] Millionär/in IV Intro (10/174)
**mime** [maɪm] pantomimisch darstellen, vorspielen II
°**mime** [maɪm] Pantomime
**mind** [maɪnd]**: Mind your own business.** Das geht dich nichts an! / Kümmere dich um deine eigenen Angelegenheiten! II **Never mind.** *etwa:* Nicht so wichtig. / Ist (doch) egal. / Das willst du gar nicht wissen. IV 3 (69)
°**mind** [maɪnd] *hier:* Kopf; Geist, Verstand
**mind map** ['maɪnd mæp] Mindmap („Gedankenkarte", „Wissensnetz") I
**mine** [maɪn] meiner, meine, meins II
**minister** ['mɪnɪstə] Pfarrer/in, Pastor/in IV 4 (81)
**minority** [maɪ'nɒrəti] Minderheit IV 2 (37)
**mints** *(pl)* [mɪnts] Pfefferminzbonbons I
**minus** ['maɪnəs] minus IV 3 (63)
**minute** ['mɪnɪt] Minute I • **Wait a minute.** Warte mal! / Moment mal! II
**mirror** ['mɪrə] Spiegel II
**miss** [mɪs]
**1.** vermissen II
**2. Miss a turn.** Einmal aussetzen. II
**Miss White** [mɪs] Frau White *(unverheiratet)* I
**missing** ['mɪsɪŋ]**: be missing** fehlen II • °**the missing information/words** die fehlenden Informationen/Wörter
**mistake** [mɪ'steɪk] Fehler I
**mix** [mɪks] mischen, mixen III °**mix up** durcheinanderbringen
**mix** [mɪks] Mix, Mischung III
**mixture** ['mɪkstʃə] Mischung III
**mobile (phone)** ['məʊbaɪl] Mobiltelefon, Handy I
**model** ['mɒdl] Modell*(-flugzeug, -schiff usw.)* I; (Foto-)Modell II
**modern** ['mɒdən] modern III
**mole** [məʊl] Maulwurf II
**mom** [mɒm, *AE:* mɑ:m] *(AE)* Mama, Mutti; Mutter III
**moment** ['məʊmənt] Moment III
**Monday** ['mʌndeɪ, 'mʌndi] Montag I • **Monday morning** Montagmorgen I
**money** ['mʌni] Geld I • **raise money (for)** [reɪz] Geld sammeln (für) IV Intro (9) • °**The money was good.** Wir haben gut verdient.
**monitor** ['mɒnɪtə] Bildschirm, Monitor III
**monkey** ['mʌŋki] Affe II
**monster** ['mɒnstə] Ungeheuer, Monster II
**month** [mʌnθ] Monat I
**monument** ['mɒnjumənt] Denkmal, Monument IV Intro (9)
°**mood** [mu:d] Stimmung
**moon** [mu:n] Mond II
**more** [mɔ:] mehr I • **lots more** viel mehr I • °**more and more** immer mehr • **more than** mehr als II • **more than me** mehr als ich II • **more boring (than)** langweiliger (als) II • **no more music** keine Musik mehr I • **not (...) any more** nicht mehr III
**morning** ['mɔ:nɪŋ] Morgen, Vormittag I • **in the morning** morgens, am Morgen I • **Monday morning** Montagmorgen I • **on Friday morning** freitagmorgens, am Freitagmorgen I
**mosque** [mɒsk] Moschee III
**most** [məʊst] (der/die/das) meiste ...; am meisten II • °**most of the time** die meiste Zeit • **most people** die meisten Leute I **(the) most boring** der/die/das langweiligste ...; am langweiligsten II
°**mostly** ['məʊstli] größtenteils
**motel** [məʊ'tel] Motel IV Intro (10)
**mother** ['mʌðə] Mutter I
**mountain** ['maʊntən] Berg II
**mouse** [maʊs]**,** *pl* **mice** [maɪs] Maus I
**mouth** [maʊθ] Mund I
**move** [mu:v]
**1.** bewegen; sich bewegen II **Move back one space.** Geh ein Feld zurück. II • **Move on one space.** Geh ein Feld vor. II
°**2.** weitergehen, weiterziehen
**3. move (to)** umziehen (nach, in) II • **move in** einziehen II • **move out** ausziehen II
°**4. move closer** näher heranrücken
**movement** ['mu:vmənt] Bewegung II
**movie** ['mu:vi] Film III
**MP3 player** [,empi:'θri: ,pleɪə] MP3-Spieler I
**Mr ...** ['mɪstə] Herr ... I
**Mrs ...** ['mɪsɪz] Frau ... I
**Ms ...** [mɪz, məz] Frau ... II
**much** [mʌtʃ] viel I • **how much?** wie viel? I • **How much is/are ...?** Was kostet/kosten ...? / Wie viel kostet/kosten ...? I • **like/love sth. very much** etwas sehr mögen / sehr lieben II
**muesli** ['mju:zli] Müsli IV 3 (58)
°**mule** [mju:l] Maultier
**multi-** ['mʌlti] viel-, mehr-; multi-, Multi- IV Intro (10) • **multi-coloured** mehrfarbig IV Intro (10) • **multi-millionaire** Multimillionär/Multimillionärin IV Intro (10/174)
**multiple choice** [,mʌltɪpl 'tʃɔɪs] Multiple-Choice II
**mum** [mʌm] Mama, Mutti; Mutter I
°**mumble** ['mʌmbl] murmeln, nuscheln
**murder** ['mɜ:də] Mord IV 4 (78)
**museum** [mju'zi:əm] Museum I
**mushroom** ['mʌʃrʊm, -ru:m] Pilz III

**music** ['mju:zɪk] Musik I • °**put on the music** Platten/CDs auflegen
**musical** ['mju:zɪkl] Musical I
**musician** [mju:'zɪʃn] Musiker/in III
**must** [mʌst]
1. müssen I
2. **mustn't do** nicht tun dürfen II
**must** [mʌst] Muss IV 1 (16)
°**mustache** [məs'tɑ:ʃ] *(AE)* Schnurrbart
**my** [maɪ] mein/e I
**myself** [maɪ'self] mir/mich (selbst) III
**mystery** ['mɪstri] Geheimnis, Rätsel IV 2 (52)

## N

**name** [neɪm] Name I • **call sb. names** jn. mit Schimpfwörtern hänseln, jm. Schimpfwörter nachrufen III • **My name is ...** Ich heiße ... / Mein Name ist ... I
**What's your name?** Wie heißt du? I
**name** [neɪm] nennen; benennen II
**name after** benennen nach IV 3 (68)
**nation** ['neɪʃn] Nation IV 4 (81)
**national** ['næʃnəl] national III
**national park** Nationalpark IV Intro (8) • °**National Guard** Nationalgarde
**Native American** [ˌneɪtɪv‿ə'merɪkən] amerikanische(r) Ureinwohner/in, Indianer/in IV Intro (9)
**natural** ['nætʃrəl] Natur-, natürlich IV Intro (9) • °**natural history** [ˌnætʃrəl 'hɪstri] Naturkunde
**near** [nɪə] in der Nähe von, nahe (bei) I
**neat** [ni:t] gepflegt II • **neat and tidy** schön ordentlich II
°**necessary** ['nesəsəri] notwendig, nötig
**need** [ni:d] brauchen, benötigen I
**needn't do** ['ni:dnt] nicht tun müssen, nicht zu tun brauchen II
**neighbour** ['neɪbə] Nachbar/in I
**nephew** ['nefju:, 'nevju:] Neffe IV 2 (51/184)
**nervous** ['nɜ:vəs] nervös, aufgeregt I
**network** ['netwɜ:k]
1. (Fernseh-/Radio-) Sendernetz IV 4 (77)
°2. (Wörter-)Netz
**never** ['nevə] nie, niemals I
**Never mind.** [ˌnevə 'maɪnd] *etwa:* Nicht so wichtig. / Ist (doch) egal. / Das willst du gar nicht wissen. IV 3 (69)
**new** [nju:] neu I
**news** *(no pl)* [nju:z] Nachrichten, Neuigkeiten III • **That's good news.** Das sind gute Nachrichten. III
**newspaper** ['nju:speɪpə] Zeitung I
**newsreader** ['nju:z,ri:də] Nachrichtensprecher/in IV 4 (78)
**next** [nekst]: **be next** der/die Nächste sein I • **the next morning/day** am nächsten Morgen/Tag I
**What have we got next?** Was haben wir als Nächstes? I
**next to** [nekst] neben II
**nice** [naɪs] schön, nett I • **Nice to meet you.** Nett, dich/euch/Sie kennenzulernen. III
**niece** [ni:s] Nichte IV 2 (51)
°**nigger** ['nɪgə] *(abwertend, beleidigend)* Nigger, Neger
**night** [naɪt] Nacht, später Abend I
**at night** nachts, in der Nacht I
**on Friday night** freitagnachts, Freitagnacht I
**nightclub** ['naɪtklʌb] Nachtklub III
**nil** [nɪl] null III
**no** [nəʊ] nein I
**no** [nəʊ] kein, keine I • **no more music** keine Musik mehr I • **no one** niemand IV 2 (34/180) • **No smoking!** Rauchen verboten! III
**No way!** Auf keinen Fall! / Kommt nicht in Frage! II • °**no longer** nicht mehr, nicht länger
**nobody** ['nəʊbədi] niemand II
**nod (-dd-)** [nɒd] nicken (mit) II
**noise** [nɔɪz] Geräusch; Lärm I
**noisy** ['nɔɪzi] laut, lärmend II
°**nominate** ['nɒmɪneɪtɪd] nominieren, ernennen
**non-violent** [ˌnɒn'vaɪələnt] gewaltlos, gewaltfrei IV 4 (76/189)
**north** [nɔ:θ] Norden; nach Norden; nördlich III
**northbound** ['nɔ:θbaʊnd] Richtung Norden III
**north-east** [ˌnɔ:θ'i:st] Nordosten; nach Nordosten; nordöstlich III
**north-west** [ˌnɔ:θ'west] Nordwesten; nach Nordwesten; nordwestlich III
**nose** [nəʊz] Nase I
**not** [nɒt] nicht I • **not (...) any** kein, keine I • **not (...) any more** nicht mehr III • **not (...) anybody** niemand II • **not (...) anything** nichts II • **not (...) anywhere** nirgendwo(hin) II • **not even** (noch) nicht einmal III • **not (...) yet** noch nicht II
**note** [nəʊt] Mitteilung, Notiz I
°**make notes** sich Notizen machen
**take notes** sich Notizen machen I
**nothing** ['nʌθɪŋ] nichts II
**notice** ['nəʊtɪs] bemerken IV 1 (27)
°**notice** ['nəʊtɪs] Notiz, Mitteilung
**notice board** Anschlagtafel, schwarzes Brett I
**November** [nəʊ'vembə] November I
**now** [naʊ] nun, jetzt I • °**now that ...** jetzt, wo ...
**number** ['nʌmbə] Zahl, Ziffer, Nummer I • **number plate** Nummernschild IV Intro (10/174)
**nut** [nʌt] Nuss IV 3 (58)

## O

**o** [əʊ] null I
°**observatory** [əb'zɜ:vətri] Aussichtsplattform
**ocean** ['əʊʃn] Ozean IV 2 (49)
**o'clock** [ə'klɒk]: **eleven o'clock** elf Uhr I
**October** [ɒk'təʊbə] Oktober I
°**odd** [ɒd]: **What word is the odd one out?** Welches Wort passt nicht dazu / gehört nicht dazu?
**of** [əv, ɒv] von I • **two kilos of oranges** zwei Kilo Orangen III
**of course** [əv 'kɔ:s] natürlich, selbstverständlich I
**off** [ɒf]: **a week/day/month ... off** eine Woche / einen Tag / einen Monat ... frei IV 3 (56) • **cut sth. off** etwas abtrennen, abschneiden III
**fall off** herunterfallen (von) II
**get off (the train/bus)** (aus dem Zug/Bus) aussteigen I • **get sth. off the ground** etwas auf den Weg bringen; etwas auf die Beine stellen III • **take sth. off** etwas ausziehen *(Kleidung)* II • **take 10 c off** 10 Cent abziehen I • **tear sth. off** etwas abreißen IV 1 (27) • **turn sth. off** etwas ausschalten III
**offer** ['ɒfə] anbieten IV 2 (52)
**offer** ['ɒfə] Angebot IV 2 (52/184)
**office** ['ɒfɪs]: **ticket office** Kasse *(für den Verkauf von Eintrittskarten)* IV 1 (16); Fahrkartenschalter III; °**principal's office** Büro des Schulleiters/der Schulleiterin
°**official** [ə'fɪʃl] offiziell
**often** ['ɒfn] oft, häufig I
**Oh dear!** [əʊ 'dɪə] Oje! II
**Oh well ...** [əʊ 'wel] Na ja ... / Na gut ... I
**oil** [ɔɪl] Öl III

**OK** [əʊ'keɪ] okay, gut, in Ordnung I **I'll/You'll/She'll/ ... be OK.** Mir/ Dir/Ihr/ ... wird nichts passieren. IV 1 (16)
**old** [əʊld] alt I • **a sixteen-year-old** ein/e Sechzehnjährige/r III **a sixteen-year-old girl** ein sechzehnjähriges Mädchen III
**old-fashioned** [ˌəʊld'fæʃnd] altmodisch III
**Olympic Games** [əˌlɪmpɪk 'geɪmz] (*kurz:* **the Olympics** [ə'lɪmpɪks]) Olympische Spiele; die Olympiade IV 4 (77)
**on** [ɒn]
**1.** auf I
**2.** an, eingeschaltet sein *(Radio, Licht usw.)* I • **turn sth. on** etwas ein-, ausschalten III
**3.** weiter • **Dream on!** Träum weiter! III • **read on** weiterlesen III **and so on** (*short:* **etc.** [et'setərə]) und so weiter (usw.) IV 3 (57) **walk on** weitergehen III • **straight on** geradeaus weiter II • **on a shift** in einer Schicht IV 1 (15) • **on 13th June** am 13. Juni I • °**on foot** zu Fuß • **on Friday** am Freitag I • **on Friday afternoon** freitagnachmittags, am Freitagnachmittag I **on Friday evening** freitagabends, am Freitagabend I • **on Friday morning** freitagmorgens, am Freitagmorgen I • **on Friday night** freitagnachts, Freitagnacht I • **on the beach** am Strand II • **on the board** an die Tafel I • **on the corner of Green Street and London Road** Green Street, Ecke London Road II • **on the internet** im Internet IV 3 (64) • **on the left** links, auf der linken Seite II • **on the phone** am Telefon I • **on the plane** im Flugzeug II • **on the radio** im Radio I • **on the right** rechts, auf der rechten Seite II **on the train** im Zug I • **on TV** im Fernsehen I • **be on** gezeigt werden, laufen *(im Fernsehen/Kino)* IV 4 (78) • **go on holiday** in Urlaub fahren II • **What page are we on?** Auf welcher Seite sind wir? I
**once** [wʌns]
**1.** einmal III
**2.** einst, früher einmal III
**once a week** einmal pro Woche III
**one** [wʌn] eins, ein, eine I • **one day** eines Tages I • **a new one** ein neuer / eine neue / ein neues II • **my old ones** meine alten II **no one** niemand IV 2 (34/180)
**one-day ticket** [ˌwʌn deɪ 'tɪkɪt] Tages(fahr)karte III
**onion** ['ʌnjən] Zwiebel III
**online** [ˌɒn'laɪn] online, Online- III
**only** ['əʊnli]
**1.** nur, bloß I
**2.** erst III
**3. the only guest** der einzige Gast I
**onto** ['ɒntə, 'ɒntʊ] auf (... hinauf) III
**open** ['əʊpən] öffnen, aufmachen I
**open** ['əʊpən] offen, geöffnet II
**open-air** [ˌəʊpən‿'eə] im Freien; Freilicht- III
**opening** ['əʊpənɪŋ]**: opening hours** Öffnungszeiten IV 1 (16/177) °**opening sentence** Einleitungssatz • °**opening titles** Vorspann *(Film)*
**opera** ['ɒprə] Oper III
**operation (on)** [ˌɒpə'reɪʃn] Operation (an) III
**opinion** [ə'pɪnjən] Meinung III • **in my opinion** meiner Meinung nach III
**opposite** ['ɒpəzɪt] Gegenteil I
**or** [ɔː] oder I
**orange** ['ɒrɪndʒ] orange(farben) I
**orange** ['ɒrɪndʒ] Orange, Apfelsine I • **orange juice** Orangensaft I
**order** ['ɔːdə] bestellen IV 1 (17)
°**order** ['ɔːdə]
**1.** Reihenfolge • **in the right order** in der richtigen Reihenfolge • **word order** Wortstellung
**2.** Befehl
**organize** ['ɔːgənaɪz] ordnen, organisieren III
**original** *(n; adj)* [ə'rɪdʒənl]
**1.** Original; Original-, IV 3 (67)
°**2.** ursprünglich
**other** ['ʌðə] andere(r, s) I • **the others** die anderen I • **the other way round** anders herum II
**Ouch!** [aʊtʃ] Autsch! I
**our** ['aʊə] unser, unsere I
**ours** ['aʊəz] unserer, unsere, unseres II
**ourselves** [aʊə'selvz] uns (selbst) III
**out** heraus, hinaus; draußen II
**out of ...** aus ... (heraus/hinaus) I °**one out of ten** einer von zehn **day out** Tagesausflug III
**outfit** ['aʊtfɪt] Outfit *(Kleidung; Ausrüstung)* II
**outside** [ˌaʊt'saɪd]
**1.** draußen I
**2.** nach draußen II
**3. outside his room** vor seinem Zimmer; außerhalb seines Zimmers I
**over** ['əʊvə]
**1.** über, oberhalb von I
**2. be over** vorbei/zu Ende sein I **over there** da drüben, dort drüben I • **over to ...** hinüber zu/nach ... II **all over the world** auf der ganzen Welt III • **from all over the UK/ the world/England** aus dem gesamten Vereinigten Königreich / aus der ganzen Welt / aus ganz England III
°**overcome** [ˌəʊvə'kʌm]**: we shall overcome** wir werden siegen *(alle Schwierigkeiten überwinden)*
**own** [əʊn]**: our own pool** unser eigenes Schwimmbad II

## P

**Pacific** [pə'sɪfɪk]**: the Pacific (Ocean)** der Pazifische Ozean, der Pazifik IV 2 (49)
**pack** [pæk] packen, einpacken II
**packet** ['pækɪt] Päckchen, Packung, Schachtel I • **a packet of mints** ein Päckchen/eine Packung Pfefferminzbonbons I
**paddle** ['pædl] paddeln III
**paddle** ['pædl] Paddel III
**pads** *(pl)* [pædz] (Knie- usw.) Schützer III
**page** [peɪdʒ] (Buch-, Heft-)Seite I **What page are we on?** Auf welcher Seite sind wir? I
**paid** [peɪd] *siehe* **pay**
**pain** [peɪn] Schmerz(en) IV 4 (91)
**painful** ['peɪnfl] schmerzhaft IV 4 (91/193)
**paint** [peɪnt] (an)malen I
**painter** ['peɪntə] Maler/in II
**pair** [peə]**: a pair (of)** ein Paar II
**palace** ['pæləs] Palast, Schloss III
°**pan** [pæn] Pfanne
**panic** ['pænɪk]**: Don't panic!** Keine Panik. / Bleib ruhig. IV 2 (48)
**pants** *(pl)* [pænts] *(AE)* Hose IV 1 (20)
**paper** ['peɪpə]
**1.** Papier I
**2.** Zeitung II • **local paper** Lokalzeitung IV 3 (59)
**paragraph** ['pærəgrɑːf] Absatz *(in einem Text)* II
**Paralympics** [ˌpærə'lɪmpɪks] Paralympische Spiele *(Olympische Spiele für Sportler/innen mit körperlicher Behinderung)* III
**paramedic** [ˌpærə'medɪk] Sanitäter/in II
**paraphrase** ['pærəfreɪz] umschreiben, anders ausdrücken III
**parcel** ['pɑːsl] Paket I

**parents** ['peərənts] Eltern I
**park** [pɑːk] Park I • **park ranger** *Ranger sind eine Art Aufseher/in in Nationalparks, die auch Führungen machen und als Wald- und Wildhüterinnen arbeiten* IV Intro (9)
**parliament** ['pɑːləmənt] Parlament III
**parrot** ['pærət] Papagei I
**part** [pɑːt] Teil I • **take part (in)** teilnehmen (an) III
**partner** ['pɑːtnə] Partner/in I
**party** ['pɑːti] Party I
**pass** [pɑːs] (herüber)reichen, weitergeben I • **pass round** herumgeben I
**past** [pɑːst] Vergangenheit I
**past** [pɑːst] vorbei (an), vorüber (an) II • **half past 11** halb zwölf (11.30/23.30) I • **quarter past 11** Viertel nach elf (11.15/23.15) I
**pasta** *(no pl)* ['pæstə] Pasta, Nudeln, Teigwaren IV 3 (58)
**path** [pɑːθ] Pfad, Weg II • **bridle path** Reitweg III
°**patrol** [pə'trəl] Patrouille, Streife °**border patrol** Grenzschutz
°**pause** [pɔːs] pausieren, Pause machen
**pavement** ['peɪvmənt] Gehweg, Bürgersteig IV 1 (14/175)
**pay (for)** [peɪ], **paid, paid** bezahlen II
**PE** [ˌpiː_'iː], **Physical Education** [ˌfɪzɪkəl_edʒu'keɪʃn] Turnen, Sportunterricht I
**pea** [piː] Erbse III
°**peaceful** ['piːsfl] friedvoll; friedfertig
**pen** [pen] Kugelschreiber, Füller I
**pence (p)** *(pl)* [pens] Pence *(Plural von „penny")*
**pencil** ['pensl] Bleistift I • **pencil case** ['pensl keɪs] Federmäppchen I • **pencil sharpener** ['pensl ʃɑːpnə] Bleistiftanspitzer I
**penny** ['peni] *kleinste britische Münze* I
**people** ['piːpl] Menschen, Leute I
**pepper** ['pepə] Pfeffer III
**per** [pɜː, pə] pro III • **per cent (%)** [pə 'sent] Prozent III
**perfect** ['pɜːfɪkt] perfekt; ideal; vollkommen IV 1 (16)
**period** ['pɪərɪəd]
1. (Unterrichts-/Schul-)Stunde IV 3 (56)
°2. **period of time** Zeitspanne, Zeitraum
**person** ['pɜːsn] Person II
**personal** ['pɜːsənl] persönliche(r, s) III

**pet** [pet] Haustier I • **pet shop** Tierhandlung I
**petrol** ['petrəl] Benzin IV Intro (10/174) **petrol station** Tankstelle IV Intro (10/174)
**phone** [fəʊn] Telefon I • **on the phone** am Telefon I • **phone call** Anruf, Telefongespräch I • **phone number** Telefonnummer I
**phone** [fəʊn] telefonieren, anrufen I
**photo** ['fəʊtəʊ] Foto I • **in the photo** auf dem Foto I • **take photos** Fotos machen, fotografieren I
°**photocopy** ['fəʊtəʊkɒpi] Fotokopie
°**phrase** [freɪz] Ausdruck, (Rede-) Wendung
**piano** [pi'ænəʊ] Klavier, Piano I **play the piano** Klavier spielen I
**pick up** [ˌpɪk_'ʌp]: **pick sb. up** jn. abholen III • **pick sth. up** etwas hochheben, aufheben II
**picnic** ['pɪknɪk] Picknick I • **have a picnic** ein Picknick machen I
**picture** ['pɪktʃə] Bild I • **in the picture** auf dem Bild I • **picture story** Bildergeschichte IV 2 (47)
°**picture sth.** sich etwas (bildlich) vorstellen
**pie** [paɪ] Obstkuchen; Pastete II
**piece** [piːs]: **a piece of** ein Stück I **a piece of paper** ein Stück Papier I
**pig** [pɪg] III
**pink** [pɪŋk] pink(farben), rosa I
°**pioneer** [ˌpaɪə'nɪə] Pionier
**pipe** [paɪp] Pfeife III
**pirate** ['paɪrət] Pirat, Piratin I
**pitch** [pɪtʃ] Spielfeld III
**pizza** ['piːtsə] Pizza I
**place** [pleɪs] Ort, Platz I • **take place** stattfinden IV 1 (15)
°**placemat** ['pleɪsmæt] Set, Platzdeckchen
**plan** [plæn] Plan I
**plan (-nn-)** [plæn] planen I
**plane** [pleɪn] Flugzeug II • **on the plane** im Flugzeug II
**planet** ['plænɪt] Planet II
**plantation** [plɑːn'teɪʃn] Plantage IV 4 (76)
**plate** [pleɪt] Teller I • **a plate of chips** ein Teller Pommes frites I **license plate** *(AE)* Nummernschild IV Intro (10) • **number plate** *(BE)* Nummernschild IV Intro (10/174)
**platform** ['plætfɔːm] Bahnsteig, Gleis III
**play** [pleɪ] spielen I • **play football** Fußball spielen I • °**play sports** Sport treiben • **play the drums** Schlagzeug spielen III • **play the fiddle** Geige spielen III • **play the guitar** Gitarre spielen I • **play the piano** Klavier spielen I

**play** [pleɪ] Theaterstück I
**player** ['pleɪə] Spieler/in I
**please** [pliːz] bitte *(in Fragen und Aufforderungen)* I
**plot** [plɒt] Handlung *(eines Romans, Films, Theaterstücks)* IV 3 (70)
**plug** [plʌg] Stecker III
**plus** [plʌs] plus IV 3 (63/187)
**pm** [ˌpiː_'em]: **7 pm** 7 Uhr abends / 19 Uhr I
**pocket** ['pɒkɪt] Tasche *(an Kleidungsstück)* II • **pocket money** Taschengeld II
**poem** ['pəʊɪm] Gedicht I
**point** [pɔɪnt] Punkt II • °**point in time** Zeitpunkt • **make a point** ein Argument vorbringen III **10.4 (ten point four)** 10,4 (zehn Komma vier) III
**point (at/to sth.)** [pɔɪnt] zeigen, deuten (auf etwas) II
**police** *(pl)* [pə'liːs] Polizei I **police station** Polizeiwache, Polizeirevier II
**policeman** [pə'liːsmən] Polizist II
**policewoman** [pə'liːswʊmən] Polizistin II
**polite** [pə'laɪt] höflich IV 3 (69)
°**politics** ['pɒlətɪks] Politik
**poltergeist** ['pəʊltəgaɪst] Poltergeist I
**ponytail** ['pəʊniteɪl] Pferdeschwanz *(Frisur)* III
**pool** [puːl] (Schwimm-)Becken III
**poor** [pɔː, pʊə] arm I • **poor Sophie** (die) arme Sophie I
**pop (music)** [pɒp] Pop(musik) III
**popcorn** ['pɒpkɔːn] Popcorn II
**popular (with)** ['pɒpjulə] populär, beliebt (bei) III
**population** [ˌpɒpju'leɪʃn] Bevölkerung, Einwohner(zahl) IV 2 (37)
**pork** [pɔːk] Schweinefleisch III
°**port** [pɔːt] Hafen(stadt)
°**position** [pə'zɪʃn] Position
**possibility** [ˌpɒsə'bɪləti] Möglichkeit, Chance IV 3 (66)
**possible** ['pɒsəbl] möglich II
**post** [pəʊst] Post *(Briefe, Päckchen, ...)* III • **post office** ['pəʊst_ɒfɪs] Postamt II
**postcard** ['pəʊstkɑːd] Postkarte II
**poster** ['pəʊstə] Poster I
**potato** [pə'teɪtəʊ], *pl* **potatoes** Kartoffel I • **potato chips** *(AE)* Kartoffelchips IV 1 (20)
**poultry** ['pəʊltri] Geflügel IV 3 (58)
**pound (£)** [paʊnd] Pfund *(britische Währung)* I

**practice** ['præktɪs] *hier:* Übungsteil I
**practise** ['præktɪs]
1. üben; trainieren I
°2. ausüben, praktizieren
**prejudice** ['predʒudɪs] Vorurteil IV 2 (37)
**prejudiced** ['predʒədɪst]: **be prejudiced (against )** voreingenommen sein (gegen), Vorurteile haben (gegenüber) IV 2 (37)
**prepare (for)** [prɪ'peə] vorbereiten; sich vorbereiten (auf)
**present** ['preznt]
1. Gegenwart I
2. Geschenk I
°**present sth. (to sb.)** [prɪ'zent] (jm.) etwas präsentieren, vorstellen
**presentation** [ˌprezn'teɪʃn] Präsentation, Vorstellung I
**presenter** [prɪ'zentə] Moderator/in II
**president** ['prezɪdənt] Präsident/in IV 4 (88)
**press** [pres] drücken III
**pretty** ['prɪti] hübsch I
**pretty healthy/good/...** ['prɪti] ziemlich gesund/gut/... II
**price** [praɪs] (Kauf-)Preis I
**prime time** ['praɪm taɪm] Hauptsendezeit IV 4 (78)
°**principal's office** [ˌprɪnsəplz‿'ɒfɪs] Büro des Schulleiters/der Schulleiterin
**print**: **bold print** [ˌbəʊld 'prɪnt] Fettdruck III
°**prison** ['prɪszn] Gefängnis
**prize** [praɪz] Preis, Gewinn I
**probably** ['prɒbəbli] wahrscheinlich II
**problem** ['prɒbləm] Problem II
**produce** [prə'dju:s] produzieren, herstellen III
**product** ['prɒdʌkt] Produkt IV 2 (36)
**production** [prə'dʌkʃn] Produktion, Herstellung IV 2 (36/180)
**profile** ['prəʊfaɪl] Porträt, Steckbrief III
**programme** ['prəʊgræm]
1. Programm I
2. (Fernseh-)Sendung IV 4 (78)
**project (about, on)** ['prɒdʒekt] Projekt (über, zu) I • **do a project** ein Projekt machen, durchführen II
**promise** ['prɒmɪs] versprechen II
°**promise** ['prɒmɪs] Versprechen, Versprechung
°**pronounce** [prə'naʊns] aussprechen
**pronunciation** [prəˌnʌnsi'eɪʃn] Aussprache I
**proof** *(no pl)* [pru:f] Beweis(e) II
**protect sb. (from sth.)** [prə'tekt] jn. (be)schützen (vor etwas) III
**protest** [prə'test] protestieren IV 3 (69)
**protest** ['prəʊtest] Protest IV 4 (81)
**proud (of sb./sth.)** [praʊd] stolz (auf jn./etwas) II
**province** ['prɒvɪns] Provinz III
**PS** [ˌpi:‿'es] **(postscript** ['pəʊstskrɪpt]**)** PS *(Nachschrift unter Briefen)* III
**pub** [pʌb] Kneipe, Lokal II
**publish** ['pʌblɪʃ] veröffentlichen III
**pull** [pʊl] ziehen I
**pullover** ['pʊləʊvə] Pullover II
**purple** ['pɜ:pl] violett; lila I
**purse** [pɜ:s] Geldbörse II
**push** [pʊʃ] drücken, schieben, stoßen I
**put (-tt-)** [pʊt], **put, put** legen, stellen, *(etwas wohin)* tun I • °**put on the music** Platten/CDs auflegen **put out a fire** ein Feuer löschen IV 1 (15) • **put sth. on** etwas anziehen *(Kleidung)* II • °**put sth. on the wall** etwas an die Wand hängen • °**put sth. together** etwas zusammenstellen, zusammenfügen • °**Put up your hand.** Heb deine Hand. / Hebt eure Hand.
**puzzled** ['pʌzld] verwirrt II
**pyjamas** *(pl)* [pə'dʒɑ:məz] Schlafanzug II
**pyramid** ['pɪrəmɪd] Pyramide IV 3 (58)

## Q

**quarter** ['kwɔ:tə]: **quarter past 11** Viertel nach 11 (11.15/23.15) I **quarter to 12** Viertel vor 12 (11.45/23.45) I
**queen** [kwi:n] Königin III
**question** ['kwestʃn] Frage I • **ask questions** Fragen stellen I °**question word** Fragewort
**queue** [kju:] *(BE)* Schlange, Reihe *(wartender Menschen)* IV 1 (14/175)
**quick** [kwɪk] schnell I
**quiet** ['kwaɪət] leise, still, ruhig I
**quite bad/quick/good ...** [kwaɪt] ziemlich schlimm/schnell/gut/... II
**quiz** [kwɪz], *pl* **quizzes** ['kwɪzɪz] Quiz, Ratespiel I
°**quotation mark** [kwəʊ'teɪʃn mɑ:k] Anführungszeichen

## R

**rabbit** ['ræbɪt] Kaninchen I
**racket** ['rækɪt]: **badminton racket** Badmintonschläger III
**radio** ['reɪdiəʊ] Radio I • **on the radio** im Radio I
**raft** [rɑ:ft] Schlauchboot *(wildwassertauglich)* IV 3 (67)
**rafting** ['rɑ:ftɪŋ] Rafting IV 3 (67)
**railway** ['reɪlweɪ] Eisenbahn II
**rain** [reɪn] Regen II
**rain** [reɪn] regnen II
**rainy** ['reɪni] regnerisch II
**raise money (for)** [reɪz] Geld sammeln (für) IV Intro (9)
**ran** [ræn] *siehe* **run**
**rang** [ræŋ] *siehe* **ring**
**ranger** ['reɪndʒə]: **(park) ranger** *eine Art Aufseher/in in Nationalparks, die auch Führungen machen und als Wald- und Wildhüterinnen arbeiten* IV Intro (9)
**rap** [ræp] Rap *(rhythmischer Sprechgesang)* I
**rapids** *(pl)* ['ræpɪdz] Stromschnellen III
**RE** [ˌɑ:r‿'i:], **Religious Education** [rɪˌlɪdʒəs‿edʒu'keɪʃn] Religion, Religionsunterricht I
**read** [ri:d], **read, read** lesen I **read on** weiterlesen III • °**read out** vorlesen • °**Read out loud.** Lies laut vor. • °**Read the poem to a partner.** Lies das Gedicht einem Partner / einer Partnerin vor.
**read** [red] *siehe* **read**
**reader** ['ri:də] Leser/in II
**ready** ['redi] bereit, fertig I • **get ready (for)** sich fertig machen (für), sich vorbereiten (auf) I • **get things ready** Dinge fertig machen, vorbereiten I
**real** ['rɪəl] echt, wirklich
**realistic** [ˌri:ə'lɪstɪk] realistisch, wirklichkeitsnah III
**reality** [ri'æləti] Wirklichkeit, Realität IV 3 (66)
**really** ['rɪəli] wirklich I
**reason** ['ri:zn] Grund, Begründung I • **for lots of reasons** aus vielen Gründen I
**receive** [rɪ'si:v] empfangen IV 4 (84)
**record** [rɪ'kɔ:d] *(Musik / einen Film)* aufnehmen III
**record** ['rekɔ:d] Schallplatte III
°**recorded message** [rɪ'kɔ:dɪd 'mesɪdʒ] (automatische) Telefonansage
**recorder** [rɪ'kɔ:də] Blockflöte III
**recording** [rɪ'kɔ:dɪŋ] Aufnahme, Aufzeichnung III

**recycled** [ˌriːˈsaɪkld] wiederverwertet, wiederverwendet, recycelt II
**recycling** [ˌriːˈsaɪklɪŋ] Wiederverwertung, Recycling II
**red** [red] rot I
**refer to (-rr-)** [rɪˈfɜː] sich beziehen auf III
°**reflex** [ˈriːfleks] Reflex
**reggae** [ˈregeɪ] Reggae III
**regular** [ˈregjələ] normal *(Größenangabe bei Getränken und Fastfood)* IV 1 (17)
**rehearsal** [rɪˈhɜːsl] Probe *(am Theater)* I
**rehearse** [rɪˈhɜːs] proben *(am Theater)* I
°**relationship** [rɪˈleɪʃnʃɪp] Beziehung
**relax** [rɪˈlæks] (sich) entspannen, sich ausruhen II
**relaxed** [rɪˈlækst] locker, entspannt III
**release** [rɪˈliːs] *(CD, Film usw.)* herausbringen, auf den Markt bringen III
°**religion** [rɪˈlɪdʒən] Religion
**remember sth.** [rɪˈmembə]
1. sich an etwas erinnern I
2. sich etwas merken I
°**3. remember sb.** jemandes gedenken
°**Remember ...** Denk dran, ...
**remote control** [rɪˌməʊt kənˈtrəʊl] Fernbedienung IV 4 (84)
**repeat** [rɪˈpiːt] Wiederholung *(einer Fernsehsendung)* IV 4 (78/190)
**report (on)** [rɪˈpɔːt] Bericht, Reportage (über) I
**report (to sb.)** [rɪˈpɔːt] (jm.) berichten II
**represent** [ˌreprɪˈzent] repräsentieren, vertreten III
**rerun** [ˈriːrʌn] *(AE)* Wiederholung *(einer Fernsehsendung)* IV 4 (78)
**rescue helicopter** [ˈreskjuː ˌhelɪkɒptə] Rettungshubschrauber II
**research (on)** *(no pl)* [rɪˈsɜːtʃ, ˈriːsɜːtʃ] Recherche, Nachforschung(en) IV 4 (81) • **do research** recherchieren IV 4 (81)
°**reservation** [ˌrezəˈveɪʃn] Reservat *(Schutzgebiet für Volksgruppen, besonders für Indianer in Nordamerika)*
°**resources** *(pl)* [rɪˈsɔːsɪz, rɪˈzɔːsɪz] Ressourcen, Rohstoffe
**rest** [rest] Rest II
**restaurant** [ˈrestrɒnt] Restaurant II
°**restart** [ˌriːˈstɑːt] *hier:* wieder in Betrieb nehmen
**result** [rɪˈzʌlt] Ergebnis, Resultat I
°**return to** [rɪˈtɜːn] zurückkehren zu, zurückgehen zu

**return ticket** [rɪˈtɜːn ˌtɪkɪt] Rückfahrkarte II
**revise** [rɪˈvaɪz]
1. überarbeiten III
2. wiederholen III
**revision** [rɪˈvɪʒn] Wiederholung *(des Lernstoffs)* I
°**rewrite** [ˌriːˈraɪt], **rewrote, rewritten** umschreiben, neu schreiben
°**rewritten** [ˌriːˈrɪtn] *siehe* **rewrite**
°**rewrote** [ˌriːˈrəʊt] *siehe* **rewrite**
**rhino** [ˈraɪnəʊ] Nashorn II
**rice** [raɪs] Reis III
**rich** [rɪtʃ] reich II
**ridden** [ˈrɪdn] *siehe* **ride**
**riddle** [ˈrɪdl] Rätsel III
**ride** [raɪd], **rode, ridden** reiten I
**go riding** reiten gehen I • **ride a bike** Rad fahren I
**ride** [raɪd]: **(bike) ride** (Rad-)Fahrt II
**take a ride** eine Fahrt machen III
°**rider** [ˈraɪdə] (Motorrad-)Fahrer/in
**right** [raɪt] richtig I • **all right** [ɔːl ˈraɪt] gut, in Ordnung II • **be right** Recht haben I • **That's right.** Das ist richtig. / Das stimmt. I • **You need a school bag, right?** Du brauchst eine Schultasche, stimmt's? / nicht wahr? I
**right** [raɪt] rechte(r, s) II • **look right** nach rechts schauen II • **on the right** rechts, auf der rechten Seite II • **turn right** (nach) rechts abbiegen II
**right** [raɪt]: **right now** jetzt sofort; jetzt gerade I • °**right here** genau hier
**right** [raɪt] Recht IV 4 (77)
**rim** [rɪm] Kante IV Intro (8)
**ring** [rɪŋ] Ring II
**ring** [rɪŋ], **rang, rung** klingeln, läuten II
**ringtone** [ˈrɪŋtəʊn] Klingelton III
°**riot** [ˈraɪət] Aufruhr
**rise** [raɪz], **rose, risen** (auf)steigen IV 4 (76)
**risen** [ˈrɪzn] *siehe* **rise**
**river** [ˈrɪvə] Fluss II
°**rm** *Abkürzung für* **room**
**RnB** [ˌɑːr‿ənˈbiː] RnB *(Rhythm and Blues; Form des Blues, in der Rhythmus eine große Rolle spielt; moderner RnB enthält Rap- und Hip Hop-Elemente)* III
**road** [rəʊd] Straße I • **Park Road** [ˌpɑːk ˈrəʊd] Parkstraße I
**rock** [rɒk] Fels, Felsen III
**rock and roll** [ˌrɒk‿ən ˈrəʊl] Rock and Roll IV 3 (69)
**rode** [rəʊd] *siehe* **ride**
**role** [rəʊl] Rolle III • **role play** [ˈrəʊl pleɪ] Rollenspiel II

**roll** [rəʊl] Brötchen I
**Roman** [ˈrəʊmən] römisch; Römer, Römerin II
**romance** [rəʊˈmæns, ˈrəʊmæns] Romanze; Romantik IV 2 (52)
**room** [ruːm] Raum, Zimmer I
°**root** [ruːt] Wurzel
**rose** [rəʊz] *siehe* **rise**
**round** [raʊnd] rund II
**round** [raʊnd] um ... (herum); in ... umher II • **the other way round** anders herum II
**route** [ruːt] Strecke, Route IV Intro (10)
**royal** [ˈrɔɪəl] königlich III
**rubber** [ˈrʌbə] Radiergummi I
**rubbish** [ˈrʌbɪʃ] (Haus-)Müll, Abfall II
**rucksack** [ˈrʌksæk] Rucksack III
**rude** [ruːd] unhöflich, unverschämt II
**rule** [ruːl] Regel, Vorschrift IV 2 (45)
**ruler** [ˈruːlə] Lineal I
**run** [rʌn] (Wett-)Lauf II
**run (-nn-)** [rʌn], **ran, run**
1. laufen, rennen I • **run around** herumrennen III
°2. verlaufen, sich erstrecken
**rung** [rʌŋ] *siehe* **ring**
**runner** [ˈrʌnə] Läufer/in II
**running** [ˈrʌnɪŋ]: **running shoes** Laufschuhe III • **running track** Laufbahn *(Sport)* III
**rush**: **rush hour** [ˈrʌʃ‿aʊə] Hauptverkehrszeit III • °**gold rush** [ˈgəʊld rʌʃ] Goldrausch
°**rush to** [rʌʃ] stürzen nach, stürmen nach

## S

**sad** [sæd]
1. traurig II
°2. *Jugendsprache:* peinlich
**saddle** [ˈsædl] Sattel III
**sadness** [ˈsædnəs] Traurigkeit IV 3 (66)
**safe (from)** [seɪf] sicher, in Sicherheit (vor) II
**safety** [ˈseɪfti] Sicherheit IV 1 (23)
**fire safety** Verhalten im Brandfall IV 1 (23)
**said** [sed] *siehe* **say**
**sailor** [ˈseɪlə] Seemann, Matrose II
**salad** [ˈsæləd] Salat *(als Gericht oder Beilage)* I
**sale** [seɪl] (Aus-, Schluss-)Verkauf IV Intro (9) • **for sale** *(auf Schild)* zu verkaufen IV Intro (9/173)
**salmon** [ˈsæmən], *pl* **salmon** Lachs III
**salt** [sɔːlt] Salz III

**same** [seɪm]**: the same ...** der-/die-/dasselbe ...; dieselben ... I • **be/look the same** gleich sein/aussehen I
**sandwich** ['sænwɪtʃ] Sandwich, *(zusammengeklapptes)* belegtes Brot I • **sandwich box** Brotdose I
**sang** [sæŋ] *siehe* **sing**
**sat** [sæt] *siehe* **sit**
**satellite** ['sætəlaɪt] Satellit IV 4 (84)
**Saturday** ['sætədeɪ, 'sætədi] Samstag, Sonnabend I
**sauna** ['sɔːnə] Sauna II • **have a sauna** in die Sauna gehen II
**sausage** ['sɒsɪdʒ] (Brat-, Bock-) Würstchen, Wurst I
**save** [seɪv]
**1.** retten II
**2.** sparen II
**saw** [sɔː] *siehe* **see**
**saxophone** ['sæksəfəʊn] Saxophon III
**say** [seɪ]**, said, said**
**1.** sagen I
°**2.** sag mal
**It says here: ...** Hier steht: ... / Es heißt hier: ... II • **say goodbye** sich verabschieden I • **Say hi to Dilip for me.** Grüß Dilip von mir. I
**say sorry** sich entschuldigen II
**scan a text (-nn-)** [skæn] einen Text schnell nach bestimmten Wörtern/Informationen absuchen II
**scared** [skeəd] verängstigt II • **be scared (of)** Angst haben (vor) I
**scarf** [skɑːf]**,** *pl* **scarves** [skɑːvs] Schal III
**scary** ['skeəri] unheimlich; gruselig I
**scene** [siːn] Szene I
**schedule** [*AE:* 'skedʒuːl, *BE:* 'ʃedjuːl] *(AE)*
**1.** Stundenplan IV 1 (20/178)
**2.** Fahrplan IV 1 (20/178)
**school** [skuːl] Schule I • **at school** in der Schule I • **school bag** Schultasche I • **school subject** Schulfach I
**science** ['saɪəns] Naturwissenschaft I
**score** [skɔː] Spielstand; Punktestand III • **final score** Endstand III • **What's the score now? – 2–0.** *(you say:* two nil) Wie steht es jetzt? *(beim Sport)* – 2:0 III
**score (a goal)** [skɔː], [gəʊl] ein Tor schießen, einen Treffer erzielen III
°**scrapbook** ['skræpbʊk] Sammelalbum
**scream** [skriːm] schreien III
**screen** [skriːn]**: flat screen** Flachbildschirm IV 4 (84)
°**script** [skrɪpt] Drehbuch
**sea** [siː] Meer, *(die)* See I
**search (for)** [sɜːtʃ] suchen (nach), durchsuchen IV 4 (81)
**search engine** ['sɜːtʃ_ˌendʒɪn] Suchmaschine *(im Internet)* IV 4 (81)
°**seat sb.** [siːt] jm. einen Sitzplatz zuweisen, jn. an seinen Platz führen
**second** ['sekənd] zweite(r, s) I
**second floor** zweiter Stock *(BE)* / erster Stock *(AE)* IV 1 (16)
► S.176 floor
**second-hand** [ˌsekənd 'hænd] gebraucht; aus zweiter Hand III
**section** ['sekʃn] Abschnitt, Teil, (Themen-)Bereich III
**see** [siː]**, saw, seen**
**1.** sehen I
**2. see sb.** jn. besuchen, jn. aufsuchen II
**See?** Siehst du? I • **See you.** Tschüs. / Bis bald. I • **Wait and see!** Wart's ab! III
**seem (to be / to do)** [siːm] (zu sein / zu tun) scheinen IV 1 (26)
**seen** [siːn] *siehe* **see**
°**see-through** ['siːθruː] durchsichtig
**segregate** ['segrɪgeɪt] trennen *(nach Rasse, Religion, Geschlecht)* IV 4 (81)
**segregation** [ˌsegrɪ'geɪʃn] (Rassen-) Trennung IV 4 (81/191)
**sell** [sel]**, sold, sold** verkaufen II
**be sold out** ausverkauft sein; vergriffen sein III
**semester** [sɪ'mestə] Semester *(Schulhalbjahr in den USA)* IV 3 (56)
**semi-final** [ˌsemi'faɪnl] Halbfinale III
°**Senate** ['senət] Senat
°**Senator** ['senətə] Senator/in
**send (to)** [send]**, sent, sent** schicken, senden (an) II
**sent** [sent] *siehe* **send**
**sentence** ['sentəns] Satz I
°**separate** ['seprət] getrennt
**September** [sep'tembə] September I
°**sequoia** [sɪ'kwɔɪə] Sequoia, Mammutbaum
**series,** *pl* **series** ['sɪəriːz] (Sende-) Reihe, Serie II
**serious** ['sɪəriəs] ernst, ernsthaft IV 2 (50)
**seriously?** ['sɪəriəsli] im Ernst? IV 2 (50)
°**serve** [sɜːv] servieren
°**set trends** [ˌset 'trendz] Trends vorgeben/setzen
°**settler** ['setlə] Siedler/in
**setup** ['setʌp] Setup II
**sex** [seks] Geschlecht III
**shadow** ['ʃædəʊ] Schatten IV 3 (69)
°**shall** [ʃəl, ʃæl]**: we shall overcome** wir werden siegen *(alle Schwierigkeiten überwinden)*
**shampoo** [ʃæm'puː] Shampoo, Haarwaschmittel III
**share sth. (with sb.)** [ʃeə] sich etwas teilen (mit jm.) I
**she** [ʃiː] sie I
**sheep,** *pl* **sheep** [ʃiːp] Schaf II
**shelf** [ʃelf]**,** *pl* **shelves** [ʃelvz] Regal(brett) I
**shift** [ʃɪft] Schicht *(bei der Arbeit)* IV 1 (15)
**shine** [ʃaɪn]**, shone, shone** scheinen *(Sonne)* II
**ship** [ʃɪp] Schiff I
**shirt** [ʃɜːt] Hemd I
**shocked** [ʃɒkt] schockiert IV 2 (47)
**shoe** [ʃuː] Schuh I
**shone** [ʃɒn] *siehe* **shine**
**shoot** [ʃuːt]**, shot, shot** schießen, erschießen III
**shop** [ʃɒp] Laden, Geschäft I
**shop assistant** ['ʃɒp_əˌsɪstənt] Verkäufer/in I • **shop window** Schaufenster II
**shop (-pp-)** [ʃɒp] einkaufen (gehen) I
**shopping** ['ʃɒpɪŋ] (das) Einkaufen I
**go shopping** einkaufen gehen I
**shopping list** Einkaufsliste I
°**shore: on shore** [ʃɔː] an Land, am Ufer
**short** [ʃɔːt] kurz I; klein *(Person)* IV 1 (16/177)
**shorts** *(pl)* [ʃɔːts] Shorts, kurze Hose I
**shot** [ʃɒt] *siehe* **shoot**
**should** [ʃəd, ʃʊd]**: Why should I ... ?** Warum sollte ich ... ? III
**shoulder** ['ʃəʊldə] Schulter I
**shout** [ʃaʊt] schreien, rufen I
**show** [ʃəʊ]
**1.** Show, Vorstellung I
°**2.** Unterhaltungssendung
**show** [ʃəʊ]**, showed, shown** zeigen I
**shower** ['ʃaʊə] Dusche I • **have a shower** (sich) duschen I
**shown** [ʃəʊn] *siehe* **show**
**shut up** [ˌʃʌt_'ʌp]**, shut, shut** den Mund halten II
**shy** [ʃaɪ] schüchtern, scheu II
**sick** [sɪk]**: I feel sick.** Mir ist schlecht. IV 1 (26) • °**I'm sick.** Mir ist schlecht.
**side** [saɪd] Seite II
**sidewalk** ['saɪdwɔːk] *(AE)* Gehweg, Bürgersteig IV 1 (14)
°**sight** [saɪt]**: within sight of** in Sichtweite von

**sights** *(pl)* [saɪts] Sehenswürdigkeiten II
**sign** [saɪn] Schild, Zeichen III
**sign** [saɪn] unterschreiben IV 3 (62)
**silence** ['saɪləns] Stille; Schweigen III • **°sit in silence** still dasitzen
**silent letter** [ˌsaɪlənt 'letə] „stummer" Buchstabe *(nicht gesprochener Buchstabe)* II
**silly** ['sɪli] albern, dumm I
**since** [sɪns]
**1.** da, weil IV 2 (51)
**2. since April 4th** seit dem 4. April IV 4 (80)
► S.191 German 'seit'
**sincerely** [sɪn'sɪəli]**: Yours sincerely** Mit freundlichen Grüßen/Herzliche Grüße *(Briefschluss bei namentlich bekanntem Empfänger)* IV 2 (45)
**sing** [sɪŋ]**, sang, sung** singen I
**singer** ['sɪŋə] Sänger/in II
**single** ['sɪŋgl] ledig, alleinstehend I **single (ticket)** einfache Fahrkarte *(nur Hinfahrt)* III
**single** ['sɪŋgl] Single III
**sink** [sɪŋk] Spüle, Spülbecken I
**sir** [sɜː, sə]**: Dear Sir or Madam** Sehr geehrte Damen und Herren *(Anrede in Briefen)* IV 2 (45)
**sister** ['sɪstə] Schwester I • **sister city** *(AE)* Partnerstadt IV 3 (59)
**sit (-tt-)** [sɪt]**, sat, sat** sitzen; sich setzen I • **sit down** sich hinsetzen II • **Sit with me.** Setz dich zu mir. / Setzt euch zu mir. I
**°situation** [ˌsɪtʃu'eɪʃn] Situation
**size** [saɪz] Größe I
**skate** [skeɪt] Inliner fahren I
**skateboard** ['skeɪtbɔːd] Skateboard I
**skater** ['skeɪtə] Skateboardfahrer/in III
**skates** *(pl)* [skeɪts] Inliner I
**sketch** [sketʃ] Sketch I
**ski** [skiː] Ski fahren/laufen III
**ski** [skiː] Ski III • **ski slope** ['skiː sləʊp] Skipiste III
**skills file** ['skɪlz faɪl] *Anhang mit Lern- und Arbeitstechniken* I
**skim a text (-mm-)** [skɪm] einen Text überfliegen *(um den Inhalt grob zu erfassen)* III
**skin** [skɪn] Haut IV 4 (81)
**skinny** ['skɪni] mager IV 2 (51)
**skirt** [skɜːt] Rock II
**sky** [skaɪ] Himmel II
**skyline** ['skaɪlaɪn] Skyline *(Horizont; Silhouette)* IV 1 (12)
**skyscraper** ['skaɪskreɪpə] Wolkenkratzer IV 1 (15)
**°skywalk** ['skaɪwɔːk] *oberirdische, wettergeschützte Fußgängerverbindung*
**slave** [sleɪv] Sklave, Sklavin II
**°slavery** ['sleɪvəri] Sklaverei
**sledge** [sledʒ] Schlitten III
**sleep** [sliːp]**, slept, slept** schlafen I
**sleep** [sliːp] Schlaf III
**sleepless** ['sliːpləs] schlaflos IV 2 (42)
**sleepover** ['sliːpəʊvə] Schlafparty III
**slept** [slept] *siehe* **sleep**
**slow** [sləʊ] langsam II
**°slur** [slɜː] lallen
**small** [smɔːl] klein I
**smart** [smɑːt] clever, schlau II
**smell** [smel] riechen II
**smell** [smel] Geruch II
**smile** [smaɪl] lächeln I • **smile at sb.** jn. anlächeln II
**smile** [smaɪl] Lächeln II
**smoke** [sməʊk] rauchen III • **No smoking!** Rauchen verboten. III
**smoke** [sməʊk] Rauch III
**snack** [snæk] Snack, Imbiss II
**snake** [sneɪk] Schlange I
**snow** [snəʊ] Schnee II
**snowball** ['snəʊbɔːl] Schneeball IV 3 (69)
**snowshoe** ['snəʊʃuː] Schneeschuh III
**snowshoeing** ['snəʊʃuːɪŋ] Schneeschuhwandern III
**so** [səʊ]
**1.** also; deshalb, daher I • **So?** Und? / Na und? II
**2. so sweet** so süß I • **so far** bisher, bis jetzt IV 4 (80)
**3. so that** sodass, damit III
**°4. So what!** Na und?
**5. Do you really think so?** Meinst du wirklich? / Glaubst du das wirklich? II
**soap** [səʊp] Seife I • **soap opera** ['səʊp‿ɒprə] *(kurz:* **soap**) Seifenoper IV 2 (49)
**soccer** ['sɒkə] Fußball IV 3 (59)
**social** ['səʊʃl] sozial, Sozial- IV 2 (52)
**sock** [sɒk] Socke, Strumpf I
**soda** ['səʊdə] *(AE)* Limonade IV 3 (58)
**sofa** ['səʊfə] Sofa I
**soft** [sɒft] weich IV 3 (65/187) • **soft drink** alkoholfreies Getränk IV 3 (65)
**software** ['sɒftweə] Software II
**sold** [səʊld] *siehe* **sell** • **be sold out** ausverkauft sein; vergriffen sein III
**soldier** ['səʊldʒə] Soldat/in IV 4 (91)
**some** [səm, sʌm] einige, ein paar I **some cheese/juice** etwas Käse/Saft I
**somebody** ['sʌmbədi] jemand I **Find/Ask somebody who ...** Finde/Frage jemanden, der ... II **somebody else** jemand anders IV 1 (15/176)
► S.176 ... else
**someone** ['sʌmwʌn] jemand IV 2 (34/180)
**something** ['sʌmθɪŋ] etwas II
**sometimes** ['sʌmtaɪmz] manchmal I
**somewhere** ['sʌmweə] irgendwo(hin) II • **somewhere else** woanders IV 1 (15/176)
► S.176 ... else
**son** [sʌn] Sohn I
**song** [sɒŋ] Lied, Song I
**soon** [suːn] bald I
**sore** [sɔː]**: have a sore throat** Halsschmerzen haben II
**sorry** ['sɒri]**: (I'm) sorry.** Entschuldigung. / Tut mir leid. I • **Sorry, I'm late.** Entschuldigung, dass ich zu spät bin/komme. I • **Sorry?** Wie bitte? I • **say sorry** sich entschuldigen II
**sort** [sɔːt] Art, Sorte II
**sound** [saʊnd] klingen, sich *(gut usw.)* anhören I
**sound** [saʊnd] Laut; Klang I **sound file** ['saʊnd faɪl] Tondatei, Soundfile III
**soup** [suːp] Suppe II
**source** [sɔːs] Quelle *(von Information, Energie usw.)* IV 4 (81)
**south** [saʊθ] Süden; nach Süden; südlich III
**southbound** ['saʊθbaʊnd] Richtung Süden III
**south-east** [ˌsaʊθ'iːst] Südosten; nach Südosten; südöstlich III
**south-west** [ˌsaʊθ'west] Südwesten; nach Südwesten; südwestlich III
**souvenir** [ˌsuːvə'nɪə] Souvenir, Mitbringsel IV Intro (10)
**space** [speɪs] Platz *(Raum)* IV 4 (90) **Move back one space.** Geh ein Feld zurück. II • **Move on one space.** Geh ein Feld vor. II
**spaghetti** [spə'geti] Spaghetti II
**°Spanish-speaking** spanischsprachig; Spanisch sprechend
**sparkling water** ['spɑːklɪŋ] Mineralwasser mit Kohlensäure, Sprudel IV 1 (17)
**speak (to)** [spiːk]**, spoke, spoken** sprechen (mit), reden (mit) II
**°speaking: Spanish-speaking** spanischsprachig; Spanisch sprechend
**special** ['speʃl]**: a special day** ein besonderer Tag I

**specific** [spə'sɪfɪk] bestimmte(r,s), spezifische(r,s) IV 2 (43)
**speech** [spi:tʃ] Rede IV 4 (81)
**make a speech** eine Rede halten IV 4 (81) • °**speech bubble** Sprechblase
**spell** [spel] buchstabieren I
**spelling** ['spelɪŋ] (Recht-)Schreibung, Schreibweise III
**spend** [spend], **spent, spent: spend money (on)** Geld ausgeben (für) II • **spend time (on)** Zeit verbringen (mit) II
**spent** [spent] *siehe* **spend**
**spicy** ['spaɪsi] würzig, scharf gewürzt III
°**spirit** ['spɪrɪt] Geist
**splash** [splæʃ] spritzen IV 4 (91)
**spoke** [spəʊk] *siehe* **speak**
**spoken** ['spəʊkən] *siehe* **speak**
**spoon** [spu:n] Löffel III
**sport** [spɔ:t] Sport; Sportart I
**do sport** *(BE)* Sport treiben I
°**play sports** *(AE)* Sport treiben
**sports centre** Sportzentrum I
**sports hall** Sporthalle III
**sportsman** ['spɔ:tsmən] Sportler IV 2 (44)
**sportswoman** ['spɔ:tswʊmən] Sportlerin IV 2 (44)
**sporty** ['spɔ:ti] sportlich III
**spot (-tt-)** [spɒt] entdecken III
**spotlight** ['spɒtlaɪt] Spotlight IV 3 (70)
**spring** [sprɪŋ] Frühling I
**spy** [spaɪ] Spion/in I
**square** [skweə] Platz III • **square km (sq km)** Quadratkilometer IV 3 (63)
**squeeze** [skwi:z] drücken; (aus-)pressen III
**squirrel** ['skwɪrəl] Eichhörnchen II
**stadium** ['steɪdiəm] Stadion III
**stage** [steɪdʒ] Bühne III
**stairs** *(pl)* [steəz] Treppe; Treppenstufen I
**stamp** [stæmp] Briefmarke I
**stand** [stænd], **stood, stood** stehen; sich (hin)stellen II
**star** [stɑ:]
**1.** Stern II
**2.** (Film-, Pop-)Star I
**start** [stɑ:t] starten, anfangen, beginnen (mit) I
**start** [stɑ:t] Start IV Intro (10)
**state** [steɪt] Staat III
**statement** ['steɪtmənt] Aussage, Feststellung III
**station** ['steɪʃn] Bahnhof I • **at the station** am Bahnhof I • **fire station** Feuerwache IV 1 (15) • **gas station** *(AE)* Tankstelle IV Intro (10)
**petrol station** *(BE)* Tankstelle IV Intro (10/174)
°**statistics** [stə'tɪstɪks] Statistik
**statue** ['stætʃu:] Statue II
**stay** [steɪ]
**1.** bleiben I • **stay out** draußen bleiben, wegbleiben III
**2.** wohnen, übernachten II • **stay with** wohnen bei III
**steak** [steɪk] Steak III
**steal** [sti:l], **stole, stolen** stehlen II
**steel** [sti:l] Stahl III • **steel drum** Steeldrum III
**step** [step]
**1.** Schritt I
**2.** Treppenstufe IV 4 (90)
**stereo** ['steriəʊ] Stereoanlage I
**stew** [stju:] Eintopf(gericht) III
**stick** [stɪk], **stuck, stuck: stick out of sth.** aus etwas herausragen, herausstehen III
**sticker** ['stɪkə] Sticker IV 1 (17)
**still** [stɪl] (immer) noch I
**stole** [stəʊl] *siehe* **steal**
**stolen** ['stəʊlən] *siehe* **steal**
**stomach** ['stʌmək] Magen II
**stomach ache** Magenschmerzen, Bauchweh II
**stone** [stəʊn] Stein II
**stood** [stʊd] *siehe* **stand**
**stop (-pp-)** [stɒp]
**1.** aufhören I
**2.** anhalten I
**Stop that!** Hör auf damit! / Lass das! I
**stop** [stɒp] Halt IV 1 (12)
**storm** [stɔ:m] Sturm; Gewitter II
**stormy** ['stɔ:mi] stürmisch II
**story** ['stɔ:ri] Geschichte, Erzählung I
**straight on** [streɪt_'ɒn] geradeaus weiter II
**strange** [streɪndʒ] seltsam, sonderbar; fremd III
°**stranger** ['streɪndʒə] Fremde(r)
**strawberry** ['strɔ:bəri] Erdbeere II
**street** [stri:t] Straße I • **at 7 Hamilton Street** in der Hamiltonstraße 7 I
**stress** [stres] Betonung III
°**stressed** [strest] betont
**strict** [strɪkt] streng III
**strike** [straɪk] Streik III • **be on strike** streiken, sich im Streik befinden III • **go on strike** streiken, in den Streik treten III
**strong** [strɒŋ]
**1.** stark II
°**2.** stabil
**structure** ['strʌktʃə] strukturieren, aufbauen II
°**structure** ['strʌktʃə] Struktur
**stuck** [stʌk] *siehe* **stick**
**student** ['stju:dənt] Schüler/in; Student/in I • **exchange student** Austauschschüler/in III
**studio** ['stju:diəʊ] Studio III
**study** ['stʌdi] studieren; sorgfältig durchlesen; lernen IV 3 (56/185)
**study hall** *Zeit zum selbstständigen Arbeiten/Lernen in der Schule* IV 3 (56) • **study skills** *(pl)* Lern- und Arbeitstechniken I
**stuff** [stʌf] Zeug, Kram II
**stupid** ['stju:pɪd] blöd, dämlich II
**subject** ['sʌbdʒɪkt]
**1.** Schulfach I
°**2.** Betreff *(in einer E-Mail)*
°**suburb** ['sʌbɜ:b] Vorort
**subway** ['sʌbweɪ]: **the subway** *(AE)* die U-Bahn II
**succeed (in sth.)** [sək'si:d] Erfolg haben, erfolgreich sein (mit etwas, bei etwas) IV 2 (37)
**success** [sək'ses] Erfolg III
**successful** [sək'sesfl] erfolgreich III
°**such a ...** [sʌtʃ_ə] so ein(e) ..., solch ein(e) ...
°**sudden** ['sʌdn]: **all of a sudden** plötzlich
**suddenly** ['sʌdnli] plötzlich, auf einmal I
**suffer (from sth.)** ['sʌfə] (an/unter etwas) leiden IV 4 (86)
**sugar** ['ʃʊgə] Zucker II
**suggestion** [sə'dʒestʃən] Vorschlag IV 3 (66)
**suitcase** ['su:tkeɪs] Koffer II
**summarize sth.** ['sʌməraɪz] etwas zusammenfassen IV 3 (67)
**summary** ['sʌməri] Zusammenfassung IV 3 (67/187)
**summer** ['sʌmə] Sommer I
**sun** [sʌn] Sonne II • °**sun-dried** ['sʌndraɪd] sonnengetrocknet
**Sunday** ['sʌndeɪ, 'sʌndi] Sonntag I
**sung** [sʌŋ] *siehe* **sing**
**sunglasses** *(pl)* ['sʌnglɑ:sɪz] (eine) Sonnenbrille I
**sunny** ['sʌni] sonnig II
**super** ['su:pə] super IV 2 (47)
**supermarket** ['su:pəmɑ:kɪt] Supermarkt II
**support** [sə'pɔ:t] unterstützen IV 4 (90) • **support a team** eine Mannschaft unterstützen; Fan einer Mannschaft sein III
**supporter** [sə'pɔ:tə] Anhänger/in, Fan III
°**supreme: the Supreme Court** [su:ˌpri:m 'kɔ:t] der Oberste Gerichtshof
**sure** [ʃʊə, ʃɔ:] klar, sicher IV 1 (15)
**be sure** sicher sein II • **make sure**

**that ...** sich vergewissern, dass ...; dafür sorgen, dass ... IV 2 (49)
**°They sure are.** (Ganz) Bestimmt.
**surf** [sɜːf]**: surf the internet** im Internet surfen III
**surfboard** ['sɜːfbɔːd] Surfbrett II
**surfing** ['sɜːfɪŋ]**: go surfing** wellenreiten gehen, surfen gehen II
**surprise** [sə'praɪz] Überraschung III
**surprise sb.** [sə'praɪz] jn. überraschen III
**surprised (at sth.)** [sə'praɪzd] überrascht (über/von etwas) III
**survey (on)** ['sɜːveɪ] Umfrage, Untersuchung (über) II
**survive** [sə'vaɪv] überleben II
**°SUV** [ˌes juː 'viː] **(sport utility vehicle** [ˌspɔːt juː'tɪləti ˌviːəkl]**)** Geländewagen
**swam** [swæm] *siehe* **swim**
**swap sth. (for sth.) (-pp-)** [swɒp] etwas (ein)tauschen (für etwas/gegen etwas) IV 3 (68)
**sweat** [swet] schwitzen IV 3 (68)
**sweat** [swet] Schweiß IV 3 (68/188)
**sweatshirt** ['swetʃɜːt] Sweatshirt I
**sweet** [swiːt] süß I
**sweetheart** ['swiːthɑːt] Liebling, Schatz II
**sweets** *(pl)* [swiːts] Süßigkeiten I
**swim (-mm-)** [swɪm]**, swam, swum** schwimmen I • **go swimming** schwimmen gehen I
**swimmer** ['swɪmə] Schwimmer/in II
**swimming** ['swɪmɪŋ]**: swimming pool** [puːl] Schwimmbad, Schwimmbecken I • **swimming trunks** *(pl)* [trʌŋks] Badehose III
**swimsuit** ['swɪmsuːt] Badeanzug III
**swum** [swʌm] *siehe* **swim**
**syllable** ['sɪləbl] Silbe I
**°symbol** ['sɪmbl] Symbole
**synonym** ['sɪnənɪm] Synonym *(Wort mit gleicher oder ähnlicher Bedeutung)* IV 2 (42)
**system** ['sɪstəm] System IV 3 (56)

# T

**table** ['teɪbl] Tisch I
**table tennis** ['teɪbl tenɪs] Tischtennis I • **table tennis bat** Tischtennisschläger III
**take** [teɪk]**, took, taken**
**1.** nehmen I
**2.** (weg-, hin)bringen I
**3.** dauern, *(Zeit)* brauchen III
**take a break** eine Pause machen IV 1 (22) • **take a ride** eine Fahrt machen III • **take notes** sich Notizen machen I • **°take off** *(infml)* sich davonmachen, sich aus dem Staub machen • **take out** herausnehmen I • **take part (in)** teilnehmen (an) III • **take photos** Fotos machen, fotografieren I
**take place** stattfinden IV 1 (15)
**°take sth. in** etwas zu sich nehmen • **take sth. off** etwas ausziehen *(Kleidung)* II • **take 10 c off** 10 Cent abziehen I • **take sth. over** etwas übernehmen; etwas in seine Gewalt bringen IV 1 (15)
**°Take turns.** Wechselt euch ab.
**°I'll take it from here.** *etwa:* Ich übernehme das jetzt. / Ich komme jetzt alleine klar. • **We'll take them.** *(beim Einkaufen)* Wir nehmen sie. I
**taken** ['teɪkən] *siehe* **take**
**talent** ['tælənt] Talent, Begabung III
**talk** [tɔːk]**: talk (about)** reden (über), sich unterhalten (über) I
**talk (to)** reden (mit), sich unterhalten (mit) I • **°talk sb. out of sth.** jm. etwas ausreden
**°talk** [tɔːk] Vortrag, Rede • **°give a talk** einen Vortrag halten
**tall** [tɔːl] hoch *(Bäume, Türme usw.)*; groß *(Person)* IV 1 (16)
**°tan** [tæn] (sonnen-)gebräunt
**tattoo** [tə'tuː] Tattoo IV 1 (27)
**taught** [tɔːt] *siehe* **teach**
**taxi** ['tæksi] Taxi III
**tea** [tiː] Tee; *(auch:) leichte Nachmittags- oder Abendmahlzeit* I
**teach** [tiːtʃ]**, taught, taught** unterrichten, lehren I
**teacher** ['tiːtʃə] Lehrer/in I • **head teacher** Schulleiter/in III
**team** [tiːm] Team, Mannschaft I
**tear** [tɪə] Träne IV 1 (27)
**tear sth. off** [teə]**, tore, torn** etwas abreißen IV 1 (27)
**teaspoon** ['tiːspuːn] Teelöffel III
**teddy** ['tedi] Teddybär III
**teen** [tiːn] Teenager-, Jugend- III
**teenager** ['tiːneɪdʒə] Teenager, Jugendliche(r) II
**teeth** [tiːθ] *Plural von „tooth"*
**telephone** ['telɪfəʊn] Telefon I
**telephone number** Telefonnummer I • **What's your telephone number?** Was ist deine Telefonnummer? I
**television (TV)** ['telɪvɪʒn] Fernsehen I
**tell (about)** [tel]**, told, told** erzählen (von), berichten (über) I • **Tell me your names.** Sagt mir eure Namen. I • **tell sb. the way** jm. den Weg beschreiben II
**temperature** ['temprətʃə] Temperatur II • **have a temperature** Fieber haben II
**tennis** ['tenɪs] Tennis I
**tense** [tens] (grammatische) Zeit, Tempus III
**tent** [tent] Zelt IV Intro (9)
**term** [tɜːm] Trimester II
**terrible** ['terəbl] schrecklich, furchtbar I
**terrified** ['terɪfaɪd]**: be terrified (of)** schreckliche Angst haben (vor) IV 4 (90)
**terrorist** ['terərɪst] Terrorist/in; Terror-, terroristisch IV 4 (79)
**test** [test] Test, Prüfung II
**text** [tekst] Text I • **text message** SMS III • **skim a text** einen Text überfliegen *(um den Inhalt grob zu erfassen)* III
**text sb.** [tekst] jm. eine SMS schicken III
**than** [ðæn, ðən] als II • **more than** mehr als II • **more than me** mehr als ich II
**thank** [θæŋk]**: Thank you.** Danke (schön). I • **Thanks.** Danke. I
**Thanks a lot!** Vielen Dank! I
**Thanks very much!** Danke sehr! / Vielen Dank! II
**that** [ðət, ðæt]
**1.** das (dort) I
**2.** jene(r, s) I
**That's me.** Das bin ich. I • **That's right.** Das ist richtig. / Das stimmt. I • **That's up to you.** Das liegt bei dir. / Das kannst/musst du (selbst) entscheiden. III • **That was close.** Das war knapp. II
**that** [ðət, ðæt] dass I • **so that** sodass, damit III
**that** [ðət, ðæt] der, die, das; die *(Relativpronomen)* III
**that far/good/bad/...** [ðæt] so weit/gut/schlecht/... III
**the** [ðə, ði] der, die, das; die I
**theatre** ['θɪətə] Theater II
**their** [ðeə] ihr, ihre *(Plural)* I
**theirs** [ðeəz] ihrer, ihre, ihrs II
**them** [ðəm, ðem] sie; ihnen I
**themselves** [ðəm'selvz] sich (selbst) III
**°theme** ['θiːm]**: theme park** Themenpark *(Freizeitpark mit Attraktionen zu einem bestimmten Thema)*
**°theme song** ['θiːm sɒŋ] Titelsong
**then** [ðen] dann, danach I
**°therapy** ['θerəpi] (Psycho-)Therapie
**there** [ðeə]
**1.** da, dort I
**2.** dahin, dorthin I
**down there** dort unten II • **over**

**there** da drüben, dort drüben I
**there are** es sind (vorhanden); es gibt I • **there's** es ist (vorhanden); es gibt I • **there isn't a ...** es ist kein/e ...; es gibt kein/e ... I
**°There you go.** *(infml) etwa:* So, das hätten wir.
**thermometer** [θəˈmɒmɪtə] Thermometer II
**°thermos** [ˈθɜːməs] Thermosflasche
**these** [ðiːz] diese, die (hier) I
**they** [ðeɪ] sie *(Plural)* I
**thief** [θiːf], *pl* **thieves** [θiːvz] Dieb/in II
**thing** [θɪŋ] Ding, Sache I • **What was the best thing about ...?** Was war das Beste an ...? II
**think** [θɪŋk], **thought, thought** glauben, meinen, denken I
**think about 1.** nachdenken über II; **2.** denken über, halten von II
**think of 1.** denken über, halten von II; **2.** denken an; sich ausdenken II
**third** [θɜːd] dritte(r, s) I
**this** [ðɪs]
**1.** dies (hier) I
**2.** diese(r, s) I
**This is Isabel.** Hier spricht Isabel. / Hier ist Isabel. *(am Telefon)* II
**this morning/afternoon/evening** heute Morgen/Nachmittag/Abend I • **this way** hier entlang, in diese Richtung II
**those** [ðəʊz] die (da), jene (dort) I
**thought** [θɔːt] *siehe* **think**
**thought** [θɔːt] Gedanke IV 3 (64)
**thousand** [ˈθaʊznd] tausend I
**threw** [θruː] *siehe* **throw**
**throat** [θrəʊt] Hals, Kehle II
**through** [θruː] durch II
**throw** [θrəʊ], **threw, thrown** werfen I • **throw up** sich übergeben IV 3 (69)
**thrown** [θrəʊn] *siehe* **throw**
**Thursday** [ˈθɜːzdeɪ, ˈθɜːzdi] Donnerstag I
**°tick** [tɪk] Häkchen
**°tick** [tɪk] ankreuzen, ein Häkchen machen
**ticket** [ˈtɪkɪt]
**1.** Eintrittskarte I
**2.** Fahrkarte II
**ticket machine** Fahrkartenautomat III • **ticket office** Kasse *(für den Verkauf von Eintrittskarten)* IV 1 (16); Fahrkartenschalter III
**one-day ticket** Tages(fahr)karte III
**return ticket** Rückfahrkarte II
**single (ticket)** einfache Fahrkarte *(nur Hinfahrt)* III
**tidy** [ˈtaɪdi] aufräumen I
**tidy** [ˈtaɪdi] ordentlich, aufgeräumt II
**°tie** [taɪ] Krawatte
**°tie** [taɪ] binden
**tiger** [ˈtaɪgə] Tiger II
**tight** [taɪt] fest IV 3 (69)
**till** [tɪl] bis *(zeitlich)* I
**time** [taɪm]
**1.** Zeit; Uhrzeit I
**2. time(s)** Mal(e); -mal II
**What's the time?** Wie spät ist es? I • **any time** jederzeit IV 1 (27/179)
**for the first time** zum ersten Mal IV 4 (91) • **in time** rechtzeitig II
**three times** dreimal III • **cross a time zone** [zəʊn] eine Zeitzone passieren IV Intro (8)
**°timeline** [ˈtaɪmlaɪn] Zeitachse, Zeitleiste
**timetable** [ˈtaɪmteɪbl]
**1.** Stundenplan I
**2.** Fahrplan II
**timing** [ˈtaɪmɪŋ]**: bad timing** schlechtes Timing III
**tip** [tɪp]
**1.** Tipp II
**2.** Spitze IV Intro (10)
**tired** [ˈtaɪəd] müde I • **be tired of sth.** genug von etwas haben, etwas satt haben IV 1 (16)
**title** [ˈtaɪtl] Titel, Überschrift I
**to** [tə, tu]
**1.** zu, nach I • **to Jenny's** zu Jenny I • **°to the front** nach vorn
**2. an e-mail to** eine E-Mail an I
**write to** schreiben an I
**3. quarter to 12** Viertel vor 12 (11.45/23.45) I
**4. try to help/to play/...** versuchen, zu helfen/zu spielen/... I
**5.** um zu II
**6. from Monday to Friday** von Montag bis Freitag III
**toast** [təʊst] Toast(brot) I
**tobacco** [təˈbækəʊ] Tabak II
**today** [təˈdeɪ] heute I
**toe** [təʊ] Zeh I
**together** [təˈgeðə] zusammen I
**toilet** [ˈtɔɪlət] Toilette I
**told** [təʊld] *siehe* **tell**
**tomato** [təˈmɑːtəʊ], *pl* **tomatoes** Tomate II
**tomorrow** [təˈmɒrəʊ] morgen I
**tomorrow's weather** das Wetter von morgen II
**tonight** [təˈnaɪt] heute Nacht, heute Abend I • **tonight's programme** das Programm von heute Abend; das heutige Abendprogramm II
**too** [tuː]**: from Bristol too** auch aus Bristol I • **Me too.** Ich auch. I
**too much/big/...** [tuː] zu viel/groß/... I
**took** [tʊk] *siehe* **take**
**tool** [tuːl] Werkzeug IV Intro (9)
**tooth** [tuːθ], *pl* **teeth** [tiːθ] Zahn I
**toothache** [ˈtuːθeɪk] Zahnschmerzen II
**toothless** [ˈtuːθləs] zahnlos IV 2 (42)
**top** [tɒp]
**1.** Spitze, oberes Ende I • **at the top (of)** oben, am oberen Ende, an der Spitze (von) I
**2.** Top, Oberteil I
**topic** [ˈtɒpɪk] Thema, Themenbereich I • **topic sentence** *Satz, der in das Thema eines Absatzes einführt* II
**tore** [tɔː] *siehe* **tear**
**torn** [tɔːn] *siehe* **tear**
**tornado** [tɔːˈneɪdəʊ] Tornado, Wirbelsturm II
**tortoise** [ˈtɔːtəs] Schildkröte I
**touch** [tʌtʃ] berühren, anfassen II
**keep in touch** in Verbindung bleiben, Kontakt halten III
**tour** [tʊə]**: tour (of the house)** Rundgang, Tour (durch das Haus) I • **tour guide** (Fremden-)Führer/in, Reiseleiter/in IV 3 (67)
**°tourism** [ˈtʊərɪzəm] Tourismus, Fremdenverkehr
**tourist** [ˈtʊərɪst] Tourist/in II
**tourist information** Fremdenverkehrsamt II
**towards sb./sth.** [təˈwɔːdz] auf jn./etwas zu II
**towel** [ˈtaʊəl] Handtuch IV 2 (52)
**tower** [ˈtaʊə] Turm I
**town** [taʊn] (Klein-)Stadt I
**track** [træk] Stück, Titel, Track *(auf einer CD)* III
**°trade** [treɪd] Handel
**tradition** [trəˈdɪʃn] Tradition IV 3 (55)
**traditional** [trəˈdɪʃənl] traditionell III
**traffic** [ˈtræfɪk] Verkehr II • **traffic jam** (Verkehrs-)Stau IV 4 (79)
**traffic light** (Verkehrs-)Ampel IV 3 (54)
**°trail** [treɪl] Pfad
**train** [treɪn] Zug I • **on the train** im Zug I • **°downtown train** Zug in Richtung Stadtmitte
**°elevated train** [ˈelɪveɪtɪd] Hochbahn
**train** [treɪn] trainieren III
**trainers** *(pl)* [ˈtreɪnəz] Turnschuhe II
**training session** [ˈseʃn] Trainingsstunde, -einheit III
**tram** [træm] Straßenbahn III
**translate (from ... into)** [trænsˈleɪt] übersetzen (aus ... ins) III

**translation** [træns'leɪʃn] Übersetzung III
**transport** ['trænspɔːt] Beförderung, Transport III
°**trash** [træʃ]: **white trash** *(AE, infml) abwertende Bezeichnung für die weiße Unterschicht*
**travel (-ll-)** ['trævl] reisen II
**Travelcard** ['trævlkɑːd] Tages-/Wochen-/Monatsfahrkarte *(der Londoner Verkehrsbetriebe)* III
**tree** [triː] Baum I
°**trend** [trend]: **set trends** Trends vorgeben/setzen
**trendy** ['trendi] modisch, schick III
°**tribute** ['trɪbjuːt] Ehrung; Würdigung
**trick** [trɪk]
**1.** (Zauber-)Kunststück, Trick I
**do tricks** (Zauber-)Kunststücke machen I
**2.** Streich II
**trip** [trɪp] Reise; Ausflug I • **go on a trip** einen Ausflug machen II
**trouble** ['trʌbl] Schwierigkeiten, Ärger II • **be in trouble** in Schwierigkeiten sein; Ärger kriegen II
**trousers** *(pl)* ['traʊzəz] Hose II
**true** [truː] wahr II
**trumpet** ['trʌmpɪt] Trompete III
**try** [traɪ]
**1.** versuchen I
**2.** probieren, kosten I
**try and do sth. / try to do sth.** versuchen, etwas zu tun I • **try on** anprobieren *(Kleidung)* I
**T-shirt** ['tiːʃɜːt] T-Shirt I
**tsunami** [tsuː'nɑːmi] Tsunami IV 2 (34)
**tube** [tjuːb]: **the Tube** *(no pl)* die Londoner U-Bahn III
**Tuesday** ['tjuːzdeɪ, 'tjuːzdi] Dienstag I
**tune** [tjuːn] Melodie III
**tunnel** ['tʌnl] Tunnel II
**turkey** ['tɜːki] Truthahn, Pute/Puter III
**turn** [tɜːn]
**1.** sich umdrehen II • **turn left/right** (nach) links/rechts abbiegen II • **turn to sb.** sich jm. zuwenden; sich an jn. wenden I
**2. turn sth. on/off** etwas ein-, ausschalten III
**3. turn sth. down/up** etwas leiser/lauter stellen IV 4 (84)
**turn** [tɜːn]: **It's your turn.** Du bist dran / an der Reihe. I • **Miss a turn.** Einmal aussetzen. II • °**Take turns.** Wechselt euch ab. • **Whose turn is it?** Wer ist dran / an der Reihe? II

**TV** [tiː'viː] Fernsehen I • **on TV** im Fernsehen I • **watch TV** fernsehen I • **TV listings** *(pl)* das Fernsehprogramm IV 4 (78)
**twice** [twaɪs] zweimal • **twice a week** zweimal pro Woche III
**twin** [twɪn]: **twin brother** Zwillingsbruder I • **twins** *(pl)* Zwillinge I
**twin town** Partnerstadt IV 3 (59)
**two all** [ˌtuː‿'ɔːl] 2 beide (2:2 unentschieden) III
**type** [taɪp] *(infml)* Typ III

## U

**unbelievable** [ˌʌnbɪ'liːvəbl] unglaublich IV 4 (79)
**uncle** ['ʌŋkl] Onkel I
**unclear** [ˌʌn'klɪə] unklar III
**uncomfortable** [ʌn'kʌmftəbl] unbequem, unbehaglich IV 2 (49/183)
**uncool** [ˌʌn'kuːl] *(infml)* uncool III
**uncountable** [ʌn'kaʊntəbl] unzählbar IV 3 (64)
**under** ['ʌndə] unter I
**underground** ['ʌndəgraʊnd]: **the underground** die U-Bahn II
°**underground** [ˌʌndə'graʊnd] unter der Erde
°**underline** [ˌʌndə'laɪn] unterstreichen
°**underlined** [ˌʌndə'laɪnd] unterstrichen
**understand** [ˌʌndə'stænd], **understood, understood** verstehen, begreifen I
**understandable** [ˌʌndə'stændəbl] verständlich IV 4 (87)
**understood** [ˌʌndə'stʊd] *siehe* **understand**
°**unemployed** [ˌʌnɪm'plɔɪd] arbeitslos
**unfair** [ˌʌn'feə] unfair, ungerecht III
**unfortunately** [ʌn'fɔːtʃənətli] leider IV 4 (80/191)
**unfriendly** [ʌn'frendli] unfreundlich III
**unhappy** [ʌn'hæpi] unglücklich III
**unhealthy** [ʌn'helθi] ungesund III
**uniform** ['juːnɪfɔːm] Uniform I
**unit** ['juːnɪt] Lektion, Kapitel I
**united**: **the United Kingdom (UK)** [juˌnaɪtɪd 'kɪŋdəm] ([ˌjuː 'keɪ]) das Vereinigte Königreich *(Großbritannien und Nordirland)* III • **the United States (US)** [juˌnaɪtɪd 'steɪts] ([ˌjuː‿'es]) die Vereinigten Staaten *(von Amerika)* III
**university** [ˌjuːnɪ'vɜːsəti] Universität IV 4 (91)

**unlock** [ˌʌn'lɒk] aufschließen; entsperren III
**unreadable** [ʌn'riːdəbl] unleserlich IV 4 (87)
**unsafe** [ʌn'seɪf] nicht sicher, gefährlich III
**untidy** [ʌn'taɪdi] unordentlich III
**until** [ən'tɪl] bis III
**up** [ʌp] hinauf, herauf, nach oben I
**up the hill** den Hügel hinauf II
**That's up to you.** Das liegt bei dir. / Das kannst/musst du (selbst) entscheiden. III
**upset (about)** [ˌʌp'set] aufgebracht, gekränkt, mitgenommen (wegen) III
**upset sb. (-tt-)** [ʌp'set], **upset, upset** jn. ärgern, kränken, aus der Fassung bringen III
°**upside down** [ˌʌpsaɪd 'daʊn] auf den Kopf gestellt
**upstairs** [ˌʌp'steəz] oben; nach oben I
**us** [əs, ʌs] uns I
**use** [juːz] benutzen, verwenden I
**useful** ['juːsfl] nützlich III
**usually** ['juːʒuəli] meistens, gewöhnlich, normalerweise I

## V

**vacation** [və'keɪʃn, *AE:* veɪ'keɪʃn] *(AE)* Urlaub, Ferien III
**valley** ['væli] Tal II
**valuable** ['væljuəbl] wertvoll IV 4 (91)
**vegetable** ['vedʒtəbl] *(ein)* Gemüse III • °**vegetable oil** Pflanzenöl
**vegetarian** [ˌvedʒə'teəriən] vegetarisch; Vegetarier/in IV 2 (43)
**version** ['vɜːʃn] Version, Fassung IV 3 (67)
**very** ['veri] sehr I • **like/love sth. very much** etwas sehr mögen/sehr lieben II • **Thanks very much!** Danke sehr! / Vielen Dank! II
**victim** ['vɪktɪm] Opfer III
**video** ['vɪdiəʊ] Video III
**view** [vjuː] Aussicht, Blick II
**viewer** ['vjuːə] Zuschauer/in IV 4 (78)
**village** ['vɪlɪdʒ] Dorf I
**violence** ['vaɪələns] Gewalt; Gewalttätigkeit IV 4 (76)
**violent** ['vaɪələnt] gewalttätig; gewaltsam IV 4 (76/189)
**violin** [ˌvaɪə'lɪn] Violine, Geige III
**visit** ['vɪzɪt] besuchen II
**visit** ['vɪzɪt] Besuch II
**visitor** ['vɪzɪtə] Besucher/in, Gast I

**vocabulary** [və'kæbjələri] Vokabelverzeichnis, Wörterverzeichnis I
**voice** [vɔɪs] Stimme IV 4 (91)
**volleyball** ['vɒlibɔ:l] Volleyball I
**volume** ['vɒlju:m] Lautstärke IV 4 (84)
**volunteer** [ˌvɒlən'tɪə] sich freiwillig melden, sich bereit erklären IV 4 (90)
**volunteer** [ˌvɒləntɪə] Freiwillige(r) IV 4 (90/193)
**vote for sb.** [vəʊt] für jn. stimmen IV 3 (68)

## W

°**wagon train** ['wægən treɪn] Planwagenkolonne, -zug
**wait (for)** [weɪt] warten (auf) I **Wait a minute.** Warte mal! / Moment mal! II • **I can't wait to see ...** ich kann es kaum erwarten, ... zu sehen I • **Wait and see!** Wart's ab! III
**waiter** ['weɪtə] Kellner II
**waiting room** ['weɪtɪŋ ru:m] Wartezimmer IV 4 (89)
**waitress** ['weɪtrəs] Kellnerin II
**wake up** [ˌweɪk_'ʌp], **woke, woken** aufwachen III • **wake sb. (up)** jn. (auf)wecken III
**walk** [wɔ:k] (zu Fuß) gehen I **walk around** herumlaufen, umherspazieren III • **walk around the town** in der Stadt umhergehen, durch die Stadt gehen III **walk off** weggehen IV 2 (49)
**walk** [wɔ:k] Spaziergang II • **a ten-kilometre walk** eine Zehn-Kilometer-Wanderung III • **go for a walk** spazieren gehen, einen Spaziergang machen II
**wall** [wɔ:l] Wand; Mauer II
°**wander** ['wɒndə] wandern; schlendern
**want** [wɒnt] (haben) wollen I **want to do** tun wollen I • **want sb. to do sth.** wollen, dass jm. etwas tut IV 4 (91)
**war** [wɔ:] Krieg IV 4 (76)
**wardrobe** ['wɔ:drəʊb] Kleiderschrank I
**warm** [wɔ:m] warm II
**warn sb. (about sth.)** [wɔ:n] jn. (vor etwas) warnen III
°**warrior** ['wɒriə] Krieger/in
**was** [wəz, wɒz]: **(I/he/she/it) was** *siehe* **be**
**wash** [wɒʃ] waschen I • **I wash my face.** Ich wasche mir das Gesicht. I
**washing machine** ['wɒʃɪŋ məˌʃi:n] Waschmaschine I
**watch** [wɒtʃ] beobachten, sich etwas ansehen; zusehen I **watch TV** fernsehen I • °**watch for** nach etwas Ausschau halten
**watch** [wɒtʃ] Armbanduhr I
**water** ['wɔ:tə] Wasser I
**wave** [weɪv] winken II
**way** [weɪ]
**1.** Weg II • **all the way** den ganzen Weg IV Intro (10) • **ask sb. the way** jn. nach dem Weg fragen II **on the way (to)** auf dem Weg (zu/nach) II • **tell sb. the way** jm. den Weg beschreiben II
**2.** Richtung II • **the other way round** anders herum II • **the wrong way** in die falsche Richtung II • **this way** hier entlang, in diese Richtung II • **which way?** in welche Richtung? / wohin? II
**3.** Art und Weise III • **the way you ...** so wie du ..., auf dieselbe Weise wie du ... IV 3 (69)
**4. by the way** übrigens II
**5. No way!** Auf keinen Fall! / Kommt nicht in Frage! II
**we** [wi:] wir I
**weak** [wi:k] schwach II
**wear** [weə], **wore, worn** tragen, anhaben *(Kleidung)* I
**weather** ['weðə] Wetter II
**webcam** ['webkæm] Webcam III
**website** ['websaɪt] Website II
**Wednesday** ['wenzdeɪ, 'wenzdi] Mittwoch I
**week** [wi:k] Woche I • **days of the week** Wochentage I • **a two-week holiday** ein zweiwöchiger Urlaub III
**weekend** [ˌwi:k'end] Wochenende I **at the weekend** am Wochenende I
**welcome** ['welkəm]
**1. Welcome (to Bristol).** Willkommen (in Bristol). I
**2. You're welcome.** Gern geschehen. / Nichts zu danken. I
**welcome sb. (to)** ['welkəm] jn. begrüßen, willkommen heißen (in) I **They welcome you to ...** Sie heißen dich in ... willkommen I
**well** [wel]
**1.** gut II
**2.** *(gesundheitlich)* gut; gesund, wohlauf II
**do well (in)** gut abschneiden (in) III • **go well** gut (ver)laufen, gutgehen III • **You did well.** Das hast du gut gemacht. II • **Oh well ...** Na ja ... / Na gut ... I • **Well, ...** Nun, ... / Also, ... I • °**Well done!** [ˌwel 'dʌn] Gut gemacht! • °**well-rounded** vielseitig interessiert/gebildet
**Welsh** [welʃ] walisisch; Walisisch II
**went** [went] *siehe* **go**
**were** [wə, wɜ:]: **(we/you/they) were** *siehe* **be**
**west** [west] Westen; nach Westen; westlich III • °**going west** *Besiedlung des Westens der USA im 19. Jh.*
**westbound** ['westbaʊnd] Richtung Westen III
**western** ['westən] westlich, West- III
**wet** [wet] nass III
**what** [wɒt]
**1.** was I
**2.** welche(r, s) I
°**What a bird!** Was für ein Vogel! **What about ...? 1.** Was ist mit ...? / Und ...? I; **2.** Wie wär's mit ...? I **What are you talking about?** Wovon redest du? I • **What colour is ...?** Welche Farbe hat ...? I **What for?** Wofür? II • **What have we got next?** Was haben wir als Nächstes? I • **What kind of car ...?** Was für ein Auto ...? III • **What page are we on?** Auf welcher Seite sind wir? I • **What's for homework?** Was haben wir als Hausaufgabe auf? I • **What's the matter?** Was ist los? / Was ist denn? II **What's the time?** Wie spät ist es? I • **What's your name?** Wie heißt du? I • **What's your telephone number?** Was ist deine Telefonnummer? I • **What was the weather like?** Wie war das Wetter? II • **I don't know what to do.** Ich weiß nicht, was ich machen soll. IV Intro (9/173) • °**So what!** Na und?
**whatever** [wɒt'evə] was (auch) immer IV 2 (49)
► S.183 whoever, whatever, whenever, wherever
**wheel** [wi:l] Rad III • **big wheel** Riesenrad III
**wheelchair** ['wi:ltʃeə] Rollstuhl I
**when** [wen] wann I • **When's your birthday?** Wann hast du Geburtstag? I
**when** [wen]
**1.** wenn I
**2.** als I
**whenever** [wen'evə] wann immer IV 2 (49/183)
► S.183 whoever, whatever, whenever, wherever

**where** [weə]
**1.** wo I
**2.** wohin I
**Where are you from?** Wo kommst du her? I

**wherever** [weər'evə] wo auch immer IV 2 (49/183)
► S.183 whoever, whatever, whenever, wherever

**which** [wɪtʃ]: **Which picture ...?** Welches Bild ...? I • **which way?** in welche Richtung? / wohin? II

**which** [wɪtʃ] der, die, das; die *(Relativpronomen)* III

**while** [waɪl] während III
► S.191 German 'während'

**whisky** ['wɪski] Whisky II

**whisper** ['wɪspə] flüstern I

**whistle** ['wɪsl] pfeifen II

**whistle** ['wɪsl] (Triller-)Pfeife III

**white** [waɪt] weiß I • °**white trash** *(AE, infml) abwertende Bezeichnung für die weiße Unterschicht*

**who** [hu:]
**1.** wer I
**2.** wen/wem II

**who** [hu:] der, die, das; die *(Relativpronomen)* III • **Find/Ask somebody who ...** Finde/Frage jemanden, der ... II

**whoever** [hu:'evə] wer auch immer IV 2 (49/183)
► S.183 whoever, whatever, whenever, wherever

**whole** [həʊl] ganze(r, s), gesamte(r, s) III

**whole-grain** ['həʊlgreɪn] Vollkorn- IV 3 (58)

**whose?** [hu:z] wessen? II • **Whose are these?** Wem gehören diese? II **Whose turn is it?** Wer ist dran / an der Reihe? II

**why** [waɪ] warum I • **Why me?** Warum ich? I • **Why should I ... ?** Warum sollte ich ... ? III

**wide** [waɪd] weit, breit IV Intro (8)

**wife** [waɪf], *pl* **wives** [waɪvz] Ehefrau II

**wild** [waɪld] wild II

**will** [wɪl]: **you'll be cold (= you will be cold)** du wirst frieren; ihr werdet frieren II • **you won't be cold** [wəʊnt] **(= you will not be cold)** du wirst nicht frieren; ihr werdet nicht frieren II

**win (-nn-)** [wɪn], **won, won** gewinnen I

**win** [wɪn] Sieg III

**wind** [wɪnd] Wind I

°**wind** [waɪnd] sich winden, schlängeln

**window** ['wɪndəʊ] Fenster I

**windy** ['wɪndi] windig I

**wine** [waɪn] Wein IV 2 (36)

°**winery** ['waɪnəri] Weingut

**wing** [wɪŋ] Flügel IV Intro (10)

**winner** ['wɪnə] Gewinner/in, Sieger/in II

**winter** ['wɪntə] Winter I

**wish** [wɪʃ]: **Best wishes** *etwa:* Alles Gute / Mit besten Grüßen *(als Briefschluss)* IV 3 (62) • °**wish** Wunsch

**with** [wɪð]
**1.** mit I
**2.** bei I
**be with sb.** mit jemandem zusammen sein IV 3 (69) • **go with** gehören zu, passen zu III • **Sit with me.** Setz dich zu mir. / Setzt euch zu mir. I

°**within sight of** [wɪ'θɪn] in Sichtweite von

**without** [wɪ'ðaʊt] ohne I

**wives** [waɪvz] *Plural von „wife"*

**woke** [wəʊk] *siehe* **wake**

**woken** ['wəʊkən] *siehe* **wake**

**wolf** [wʊlf], *pl* **wolves** [wʊlvz] Wolf II

**woman** ['wʊmən], *pl* **women** ['wɪmɪn] Frau I

**won** [wʌn] *siehe* **win**

**wonder** ['wʌndə] sich fragen, gern wissen wollen II

**won't** [wəʊnt]: **you won't be cold (= you will not be cold)** du wirst nicht frieren; ihr werdet nicht frieren II

**wood** [wʊd] Holz III

**woodpecker** ['wʊdpekə] Specht II

**woods** *(pl)* [wʊdz] Wald, Wälder III

**word** [wɜ:d] Wort I • **word building** Wortbildung II
°**word order** Wortstellung

**wore** [wɔ:] *siehe* **wear**

**work** [wɜ:k]
**1.** arbeiten I
**2.** funktionieren III
**work hard** hart arbeiten II
**work on sth.** an etwas arbeiten I
**work out** gut ausgehen IV 2 (51)
**work sth. out** etwas herausarbeiten, herausfinden IV 1 (23) • °**work sth. through** etwas durcharbeiten

**work** [wɜ:k] Arbeit I • **at work** bei der Arbeit / am Arbeitsplatz I

**worker** ['wɜ:kə] Arbeiter/in II

**workplace** ['wɜ:kpleɪs] Arbeitsplatz IV 4 (79)

**worksheet** ['wɜ:kʃi:t] Arbeitsblatt I

**workshop** ['wɜ:kʃɒp] Workshop, Lehrgang III

**world** [wɜ:ld] Welt I • **all over the world** auf der ganzen Welt III **from all over the world** aus der ganzen Welt III • **in the world** (auf) der Welt IV 1 (25)

**worn** [wɔ:n] *siehe* **wear**

**worried (about)** ['wʌrid] beunruhigt (wegen), besorgt (wegen/um) IV 3 (59)

**worry** ['wʌri] Sorge, Kummer II

**worry (about)** ['wʌri] sich Sorgen machen (wegen, um) I • **Don't worry.** Mach dir keine Sorgen. I

**worse** [wɜ:s] schlechter, schlimmer II

**worst** [wɜ:st]: **(the) worst** am schlechtesten, schlimmsten; der/die/das schlechteste, schlimmste II

**would** [wəd, wʊd]: **I/you/... would ...** ich würde / du würdest / ... III • **I'd like ... (= I would like ...)** Ich hätte gern ... / Ich möchte gern ... I **Would you like ...?** Möchtest du ...? / Möchten Sie ...? I • **Would you like some?** Möchtest du etwas/ein paar? / Möchten Sie etwas/ein paar? I • **I'd like to talk about ... (= I would like to talk about ...)** Ich möchte über ... reden / Ich würde gern über ... reden I

**write** [raɪt], **wrote, written** schreiben I • **write down** aufschreiben I • **write to** schreiben an I

**writer** ['raɪtə] Schreiber/in; Schriftsteller/in II

**written** ['rɪtn] *siehe* **write**

**wrong** [rɒŋ] falsch, verkehrt I • **be wrong 1.** falsch sein I; **2.** sich irren, Unrecht haben II • **the wrong way** in die falsche Richtung II

**wrote** [rəʊt] *siehe* **write**

## Y

**yard** [jɑ:d] Hof II • **in the yard** auf dem Hof II

**yawn** [jɔ:n] gähnen II

**year** [jɪə]
**1.** Jahr I
**2.** Jahrgangsstufe I
**a sixteen-year-old** ein/e Sechzehnjährige/r III • **a sixteen-year-old girl** ein sechzehnjähriges Mädchen III

**yellow** ['jeləʊ] gelb I

**yes** [jes] ja I

**yesterday** ['jestədeɪ, 'jestədi] gestern I • **yesterday morning/afternoon/evening** gestern Morgen/Nachmittag/Abend I • **yesterday's homework** die Hausaufgaben von gestern II

**yet** [jet]: **not (...) yet** noch nicht II
**yet?** schon? II
°**Yiddish** ['jɪdɪʃ] Jiddisch; jiddisch
°**yo** [jəʊ] *(infml)* hey
**yoga** ['jəʊgə] Yoga I
**you** [ju:]
**1.** du; Sie I
**2.** ihr I • **you two** ihr zwei I
**3.** dir; dich; euch I
**4.** man III
**young** [jʌŋ] jung I
**your** [jɔ:]
**1.** dein/e I
**2.** Ihr I
**3.** euer/eure I
**yours** [jɔ:z]
**1.** deiner, deine, deins II
**2.** Ihrer, Ihre, Ihrs II
**3.** eurer, eure, eures II
**yourself** [jɔ:'self] dir/dich (selbst) III
**yourselves** [jɔ:'selvz] euch (selbst) III
**youth** [ju:θ] Jugend, Jugend- III
**youth group** Jugendgruppe IV Intro (9) • **youth hostel** Jugendherberge III
**yuck** [jʌk] igitt III

## Z

**zebra** ['zebrə] Zebra II
**zero** ['zɪərəʊ] null I • °**Ground Zero** [ˌgraʊnd 'zɪərəʊ] Bodennullpunkt *(Bezeichnung für das zerstörte World Trade Center in New York; ursprünglich: Explosionsstelle einer Bombe oder Rakete über dem Boden)*
**zone** [zəʊn] Zone, Gebiet IV Intro (8)
**zoo** [zu:] Zoo IV 1 25

## English sounds (Englische Laute)

Die Lautschrift in den eckigen Klammern zeigt dir, wie ein Wort ausgesprochen wird.
In der folgenden Übersicht findest du alle Lautzeichen.

| Vokale (Selbstlaute) | | | | Konsonanten (Mitlaute) | | | |
|---|---|---|---|---|---|---|---|
| [i:] | green | [eɪ] | skate | [b] | box | [f] | full |
| [i] | happy | [aɪ] | time | [p] | play | [v] | very |
| [ɪ] | in | [ɔɪ] | boy | [d] | dad | [s] | sister |
| [e] | yes | [əʊ] | old | [t] | ten | [z] | please |
| [æ] | black | [aʊ] | now | [g] | good | [ʃ] | shop |
| [ɑ:] | park | [ɪə] | here | [k] | cat | [ʒ] | television |
| [ɒ] | song | [eə] | where | [m] | mum | [tʃ] | teacher |
| [ɔ:] | morning | [ʊə] | tour | [n] | no | [dʒ] | Germany |
| [u:] | blue | | | [ŋ] | sing | [θ] | thanks |
| [ʊ] | book | | | [l] | hello | [ð] | this |
| [ʌ] | mum | | | [r] | red | [h] | he |
| [ɜ:] | T-shirt | | | [w] | we | | |
| [ə] | a partner | | | [j] | you | | |

## The English alphabet (Das englische Alphabet)

| | | | | | | | |
|---|---|---|---|---|---|---|---|
| a | [eɪ] | h | [eɪtʃ] | o | [əʊ] | v | [vi:] |
| b | [bi:] | i | [aɪ] | p | [pi:] | w | ['dʌblju:] |
| c | [si:] | j | [dʒeɪ] | q | [kju:] | x | [eks] |
| d | [di:] | k | [keɪ] | r | [ɑ:] | y | [waɪ] |
| e | [i:] | l | [el] | s | [es] | z | [zed] |
| f | [ef] | m | [em] | t | [ti:] | | |
| g | [dʒi:] | n | [en] | u | [ju:] | | |

Das **German – English Dictionary** enthält den **Lernwortschatz** der Bände 1 bis 4 von *English G 21*. Es kann dir eine erste Hilfe sein, wenn du vergessen hast, wie etwas auf Englisch heißt.

Wenn du wissen möchtest, wo das englische Wort zum ersten Mal in *English G 21* vorkommt, dann kannst du im **English – German Dictionary** (S. 194–224) nachschlagen.

Im **German – English Dictionary** werden folgende **Abkürzungen** und **Symbole** verwendet:

| | | | | |
|---|---|---|---|---|
| jm. = jemandem | sb. = somebody | *pl = plural* | *BE = British English* | *infml = informal* |
| jn. = jemanden | sth. = something | *no pl = no plural* | *AE = American English* | |

▶ Der Pfeil verweist auf Kästchen im Vocabulary (S. 172–193), in denen du weitere Informationen findest.

## A

**abbiegen: (nach) links/rechts abbiegen** turn left/right [tɜːn]
**Abend** evening ['iːvnɪŋ]; *(später Abend)* night [naɪt] • **am Abend, abends** in the evening
**Abendbrot, -essen** dinner ['dɪnə]
**Abendbrot essen** have dinner
**zum Abendbrot** for dinner
**Abenteuer** adventure [əd'ventʃə]
**aber** but [bət, bʌt] • **aber egal, ...** *(wie auch immer, ...; wie dem auch sei, ...; na ja, ...)* anyway, ... ['eniweɪ]
**abfahren** *(wegfahren)* leave [liːv]
**Abfahrt** *(Abreise)* departure (dep) [dɪ'pɑːtʃə]
**Abfall** rubbish ['rʌbɪʃ] *(BE)*; garbage ['gɑːbɪdʒ] *(AE)*
**Abflug** departure (dep) [dɪ'pɑːtʃə]
**Abgemacht!** It's a deal. [diːl]
**abhängen (mit Freunden/Freundinnen)** *(rumhängen)* hang out (with friends) [ˌhæŋ_'aʊt]
**abholen: jn. abholen** pick sb. up [ˌpɪk_'ʌp]
**Abkommen: ein Abkommen treffen** make a deal [diːl]
**Abmachung: eine Abmachung treffen** make a deal [diːl]
**Abreise** departure (dep) [dɪ'pɑːtʃə]
**abreißen** tear off [ˌteər_'ɒf]
**Absatz** *(in einem Text)* paragraph ['pærəgrɑːf]
**abschließen** lock [lɒk]
**Abschluss** *(einer Geschichte, eines Films usw.)* ending ['endɪŋ]
**abschneiden: etwas abschneiden** cut sth. off [ˌkʌt_'ɒf]
**Abschnitt** section ['sekʃn]
**abschreiben** *(kopieren)* copy ['kɒpi]
**absetzen: jn. absetzen** *(aussteigen lassen)* drop sb. off [ˌdrɒp_'ɒf]
**abtrennen: etwas abtrennen** *(abschneiden)* cut sth. off [ˌkʌt_'ɒf]
**abziehen: 10 Cent abziehen** take 10 c off [ˌteɪk_'ɒf]
**achten: auf etwas achten** *(horchen)* listen for sth. ['lɪsn]
**Acker** field [fiːld]
**addieren (zu)** add (to) [æd]
**Adresse** address [ə'dres]
**Affe** monkey ['mʌŋki]
**Afro-Amerikaner/in** African American [ˌæfrɪkən_ə'merɪkən]
**afro-amerikanisch** African American [ˌæfrɪkən_ə'merɪkən]
**aktiv** active ['æktɪv]
**Aktivität** activity [æk'tɪvəti]
**Akzent** accent ['æksənt]
**albern** silly ['sɪli]
**Album** album ['ælbəm]
**alkoholfreies Getränk** soft drink [ˌsɒft 'drɪŋk]
**alle** *(die ganze Gruppe)* all [ɔːl]; *(jeder)* everyone ['evriwʌn]
**Allee** avenue ['ævənjuː]
**allein** alone [ə'ləʊn]
**alleinstehend** single ['sɪŋgl]
**alles** everything ['evriθɪŋ]; all [ɔːl]; *(was es auch sei / egal was)* anything ['eniθɪŋ] • **Alles Gute** *(als Briefschluss)* Best wishes ['wɪʃɪz]
**allgemeine(r, s)** general ['dʒenrəl]
**alltägliche(r, s), Alltags-** everyday ['evrideɪ]
**Alphabet** alphabet ['ælfəbet]
**als 1.** *(zeitlich)* when [wen]; *(während)* as [əz, æz]
**2. als ob** as if [əz_'ɪf]
**3. als Feuerwehrfrau, -mann** as a firefighter
**4. größer/teurer als** bigger/more expensive than [ðæn, ðən]
**also** *(daher, deshalb)* so [səʊ]
Also, ... Well, ... [wel]
**alt** old [əʊld]
**Alter** age [eɪdʒ]
**altmodisch** old-fashioned [ˌəʊld'fæʃnd]
**am 1. am Bahnhof** at the station
**am oberen Ende (von)** at the top (of) • **am Strand** on the beach
**am Telefon** on the phone • **am unteren Ende (von)** at the bottom (of) ['bɒtəm]
**2.** *(nahe bei)* **am Meer** by the sea
**3.** *(zeitlich)* **am 13. Juni** on 13th June • **am Morgen/Nachmittag/Abend** in the morning/afternoon/evening • **am Ende (von)** at the end (of) • **am Freitag** on Friday
**am Freitagmorgen** on Friday morning • **am nächsten Morgen/Tag** the next morning/day • **am Wochenende** at the weekend
**Amerikanische(r) Ureinwohner/in** Native American [ˌneɪtɪv_ə'merɪkən]
**Amnestie** amnesty ['æmnəsti]
**Ampel** traffic light ['træfɪk laɪt]
**amüsieren: sich amüsieren** have fun [hæv 'fʌn] • **Amüsier dich gut!** Enjoy yourself.
**an 1. an dem/den Tisch (dort)** at that table • **an der Spitze** at the top (of) • **an der/die Tafel** on the board • **an jn. schreiben** write to sb.
**2.** *(nahe bei)* **an der See** by the sea
**3. Was war das Beste an ...?** What was the best thing about ...?
**4. an sein** *(Radio, Licht usw.)* be on
**anbauen** *(Getreide usw.)* grow [grəʊ]
**anbieten** offer ['ɒfə]
**andere(r, s)** other ['ʌðə] • **die anderen** the others
**ändern: (sich) ändern** change [tʃeɪndʒ]
▶ S.186 (to) change – change
**anders (als)** different (from) ['dɪfrənt]
**anders ausdrücken** *(umschreiben)* paraphrase ['pærəfreɪz] • **anders herum** the other way round
**jemand anders** sombebody else
▶ S.176 ... else
**Änderung** change [tʃeɪndʒ]
▶ S.186 (to) change – change
**Anfang** beginning [bɪ'gɪnɪŋ] • **am Anfang** at first
**anfangen (mit)** begin [bɪ'gɪn]; start [stɑːt]
**anfassen** touch [tʌtʃ]

**anfühlen: sich gut anfühlen** feel good [fi:l]
**Anführer/in** leader ['li:də]
**Angebot** offer ['ɒfə]
**angeln** fish [fɪʃ]
**angreifen** attack [ə'tæk]
**Angriff** attack [ə'tæk]
**Angst haben (vor)** be afraid (of) [ə'freɪd]; be scared (of) [skeəd] **schreckliche Angst haben (vor)** be terrified (of) ['terɪfaɪd]
**anhaben** *(Kleidung)* wear [weə]
**anhalten** stop [stɒp]
**Anhänger/in** *(Fan)* supporter [sə'pɔ:tə]
**anhören 1. sich etwas anhören** listen to sth. ['lɪsn] **2. sich gut anhören** sound good [saʊnd]
**anklicken: etwas anklicken** click on sth. [klɪk]
**ankommen** arrive [ə'raɪv]
**ankündigen** announce [ə'naʊns]
**Ankündigung** announcement [ə'naʊnsmənt]
**Ankunft** arrival (arr) [ə'raɪvl]
**anlächeln: jn. anlächeln** smile at sb. [smaɪl]
**Anleitung(en)** *(Gebrauchsanweisungen)* instructions *(pl)* [ɪn'strʌkʃnz]
**anmailen: jn. anmailen** mail sb. [meɪl]
**anmalen** paint [peɪnt]; *(bunt ausmalen)* colour ['kʌlə]
**Anorak** anorak ['ænəræk]
**anpassen: sich anpassen** fit in [ˌfɪt‿'ɪn]
**anpflanzen** *(Getreide usw.)* grow [grəʊ]
**anprobieren** *(Kleidung)* try on [ˌtraɪ‿'ɒn]
**Anruf** call; phone call ['fəʊn kɔ:l]
**anrufen** call [kɔ:l]; phone [fəʊn]
**Ansage** *(Durchsage)* announcement [ə'naʊnsmənt]
**anschauen** look at [lʊk]
**Anschlagtafel** notice board ['nəʊtɪs bɔ:d] *(BE)*; bulletin board ['bʊlətɪn bɔ:d] *(AE)*
**anschließen: sich jm. anschließen** join sb. [dʒɔɪn]
**Anschrift** address [ə'dres]
**ansehen: sich etwas ansehen** look at sth. [lʊk]; watch sth. [wɒtʃ]; have a look at sth.
**Antwort (auf)** answer (to) ['ɑ:nsə]
**antworten** answer ['ɑ:nsə]
**Anweisung(en)** *(Gebrauchsanweisungen)* instructions *(pl)* [ɪn'strʌkʃnz]
**anziehen: etwas anziehen** *(Kleidung)* put sth. on [ˌpʊt‿'ɒn] • **sich anziehen** get dressed [get 'drest]
**Apfel** apple ['æpl]
**Apfelsine** orange ['ɒrɪndʒ]
**Apotheke** chemist ['kemɪst]
**Apotheker: beim Apotheker** at the chemist's
**Appetit** appetite ['æpɪtaɪt]
**April** April ['eɪprəl]
**Arbeit** work [wɜ:k] • **bei der Arbeit/am Arbeitsplatz** at work • **gute Arbeit leisten** do a good job
**arbeiten (an)** work (on) [wɜ:k]
**Arbeiter/in** worker ['wɜ:kə]
**Arbeitsblatt** worksheet ['wɜ:kʃi:t]
**arbeitslos** jobless ['dʒɒbləs]
**Arbeitsplatz** *(Ort)* workplace ['wɜ:kpleɪs]
**Arbeits- und Lerntechniken** study skills ['stʌdi skɪlz]
**Archiv** archive ['ɑ:kaɪv]
**Ärger** *(Schwierigkeiten)* trouble ['trʌbl] • **Ärger kriegen** be in trouble
**ärgern: jn. ärgern** *(kränken)* upset sb. [ʌp'set]
**Argument** argument ['ɑ:gjumənt] **ein Argument vorbringen** make a point
**Argumentation** argument ['ɑ:gjumənt]
**arm** poor [pɔ:, pʊə]
**Arm** arm [ɑ:m]
**Armbanduhr** watch [wɒtʃ]
**Art 1.** *(Sorte)* sort (of) [sɔ:t]; kind (of) [kaɪnd] **2. Art und Weise** way [weɪ]
**Artikel** article ['ɑ:tɪkl]
**Arzt/Ärztin** doctor ['dɒktə] • **zum Arzt** to the doctor's
**Atlantik** Atlantic (Ocean) [ətˌlæntɪk‿'əʊʃn]
**Atlantischer Ozean** Atlantic (Ocean) [ətˌlæntɪk‿'əʊʃn]
**Attraktion** attraction [ə'trækʃən]
**auch: auch aus Bristol** from Bristol too [tu:]; also from Bristol ['ɔ:lsəʊ] **Ich auch.** Me too.
**auf** on [ɒn] • **auf (... hinauf)** onto ['ɒntə, 'ɒntʊ] • **auf dem Bild/Foto** in the picture/photo • **auf dem Feld** in the field • **auf dem Hof** in the yard • **auf dem Land** *(im Gegensatz zur Stadt)* in the country; *(nicht auf dem Wasser)* on land **auf dem Weg (zu/nach)** on the way (to) • **auf der Erde** on earth **auf der ganzen Welt** all over the world • **auf der Welt** in the world **auf einmal** suddenly ['sʌdnli] • **auf Englisch** in English • **Auf geht's!** Let's go. • **auf jn./etwas zu** towards sb./sth. [tə'wɔ:dz] • **Auf keinen Fall!** No way! • **Auf welcher Seite sind wir?** What page are we on? • **Auf Wiedersehen.** Goodbye. [ˌgʊd'baɪ]
**aufbewahren** keep [ki:p]
**aufführen** *(Szene, Dialog)* act [ækt]
**Aufgabe** *(im Schulbuch)* exercise ['eksəsaɪz]; *(Job)* job [dʒɒb]
**aufgeben** *(nicht mehr weitermachen)* give up
**aufgebracht** (wegen) upset (about) [ˌʌp'set]
**aufgeräumt** *(ordentlich)* tidy ['taɪdi]
**aufgeregt** *(nervös)* nervous ['nɜ:vəs]; *(begeistert)* excited [ɪk'saɪtɪd]
**aufheben: etwas aufheben** *(hochheben)* pick sth. up [ˌpɪk‿'ʌp]
**aufhören** stop [stɒp]
**auflegen** *(Musik/CDs/Platten; in der Disko)* DJ ['di:dʒeɪ]
**auflisten** list [lɪst]
**aufmachen** open ['əʊpən]
**Aufnahme** *(Aufzeichnung)* recording [rɪ'kɔ:dɪŋ]
**aufnehmen** *(Musik / einen Film)* record [rɪ'kɔ:d]
**aufpassen: auf etwas/jn. aufpassen** look after sth./sb. [ˌlʊk‿'ɑ:ftə]
**aufräumen** tidy ['taɪdi]
**aufregend** exciting [ɪk'saɪtɪŋ]
**Aufsatz** essay ['eseɪ]
**aufschauen (von)** look up (from) [ˌlʊk‿'ʌp]
**aufschließen** unlock [ˌʌn'lɒk]
**aufschreiben** write down [ˌraɪt 'daʊn]
**Aufseher/in** *(in Nationalparks, die auch Führungen machen und als Wald- und Wildhüterinnen arbeiten)* park ranger ['pɑ:k reɪndʒə]
**aufstehen** get up [ˌget‿'ʌp]
**aufsteigen** *(hochsteigen, in die Luft steigen)* rise [raɪz]
**aufsuchen: jn. aufsuchen** see sb. [si:]
**Auftritt** *(Konzert)* gig [gɪg] *(infml)* **einen Auftritt haben** *(ein Konzert geben)* do a gig
**aufwachen** wake up [ˌweɪk‿'ʌp]
**aufwachsen** grow up [ˌgrəʊ‿'ʌp]
**aufwecken: jn. aufwecken** wake sb. up [ˌweɪk‿'ʌp]
**aufzählen** *(auflisten)* list [lɪst]
**Aufzeichnung** *(Aufnahme)* recording [rɪ'kɔ:dɪŋ]
**Aufzug** lift [lɪft] *(BE)*; elevator ['elɪveɪtə] *(AE)*
**Auge** eye [aɪ]
**August** August ['ɔ:gəst]
**aus: Ich komme/bin aus ...** I'm from ... [frəm, frɒm] • **aus ... (heraus/hinaus)** out of ... ['aʊt‿əv] • **aus der ganzen Welt** from all over the world • **aus dem Zug/Bus aussteigen** get off the train/bus

**aus vielen Gründen** for lots of reasons • **aus zweiter Hand** *(gebraucht)* second-hand [ˌsekənd ˈhænd]
**ausdenken: sich etwas ausdenken** think of sth. [θɪŋk]
**ausdrücken: anders ausdrücken** *(umschreiben)* paraphrase [ˈpærəfreɪz]
**auseinander** *(getrennt)* apart [əˈpɑːt]
**Ausflug** trip [trɪp] • **einen Ausflug machen** go on a trip
**ausgeben: Geld ausgeben (für)** spend money (on) [spend]
**Ausgehverbot haben** be grounded [ˈgraʊndɪd]
**ausgestellt sein/werden** be on display [dɪˈspleɪ]
**ausgezeichnet** *(hervorragend)* excellent [ˈeksələnt]
► S.185 US school grades
**auslachen** laugh at
**ausländisch** foreign [ˈfɒrən]
**auslassen: etwas auslassen** *(weglassen)* leave sth. out [ˌliːv_ˈaʊt]
**ausmalen** *(bunt anmalen, kolorieren)* colour [ˈkʌlə]
**auspressen** squeeze [skwiːz]
**ausruhen: sich ausruhen** relax [rɪˈlæks]
**Ausrüstung** *(Ausrüstungsgegenstände)* equipment [ɪˈkwɪpmənt]; *(Ausrüstungsgegenstände oder Kleidung für eine bestimmte Aktivität)* gear [gɪə]
**Aussage** statement [ˈsteɪtmənt]
**ausschalten** turn off [tɜːn]
**aussehen: anders/toll/alt aussehen** look different/great/old [lʊk]
**fürchterlich aussehen** be a mess [mes]
**außer** except [ɪkˈsept]
**außerhalb seines Zimmers** outside his room [ˌaʊtˈsaɪd]
**aussetzen: Einmal aussetzen.** Miss a turn. [tɜːn]
**Aussicht (auf)** *(Blick)* view (of) [vjuː]
**Aussprache** pronunciation [prəˌnʌnsiˈeɪʃn]
**aussteigen (aus dem Zug/Bus)** get off (the train/bus) [ˌget_ˈɒf] • **jn. aussteigen lassen** drop sb. off [ˌdrɒp_ˌɒf]
**aussuchen: (sich) etwas aussuchen** choose sth. [tʃuːz]
**Austauschschüler/in** exchange student [ɪksˈtʃeɪndʒ ˌstjuːdnt]
**Ausverkauf** sale [seɪl]
**ausverkauft sein** be sold out [ˌsəʊld_ˈaʊt]
**auswählen** choose [tʃuːz]
**ausziehen 1.** *(aus Wohnung)* move out [ˌmuːv_ˈaʊt]
**2. etwas ausziehen** *(Kleidung)* take sth. off [ˌteɪk_ˈɒf]
**Auto** car [kɑː]; auto [ˈɔːtəʊ] *(AE)*
**Autofahrt** drive [draɪv]
**Autsch!** Ouch! [aʊtʃ]

## B

**Baby** baby [ˈbeɪbi] • **ein Baby bekommen** have a baby
**Bäckerei** bakery [ˈbeɪkəri]
**Badeanzug** swimsuit [ˈswɪmsuːt]
**Badehose** swimming trunks *(pl)* [trʌŋks]
**baden** *(ein Bad nehmen)* have a bath [bɑːθ]
**Badewanne** bath [bɑːθ]
**Badezimmer** bathroom [ˈbɑːθruːm]
**Badminton** badminton [ˈbædmɪntən]
**Badmintonschläger** badminton racket [ˈrækɪt]
**Bahnhof** station [ˈsteɪʃn] • **am Bahnhof** at the station
**Bahnsteig** *(Gleis)* platform [ˈplætfɔːm]
**bald** soon [suːn] • **Bis bald.** See you. [ˈsiː juː]
**Ball 1.** ball [bɔːl]
**2.** *(Tanzveranstaltung)* ball [bɔːl]
**Banane** banana [bəˈnɑːnə]
**Band** *(Musikgruppe)* band [bænd]
**Bank 1.** *(Sparkasse)* bank [bæŋk]
**2.** *(Sitzbank)* bench [bentʃ]
**Bankräuber/in** bank robber [ˈrɒbə]
**Bar** bar [bɑː]
**Bär** bear [beə]
**Bart** beard [bɪəd]
**Baseball** baseball [ˈbeɪsbɔːl]
**Baseballmütze** baseball cap [kæp]
**Basketball** basketball [ˈbɑːskɪtbɔːl]
**Bauchweh** stomach ache [ˈstʌmək_eɪk]
**bauen** build [bɪld]
**Bauer/Bäuerin** farmer [ˈfɑːmə]
**Bauernhaus** farmhouse [ˈfɑːmhaʊs]
**Bauernhof** farm [fɑːm]
**Baum** tree [triː]
**Baumwolle** cotton [ˈkɒtn]
**beantworten** answer [ˈɑːnsə]
**Becken** *(Schwimmbecken)* pool [puːl]
**bedeuten** mean [miːn]
**Bedeutung** meaning [ˈmiːnɪŋ]
**bedeutungsähnliches Wort** synonym [ˈsɪnənɪm]
**beeilen: sich beeilen** hurry [ˈhʌri]; hurry up [ˌhʌri_ˈʌp]
**beeindruckt** impressed [ɪmˈprest]
**beenden** finish [ˈfɪnɪʃ]; end [end]
**Beförderung** *(Transport)* transport [ˈtrænspɔːt]
**Begabung** talent [ˈtælənt]
**begeistert** *(aufgeregt)* excited [ɪkˈsaɪtɪd]
**Beginn** beginning [bɪˈgɪnɪŋ]
**beginnen (mit)** begin [bɪˈgɪn]; start [stɑːt]
**Begnadigung** amnesty [ˈæmnəsti]
**begreifen** understand [ˌʌndəˈstænd]
**Begründung** *(Grund)* reason [ˈriːzn]; *(Argument)* argument [ˈɑːgjumənt]
**behaglich** comfortable [ˈkʌmftəbl]
**behalten** keep [kiːp]
**behindert** disabled [dɪsˈeɪbld]
**bei: bei den Shaws zu Hause** at the Shaws' house • **bei der Arbeit** at work • **Englisch bei Mr Kingsley** English with Mr Kingsley
**beide** both [bəʊθ] • **2 beide** *(2:2 unentschieden)* 2 all [ˌtuː_ˈɔːl]
**Beifall klatschen** *(laut jubelnd)* cheer [tʃɪə]; clap [klæp]
**Bein** leg [leg] • **etwas auf die Beine stellen** get sth. off the ground
**beinahe** almost [ˈɔːlməʊst]
**Beispiel** example [ɪgˈzɑːmpl] • **zum Beispiel** for example
**bekannt** known [nəʊn]
**Bekanntgabe** announcement [əˈnaʊnsmənt]
**bekanntgeben** announce [əˈnaʊns]
**beklagen: sich (über etwas) beklagen** complain (about sth.) [kəmˈpleɪn]
**bekommen** get [get] • **ein Baby bekommen** have a baby
**belästigen: jn. belästigen** annoy sb. [əˈnɔɪ ]
**belebt** *(Straße, Ort)* busy [ˈbɪzi]
**beliebig: jede(r) (Beliebige)** anybody [ˈenibɒdi]; anyone [ˈeniwʌn]
**jede(r) (beliebige) ...** any [ˈeni]
► S.179 any
**beliebt** popular [ˈpɒpjələ]
**bemerken 1.** notice [ˈnəʊtɪs]
**2.** *(erkennen)* realize [ˈriːəlaɪz]
**3.** *(sagen)* mention [ˈmenʃən]
**Bemerkung** *(Kommentar)* comment [ˈkɒment]
**benachteiligen: jn. benachteiligen** discriminate against sb. [dɪˈskrɪmɪneɪt]
**Benachteiligung (von)** discrimination (against) [dɪˌskrɪmɪˈneɪʃn]
**benennen** name [kɔːl]
**benötigen** need [niːd]
**benutzen** use [juːz]
**Benzin** petrol [ˈpetrəl] *(BE);* gas [gæs] *(AE)*
**beobachten** watch [wɒtʃ]
**bequem** comfortable [ˈkʌmftəbl]
**Machs dir bequem.** Make yourself comfortable. [ˈkʌmftəbl]

**Bereich** area ['eəriə]; section ['sekʃn]
**bereit** ready ['redi] **bereits** already [ɔ:l'redi]
**Berg** mountain ['maʊntən]
**Bericht (über)** report (on) [rɪ'pɔ:t]
**berichten (über)** tell (about) [tel] **(jm.) etwas berichten** report sth. (to sb.) [rɪ'pɔ:t]
**berichtigen** correct [kə'rekt]
**beruhigen: sich beruhigen** calm down [ˌkɑ:m 'daʊn]
**berühmt** famous ['feɪməs]
**berühren** touch [tʌtʃ]
**Bescheid: über etwas Bescheid wissen** know about sth. [nəʊ]
**beschließen** decide (on) [dɪ'saɪd]
**beschreiben: (jm.) etwas beschreiben** describe sth. (to sb.) [dɪ'skraɪb] **jm. den Weg beschreiben** tell sb. the way
**Beschreibung** description [dɪ'skrɪpʃn]
**beschweren: sich (über etwas) beschweren** complain (about sth.) [kəm'pleɪn]
**besiegen** beat [bi:t]
**besitzen** have [həv, hæv]
**besondere(r, s)** special ['speʃl] • **ein besonderer Tag** a special day
**besonders** especially [ɪ'speʃəli]
**besorgen** *(holen)* get [get]
**besorgt (wegen/um)** worried (about) ['wʌrid]
**Besprechung** meeting ['mi:tɪŋ]
**besser** better ['betə]
**beste: am besten** (the) best [best] **der/die/das beste ...; die besten ...** the best ... • **Was war das Beste an ...?** What was the best thing about ...?
**bestellen** order ['ɔ:də]
**bestimmte(r,s)** specific [spə'sɪfɪk]
**Besuch** visit ['vɪzɪt]
**besuchen: jn. besuchen** visit sb. ['vɪzɪt]; see sb. [si:]
**Besucher/in** visitor ['vɪzɪtə]
**beteiligen: sich beteiligen (an)** get involved (in) [ɪn'vɒlvd]
**betteln (um)** beg (for) [beg]
**Betonung** stress [stres]
**betreten** enter ['entə]
**Bett** bed [bed] • **ins Bett gehen** go to bed
**beunruhigt (wegen)** worried (about) ['wʌrid]
**beurteilen (nach)** judge (by) [dʒʌdʒ]
**Beutel** bag [bæg]
**Bevölkerung** population [ˌpɒpju'leɪʃn]
**bevor** before [bɪ'fɔ:]
**bewegen: sich bewegen** move [mu:v]
**Bewegung** movement ['mu:vmənt]; *(körperliche Bewegung)* exercise ['eksəsaɪz] *(no pl)*
**Beweis(e)** proof *(no pl)* [pru:f]
**bewölkt** cloudy ['klaʊdi]
**bezahlen: etwas bezahlen** pay for sth. [peɪ]
**beziehen: sich beziehen auf** refer to [rɪ'fɜ:]
**Bezirk** *(Stadtbezirk)* borough ['bʌrə, *(AE:* 'bɜ:rəʊ)]
► S.175 New York: the five boroughs
**Bibliothek** library ['laɪbrəri]
**Bild** picture ['pɪktʃə] • **auf dem Bild** in the picture
**Bildergeschichte** picture story
**Bildschirm** monitor ['mɒnɪtə]
**Bildung** education [ˌedʒʊ'keɪʃn]
**Bildunterschrift** caption ['kæpʃn]
**billig** cheap [tʃi:p]
**Bindewort** linking word ['lɪŋkɪŋ wɜ:d]
**Biografie** biography [baɪ'ɒgrəfi]
**Biologie** biology [baɪ'ɒlədʒi]
**bis** *(zeitlich)* until [ən'tɪl]; till [tɪl] **Bis bald.** See you. ['si: ju:] • **bis jetzt** so far • **bis (spätestens) zehn Uhr** by ten o'clock • **von Montag bis Freitag** from Mondays to Fridays
**bisher** so far
**bisschen: ein bisschen** a bit [bɪt]
**bitte 1.** *(in Fragen und Aufforderungen)* please [pli:z]
**2. Bitte sehr. / Hier bitte.** Here you are.
**3. Bitte, gern geschehen.** You're welcome. ['welkəm]
**4. Wie bitte?** Sorry? ['sɒri]
**bitten: (eindringlich) bitten (um)** beg (for) [beg]
**blasen** blow [bləʊ]
**blau** blue [blu:]
**bleiben** stay [steɪ] • **draußen bleiben** stay out • **in Verbindung bleiben** keep in touch [ˌki:p‿ɪn 'tʌtʃ] **Bleib ruhig.** Don't panic! ['pænɪk]
**Bleistift** pencil ['pensl]
**Bleistiftanspitzer** pencil sharpener ['pensl ʃɑ:pnə]
**Blick** *(Aussicht)* view [vju:] • **einen Blick werfen auf etwas** have a look at sth.
**Blitz** *(Lichtblitz)* flash [flæʃ]
**Block** *(Häuser-, Wohnblock)* block [blɒk]
**Blockflöte** recorder [rɪ'kɔ:də]
**blöd** stupid ['stju:pɪd]
**Blog** *(Internet-Tagebuch)* blog *(von web log)* [blɒg]
**blond** blond [blɒnd]
**bloß** just [dʒʌst]; only ['əʊnli]
**Blut** blood [blʌd]
**Boden** *(Erdboden)* ground [graʊnd]
**Bodyguard** bodyguard ['bɒdigɑ:d]
**Bohne** bean [bi:n]
**Boot** boat [bəʊt]
**böse sein (auf jn.)** be cross (with sb.) [krɒs]; be angry (with sb.) ['æŋgri] **böse sein (über etwas)** be angry (about sth.)
**Boss** boss [bɒs]
**brainstormen** *(so viele Ideen wie möglich sammeln)* brainstorm ['breɪnstɔ:m]
**Brand** fire ['faɪə]
**brauchen** need [ni:d]; *(Zeit brauchen, dauern)* take [teɪk] • **nicht zu tun brauchen** needn't do ['ni:dnt]
**braun** brown [braʊn]
**brav** good [gʊd]
**Breakdance** breakdance ['breɪkdɑ:ns]
**brechen** break [breɪk]
**breit** *(weit)* wide [waɪd]
**brennen** burn [bɜ:n]
**Brett: schwarzes Brett** bulletin board *(AE)* ['bʊlətɪn bɔ:d]
**Brief (an)** letter (to) ['letə]
**Briefmarke** stamp [stæmp]
**Brille: (eine) Brille** glasses *(pl)* ['glɑ:sɪz]
**bringen: (mit-, her)bringen** bring [brɪŋ] • **(weg-, hin)bringen** take [teɪk] • **alles in Unordnung bringen** make a mess • **etwas auf den Weg bringen** get sth. off the ground
**britisch; Brite, Britin** British ['brɪtɪʃ]
**Broschüre** brochure ['brəʊʃə]
**Brot** bread *(no pl)* [bred]
**Brötchen** roll [rəʊl]
**Brotdose** sandwich box ['sænwɪtʃ bɒks]
**Brücke** bridge [brɪdʒ]
**Bruder** brother ['brʌðə]
**Buch** book [bʊk]
**Bücherei** library ['laɪbrəri]
**Buchstabe** letter ['letə]
**buchstabieren** spell [spel]
**Bucht** bay [beɪ]
**Bühne** stage [steɪdʒ]
**bunt an-, ausmalen** colour ['kʌlə]
**Burg** castle ['kɑ:sl]
**Burger** burger ['bɜ:gə]
**Bürger/in** citizen ['sɪtɪzn]
**Bürgerkrieg** civil war [ˌsɪvl 'wɔ:]
**Bürgermeister/in** mayor ['meə]
**Bürgerrechte** civil rights *(pl)* [ˌsɪvl 'raɪts]
**Bürgersteig** pavement ['peɪvmənt] *(BE)*; sidewalk *(AE)* ['saɪdwɔ:k]
**Bus** bus [bʌs]
**Bushaltestelle** bus stop ['bʌs stɒp]
**Butter** butter ['bʌtə]

## C

**Café** café ['kæfeɪ]
**Cafeteria** cafeteria [ˌkæfə'tɪəriə]
**Camp** camp [kæmp]
**Cartoon** cartoon [kɑː'tuːn]
**CD** CD [ˌsiː'diː] • **CD-Spieler** CD player [ˌsiː'diː ˌpleɪə]
**Celsius** Celsius (C) ['selsiəs]
**Cent** cent (c) [sent]
**Chance** chance [tʃɑːns]; possibility [ˌpɒsə'bɪləti]
**Charakter** character ['kærəktə]
**Charts** charts [tʃɑːts]
**Chatroom** chat room ['tʃæt ruːm]
**chatten** chat [tʃæt]
**Chef/in** boss [bɒs]
**Chor** choir ['kwaɪə]
**clever** clever ['klevə]; smart [smɑːt]
**Clique** crowd *(infml)* [kraʊd]
**Clown/in** clown [klaʊn]
**Cola** cola ['kəʊlə]
**Comic-Heft** comic ['kɒmɪk]
**Computer** computer [kəm'pjuːtə]
**cool** cool [kuːl]
**Cornflakes** cornflakes ['kɔːnfleɪks]
**Countdown** countdown ['kaʊntdaʊn]
**Court** *(für Squash, Badminton)* court [kɔːt]
**Cousin, Cousine** cousin ['kʌzn]
**Creme** cream [kriːm]
**Curry(gericht)** curry ['kʌri]

## D

**da, dahin** *(dort, dorthin)* there [ðeə] **da drüben** over there [ˌəʊvə 'ðeə]
**da** *(weil)* since [sɪns]
**daheim** at home [ət 'həʊm]
**daher** so [səʊ]
**damit** *(sodass)* so that
**dämlich** stupid ['stjuːpɪd]
**danach** *(zeitlich)* after that [ˌɑːftə 'ðæt]
**dankbar** thankful ['θæŋkfl]; *(froh)* glad [glæd]
**Danke.** Thank you. ['θæŋk juː]; Thanks. • **Danke sehr!** Thanks very much! • **Vielen Dank!** Thanks a lot!
**dann** then [ðen]
**darstellende Kunst** drama ['drɑːmə]
**das 1.** *(Artikel)* the [ðə, ði] **2.** *(Relativpronomen)* **das Mädchen, das ...** the girl who ... / the girl that ... • **das Auto, das ...** the car that ... / the car which ...
**das (dort)** *(Singular)* that [ðət, ðæt]; *(Plural)* those [ðəʊz] • **Das bin ich.** That's me.
**dass** that [ðət, ðæt]
**dasselbe** the same [seɪm]
**Datum** date [deɪt]
**dauern** last (for) [lɑːst]; *(Zeit brauchen)* take [teɪk]
**dazu: jn. dazu bringen, etwas zu tun** make sb. do sth.
**Debatte** debate [dɪ'beɪt]
**debattieren** debate [dɪ'beɪt]
**decken: den Tisch decken** lay the table [ˌleɪ ðə 'teɪbl]
**dein(e) ...** your ... [jɔː]
**deiner, deine, deins** yours [jɔːz]
**Deli** deli ['deli]
**Demonstration** march [mɑːtʃ]
**denken** think [θɪŋk] • **denken an** think of • **Was denkst du über ...?** What do you think about/of ...?
**Denkmal** monument ['mɒnjumənt]
**deprimierend** depressing [dɪ'presɪŋ]
**der 1.** *(Artikel)* the [ðə, ði] **2.** *(Relativpronomen)* **der Mann, der ...** the man who ... / the man that ... • **der Laden, der ...** the shop that ... / the shop which ...
**derselbe** the same [seɪm]
**deshalb** so [səʊ]
**Detail** detail ['diːteɪl]
**Detektiv/in** detective [dɪ'tektɪv]
**deuten (auf etwas)** *(zeigen)* point (at/to sth.) [pɔɪnt]
**deutlich** clear [klɪə]
**Deutsch; deutsch; Deutsche(r)** German ['dʒɜːmən]
**Deutschland** Germany ['dʒɜːməni]
**Dezember** December [dɪ'sembə]
**dich** you [juː] • **dich (selbst)** *(Reflexivpronomen)* yourself [jə'self, jɔː'self]
**die 1.** *(Artikel)* the [ðə, ði] **2.** *(Relativpronomen)* **die Frau, die ...** the woman who ... / the woman that ... • **die Jacke, die ...** the jacket that ... / the jacket which ...
**die (dort)** *(Singular)* that [ðət, ðæt]; *(Plural)* those [ðəʊz] • **die (hier)** *(Singular)* this [ðɪs]; *(Plural)* these [ðiːz]
**Dieb/in** thief [θiːf], *pl* thieves [θiːvz]
**Diele** hall [hɔːl]
**Dienstag** Tuesday ['tjuːzdeɪ, 'tjuːzdi] *(siehe auch unter „Freitag")*
**dies (hier); diese(r, s)** *(Singular)* this [ðɪs]; *(Plural)* these [ðiːz]
**dieselbe(n)** the same [seɪm]
**Ding** thing [θɪŋ]
**Dinosaurier** dinosaur ['daɪnəsɔː]
**dir** you [juː]
**Diskjockey** DJ ['diːdʒeɪ]
**Disko** disco ['dɪskəʊ]
**diskriminieren: jn. diskriminieren** discriminate against sb. [dɪ'skrɪmɪneɪt]
**Diskriminierung (von)** discrimination (against) [dɪˌskrɪmɪ'neɪʃn]
**Diskussion** discussion [dɪ'skʌʃn]
**Doktor** doctor ['dɒktə]
**Dokumentarbeitrag** documentary [ˌdɒkju'mentri]
**Dokumentarfilm** documentary [ˌdɒkju'mentri]
**Dollar** dollar ($) ['dɒlə]
**Dom** cathedral [kə'θiːdrəl]
**Donnerstag** Thursday ['θɜːzdeɪ, 'θɜːzdi] *(siehe auch unter „Freitag")*
**doppelt, Doppel-** double ['dʌbl]
**Dorf** village ['vɪlɪdʒ]
**dort, dorthin** there [ðeə] • **dort drüben** over there [ˌəʊvə 'ðeə] **dort unten** down there
**Dossier** dossier ['dɒsieɪ]
**downloaden** *(runterladen)* download [ˌdaʊn'ləʊd]
**Drachen** kite [kaɪt]
**Drama** drama ['drɑːmə]
**dran: Ich bin dran.** It's my turn. [tɜːn]
**draußen** outside [ˌaʊt'saɪd]; out [aʊt] **nach draußen** outside • **draußen bleiben** stay out
**dreimal** three times
**drinnen** inside [ˌɪn'saɪd] • **hier drinnen** in here [ˌɪn 'hɪə] • **nach drinnen** inside
**dritte(r, s)** third [θɜːd]
**Droge** drug [drʌg] • **Drogen nehmen** be on drugs
**Drogerie** chemist ['kemɪst]
**drüben: da/dort drüben** over there [ˌəʊvə 'ðeə]
**drücken** push [pʊʃ]; *(pressen)* press [pres]; squeeze [skwiːz]
**du** you [juː]
**dumm** *(albern)* silly ['sɪli]
**dunkel** dark [dɑːk]
**durch** through [θruː]; *(in...umher)* around [ə'raʊnd] • **durch die Stadt** around the town
**durcheinander: alles durcheinanderbringen** make a mess [ˌmeɪk‿ə 'mes]
**durchführen: ein Projekt durchführen** do a project
**durchqueren** cross [krɒs]
**Durchsage** *(Ansage)* announcement [ə'naʊnsmənt]
**Durchschnitt; Durchschnitts-** average ['ævərɪdʒ]
**durchschnittlich** average ['ævərɪdʒ] ► S.185 US school grades
**durchsuchen** search (for) [sɜːtʃ]
**dürfen** can [kən, kæn]; may [meɪ]; be allowed to [ə'laʊd] • **nicht dürfen** mustn't ['mʌsnt]
**Dusche** shower ['ʃaʊə]

**duschen; sich duschen** have a shower ['ʃaʊə]
**DVD** DVD [ˌdiː viː' diː]

## E

**echt** real [rɪəl]
**Ecke** corner ['kɔːnə] • **Green Street, Ecke London Road** on the corner of Green Street and London Road
**egal: Ist (doch) egal.** Never mind. [ˌnevə 'maɪnd]
**Ehefrau** wife [waɪf], *pl* wives [waɪvz]
**Ehemann** husband ['hʌzbənd]
**Ei** egg [eg]
**Eichhörnchen** squirrel ['skwɪrəl]
**Eifersucht** jealousy ['dʒeləsi]
**eifersüchtig (auf)** jealous (of) ['dʒeləs]
**eigene(r, s): unser eigenes Schwimmbad** our own pool [əʊn]
**eigentlich** *(in Wirklichkeit)* actually ['æktʃuəli]
**Eile: in Eile sein** be in a hurry ['hʌri]
**eilen** *(sich beeilen)* hurry ['hʌri]
**eilig: es eilig haben** be in a hurry ['hʌri]
**ein(e)** a, an [ə, ən]; one [wʌn] **ein(e) andere(r, s) ...** another ... [ə'nʌðə] • **eine Menge** a lot (of) [lɒt]; lots (of) [lɒts] • **ein neuer / eine neue / ein neues** a new one [wʌn] • **ein paar** some [səm, sʌm] **eines Tages** one day
**einander** *(sich gegenseitig)* each other [iːtʃ‿'ʌðə]
**einfach** *(nicht schwierig)* easy ['iːzi] **einfach nur** just [dʒʌst] • **einfache Fahrkarte** *(nur Hinfahrt)* single (ticket) ['sɪŋgl]
**Einfall** *(Idee)* idea [aɪ'dɪə]
**einfügen: sich einfügen** *(sich anpassen)* fit in [ˌfɪt‿'ɪn]
**Einführung (in)** introduction (to) [ˌɪntrə'dʌkʃn]
**eingeschaltet sein** *(Licht usw.)* be on
**einige** some [səm, sʌm]; *(einige wenige)* a few [fjuː]
**einigen: sich einigen (auf)** agree (on) [ə'griː]
**einkaufen** shop [ʃɒp] • **einkaufen gehen** go shopping; shop
**Einkaufen** shopping ['ʃɒpɪŋ]
**Einkaufsliste** shopping list
**einladen (zu)** invite (to) [ɪn'vaɪt]
**Einladung (zu)** invitation (to) [ˌɪnvɪ'teɪʃn]
**einmal** once [wʌns] • **einmal pro Woche** once a week • **auf einmal** suddenly ['sʌdnli] • **Einmal aussetzen.** Miss a turn. [tɜːn] • **früher einmal** once • **(noch) nicht einmal** not even
**einpacken** pack [pæk]
**eins, ein, eine** one ['wʌn]
**einsam** lonely ['ləʊnli]
**Einsatzort** location [ləʊ'keɪʃn]
**einschalten** *(Computer usw.)* turn on [ˌtɜːn‿'ɒn]
**einschätzen (nach)** judge (by) [dʒʌdʒ]
**einschüchtern** bully ['bʊli]
**einst** *(früher einmal)* once [wʌns]
**einsteigen (in den Zug/Bus)** get on (the train/bus) [ˌget‿'ɒn]
**Einstellung (zu, gegenüber)** attitude (to, towards) ['ætɪtjuːd]
**eintauschen: etwas eintauschen (für etwas / gegen etwas)** swap sth. (for sth.) [swɒp]
**Eintopf(gericht)** stew [stjuː]
**Eintrag** *(in Wörterbuch/Tagebuch)* entry ['entri]
**Eintragung** *(in Tagebuch)* entry ['entri]
**eintreffen** *(ankommen)* arrive [ə'raɪv]
**eintreten (in)** enter ['entə]
**Eintritt** *(Eintrittspreis)* admission [əd'mɪʃn]
**Eintrittskarte** ticket ['tɪkɪt]
**Eintrittspreis** admission [əd'mɪʃn]
**Einwanderer/Einwanderin** immigrant ['ɪmɪgrənt]
**Einwohner(zahl)** population [ˌpɒpju'leɪʃn]
**Einzelheit** detail ['diːteɪl]
**einziehen** *(in Wohnung)* move in [ˌmuːv‿'ɪn]
**einzig: der einzige Gast** the only guest ['əʊnli]
**Eis** ice [aɪs]; *(Speiseeis)* ice cream [ˌaɪs 'kriːm]
**Eisenbahn** railway ['reɪlweɪ]
**Eishockey** ice hockey ['aɪs hɒki]
**Elefant** elephant ['elɪfənt]
**elektrisch** electric [ɪ'lektrɪk]
**Elektrizität** electricity [ɪˌlek'trɪsəti]
**Elektro-** electric [ɪ'lektrɪk]
**elektronisch** electronic [ɪˌlek'trɒnɪk]
**Eltern** parents ['peərənts]
**E-Mail (an)** e-mail (to) ['iːmeɪl]
**empfangen** receive [rɪ'siːv]
**End-** *(letzte/r/s)* final ['faɪnl]
**Ende 1.** end [end]; *(einer Geschichte, eines Films usw.)* ending ['endɪŋ] **am Ende (von)** at the end (of) **zu Ende machen** finish ['fɪnɪʃ] • **zu Ende gehen** end [end] • **zu Ende sein** be over ['əʊvə] **2. oberes Ende** *(Spitze)* top [tɒp] **am oberen Ende** at the top **3. unteres Ende** bottom ['bɒtəm] **am unteren Ende** at the bottom ['bɒtəm]
**enden** finish ['fɪnɪʃ]; end [end]
**endlich** at last [ət 'lɑːst]
**endlos** endless ['endləs]
**Endstand** *(beim Sport)* final score [ˌfaɪnl 'skɔː]
**engagieren: sich engagieren (für, bei)** get involved (in) [ɪn'vɒlvd]
**Engel** angel ['eɪndʒl]
**Englisch; englisch** English ['ɪŋglɪʃ]
**Enkel/in** grandchild ['græntʃaɪld], *pl* grandchildren ['græntʃɪldrən]
**entdecken** discover [dɪ'skʌvə]; spot [spɒt]
**Entdecker/in** *(Forscher/in)* explorer [ɪk'splɔːrə]
**Entführer/in** *(eines Flugzeugs)* hijacker ['haɪdʒækə]
**enthalten** contain [kən'teɪn]
**entkommen** escape [ɪ'skeɪp]
**entlang der Straße / die Straße entlang** along the street [ə'lɒŋ]
**entscheiden: sich entscheiden (für)** decide (on) [dɪ'saɪd] • **Das kannst/ musst du (selbst) entscheiden.** That's up to you.
**entschuldigen: sich entschuldigen** say sorry ['sɒri]
**Entschuldigung 1.** *(Tut mir leid.)* I'm sorry. ['sɒri] • **Entschuldigung, dass ich zu spät bin/komme.** Sorry, I'm late. **2. Entschuldigung, ... / Entschuldigen Sie, ...** *(Darf ich mal stören?)* Excuse me, ... [ɪk'skjuːz miː]
**entspannen; sich entspannen** relax [rɪ'læks]
**entspannt** relaxed [rɪ'lækst]
**entsperren** unlock [ˌʌn'lɒk]
**enttäuschen** disappoint [ˌdɪsə'pɔɪnt]
**enttäuscht (von/über)** disappointed (about) [ˌdɪsə'pɔɪntɪd]
**entwerfen** design [dɪ'zaɪn]
**er 1.** *(männliche Person)* he [hiː] **2.** *(Ding, Tier)* it [ɪt]
**Erbse** pea [piː]
**Erdbeben** earthquake ['ɜːθkweɪk]
**Erdbeere** strawberry ['strɔːbəri]
**Erdboden** ground [graʊnd]
**Erde** earth [ɜːθ] • **auf der Erde** on earth
**Erdgeschoss** ground floor *(BE)*; first floor *(AE)* ► S.176 floor
**Erdkunde** geography [dʒi'ɒgrəfi]
**Ereignis** event [ɪ'vent]
**erfahren** *(erleben)* experience [ɪk'spɪəriəns] • **etwas über etwas erfahren** learn sth. about sth. [lɜːn]
**Erfahrung(en)** experience [ɪk'spɪəriəns] • **meiner Erfahrung nach** in my experience

**Erfolg** success [sək'ses] • **Erfolg haben (mit etwas, bei etwas)** succeed (in sth.) [sək'si:d]
**erfolgreich** successful [sək'sesfl]
**erfolgreich sein (mit etwas, bei etwas)** succeed (in sth.) [sək'si:d]
**erforschen** explore [ɪk'splɔ:]
**ergänzen** add (to) [æd]
**Ergebnis** result [rɪ'zʌlt]
**erinnern: sich erinnern (an)** remember [rɪ'membə]
**erkältet sein** have a cold [kəʊld]
**Erkältung** cold [kəʊld] • **eine Erkältung haben** have a cold
**erklären: jm. etwas erklären** explain sth. to sb. [ɪk'spleɪn] • **sich bereit erklären** volunteer [ˌvɒlən'tɪə]
**Erklärung** explanation [ˌeksplə'neɪʃn]
**erkunden** explore [ɪk'splɔ:]
**erlauben: jm. erlauben, etwas zu tun** let sb. do sth. [let]
**erlaubt sein** be allowed
**erläutern: jm. etwas erläutern** explain sth. to sb. [ɪk'spleɪn]
**erleben** experience [ɪk'spɪəriəns]
**Erlebnis** experience [ɪk'spɪəriəns]
**ernst** serious ['sɪəriəs]
**Ernst: im Ernst?** seriously? ['sɪəriəsli]
**ernsthaft** serious ['sɪəriəs]
**erraten** guess [ges]
**erschießen** shoot [ʃu:t]
**erst** only ['əʊnli]
**erstaunlich** amazing [ə'meɪzɪŋ]
**erste(r, s)** first [fɜ:st] • **als Erstes** first • **der erste Tag** the first day **der/die Erste sein** be first • **zum ersten Mal** for the first time
**erwachsen werden** grow up [ˌgrəʊ‿'ʌp]
**Erwachsene(r)** adult ['ædʌlt]
**erwarten** expect [ɪk'spekt] • **ich kann es kaum erwarten, ... zu sehen** I can't wait to see ... [weɪt]
**erwischen** *(fangen)* catch [kætʃ]
**erzählen (von)** tell (about) [tel]
**Erzählung** story ['stɔ:ri]
**erzielen: einen Treffer erzielen** *(ein Tor schießen)* score (a goal) [skɔ:], [gəʊl]
**es** it [ɪt] • **es gibt** *(es ist vorhanden)* there's; *(es sind vorhanden)* there are
**Essen** food [fu:d]; *(Mahlzeit)* meal [mi:l]
**essen** eat [i:t] • **Abendbrot essen** have dinner • **Toast zum Frühstück essen** have toast for breakfast
**Esszimmer** dining room ['daɪnɪŋ ru:m]
**Etagenbett** bunk (bed) [bʌŋk]
**ethnisch** ethnic ['eθnɪk]
**etwas** something ['sʌmθɪŋ]; *(irgendetwas)* anything ['eniθɪŋ]; *(ein bisschen)* a bit [bɪt] • **etwas Käse** some cheese [səm, sʌm]
**euch** you [ju:] • **euch (selbst)** yourselves [jə'selvz, jɔ:'selvz]
**euer, eure ...** your ... [jɔ:]
**eurer, eure, eures** yours [jɔ:z]
**Euro** euro ['jʊərəʊ]
**exakt** exact [ɪg'zækt]
**Exemplar** copy ['kɒpi]
**Explosion** explosion [ɪk'spləʊʒn]

## F

**Fabrik** factory ['fæktri]
**fähig sein, etwas zu tun** be able to do sth. ['eɪbl]
**Fähre** ferry ['feri]
**fahren** go [gəʊ]; *(ein Auto / mit dem Auto)* drive [draɪv] • **in Urlaub fahren** go on holiday • **mit dem Auto/Zug/Rad/... fahren** go by car/train/bike/... • **Inliner/Skateboard fahren** skate [skeɪt] • **Rad fahren** cycle ['saɪkl]; ride a bike [ˌraɪd‿ə 'baɪk]
**Fahrer/in** driver ['draɪvə]
**Fahrkarte** ticket ['tɪkɪt] • **einfache Fahrkarte** *(nur Hinfahrt)* single (ticket) ['sɪŋgl]
**Fahrkartenautomat** ticket machine ['tɪkɪt məˌʃi:n]
**Fahrkartenschalter** ticket office ['tɪkɪt‿ˌɒfɪs]
**Fahrplan** timetable ['taɪmteɪbl] *(BE)*; schedule [*AE:* 'skedʒu:l, *BE:* 'ʃedju:l] *(AE)*
**Fahrrad** bike [baɪk]
**Fahrstuhl** lift [lɪft] *(BE)*; elevator ['elɪveɪtə] *(AE)*
**Fahrt** journey ['dʒɜ:ni] • **(Auto-)Fahrt** drive [draɪv] • **(Rad-)Fahrt** (bike) ride [raɪd] • **eine Fahrt machen** take a ride [raɪd]
**fair** fair [feə]
**Fakt** *(Tatsache)* fact [fækt]
**Fall** *(Kriminalfall)* case [keɪs]
**fallen** fall [fɔ:l]
**fallen lassen** drop [drɒp]
**falls** if [ɪf]
**falsch** wrong [rɒŋ]; false [fɔ:ls] • **in die falsche Richtung** the wrong way
**Familie** family ['fæməli]
**Fan** fan [fæn]; *(Unterstützer/in)* supporter [sə'pɔ:tə] • **Fan einer Mannschaft sein** support a team [sə'pɔ:t]
**fangen** catch [kætʃ]
**Fantasie** imagination [ɪˌmædʒɪ'neɪʃn]
**fantastisch** fantastic [fæn'tæstɪk]
**Farbe** colour ['kʌlə] • **Welche Farbe hat ...?** What colour is ...?
**färben** *(bunt an-, ausmalen)* colour ['kʌlə]
**Farm** farm [fɑ:m]
**Farmhaus** farmhouse ['fɑ:mhaʊs]
**Fassung** *(Version)* version ['vɜ:ʃn]
**jd. aus der Fassung bringen** upset sb. [ʌp'set]
**fast** almost ['ɔ:lməʊst]
**Fastfood** fast food [ˌfɑ:st 'fu:d]
**Faust** fist [fɪst]
**Februar** February ['februəri]
**Federball** badminton ['bædmɪntən]
**Federmäppchen** pencil case ['pensl keɪs]
**fehlen** be missing ['mɪsɪŋ]
**Fehler** mistake [mɪ'steɪk]
**Feind/in** enemy ['enəmi]
**Feiertag** holiday ['hɒlədeɪ]
**Feld 1.** field [fi:ld] • **auf dem Feld** in the field
**2.** *(bei Brettspielen)* **Geh ein Feld vor.** Move on one space. [speɪs] **Geh ein Feld zurück.** Move back one space.
**Fels, Felsen** rock; *(Klippe)* cliff [klɪf]
**Fenster** window ['wɪndəʊ]
**Ferien** holidays ['hɒlədeɪz] *(BE)*; vacation [və'keɪʃn, *AE:* veɪkeɪʃn] *(AE)*
**Ferienlager** camp [kæmp]
**Ferienwohnung** holiday flat ['hɒlədeɪ flæt]
**Fernbedienung** remote control [rɪˌməʊt kən'trəʊl]
**Fernsehen** television ['telɪvɪʒn]; TV [ti:'vi:] • **im Fernsehen** on TV
**fernsehen** watch TV [ˌwɒtʃ ti:'vi:]
**Fernsehkanal** channel ['tʃænl]
**Fernsehprogramm** TV listings *(pl)* ['lɪstɪŋ]; *(Fernsehkanal)* channel ['tʃænl]
**Fernsehsendung** programme ['prəʊgræm]
**Fernsehspiel** drama ['drɑ:mə]
**Fernstraße** *(in den USA, oft mit vier oder mehr Spuren)* highway ['haɪweɪ]
**fertig** *(bereit)* ready ['redi] • **sich fertig machen (für)** *(sich vorbereiten)* get ready (for) • **Dinge fertig machen (für)** *(vorbereiten)* get things ready (for)
**fest** tight [taɪt]
**Fest, Festival** festival ['festɪvl]
**Festspiele** festival ['festɪvl]
**fett** fat [fæt]
**Fettdruck** bold print [ˌbəʊld 'prɪnt]
**Feuer** fire ['faɪə] • **ein Feuer löschen** put out a fire
**Feuerwache** fire station ['faɪə steɪʃn]

**Feuerwehrfrau** firewoman ['faɪə,wʊmən]; firefighter ['faɪəfaɪtə]
**Feuerwehrmann** fireman ['faɪəmən]; firefighter ['faɪəfaɪtə]
**Fieber haben** have a temperature ['temprətʃə]
**Fiedel** fiddle ['fɪdl] *(infml)* • **Fiedel spielen** play the fiddle
**Figur** *(in Roman, Film, Theaterstück)* character ['kærəktə]
**Film** film [fɪlm]; movie ['mu:vi]
**Filmemacher** film-maker ['fɪlmmeɪkə]
**filmen** film [fɪlm]
**Filmstar** film star ['fɪlm stɑ:]
**Filmstudio** film studio ['fɪlm ,stju:diəʊ]
**Filzstift** felt tip ['felt tɪp]
**Finale** final ['faɪnl]
**finden** *(entdecken)* find [faɪnd]
**Finder** finder ['faɪndə]
**Finger** finger ['fɪŋgə]
**Firma** company ['kʌmpəni]
**Fisch** fish, *pl* fish [fɪʃ]
**fischen** fish [fɪʃ]
**Fischzüchter/in** farmer ['fɑ:mə]
**Fitness** fitness ['fɪtnəs]
**Fitnessstudio** gym [dʒɪm]
**Flachbildschirm** flat screen ['flæt skri:n]
**Flasche** bottle ['bɒtl] • **eine Flasche Milch** a bottle of milk
**Fleisch** meat [mi:t]
**Fleischer** butcher ['bʊtʃə] • **beim Fleischer** at the butcher's
**fleißig** hard-working [,hɑ:d'wɜ:kɪŋ]
**fliegen** fly [flaɪ]
**fliehen (vor jm. / aus etwas)** escape (from sb./sth.) [ɪ'skeɪp]
**Flug** flight [flaɪt] • **ein 14-stündiger Flug, ein 14-Stunden-Flug** a 14-hour flight
**Flügel** *(bei einem Vogel, Flugzeug)* wing [wɪŋ]
**Flughafen** airport ['eəpɔ:t]
**Flugsteig** gate [geɪt]
**Flugzeug** plane [pleɪn] • **im Flugzeug** on the plane
**Flugzeugentführer/in** hijacker ['haɪdʒækə]
**Flur** hall [hɔ:l]
**Fluss** river ['rɪvə]
**Flusspferd** hippo ['hɪpəʊ]
**flüstern** whisper ['wɪspə]
**folgen** follow ['fɒləʊ]
**Folk** folk (music) ['fəʊk ,mju:zɪk]
**Football** American football [ə,merɪkən 'fʊtbɔ:l]
**Forscher/in** explorer [ɪk'splɔ:rə]
**fort** away [ə'weɪ]
**Foto** photo ['fəʊtəʊ] • **auf dem Foto** in the photo • **Fotos machen** take photos
**Fotoapparat** camera ['kæmərə]
**fotografieren** take photos [teɪk 'fəʊtəʊz]
**Frage** question ['kwestʃn] • **Fragen stellen** ask questions • **Kommt nicht in Frage!** No way!
**fragen** ask [ɑ:sk] • **nach etwas fragen** ask about sth. • **jn. nach dem Weg fragen** ask sb. the way; ask sb. for directions • **sich fragen** wonder ['wʌndə]
**Französisch** French [frentʃ]
**Frau** woman ['wʊmən], *pl* women ['wɪmɪn] • **Frau Brown** Mrs Brown ['mɪsɪz]; Ms Brown [mɪz, məz] • **Frau White** *(unverheiratet)* Miss White [mɪs]
**frei** free [fri:] • **freie Zeit** free time **im Freien** *(Freilicht-)* open-air [,əʊpən_'eə] • **eine Woche / einen Tag / einen Monat ... frei** a week/ day/month ... off
**Freilicht-** open-air [,əʊpən_'eə]
**Freitag** Friday ['fraɪdeɪ, 'fraɪdi] **freitagabends, am Freitagabend** on Friday evening • **freitagnachts, Freitagnacht** on Friday night
**freiwillig: sich freiwillig melden** volunteer [,vɒlən'tɪə]
**Freiwillige(r)** volunteer [,vɒlən'tɪə]
**Freizeit** free time [,fri: 'taɪm]
**Freizeitzentrum, -park** leisure centre ['leʒə sentə]
**fremd** strange [streɪndʒ]; *(ausländisch)* foreign ['fɒrən]
**Fremdenführer/in** (tour) guide [gaɪd]
**Fremdenverkehrsamt** tourist information ['tʊərɪst_ɪnfə,meɪʃn]
**Fremdsprache** foreign language [,fɒrən 'læŋgwɪdʒ]
**freuen: sich auf etwas freuen** look forward to ['fɔ:wəd]
**Freund** friend [frend]; *(Kumpel)* mate [meɪt] *(infml)*; *(fester Freund)* boyfriend ['bɔɪfrend]
**Freundin** friend [frend]; *(Kumpel)* mate [meɪt] *(infml)*; *(feste Freundin)* girlfriend ['gɜ:lfrend]
**freundlich** friendly ['frendli]
**Freundlichkeit** friendliness ['frendlinəs]
**frieren** be cold [kəʊld]
**frisch** fresh [freʃ]
**Frischkäse** cream cheese [,kri:m 'tʃi:z]
**Friseur/in** hairdresser ['heədresə] **beim Friseur** at the hairdresser's
**froh** happy ['hæpi]; glad [glæd]
**Frosch** frog [frɒg]
**Frucht, Früchte** fruit [fru:t]
**früh** early ['ɜ:li]
**früher** *(einst, früher einmal)* once [wʌns]
**Frühling** spring [sprɪŋ]
**Frühstück** breakfast ['brekfəst] **zum Frühstück** for breakfast
**frühstücken** have breakfast
**Frühstückspension** Bed and Breakfast (B&B) [,bed_ən 'brekfəst]
**Fuchs** fox [fɒks]
**fühlen; sich fühlen** feel [fi:l]
**Führer/in** (Leiter/in, Anführer/in) leader ['li:də]; *(Fremdenführer/in)* (tour) guide [gaɪd]
**Füller** pen [pen]
**funktionieren** work [wɜ:k]
**für** for [fə, fɔ:] • **Was für ein Auto ...?** What kind of car ...?
**furchtbar** terrible ['terəbl]; awful ['ɔ:fl]
**fürchterlich aussehen** be a mess [mes]
**Fuß** foot [fʊt], *pl* feet [fi:t]; *(Längenmaß; 1 Fuß = 30,48 cm)* foot [fʊt]
**Fußball** football ['fʊtbɔ:l] • **Fußball spielen** play football
**Fußballplatz** pitch [pɪtʃ]
**Fußballschuhe, -stiefel** football boots ['fʊtbɔ:l bu:ts]
**Fußboden** floor [flɔ:]
**Futter** food [fu:d]
**füttern** feed [fi:d]

## G

**Gabel** fork [fɔ:k]
**gähnen** yawn [jɔ:n]
**ganze(r, s)** whole [həʊl] • **auf der ganzen Welt** all over the world **aus der ganzen Welt** from all over the world • **den ganzen Tag (lang)** all day • **den ganzen Weg** all the way • **die ganze Zeit** all the time **Das ist ganz falsch.** This is all wrong.
**Garage** garage ['gærɑ:ʒ]
**Garten** garden ['gɑ:dn]
**Gärtner/in** gardener ['gɑ:dnə]
**Gas** gas [gæs]
**Gasse** lane [leɪn]
**Gast** guest [gest]; *(Besucher/in)* visitor ['vɪzɪtə]
**Gebäude** building ['bɪldɪŋ]
**geben** give [gɪv] • **es gibt** *(es ist vorhanden)* there's; *(es sind vorhanden)* there are • **jm. die Schuld geben (an)** blame sb. (for) [bleɪm]
**geboren sein/werden** be born [bɔ:n]
**gebraucht** *(aus zweiter Hand)* second-hand [,sekənd 'hænd]
**gebrochen** *(Arm, Bein)* broken ['brəʊkən]

**Geburtstag** birthday ['bɜ:θdeɪ] **Herzlichen Glückwunsch zum Geburtstag.** Happy birthday. **Ich habe im Mai / am 13. Juni Geburtstag.** My birthday is in May / on 13th June. • **Wann hast du Geburtstag?** When's your birthday?
**Gedanke** thought [θɔ:t]
**Gedicht** poem ['pəʊɪm]
**geehrt: Sehr geehrte Damen und Herren** *(Anrede in Briefen)* Dear Sir or Madam [sɜ:; 'mædəm]
**Gefahr** danger ['deɪndʒə]
**gefährlich** dangerous ['deɪndʒərəs]; *(nicht sicher)* unsafe [ʌn'seɪf]
**Gefallen: Würdest du mir einen Gefallen tun?** Would you do me a favour? ['feɪvə]
**Gefängnis** jail [dʒeɪl]
**Geflügel** poultry ['pəʊltri]
**Gefühl** feeling ['fi:lɪŋ]
**gegen** against [ə'genst] • **gegen sechs** *(um sechs Uhr herum)* around six
**gegenseitig: sich gegenseitig** each other [i:tʃ_'ʌðə]
**Gegenteil** opposite ['ɒpəzɪt]
**Gegenwart** present ['preznt]
**Geheimnis** mystery ['mɪstri]
**gehen 1.** go [gəʊ]; *(zu Fuß gehen)* walk [wɔ:k]; *(weggehen)* leave [li:v] **Auf geht's!** Let's go. • **einkaufen gehen** go shopping; shop [ʃɒp] **Geh ein Feld vor.** Move on one space. [speɪs] • **Geh ein Feld zurück.** Move back one space. • **in die Sauna gehen** have a sauna **ins Bett gehen** go to bed • **ins Kino gehen** go to the cinema **nach Hause gehen** go home **reiten/schwimmen gehen** go riding/swimming • **spazieren gehen** go for a walk [wɔ:k] **2. Es geht mir/ihm gut.** I'm/He's fine. [faɪn] **3. Es geht um Mr Green.** This is about Mr Green. **4. Das geht dich nichts an!** Mind your own business. [,maɪnd jər_,əʊn 'bɪznəs]
**gehören 1. jm. gehören/zu jm. gehören** belong to [bɪ'lɒŋ] • **Wem gehören diese?** Whose are these? **2. gehören zu** *(passen zu)* go with
**Gehweg** pavement ['peɪvmənt] *(BE)*; sidewalk ['saɪdwɔ:k] *(AE)*
**Geige** violin [,vaɪə'lɪn]; fiddle *(infml)* ['fɪdl]
**Geist** *(Gespenst)* ghost [gəʊst]
**gekränkt (wegen)** upset (about) [,ʌp'set]
**Gelächter** laughter ['lɑ:ftə]
**gelangen** *(hinkommen)* get [get]
**gelangweilt sein** get bored [bɔ:d]
**gelassen** *(locker)* easy-going [,i:zi'gəʊɪŋ]
**gelb** yellow ['jeləʊ]
**Geld** money ['mʌni] • **Geld ausgeben (für)** spend money (on) [spend]
**Geldbörse** purse [pɜ:s]
**Gemeindehalle, -saal** community hall [kə'mju:nəti]
**Gemeinschaftshalle, -saal** community hall [kə'mju:nəti]
**Gemüse:** *(ein)* **Gemüse** vegetable ['vedʒtəbl]
**genannt werden** *(heißen)* be called [kɔ:ld]
**genau 1.** *(Adjektiv)* exact [ɪg'zækt] **2.** *(Adverb)* exactly [ɪg'zæktli] **genau in dem Moment** just then **genau wie du** just like you
**genial** brilliant ['brɪliənt]
**genießen** enjoy [ɪn'dʒɔɪ]
**genug** enough [ɪ'nʌf] • **genug von etwas haben** be tired of sth.
**geöffnet** open ['əʊpən]
**Geografie** geography [dʒi'ɒgrəfi]
**gepflegt** neat [ni:t]
**gerade** at the moment; *(eben, soeben)* just [dʒʌst] • **gerade dann** *(genau in dem Moment)* just then **jetzt gerade** *(in diesem Moment)* right now [raɪt 'naʊ]
**geradeaus weiter** straight on [streɪt_'ɒn]
**Gerät** *(Maschine)* machine [mə'ʃi:n]
**Geräusch** noise [nɔɪz]
**gerecht** fair [feə]
**Gericht** *(Speise)* dish [dɪʃ]
**Gericht(shof)** court [kɔ:t]
**gern: Ich hätte gern ... / Ich möchte gern ...** I'd like ... (= I would like ...) **Ich schwimme/tanze/... gern.** I like swimming/dancing/... • **Ich würde gern über ... reden** I'd like to talk about ... • **Gern geschehen.** You're welcome. ['welkəm]
**gernhaben** like [laɪk]
**Geruch** smell
**gesamte(r, s)** whole [həʊl] • **aus dem gesamten Vereinigten Königreich** from all over the United Kingdom
**Geschäft** shop [ʃɒp]
**Geschäft(e)** *(Handel)* business ['bɪznəs]
**geschehen (mit)** happen (to) ['hæpən]
**Geschenk** present ['preznt]
**Geschichte 1.** story ['stɔ:ri] **2.** *(vergangene Zeiten)* history ['hɪstri]
**geschieden** divorced [dɪ'vɔ:st]
**Geschirrspülmaschine** dishwasher ['dɪʃwɒʃə]
**Geschlecht** sex [seks]
**geschlossen** closed [kləʊzd]
**Gesellschaft** *(Firma)* company ['kʌmpəni]
**Gesetz** law [lɔ:]
**gesetzlich** legal ['li:gl]
**Gesicht** face [feɪs]
**Gespenst** *(Geist)* ghost [gəʊst]
**Gespräch** conversation [,kɒnvə'seɪʃn]
**gestalten** design [dɪ'zaɪn]
**gestern** yesterday ['jestədeɪ, 'jestədi] **gestern Morgen/Nachmittag/Abend** yesterday morning/afternoon/evening • **die Hausaufgaben von gestern** yesterday's homework
**gesund** healthy ['helθi]; well [wel]
**Gesundheit** health [helθ]
**Gesundheitslehre** health [helθ]
**Getränk** drink [drɪŋk]; *(alkoholfrei)* soft drink [,sɒft 'drɪŋk]
**getrennt** apart [ə'pɑ:t]
**Gewalt** violence ['vaɪələns] • **etwas in seine Gewalt bringen** take sth. over
**gewaltfrei** non-violent [nɒn]
**gewaltlos** non-violent [,nɒn'vaɪələnt]
**gewaltsam** violent ['vaɪələnt]
**gewalttätig** violent ['vaɪələnt]
**Gewalttätigkeit** violence ['vaɪələns]
**Gewehr** gun [gʌn]
**Gewinn** prize [praɪz]
**gewinnen** win [wɪn]
**Gewinner/in** winner ['wɪnə]
**Gewitter** storm [stɔ:m]
**gewöhnlich** usually ['ju:ʒuəli]
**gezeigt werden** *(im Fernsehen/Kino)* be on
**Giraffe** giraffe [dʒə'rɑ:f]
**Gitarre** guitar [gɪ'tɑ:] • **Gitarre spielen** play the guitar
**Glas** glass [glɑ:s] • **ein Glas Wasser** a glass of water
**glauben** think [θɪŋk]; believe [bɪ'li:v] **Glaubst du das wirklich?** Do you really think so?
**gleich sein/aussehen** be/look the same [seɪm]
**Gleis** *(Bahnsteig)* platform ['plætfɔ:m]
**Glocke** bell [bel]
**Glück: Glück haben (mit)** be lucky (with) ['lʌki] • **Viel Glück (bei/mit ...)!** Good luck (with ...)! [gʊd 'lʌk] • **zum Glück** *(glücklicherweise)* fortunately ['fɔ:tʃənətli]; luckily ['lʌkɪli]
**glücklich** happy ['hæpi]
**glücklicherweise** luckily ['lʌkɪli]
**Gold** gold [gəʊld]

**goldene(r,s)** golden ['gəʊldən]
**Golf** golf [gɒlf]
**Gouverneur/in** *(Oberhaupt eines US-Bundesstaates)* governor ['gʌvənə]
**Grad** degree [dɪ'gri:]
**Grammatik** grammar ['græmə]
**grau** grey [greɪ]
**grauenhaft** horrible ['hɒrəbl]
**grausam** cruel ['kru:əl]
**Grenze** border ['bɔ:də]
**groß** big [bɪg]; large [lɑ:dʒ]; *(riesig)* huge [hju:dʒ]; *(Personen, Körpergröße)* tall [tɔ:l]
**Großbuchstabe** capital letter [,kæpɪtl 'letə]
**großartig** great [greɪt]; awesome ['ɔ:səm] *(AE, infml)*
**Größe** *(Schuhgröße usw.)* size [saɪz]
**Großeltern** grandparents ['grænpeərənts]
**Großmutter** grandmother ['grænmʌðə]
**Großstadt** city ['sɪti]
**Großvater** grandfather ['grænfɑ:ðə]
**grün** green [gri:n]
**Grund** reason ['ri:zn]; *(Ursache)* cause [kɔ:z] • **aus vielen Gründen** • for lots of reasons
**gründen** found [faʊnd]
**Grundschule** *(für 6- bis 11-Jährige in den USA)* elementary school [,elɪ'mentri sku:l]
**Gruppe** group [gru:p]; *(Musikgruppe)* band [bænd]; *(Clique)* crowd *(infml)* [kraʊd]
**gruselig** scary ['skeəri]
**Gruß: Liebe Grüße, ...** *(Briefschluss)* Love ... [lʌv] • **Mit besten Grüßen** *(als Briefschluss)* Best wishes ['wɪʃɪz] • **Mit freundlichen Grüßen** *(bei namentlich unbekanntem Empfänger)* Yours faithfully ['feɪθfəli]; *(bei namentlich bekanntem Empfänger)* Yours sincerely [sɪn'sɪəli]
**Grüß Dilip von mir.** Say hi to Dilip for me.
**gucken** look [lʊk]
**gut** good [gʊd]; *(okay)* OK [əʊ'keɪ]; *(in Ordnung)* all right [ɔ:l 'raɪt]; *(gesundheitlich gut, wohlauf)* well [wel]; fine [faɪn] • **Alles Gute** *(als Briefschluss)* Best wishes ['wɪʃɪz] **Es geht mir/ihm gut.** I'm/He's fine. • **gute Arbeit leisten** do a good job • **Guten Morgen.** Good morning. • **Guten Tag.** Hello.; *(nachmittags)* Good afternoon. **gut abschneiden (in)** do well (in) **gut ausgehen** work out [,wɜ:k_'aʊt] **gut in etwas sein/etwas gut können** be good at sth. • **gut (ver)laufen** *(gutgehen, klappen)* go well **Das hast du gut gemacht.** You did well. • **gutgehen** *(gut (ver)laufen, klappen)* go well

## H

**Haar, Haare** hair *(no pl)* [heə]
**Haarwaschmittel** shampoo [ʃæm'pu:]
**haben** have got ['hæv gɒt]; have [həv, hæv] • **Ich habe keinen Stuhl.** I haven't got a chair. • **Ich habe am 13. Juni/im Mai Geburtstag.** My birthday is on 13th June/in May. **Wann hast du Geburtstag?** When's your birthday? • **haben wollen** want [wɒnt] • **Was haben wir als Hausaufgabe auf?** What's for homework?
**Hafen** harbour ['hɑ:bə]
**Hähnchen** chicken ['tʃɪkɪn]
**halb: eine halbe Stunde** half an hour [,hɑ:f_ən_'aʊə] • **halb zwölf** half past 11 [hɑ:f]
**Halbfinale** semi-final [,semi'faɪnl]
**Halbzeit** half • **die erste Halbzeit** the first half • **Halbzeit(pause)** half-time [,hɑ:f 'taɪm]
**Halfpipe** half-pipe ['hɑ:fpaɪp]
**Hälfte** half [hɑ:f], *pl* halves [hɑ:vs] **die Hälfte der/des** half of
**Hallo!** Hi! [haɪ]; Hello. [hə'ləʊ]; Hey! [heɪ]
**Hals** throat [θrəʊt]
**Halsschmerzen haben** have a sore throat [sɔ: 'θrəʊt]
**Halt** stop [stɒp]
**halten 1.** hold [həʊld]
**2.** *(aufbewahren)* keep [ki:p] **etwas warm/kühl/offen/... halten** keep sth. warm/cool/open/...
**3.** *(behalten)* keep • **Kontakt halten** keep in touch [,ki:p_ɪn 'tʌtʃ]
**4. Halt den Mund!** Shut up. [,ʃʌt_'ʌp]
**5. Was hältst du von ...?** What do you think about/of ...?
**6. eine Rede/halten** make a speech [spi:tʃ]
**Haltung (gegenüber)** attitude (to, towards) ['ætɪtju:d]
**Hamburger** hamburger ['hæmbɜ:gə]
**Hamster** hamster ['hæmstə]
**Hand** hand [hænd] • **aus zweiter Hand** *(gebraucht)* second-hand
**Handball** handball ['hændbɔ:l]
**Handel** *(Geschäft)* business ['bɪznəs]
**Handlung** *(eines Romans, Films, Theaterstücks)* plot [plɒt]
**Handtuch** towel ['taʊəl]
**Handy** mobile (phone) ['məʊbaɪl]
**hänseln: jn. mit Schimpfwörtern hänseln** call sb. names
**Happyend** happy ending [,hæpi_'endɪŋ]
**hart** hard [hɑ:d] • **hart arbeiten** work hard
**hassen** hate [heɪt]
**häufig** often ['ɒfn]
**Haupt-** main [meɪn]
**Hauptsendezeit** prime time ['praɪm taɪm]
**Hauptstadt** capital ['kæpɪtl]
**Hauptverkehrszeit** rush hour ['rʌʃ_aʊə]
**Haus** house [haʊs] • **im Haus der Shaws / bei den Shaws zu Hause** at the Shaws' house • **nach Hause gehen** go home [həʊm] • **nach Hause kommen** come home; get home • **zu Hause** at home
**Hausarrest haben** be grounded ['graʊndɪd]
**Hausaufgabe(n)** homework *(no pl)* ['həʊmwɜ:k] • **die Hausaufgabe(n) machen** do homework • **Was haben wir als Hausaufgabe auf?** What's for homework?
**Häuserblock** block [blɒk]
**Hausmeister/in** caretaker ['keəteɪkə]
**Haustier** pet [pet]
**Haustür** front door [,frʌnt 'dɔ:]
**Haut** skin [skɪn]
**Heim** home [həʊm]
**heiß** hot [hɒt]
**heißen 1.** *(genannt werden)* be called [kɔ:ld] • **Ich heiße ...** My name is ... • **Wie heißt du?** What's your name?
**2. Sie heißen dich in ... willkommen** They welcome you to ... ['welkəm]
**helfen** help [help]
**Helikopter** helicopter ['helɪkɒptə]
**hell** *(leuchtend)* bright [braɪt]; *(Haare)* blond [blɒnd]
**Helm** helmet ['helmɪt]
**Hemd** shirt [ʃɜ:t]
**herauf** up [ʌp]
**heraus** out [aʊt] • **aus ... heraus** out of ... ['aʊt_əv]
**herausarbeiten: etwas herausarbeiten** *(herausfinden)* work sth. out
**herausbringen** *(Buch, CD, Film usw. auf den Markt bringen)* release [rɪ'li:z]
**herausfinden** find out [,faɪnd_'aʊt]; *(entdecken)* discover [dɪ'skʌvə] **etwas über etwas herausfinden** learn sth. about sth. [lɜ:n] • **etwas herausfinden** *(herausarbeiten)* work sth. out
**herausnehmen** take out [,teɪk_'aʊt]

**herausragen aus etwas** stick out of sth. [stɪk]
**herausstehen aus etwas** *(herausragen)* stick out of sth. [stɪk]
**Herberge** hostel ['hɒstl]
**herbringen** bring [brɪŋ]
**Herbst** autumn ['ɔ:təm]
**Herd** cooker ['kʊkə]
**hereinkommen** come in [ˌkʌm_'ɪn]
**Herr Brown** Mr Brown ['mɪstə]
**herstellen** produce [prə'dju:s]
**Herstellung** production [prə'dʌkʃn]
**herum: anders herum** the other way round [raʊnd] • **um ... herum** round, around • **um sechs Uhr herum** *(gegen sechs)* • around six
**herum-: etwas herumgeben** pass sth. round [ˌpɑ:s 'raʊnd] • **herumgehen** walk around [ə'raʊnd] **herumrennen** run around **herumspringen** jump around
**herunter** down [daʊn]
**herunterfallen (von)** fall off [ˌfɔ:l_'ɒf]
**herunterladbar** downloadable [ˌdaʊn'ləʊdəbl]
**hervorragend** excellent ['eksələnt] ▶ S.185 US school grades
**Herz** heart [hɑ:t]
**Herzlichen Glückwunsch zum Geburtstag.** Happy birthday. [ˌhæpi 'bɜ:θdeɪ]
**heute** today [tə'deɪ] • **heute Morgen/Nachmittag/Abend** this morning/afternoon/evening **heute Nacht** tonight [tə'naɪt] **das Programm von heute** today's programme
**heutig: das heutige Programm** today's programme
**hier** here [hɪə] • **Hier bitte.** *(Bitte sehr.)* Here you are. • **hier drinnen** in here [ˌɪn 'hɪə] • **hier entlang** this way ['ðɪs weɪ] • **Hier spricht Isabel. / Hier ist Isabel.** *(am Telefon)* This is Isabel. • **Hier steht: ... / Es heißt hier: ...** *(im Text)* It says here: ...
**hierher** here [hɪə]
**Hilfe** help [help]
**hilflos** helpless ['helpləs]
**hilfreich** helpful ['helpfl]
**Himmel** sky [skaɪ]; *(im religiösen Sinn)* heaven ['hevn] • **am Himmel** in the sky
**hinauf** up [ʌp] • **den Hügel hinauf** up the hill • **auf ... hinauf** onto ['ɒntə, 'ɒntʊ]
**hinaufklettern (auf)** climb [klaɪm]
**hinaus** out [aʊt] • **aus ... hinaus** out of ... ['aʊt_əv]
**hinein: in ... hinein** into ... ['ɪntə, 'ɪntʊ]
**hineinfahren (in)** crash (into) [kræʃ]
**hineinpassen** fit in [ˌfɪt_'ɪn]
**hinfallen** fall [fɔ:l]; fall down
**hinkommen** *(gelangen)* get [get]
**hinsetzen: sich hinsetzen** sit down
**hinstellen: sich hinstellen** stand [stænd]
**hinter** behind [bɪ'haɪnd]
**Hintergrund** background ['bækgraʊnd]
**Hintertür** back door
**hinüber zu/nach ...** over to ... ['əʊvə]
**hinunter** down [daʊn]
**hinzufügen (zu)** add (to) [æd]
**Hirsch** deer, *pl* deer [dɪə]
**Hit** hit [hɪt]
**Hitliste** charts [tʃɑ:ts]
**Hobby** hobby ['hɒbi], *pl* hobbies
**hoch** high [haɪ]; *(Bäume, Türme usw.)* tall [tɔ:l]
**hochheben: etwas hochheben** pick sth. up [ˌpɪk_'ʌp]
**hochsehen (von)** look up (from) [ˌlʊk_'ʌp]
**Hockey** hockey ['hɒki]
**Hockeyplatz, -feld** hockey pitch ['hɒki pɪtʃ]
**Hockeyschuhe** hockey shoes ['hɒki ʃu:z]
**Hof** yard [jɑ:d] • **auf dem Hof** in the yard
**hoffen** hope [həʊp]
**Hoffnung** hope [həʊp]
**höflich** polite [pə'laɪt]
**holen** *(besorgen)* get [get]
**Holz** wood [wʊd]
**horchen: auf etwas horchen** *(achten)* listen for sth. ['lɪsn]
**hören** hear [hɪə] • **Na hör mal!** Come on. [ˌkʌm_'ɒn]
**Hose** trousers *(pl)* ['traʊzəz] *(BE)*; pants *(pl)* [pænts] *(AE)*
**Hotel** hotel [həʊ'tel]
**Hotline** hotline ['hɒtlaɪn]
**hübsch** pretty ['prɪti]
**Hubschrauber** helicopter ['helɪkɒptə]
**Hügel** hill [hɪl]
**hügelig** hilly ['hɪli]
**Huhn** chicken ['tʃɪkɪn]
**Hülle** cover ['kʌvə]
**Hund** dog [dɒg]
**hundert** hundred ['hʌndrəd]
**Hunger haben** be hungry ['hʌŋgri]
**hungrig sein** be hungry ['hʌŋgri]
**Hurra!** Hooray! [hu'reɪ]
**Hut** hat [hæt]
**Hütte** cabin ['kæbɪn]

## I

**ich** I [aɪ] • **Ich auch.** Me too. [ˌmi: 'tu:] • **Das bin ich.** That's me. **Warum ich?** Why me?
**ideal** perfect ['pɜ:fɪkt]
**Idee** idea [aɪ'dɪə] • **Ideen sammeln** brainstorm ['breɪnstɔ:m]
**Igel** hedgehog ['hedʒhɒg]
**igitt** yuck [jʌk]
**ihm** him; *(bei Dingen, Tieren)* it
**ihn** him; *(bei Dingen, Tieren)* it
**ihnen** them [ðəm, ðem]
**Ihnen** *(höfliche Anrede)* you [ju:]
**ihr** *(Plural von „du")* you [ju:] • **ihr zwei** you two [ˌju: 'tu:]
**ihr: Hilf ihr.** Help her. [hə, hɜ:]
**ihr(e)** *(besitzanzeigend)* *(zu „she")* her [hə, hɜ:]; *(zu „they")* their [ðeə]
**Ihr(e)** *(höfliche Anrede)* your [jɔ:]
**ihrer, ihre, ihrs** *(zu „she")* hers [hɜ:z]; *(zu „they")* theirs [ðeəz]
**Ihrer, Ihre, Ihrs** *(höfliche Anrede)* **yours** [jɔ:z]
**illegal** illegal [ɪ'li:gl]
**im: im Fernsehen** on TV • **im Flugzeug** on the plane • **im Jahre 1919** in 1919 • **im Haus der Shaws** at the Shaws' house • **im Mai** in May • **im Radio** on the radio • **im Zug** on the train
**Imbiss** snack [snæk]
**Imbissstube** café ['kæfeɪ]
**immer 1.** always ['ɔ:lweɪz] • **immer noch** still [stɪl] **2. wann (auch) immer** whenever [wen'evə] • **was (auch) immer** whatever [wɒt'evə] • **wer/wen/wem (auch) immer** whoever [hu:'evə] • **wo (auch) immer** wherever [weər'evə] • **wohin (auch) immer** wherever ▶ S.183 whoever, whatever, whenever, wherever
**in** in • **in ... (hinein)** into ... ['ɪntə, 'ɪntʊ] • **in den Zug/Bus einsteigen** get on the train/bus • **in der Stadt umher** around the town • **in der ...straße** in ... Street • **in der Hamiltonstraße 7** at 7 Hamilton Street • **in der Nacht** at night **in der Nähe von** near • **in der Pause** *(zwischen Schulstunden)* at break • **in der Schule** at school **in die falsche Richtung** the wrong way • **in die Sauna gehen** have a sauna • **in Eile sein** be in a hurry **ins Bett gehen** go to bed • **ins Kino gehen** go to the cinema • **in Urlaub fahren** go on holiday • **in Verbindung bleiben** keep in touch **in welche Richtung?** which way? **in Wirklichkeit** *(eigentlich)* actually ['æktʃuəli]
**Indianer/in** Native American [ˌneɪtɪv_ə'merɪkən]
**Industrie** industry ['ɪndəstri]

**industriell** industrial [ɪn'dʌstriəl]
**Information(en) (über)** information (about/on) *(no pl)* [ˌɪnfə'meɪʃn]
**Informationsquelle** source [sɔ:s]
**Ingenieur/in** engineer [ˌendʒɪ'nɪə]
**Inliner** skates [skeɪts] • **Inliner fahren** skate
**innen (drin)** inside [ˌɪn'saɪd]
**Innenstadt** city centre [ˌsɪti 'sentə]
**innerhalb** inside [ˌɪn'saɪd]
**Insel** island ['aɪlənd]
**installieren** install [ɪn'stɔ:l]
**Instrument** instrument ['ɪnstrəmənt]
**interessant** interesting ['ɪntrəstɪŋ]
**interessieren: sich interessieren (für)** be interested (in) ['ɪntrəstɪd]
**interessiert sein (an)** be interested (in) ['ɪntrəstɪd]
**international** international [ˌɪntə'næʃnəl]
**Internet** internet ['ɪntənet] • **im Internet** on the internet • **im Internet surfen** surf the internet [sɜ:f]
**Interview** interview ['ɪntəvju:]
**interviewen** interview ['ɪntəvju:]
**irgendein(e)** any ['eni]
► S.179 any
**irgendetwas** anything ['eniθɪŋ]
**irgendetwas anderes** anything else [els]
► S.179 any ► S.176 ... else
**irgendjemand** anybody ['enibɒdi]; anyone ['eniwʌn] • **irgendjemand anderes** anybody/anyone else
► S.179 any ► S.176 ... else
**irgendwelche** any ['eni]
**irgendwo(hin)** somewhere ['sʌmweə]; anywhere ['eniweə]
**irren: sich irren** be wrong [rɒŋ]

## J

**ja** yes [jes]
**Jacke, Jackett** jacket ['dʒækɪt]
**Jagd** hunt [hʌnt]
**jagen** hunt [hʌnt]
**Jahr** year [jɪə]
**Jahrestag** *(Jubiläum)* anniversary [ˌænɪ'vɜ:səri]
**Jahrgangsstufe** year [jɪə] *(BE)*; grade [greɪd] *(AE)*
**Jahrhundert** century ['sentʃəri]
**...jährig: ein(e) Sechzehnjährige(r)** a sixteen-year-old • **ein sechzehnjähriges Mädchen** a sixteen-year-old girl
**Januar** January ['dʒænjuəri]
**Jazz** jazz [dʒæz]
**je?** *(jemals?)* ever? ['evə]
**Jeans** jeans *(pl)* [dʒi:nz]
**jede(r, s) ...** *(Begleiter)* **1.** every ... ['evri]
**2.** *(jeder einzelne)* each ... [i:tʃ]
**3.** *(jeder beliebige)* any ... ['eni]
► S.179 any
**jeder** *(Pronomen)* **1.** everybody ['evribɒdi]; everyone ['evriwʌn]
**2.** *(jeder Beliebige)* anybody ['enibɒdi]; anyone ['eniwʌn]
► S.179 any
**jederzeit** any time
► S.179 any
**jemals?** ever? ['evə]
**jemand** **1.** somebody ['sʌmbədi]; someone ['sʌmwʌn] • **jemand anders** sombebody/someone else
**2.** *(irgendjemand)* anybody ['enibɒdi]; anyone ['eniwʌn] • **sonst noch jemand?** anybody/anyone else?
► S.179 any ► S.176 ... else
**jene(r, s)** *(Singular)* that [ðət, ðæt]; *(Plural)* those [ðəʊz]
**jetzt** now [naʊ] • **jetzt gerade, jetzt sofort** right now • **bis jetzt** so far
**Job** job [dʒɒb]
**Journalist/in** journalist ['dʒɜ:nəlɪst]
**jubeln** cheer [tʃɪə]
**Jubiläum** anniversary [ˌænɪ'vɜ:səri]
**jüdisch** Jewish ['dʒu:ɪʃ]
**Judo** judo ['dʒu:dəʊ] • **Judo machen** do judo
**Jugend** youth [ju:θ]
**Jugend-** junior ['dʒu:niə]; *(Teenager-)* teen [ti:n]
**Jugendgruppe** youth group
**Jugendherberge** youth hostel ['ju:θˌhɒstl]
**Jugendliche(r)** kid [kɪd]; teenager ['ti:neɪdʒə]
**Juli** July [dʒu'laɪ]
**jung** young [jʌŋ]
**Junge** boy [bɔɪ]
**Juni** June [dʒu:n]
**Junioren-** junior ['dʒu:niə]
**Journalist/in** journalist ['dʒɜ:nəlɪst]

## K

**Kabel** *(auch kurz für Kabelfernsehen)* cable ['keɪbl]
**Kaffee** coffee ['kɒfi] • **Kaffe zum Mitnehmen** coffee to go [kɒfi tə 'gəʊ]
**Käfig** cage [keɪdʒ]
**Kalender** calendar ['kælɪndə]
**Kalorie** calorie ['kæləri]
**kalt** cold [kəʊld]
**Kälte** cold [kəʊld]
**Kamel** camel ['kæml]
**Kamera** camera ['kæmərə]
**Kampf** fight [faɪt]
**kämpfen (für, um)** fight (for) [faɪt]
**Kanal** **1.** canal [kə'næl]
**2.** *(Fernsehsender)* channel ['tʃænl]
**Känguru** kangaroo [ˌkæŋgə'ru:]
**Kaninchen** rabbit ['ræbɪt]
**Kante** rim [rɪm]
**Kantine** canteen [kæn'ti:n]
**Kanu** canoe [kə'nu:] • **Kanu fahren** canoe [kə'nu:]
**Kappe** cap [kæp]
**kaputt** broken ['brəʊkən] • **kaputt gehen** break [breɪk]
**Karotte** carrot ['kærət]
**Karriere** career [kə'rɪə]
**Karte** *(Post-, Spielkarte)* card [kɑ:d]
**Kartoffel** potato [pə'teɪtəʊ], *pl* -toes
**Kartoffelchips** crisps *(pl)* [krɪsps] *(BE)*; potato chips *(pl)* [tʃɪps] *(AE)*
**Käse** cheese [tʃi:z]
**Kasse** *(für den Verkauf von Eintrittskarten)* ticket office ['tɪkɪt‿ɒfɪs]
**Kästchen, Kasten** box [bɒks]
**Kathedrale** cathedral [kə'θi:drəl]
**Katze** cat [kæt]
**kaufen** buy [baɪ]
**Kaufhaus** department store [dɪ'pɑ:tmənt stɔ:]
**Kehle** throat [θrəʊt]
**kein(e)** no; not a; not (...) any • **Ich habe keinen Stuhl.** I haven't got a chair. • **keine Musik mehr** no more music
**Keks** biscuit ['bɪskɪt] *(BE)*; cookie ['kʊki] *(AE)*
**Kellner** waiter ['weɪtə]
**Kellnerin** waitress ['weɪtrəs]
**kennen** know [nəʊ]
**kennenlernen: jn. kennenlernen** get to know sb.; *(zum ersten Mal treffen)* meet sb. [mi:t] • **Nett, dich/euch/Sie kennenzulernen.** Nice to meet you.
**kennzeichnen** mark up [ˌmɑ:k‿'ʌp]
**Kerl** guy *(infml)* [gaɪ]
**Keyboard** *(elektronisches Tasteninstrument)* keyboard ['ki:bɔ:d]
**Kilogramm, Kilo (kg)** kilogram (kg) ['ki:ləgræm], kilo ['ki:ləʊ] • **ein 150 Kilogramm schwerer Bär** a 150-kilogram bear
**Kilometer (km)** kilometre (km) ['kɪləmi:tə] • **eine Zehn-Kilometer-Wanderung** a ten-kilometre walk
**Kind** child [tʃaɪld], *pl* children ['tʃɪldrən]; kid [kɪd] • **ein Kind bekommen** have a child
**Kindergarten** kindergarten ['kɪndəgɑ:tn]
**Kino** cinema ['sɪnəmə] • **ins Kino gehen** go to the cinema
**Kirche** church [tʃɜ:tʃ]
**Kirsche** cherry ['tʃeri]

**Kiste** box [bɒks]
**Kiwi** kiwi ['ki:wi:]
**Klang** sound [saʊnd]
**klar** 1. clear [klɪə]
2. *(sicher, kein Problem)* sure [ʃʊə, ʃɔ:]
**Klasse** class [klɑ:s]; form [fɔ:m]; grade [greɪd] *(AE)*
**klasse** awesome *(AE, infml)* ['ɔ:səm]
**Klassenkamerad/in** classmate ['klɑ:smeɪt]
**Klassenlehrer/in** class teacher; form teacher
**Klassenzimmer** classroom ['klɑ:sru:m]
**klassisch** classical ['klæsɪkl]
**klatschen** clap [klæp]
**Klavier** piano [pi'ænəʊ] • **Klavier spielen** play the piano
**kleben: (auf-, ein)kleben** glue [glu:]
**Klebestift** glue stick ['glu: stɪk]
**Klebstoff** glue [glu:]
**Kleid** dress [dres]
**Kleider** *(Kleidungsstücke)* clothes *(pl)* [kləʊðz, kləʊz]
**Kleiderordnung** dress code ['dres kəʊd]
**Kleiderschrank** wardrobe ['wɔ:drəʊb]
**Kleidung(sstücke)** clothes *(pl)* [kləʊðz, kləʊz]
**klein** little ['lɪtl]; small [smɔ:l]; *(Körpergröße)* short [ʃɔ:t]
**Kleingeld** change [tʃeɪndʒ]
► S.186 (to) change – change
**Kleinstadt** town [taʊn]
**klettern** climb [klaɪm] • **Klettere auf einen Baum.** Climb a tree.
**Klingel** bell [bel]
**klingeln** ring [rɪŋ]
**Klingelton** ringtone ['rɪŋtəʊn]
**klingen** sound [saʊnd]
**Klinik** clinic ['klɪnɪk]
**Klippe** cliff [klɪf]
**Klon** clone [kləʊn]
**Klub** club [klʌb]
**klug** clever ['klevə]
**Klugheit** cleverness ['klevənəs]
**knapp: Das war knapp.** That was close. [kləʊs]
**Kneipe** pub [pʌb]
**Knie** knee [ni:]
**Knieschützer** *(pl)* pads *(pl)* [pædz]
**Knopf** button ['bʌtn]
**Koch** cook [kʊk]
**kochen** cook [kʊk]
**Köchin** cook [kʊk]
**Koffer** suitcase ['su:tkeɪs]
**Koje** *(Etagenbett)* bunk (bed) [bʌŋk]
**kolorieren** colour ['kʌlə]
**komisch** funny ['fʌni]
**Komma: 10,4 (zehn Komma vier)** 10.4 (ten point four)
**kommen** come [kʌm]; *(hinkommen)* get [get] • **Ich komme aus …** I'm from … • **Wo kommst du her?** Where are you from? • **nach Hause kommen** come home; get home • **zu spät kommen** be late **Kommt nicht in Frage!** No way! **Ach komm!** Come on. [ˌkʌm_'ɒn] **Na los, komm.** Come on.
**Kommentar** comment ['kɒment]
**Komödie** comedy ['kɒmədi]
**König** king [kɪŋ]
**Königin** queen [kwi:n]
**königlich** royal ['rɔɪəl]
**Königreich: das Vereinigte Königreich** *(Großbritannien und Nordirland)* the United Kingdom (UK) [juˌnaɪtɪd 'kɪŋdəm, ju:'keɪ]
**können** can [kən, kæn]; be able to ['eɪbl] • **etwas gut/schlecht können** be good/bad at sth. • **ich kann nicht …** I can't … [kɑ:nt] **Kann ich Ihnen helfen? / Was kann ich für Sie tun?** *(im Laden)* Can I help you?
**könnte(n): ich/er könnte …** I/he could … [kəd, kʊd] • **du könntest (vielleicht) Hilfe brauchen** you might need help [maɪt]
**konnte(n): ich/er konnte …** I/he could … [kəd, kʊd]
**Kontakt halten** keep in touch [ˌki:p_ɪn 'tʌtʃ]
**Kontext** context ['kɒntekst]
**kontrollieren** *(überprüfen)* check [tʃek]
**Konzert** concert ['kɒnsət] • **ein Konzert geben** *(einen Auftritt haben)* do a gig *(infml)*
**Kopf** head [hed]
**Kopfhörer** headphones *(pl)* ['hedfəʊnz]
**kopflos** headless ['hedləs]
**Kopfschmerzen** headache ['hedeɪk]
**Kopie** copy ['kɒpi]
**kopieren** copy ['kɒpi]
**Korb** basket ['bɑ:skɪt] • **ein Korb Äpfel** a basket of apples
**Korn** grain [greɪn]
**Körper** body ['bɒdi]
**körperliche Bewegung** exercise *(no pl)*
**korrigieren** correct [kə'rekt]
**kosten** 1. cost [kɒst] • **Er/Sie/Es kostet 1 Pfund.** It's £1. • **Sie kosten 35 Pence.** They are 35p. • **Wie viel kostet/kosten …?** How much is/are …?
2. *(Essen probieren)* try [traɪ]
**kostenlos** free [fri:]
**köstlich** delicious [dɪ'lɪʃəs]
**Kram** stuff [stʌf]
**krank** ill [ɪl]
**kränken: jd. kränken** *(aus der Fassung bringen)* upset sb. [ʌp'set]
**Krankenhaus** hospital ['hɒspɪtl]
**Krankheit** illness ['ɪlnəs]
**Krankenwagen** ambulance ['æmbjələns]
**Kreis** circle ['sɜ:kl]
**Krieg** war [wɔ:]
**kriegen** get [get]
**Krimi** crime film ['kraɪm fɪlm]; crime story ['kraɪm ˌstɔ:ri]
**Kriminalität** crime [kraɪm]
**Krimiserie** crime series ['kraɪm ˌsɪəri:z]
**Krokodil** crocodile ['krɒkədaɪl]
**Krug** jug [dʒʌg] • **ein Krug Orangensaft** a jug of orange juice
**Küche** kitchen ['kɪtʃɪn]
**Kuchen** cake [keɪk]
**Kugelschreiber** pen [pen]
**Kuh** cow [kaʊ]
**kühl** cool [ku:l]
**Kühlschrank** fridge [frɪdʒ]
**Kultur** culture ['kʌltʃə]
**Kummer** worry ['wʌri]
**kümmern** 1. **sich um etwas/jn. kümmern** look after sth./sb. [ˌlʊk_'ɑ:ftə]
2. **Kümmere dich um deine eigenen Angelegenheiten!** Mind your own business. [ˌmaɪnd jər_ˌəʊn 'bɪznəs]
**Kumpel** mate [meɪt]
**Kunde, Kundin** customer ['kʌstəmə]
**Kunst** art [ɑ:t]
**Künstler/in** artist ['ɑ:tɪst]
**künstlich** artificial [ˌɑ:tɪ'fɪʃl]
**Kurs** *(Lehrgang)* course [kɔ:s]; *(Unterrichtsstunde)* class
**kurz** short [ʃɔ:t] • **kurze Hose** shorts *(pl)* [ʃɔ:ts]
**Kuss** kiss [kɪs]
**küssen** kiss [kɪs]
**Küste** coast [kəʊst]

## L

**lächeln** smile [smaɪl]
**Lächeln** smile [smaɪl]
**lachen** laugh [lɑ:f]
**lächerlich** laughable ['lɑ:fəbl]
**Lachs** salmon ['sæmən]
**Laden** *(Geschäft)* shop [ʃɒp]
**Ladentisch** counter ['kaʊntə]
**Lage: in der Lage sein, etwas zu tun** be able to do sth. ['eɪbl]
**Lager** *(Ferienlager)* camp [kæmp]
**Lamm(fleisch)** lamb [læm]
**Lampe** lamp [læmp]
**Land** *(auch als Gegensatz zur Stadt)* country ['kʌntri]; countryside ['kʌntrisaɪd]; *(Grund und Boden)* land [lænd] • **auf dem Land** *(im Gegen-*

*satz zur Stadt)* in the country; *(nicht auf dem Wasser)* on land
**landen** land [lænd]
**Landkarte** map [mæp]
**Landschaft** countryside ['kʌntrisaɪd]
**Landwirt/in** farmer ['fɑ:mə]
**Landwirtschaft** farming ['fɑ:mɪŋ]
**lang** long [lɒŋ] • **drei Tage lang** for three days • **Wie lange?** how long?
**langsam** slow [sləʊ]
**langweilen: sich langweilen** get bored [bɔ:d]
**langweilig** boring ['bɔ:rɪŋ]
**Lärm** noise [nɔɪz]
**lärmend** noisy ['nɔɪzi]
**Lasagne** lasagne [lə'zænjə]
**lassen** let [let] • **Lass uns ... / Lasst uns ...** Let's ... • **Lass das!** Stop that!
**lässig** easy-going [,i:zi'gəʊɪŋ]
**Lastkraftwagen** lorry ['lɒri]
**Lauf** run [rʌn]
**Laufbahn** *(Sport)* running track [træk]
**laufen 1.** run [rʌn] **2.** *(im Fernsehen/Kino)* to be on
**Läufer/in** runner ['rʌnə]
**Laufschuhe** running shoes
**laut** loud [laʊd]; *(lärmend)* noisy ['nɔɪzi] • **etwas lauter stellen** turn sth. up
**Laut** sound [saʊnd]
**läuten** ring [rɪŋ]
**Lautstärke** volume ['vɒlju:m]
**leben** live [lɪv]
**Leben** life [laɪf], *pl* lives [laɪvz] • **am Leben** alive [ə'laɪv]
**lebendig** alive [ə'laɪv]
**Lebensmittel** food [fu:d]
**lecker** delicious [dɪ'lɪʃəs]
**Leder** leather ['leðə]
**ledig** single ['sɪŋgl]
**leer** empty ['empti]
**legal** legal ['li:gl]
**legen** *(hin-, ablegen)* put [pʊt]
**lehren** teach [ti:tʃ]
**Lehrer/in** teacher ['ti:tʃə]
**Lehrgang** *(Kurs, Seminar)* workshop ['wɜ:kʃɒp]; course [kɔ:s]
**Leibwächter/in** bodyguard ['bɒdigɑ:d]
**leicht** *(nicht schwierig)* easy ['i:zi]
**Leichtathletik** athletics [æθ'letɪks]
**leiden: (an/unter etwas) leiden** suffer (from sth.) ['sʌfə]
**leider** I'm afraid [ə'freɪd]; unfortunately [ʌn'fɔ:tʃənətli]
**leidtun: Tut mir leid.** I'm sorry. ['sɒri]
**leise** quiet ['kwaɪət] • **etwas leiser stellen** turn sth. down
**Leiter/in** *(Anführer/in)* leader ['li:də]
**Lektion** *(im Schulbuch)* unit ['ju:nɪt]
**lernen** learn [lɜ:n]; *(für die Schule arbeiten)* study ['stʌdi]
**Lern- und Arbeitstechniken** study skills ['stʌdi skɪlz]
**lesen** read [ri:d]
**Leser/in** reader ['ri:də]
**letzte(r, s)** last [lɑ:st]; final ['faɪnl]
**leuchtend** bright [braɪt]
**Leute** people ['pi:pl]; guys [gaɪz] *(AE, infml)*
**Licht** light [laɪt]
**Lichtblitz** flash [flæʃ]
**Liebe** love [lʌv]
**Liebe Grüße, ...** *(Briefschluss)* Love ... [lʌv]
**lieben** love [lʌv]
**liebenswert** likeable ['laɪkəbl]
**Lieber Jay, ...** Dear Jay ... [dɪə]
**lieber: etwas lieber mögen** like sth. better
**Liebling** dear [dɪə]; sweetheart ['swi:thɑ:t]
**Lieblings-: meine Lieblingsfarbe** my favourite colour ['feɪvərɪt]
**Lied** song [sɒŋ]
**Liedtext** lyrics *(pl)* ['lɪrɪks]
**liegen** lie [laɪ] • **Das liegt bei dir.** *(Das kannst/musst du (selbst) entscheiden.)* That's up to you.
**lila** purple ['pɜ:pl]
**Limonade** lemonade [,lemə'neɪd] *(BE)*; soda ['səʊdə] *(AE)*
**Lineal** ruler ['ru:lə]
**Linie: (U-Bahn-)Linie** line [laɪn]
**linke(r, s)** left [left] • **links, auf der linken Seite** on the left • **(nach) links abbiegen** turn left • **nach links schauen** look left
**Liste** list [lɪst]
**Livemusik** live music [laɪv]
**Loch** hole [həʊl]
**Löffel** spoon [spu:n]
**Logo** logo ['ləʊgəʊ], *pl* logos
**Lokal** *(Kneipe)* pub [pʌb]
**Lokal-** *(örtlich)* local ['ləʊkl] • **Lokalzeitung** local paper ['ləʊkl]
**löschen: ein Feuer löschen** put out a fire
**Löwe** lion ['laɪən]
**Luft** air [eə]

## M

**machbar** doable ['du:əbl]
**machen** do [du:]; make [meɪk] • **die Hausaufgabe(n) machen** do homework • **einen Ausflug machen** go on a trip • **eine Pause machen** take a break • **einen Spaziergang machen** go for a walk • **eine Spritztour/Fahrt machen** take a ride • **eine Übung machen** do an exercise • **ein Picknick machen** have a picnic • **Fotos machen** take photos • **jm. Vorwürfe machen (wegen)** blame sb. (for) **Judo machen** do judo • **sich Notizen machen** take notes • **sich Sorgen machen (um, wegen)** worry (about) ['wʌri] • **(Zauber-)Kunststücke machen** do tricks • **Machen Sie es sich bequem. / Mach es dir bequem.** Make yourself comfortable. • **Reiten macht Spaß.** Riding is fun.
**Mädchen** girl [gɜ:l]
**Magazin** *(Zeitschrift)* magazine [,mægə'zi:n]
**Magen** stomach ['stʌmək]
**Magenschmerzen** stomach ache ['stʌmək_eɪk]
**mager** skinny ['skɪni]
**Magst du ...?** Do you like ...? [laɪk] *(siehe auch unter „mögen")*
**mähen: Rasen mähen** cut the grass [grɑ:s]
**Mahlzeit** meal [mi:l]
**Mai** May [meɪ]
**mailen: jm. etwas mailen** mail sb. sth. [meɪl]
**Make-up** make-up ['meɪkʌp]
**Mal(e); -mal** time(s) [taɪm(z)] • **zum ersten Mal** for the first time
**malen** paint [peɪnt]
**Maler/in** painter ['peɪntə]
**Mama** mum [mʌm] *(BE)*; mom [mɒm, *AE:* mɑ:m] *(AE)*
**man** you [ju:]
**Manager/in** manager ['mænədʒə]
**manchmal** sometimes ['sʌmtaɪmz]
**Mann** man [mæn], *pl* men [men]
**männlich** male [meɪl]
**Mannschaft** team [ti:m]
**Mappe** *(des Sprachenportfolios)* dossier ['dɒsieɪ]
**markieren** mark up [,mɑ:k_'ʌp]
**Markt** market ['mɑ:kɪt]
**Marmelade** *(Orangenmarmelade)* marmalade ['mɑ:məleɪd]
**Marsch** march [mɑ:tʃ]; *(Wanderung)* hike [haɪk]
**März** March [mɑ:tʃ]
**Maschine** machine [mə'ʃi:n]
**Masse** *(Menschenmasse)* crowd [kraʊd]
**Mathematik** maths [mæθs]
**Matrose** sailor ['seɪlə]
**Mauer** wall [wɔ:l]
**Maulwurf** mole [məʊl]
**Maus** mouse [maʊs], *pl* mice [maɪs]
**Medaille** medal ['medl]

**Mediation** *(Sprachmittlung)* mediation [ˌmiːdiˈeɪʃn]
**Medien** media *(pl)* [ˈmiːdiə]
**Medikament** drug [drʌg]
**Meer** sea [siː]
**Meerschweinchen** guinea pig [ˈgɪni pɪg]
**mehr** more [mɔː] • **mehr als** more than • **mehr als ich** more than me • **nicht mehr** not ... any more **viel mehr** lots more • **keine Musik mehr** no more music
**mehrfarbig** multi-coloured [ˈmʌltiˌkʌləd]
**Mehrheit** majority [məˈdʒɒrəti]
**Meile** *(= ca. 1,6 km)* mile [maɪl]
**meilenweit** for miles [maɪlz]
**mein(e) ...** my ... [maɪ] • **meine neuen** my new ones [wʌnz]
**meinen** think [θɪŋk]; *(sagen wollen)* mean [miːn] • **Meinst du wirklich?** Do you really think so?
**meiner, meine, meins** mine [maɪn]
**Meinung** opinion [əˈpɪnjən] • **anderer Meinung sein (als)** disagree (with) [ˌdɪsəˈgriː] • **meiner Meinung nach** in my opinion
**meist: (der/die/das) meiste ...; am meisten** most [məʊst] • **die meisten Leute** most people
**meistens** usually [ˈjuːʒuəli]
**Meister/in** *(Champion)* champion [ˈtʃæmpiən]
**Meisterschaft** championship [ˈtʃæmpiənʃɪp]
**melden: sich freiwillig melden** volunteer [ˌvɒlənˈtɪə]
**Melodie** tune [tjuːn]
**Menge** *(Menschenmenge)* crowd [kraʊd]
**Menschen** people [ˈpiːpl]
**Menschen-** human [ˈhjuːmən]
**Menschenmenge** crowd [kraʊd]
**menschlich** human [ˈhjuːmən]
**merken: sich etwas merken** remember sth. [rɪˈmembə]
**Messer** knife [naɪf], *pl* knives [naɪvz]
**Meter** metre [ˈmiːtə]
**Metzger** butcher [ˈbʊtʃə] • **beim Metzger** at the butcher's
**mich** me [miː] • **mich (selbst)** myself [maɪˈself]
**Mikrofon** microphone [ˈmaɪkrəfəʊn]
**Milch** milk [mɪlk]
**mild** mild [maɪld]
**Million** million [ˈmɪljən]
**Millionär/in** millionaire [ˌmɪljəˈneə]
**Minderheit** minority [maɪˈnɒrəti]
**Mindmap** mind map [ˈmaɪnd mæp]
**Mineralwasser mit Kohlensäure** sparkling water [ˈspɑːklɪŋ]
**minus** minus [ˈmaɪnəs]
**Minute** minute [ˈmɪnɪt]
**mir** me [miː]
**mischen** mix [mɪks]
**Mischung** mix [mɪks]; mixture [ˈmɪkstʃə]
**mit** with [wɪð] • **mit dem Auto/Zug/Rad/... fahren** go by car/train/bike/... • **Mit besten Grüßen** *(als Briefschluss)* Best wishes [ˈwɪʃɪz] • **Mit freundlichen Grüßen** *(freundliche, aber formelle Grußformel in Briefen)* Yours faithfully [ˈfeɪθfəli] • **Mit freundlichen/herzlichen Grüßen** *(freundliche Grußformel in Briefen)* Yours sincerely [sɪnˈsɪəli]
**mitbringen** bring [brɪŋ]
**Mitbringsel** souvenir [ˌsuːvəˈnɪə]
**Mitglied (von, in)** member (of) [ˈmembə]
**mitmachen: bei etwas/jm. mitmachen** join sth./sb. [dʒɔɪn]
**mitnehmen: Kaffee zum Mitnehmen** coffee to go [kɒfɪ tə ˈgəʊ]
**Mitschüler/in** classmate [ˈklɑːsmeɪt]
**Mittagessen** lunch [lʌntʃ] • **zum Mittagessen** for lunch
**Mittagspause** lunch break [ˈlʌntʃ breɪk]
**Mitte** centre [ˈsentə]; middle (of) [ˈmɪdl]
**Mitteilung** *(Notiz)* note [nəʊt]
**Mittel-** *(Zentral-)* central [ˈsentrəl]
**mittel(groß)** medium [ˈmiːdiəm]
**Mittelteil** middle [ˈmɪdl]
**Mitternacht** midnight [ˈmɪdnaɪt]
**Mittwoch** Wednesday [ˈwenzdeɪ, ˈwenzdi] *(siehe auch unter „Freitag")*
**Mix** mix [mɪks]
**mixen** mix [mɪks]
**Mobiltelefon** mobile phone [ˌməʊbaɪl ˈfəʊn]; mobile [ˈməʊbaɪl]
**möchte: Ich möchte gern ... (haben)** I'd like ... (= I would like ...) • **Ich möchte über ... reden** I'd like to talk about ... • **Möchtest du etwas (Saft) / ein paar (Kekse)?** Would you like some (juice/biscuits)?
**Mode** fashion [ˈfæʃn]
**Modell** *(-auto, -schiff; Fotomodell)* model [ˈmɒdl]
**Moderator/in** presenter [prɪˈzentə]
**modern** modern [ˈmɒdən]
**modisch** *(schick, im Trend)* trendy [ˈtrendi]
**mögen** like [laɪk]; *(sehr mögen)* love [lʌv] • **etwas lieber mögen** like sth. better
**möglich** possible [ˈpɒsəbl]
**Möglichkeit** possibility [ˌpɒsəˈbɪləti]; *(Gelegenheit, Chance)* chance [tʃɑːns]
**Möhre** carrot [ˈkærət]
**Moment** moment [ˈməʊmənt] **genau in dem Moment** just then • **Moment mal!** Wait a minute. [ˈmɪnɪt]
**Monat** month [mʌnθ]
**Mond** moon [muːn]
**Monitor** monitor [ˈmɒnɪtə]
**Monster** monster [ˈmɒnstə]
**Montag** Monday [ˈmʌndeɪ, ˈmʌndi] *(siehe auch unter „Freitag")*
**Monument** monument [ˈmɒnjumənt]
**Mord** murder [ˈmɜːdə]
**morgen** tomorrow [təˈmɒrəʊ] • **das Wetter von morgen** tomorrow's weather
**Morgen** morning [ˈmɔːnɪŋ] • **am Morgen, morgens** in the morning **Guten Morgen.** Good morning. **Montagmorgen** Monday morning
**Moschee** mosque [mɒsk]
**Motel** motel [məʊˈtel]
**MP3-Spieler** MP3 player [ˌempiːˈθriː ˌpleɪə]
**müde** tired [ˈtaɪəd]
**Müll** rubbish [ˈrʌbɪʃ] *(BE)*; garbage [ˈgɑːbɪdʒ] *(AE)*
**Mülltonne** bin [bɪn]; dustbin [ˈdʌstbɪn]
**multi-, Multi-** multi- [ˈmʌlti] • **Multimillionär/in** multi-millionaire [ˌmʌltiˌmɪljəˈneə]
**Multiple-Choice** multiple choice [ˌmʌltɪpl ˈtʃɔɪs]
**Mund** mouth [maʊθ] • **Halt den Mund!** Shut up. [ˌʃʌt‿ˈʌp]
**murren** grumble [ˈgrʌmbl]
**Museum** museum [mjuˈziːəm]
**Musical** musical [ˈmjuːzɪkl]
**Musik** music [ˈmjuːzɪk]
**Musiker/in** musician [mjuːˈzɪʃn]
**Müsli** muesli [ˈmjuːzli]
**Muss** must [mʌst]
**müssen** have to; must [mʌst] **nicht müssen** needn't [ˈniːdnt]
**mutig** brave [breɪv]
**Mutter** mother [ˈmʌðə]
**Mutti** mum [mʌm] *(BE)*; mom [mɒm, *AE:* mɑːm] *(AE)*
**Mütze** cap [kæp]

## N

**Na ja ... / Na gut ...** Oh well ... [əʊ ˈwel]; anyway [ˈeniweɪ]
**Na und?** So? [səʊ]
**nach 1.** *(örtlich)* to [tə, tu] • **nach draußen** outside • **nach drinnen** inside • **nach Hause gehen** go home • **nach Hause kommen** come home; get home • **nach oben** up; *(im Haus)* upstairs

[ˌʌp'steəz] • **nach unten** down; *(im Haus)* downstairs [ˌdaʊn'steəz]
**2.** *(zeitlich)* after ['ɑːftə] • **Viertel nach 11** quarter past 11 [pɑːst]
**3. nach etwas fragen** ask about sth. [ə'baʊt]
**Nachbar/in** neighbour ['neɪbə]
**nachdem** after ['ɑːftə]
**nachdenken über** think about
**Nachforschung(en)** *(Recherche)* research (on) *(no pl)* [rɪ'sɜːtʃ, 'riːsɜːtʃ]
**Nachmittag** afternoon [ˌɑːftə'nuːn]
**am Nachmittag, nachmittags** in the afternoon
**Nachricht** message ['mesɪdʒ]
**Nachrichten** *(im Fernsehen, Radio; Neuigkeiten)* news *(no pl)* [njuːz]
**Das sind gute Nachrichten.** That's good news.
**Nachrichtensprecher/in** newsreader ['njuːzˌriːdə]
**nachrufen: jm. Schimpfwörter nachrufen** call sb. names
**nachschlagen: etwas nachschlagen** look sth. up [ˌlʊk‿'ʌp]
**nächste(r, s): am nächsten Tag** the next day [nekst] • **der Nächste sein** be next • **Was haben wir als Nächstes?** What have we got next?
**Nacht** night [naɪt] • **heute Nacht** tonight [tə'naɪt] • **in der Nacht, nachts** at night
**Nachteil** disadvantage [ˌdɪsəd'vɑːntɪdʒ]
**Nachtklub** nightclub ['naɪtklʌb]
**nahe (bei)** near [nɪə]; close (to) [kləʊs]
**Nähe: in der Nähe von** near [nɪə]
**Name** name [neɪm]
**Nase** nose [nəʊz] • **die Nase voll haben (von etwas)** be fed up (with sth.) [ˌfed‿'ʌp]
**Nashorn** rhino ['raɪnəʊ]
**nass** wet [wet]
**Nation** nation ['neɪʃn]
**national** national ['næʃnəl]
**Nationalpark** national park [ˌnæʃnəl 'pɑːk]
**Natur** *(Landschaft)* countryside ['kʌntrisaɪd]
**Natur-** natural ['nætʃrəl]
**natürlich 1.** *(nicht künstlich)* natural ['nætʃrəl]
**2.** *(selbstverständlich)* of course [əv 'kɔːs]
**Naturwissenschaft** science ['saɪəns]
**Nebel** fog [fɒg]
**neben** next to ['nekst tə]
**nebenbei bemerkt** actually ['æktʃuəli]
**neblig** foggy ['fɒgi]
**Neffe** nephew ['nefjuː, 'nevjuː]
**nehmen** take [teɪk] • **Wir nehmen es.** *(beim Einkaufen)* We'll take it.
**neidisch (auf)** jealous (of) ['dʒeləs]
**nein** no [nəʊ]
**nennen** *(rufen, bezeichnen)* call [kɔːl]; *(benennen)* name [neɪm]
**nerven: jn. nerven** annoy sb. [ə'nɔɪ]
**Nerven: Mein Vater geht mir auf die Nerven.** My dad is annoying. [ə'nɔɪɪŋ]
**nervös** nervous ['nɜːvəs]
**nett** nice [naɪs]; *(liebenswert)* likeable ['laɪkəbl]
**neu** new [njuː]
**neueste(r, s)** latest ['leɪtɪst]
**Neuigkeiten** news [njuːz]
**nicht** not [nɒt] • **nicht mehr** not (...) any more • **Nicht so wichtig.** Never mind. [ˌnevə 'maɪnd] • **Du brauchst eine Schultasche, nicht wahr?** You need a school bag, right? [raɪt] • **Ich weiß es nicht.** I don't know. [ˌdəʊnt 'nəʊ] • **noch nicht** not (...) yet [jet] • **(noch) nicht einmal** not even ['iːvn]
**Nichte** niece [niːs]
**nichts** nothing ['nʌθɪŋ]; not (...) anything ['eniθɪŋ] • **Nichts zu danken.** You're welcome. ['welkəm]
**nicken (mit)** nod [nɒd]
**nie, niemals** never ['nevə]
**niemand** nobody ['nəʊbədi]; no one ['nəʊ‿wʌn]; not (...) anybody/anyone ['enibɒdi, 'eniwʌn]
**nirgendwo(hin)** not (...) anywhere ['eniweə]
**noch: noch ein(e) ...** another ... [ə'nʌðə] • **noch 45 Pence** another 45 p • **noch einmal** again [ə'gen]
**noch nicht** not (...) yet [jet] • **noch nicht einmal** not even [iːvn]
**(immer) noch** still [stɪl] • **sonst noch etwas?** anything else
**sonst noch jemand?** anybody else? • **was ... (sonst) noch?** what else? • **wen ... (sonst) noch?** who else?
▸ S.176 ... else
**Norden** north [nɔːθ] • **nach Norden** north • **Richtung Norden** *(Fahrtrichtung)* northbound ['nɔːθbaʊnd]
**nördlich** north [nɔːθ]
**Nordosten** north-east [ˌnɔːθ'iːst]
**nach Nordosten** north-east
**nordöstlich** north-east [ˌnɔːθ'iːst]
**Nordwesten** north-west [ˌnɔːθ'west]
**nach Nordwesten** north-west
**nordwestlich** north-west [ˌnɔːθ'west]
**nörgeln** grumble ['grʌmbl]
**normal** *(Größenangabe bei Getränken)* regular ['regjələ]
**normalerweise** usually ['juːʒuəli]
**Note** *(Zensur)* grade [greɪd] *(BE auch:* mark [mɑːk])
**Notiz** note [nəʊt] • **sich Notizen machen** take notes
**November** November [nəʊ'vembə]
**null** o [əʊ]; zero ['zɪərəʊ]; *(beim Sport)* nil [nɪl]
**Nummer** number ['nʌmbə]
**Nummernschild** number plate ['nʌmbə pleɪt] *(BE)*; license plate ['laɪsns pleɪt] *(AE)*
**nun** now [naʊ] • **Nun, ...** Well, ... [wel]
**nur** only ['əʊnli]; just [dʒʌst] • **nur zum Spaß** just for fun
**Nuss** nut [nʌt]
**nützlich** useful ['juːsfl]; *(hilfreich)* helpful ['helpfl]; *(wertvoll)* valuable ['væljuəbl]

## O

**ob** if [ɪf]
**obdachlos** homeless ['həʊmləs]
**oben** above [ə'bʌv]; *(an der Spitze)* at the top (of) [tɒp]; *(im Haus)* upstairs [ˌʌp'steəz] • **nach oben** up; *(im Haus)* upstairs
**Oberbegriff** group word ['gruːp wɜːd]
**oberhalb von** over ['əʊvə]; above [ə'bʌv]
**Oberteil** top [tɒp]
**Obst** fruit [fruːt]
**Obstkuchen** pie [paɪ]
**Obstsalat** fruit salad ['fruːt ˌsæləd]
**obwohl** although [ɔːl'ðəʊ]
**oder** or [ɔː] • **Das ist nicht dein Ernst, oder?** You're joking, aren't you?
**offen** open ['əʊpən]
**öffnen** open ['əʊpən]
**Öffnungszeiten** (opening) hours *(pl)*
**oft** often ['ɒfn]
**ohne** without [wɪ'ðaʊt]
**Ohr** ear [ɪə]
**Ohrenschmerzen** earache ['ɪəreɪk]
**Ohrring** earring ['ɪərɪŋ]
**Oje!** Oh dear! [əʊ 'dɪə]
**okay** OK [əʊ'keɪ]
**Oktober** October [ɒk'təʊbə]
**Öl** oil [ɔɪl]
**Olympiade** Olympic Games (*or:* the Olympics) [əˌlɪmpɪk 'geɪmz (ə'lɪmpɪks)]
**Olympische Spiele** Olympic Games (*or:* the Olympics) [əˌlɪmpɪk 'geɪmz (ə'lɪmpɪks)]
**Oma** grandma ['grænmɑː]; granny ['græni]
**Onkel** uncle ['ʌŋkl]
**online, Online-** online [ˌɒn'laɪn]

**Opa** grandpa ['grænpɑ:]; grandad ['grændæd]
**Oper** opera ['ɒprə]
**Operation (an)** operation (on) [,ɒpə'reɪʃn]
**Opfer** victim ['vɪktɪm]
**Orange** orange ['ɒrɪndʒ]
**orange(farben)** orange ['ɒrɪndʒ]
**Orangenmarmelade** marmalade ['mɑ:məleɪd]
**Orangensaft** orange juice ['ɒrɪndʒ dʒu:s]
**ordentlich** tidy ['taɪdi]
**Ordnung: in Ordnung** all right [ɔ:l 'raɪt]; fine [faɪn]
**organisieren** organize ['ɔ:gənaɪz]
**Original; Original-** original *(n; adj)* [ə'rɪdʒənl]
**Ort** place [pleɪs]; *(Veranstaltungs-, Wohnort)* location [ləʊ'keɪʃn]
**Orts-, örtlich** local ['ləʊkl]
**Osten** east [i:st] • **nach Osten** east [i:st] • **Richtung Osten** eastbound ['i:stbaʊnd]
**Oster-** Easter ['i:stə]
**Ostern** Easter ['i:stə]
**östlich** east [i:st]
**Outfit** *(Kleidung; Ausrüstung)* outfit ['aʊtfɪt]
**Ozean** ocean ['əʊʃn]

## P

**paar: ein paar** some [səm, sʌm]; *(einige wenige)* a few [fju:] • **ein paar Wochen/Tage/...** a couple of weeks/days/... ['kʌpl]
**Paar: ein Paar** a pair (of) [peə]
**Päckchen** packet ['pækɪt] • **ein Päckchen Pfefferminzbonbons** a packet of mints
**packen** pack [pæk]
**Packung** packet ['pækɪt] • **eine Packung Pfefferminzbonbons** a packet of mints
**Paddel** paddle ['pædl]
**paddeln** paddle ['pædl]; canoe [kə'nu:]
**Paket** parcel ['pɑ:sl]
**Palast** palace ['pæləs]
**Panik: Keine Panik.** Don't panic! ['pænɪk]
**pantomimisch darstellen** mime [maɪm]
**Papa** dad [dæd]
**Papagei** parrot ['pærət]
**Papier** paper ['peɪpə]
**Paralympische Spiele** *(Olympische Spiele für Sportler/innen mit körperlicher Behinderung)* Paralympics [,pærə'lɪmpɪks]
**Park** park [pɑ:k]
**Parken: das Parken** parking ['pɑ:kɪŋ]
**Parkplatz** *(für viele Autos)* car park ['kɑ: pɑ:k]
**Parlament** parliament ['pɑ:ləmənt]
**Partner/in** partner ['pɑ:tnə]
**Partnerstadt** twin town [,twɪn 'taʊn] *(BE)*; sister city *(AE)*
**Party** party ['pɑ:ti]
**passen** fit [fɪt] • **passen zu** go with
**passieren (mit)** **1.** happen (to) ['hæpən] • **Mir/Dir/Ihr/... wird nichts passieren.** I'll/You'll/She'll/... be OK.
**2.** *(durchqueren)* cross [krɒs]
**Pasta** *(Nudeln, Teigwaren)* pasta *(no pl)* ['pæstə]
**Pastor/in** minister ['mɪnɪstə]
**Pause** break [breɪk] • **in der Pause** *(zwischen Schulstunden)* at break **eine Pause machen** take a break
**Pazifik** Pacific (Ocean) [pə,sɪfɪk_'əʊʃn]
**Pazifischer Ozean** Pacific Ocean [pə,sɪfɪk_'əʊʃn]
**peinlich: Es ist mir peinlich.** I'm embarrassed. [ɪm'bærəst]
**Pence** pence (p) [pens]
**perfekt** perfect ['pɜ:fɪkt]
**Person** person ['pɜ:sn]; *(in Roman, Film, Theaterstück)* character ['kærəktə]
**persönliche(r, s)** personal ['pɜ:sənl]
**Pfad** path [pɑ:θ]
**Pfarrer/in** minister ['mɪnɪstə]
**Pfeffer** pepper ['pepə]
**Pfefferminzbonbons** mints [mɪnts]
**Pfeife** **1.** *(zum Rauchen; Orgelpfeife)* pipe [paɪp]
**2.** *(Trillerpfeife)* whistle ['wɪsl]
**pfeifen** whistle ['wɪsl]
**Pferd** horse [hɔ:s]
**Pferdeschwanz** *(Frisur)* ponytail ['pəʊniteɪl]
**Pfund** *(britische Währung)* pound (£) [paʊnd] • **Es kostet 1 Pfund.** It's £1.
**Piano** piano [pi'ænəʊ]
**Picknick** picnic ['pɪknɪk] • **ein Picknick machen** have a picnic
**piepsen** bleep [bli:p]
**Piepton** bleep [bli:p]
**Pilz** mushroom ['mʌʃrʊm, -ru:m]
**pink(farben)** pink [pɪŋk]
**Pirat/in** pirate ['paɪrət]
**Pizza** pizza ['pi:tsə]
**PKW** car [kɑ:] *(BE)*; auto *(AE)* ['ɔ:təʊ]
**Plan** plan [plæn]
**planen** plan [plæn]
**Planet** planet ['plænɪt]
**Plantage** plantation [plɑ:n'teɪʃn]
**Platz** *(Ort, Stelle)* place [pleɪs]; *(Raum)* space [speɪs]; *(in der Stadt)* square [skweə]; *(runder Platz in der Stadt)* circus ['sɜ:kəs]; *(für Squash, Badminton)* court [kɔ:t]; *(Einsatzort)* location [ləʊ'keɪʃn]
**Plätzchen** biscuit ['bɪskɪt]
**plaudern** chat [tʃæt]
**plötzlich** suddenly ['sʌdnli]
**plus** plus [plʌs]
**Pokal** cup [kʌp]
**Polizei** police *(pl)* [pə'li:s]
**Polizeiwache, Polizeirevier** police station [pə'li:s steɪʃn]
**Polizist/in** policeman [pə'li:smən]/ policewoman [pə'li:swʊmən]
**Poltergeist** poltergeist ['pəʊltəgaɪst]
**Pommes frites** chips *(pl)* [tʃɪps] *(BE)*; French fries *(pl)* [fraɪz] *(AE)*
**Popcorn** popcorn ['pɒpkɔ:n]
**Pop(musik)** pop (music) [pɒp]
**populär (bei)** popular (with) ['pɒpjələ]
**Porträt** *(Steckbrief)* profile ['prəʊfaɪl]
**Post** *(Briefe, Päckchen, ...)* post [pəʊst]; *(Postamt)* post office ['pəʊst_ɒfɪs]
**Postamt** post office ['pəʊst_ɒfɪs]
**Poster** poster ['pəʊstə]
**Postkarte** postcard ['pəʊstkɑ:d]
**Präsentation** presentation [,prezn'teɪʃn]
**Präsident/in** president ['prezɪdənt]
**Preis** *(Kaufpreis)* price [praɪs]; *(Gewinn)* prize [praɪz]
**pressen** squeeze [skwi:z]
**pro** per [pɜ:, pə] • **einmal pro Woche** once a week / once per week
**Probe** *(am Theater)* rehearsal [rɪ'hɜ:sl]
**proben** *(am Theater)* rehearse [rɪ'hɜ:s]
**probieren** try [traɪ]
**Problem** problem ['prɒbləm] • **kein Problem** *(klar, sicher)* sure [ʃʊə, sɔ:]
**Produkt** product ['prɒdʌkt]
**Produktion** production [prə'dʌkʃn]
**produzieren** produce [prə'dju:s]
**Programm** programme ['prəʊgræm]; *(Kanal im Fernsehen, Radio)* channel ['tʃænl]
**Projekt (über, zu)** project (on, about) ['prɒdʒekt] • **ein Projekt machen, durchführen** do a project
**Prospekt** brochure ['brəʊʃə]
**Protest** protest ['prəʊtest]
**protestieren** protest [prəʊ'test]
**Provinz** province ['prɒvɪns]
**Prozent** per cent (%) [pə 'sent]
**prüfen** *(überprüfen)* check [tʃek]
**Prüfung** test [test]
**PS** *(Nachschrift unter Briefen)* PS [,pi:_'es] (postscript ['pəʊstskrɪpt])
**Publikum** audience ['ɔ:diəns]
**Pullover** pullover ['pʊləʊvə]

**Punkt** *(bei Test, Quiz)* point [pɔɪnt]
**Punktestand** *(Spielstand)* score [skɔː]
**Pute/Puter** turkey ['tɜːki]
**putzen** clean [kliːn] • **Ich putze mir die Zähne.** I clean my teeth.
**Putzfrau, -mann** cleaner ['kliːnə]
**Pyramide** pyramid ['pɪrəmɪd]

## Q

**Quadratkilometer** square km (sq km) [skweə ]
**Quelle** *(von Information, Energie usw.)* source [sɔːs]
**Querflöte** flute [fluːt]
**Quiz** quiz [kwɪz], *pl* quizzes ['kwɪzɪz]

## R

**Rad 1.** wheel ['wiːl] **2.** *(Fahrrad)* bike [baɪk]
**Rad fahren** cycle ['saɪkl]; ride a bike [ˌraɪd‿ə 'baɪk]
**Radfahrt** bike ride ['baɪk raɪd]
**Radiergummi** rubber ['rʌbə] *(BE)*; eraser [ɪ'reɪzə, *AE:* ɪ'reɪsər] *(AE)*
**Radio** radio ['reɪdiəʊ] • **im Radio** on the radio
**Radiokanal** channel ['tʃænl]
**Radioprogramm** *(Radiokanal)* channel ['tʃænl]
**Radio-Sendernetz** network ['netwɜːk]
**Radweg** cycle path ['saɪkl pɑːθ]
**Rafting** rafting ['rɑːftɪŋ]
**Rap** rap [ræp]
**Rasen** grass [grɑːs] • **Rasen mähen** cut the grass
**raten** *(erraten, schätzen)* guess [ges]
**Ratespiel** quiz [kwɪz], *pl* quizzes ['kwɪzɪz]
**Rätsel** riddle ['rɪdl]; *(Geheimnis)* mystery ['mɪstri]
**Rauch** smoke [sməʊk]
**rauchen** smoke [sməʊk] • **Rauchen verboten.** No smoking.
**Raum** room [ruːm, rʊm]
**Rauschgift** drug [drʌg]
**Realität** reality [riː'æləti]
**realistisch** realistic [ˌriːə'lɪstɪk]
**Recherche (zu)** research (on) *(no pl)* [rɪ'sɜːtʃ, 'riːsɜːtʃ]
**recherchieren** do research [rɪ'sɜːtʃ]
**Rechnung** bill [bɪl]
**Recht** right [raɪt] • **Recht haben** be right [raɪt]
**rechte(r, s)** right [raɪt] • **rechts, auf der rechten Seite** on the right **(nach) rechts abbiegen** turn right **nach rechts schauen** look right
**Rechtschreibung** spelling ['spelɪŋ]
**rechtzeitig** in time [ɪn 'taɪm]
**recycelt** recycled [ˌriː'saɪkld]
**Recycling** recycling [ˌriː'saɪklɪŋ]
**Redakteur/in** editor ['edɪtə]
**Rede** speech [spiːtʃ] • **eine Rede halten** make a speech [spiːtʃ]
**reden (mit, über)** talk (to, about) [tɔːk]; speak (to, about) [spiːk] **Wovon redest du?** What are you talking about?
**Refrain** chorus ['kɔːrəs]
**Regal(brett)** shelf [ʃelf], *pl* shelves [ʃelvz]
**Regel** *(Vorschrift)* rule [ruːl]
**Regen** rain [reɪn]
**Reggae** reggae [re'geɪ]
**regieren** govern ['gʌvən]
**Regierung** government ['gʌvənmənt]
**Regisseur/in** film director ['fɪlm dəˌrektə]
**regnen** rain [reɪn]
**regnerisch** rainy ['reɪni]
**Reh** deer, *pl* deer [dɪə]
**reich** rich [rɪtʃ]
**reichen** *(weitergeben)* pass [pɑːs]
**Reihe 1.** *(wartende Menschen)* queue [kjuː] *(BE)*; line [laɪn] *(AE)* **2.** *(Sendereihe, Serie)* series, *pl* series ['sɪəriːz] **3. Du bist an der Reihe.** It's your turn. [tɜːn] • **Wer ist an der Reihe?** Whose turn is it? [huːz]
**Reis** rice [raɪs]
**Reise** trip [trɪp]; *(Fahrt)* journey ['dʒɜːni] • **eine Reise unterbrechen** break a journey
**Reiseleiter/in** (tour) guide [gaɪd]
**reisen** travel ['trævl]
**reiten** ride [raɪd] • **reiten gehen** go riding
**Reitweg** bridle path ['braɪdl pɑːθ]
**Religion** *(Religionsunterricht)* RE [ˌɑːr‿'iː], Religious Education [rɪˌlɪdʒəs‿edʒu'keɪʃn]
**rennen** run [rʌn]
**Reportage (über)** report (on) [rɪ'pɔːt]
**repräsentieren** represent [ˌreprɪ'zent]
**resignieren** give up
**Rest** rest [rest]
**Restaurant** restaurant ['restrɒnt]; *(Imbissstube, Café)* café ['kæfeɪ]
**Resultat** result [rɪ'zʌlt]
**retten** save [seɪv]
**Rettungshubschrauber** rescue helicopter ['reskjuː ˌhelɪkɒptə]
**richtig** right [raɪt]; *(korrekt)* correct [kə'rekt]
**Richtung** way [weɪ] • **in diese Richtung** this way • **in die falsche Richtung** the wrong way • **in welche Richtung?** which way? **Richtung Norden** northbound ['nɔːθbaʊnd] • **Richtung Osten** eastbound ['iːstbaʊnd] • **Richtung Süden** southbound ['saʊθbaʊnd] **Richtung Westen** westbound ['westbaʊnd]
**riechen** smell [smel]
**Riesenrad** big wheel [ˌbɪg 'wiːl]
**riesig** huge [hjuːdʒ]
**Rindfleisch** beef [biːf]
**Ring** ring [rɪŋ]
**Rock** skirt [skɜːt]
**Rock and Roll** rock and roll [ˌrɒk‿ən 'rəʊl]
**Rolle** role [rəʊl]
**Rollenspiel** role play ['rəʊl pleɪ]
**Rollstuhl** wheelchair ['wiːltʃeə]
**Romantik** romance [rəʊ'mæns, 'rəʊmæns]
**Romanze** romance [rəʊ'mæns, 'rəʊmæns]
**römisch; Römer, Römerin** Roman ['rəʊmən]
**rosa** pink [pɪŋk]
**rot** red [red]
**Route** route [ruːt]
**Rückfahrkarte** return ticket [rɪ'tɜːn ˌtɪkɪt]
**Rucksack** rucksack ['rʌksæk] *(BE)*; backpack ['bækpæk] *(AE)*
**rufen** call [kɔːl]; shout [ʃaʊt] • **die Polizei rufen** call the police
**ruhig** quiet ['kwaɪət] • **Bleib ruhig.** Don't panic! ['pænɪk]
**rumhängen (mit Freunden/Freundinnen)** *(abhängen)* hang out (with friends) [ˌhæŋ‿'aʊt]
**rund** round [raʊnd]
**Rundgang (durch das Haus)** tour (of the house) [tʊə]
**runterladen** *(downloaden)* download [ˌdaʊn'ləʊd]

## S

**Sache** thing [θɪŋ]
**Saft** juice [dʒuːs]
**sagen** say [seɪ] • **Sagt mir eure Namen.** Tell me your names. [tel]
**Sahne** cream [kriːm]
**Salat 1.** *(Kopfsalat)* lettuce ['letɪs] **2.** *(Gericht, Beilage)* salad ['sæləd]
**Salz** salt [sɔːlt]
**sammeln** collect [kə'lekt] • **Ideen sammeln** brainstorm ['breɪnstɔːm]
**Sammler/in** collector [kə'lektə]
**Sammlung** collection [kə'lekʃn]
**Samstag** Saturday ['sætədeɪ, 'sætədi] *(siehe auch unter „Freitag")*
**Sandwich** sandwich ['sænwɪtʃ, '-wɪdʒ]
**Sänger/in** singer ['sɪŋə]

**Sanitäter/in** paramedic [ˌpærəˈmedɪk]
**Satellit** satellite [ˈsætəlaɪt]
**satt: etwas satt haben** be tired of sth. [ˈtaɪəd]
**Sattel** saddle [ˈsædl]
**Satz** sentence [ˈsentəns]
**sauber** clean [kliːn] • **sauber machen** clean
**sauer sein (auf)** be cross (with) [krɒs]
**Säule** column [ˈkɒləm]
**Sauna** sauna [ˈsɔːnə] • **in die Sauna gehen** have a sauna
**Saxophon** saxophone [ˈsæksəfəʊn]
**Schachtel** packet [ˈpækɪt]; box [bɒks]
**Schaf** sheep, *pl* sheep [ʃiːp]
**Schal** scarf [skɑːf], *pl* scarves [skɑːvz]
**Schale** bowl [bəʊl] • **eine Schale Cornflakes** a bowl of cornflakes
**Schallplatte** record [ˈrekɔːd]
**scharf** *(würzig)* spicy [ˈspaɪsi]
**Schatten** shadow [ˈʃædəʊ]
**Schatz** dear [dɪə]; sweetheart [ˈswiːthɑːt]
**schätzen** *(raten, erraten)* guess [ges]
**schauen** look [lʊk] • **nach links/rechts schauen** look left/right
**Schaufenster** shop window [ˌʃɒp ˈwɪndəʊ]
**Schauspiel** drama [ˈdrɑːmə]
**Schauspieler/in** actor [ˈæktə]
**scheinen 1.** *(Sonne)* shine [ʃaɪn] **2. zu sein/zu tun scheinen** seem to be/to do [siːm]
**scherzen** joke [dʒəʊk]
**scheu** shy [ʃaɪ]
**scheußlich** horrible [ˈhɒrəbl]
**Schicht** *(bei der Arbeit)* shift [ʃɪft] **in einer Schicht** on a shift
**schick** *(modisch, im Trend)* trendy [ˈtrendi]
**schicken (an)** *(Post, E-Mail)* send (to) [send]; mail (to) [meɪl] • **jm. eine SMS schicken** text sb. [tekst]
**schieben** push [pʊʃ]
**schießen** shoot [ʃuːt]; *(ein Tor schießen)* score (a goal) [skɔː], [gəʊl]
**Schiff** boat [bəʊt]; ship [ʃɪp]
**Schild** sign [saɪn]
**Schildkröte** tortoise [ˈtɔːtəs]
**Schimpfwort: jn. mit Schimpfwörtern hänseln, jm. Schimpfwörter nachrufen** call sb. names
**Schinkenspeck** bacon [ˈbeɪkən]
**Schlaf** sleep [sliːp]
**Schlafanzug** pyjamas *(pl)* [pəˈdʒɑːməz]
**schlafen** sleep [sliːp]; *(nicht wach sein)* be asleep [əˈsliːp]
**schlaflos** sleepless [ˈsliːpləs]
**Schlafparty** sleepover [ˈsliːpəʊvə]
**Schlafzimmer** bedroom [ˈbedruːm]

**schlagen** hit [hɪt]; *(besiegen)* beat [biːt] • **gegen/auf die Windschutzscheibe schlagen** hit the windscreen [ˈwɪndskriːn]
**Schlägerei** fight [faɪt]
**Schlagzeile** headline [ˈhedlaɪn]
**Schlagzeug** drums *(pl)* [drʌmz] **Schlagzeug spielen** play the drums
**Schlange 1.** snake [sneɪk] **2.** *(wartende Menschen)* queue [kjuː] *(BE)*, line [laɪn] *(AE)*
**schlau** clever [ˈklevə]; smart [smɑːt]
**Schlauchboot** *(wildwassertauglich)* raft
**Schlauheit** cleverness [ˈklevənəs]
**schlecht** bad [bæd] • **schlechter** worse [wɜːs] • **am schlechtesten; der/die/das schlechteste** (the) worst [wɜːst] • **schlecht abschneiden (in)** do badly (in) • **schlecht in etwas sein; etwas schlecht können** be bad at sth. • **schlechtes Timing** bad timing • **Mir ist schlecht.** I feel sick. [sɪk]
**Schleuse** lock [lɒk]
**schließen** *(zumachen)* close [kləʊz]
**schließlich** at last [ət ˈlɑːst]; *(zum Schluss)* in the end
**schlimm** bad [bæd] • **schlimmer** worse [wɜːs] • **am schlimmsten; der/die/das schlimmste** (the) worst [wɜːst]
**Schlitten** sledge [sledʒ]
**Schlittschuhbahn** ice rink [ˈaɪs rɪŋk]
**Schloss** castle [ˈkɑːsl]; *(Palast)* palace [ˈpæləs]
**Schlucht** canyon [ˈkænjən]
**Schluss 1.** end [end] • **zum Schluss** in the end **2.** *(einer Geschichte, eines Films usw.)* ending [ˈendɪŋ] **3. Schlüsse ziehen** draw conclusions [ˌdrɔː kənˈkluːʒnz]
**schlussfolgern** draw conclusions [ˌdrɔː kənˈkluːʒnz]
**Schlüssel** key [kiː]
**Schlüsselring** key ring [ˈkiː rɪŋ]
**Schlüsselwort** key word [ˈkiː wɜːd]
**Schlussverkauf** sale [seɪl]
**Schmerz(en)** pain [peɪn]
**schmerzhaft** painful [ˈpeɪnfl]
**schmutzig** dirty [ˈdɜːti]
**schnappen** grab sth. [græb]
**Schnee** snow [snəʊ]
**Schneeball** snowball [ˈsnəʊbɔːl]
**Schneeschuh** snowshoe [ˈsnəʊʃuː]
**Schneeschuhwandern** snowshoeing [ˈsnəʊʃuːɪŋ]
**schneiden** cut [kʌt]
**schnell** quick [kwɪk]; fast [fɑːst]
**schockiert** shocked [ʃɒkt]

**Schokolade** chocolate [ˈtʃɒklət]
**schon** already [ɔːlˈredi] • **schon?** yet? [jet] • **schon mal?** ever? [ˈevə]
**schön** beautiful [ˈbjuːtɪfl]; *(nett)* nice [naɪs]; *(gut, in Ordnung)* fine [faɪn] **schön ordentlich** neat and tidy **Schön, dass du wieder da bist.** Good to have you back.
**Schönheit** beauty [ˈbjuːti]
**Schrank** cupboard [ˈkʌbəd]; *(Kleiderschrank)* wardrobe [ˈwɔːdrəʊb]
**schrecklich** terrible [ˈterəbl]; awful [ˈɔːfl] • **schreckliche Angst haben (vor)** be terrified (of) [ˈterɪfaɪd]
**schreiben (an)** write (to) [raɪt]
**Schreiber/in** writer [ˈraɪtə]
**Schreibtisch** desk [desk]
**Schreibung** *(Rechtschreibung, Schreibweise)* spelling [ˈspelɪŋ]
**schreien** shout [ʃaʊt]; scream [skriːm]
**Schriftsteller/in** writer [ˈraɪtə]
**Schritt** step [step]
**schüchtern** shy [ʃaɪ]
**Schuh** shoe [ʃuː]
**Schuld: Das ist nicht meine Schuld.** It's not my fault. [fɔːlt] • **jm. die Schuld geben (an)** blame sb. (for) [bleɪm]
**schuldbewusst** guilty [ˈgɪlti]
**schuldig** guilty [ˈgɪlti]
**Schule** school [skuːl] • **in der Schule** at school
**Schüler/in** student [ˈstjuːdənt]
**Schulfach** (school) subject [ˈsʌbdʒɪkt]
**Schulheft** exercise book [ˈeksəsaɪz bʊk]
**Schulleiter/in** head teacher [ˌhed ˈtiːtʃə]
**Schulmensa** canteen [kænˈtiːn] *(BE)*; cafeteria [ˌkæfəˈtɪəriə] *(AE)*
**Schulnote** grade [greɪd] *(BE auch:* mark [mɑːk]*)*
**Schulstunde** lesson [ˈlesn] *(BE)*; period [ˈpɪəriəd] *(AE)*
**Schultasche** school bag [ˈskuːl bæg]
**Schulter** shoulder [ˈʃəʊldə]
**Schulterpolster** *(beim American Football)* pad [pæd]
**Schüssel** bowl [bəʊl]
**schützen: jn. (vor etwas) schützen** protect sb. (from sth.) [prəˈtekt]
**Schützer** *(Knieschützer usw. für Inlineskater)* pad [pæd]
**schwach** weak [wiːk]
**schwarz** black [blæk] • **schwarzes Brett** *(Anschlagtafel)* notice board [ˈnəʊtɪs bɔːd] *(BE)*; bulletin board [ˈbʊlətɪn bɔːd] *(AE)*
**Schweigen** silence [ˈsaɪləns]
**Schwein** pig [pɪg]
**Schweinefleisch** pork [pɔːk]
**Schweiß** sweat [swet]

**schwer** **1.** *(Gewicht)* heavy ['hevi]
**ein 150 Kilogramm schwerer Bär** a 150-kilogram bear
**2.** *(schwierig)* difficult ['dɪfɪkəlt]; hard [hɑːd]
**3.** *(anstrengend)* hard [hɑːd]
**Schwester** sister ['sɪstə]
**schwierig** difficult ['dɪfɪkəlt]; hard [hɑːd]
**Schwierigkeiten** trouble ['trʌbl] • **in Schwierigkeiten sein** be in trouble
**Schwimmbad, -becken** swimming pool ['swɪmɪŋ puːl]
**schwimmen** swim [swɪm]
**schwimmen gehen** go swimming
**Schwimmer/in** swimmer ['swɪmə]
**schwitzen** sweat [swet]
**See** **1.** *(Binnensee)* lake [leɪk]
**2.** *(die See, das Meer)* sea [siː]
**Seemann** sailor ['seɪlə]
**sehen** see [siː] • **Siehst du?** See?
**Sehenswürdigkeiten** sights *(pl)* [saɪts]
**sehr** very ['veri] • **Danke sehr!** Thanks very much! • **Er mag sie sehr.** He likes her a lot. [ə 'lɒt]
**etwas sehr mögen / sehr lieben** like/love sth. very much
**Seife** soap [səʊp]
**Seifenoper** soap (opera) ['səʊp (ɒprə)]
**sein** *(Verb)* be [biː]
**sein(e)** *(besitzanzeigend)* *(zu „he")* his; *(zu „it")* its
**seiner, seine, seins** his [hɪz]
**seit** **1.** *(mit Zeitraum)* **seit 20 Minuten** for 20 minutes
**2.** *(mit Zeitpunkt)* **seit dem 4. April** since April 4th [sɪns]
**Seit wann ...?** How long ...?
► S.191 German 'seit'
**Seite** **1.** side [saɪd] • **auf der linken Seite** on the left • **auf der rechten Seite** on the right
**2.** *(Buch-, Heftseite)* page [peɪdʒ]
**Auf welcher Seite sind wir?** What page are we on?
**selbst: über dich selbst** about yourself [jə'self, jɔː'self]
**selbstverständlich** of course [əv 'kɔːs]
**seltsam** *(sonderbar; fremd)* strange [streɪndʒ]
**Semester** *(Schulhalbjahr in den USA)* semester [sɪ'mestə]
**senden (an)** *(Post, E-Mail)* send (to) [send]; mail to [meɪl]
**Sendernetz** *(im Radio und Fernsehen)* network ['netwɜːk]
**Sendereihe** series, *pl* series ['sɪəriːz]
**Sendung** *(im Fernsehen, Radio)* programme ['prəʊgræm]
**September** September [sep'tembə]

**Serie** *(Sendereihe)* series, *pl* series ['sɪəriːz]
**Sessel** armchair ['ɑːmtʃeə]
**Setup** setup ['setʌp]
**setzen: sich setzen** sit [sɪt] • **Setz dich / Setzt euch zu mir.** Sit with me.
**Shampoo** shampoo [ʃæm'puː]
**Shorts** shorts *(pl)* [ʃɔːts]
**Show** show [ʃəʊ]
**sich (selbst)** **1.** *(zu „she")* herself [hə'self, hɜː'self]
**2.** *(zu „he")* himself [hɪm'self]
**3.** *(zu „it")* itself [ɪt'self]
**4.** *(zu „they")* themselves [ðəm'selvz]
**5. sich (gegenseitig)** *(einander)* each other [iːtʃ_'ʌðə]; one another [wʌn_ə'nʌðə]
**sicher** **1.** *(in Sicherheit)* safe (from) [seɪf] • **nicht sicher** unsafe [ʌn'seɪf]
**2. sicher sein** *(nicht zweifeln)* be sure [ʃʊə, ʃɔː]
**3. sicher** *(kein Problem, klar)* sure [ʃʊə, ʃɔː]
**Sicherheit** *(das Sichersein vor Gefahr)* safety ['seɪfti]; *(Sicherheitsvorkehrungen)* security [sɪ'kjʊərəti] • **in Sicherheit (vor)** safe (from) [seɪf]
**sie** **1.** *(weibliche Person)* she [ʃiː]
**Frag sie.** Ask her. [hə, hɜː]
**2.** *(Ding, Tier)* it [ɪt]
**3.** *(Plural)* they [ðeɪ] • **Frag sie.** Ask them. [ðəm, ðem]
**Sie** *(höfliche Anrede)* you [juː]
**Sieg** win [wɪn]
**Sieger/in** winner ['wɪnə]
**Silbe** syllable ['sɪləbl]
**singen** sing [sɪŋ]
**Single** single ['sɪŋgl]
**sitzen** sit [sɪt]
**Skateboard** skateboard ['skeɪtbɔːd]
**Skateboard fahren** skate [skeɪt]
**skaten** skate [skeɪt]
**Skater** skater ['skeɪtə]
**Sketch** sketch [sketʃ]
**Ski** ski [skiː] • **Ski fahren/laufen** ski [skiː]
**Skipiste** ski slope ['skiː sləʊp]
**Sklave, Sklavin** slave [sleɪv]
**Skyline** *(Horizont; Silhouette)* skyline ['skaɪlaɪn]
**SMS** text message ['tekst ˌmesɪdʒ]
**jm. eine SMS schicken** text sb. [tekst]
**Snack** snack [snæk]
**so:** **1. so weit/gut/schlecht/...** that far/good/bad/... • **so süß** so sweet [səʊ]
**2. so alt/groß wie** as old/big as
**3. so, wie sie es mag** the way she likes it
**4. Es ist immer so.** It's always like this.

**Soap** soap [səʊp]
**Soapopera** soap opera ['səʊp_ˌɒprə]
**Socke** sock [sɒk]
**sodass** so that
**soeben** just [dʒʌst]
**Sofa** sofa ['səʊfə]
**sofort** immediately [ɪ'miːdiətli]
**Software** software ['sɒftweə]
**sogar** even ['iːvn] • **sogar wenn** even if
**Sohn** son [sʌn]
**Soldat/in** soldier ['səʊldʒə]
**sollte(n): Warum sollte ich ...?** Why should I ...? [ʃəd, ʃʊd]
**Sommer** summer ['sʌmə]
**sonderbar** *(fremd; seltsam)* strange [streɪndʒ]
**sondern** but
**Song** song [sɒŋ]
**Sonnabend** Saturday ['sætədeɪ, 'sætədi]
*(siehe auch unter „Freitag")*
**Sonne** sun [sʌn]
**Sonnenbrille: (eine) Sonnenbrille** sunglasses *(pl)* ['sʌnglɑːsɪz]
**sonnig** sunny ['sʌni]
**Sonntag** Sunday ['sʌndeɪ, 'sʌndi]
*(siehe auch unter „Freitag")*
**sonst: sonst noch etwas?** anything else? • **sonst noch jemand?** anybody else? • **was ... sonst noch?** what else? • **wen ... sonst noch?** who else?
► S.176 ... else
**Sorge** worry ['wʌri] • **sich Sorgen machen (wegen, um)** worry (about) • **Mach dir keine Sorgen.** Don't worry.
**sorgen: dafür sorgen, dass ...** make sure that ...
**sorgfältig** careful ['keəfl]
**Sorte** sort [sɔːt]
**Soundfile** sound file ['saʊnd faɪl]
**Souvenir** souvenir [ˌsuːvə'nɪə]
**sowieso** anyway ['eniweɪ]
**Sozial-; sozial** social ['səʊʃl]
**Spaghetti** spaghetti [spə'geti]
**spannend** exciting [ɪk'saɪtɪŋ]
**sparen** save [seɪv]
**Spaß** fun [fʌn] • **Spaß haben** have fun • **nur zum Spaß** just for fun
**Reiten macht Spaß.** Riding is fun.
**Viel Spaß!** Have fun! / Enjoy yourself.
**spät** late [leɪt] • **Wie spät ist es?** What's the time? • **zu spät sein/kommen** be late
**später** later ['leɪtə]
**spätestens: bis spätestens 10 (Uhr)** by ten (o'clock)
**spazieren gehen** go for a walk [wɔːk]
**Spaziergang** walk [wɔːk] • **einen Spaziergang machen** go for a walk

**Specht** woodpecker ['wʊdpekə]
**Speise** dish [dɪʃ]
**Speisekarte** menu ['menju:]
**sperren** lock [lɒk]
**spezifische(r,s)** specific [spə'sɪfɪk]
**Spiegel** mirror ['mɪrə]
**Spiel** game [geɪm]; *(Wettkampf)* match [mætʃ]
**spielen** play [pleɪ]; *(Szene, Dialog)* act [ækt] • **Fußball spielen** play football • **Gitarre/Klavier spielen** play the guitar/the piano
**Spieler/in** player ['pleɪə]
**Spielstand** *(Punktestand)* score [skɔ:]
**Spion/in** spy [spaɪ]
**Spitze** *(oberes Ende)* top [tɒp]; *(Flügel-, Schuhspitze)* tip [tɪp] • **an der Spitze (von)** at the top (of)
**Sport; Sportart** sport [spɔ:t] • **Sport treiben** do sport
**Sportler, Sportlerin** sportsman, sportswoman ['spɔ:tsmən, -ˌwʊmən]
**Sporthalle** gym [dʒɪm]; sports hall ['spɔ:ts hɔ:l]
**sportlich** sporty ['spɔ:ti]
**Sportunterricht** PE [ˌpi:‿'i:], Physical Education [ˌfɪzɪkəl‿edʒu'keɪʃn]
**Sportzentrum** sports centre ['spɔ:ts ˌsentə]
**Sprache** language ['læŋgwɪdʒ]
**Sprachmittlung** *(Mediation)* mediation [ˌmi:di'eɪʃn]
**sprechen (mit)** speak (to) [spi:k]
**Hier spricht Isabel.** *(am Telefon)* This is Isabel.
**springen** jump [dʒʌmp]
**spritzen** *(mit Wasser)* splash [splæʃ]
**Sprudel** sparkling water ['spɑ:klɪŋ]
**Spülbecken, Spüle** sink [sɪŋk]
**Staat** state [steɪt] • **die Vereinigten Staaten (von Amerika)** the United States (US) [juˌnaɪtɪd 'steɪts], [ˌju:‿'es]
**Staatsangehörige(r)** citizen ['sɪtɪzn]
**Staatsbürger/in** citizen ['sɪtɪzn]
**Stadion** stadium ['steɪdiəm]
**Stadt** *(Großstadt)* city ['sɪti]; *(Kleinstadt)* town [taʊn]
**Stadtbezirk** borough ['bʌrə, *AE:* 'bɜ:rəʊ]
► S.175 New York: the five boroughs
**Stadtplan** map [mæp]
**Stadtzentrum** city centre [ˌsɪti 'sentə] *(BE)*; downtown [ˌdaʊn'taʊn] *(AE)*
**der Bus in Richtung Stadtzentrum** the downtown bus *(AE)* • **im/in das Stadtzentrum** downtown *(AE)*
**Stahl** steel [sti:l]
**Stall** *(für Kaninchen)* hutch [hʌtʃ]
**Stammbaum** family tree ['fæməli tri:]
**Standort** location [ləʊ'keɪʃn]
**Star** *(Film-, Popstar)* star [stɑ:]
**stark** strong [strɒŋ]
**Start** start [stɑ:t]
**starten** start [stɑ:t]
**Statue** statue ['stætʃu:]
**Stau** traffic jam ['træfɪk dʒæm]
**Steak** steak [steɪk]
**Steckbrief** *(Beschreibung)* profile ['prəʊfaɪl]
**Stecker** plug [plʌg]
**Steeldrum** steel drum [ˌsti:l 'drʌm]
**stehen** stand [stænd] • **Hier steht: ...** *(im Text)* It says here: ... • **Wie steht es?** *(beim Sport)* What's the score?
**stehlen** steal [sti:l]
**steigen** *(aufsteigen)* rise [raɪz]
**Steigerung** comparison [kəm'pærɪsn]
**Stein** stone [stəʊn]
**stellen** *(hin-, abstellen)* put [pʊt]
**Fragen stellen** ask questions
**sich (hin)stellen** stand [stænd]
**etwas auf die Beine stellen** get sth. off the ground • **etwas leiser/lauter stellen** turn sth. down/up • **Stell dir vor! / Stellt euch vor!** Guess what! [ˌges 'wɒt]
**sterben (an)** die (of) [daɪ]
**Stereoanlage** stereo ['steriəʊ]
**Stern** star [stɑ:]
**Stichwort** *(Schlüsselwort)* key word ['ki: wɜ:d]
**Sticker** sticker ['stɪkə]
**Stiefel** boot [bu:t]
**still** quiet ['kwaɪət]
**Stille** silence ['saɪləns]
**Stimme** voice [vɔɪs]
**stimmen 1. Das stimmt.** That's right. [raɪt] • **..., stimmt's?** ..., right?
**2. für jn. stimmen** vote for sb. [vəʊt]
**Stock** *(Stockwerk)* floor [flɔ:] • **erster Stock** first floor *(BE)*; second floor *(AE)* • **im ersten Stock** on the first floor *(BE)*; on the second floor *(AE)*
► S.176 floor
**Stockwerk** floor [flɔ:]
► S.176 floor
**stolz (auf jn./etwas)** proud (of sb./sth.) [praʊd]
**stoßen** push [pʊʃ]
**Strand** beach [bi:tʃ] • **am Strand** on the beach
**Straße** road [rəʊd]; street [stri:t]
**Straßenbahn** tram [træm]
**Strecke** *(Route)* route [ru:t]
**Streich** trick [trɪk]
**Streik** strike [straɪk] • **in den Streik treten** go on strike • **sich im Streik befinden** be on strike
**streiken 1.** *(sich im Streik befinden)* be on strike [straɪk]
**2.** *(in den Streik treten)* go on strike
**Streit** argument ['ɑ:gjumənt]
**streiten; sich streiten** argue ['ɑ:gju:]
**streng** strict [strɪkt]
**Strom** electricity [ɪˌlek'trɪsəti]
**Stromschnellen** rapids *(pl)* ['ræpɪdz]
**strukturieren** structure ['strʌktʃə]
**Strumpf** sock [sɒk]
**Stück 1.** piece [pi:s] • **ein Stück Papier** a piece of paper
**2.** *(Titel auf einer CD)* track [træk]
**Student/in** student ['stju:dənt]
**studieren** study ['stʌdi]
**Studio** studio ['stju:diəʊ]
**Stuhl** chair [tʃeə]
**stumm: „stummer" Buchstabe** *(nicht gesprochener Buchstabe)* silent letter [ˌsaɪlənt 'letə]
**Stunde** hour ['aʊə]; *(Schulstunde)* lesson ['lesn]; period ['pɪəriəd] • **eine halbe Stunde** half an hour [ˌhɑ:f‿ən‿'aʊə] • **ein 14-Stunden-Flug** a 14-hour flight • **ein Supermarkt, der 24 Stunden geöffnet ist** a 24-hour supermarket
**Stundenplan** timetable ['taɪmteɪbl] *(BE)*; schedule [*AE:* 'skedʒu:l, *BE:* 'ʃedju:l] *(AE)*
**...stündig: ein 14-stündiger Flug** a 14-hour flight
**Sturm** storm [stɔ:m]
**stürmisch** stormy ['stɔ:mi]
**stürzen** *(hinfallen)* fall [fɔ:l]
**suchen: etwas suchen** look for sth. ['lʊk fɔ:]; search (for) sth. [sɜ:tʃ]
**Suchmaschine** *(im Internet)* search engine ['sɜ:tʃ‿endʒɪn]
**Süden** south [saʊθ] • **nach Süden** south • **Richtung Süden** *(Fahrtrichtung)* southbound ['saʊθbaʊnd]
**südlich** south [saʊθ]
**Südosten** south-east [ˌsaʊθ'i:st]
**nach Südosten** south-east
**südöstlich** south-east [ˌsaʊθ'i:st]
**Südwesten** south-west [ˌsaʊθ'west]
**nach Südwesten** south-west
**südwestlich** south-west [ˌsaʊθ'west]
**super** super ['su:pə]
**Supermarkt** supermarket ['su:pəmɑ:kɪt]
**Suppe** soup [su:p]
**Surfbrett** surfboard ['sɜ:fbɔ:d]
**surfen** surf [sɜ:f] • **im Internet surfen** surf the internet [sɜ:f]
**süß** sweet [swi:t]
**Süßigkeiten** sweets *(pl)* [swi:ts]
**Sweatshirt** sweatshirt ['swetʃɜ:t]
**sympathisch** likeable ['laɪkəbl]
**Synonym** synonym ['sɪnənɪm]
**System** system ['sɪstəm]
**Szene** scene [si:n]

# T

**Tabak** tobacco [tə'bækəʊ]
**Tafel** *(Wandtafel)* board [bɔ:d] • **an der/die Tafel** on the board
**Tag** day [deɪ] • **drei Tage (lang)** for three days • **eines Tages** one day **Guten Tag.** Hello.; *(nachmittags)* Good afternoon. [gʊd‿ɑ:ftə'nu:n]
**Tagebuch** diary ['daɪəri]
**Tagesausflug** a day out
**Tagesfahrkarte** all-day ticket; *(der Londoner Verkehrsbetriebe)* Travelcard ['trævlkɑ:d]
**täglich** daily ['deɪli]
**Tal** valley ['væli]
**Talent** talent ['tælənt]
**Tankstelle** petrol station *(BE)*; gas station *(AE)*
**Tante** aunt [ɑ:nt]; auntie ['ɑ:nti]
**Tanz** dance [dɑ:ns]
**Tanzfläche** dance floor ['dɑ:ns flɔ:]
**tanzen** dance [dɑ:ns]
**Tanzen** dancing ['dɑ:nsɪŋ]
**Tänzer/in** dancer ['dɑ:nsə]
**Tanzstunden, Tanzunterricht** dancing lessons ['dɑ:nsɪŋ ˌlesnz]
**Tasche** *(Tragetasche, Beutel)* bag [bæg]; *(Hosentasche, Jackentasche)* pocket ['pɒkɪt]
**Taschengeld** pocket money ['pɒkɪt mʌni]
**Tasse** cup [kʌp] • **eine Tasse Tee** a cup of tea
**tätig** *(aktiv)* active ['æktɪv]
**Tätigkeit** activity [æk'tɪvəti]
**Tatsache** fact [fækt]
**Tattoo** tattoo [tə'tu:]
**tauschen: etwas tauschen (für etwas/gegen etwas)** swap sth. (for sth.) [swɒp]
**tausend** thousand ['θaʊznd]
**Taxi** taxi ['tæksi] ; cab [kæb] • **ein Taxi nehmen** get a taxi/cab
**Team** team [ti:m]
**Teddy** teddy ['tedi]
**Tee** tea [ti:]
**Teelöffel** teaspoon ['ti:spu:n]
**Teenager** teenager ['ti:neɪdʒə]
**Teenager-** *(Jugend-)* teen [ti:n]
**Teil** part [pɑ:t]; *(Abschnitt)* section ['sekʃn]
**teilen: sich etwas teilen (mit jm.)** share sth. (with sb.) [ʃeə]
**teilnehmen (an)** take part (in) [teɪk 'pɑ:t]
**Telefon** (tele)phone ['telɪfəʊn] • **am Telefon** on the phone
**telefonieren** phone [fəʊn]
**Telefonnummer** (tele)phone number ['telɪfəʊn ˌnʌmbə]
**Teller** plate [pleɪt] • **ein Teller Pommes frites** a plate of chips
**Temperatur** temperature ['temprətʃə]
**Tempus** *(grammatische Zeit)* tense [tens]
**Tennis** tennis ['tenɪs]
**Termin** appointment [ə'pɔɪntmənt]
**Terminkalender** diary ['daɪəri]
**Terror-** terrorist ['terərɪst]
**Terrorist/in** terrorist ['terərɪst]
**terroristisch** terrorist ['terərɪst]
**Test** test [test]
**teuer** expensive [ɪk'spensɪv]
**Text** text [tekst]; *(Liedtext)* lyrics *(pl)* ['lɪrɪks]
**Textquelle** source [sɔ:s]
**Theater** theatre ['θɪətə]
**Theaterstück** play [pleɪ]
**Theke** counter ['kaʊntə]
**Thema, Themenbereich** topic ['tɒpɪk]
**Thermometer** thermometer [θə'mɒmɪtə]
**tief** deep [di:p]
**Tier** animal ['ænɪml]; *(Haustier)* pet [pet]
**Tierhandlung** pet shop ['pet ʃɒp]
**Tiger** tiger ['taɪgə]
**Timing: schlechtes Timing** bad timing ['taɪmɪŋ]
**Tipp** tip [tɪp]
**Tisch** table ['teɪbl]
**Tischtennis** table tennis ['teɪbl tenɪs]
**Tischtennisschläger** table tennis bat [bæt]
**Titel 1.** *(Überschrift)* heading ['hedɪŋ] **2.** title ['taɪtl]; *(Musikstück auf einer CD)* track [træk]
**Toast(brot)** toast [təʊst]
**Tochter** daughter ['dɔ:tə]
**Tod** death [deθ]
**Todestag: jemandes Todestag** anniversary of sb.'s death [ˌænɪ'vɜ:səri]
**Toilette** toilet ['tɔɪlət]
**toll** fantastic [fæn'tæstɪk]; great [greɪt]; brilliant ['brɪliənt]
**Tomate** tomato [tə'mɑ:təʊ], *pl* tomatoes
**Tondatei** sound file ['saʊnd faɪl]
**Top** *(Oberteil)* top [tɒp]
**Tor** gate [geɪt]; *(im Sport)* goal [gəʊl] **ein Tor schießen** score (a goal) [skɔ:]
**Torfrau, Torwart** goalkeeper ['gəʊlki:pə]
**Tornado** tornado [tɔ:'neɪdəʊ]
**Torte** cake [keɪk]
**tot** dead [ded]
**töten** kill [kɪl]
**Tour (durch das Haus)** tour (of the house) [tʊə]
**Tourist/in** tourist ['tʊərɪst]
**Track** *(auf einer CD)* track [træk]
**Tradition** tradition [trə'dɪʃn]
**traditionell** traditional [trə'dɪʃənl]
**tragen** *(Kleidung)* wear [weə]
**Trainer/in** coach [kəʊtʃ]
**trainieren** practise ['præktɪs]; train [treɪn]
**Training** *(körperliche Bewegung)* exercise *(no pl)*
**Trainingsstunde, -einheit** training session ['seʃn]
**Träne** tear [tɪə]
**Transport** *(Beförderung)* transport ['trænspɔ:t]
**Traum** dream [dri:m]
**träumen (von)** dream (of, about), [dri:m] • **Träum weiter!** Dream on!
**Traumhaus** dream house
**traurig** sad [sæd]
**Traurigkeit** sadness ['sædnəs]
**treffen; sich treffen** meet [mi:t] **ein Abkommen / eine Abmachung treffen** make a deal [di:l]
**Treffer: einen Treffer erzielen** score (a goal) [skɔ:], [gəʊl]
**trennen** *(nach Rasse, Religion, Geschlecht)* segregate ['segrɪgeɪt]
**Trennung** *(von Gruppen etc.)* segregation [ˌsegrɪ'geɪʃn]
**Treppe** stairs *(pl)* [steəz]
**Treppenstufe** step [step]
**treten** kick [kɪk]
**Trick** *(Zauberkunststück)* trick [trɪk]
**Trillerpfeife** whistle ['wɪsl]
**Trimester** term [tɜ:m]
**trinkbar** drinkable ['drɪŋkəbl]
**trinken** drink [drɪŋk] • **Milch zum Frühstück trinken** have milk for breakfast
**Trommel** drum [drʌm]
**Trompete** trumpet ['trʌmpɪt]
**trostlos** depressing [dɪ'presɪŋ]
**trotzdem** anyway ['eniweɪ]
**Truthahn** turkey ['tɜ:ki]
**Tschüs.** Bye. [baɪ]; See you. ['si: ju:]
**T-Shirt** T-shirt ['ti:ʃɜ:t]
**Tsunami** tsunami [tsu:'nɑ:mi]
**tüchtig** hard-working [ˌhɑ:d'wɜ:kɪŋ]
**tun** do [du:] • **Tue, was ich tue.** Do what I do. • **tun müssen** have to do • **tun wollen** want to do [wɒnt] **Tut mir leid.** I'm sorry. ['sɒri]
**Tunnel** tunnel ['tʌnl]
**Tür** door [dɔ:]
**Türklingel** doorbell ['dɔ:bel]
**Turm** tower ['taʊə]
**Turnen** *(Sportunterricht)* PE [ˌpi:‿'i:], Physical Education [ˌfɪzɪkəl‿edʒu'keɪʃn]
**Turnhalle** gym [dʒɪm]
**Turnschuhe** trainers *(pl)* ['treɪnəz]

**Tut mir leid.** I'm sorry. ['sɒri]
**Tüte** bag [bæg]
**Typ** type [taɪp] *(infml)*; *(Kerl)* guy [gaɪ] *(infml)*
**Tyrann** *(Schultyrann)* bully ['bʊli]
**tyrannisieren** bully ['bʊli]

# U

**U-Bahn: die U-Bahn** the underground ['ʌndəgraʊnd] *(BE)*; the subway ['sʌbweɪ] *(AE)*; *(in London)* the Tube *(no pl)* [tju:b]
**U-Bahnlinie** line [laɪn]
**üben** practise ['præktɪs]
**über 1.** about [ə'baʊt] • **über dich selbst** about yourself
**2.** *(räumlich)* over ['əʊvə]; *(quer über)* across [ə'krɒs]; *(oberhalb von)* above [ə'bʌv]
**überall** everywhere ['evriweə]
**überarbeiten** revise [rɪ'vaɪz]
**übereinstimmen: mit jm./etwas übereinstimmen** agree with sb./sth. [ə'gri:]
**überfliegen: einen Text überfliegen** *(um den Inhalt grob zu erfassen)* skim a text [skɪm]
**überfüllt** crowded ['kraʊdɪd]
**übergeben: sich übergeben** *(spucken)* throw up [ˌθrəʊ_'ʌp]
**überleben** survive [sə'vaɪv]
**übernachten** *(über Nacht bleiben)* stay [steɪ]
**übernehmen: etwas übernehmen** take sth. over [ˌteɪk_'əʊvə]
**überprüfen** check [tʃek]
**überqueren** cross [krɒs]
**überraschen: jn. überraschen** surprise sb. [sə'praɪz]
**überrascht (über etwas)** surprised (at sth.) [sə'praɪzd]
**Überraschung** surprise [sə'praɪz]
**Überschrift** title ['taɪtl]; heading ['hedɪŋ]
**übersetzen (aus ... ins)** translate (from ... into) [træns'leɪt]
**Übersetzung** translation [træns'leɪʃn]
**übrigens** *(nebenbei bemerkt)* by the way [ˌbaɪ ðə 'weɪ]; actually ['æktʃuəli]
**Übung** *(im Schulbuch)* exercise ['eksəsaɪz] • **eine Übung machen** do an exercise
**Übungsheft** exercise book ['eksəsaɪz bʊk]
**Uhr 1.** *(Armbanduhr)* watch [wɒtʃ]; *(Wand-, Stand-, Turmuhr)* clock [klɒk]
**2. elf Uhr** eleven o'clock • **7 Uhr morgens/vormittags** 7 am [ˌeɪ_'em]
**7 Uhr nachmittags/abends** 7 pm [ˌpi:_'em] • **um 8 Uhr 45** at 8.45
**Uhrzeit** time [taɪm]
**um 1.** *(örtlich)* **um ... (herum)** round [raʊnd]; around [ə'raʊnd] • **um den See (herum)** around the lake
**ganz um die Burg herum** all around the castle
**2.** *(zeitlich)* **um 8.45** at 8.45 • **um sechs herum** *(gegen sechs)* around six
**3. Es geht um Mr Green.** This is about Mr Green.
**4. um zu** to
**umdrehen: sich umdrehen** turn [tɜ:n]
**Umfrage (über)** survey (on) ['sɜ:veɪ]
**umher: in ... umher** round [raʊnd]; around [ə'raʊnd] • **in der Stadt umher** around the town
**umher-: umhergehen; umherspazieren** walk around • **umherrennen** run around • **umherspringen** jump around
**umschreiben** *(anders ausdrücken)* paraphrase ['pærəfreɪz]
**umsehen: sich umsehen** look round [ˌlʊk 'raʊnd]
**umsteigen** change [tʃeɪndʒ]
▶ S.186 (to) change – change
**umziehen 1. sich umziehen** change [tʃeɪndʒ]
**2. umziehen (nach, in)** *(die Wohnung wechseln)* move (to) [mu:v]
▶ S.186 (to) change – change
**unbehaglich** uncomfortable [ʌn'kʌmftəbl]
**unbequem** uncomfortable [ʌn'kʌmftəbl]
**uncool** uncool [ˌʌn'ku:l] *(infml)*
**und** and [ənd, ænd] • **Und? / Na und?** So? [səʊ] • **und so weiter (usw.)** and so on (etc. [et'setərə])
**unentschieden: 2:2 unentschieden** 2 all
**Unentschieden** draw [drɔ:]
**unfair** unfair [ˌʌn'feə]
**Unfall** accident ['æksɪdənt]
**unfreundlich** unfriendly [ʌn'frendli]
**ungefähr** about [ə'baʊt]
**Ungeheuer** monster ['mɒnstə]
**ungenügend** *(Schulnote)* failure ['feɪljə]
▶ S.185 US school grades
**ungerecht** unfair [ˌʌn'feə]
**ungesetzlich** illegal [ɪ'li:gl]
**ungesund** unhealthy [ʌn'helθi]
**unglaublich** unbelievable [ˌʌnbɪ'li:vəbl]; *(sehr erstaunlich)* amazing [ə'meɪzɪŋ]
**unglücklich** unhappy [ʌn'hæpi]
**unheimlich** scary ['skeəri]
**unhöflich** rude [ru:d]
**Uniform** uniform ['ju:nɪfɔ:m]
**Universität** university [ˌju:nɪ'vɜ:səti]
**unklar** unclear [ˌʌn'klɪə]
**unleserlich** unreadable [ʌn'ri:dəbl]
**unmöglich** impossible [ɪm'pɒsəbl]
**unordentlich** untidy [ʌn'taɪdi] • **sehr unordentlich sein** *(Zimmer)* be a mess [mes]
**Unordnung: alles in Unordnung bringen** make a mess [ˌmeɪk_ə 'mes]
**Unrecht haben** be wrong [rɒŋ]
**uns** us [əs, ʌs] • **uns (selbst)** ourselves [aʊə'selvz]
**unser(e) ...** our ... ['aʊə] • **unser eigenes Schwimmbad** our own pool [əʊn]
**unserer, unsere, unseres** ours ['aʊəz]
**unten** below [bɪ'ləʊ]; *(im Haus)* downstairs [ˌdaʊn'steəz] • **am unteren Ende (von)** at the bottom (of) ['bɒtəm] • **dort unten** down there • **nach unten** down; *(im Haus)* downstairs
**unter** under ['ʌndə]; *(unterhalb von)* below [bɪ'ləʊ]
**unterbrechen: eine Reise unterbrechen** break a journey [ˌbreɪk_ə 'dʒɜ:ni]
**unterhalb (von)** below [bɪ'ləʊ]
**unterhalten: sich unterhalten (mit, über)** talk (to, about) [tɔ:k]
**Unterhaltung** *(Gespräch)* conversation [ˌkɒnvə'seɪʃn]
**Unterricht** lessons *(pl)* ['lesnz] • **im Unterricht** in class [klɑ:s]
**unterrichten** teach [ti:tʃ]
**Unterrichtsstunde** lesson ['lesn] *(BE)*; period ['pɪəriəd] *(AE)*
**unterschiedlich** different ['dɪfrənt]
**unterstützen** support [sə'pɔ:t]
**Untersuchung (über)** *(Umfrage)* survey (on) ['sɜ:veɪ]
**unverschämt** rude [ru:d]
**unzählbar** uncountable [ʌn'kaʊntəbl]
**Ureinwohner(in): Amerikanische(r) Ureinwohner/in** Native American [ˌneɪtɪv_ə'merɪkən]
**Urgroßmutter** great-grandmother [ˌgreɪt'grænmʌðə]
**Urgroßvater** great-grandfather [ˌgreɪt'grænfɑ:ðə]
**Urlaub** holiday ['hɒlədeɪ] *(BE)*; vacation [və'keɪʃn, *AE:* veɪ'keɪʃn] *(AE)* • **in Urlaub fahren** go on holiday • **in Urlaub sein** be on holiday • **ein zweiwöchiger Urlaub** a two-week holiday
**Ursache** cause [kɔ:z]
**usw.** *(und so weiter)* etc. [et'setərə]

# V

**Vater** father ['fɑ:ðə]
**Vati** dad [dæd]
**Vegetarier/in** vegetarian [ˌvedʒə'teəriən]
**vegetarisch** vegetarian [ˌvedʒə'teəriən]
**Verabredung** appointment [ə'pɔɪntmənt]
**verabschieden: sich verabschieden** say goodbye [ˌseɪ gʊd'baɪ]
**verändern; sich verändern** change [tʃeɪndʒ]
▶ S.186 (to) change – change
**Veränderung** change [tʃeɪndʒ]
▶ S.186 (to) change – change
**Veranstaltung** event [ɪ'vent]
**verängstigt** scared [skeəd]
**Veranstaltungsort** location [ləʊ'keɪʃn]
**verbessern** *(besser machen)* improve [ɪm'pru:v]; *(korrigieren)* correct [kə'rekt]
**verbinden** *(einander zuordnen)* link [lɪŋk]
**Verbindung** *(Verknüfung)* link [lɪnk] • **in Verbindung bleiben** keep in touch [ˌki:p‿ɪn 'tʌtʃ]
**verboten: Rauchen verboten.** No smoking.
**Verbrechen** crime [kraɪm]
**verbrennen** burn [bɜ:n]
**verbringen: Zeit verbringen (mit)** spend time (on) [spend]
**verdienen** earn [ɜ:n]
**Verein** club [klʌb]
**vereinigt: das Vereinigte Königreich** *(Großbritannien und Nordirland)* the United Kingdom (UK) [juˌnaɪtɪd 'kɪŋdəm], [ˌju:'keɪ] • **die Vereinigten Staaten (von Amerika)** the United States (US) [juˌnaɪtɪd 'steɪts], [ju:‿'es]
**verfolgen** follow ['fɒləʊ]
**vergeben** forgive [fə'gɪv]
**vergessen** forget [fə'get]
**vergewissern: sich vergewissern, dass ...** make sure that ...
**Vergleich** comparison [kəm'pærɪsn]
**vergleichen** compare [kəm'peə]
**vergriffen sein** *(ausverkauft sein)* be sold out [ˌsəʊld‿'aʊt]
**verhalten: sich verhalten** act [ækt]
**Verhalten im Brandfall** fire safety ['faiə seɪfti]
**verheiratet (mit)** married (to) ['mærɪd]
**Verkauf** sale [seɪl] • **zum Verkauf** for sale [seɪl]
**verkaufen** sell [sel] • **zu verkaufen** for sale [seɪl]
**Verkäufer/in** *(im Geschäft)* shop assistant ['ʃɒp‿əˌsɪstənt]
**Verkehr** traffic ['træfɪk]
**Verkehrsampel** traffic light ['træfɪk laɪt]
**Verkehrsmittel** transport *(no pl)* ['trænspɔ:t]
**verkehrsreich** *(Straße)* busy ['bɪzi]
**Verkehrsstau** traffic jam ['træfɪk dʒæm]
**verkehrt** *(falsch)* wrong [rɒŋ]
**verknallt: in jn. verknallt sein** have a crush on sb. [krʌʃ]
**verknüpfen** *(einander zuordnen)* link [lɪŋk]
**Verknüpfung** link [lɪŋk]
**verlassen** leave [li:v]
**verletzen** hurt [hɜ:t]
**verletzt** hurt [hɜ:t]
**verlieben: sich verlieben (in jn.)** fall in love (with sb.)
**verlieren** lose [lu:z]
**vermissen** miss [mɪs]
**Vermittlung** *(Sprachmittlung, Mediation)* mediation [ˌmi:di'eɪʃn]
**veröffentlichen** publish ['pʌblɪʃ]
**verrückt** mad [mæd]; crazy ['kreɪzi]
**verrückt nach/auf etwas sein** be mad about sth.
**Versammlung** meeting ['mi:tɪŋ]; *(morgendliche Schulversammlung, oft mit Andacht)* Assembly [ə'sembli]
**verschieden** *(anders)* different ['dɪfrənt]
**verschwinden** disappear [ˌdɪsə'pɪə]
**Version** version ['vɜ:ʃn]
**versprechen** promise ['prɒmɪs]
**verständlich** understandable [ˌʌndə'stændəbl]
**verstecken; sich verstecken** hide [haɪd]
**verstehen 1.** understand [ˌʌndə'stænd] **2. sich gut/schlecht mit jm. verstehen** get on well/badly with sb.
**versuchen** try [traɪ] • **versuchen zu tun** try and do / try to do
**vertreten** *(repräsentieren)* represent [ˌreprɪ'zent]
**verursachen** cause [kɔ:z]
**verwenden** use [ju:z]
**verwirrt** puzzled ['pʌzld]
**verzeihen** forgive [fə'gɪv]
**Video** video ['vɪdiəʊ]
**viel** a lot (of) [lɒt]; lots (of) [lɒts]; much [mʌtʃ] • **viele** a lot (of) [lɒt]; lots (of) [lɒts]; many ['meni] • **Viel Glück (bei/mit ...)!** Good luck (with ...)! • **viel mehr** lots more **Viel Spaß!** Have fun! / Enjoy yourself. • **wie viel?** how much? • **wie viele?** how many? • **Vielen Dank!** Thanks a lot!
**vielfarbig** multi-coloured ['mʌltiˌkʌləd]
**vielleicht** maybe ['meɪbi] • **du könntest vielleicht Hilfe brauchen** you might need help [maɪt]
**Viertel: Viertel nach 11** quarter past 11 ['kwɔ:tə] • **Viertel vor 12** quarter to 12
**violett** purple ['pɜ:pl]
**Violine** violin [ˌvaɪə'lɪn]
**Vogel** bird [bɜ:d]
**Vokabelverzeichnis** vocabulary [və'kæbjələri]
**Volks-** ethnic ['eθnɪk]
**voll** full [fʊl]; *(überfüllt)* crowded ['kraʊdɪd] • **die Nase voll haben (von etwas)** be fed up (with sth.) [ˌfed‿'ʌp]
**Volleyball** volleyball ['vɒlibɔ:l]
**vollkommen** perfect ['pɜ:fɪkt]
**Vollkorn-** whole-grain ['həʊlgreɪn]
**von** of [əv, ɒv]; from [frəm, frɒm] **ein Aufsatz von ...** an essay by ... [baɪ] • **von Montag bis Freitag** from Mondays to Fridays
**vor 1.** *(räumlich)* in front of [ɪn 'frʌnt‿əv] **2.** *(zeitlich)* **vor dem Abendessen** before dinner [bɪ'fɔ:] • **vor einer Minute** a minute ago [ə'gəʊ] **Viertel vor 12** quarter to 12
**vorankommen: Wie komme ich voran?** *(Wie sind meine Fortschritte?)* How am I doing?
**vorbei (an)** *(vorüber)* past [pɑ:st]
**vorbei sein** be over ['əʊvə]
**vorbereiten** prepare [prɪ'peə] • **sich vorbereiten (auf)** prepare (for); get ready (for) ['redi] • **Dinge vorbereiten** get things ready
**vorbringen: ein Argument vorbringen** make a point [pɔɪnt]
**Vordergrund** foreground ['fɔ:graʊnd]
**voreingenommen sein (gegen),** be prejudiced (against ) ['predʒədɪst]
**Vorhang** curtain ['kɜ:tn]
**Vormittag** morning ['mɔ:nɪŋ]
**Vorschlag** suggestion [sə'dʒestʃən]
**Vorschrift** rule [ru:l]
**Vorschule** *(in den USA für 5- bis 6-Jährige)* kindergarten ['kɪndəgɑ:tn]
**vorsichtig** careful ['keəfl]
**vorspielen** *(pantomimisch darstellen)* mime [maɪm]
**vorstellen: sich etwas vorstellen** imagine sth. [ɪ'mædʒɪn] • **Stell dir vor! / Stellt euch vor!** Guess what! [ˌges 'wɒt]
**Vorstellung 1.** *(Präsentation)* presentation [ˌprezn'teɪʃn]; *(Show)* show [ʃəʊ] **2.** *(Fantasie)* imagination [ɪˌmædʒɪ'neɪʃn]

**Vorteil (gegenüber jm./etwas)** advantage (over sb./sth.) [əd'vɑ:ntɪdʒ]
**vorüber (an)** *(vorbei)* past [pɑ:st]
**Vorurteil** prejudice ['predʒudɪs]
**Vorurteile haben (gegenüber)** be prejudiced (against) ['predʒədɪst]
**Vorwürfe: jm. Vorwürfe machen (wegen)** blame sb. (for) [bleɪm]

## W

**Wahl** *(von Kandidaten bei einer Abstimmung)* election [ɪ'lekʃn]
**wählen 1.** *(auswählen)* choose [tʃu:z] **2. jn. zu etwas wählen** elect sb. sth. [ɪ'lekt]
**wahr** true [tru:]
**während 1.** *(vor Nomen)* during ['djʊərɪŋ] • **während des Spiels** during the match **2.** *(vor Nebensatz)* as [əz, æz]; while [waɪl] • **während wir zuschauten** as/while we were watching
► S.189 German 'während'
**wahrscheinlich** probably ['prɒbəbli]
**Wald** forest ['fɒrɪst]; woods *(pl)* [wʊdz]
**walisisch; Walisisch** Welsh [welʃ]
**Wand** wall [wɔ:l]
**wandern** hike [haɪk] • **wandern gehen** go on a hike
**Wanderung** hike [haɪk]
**Wange** cheek [tʃi:k]
**wann** when [wen] • **wann immer** whenever [wen'evə] • **Seit wann?** how long?
► S.183 whoever, whatever, whenever, wherever
► S.191 German 'seit'
**warm** warm [wɔ:m]
**warnen: jn. (vor etwas) warnen** warn sb. (about sth.) [wɔ:n]
**warten (auf)** wait (for) [weɪt]
**Warte mal!** Wait a minute. ['mɪnɪt]
**Wart's ab!** Wait and see!
**Warteschlange** queue [kju:] *(BE)*; line [laɪn] *(AE)*
**Wartezimmer** waiting room
**warum** why [waɪ] • **Warum ich?** Why me?
**was** what [wɒt] • **was auch immer** whatever [wɒt'evə] • **Was für ein Auto ...?** What kind of car ...?
**Was haben wir als Hausaufgabe auf?** What's for homework?
**Was haben wir als Nächstes?** What have we got next? • **Was ist los? / Was ist denn?** What's the matter? ['mætə] • **Was ist mit ...?** What about ...? • **Was kostet/kosten ...?** How much is/are ...?
**was ... (sonst) noch?** what else?
**Was war das Beste an ...?** What was the best thing about ...?
**Ich weiß nicht, was ich machen soll.** I don't know what to do.
► S.173 Question words + to-infinitive: how to ... / what to ... / ...
► S.176 ... else
► S.183 whoever, whatever, whenever, wherever
**waschen** wash [wɒʃ] • **Ich wasche mir das Gesicht.** I wash my face.
**Waschmaschine** washing machine ['wɒʃɪŋ mə,ʃi:n]
**Wasser** water ['wɔ:tə]
**Webcam** webcam ['webkæm]
**Website** website ['websaɪt]
**Wechsel** *(Veränderung)* change [tʃeɪndʒ]
► S.186 (to) change – change
**wechseln** change [tʃeɪndʒ]
► S.186 (to) change – change
**Wechselgeld** change [tʃeɪndʒ]
► S.186 (to) change – change
**weg** away [ə'weɪ]
**Weg** way [weɪ]; *(Pfad)* path [pɑ:θ]; *(Gasse)* lane [leɪn] • **auf dem Weg (zu/nach)** on the way (to)
**den ganzen Weg** all the way
**jm. den Weg beschreiben** tell sb. the way • **jn. nach dem Weg fragen** ask sb. the way / ask sb. for directions [də'rekʃnz] • **etwas auf den Weg bringen** get sth. off the ground
**Wegbeschreibung** directions *(pl)* [də'rekʃnz] • **jn. um eine Wegbeschreibung bitten** ask sb. for directions
**wegbleiben** *(draußen bleiben)* stay out [,steɪ_'aʊt]
**wegen** because of [bɪ'kɒz_əv]
**weggehen** leave [li:v]
**weglassen: etwas weglassen** *(auslassen)* leave sth. out [,li:v_'aʊt]
**wehen** blow [bləʊ]
**wehtun** hurt [hɜ:t]; ache [eɪk] • **jm. wehtun** hurt sb.
**weiblich** female ['fi:meɪl]
**weich** soft [sɒft]
**Weide** field [fi:ld]
**Weihnachten** Christmas ['krɪsməs]
**weil** because [bɪ'kɒz]; since [sɪns]
**Wein** wine [waɪn]
**weinen** cry [kraɪ]
**Weintraube** grape [greɪp]
**Weise** *(Art und Weise)* way [weɪ]
**weiß** white [waɪt]
**weit 1. weit (entfernt)** far [fɑ:] **2.** *(breit)* wide [waɪd]
**weiter: geradeaus weiter** straight on [streɪt_'ɒn] • **und so weiter (usw.)** and so on (etc. [et'setərə])
**weitere(r, s): weitere 45 Pence** another 45 p [ə'nʌðə]
**weiter-: weitergeben** pass [pɑ:s]
**weitergehen** walk on • **weiterlesen** read on • **weitermachen** go on • **weiterreden** go on
**weiterträumen** dream on
**welche(r, s)** which [wɪtʃ] • **Auf welcher Seite sind wir?** What page are we on? [wɒt] • **Welche Farbe hat ...?** What colour is ...?
**wellenreiten gehen** go surfing ['sɜ:fɪŋ]
**Wellensittich** budgie ['bʌdʒi]
**Welt** world [wɜ:ld] • **(auf) der Welt** in the world • **auf der ganzen Welt** all over the world • **aus der ganzen Welt** from all over the world
**wem?** who? [hu:] • **Wem gehören diese?** Whose are these? [hu:z]
**wen?** who? [hu:] • **wen (sonst) noch?** who else?
► S.176 ... else
**wenden: sich an jn. wenden** turn to sb. [tɜ:n]
**wenig 1.** *(mit nicht zählbaren Nomen)* **wenig Zeit/Wasser** little time/water ['lɪtl] • **ein wenig** *(ein bisschen)* a little • **weniger** less [les] • **am wenigsten** least [li:st]
**2.** *(mit zählbaren Nomen im Plural)* **wenige Stunden/Flaschen** few hours/bottles [fju:]; *(ein paar)* a few hours/bottles • **weniger** fewer ['fju:ə] • **am wenigsten** fewest ['fju:ɪst]
► S.182 little („wenig") – few („wenige")
**wenigstens** at least [ət 'li:st]
**wenn 1.** *(zeitlich)* when [wen] **2.** *(falls)* if [ɪf]
**wer?** who? [hu:] • **wer auch immer** whoever [hu:'evə] • **Wer ist dran / an der Reihe?** Whose turn is it? [hu:z]
► S.183 whoever, whatever, whenever, wherever
**werden** become [bɪ'kʌm] • **wütend/heiß/... werden** get angry/hot/...
**du wirst frieren; ihr werdet frieren** you'll be cold (= you will be cold) [wɪl] • **du wirst nicht frieren; ihr werdet nicht frieren** you won't be cold (= you will not be cold) [wəʊnt]
**werfen** throw [θrəʊ] • **einen Blick werfen auf etwas** have a look at sth. [lʊk]
**Werkzeug** tool [tu:l]
**wertvoll** valuable ['væljuəbl]

**Wesen** *(Charakter)* character ['kærəktə]
**wessen?** whose? [hu:z]
**West-** western ['westən]
**Westen** west [west] • **nach Westen** west • **Richtung Westen** *(Fahrtrichtung)* westbound ['westbaʊnd]
**westlich** *(westlich von)* west [west]; *(Gebiet)* western ['westən]
**Wettbewerb** competition [ˌkɒmpə'tɪʃn]
**Wetter** weather ['weðə]
**Wettkampf** competition [ˌkɒmpə'tɪʃn]; match [mætʃ]
**Whisky** whisky ['wɪski]
**wichtig** important [ɪm'pɔ:tnt] • **Nicht so wichtig.** Never mind. [ˌnevə 'maɪnd]
**wie 1.** *(Fragewort)* how [haʊ] • **Wie bitte?** Sorry? ['sɒri] • **Wie geht es dir/Ihnen/euch?** How are you? [ˌhaʊ_'ɑ: jʊ] • **Wie heißt du?** What's your name? • **Wie komme ich voran?** *(Wie sind meine Fortschritte?)* How am I doing? • **Wie lange?** how long? • **wie man etwas tut/ tun kann/ tun soll** how to do sth. • **Wie spät ist es?** What's the time? • **Wie steht es jetzt?** *(beim Sport)* What's the score? • **wie viel?** how much? **wie viele?** how many? • **Wie war ...?** How was ...? • **Wie war das Wetter?** What was the weather like? • **Wie wär's mit ...?** What about ...?
**2. so alt/groß wie** as old/big as [əz, æz]
**3. wie ein Filmstar** like a film star [laɪk]
**4. wie auch immer, ... / wie dem auch sei, ...** anyway, ... ['eniweɪ]
► S.173 Question words + to-infinitive: how to ... / what to ... / ...
**wieder** again [ə'gen]
**wiederholen** *(Lernstoff)* revise [rɪ'vaɪz]
**Wiederholung** *(des Lernstoffs)* revision [rɪ'vɪʒn]; *(einer Fernsehsendung)* repeat [rɪ'pi:t] *(BE)*; rerun ['ri:rʌn] *(AE)*
**Wiedersehen: Auf Wiedersehen.** Goodbye. [ˌgʊd'baɪ]
**wiederverwendet/-verwertet** recycled [ˌri:'saɪkld]
**Wiederverwertung** recycling [ˌri:'saɪklɪŋ]
**wild** wild [waɪld]
**willkommen: Willkommen (in Bristol).** Welcome (to Bristol). ['welkəm] • **Sie heißen dich in ... willkommen** They welcome you to ...
**Wind** wind [wɪnd]
**windig** windy ['wɪndi]
**Windjacke** anorak ['ænəræk]
**winken** wave [weɪv]
**Winter** winter ['wɪntə]
**wir** we [wi:]
**Wirbelsturm** tornado [tɔ:'neɪdəʊ]
**wirklich 1.** *(tatsächlich)* really ['rɪəli] **Meinst du wirklich? / Glaubst du das wirklich?** Do you really think so?
**2.** *(echt)* real [rɪəl]
**Wirklichkeit** reality • **in Wirklichkeit** *(eigentlich)* actually ['æktʃuəli]
**wirklichkeitsnah** realistic [ˌri:ə'lɪstɪk]
**wissen** know [nəʊ] • **wissen wollen** wonder ['wʌndə] • **Das willst du gar nicht wissen.** Never mind. [ˌnevə 'maɪnd] • **Ich weiß es nicht.** I don't know. • **von etwas wissen; über etwas Bescheid wissen** know about sth. • **..., wissen Sie. / ..., weißt du.** ..., you know. • **Weißt du was, Sophie?** You know what, Sophie? • **Woher weißt du ...?** How do you know ...?
**Witz** joke [dʒəʊk] • **Witze machen** joke
**witzig** funny ['fʌni]
**wo** where [weə] • **Wo kommst du her?** Where are you from? • **wo auch immer** wherever [weər'evə]
► S.183 whoever, whatever, whenever, wherever
**woanders** somewhere else
► S.176 ... else
**Woche** week [wi:k]
**Wochenende** weekend [ˌwi:k'end] **am Wochenende** at the weekend
**Wochentage** days of the week
**...wöchig: ein zweiwöchiger Urlaub** a two-week holiday
**Wofür?** What for? [ˌwɒt 'fɔ:]
**Woher weißt du ...?** How do you know ...? [nəʊ]
**wohin** where [weə]; *(in welche Richtung)* which way
**wohlauf** *(gesund)* well [wel]
**Wohltätigkeitsbasar** jumble sale ['dʒʌmbl seɪl]
**Wohnblock** block [blɒk]
**wohnen** live [lɪv] • **bei jm. wohnen** stay with sb. [steɪ]
**Wohnheim** hostel ['hɒstl]
**Wohnort** location [ləʊ'keɪʃn]
**Wohnung** flat [flæt] *(BE)*; apartment [ə'pɑ:tmənt] *(AE)*
**Wohnungstür** front door [ˌfrʌnt 'dɔ:]
**Wohnwagen** caravan ['kærəvæn]
**Wohnzimmer** living room ['lɪvɪŋ ru:m]
**Wolf** wolf, *pl* wolves [wʊlf, wʊlvz]
**Wolke** cloud [klaʊd]
**Wolkenkratzer** skyscraper ['skaɪskreɪpə]
**wolkenlos** cloudless ['klaʊdləs]
**wollen** *(haben wollen)* want [wɒnt] **tun wollen** want to do • **wollen, dass jm. etwas tut** want sb. to do sth.
**Workshop** workshop ['wɜ:kʃɒp]
**Wort** word [wɜ:d]
**Wortbildung** word building ['wɜ:d ˌbɪldɪŋ]
**Wörterbuch** dictionary ['dɪkʃənri]
**Wörterverzeichnis** vocabulary [və'kæbjələri]; *(alphabetisches)* dictionary ['dɪkʃənri]
**Wovon redest du?** What are you talking about?
**würden: ich würde ... / du würdest ...** I would ... / you would ... [wəd, wʊd]
**Würfel** dice, *pl* dice [daɪs]
**Wurst, Würstchen** sausage ['sɒsɪdʒ]
**würzig** *(scharf gewürzt)* spicy ['spaɪsi]
**wütend (über etwas/auf jn.)** angry (about sth./with sb.) ['æŋgri]

## Y

**Yoga** yoga ['jəʊgə]

## Z

**Zahl** number ['nʌmbə]
**zählbar** countable ['kaʊntəbl]
**zählen** count [kaʊnt]
**Zahn** tooth [tu:θ], *pl* teeth [ti:θ] • **Ich putze mir die Zähne.** I clean my teeth.
**Zahnarzt, -ärztin** dentist ['dentɪst]
**zahnlos** toothless ['tu:θləs]
**Zahnschmerzen** toothache ['tu:θeɪk]
**zanken; sich zanken** argue ['ɑ:gju:]
**zappen** hop channels [ˌhɒp 'tʃænəlz]
**Zauberkunststück** trick [trɪk] **Zauberkunststücke machen** do tricks
**Zaun** fence [fens]
**Zebra** zebra ['zebrə]
**Zeh** toe [təʊ]
**Zeichen** *(Schild)* sign [saɪn]
**zeichnen** draw [drɔ:]
**Zeichnung** drawing ['drɔ:ɪŋ]
**zeigen** show [ʃəʊ] • **auf etwas zeigen** point at/to sth. [pɔɪnt] **gezeigt werden** *(im Fernsehen/Kino)* to be on
**Zeile** line [laɪn]

**Zeit** time [taɪm]; *(grammatische Zeit, Tempus)* tense [tens] • **Zeit verbringen (mit)** spend time (on) [spend]
**Zeitschrift** magazine [ˌmægəˈziːn]
**Zeitung** newspaper [ˈnjuːspeɪpə]; paper [ˈpeɪpə]
**Zeitungsartikel** article [ˈɑːtɪkl]
**Zeitzone** time zone [zəʊn] • **eine Zeitzone passieren** cross a time zone
**Zelt** tent [tent]
**zelten** camp [kæmp]
**Zensur** *(Schulnote)* grade [greɪd] (*BE auch:* mark [mɑːk])
**Zentimeter** centimetre (cm) [ˈsentɪmiːtə]
**Zentral-** *(Mittel-)* central [ˈsentrəl]
**Zentrum** centre [ˈsentə]
**zerbrechen** break [breɪk]
**zerbrechlich** breakable [ˈbreɪkəbl]
**zerbrochen** broken [ˈbrəʊkən]
**zerstören** destroy [dɪˈstrɔɪ]
**Zeug** *(Kram)* stuff [stʌf]
**ziehen** pull [pʊl] • **Schlüsse ziehen** draw conclusions [ˌdrɔː kənˈkluːʒnz]
**ziemlich gut** pretty good [ˈprɪti]; quite good [kwaɪt]
**Ziffer** number [ˈnʌmbə]
**Zimmer** room [ruːm, rʊm]
**Zitrone** lemon [ˈlemən]
**Zoo** zoo [zuː]
**zu 1.** *(örtlich)* to [tə, tu] • **zu Jenny** to Jenny's • **zu Hause** at home **zum Arzt** to the doctor's • **Setz dich zu mir.** Sit with me. • **auf jn./etwas zu** towards sb./sth. [təˈwɔːdz]
**2. zum Beispiel** for example [ˌfər‿ɪgˈzɑːmpl] • **zum Frühstück/ Mittagessen/Abendbrot** for breakfast/lunch/dinner [fə, fɔː]
**zum Schluss** in the end
**3. zu viel** too much [tuː] • **zu spät sein/kommen** be late
**4. versuchen zu tun** try and do / try to do
**5.** *(geschlossen)* closed [kləʊzd]
**zubereiten** *(kochen)* cook [kʊk]
**Zucker** sugar [ˈʃʊgə]
**zuerst** *(als Erstes)* first [fɜːst]; *(zu Beginn)* at first
**Zug** train [treɪn] • **im Zug** on the train
**Zuhause** home [həʊm]
**zuhören** listen (to) [ˈlɪsn]
**Zuhörer/in** listener [ˈlɪsənə]
**Zuhörer/innen** *(Publikum)* audience [ˈɔːdɪəns]
**zulassen, dass jd. etwas tut** *(erlauben)* let sb. do sth. [let]
**zum** *siehe „zu"*
**zumachen** close [kləʊz]
**zumindest** at least [ət ˈliːst]
**zurück (nach)** back (to) [bæk]
**zurücklassen** leave [liːv]
**zusammen** together [təˈgeðə] • **mit jm. zusammen sein** to be with sb.
**zusammenfassen: etwas zusammenfassen** summarize sth. [ˈsʌməraɪz]
**Zusammenfassung** summary [ˈsʌməri]
**Zusammenhang** context [ˈkɒntekst]
**zusammenpassen, -gehören** go together
**zusammenstoßen (mit)** crash (into) [kræʃ]
**zusätzlich** extra [ˈekstrə]
**Zuschauer/in** viewer [ˈvjuːə]
**Zuschauer/innen** *(Publikum)* audience [ˈɔːdɪəns]
**zusehen** watch [wɒtʃ]
**zustimmen: jm./etwas zustimmen** agree with sb./sth. [əˈgriː] • **nicht zustimmen** disagree [ˌdɪsəˈgriː]
**zuwenden: sich jm. zuwenden** turn to sb. [tɜːn]
**zwanglos** *(entspannt)* relaxed [rɪˈlækst]
**zweimal** twice [twaɪs]
**zweite(r, s)** second [ˈsekənd]
**Zwiebel** onion [ˈʌnjən]
**Zwillinge** twins *(pl)* [twɪnz]
**Zwillingsbruder** twin brother [ˈtwɪn ˌbrʌðə]
**zwischen** between [bɪˈtwiːn]

## First names (Vornamen)

**Abraham** ['eɪbrəhæm]
**Adriana** [ˌeɪdri'ɑ:nə]
**Alicia** [ə'lɪʃə, ə'lɪʃiə]
**Angus** ['æŋgəs]
**Anthony** ['æntəni, 'ænθəni]
**Aretha** [ə'ri:θə]
**Ashley** ['æʃli]
**Barack** [bə'rɑ:k]
**Bart** [bɑ:t]
**Bert** [bɜ:t]
**Bertha** ['bɜ:θə]
**Beyoncé** [bi'jɒnseɪ]
**Brad** [bræd]
**Bruce** [bru:s]
**Buddy** ['bʌdi]
**Caitlin** ['keɪtlɪn, 'kætlɪn]
**Carrie** ['keri, 'kæri]
**Chris** [krɪs]
**Chuck** [tʃʌk]
**Cindy** ['sɪndi]
**Coretta** [kə'retə]
**Cruz** [kru:z]
**Dan** [dæn]
**David** ['deɪvɪd]
**Diego** [di'eɪgəʊ]
**Domino** ['dɒmɪnəʊ]
**Donna** ['dɒnə]
**Earl** [ɜ:l]
**Eileen** ['aɪli:n]
**Ellis** ['elɪs]
**Ernie** ['ɜ:ni]
**Errol** ['erəl]
**Erykah** ['erɪkə]
**George** [dʒɔ:dʒ]
**Jake** [dʒeɪk]
**James** [dʒeɪmz]
**Jane** [dʒeɪn]
**Jelly** ['dʒeli]
**Johnny** ['dʒɒni]
**Joseph** ['dʒəʊzɪf, 'dʒəʊsəf]
**Josephine** ['dʒəʊzəfi:n, 'dʒəʊsəfi:n]
**Josh** [dʒɒʃ]
**Kelly** ['keli]
**Langston** ['læŋstən]
**Lara** ['lɑ:rə]
**Larry** ['læri, 'leri]
**Lauryn** ['lɒrən]
**LeBron** [lə'brɒn]
**Louie** ['lu:i]
**Louis** ['lu:ɪs, 'lu:i]
**Luis** [lu:'i:s, 'lu:ɪs]
**Luke** [lu:k]
**Madison** ['mædɪsn]
**Marco** ['mɑ:kəʊ]
**Margaret** ['mɑ:grət]
**Marge** [mɑ:dʒ]
**Maria** [mə'ri:ə]
**Martin** ['mɑ:tɪn]
**Marvin** ['mɑ:vɪn]
**Melba** ['melbə]
**Melissa** [mə'lɪsə]
**Morton** ['mɔ:tən]
**Myron** ['maɪrən]
**Nate** [neɪt]
**Ray** [reɪ]
**Ricardo** [rɪ'kɑ:dəʊ]
**Richard** ['rɪtʃəd]
**Rick** [rɪk]
**Robert** ['rɒbət]
**Rodney** ['rɒdni]
**Ruth** [ru:θ]
**Ryan** ['raɪən]
**Shirley** ['ʃɜ:li]
**Stephon** ['sti:vn]
**Sullivan** ['sʌlɪvən]
**Theodore** ['θi:ədɔ:]
**Thomas** ['tɒməs]
**Todd** [tɒd, tɑ:d]
**Wayne** [weɪn]

## Family names (Familiennamen)

**Alvarez** ['ælvərez]
**Armstrong** ['ɑ:mstrɒŋ]
**Badu** [bə'du:]
**Ballou** [bə'lu:]
**Bertanelli** [ˌbɜ:tə'neli]
**Bethune** [be'θu:n]
**Berry** ['beri]
**Bolden** ['bəʊldən]
**Callahan** ['kæləhən]
**Campbell** ['kæmbəl]
**Carter** ['kɑ:tə]
**Charles** [tʃɑ:lz]
**Clinton** ['klɪntən]
**Columbus** [kə'lʌmbəs]
**Cooke** [kʊk]
**Crutcher** ['krʌtʃə]
**D'Agostino** [ˌdægə'sti:nəʊ]
**Devlin** ['devlɪn]
**Diddley** ['dɪdli]
**Ebb** [eb]
**Flynn** [flɪn]
**Franklin** ['fræŋklɪn]
**Fuentes** [fu'entez, 'fwentes]
**Goode** [gʊd]
**Hawley** ['hɔ:li]
**Hughes** [hju:z]
**Ignatow** [ɪg'nɑ:təʊ]
**Jefferson** ['dʒefəsn]
**Johnson** ['dʒɒnsn]
**Kennedy** ['kenədi]
**Kruger** ['kru:gə]
**Langer** ['læŋgə]
**Lawrence** ['lɒrəns]
**Lee** [li:]
**Lefevre** [lə'fi:və]
**Levoy** ['li:vɔɪ]
**Lincoln** ['lɪŋkən]
**Lloyd** [lɔɪd]
**Lucas** ['lu:kəs]
**Luther** ['lu:θə]
**Marbury** ['mɑ:bəri]
**Marshall** ['mɑ:ʃl]
**McCourt** [mə'kɔ:t]
**Meerbusch** ['mɪəbʊʃ]
**Mitchell** ['mɪtʃəl]
**Morales** [mə'rɑ:lez, mə'ræləs]
**Muir** [mjʊə]
**Nielson** ['ni:lsən]
**Obama** [əʊ'bɑ:mə]
**Pattillo** [pə'tɪləʊ]
**Pemberton** ['pembətən]
**Pitt** [pɪt]
**Polo** ['pəʊləʊ]
**Rainey** ['reɪni]
**Roll** [rəʊl]
**Roosevelt** ['rəʊzəvelt]
**Salgado** [sæl'gɑ:dəʊ]
**Sanford** ['sænfəd]
**Scott** [skɒt]
**Sheckler** ['ʃeklə]
**Simpson** ['sɪmpsən]
**Smith** [smɪθ]
**Springsteen** ['sprɪŋsti:n]
**Strauss** [straʊs]
**Viotti** [vi'ɒti]
**Washington** ['wɒʃɪŋtən]
**Wilkins** ['wɪlkɪnz]
**William** ['wɪljəm, 'wɪliəm]

## Place names (Ortsnamen)

*(siehe auch S. 263:* The United States of America)

**Atlanta** [ət'læntə]
**Avenida Pico** [ˌɑ:və'ni:də 'pi:kəʊ, ˌævə'ni:də 'pi:kəʊ]
**Battery Place** ['bætri, bætəri pleɪs]
**Berlin** [bɜ:'lɪn]
**Broadway** ['brɔ:dweɪ]
**Bronx** [brɒŋks]
**Brooklyn** ['brʊklɪn]
**Brownsville** ['braʊnsvɪl]
**Castor River** [ˌkɑ:stə 'rɪvə]
**Chicago** [ʃɪ'kɑ:gəʊ]
**Chinatown** ['tʃaɪnətaʊn]
**Coloma** [kə'ləʊmə]
**Coney Island** [ˌkəʊni‿'aɪlənd]
**Dahlonega** [də'lɒnəgə]
**Dublin** ['dʌblɪn]
**Eiffel Tower** [ˌaɪfl 'taʊə]
**Ellis Island** [ˌelɪs‿'aɪlənd]
**Empire State Building** [ˌempaɪə 'steɪt ˌbɪldɪŋ]
**Eureka** [ju'ri:kə]
**Fort Lincoln** [ˌfɔ:t 'lɪŋkən]
**Gateway Arch** [ˌgeɪtweɪ‿'ɑ:tʃ]
**Grand Canyon** [ˌgrænd 'kænjən]
**Hayden Street** ['heɪdn stri:t]
**Herald Square** [ˌherəld 'skweə]
**Hermann** ['hɜ:mən]
**Hermannthal Winery** [ˌhɜ:məntɑ:l 'waɪnəri]
**Holbrook** ['həʊlbrʊk]
**Hollywood** ['hɒliwʊd]
**Inglewood** ['ɪŋglwʊd]
**Jamestown** ['dʒeɪmztaʊn]
**Las Vegas** [læs 'veɪgəs]
**Lexington Avenue** [ˌleksɪŋtən 'ævənju:]
**Los Angeles** [lɒs‿'ændʒəli:z]
**Macy's** ['meɪsiz]
**Malibu** ['mælɪbu:]
**Manhattan** [mæn'hætn]
**Mission Viejo** [ˌmɪʃn vi'eɪhəʊ]
**Napa Valley** [ˌnæpə 'væli]
**Nathan's** ['neɪθnz]
**New Echota** [ˌnju:‿i'kəʊtə]
**New York** [ˌnju: 'jɔ:k]
**Paces Ferry Road** [ˌpeɪsɪz ˌferi 'rəʊd]
**Purdue University** [ˌpɜ:dju: ju:nɪ'vɜ:səti]
**Queens** [kwi:nz]
The **Ramble** ['ræmbl]
**Rome** [rəʊm]
**Sacramento** [ˌsækrə'mentəʊ]
**San Clemente** [ˌsæn klə'menti]
**San Diego** [ˌsæn di'eɪgəʊ]
**San Francisco** [ˌsæn frən'sɪskəʊ]
**Santa Monica** [ˌsæntə 'mɒnɪkə]
**Santa Rosa** [ˌsæntə 'rəʊzə]
**Savannah** [sə'vænə]
**Sequoia National Park** [sɪˌkwɔɪə ˌnæʃnəl 'pɑ:k]
**Shorecliffs Middle School** ['ʃɔ:klɪfs]
**Sicily** ['sɪsəli]
**Silicon Valley** [ˌsɪlɪkən 'væli]
**Sinaloa** [ˌsɪnə'ləʊə]
**Staten Island** [ˌstætn‿'aɪlənd]
**St. Louis** [sənt 'lu:ɪs]
**Tucumcari** [ˌtu:kəm'keəri]
**Tulsa** ['tʌlsə]
**Washington** ['wɒʃɪŋtən]
**Watsonville** ['wɒtsnvɪl]
**World Trade Center** [ˌwɜ:ld 'treɪd ˌsentə]
**Yankee Stadium** [ˌjæŋki 'steɪdiəm]
**Yosemite** [jəʊ'seməti]

## Other names (Andere Namen)

**Bearcats** ['beəkæts]
**Bellagio** [bə'lɑ:dʒɪəʊ]
**Billboard** ['bɪlbɔ:d]
**Cherokees** ['tʃerəki:z]
**Colorado** [ˌkɒlə'rɑ:dəʊ]
**Harlem Globetrotters** [ˌhɑ:ləm 'gləʊbˌtrɒtəz]
**Hualapai** ['wæləpaɪ]
**Kool** [ku:l]
**LeToya** [lə'tɔɪə]
The **Mets** [mets]
**Militia Act** [mɪ'lɪʃə ˌækt]
**Mississippi** [ˌmɪsɪ'sɪpi]
**Ne-Yo** ['ni:əʊ]
**Rhine** [raɪn]
**Rushmore** ['rʌʃmɔ:]
**Sledge** [sledʒ]
**Usher** ['ʌʃə]
**Yankees** ['jæŋkiz]

| Country/Continent | Adjective | Person | People |
|---|---|---|---|
| **Africa** ['æfrɪkə] *Afrika* | African ['æfrɪkən] | an African | the Africans |
| **America** [ə'merɪkə] *Amerika* | American [ə'merɪkən] | an American | the Americans |
| **Asia** ['eɪʃə, 'eɪʒə] *Asien* | Asian ['eɪʃn, 'eɪʒn] | an Asian | the Asians |
| **Australia** [ɒ'streɪliə] *Australien* | Australian [ɒ'streɪliən] | an Australian | the Australians |
| **Austria** ['ɒstriə] *Österreich* | Austrian ['ɒstriən] | an Austrian | the Austrians |
| **Belgium** ['beldʒəm] *Belgien* | Belgian ['beldʒən] | a Belgian | the Belgians |
| **Canada** ['kænədə] *Kanada* | Canadian [kə'neɪdiən] | a Canadian | the Canadians |
| **China** ['tʃaɪnə] *China* | Chinese [ˌtʃaɪ'ni:z] | a Chinese | the Chinese |
| **Croatia** [krəʊ'eɪʃə] *Kroatien* | Croatian [krəʊ'eɪʃn] | a Croatian | the Croatians |
| **the Czech Republic** [ˌtʃek rɪ'pʌblɪk]<br>*Tschechien, die Tschechische Republik* | Czech [tʃek] | a Czech | the Czechs |
| **Denmark** ['denmɑ:k] *Dänemark* | Danish ['deɪnɪʃ] | a Dane [deɪn] | the Danes |
| **England** ['ɪŋglənd] *England* | English ['ɪŋglɪʃ] | an Englishman/-woman | the English |
| **Europe** ['jʊərəp] *Europa* | European [ˌjʊərə'pi:ən] | a European | the Europeans |
| **Finland** ['fɪnlənd] *Finnland* | Finnish ['fɪnɪʃ] | a Finn [fɪn] | the Finns |
| **France** [frɑ:ns] *Frankreich* | French [frentʃ] | a Frenchman/-woman | the French |
| **Georgia** ['dʒɔ:dʒə] *Georgien* | Georgian ['dʒɔ:dʒən] | a Georgian | the Georgians |
| **Germany** ['dʒɜ:məni] *Deutschland* | German ['dʒɜ:mən] | a German | the Germans |
| **(Great) Britain** ['brɪtn] *Großbritannien* | British ['brɪtɪʃ] | a Briton ['brɪtn] | the British |
| **Greece** [gri:s] *Griechenland* | Greek [gri:k] | a Greek | the Greeks |
| **Holland** ['hɒlənd] *Holland, die Niederlande* | Dutch [dʌtʃ] | a Dutchman/-woman | the Dutch |
| **Hungary** ['hʌŋgəri] *Ungarn* | Hungarian [hʌŋ'geəriən] | a Hungarian | the Hungarians |
| **India** ['ɪndiə] *Indien* | Indian ['ɪndiən] | an Indian | the Indians |
| **Ireland** ['aɪələnd] *Irland* | Irish ['aɪrɪʃ] | an Irishman/-woman | the Irish |
| **Italy** ['ɪtəli] *Italien* | Italian [ɪ'tæliən] | an Italian | the Italians |
| **Japan** [dʒə'pæn] *Japan* | Japanese [ˌdʒæpə'ni:z] | a Japanese | the Japanese |
| **Korea** [kə'riə] *Korea* | Korean [kə'riən] | a Korean | the Koreans |
| **the Netherlands** ['neðələndz]<br>*die Niederlande, Holland* | Dutch [dʌtʃ] | a Dutchman/-woman | the Dutch |
| **New Zealand** [ˌnju: 'zi:lənd] *Neuseeland* | New Zealand [ˌnju: 'zi:lənd] | a New Zealander | the New Zealanders |
| **Norway** ['nɔ:weɪ] *Norwegen* | Norwegian [nɔ:'wi:dʒən] | a Norwegian | the Norwegians |
| **Pakistan** [ˌpækɪ'stæn, ˌpɑ:kɪ'stɑ:n] *Pakistan* | Pakistani<br>[ˌpækɪ'stæni, ˌpɑ:kɪ'stɑ:ni] | a Pakistani | the Pakistanis |
| **the Philippines** ['fɪlɪpi:nz] *die Philippinen* | Philippine ['fɪlɪpi:n] | a Filipino [ˌfɪlɪ'pi:nəʊ]/<br>Filipina [ˌfɪlɪ'pi:nə] | the Filipinos/<br>Filipinas |
| **Poland** ['pəʊlənd] *Polen* | Polish ['pəʊlɪʃ] | a Pole [pəʊl] | the Poles |
| **Portugal** ['pɔ:tʃʊgl] *Portugal* | Portuguese [ˌpɔ:tʃu'gi:z] | a Portuguese | the Portuguese |
| **Puerto Rico** [ˌpwɜ:təʊ 'ri:kəʊ] *Puerto Rico* | Puerto Rican [ˌpwɜ:təʊ 'ri:kən] | a Puerto Rican | the Puerto Ricans |
| **Russia** ['rʌʃə] *Russland* | Russian ['rʌʃn] | a Russian | the Russians |
| **Scotland** ['skɒtlənd] *Schottland* | Scottish ['skɒtɪʃ] | a Scotsman/-woman,<br>a Scot [skɒt] | the Scots,<br>the Scottish |
| **Slovakia** [sləʊ'vɑ:kiə, sləʊ'vækiə]<br>*die Slowakei* | Slovak ['sləʊvæk] | a Slovak | the Slovaks |
| **Slovenia** [sləʊ'vi:niə] *Slowenien* | Slovenian [sləʊ'vi:niən],<br>Slovene ['sləʊvi:n] | a Slovene,<br>a Slovenian | the Slovenes,<br>the Slovenians |
| **Spain** [speɪn] *Spanien* | Spanish ['spænɪʃ] | a Spaniard ['spænɪəd] | the Spaniards |
| **Sweden** ['swi:dn] *Schweden* | Swedish ['swi:dɪʃ] | a Swede [swi:d] | the Swedes |
| **Switzerland** ['swɪtsələnd] *die Schweiz* | Swiss [swɪs] | a Swiss | the Swiss |
| **Turkey** ['tɜ:ki] *die Türkei* | Turkish ['tɜ:kɪʃ] | a Turk [tɜ:k] | the Turks |
| **the United Kingdom (the UK)**<br>[juˌnaɪtɪd 'kɪŋdəm, ju:'keɪ]<br>*das Vereinigte Königreich*<br>*(Großbritannien und Nordirland)* | British ['brɪtɪʃ] | a Briton ['brɪtn] | the British |
| **the United States of America**<br>**(the USA)**<br>[juˌnaɪtɪd ˌsteɪts_əv_ə'merɪkə,<br>ˌju:_es_'eɪ]<br>*die Vereinigten Staaten von Amerika* | American [ə'merɪkən] | an American | the Americans |
| **Wales** [weɪlz] *Wales* | Welsh [welʃ] | a Welshman/-woman | the Welsh |

## 7 Questions and answers ▸ Unit 5 (p. 100)

*If you are a **suspect**, you have to answer some questions.*

### Role card **SCENE 1**, Sam

**Why do you think you (Sam) got a good grade on the test?**
**You:** Since I was a little girl, my grandmother has told me about Martin Luther King. She met him once. I have got a photo of Grandma and Dr King. I wanted to show it to Mr Bell. I didn't need to study for the test. I knew it all from my grandmother.

**Did you want to win Jacko's MP3 player?**
**You:** No, I've already got one. I think CJ likes the same music as Jacko. Ask her.

**Were you in school after class on Wednesday?**
**You:** No, I went home after the last class.

### Role card **SCENE 1**, Nat

**Why do you think Sam got a good grade on the test?**
**You:** I don't know. That was a big surprise. She never gets good grades. But I don't want to say anything. Ask Sam.

**Did you want to win Jacko's MP3 player?**
**You:** No, I've already got one. Try someone else.

**Were you in school after class on Wednesday?**
**You:** Yes, I was working in the library. I went to get a drink and I saw Scott and Flash. Then I went back to the library and stayed there until it closed. Then I went home.

### Role card **SCENE 1**, Jacko

**Why do you think Sam got a good grade on the test?**
**You:** Well, it was a surprise, but how should I know? Ask Sam!

**Did you want to win Jacko's MP3 player?**
**You:** I am Jacko, remember. It was my MP3 player. Ask the others.

**Were you in school after class on Wednesday?**
**You:** Of course not. I went home after the last class and studied for the test. I had to get a good grade because I didn't want to lose my MP3 player.

### Role card **SCENE 1**, Scott

**Why do you think Sam got a good grade on the test?**
**You:** I think she was very interested in Martin Luther King's story. Cindy told me something about a photo.

**Did you want to win Jacko's MP3 player?**
**You:** No. I've already got an MP3 player. CJ told me Jacko's got a good playlist. Ask her.

**Were you in school after class on Wednesday?**
**You:** Yes, I came back to get a book for homework. I saw Flash and he tried to get me into trouble but I walked away. I didn't have time. I work at the burger bar on Wednesday nights. I had to finish my homework before work.

Role card **SCENE 1**, **Flash**

**Why do you think Sam got a good grade on the test?**
**You:** I don't know. Anyway, she's not one of my friends. I don't really know her and I don't care. Ask Sam.

**Did you want to win Jacko's MP3 player?**
**You:** No. My MP3 player is much better. It cost a lot of money.

**Were you in school after class on Wednesday?**
**You:** Yes, I was at basketball practice – I train for two hours every day after school – that's why I'm the star of the team.

Role card **SCENE 1**, **Cindy**

**Why do you think Sam got a good grade on the test?**
**You:** She showed me a photo of her grandmother and Martin Luther King. I think she knew a lot about him.

**Did you want to win Jacko's MP3 player?**
**You:** No, I've already got one and I hate Jacko's music. It's so loud and fast! Only CJ likes the same music as Jacko.

**Were you in school after class on Wednesday?**
**You:** No, I wasn't. Scott came back to get a book for homework. I waited for him outside the school.

Role card **SCENE 1**, **CJ**

**Why do you think Sam got a good grade on the test?**
**You:** I'm new in this class. I don't know. Ask Sam!

**Did you want to win Jacko's MP3 player?**
**You:** Well, I've already got an MP3 player. But sometimes it's boring to listen to the same music. Jacko's got a great playlist on his MP3. And he's got such a big mouth. So the true answer is yes, I did want to win it ... but I didn't cheat.

**Were you in school after class on Wednesday?**
**You:** No, I went home after the last class.

Role card **SCENE 1**, **Mr Bell**

**Why do you think Sam got a good grade on the test?**
**You:** She showed me a photo of Martin Luther King and her grandmother. I think her grandmother told her a lot of interesting things about him.

**Did you want to win Jacko's MP3 player?**
**You:** No, I'm the teacher, remember. Ask one of the students.

**Were you in school after class on Wednesday?**
**You:** No. I went home at 3.15.

## 10 Questions and answers ▸ Unit 5 (p. 104)

*If you are a **suspect**, you have to answer some questions.*

Role card **SCENE 2**, Sam

**Why did Nat start to cry in the test?**
**You:** I know she's stressed because her parents give her a hard time about schoolwork. But I don't really know why Nat started to cry. Ask her.

**Do you want to take the test again?**
**You:** No! Of course not! I got an A! My grandmother will be very proud of me. That was my first A in History! I don't think I can do that again.

**Who do you think did it?**
**You:** I don't know. Maybe it was Mr Bell. I think he's worried about what the principal will say.

Role card **SCENE 2**, Nat

**Why did you start to cry in the test?**
**You:** I worked really hard for the test. I wanted my parents to be proud of me. Then, when I looked at the paper, I panicked. I couldn't remember anything. That's why I cried.

**Do you want to take the test again?**
**You:** No! I hate tests. I get so stressed! I don't want to do it again! But maybe it's not such a bad idea. I could get a better grade. But then there would be the stress again.

**Who do you think did it?**
**You:** I don't know. I don't think it was Mr Bell. It must be one of the students. But I don't know who.

Role card **SCENE 2**, Jacko

**Why did Nat start to cry in the test?**
**You:** Did she cry? I don't know. I didn't see anything. She takes school too seriously. You have to ask Nat.

**Do you want to take the test again?**
**You:** No! I worked hard to get the best grade. Of course I don't want to take the test again. It was too much work at the first time!

**Who do you think did it?**
**You:** I don't know. Maybe it was Mr Bell. That would be so funny!

Role card **SCENE 2**, Scott

**Why did Nat start to cry in the test?**
**You:** I don't know. I know that Cindy was worried about her. Cindy is very sweet. She worries about everyone! I think you have to ask Nat.

**Do you want to take the test again?**
**You:** Well, I got a B. Maybe I'd get an A if I did it again. But I don't have time to study. No, I don't want to take the test again.

**Who do you think did it?**
**You:** It must be Flash. He's trying to get me into trouble.

Role card **SCENE 2**, **Flash**

**Why did Nat start to cry in the test?**

**You:** I don't know. Nat's always stressed. Ask her.

**Do you want to take the test again?**

**You:** No, not really. But I don't really care. You know that I'm not interested in tests and grades. I got a D on the test. That's OK for me.

**Who do you think did it?**

**You:** Scott. I'm sure it was him ... well, I hope it was him! Then Cindy can see that he is not so perfect. That would be really great.

Role card **SCENE 2**, **Cindy**

**Why did Nat start to cry in the test?**

**You:** She's very stressed. Maybe she was crying because she couldn't answer any of the questions. Maybe you should ask her.

**Do you want to take the test again?**

**You:** No, not really. I'm happy with my grade.

**Who do you think did it?**

You: I don't know. I know that I didn't do it and of course I know that Scott didn't do it. He would never do such a thing. Maybe it was Flash. He isn't very nice to Scott.

Role card **SCENE 2**, **CJ**

**Why did Nat start to cry in the test?**

**You:** I have no idea. I don't know what her problem is. She is strange. Ask her.

**Do you want to take the test again?**

**You:** No. What a boring idea! But I'm sure I would get a good grade in another test.

**Who do you think did it?**

**You:** No idea. I only know it wasn't me and I didn't have anything to do with the problem at my old school. I came here because my mom got a new job and my family moved here.

Role card **SCENE 2**, **Mr Bell**

**Why did Nat start to cry in the test?**

**You:** I don't know. I worry about Nat. She's a good student but she panicks about her work. She studies too hard. She's always in the library. She went there again after the test.

**Do you want to take the test again?**

**You:** Well, most of the students got really bad grades. Maybe they need another chance. But another test would be a lot of work. No, I don't want to read all the test papers again.

**Who do you think did it?**

**You:** I don't know. I really don't know!

| Infinitive | Simple past form | Past participle | |
|---|---|---|---|
| (to) **be** | **was/were** | **been** | sein |
| (to) **beat** | **beat** | **beaten** | schlagen; besiegen |
| (to) **become** | **became** | **become** | werden |
| (to) **begin** | **began** | **begun** | beginnen, anfangen (mit) |
| (to) **blow** | **blew** | **blown** | wehen, blasen |
| (to) **break** | **broke** | **broken** | (zer)brechen; kaputt gehen |
| (to) **bring** | **brought** | **brought** | (mit-, her)bringen |
| (to) **build** | **built** | **built** | bauen |
| (to) **buy** | **bought** | **bought** | kaufen |
| (to) **catch** | **caught** | **caught** | fangen; erwischen |
| (to) **choose** [uː] | **chose** [əʊ] | **chosen** [əʊ] | (aus)wählen; (sich) aussuchen |
| (to) **come** | **came** | **come** | kommen |
| (to) **cost** | **cost** | **cost** | kosten |
| (to) **cut** | **cut** | **cut** | schneiden |
| (to) **do** | **did** | **done** [ʌ] | tun, machen |
| (to) **draw** | **drew** | **drawn** | zeichnen |
| (to) **drink** | **drank** | **drunk** | trinken |
| (to) **drive** [aɪ] | **drove** | **driven** [ɪ] | *(ein Auto)* fahren |
| (to) **eat** | **ate** [et, eɪt] | **eaten** | essen |
| (to) **fall** | **fell** | **fallen** | (hin)fallen, stürzen |
| (to) **feed** | **fed** | **fed** | füttern |
| (to) **feel** | **felt** | **felt** | (sich) fühlen; sich anfühlen |
| (to) **fight** | **fought** | **fought** | kämpfen |
| (to) **find** | **found** | **found** | finden |
| (to) **fly** | **flew** | **flown** | fliegen |
| (to) **forget** | **forgot** | **forgotten** | vergessen |
| (to) **forgive** | **forgave** | **forgiven** | vergeben, verzeihen |
| (to) **get** | **got** | **got** | bekommen; holen; werden; (hin)kommen |
| (to) **give** | **gave** | **given** | geben |
| (to) **go** | **went** | **gone** [ɒ] | gehen, fahren |
| (to) **grow** | **grew** | **grown** | wachsen; anbauen, anpflanzen |
| (to) **hang out** *(infml)* | **hung out** | **hung out** | rumhängen, abhängen |
| (to) **have (have got)** | **had** | **had** | haben, besitzen |
| (to) **hear** [ɪə] | **heard** [ɜː] | **heard** [ɜː] | hören |
| (to) **hide** [aɪ] | **hid** [ɪ] | **hidden** [ɪ] | (sich) verstecken |
| (to) **hit** | **hit** | **hit** | schlagen |
| (to) **hold** | **held** | **held** | halten |
| (to) **hurt** | **hurt** | **hurt** | wehtun; verletzen |
| (to) **keep** | **kept** | **kept** | (be)halten |
| (to) **know** [nəʊ] | **knew** [njuː] | **known** [nəʊn] | wissen; kennen |
| (to) **lay** the table | **laid** | **laid** | den Tisch decken |
| (to) **leave** | **left** | **left** | (weg)gehen; abfahren; verlassen; zurücklassen |

| Infinitive | Simple past form | Past participle | |
|---|---|---|---|
| (to) **let** | **let** | **let** | lassen |
| (to) **lie** [aɪ] | **lay** [eɪ] | **lain** [eɪ] | liegen |
| (to) **lose** [uː] | **lost** [ɒ] | **lost** [ɒ] | verlieren |
| (to) **make** | **made** | **made** | machen; bauen; bilden |
| (to) **mean** [iː] | **meant** [e] | **meant** [e] | bedeuten; meinen |
| (to) **meet** | **met** | **met** | (sich) treffen |
| (to) **pay** | **paid** | **paid** | bezahlen |
| (to) **put** | **put** | **put** | legen, stellen, *(wohin)* tun |
| (to) **read** [iː] | **read** [e] | **read** [e] | lesen |
| (to) **ride** [aɪ] | **rode** | **ridden** [ɪ] | reiten; *(Rad)* fahren |
| (to) **ring** | **rang** | **rung** | klingeln, läuten |
| (to) **rise** [aɪ] | **rose** | **risen** [ɪ] | (auf)steigen |
| (to) **run** | **ran** | **run** | rennen, laufen |
| (to) **say** [eɪ] | **said** [e] | **said** [e] | sagen |
| (to) **see** | **saw** | **seen** | sehen; besuchen, aufsuchen |
| (to) **sell** | **sold** | **sold** | verkaufen |
| (to) **send** | **sent** | **sent** | schicken, senden |
| (to) **shine** | **shone** [ɒ] | **shone** [ɒ] | scheinen *(Sonne)* |
| (to) **shoot** [uː] | **shot** | **shot** | schießen, erschießen |
| (to) **show** | **showed** | **shown** | zeigen |
| (to) **shut up** | **shut** | **shut** | den Mund halten |
| (to) **sing** | **sang** | **sung** | singen |
| (to) **sit** | **sat** | **sat** | sitzen; sich setzen |
| (to) **sleep** | **slept** | **slept** | schlafen |
| (to) **speak** | **spoke** | **spoken** | sprechen |
| (to) **spend** | **spent** | **spent** | *(Zeit)* verbringen; *(Geld)* ausgeben |
| (to) **stand** | **stood** | **stood** | stehen; sich (hin)stellen |
| (to) **steal** | **stole** | **stolen** | stehlen |
| (to) **stick** | **stuck** | **stuck** | herausragen, herausstehen |
| (to) **swim** | **swam** | **swum** | schwimmen |
| (to) **take** | **took** | **taken** | nehmen; (weg-, hin)bringen; dauern, *(Zeit)* brauchen |
| (to) **teach** | **taught** | **taught** | unterrichten, lehren |
| (to) **tear sth. off** [eə] | **tore** | **torn** | etwas abreißen |
| (to) **tell** | **told** | **told** | erzählen, berichten |
| (to) **think** | **thought** | **thought** | denken, glauben, meinen |
| (to) **throw** | **threw** | **thrown** | werfen |
| (to) **understand** | **understood** | **understood** | verstehen |
| (to) **upset** | **upset** | **upset** | ärgern, kränken, aus der Fassung bringen |
| (to) **wake** up | **woke** | **woken** | aufwachen; wecken |
| (to) **wear** [eə] | **wore** [ɔː] | **worn** [ɔː] | tragen *(Kleidung)* |
| (to) **win** | **won** [ʌ] | **won** [ʌ] | gewinnen |
| (to) **write** | **wrote** | **written** | schreiben |

## Key to the self-assessment tests

### Unit 1 ▸ p. 29

1 C boroughs
2 B Manhattan
3 C in the south of Manhattan
4 B the World Trade Center
5 D a cellphone
6 B Ellis Island
7 cellphone – pants – sidewalk – potato chips
8 lift – queue – underground – holiday(s)
9 B awful
10 C put out
11 B blocks
12 D deli
13 C Hiking
14 D playing
15 a) If you had lots of money, you could fly to New York in your next holidays.
b) If I ever go to New York, I want to go up the Empire State Building.
c) When I was in New York last June, I saw Times Square.

### Unit 2 ▸ p. 53

1 A the Golden State
2 C Silicon Valley
3 D Spanish
4 B illegal
5 C the Golden Gate Bridge
6 D read every word
7 C specific information
8 C Yours faithfully
9 C companies
10 B industrial
11 A ethnic group
12 D experienced
13 B prejudiced
14 D are made
15 A was discovered
16 B by
17 C Someone stole my camera.

### Unit 3 ▸ p. 71

1 D middle
2 B industry
3 C river
4 elementary school
5 grade
6 extracurricular activities/extracurriculars
7 A (excellent)
8 the British English words are:
a) notice board b) timetable c) lesson
9 a) seven point nine b) degree Celsius
10 In the US cola and lemonade are often called soda.
11 To keep fit, eat the right food and do daily exercise.
12 Chicken and turkey are a kind of meat we call poultry.
13 Statement C is not true:
C lots of details from the original text.
14 a) I need some information.
b) Can I have a glass of milk, please?
– Of course, there's some milk in the fridge.
c) Would you like some fruit with your sandwich?
– Yes, an apple would be nice.
15 a) The students talked about food in their Health class. They agreed that the food they eat isn't very healthy.
b) Is life in Hermann quiet? – Yes, but the life of the local newspaper reporter is quite busy.
16 C Timo couldn't open the door.
He had lost his key.
17 D When I saw Jake at 11 o'clock, he hadn't eaten his breakfast yet.

Key to the self-assessment tests

## Unit 4

▸ p. 93

(One point for each correct answer to question 1–11, two points for each correct sentence to question 12.)

1 B states in the north and in the south
2 D discrimination against blacks
3 A the White House
4 a) series
b) reality show
c) comedy
d) prime time
e) documentary
5 D books
6 C the TV listings
7 C When you do research, you should use more than one source.
8 D In your notes you should never copy whole sentences, use your own words.
9 When do you have to draw conclusions?
D The information is given indirectly.
10 a) We have lived in the same flat for six years.
b) I've had English with Frau Marx since the beginning of last year.
11 a) since kindergarten
b) for an hour
c) since 9/11
d) since the accident
e) for a long time
12 a) Yes, I've known him for two years. 2 points
b) Yes, he has been in hospital since Monday. 2 points

## Illustrationen

**Silke Bachmann**, Hamburg (30; 49–51; 68–70; 79; 80; 118); **Roland Beier**, Berlin (23; 29; 40; 42; 48; 53; 56; 58; 64; 66; 71; 93; 96-105; 133; 143-193); **Dr. Volkhard Binder**, Berlin (S. 131); **Carlos Borrell**, Berlin (vordere u. hintere Umschlaginnenseite; 8-11; 13; 20 oben (u. 106); 54; 54-55 (Hintergrund); 55; 60; 61 oben; 120; 121; 123; 133; 140); **Stéphane Gamain/NB Illustration**, London (20 Mitte, unten; 24; 26-28; 38; 46; 47(u. 108); **Jörn Hennig**, Berlin (136–137)

## Bildquellen

**Michelle Abesamis**, New York (S. 23 zoo); **Agentur Focus**, Hamburg (S. 89 Mitte li.: Magnum Photos/Elliott Erwitt); **Alamy**, Abingdon (Inhaltsverz. Caitlin (u. 8 oben li.): Geoff du Feu (RF); Luis (u. 9): David R. Frazier Photolibrary, Inc., skyline (M) (u. 12/13): JUPITERIMAGES/ Thinkstock (RF), surfers (M) (u. 34): Juice Images Limited (RF); S. 9 Mitte school bus: Directphoto.org; S. 9 Mitte pool: Radius Images; S. 10 oben li.: Robert Harding Picture Library Ltd, condor: John Cancalosi, Route 66 logo: wendy connett; S. 12 Bild A: Jon Arnold Images Ltd., Bild B: Tetra Images; S. 13 Bild F: Jochen Tack, Bild H: Yadid Levy; S. 14 oben girls (M): Andrew Rubtsov, Bild 1: fStop (RF), Bild 2: Dieter Melhorn, Bild 3: John Taylor, Bild 6: Stockbyte(RF); S. 15 oben: Picture Partners, Mitte: eStock Photo/Gg; S. 17 oben: Sandra Baker, unten li.: Arcaid/G Jackson, unten re.: PCL; S. 18 unten re.: Jeff Greenberg; S. 19 unten: Mary Evans Picture Library; S. 21 shop assistant: John Sturrock, hairdresser: Tetra Images (RF); S. 34 Bild A (M) beach: Stephen Saks Photography, Bild C (M) sign: Frank Vetere, highway 101: Stock Connection Blue; S. 35 Bild F: Richard Broadwell; S. 36 strawberries: Tony Hertz, vineyard: Fabian Gonzales, Google HQ: Rodolfo Arpia, Magic Mountain: LHB Photo; S. 39 oben li.: North Wind Picture Archives, oben re.: ABN Stock Images, Mitte: Russ Bishop, unten li.: Pick and Mix Images, unten re.: Horizon International Images Limited; S. 44 unten (u. 112): Chuck Nacke; S. 45 Bild 4 (u. 113): Pick and Mix Images; S. 46 Bild 3 li.: History Archive, re.: INTERFOTO Pressebildagentur; S. 54 Bild B: Danita Delimont; S. 56: Richard G. Bingham II; S. 57 Mitte: GPI Stock; S. 61 unten: Don Smetzer; S. 85 unten: Helene Rogers; S. 86: VStock (RF); S. 102 earpiece, ear: Steve Hamblin, iPod Shuffle: colinspics; S. 106 re.: Ambient Images Inc.; S. 107 helicopter: Mary Evans Picture Library; S. 116: Steve Skjold; S. 120 unten re.: Deco; S. 121 slave ship, unten: North Wind Pictures Archives; 123 oben li.: Chris A Crumley; S. 124 oben re.: LOOK Die Bildagentur der Fotografen GmbH/Konrad Wothe; S. 125 Mitte: Gavin Gough; S. 127 oben li.: Gail Mooney-Kelly, oben re.: Chuck Eckert; S. 129 helmet: Photodisc (RF), knee pads: Studiomode; S. 134 observation room: Andre Jenny, park: Rich Iwasaki; S. 138 oben re.: Content Mine International, Mitte re.: Factoryhill unten re.: Pictorial Press; S. 139 oben li.: Pictorial Press, unten: Scott London, oben Mitte: Allstar Picture Library); **Animal Planet**, München (S. 78 Animal Planet logo); **Arteaga Photos LTD.**, St. Louis (S. 135 Bild 1 u. 3); **Associated Press**, Frankfurt/Main (S. 35 Bild G: PAUL SAKUMA); S. 89 oben re.; S. 90 oben; S. 92 oben: Danny Johnston; S. 130: Amy Sancetta); **Britta Bensmann**, Berlin (S. 129 elbow pads); **Dave Briccetti**, Lafayette (S. 43 unten); **Bridgeman**, Berlin (S. 121 ships: Private Collection/ Look and Learn/ BridgemanArt.de); **Brown Brothers**, Sterling, PA. (S. 19 oben); **Jan Burwick**, Hamburg (S. 131); **Cable News Network. A Time Warner Company**, Atlanta (S. 78 CNN logo); **CBS Broadcasting Inc.**, Los Angeles (S. 78 CBS logo: Use of logo from CBS Eye Logos - Courtesy of CBS Broadcasting Inc., Los Angeles); **Cinetext**, Frankfurt/Main (S. 45 Bild 3 (u. 113): Cinetext Bildarchiv; S. 47 Bild 1: Cinetext Bildarchiv; S. 48 Ratatouille: Buena Vista, Jesse James: Warner Bros.; S. 85 oben: 20th Century Fox); **The Coca-Cola Company**, Atlanta (S. 76 unten Mitte); **Corbis**, Düsseldorf (S. 7 (u. 147): Reuters/Jeff Topping; S. 57 unten: Charles Gupton; S. 77 unten re.: Franz-Marc Frei; S. 81 unten: Bettmann; S. 82 oben: Comstock (RF); S. 89 Mitte re.: Bettmann; S. 90 oben re.: Bettmann; unten re.: Bettmann; 91 oben, unten li.: Bettmann; S. 107 Bild 8 li.: Adam Woolfitt; S. 127 unten: Stringer/Henny Abrams/Reuter; S. 128: Bo Bridges; S. 132 unten li.: Lloyd Cluff, unten re.: Grant Smith; S. 129 unten re.: Steve Boyle/ NewSport; S. 135 Bild 2, Bild 4: Bettmann; S. 142: Bettmann/William Horace Smith; S. 139 Mitte re.: Tim Mosenfelder, Mitte: Laura Levine); **Angel & Wilma Delgadillo's Route 66 Gift Shop & Visitor's Center**, Seligman (S. 10 license plate); **Denver Public Library**, Denver (S. 60 unten: Colorado Historical Society & Denver Art Museum); **FDNY/NYC & Company**, New York (S. 23 FDNY logos: All New York City logos and marks depicted herein are the property of the City of New York and may not be used without prior written consent); **First National Bank of Atlanta**, Atlanta (Inhaltsverz. (u. 76 (M)): Atlanta burning photo: Taken from "Atlanta Rusurgens". Written and published by the First National Bank of Atlanta. November 1971, Atlanta. Photo: Metro-Goldwyn-Mayer); **FOX Broadcasting Company**, Los Angeles (S. 78 FOX logo: FOX is the trademark of FOX Broadcasting Company and is used with permission of FOX Broadcasting Company); **Fricke Studio**, Hermann (Inhaltsverz. Jake (u. 10 oben); S. 54 Bild B, Bild D, Bild E; S. 55 Bild F, Bild G, Bild H; S. 57 oben; S. 59 oben, unten); **Getty Images**, München (S. 6, S. 11 skywalk: David McNew; S. 8 oben: Richard Price, unten re.: Michael Clark; S. 15 unten: Aurora/Ian Shive; S. 18 oben li.: Stone/Archive Holdings Inc.; S. 21 firefighter: Getty Images News/Gilles Mingasson; S. 32: AFP/Stan Honda; S. 38 li.: Getty Images News/ Chip Somodevilla; S. 41 oben li.: Photographer's Choice/Grant Faint; S. 43 oben: Justin Sullivan; S. 61 oben: The Bridgeman Art Library/Charles Marion Russell; S. 65: Justin Sullivan; S. 73: Image Source (RF); S. 77 unten Mitte: Hulton Archive/Agence France Presse, unten li.: WireImage; S. 81 oben: München: Popperfoto/Rolls Press; S. 82 unten: CNN/ Handout; S. 83 Mitte: NBAE/David Liam Kyle; S. 89 oben li.: Hulton Archive/ William Lovelace; S. 90 Mitte li.: Hulton Archive/Moore; S. 95 unten Martin Luther King (M): Hulton Archive/Agence France Presse; S. 109 oben: Photographer's Choice/Louis Schwartzberg; S. 124 li.: Mitchell Funk, unten re.: Mario Tama; S. 128: Peter Kramer; S. 132 oben: Cindy Karp; S. 138 oben li.: FPG, Mitte: Michael Ochs Archives); **www.Gleis4.de** (S. 62); **Grand Canyon NP Museum Collection**, Grand Canyon (S. 21 ranger); **Howard Architectural Models, Inc.**, Toldedo (S. 125 oben li.); **iStockphoto**, Calgary (S. 47 Bild 3: Greg Nicholas; S. 75 Bild 4: dwphotos, Bild 7: Sergia Kishan, Bild 8: Lisa Fletcher; **Chris Junker**, Portland (S. 135 Arch skin); **jupiterimages**, Ottobrunn/München (Inhaltsverz. Madison (u. 11; 87): Polka Dot Images (RF)); **Adam Kuban**, New York (S. 125 oben re.); **Elliot Larson**, Walnut Creek (S. 17 oben); **Major League Baseball Properties, Inc.** (S. 126 oben: Major League Baseball trademarks and copyrights are used with permission of Major League Baseball Properties, Inc.); **Massachusetts Commandery Military Order of the Loyal Legion and the U.S. Army Military History Institute** (S. 141); **mauritius images**, Mittenwald (S. 11 mule train: Jeff O'Brien; S. 13 Bild G: age; S. 14 oben street (M): age); **MTV Networks Germany GmbH**, Berlin (S. 78 MTV logo); **Peter Newcomb Photography**, St. Louis (Inhaltsverz.: Hermann (u. 54); **Barack Obama Office**, Washington D.C. (S. 83 unten re.); **Thomas Parker**, Vienna, Missouri, USA (S. 55 Bild F); Photolibrary, London (Atlanta (M) Inhaltsverz. (u. S. 77): Jon Arnold Travel/ Walter Bibikow; S. 63: Owaki-Kulla); **Picture-Alliance**, Frankfurt/Main (S. 9 unten: dpa/Jörg Schmitt; S. 10 unten re.: MAXPPP/Marianna Day Massey; S. 23 unten li.: dpa-Report/PA Magdalena Mayo; S. 35 Bild G: dpa-Report/Ken James; S. 38 re.: dpa/ Jerzy Dabrowski; S. 45 Bild 6 (u. 113): dpa-Fotoreport/epa afp Scott Nelson; S. 46 Bild 4 li.: united archives, re.: dpa; S. 76 unten li.: akg-images; S. 80: dpaweb, dpa-Report/Thomas S. England; S. 83 unten li. (u. 139): Sven Simon, unten re.: dpa-Report/ epa Peter Fowley; S. 106 li.: HB-Verlag/Martin Sasse; S. 149: HB-Verlag/ Martin Sasse); **Marion Schönenberger**, Berlin (Inhaltsverz. Teenagers (u. 95); S. 94-105); **Redferns**, London (S. 138 unten li.: Deltahaze Corporation); **Ohad Shahar/ PhotoStock-Israel**: www.photographersdirect.com (S. 134 tram); **Shutterstock**, New York (Inhaltsverz. Statue of Liberty (M) (u. 12): gary718, homeless (M) (u. 34): Nikita Rogul, fire (M) (u. 80/81): David Lee; S. 10 book (M): Martina I. Meyer, key ring: Tina Rencelj; S. 11 Bellagio: Andy Z.; S. 12 Bild C: Marcin Wasilewski; S. 13 Bild E: Sandy Maya Matzen; S. 14 Bild 5: emin kuliyev; S. 17 Mitte: Hannamariah, unten li.: Scott Rothstein; S. 21 Mitte (u. 110): Steven Pepple; S. 22 (u. 111): Vladimir Korostyshevskiy; S. 25 unten Mitte: Bill Kennedy, unten re.: Ilja Mašík; S. 33 Bild 1: Yobidaba, Bild 2: Jason Kasumovic, Bild 3: cardiae, Bild 4: Jostein Hauge, Bild 5: Christa DeRidder, Bild 6: Miguel Angel Salinas Salinas, Bild 7: sonya etchison, Bild 8: Max Blain, Bild 9: erikdegraaf fotografie; S. 34 Bild A sign (M): Michael Ledray, Bild D: Michal G Smith; S. 35 Bild E: Chee-Onn Leong; S. 36 strawberries: Norman Chan; S. 37: MANDYGIDBEHEAR; S. 40/41: Brandon Holmes; S. 40 oben: Albo; S. 41 oben li.: Rena Schild, Mitte: Byron W.Moore, unten li.: David Alexander Liu, Oscar: Oliver Johannes Uhrig; S. 44 oben (u. 112): slowfish; S. 45 (u. 113) Bild 1: Feverpitched, Bild 2: Stas Volik; Bild 5: crystalfoto; S. 46 Bild 1 li.: Guus van Raaphorst; S. 47 Bild 2: stocksnapp, Bild 4: Ivan Stevanovic; S. 67: Ron Hilton; S. 75 Bild 1: Maxim Petrichuk, Bild 2: Palto, Bild 3: Jose Marines; Bild 5: B. Speckart, Bild 6: Olga Chernetskaya, Bild 9: Glenda M. Powers; S. 79 unten: Monkey Business Images; S. 82/83 US flag background: Goxy; S. 83 Mitte re.: James M phelps, Jr; S. 84 unten re.: Kutlazev Dmitry, unten li.: Andryej Petelski, oben: Lee Torrens; S. 86 (u. 121): Condor 36; S. 93 oben re.: Remus; S.111 (u. 22): Vladimir Korostyshevskiy; S. 107 Bild 5 li.: Alex Staroseltsev, re.: luchschen; S. 107 unten: David Alexander Liu; S. 109 unten: iofoto; 110 (u. 21); Steven Pepple; S. 120 oben li.: Goxy, oben re.: Mario Bruno, unten li.: ifoto; S. 121 oben re.: Oralleff; S. 123 unten li.: Chee-Onn Leong, unten re.: Tomasz Szymanski); S. 127 Mitte re.: WITTY234; S. 129 wrist guard: triaphoto; **Stone Hill Winery**, Hermann (S. 60 oben); **Makoto Takami**, Japan (S. 14 Bild 4); **Topeka Room, Topeka & Shawnee County Public Library**, Topeka (S. 89 Mitte re.); **ullstein bild**, Berlin (S. 18 unten li.: histopics; S. 40 unten: Peter Arnold Inc.; S. 46 Bild 1 re.: Granger Collection, Bild 2 li.: AISA, re.: Granger Collection, Bild 4 li.: Granger Collection; S. 76 unten re.: dpa; S. 78 NBC logo: Keith (used by permission of NBC Universal, Inc., New York); S. 107 Bild 6 li.: TopFoto, re.: Granger Collection, Bild 7 li.: Imagebroker.net, Bild 8 re.: AP; S.121 trail of tears: Granger Collection; S. 121 unten: CARO/Muhs; S. 122 oben, Mitte, unten: Granger Collection; S. 133: Still Pictures; S. 138 unten Mitte: Carl Van Vechten); **U.S. Department of the Interior, National Park Service** (S. 134/135 Gateway Arch (Artist: David Leech); S. 134 Gateway Arch triangle detail (Artist David Leech); S. 135 construction progress (Artist: David Leech))

## Titelbild

**Corbis**, Düsseldorf (yellow cab (M): image100 (RF), Times Square (M): Jose Fuste Raga); **Corel Library**: (US Flag Hintergrund (M))

## Textquellen

S. 26–28: *You can tell me.* Adapted from "Kelly 'n' Me" by Myron Levoy. Published by iUniverse.com, Inc. Lincoln. All Rights Reserved © 1992, 2000 by Myron Levoy. Reprinted by arrangement with the author and Writers House LLC, acting as agent for the author; S. 68–70: *Angus Bethune's moment.* Adapted from „Telephone Man" from "Athletic Shorts" © 1989, 1991 by Chris Crutcher. Printed with permission from Greenwillow Books, an imprint of HarperCollins Publishers; S. 90–91: *Melba's story.* Excerpts taken from „Warriors don't Cry. The Searing Memoir of the Battle to Integrate Little Rock's Central High" by Melba Pattillo Beals. Abridged edition. Simon Pulse, 1995; S. 124: *The City* by David Ignatow. Reprinted with permission from the March 17, 1969 issue of "The Nation". For subscription information, call 1-800-333-8563. Portions of each week's Nation magazine can be accessed at http://www.thenation.com; S. 124: *Skyscraper* by Dennis Lee. From "Alligator Pie" (Macmillan of Canada, 1974; Key Porter Books, 2001). Copyright © 1974 Dennis Lee. With permission of the author; S. 124: *Subway rush hour* © 1994 by the Estate of Langston Hughes; S. 125: *To the visitor.* © 2003 Frank McCourt; S. 130: *Child labour on the US-Mexican border.* Abridged and adapted from "Illegal child labor in Mexico puts food on tables of Americans" by Chris Hawley. The Arizona Republic, May 9, 2008; S. 145: Auszug von S. 582 aus „English G 2000 Wörterbuch - Das Wörterbuch zum Lehrwerk". Herausgegeben von der Langenscheidt-Redaktion Wörterbücher und der Cornelsen-Redaktion Englisch. © 2002 Cornelsen Verlag GmbH & Co. OHG, Berlin und Langenscheidt KG, Berlin und München.

## Liedquellen

S. 17: *A heart in New York*: K+T: Gallagher, Benny/Lyle, Graham. © Good Single Ltd./Imagem Songs Ltd. Tj musicservice GmbH, Hamburg. Imagem Music GmbH, Hamburg; S. 125: *New York, New York*: K+T: Ebb, Fred. © by EMI Unart Catalog Inc. D/A/CH/Osteuropäische Länder: EMI Partnership Musikverlag GmbH, Hamburg

| Staat | | Abkürzung | Hauptstadt | |
|---|---|---|---|---|
| **Alabama** | [ˌælə'bæmə] | **AL** | **Montgomery** | [mənt'gʌməri] |
| **Alaska** | [ə'læskə] | **AK** | **Juneau** | ['dʒu:nəʊ] |
| **Arizona** | [ˌærɪ'zəʊnə] | **AZ** | **Phoenix** | ['fi:nɪks] |
| **Arkansas** | ['ɑ:kənsɔ:] | **AR** | **Little Rock** | [ˌlɪtl 'rɒk] |
| **California** | [ˌkælə'fɔ:niə] | **CA** | **Sacramento** | [ˌsækrə'mentəʊ] |
| **Colorado** | [ˌkɒlə'rɑ:dəʊ] | **CO** | **Denver** | ['denvə] |
| **Connecticut** | [kə'netɪkət] | **CT** | **Hartford** | ['hɑ:tfəd] |
| **Delaware** | ['deləweə] | **DE** | **Dover** | ['dəʊvə] |
| **Florida** | ['flɒrɪdə] | **FL** | **Tallahassee** | [ˌtælə'hæsi] |
| **Georgia** | ['dʒɔ:dʒə] | **GA** | **Atlanta** | [ət'læntə] |
| **Hawaii** | [hə'waɪi] | **HI** | **Honolulu** | [ˌhɒnə'lu:lu:] |
| **Idaho** | ['aɪdəhəʊ] | **ID** | **Boise** | ['bɔɪzi] |
| **Illinois** | [ˌɪlə'nɔɪ] | **IL** | **Springfield** | ['sprɪŋfi:ld] |
| **Indiana** | [ˌɪndi'ænə] | **IN** | **Indianapolis** | [ˌɪndiə'næpəlɪs] |
| **Iowa** | ['aɪəwə] | **IA** | **Des Moines** | [də 'mɔɪn] |
| **Kansas** | ['kænzəs] | **KS** | **Topeka** | [təʊ'pi:kə] |
| **Kentucky** | [ken'tʌki] | **KY** | **Frankfort** | ['fræŋkfət] |
| **Louisiana** | [luˌi:zi'ænə] | **LA** | **Baton Rouge** | [ˌbætn 'ru:ʒ] |
| **Maine** | [meɪn] | **ME** | **Augusta** | [ɔ:'gʌstə] |
| **Maryland** | ['meərilənd] | **MD** | **Annapolis** | [ə'næpəlɪs] |
| **Massachusetts** | [ˌmæsə'tʃu:sɪts] | **MA** | **Boston** | ['bɒstən] |
| **Michigan** | ['mɪʃɪgən] | **MI** | **Lansing** | ['lɑ:nsɪŋ] |
| **Minnesota** | [ˌmɪnɪ'səʊtə] | **MN** | **Saint Paul** | [sənt 'pɔ:l] |
| **Mississippi** | [ˌmɪsɪ'sɪpi] | **MS** | **Jackson** | ['dʒæksən] |
| **Missouri** | [mɪ'zʊəri] | **MO** | **Jefferson City** | [ˌdʒefəsən 'sɪti] |
| **Montana** | [mɒn'tænə] | **MT** | **Helena** | ['helənə] |
| **Nebraska** | [nə'bræskə] | **NE** | **Lincoln** | ['lɪŋkən] |
| **Nevada** | [nə'vɑ:də] | **NV** | **Carson City** | [ˌkɑ:sn 'sɪti] |
| **New Hampshire** | [ˌnju: 'hæmpʃə] | **NH** | **Concord** | ['kɒŋkɔ:d, 'kɒŋkəd] |
| **New Jersey** | [ˌnju: 'dʒɜ:zi] | **NJ** | **Trenton** | ['trentən] |
| **New Mexico** | [ˌnju: 'meksɪkəʊ] | **NM** | **Santa Fe** | [ˌsæntə 'feɪ] |
| **New York** | [ˌnju: 'jɔ:k] | **NY** | **Albany** | ['ɔ:lbəni] |
| **North Carolina** | [ˌnɔ:θ kærə'laɪnə] | **NC** | **Raleigh** | ['rɔ:li] |
| **North Dakota** | [ˌnɔ:θ də'kəʊtə] | **ND** | **Bismarck** | ['bɪzmɑ:k] |
| **Ohio** | [əʊ'haɪəʊ] | **OH** | **Columbus** | [kə'lʌmbəs] |
| **Oklahoma** | [ˌəʊklə'həʊmə] | **OK** | **Oklahoma City** | [ˌəʊkləˌhəʊmə 'sɪti] |
| **Oregon** | ['ɒrɪgən] | **OR** | **Salem** | ['seɪləm] |
| **Pennsylvania** | [ˌpensl'veɪniə] | **PA** | **Harrisburg** | ['hærɪsbɜ:g] |
| **Rhode Island** | [ˌrəud_'aɪlənd] | **RI** | **Providence** | ['prɒvɪdəns] |
| **South Carolina** | [ˌsaʊθ kærə'laɪnə] | **SC** | **Columbia** | [kə'lʌmbiə] |
| **South Dakota** | [ˌsaʊθ də'kəʊtə] | **SD** | **Pierre** | [pɪə] |
| **Tennessee** | [ˌtenə'si:] | **TN** | **Nashville** | ['næʃvɪl] |
| **Texas** | ['teksəs] | **TX** | **Austin** | ['ɒstɪn] |
| **Utah** | ['ju:tɑ:] | **UT** | **Salt Lake City** | [ˌsɔ:lt leɪk 'sɪti] |
| **Vermont** | [və'mɒnt] | **VT** | **Montpelier** | [mɒnt'pi:liə] |
| **Virginia** | [və'dʒɪniə] | **VA** | **Richmond** | ['rɪtʃmənd] |
| **Washington** | ['wɒʃɪŋtən] | **WA** | **Olympia** | [ə'lɪmpiə] |
| **West Virginia** | [ˌwest və'dʒɪniə] | **WV** | **Charleston** | ['tʃɑ:lstən] |
| **Wisconsin** | [wɪs'kɒnsɪn] | **WI** | **Madison** | ['mædɪsən] |
| **Wyoming** | [waɪ'əʊmɪŋ] | **WY** | **Cheyenne** | [ˌʃaɪ'æn] |

# Classroom English

| Was *du* im Klassenzimmer sagen kannst | What *you* can say in the classroom |
|---|---|
| **Du brauchst Hilfe** | **You need help** |
| Können Sie mir bitte helfen? | **Can you help me, please?** |
| Auf welcher Seite sind wir, bitte? | **What page are we on, please?** |
| Was heißt ... auf Englisch/Deutsch? | **What's ... in English/German?** |
| Wie spricht man das erste Wort in Zeile 2 aus? | **How do you say the first word in line 2?** |
| Können Sie bitte ... buchstabieren? | **Can you spell ..., please?** |
| Können Sie es bitte an die Tafel schreiben? | **Can you write it on the board, please?** |
| Kann ich es auf Deutsch sagen? | **Can I say it in German?** |
| Können Sie/Kannst du bitte lauter sprechen? | **Can you speak louder, please?** |
| Können Sie/Kannst du das bitte noch mal sagen? | **Can you say that again, please?** |
| **Über Texte und Themen sprechen** | **Talking about texts and topics** |
| Ich finde die Geschichte ... | **I think the story is ...** |
| schön/interessant/langweilig/schrecklich/.... | **nice/interesting/boring/terrible/...** |
| Es war lustig/gruselig/langweilig/..., als ... | **It was funny/scary/boring/... when ...** |
| Ich fand es gut/nicht gut, als ... | **I liked it/didn't like it when ...** |
| Ich finde, Tom hat recht/nicht recht, weil ... | **I think Tom is right/wrong because ...** |
| Ich bin mir nicht sicher. Vielleicht ... | **I'm not sure. Maybe ...** |
| Was meinst du? | **What do you think?** |
| Ich stimme ... zu/nicht zu, weil ... | **I agree/disagree (with ...) because ...** |
| **Hausaufgaben und Übungen** | **Homework and exercises** |
| Tut mir leid, ich habe mein Schulheft nicht dabei, Herr ... | **Sorry, I haven't got my exercise book, Mr ...** |
| Ich habe meine Hausaufgaben vergessen, Frau ... | **I've forgotten my homework, Mrs/Ms/Miss ...** |
| Ich kann Nummer 3 nicht lösen. | **I can't do number 3.** |
| Entschuldigung, ich bin noch nicht fertig. | **Sorry, I haven't finished yet.** |
| Ich habe ... Ist das auch richtig? | **I've got ... Is that right too?** |
| Tut mir leid, das weiß ich nicht. | **Sorry, I don't know.** |
| Was haben wir (als Hausaufgabe) auf? | **What's for homework?** |
| **Bei der Partnerarbeit** | **Work with a partner** |
| Kann ich mit Julian arbeiten? | **Can I work with Julian?** |
| Wer ist dran? – Du bist dran. | **Whose turn is it? – It's your turn.** |
| Ich finde, wir sollten/könnten ... | **I think we should/could ...** |
| Was machen wir zuerst? | **What are we going to do first?** |
| **What your teacher says** | **Was dein/e Lehrer/in sagt** |
| **Open your books at page 24, please.** | Schlagt bitte Seite 24 auf. |
| **Look at the picture/line 8/... on page 24.** | Seht euch das Bild/Zeile 8/... auf Seite 24 an. |
| **Copy/Complete the chart/network/...** | Übertragt/Vervollständigt die Tabelle/das Wörternetz/... |
| **Correct the mistakes.** | Verbessert die Fehler. |
| **Take notes.** | Macht euch Notizen. |
| **Do exercise 3 for homework, please.** | Macht bitte Übung 3 als Hausaufgabe. |
| **Have you finished?** | Seid ihr fertig? / Bist du fertig? |
| **Switch off your mobile phones.** | Schaltet eure Handys aus. |
| **Walk around the class and ask other students.** | Geht durch die Klasse und fragt andere Schüler/innen. |
| **Discuss ... with ...** | Diskutiere/Diskutiert ... mit ... |
| **Give a presentation about ...** | Halte/Haltet einen Vortrag über ... |
| **Report to the class.** | Berichte/Berichtet der Klasse. |